D0760944

# Taking Psychology
# and Law into
# the Twenty-First Century

# Perspectives in

# Law & Psychology

Sponsored by the American Psychology-Law Society / Division 41 of the American Psychological Association

**Series Editor**: Ronald Roesch, *Simon Fraser University, Burnaby, British Columbia, Canada*

**Editorial Board**: Jane Goodman-Delahunty, Thomas Grisso, Stephen D. Hart, Marsha Liss, Edward P. Mulvey, James R. P. Ogloff, Norman G. Poythress, Jr., Don Read, Regina Schuller, and Patricia Zapf

# Taking Psychology and Law into the Twenty-First Century

### Edited by

## James R. P. Ogloff

*Monash University and Victorian Institute of Forensic Mental Health (Forensicare)*
*Melbourne, Victoria, Australia*

KLUWER ACADEMIC / PLENUM PUBLISHERS
NEW YORK/BOSTON/DORDRECHT/LONDON/MOSCOW

Library of Congress Cataloging-in-Publication Data

Taking psychology and law into the twenty-first century/edited by James R.P. Ogloff.
    p.   ; cm.—(Perspectives in law & psychology; v. 14)
    Includes bibliographical references and index.
    ISBN 0-306-46760-7
    1. Law—Psychological aspects.  2. Psychology, Forensic.  3. Sociological jurisprudence.
I. Ogloff, James R. P.  II. Series.

K346 .T35 2002
340'.01'9—dc21

2002023006

ISBN 0-306-46760-7

©2002 Kluwer Academic / Plenum Publishers, New York
233 Spring Street, New York, New York 10013

http://www.wkap.nl/

10  9  8  7  6  5  4  3  2  1

A C.I.P. record for this book is available from the Library of Congress

To my students …

Marie Achille, Liz Bannerman, Georgia Bekiou,
Lisa Brown, Rachel Campbell, Shirley Chau, Sonia Chopra,
Margaret Clingwall Pfoh, Michael Davis, Kevin Douglas, Kelly Frame,
Nathalie Gagnon, Jennifer Honeyman, Lindsey Jack, Ken Kroeker,
David Lyon, Andrea McEachran, Rachel McKenzie, Bronwyn McKeon,
Lynda Murdoch, Tonia Nicholls, Olga Nikonova, Maureen Olley,
Heather Rhodes, Marc Rogers, Gordon Rose, Karen Salekin,
Randy Salekin, Kerry Smith, Lynne Sullivan, Darryl Ternowski,
Sandra Vermeulen, Gina Vincent, Tristin Wayte, Andrew Welsh,
and Karen Whittemore

and to all the students of law and psychology.
You are the future of the discipline.

# Contributors

RANDY BORUM • Department of Mental Health Law & Policy, Florida Mental Health Institute, University of South Florida, Tampa, Florida 33612

BETTE L. BOTTOMS • Department of Psychology, University of Illinois at Chicago, Chicago, Illinois 60607-7137

JOHN C. BRIGHAM • Department of Psychology, Florida State University, Tallahassee, Florida 32306

ELIZABETH C. A. BRIMACOMBE • Department of Psychology, University of Victoria, Victoria, British Columbia, Canada V8W 3P5

SONIA R. CHOPRA • Department of Psychology, Simon Fraser University, Burnaby, British Columbia V5A 1S6

JOHN DARLEY • Psychology Department, Princeton University, Princeton, New Jersey 08544-1010

KEVIN S. DOUGLAS • Department of Mental Health Law and Policy, Florida Mental Health Institute, University of South Florida, Tampa, Florida 33612

SOLOMON FULERO • Department of Psychology, Sinclair College, Dayton, Ohio 45402

EDITH GREENE • Department of Psychology, University of Colorado, Colorado Springs, Colorado 80933

AMY HACKNEY • Department of Psychology, Saint Louis University, Saint Louis, Missouri 63101

CRAIG HANEY • Department of Psychology, University of California—Santa Cruz, Santa Cruz, California 95064

STEPHEN D. HART • Department of Psychology, Simon Fraser University, Burnaby, British Columbia, Canada V5A 1S6

KIRK HEILBRUN • Department of Clinical and Health Psychology, MCP Hahnemann University, Philadelphia, Philadephia 19102

JAMES HEMPHILL • Department of Psychology, Simon Fraser University, Burnaby, British Columbia, Canada V5A 1S6

LARRY HEUER • Department of Psychology, Barnard College, 415 Milbank Hall, Columbia University, New York, New York 10027

KAREN KADELA • Department of Psychology, Saint Louis University, Saint Louis, Missouri 63101

WILLIAM J. KOCH • Health Psychology Clinic, University of British Columbia Psychiatry, University of British Columbia Hospital, 2211 Wesbrook Mall, Vancouver, British Columbia, Canada V6T 2B5

MARGARET BULL KOVERA • Florida International University, North Miami, Florida 33181

RODERICK C. LINDSAY • Department of Psychology, Queen's University, Kingston, Ontario, Canada K7L 3N6

DAVID R. LYON • Department of Psychology, Simon Fraser University, Burnaby, British Columbia, Canada V5A 1S6

DALE E. MCNIEL • Department of Psychiatry, School of Medicine, University of California, San Francisco, California 94143-0984

KARI L. NYSSE-CARRIS • Department of Psychology, University of Illinois at Chicago, Chicago, Illinois 60607-7137

JAMES R. P. OGLOFF • School of Psychology, Psychiatry and Psychological Medicine, Monash University and Victorian Institute of Forensic Mental Health (Forensicare), Thomas Embling Hospital, Fairfield, Victoria 3078, Australia

RANDY K. OTTO • Department of Mental Health Law and Policy, Louis de la Parte Florida Mental Health Center, University of South Florida, Tampa, Florida 33612-3899

STEVEN D PENROD • Department of Psychology, John Jay College of Criminal Justice, The City University of New York, New York, New York 10019-1199

NORMAN G. POYTHRESS • Department of Mental Health Law & Policy, University of South Florida, Tampa, Florida 33612-3899

SHANNON RAUCH • Department of Psychology, Saint Louis University, Saint Louis, Missouri 63101

N. DICKON REPPUCCI • Department of Psychology, Gilmer Hall, University of Virginia, Charlottesville, Virginia 22904-4400

JENNIFER K. ROBBENNOLT • Faculty of Law, University of Missouri-Columbia, School of Law, Columbia, Missouri 65211

RONALD ROESCH • Mental Health, Law, and Policy Institute, Simon Fraser University, Burnaby, British Columbia, Canada V5A 1S6

MELANIE ROGERS • Department of Psychology, Brooklyn College and Graduate Center, Bedford Avenue and Avenue H, Brooklyn, New York 11210

RICHARD ROGERS • Department of Psychology, University of North Texas, Denton, Texas 76203-3587

V. GORDON ROSE • Program in Law and Forensic Psychology, Simon Fraser University, Burnaby, British Columbia, Canada V5A 1S6

JOTI SAMRA • Department of Psychiatry & Behavioral Sciences, University of Washington School of Medicine, Seattle, Washington 98195

REGINA A. SCHULLER • Department of Psychology, York University, Toronto, Ontario, Canada M3J 1P3

HOPE SEIB • Department of Psychology, Saint Louis University, Saint Louis, Missouri 63101

CHRISTINA ANN STUDEBAKER • Research Division, Federal Judicial Center, Washington, DC 20002

LYNNE E. SULLIVAN • Child Study and Treatment Center and University of Washington, Tacoma, Washington 98498

JENNIFER A. TWEED • Department of Psychology, University of Virginia, Charlottesville, Virginia 22904-4400

TOM TYLER • Department of Psychology, New York University, New York, New York 10003

JODI L. VILJOEN • Department of Psychology, Simon Fraser University, Burnaby, Birtish Columbia, Canada V5A 1S6

LAURA WARREN • Department of Psychology, Saint Louis University, St. Louis, Missouri 63101

TRISTIN WAYTE • Department of Psychology, Simon Fraser University, Burnaby, British Columbia, Canada V5A 1S6

GARY L. WELLS • Psychology Department, Iowa State University, Ames, Iowa 50011

KAREN E. WHITTEMORE • Forensic Psychiatric Services Commission, Surrey, British Columbia, Canada V3V 4B8

RICHARD WIENER • Department of Psychology, Baruch College and Graduate Center, City University of New York, New York, New York 10010

RYAN WINTER • Department of Psychology, Brooklyn College and Graduate Center, Brooklyn, New York 11210

PATRICIA A. ZAPF • Department of Psychology, University of Alabama, Tuscaloosa, Alabama 35401-0348

# Preface

This book is the culmination of a review of the field of law and psychology that was undertaken by the American Psychology Law Society as part of my presidential initiative. The purpose of the initiative was to determine both where we have been and where we should be going in the new millennium. As we entered the new millennium, the American Psychology Law Society (APLS) was just over thirty years old. In that time, we had grown, as has the field of law and psychology. Article I(2) of our by-laws specify that "the purposes of the Society shall be:

a. To advance the contributions of psychology to the understanding of law and legal institutions through basic and applied research;
b. To promote the education of psychologists in matters of law and the education of legal personnel in matters of psychology, including the appropriate use of psychologists in the legal system; and
c. To inform the psychological and legal communities and the general public of current research, educational, and service activities in the field of psychology and law.

As the above purposes indicate, APLS exists both as a collegial organization that enhances the interaction of scholar and practitioners in our field and as a mechanism for driving our field. While we have grown, we have developed many programs to facilitate these ends; however, the new millennium offers an opportunity to re-evaluate our society and our field.

Although the field has grown at a considerable rate, few have taken advantage of the opportunity to step back and review some of the major areas of the field. Such a review was seen as an important process because the discipline of psychology and law has developed more by accident than by plan. While some could argue that this has served us well, the simple fact is that our discipline has been relatively ineffective in the law. Of more concern, perhaps, is that we have been at least as ineffective in influencing psychology more generally. As the first purpose of APLS, as provided in Article I(2), is "to advance the contributions of psychology to the understanding of law and legal institutions through basic and applied research," we took advantage of the opportunity to explore the developments and limitations of several areas of the field.

The initiative I led drew upon the "state of the discipline" project that Gary Melton initiated in the 1980s while he was the president of APLS. While the initiative was consistent with that proposed by Gary Melton, the chapters that were ultimately completed for this book serve as reviews of the areas that bridge the generations of researchers. The project began with a meeting of most chapter authors in Vancouver in the spring of 1999. Although there was some variation in the final products, each working group began with a mixture of senior scholars, more junior, but well recognized, scholars, and graduate students in the areas. Following the meeting, each group prepared an overview of a chapter. These products were presented at the Biennial Meeting of the American Psychology Law Society in New Orleans in March, 2000. Finally, APLS members were invited to discuss the topics with chapter authors at the APA annual meeting in 2000.

In addition to the presidential initiative, a review of *Law and Human Behavior* was conducted. With respect to the review of *Law and Human Behavior*, Richard Wiener independently applied for and received a grant from the National Science Foundation to fund a weekend workshop to evaluate past, current, and future directions of the journal. Dr. Wiener and his colleagues have prepared a chapter following this review for this volume.

James R. P. Ogloff
Melbourne, Victoria, Australia
December 2001

# Acknowledgements

In many respects, the idea for the presidential initiative that led to this book came from my doctoral supervisor, Gary Melton. He had a similar idea when he served as president of the American Psychology Law Society in the 1980s. Gary has been a great influence to me and to the field and for that I am particularly grateful. I extend my thanks to all of the authors of the chapters for their diligence and for their excellent work. I would like to thank members of the steering committee for my presidential initiative that culminated in this book, Shari Diamond, Norman Finkel, Jane Goodman-Delahunty, David Faigman, Murray Levine, Mark Small, and Richard Wiener. The presidential initiative was sponsored and funded by the American Psychology Law Society (Division 41 of the American Psychological Association) and supported by the Executive Committee. I very much appreciated the support of the Executive Committee and hope that this book is a worthy product for our members. I would like to express my deep gratitude to Jennifer van Rassel, the Program Assistant for the Program in Law and Forensic Psychology at Simon Fraser University. She spent many hours formatting and making edits to the chapters. As always, I appreciate Ron Roesch's excellent editorial skills, his guidance, and his dedication to the books in this book series. Finally, this book was completed while I was in the Department of Psychology at Simon Fraser University. I very much appreciate the support I received from the department and the university throughout this project.

# Contents

CHAPTER 2. PSYCHOLOGICAL JURISPRUDENCE:
TAKING PSYCHOLOGY AND LAW INTO THE TWENTY-FIRST CENTURY

*John Darley, Sol Fulero, Craig Haney, and Tom Tyler*

CHAPTER 3. CHILDREN, PSYCHOLOGY, AND LAW: REFLECTIONS ON
PAST AND FUTURE CONTRIBUTIONS TO SCIENCE AND POLICY

*Bette L. Bottoms, N. Dickon Reppucci, Jennifer A. Tweed, and
Kari L. Nysse-Carris*

CHAPTER 4. FORENSIC ASSESSMENT: CURRENT STATUS AND
FUTURE DIRECTIONS

*Kirk Heilbrun, Richard Rogers, and Randy Otto*

CHAPTER 5. RISK ASSESSMENT

*Dale E. McNiel, Randy Borum, Kevin S. Douglas, Stephen D. Hart,
David Lyon, Lynne E. Sullivan, and James F. Hemphill*

CHAPTER 6. COMPETENCY: PAST, PRESENT, AND FUTURE

*Patricia A. Zapf, Jodi L. Viljoen, Karen E. Whittemore,
Norman G. Poythress, and Ronald Roesch*

CHAPTER 7. EYEWITNESS RESEARCH

*R. C. L. Lindsay, John C. Brigham, C. A. Elizabeth Brimacombe
and, Gary L. Wells*

CHAPTER 8. JURORS AND JURIES: A REVIEW OF THE FIELD

*Edith Greene, Sonia R. Chopra, Margaret Bull Kovera, Steven D. Penrod, V. Gordon Rose, Regina Schuller, and Christina A. Studebaker*

CHAPTER 9. THE MONETARY WORTH OF PSYCHOLOGICAL INJURY:
WHAT ARE LITIGANTS SUING FOR?

*Joti Samra and William J. Koch*

CHAPTER 10. PSYCHOLOGICAL ISSUES IN CIVIL LAW

*Tristin Wayte, Joti Samra, Jennifer K. Robbennolt, Larry Heuer, and
William J. Koch*

CHAPTER 11. EVALUATING PUBLISHED RESEARCH IN PSYCHOLOGY
AND LAW: A GATEKEEPER ANALYSIS OF *LAW AND HUMAN BEHAVIOR*

*Richard L. Wiener, Ryan J. Winter, Melanie Rogers, Hope Seib,*
*Shannon Rauch, Karen Kadela, Amy Hackney, and Laura Warren*

# Two Steps Forward and One Step Backward[1]

## The Law and Psychology Movement(s) in the 20th Century

### JAMES R. P. OGLOFF

> The development of the synthesis of law and psychology will be a long and perhaps a tedious process; but it is a process, however much patience it may require, which for the law will yield a fruitful harvest. (Cairns, 1935, p. 219)

As we enter the waning months of the 20th century, it seems appropriate to look back at the two law and psychology movements that have occurred this century. It is fitting, too, that I should be giving this speech in Boston where just over a century ago the soil was tilled at Harvard Law School to allow for the roots of the law and psychology movement to be planted. It was at Harvard University more than a century ago, under the direction of University President Charles Eliot and Law School Dean Christopher Columbus Langdell, that the 3-year postgraduate law school curriculum was initiated. The change from a 1- or 2-year undergraduate

[1]This paper was presented as the author's Presidential Address of the American Psychology-Law Society (Division 41 of the American Psychological Association). Originally published in *Law and Human Behavior*, 24(4) (2000); 457–483.

JAMES R. P. OGLOFF • Foundation Professor of Clinical Forensic Psychology, School of Psychology, Psychiatry and Psychological Medicine, Monash University and Director Psychological Services, Victorian Institute of Forensic Mental Health (Forensicare), Thomas Embling Hospital, Fairfield, Victoria 3078, Australia.

program to one which required that students hold a baccalaureate degree before beginning the study of law ensured that law students would begin their studies with a formal background in another field—and in many cases a degree in a social science (Ogloff, Tomkins, & Bersoff, 1996).

Once the academic soil was tilled, just over 90 years ago, Prof. H. Munsterberg—again of Harvard University—published his seminal book, *On the Witness Stand* (1908), which helped plant the seeds that grew into the initial law and psychology movement. Unfortunately, as I will note below, Munsterberg's book was not received openly by either lawyers or social scientists. Indeed, in a book arguing for the advancement of social science, including psychology, in the law Cairns (1935) referred to *On the witness stand* as a "rash and presumptuous little book" (p. 169).

While I decided that it would be appropriate to reflect back on the development of law and psychology this century, I decided that I would not just merrily list our many accomplishments.[2] Rather, my goal is to be more critical in looking back in order to learn from what we have done, and failed to do. Such a perspective, it is hoped, will help ensure the continued growth and success of our field into the 21st century. Because this paper is somewhat cynical and even critical, it is important to put it into perspective by briefly highlighting some of the many advances we have made in the field of law and psychology in the latter part of this century.

Just 30 years ago, there was no journal dedicated to the study of law and psychology, there had not yet been a convention of the American Psychology-Law Society, there were fewer than 500 articles catalogued in *Psychological Abstracts* on topics broadly related to our field, very few sessions at the APA convention were in law and psychology (only one in 1965, for example), APLS was newly formed (with 101 charter members listed in the first membership directory published in 1969), and there were no formal graduate or joint degree training programs in the field (see generally, Fulero, in press; Grisso, 1991; Monahan & Loftus, 1982; Tapp, 1976).

Despite our growth, the development of the law and psychology movement has occurred more by chance than by planning and we have had far less influence on the legal system than we tend to believe. Indeed, as Melton (1990) detailed, the course of psycholegal studies (or whatever you want to call "it") has not been particularly well plotted.

---

[2]Given the limited space here, I shall not detail the advances that have been made in the field of law and psychology. I want to emphasize that while I take a decidedly critical perspective in this article, I fully appreciate the many advances that have been made in our field. Those advances have been well documented elsewhere (see, e.g., Brigham, 1999; Grisso, 1991; Melton, 1990; Ogloff, 1992; Ogloff, Tomkins, & Bersoff, 1996; Roesch, Hart, & Ogloff, 1999).

One would be hard pressed to find a common theme—let alone a common course—in the research and application of psychology to the legal system. The movement largely has been driven by psychologists, often with little knowledge of the law, conducting studies or practicing in areas of interest to them, based on their own disciplinary pedagogy. Only recently have those in the area really begun to develop an integrated approach to the study of the law and legal systems. To a large extent, the success and impact of the law and psychology movement depends on the quality and diversity of our scholarship, and our ability to apply that knowledge to the legal system. Although the number of psychologists working in areas relevant to the law has grown, and the areas investigated have been expanded somewhat, the law and psychology movement still is relatively obscure, especially within the law. It is worth pointing out that in 1971, 40% of APLS members were lawyers (Fulero, in press). Now, one is hard-pressed to identify more than a handful of APLS members who are lawyers without also holding doctorates in psychology.[3]

Why should we care about having our findings and our work influence the law? The law is among the most pervasive forces in society. For psychology to have an impact on society, it is crucial for psychology to have an impact on the law. Given the power that the law has over people and society, and the extent to which the broad range of research and practice in psychology leads to a better and more sophisticated understanding of human behavior and mental processes, the overlap between psychology and law is expansive. As has been discussed in considerable detail, the knowledge generated in psychology has much to offer the law (e.g., Loh, 1981; Melton, 1987b; Ogloff, 1990, 1992; Ogloff et al., 1996; Small, 1993; Tapp, 1976; Wiener, 1993).

In this article, I will discuss the two psychology movements that have occurred during the 20th century. The first movement occurred from the turn of the century until approximately 1940 and the second began in the late 1960s and exists to this day. I will then reflect on the "step backward"—the eventual fading of psychology and law from approximately 1940 until the late 1960s. Following the discussion of the "two steps forward and one step back," I will present 12 points that we must consider, address, and ideally rectify to ensure that our field does not take yet another step back as we bridge the new millennium.

---

[3]While the actual number of lawyer members is not available, lawyers cannot be members of APA. As such, the lawyer members are Members at Large of the American Psychology-Law Society (not members of Division 41). As of August 1999, there were only 175 Members at Large. Therefore, even if all of the Members at Large were lawyers (which they most certainly are not), the percentage of lawyer-members would still be less than 7%.

## THE FIRST STEP FORWARD—THE GERMINATION AND
## SPROUTING OF LAW AND PSYCHOLOGY[4]

> The life of the law has not been logic: it has been experience. The felt necessi-
> ties of the time, the prevalent moral and political theories, intuitions of public
> policy, avowed or unconscious, even the prejudices which judges share with
> their fellowmen, have had a good deal more to do than the syllogism in deter-
> mining the rules by which men should be governed. (Holmes, 1881, p. 1)

As alluded to in the introduction, the very possibility of having a law
and psychology movement occurred when, late in the 19th century, legal
education evolved from an apprenticeship model to a university-based
system (Ogloff et al., 1996; Stevens, 1983).[5] It was at that time that legal
scholars began to insist that to fully understand the law, one must examine and understand the social contexts from which the law was derived
and that ultimately are influenced by the law (Friedman, 1985; Purcell,
1973). This perspective, which came to be known as sociological jurisprudence, "insisted ... [on] empirical observations of changing social conditions and [the replacement of] pseudologic with 'experience'" (White,
1976, p. 252). It was no longer enough to "know the law" by studying
judicial opinions, the method that had become the cornerstone of legal
systems in North America that were based on English common law.
Indeed, Oliver Wendell Holmes (1897) wrote that "for the rational study
of law ... the black-letter man may be the man of the present, but the man
of the future is the man of statistics and the master of economics" (p. 469).
In addition to this well-known quote, Holmes in some of his thinking was
apparently directly influenced by psychology. Indeed, he adopted the
term "volition" to describe voluntary acts—a term introduced into psychology by Wundt (Cairns, 1935; O. W. Holmes, 1881).

Following sociological jurisprudence, other movements evolved that
also challenged the law to be aware of social and legal "realities" (Purcell,
1973; Schlegel, 1979, 1980; Tomkins & Oursland, 1991; Twining, 1973;
White, 1972). These groups, such as the legal realists, advocated drawing
upon the social sciences for methodologies and perspectives from which

---

[4]It must be emphasized, of course, that due to the space limitations here, the historical
review presented is by no means exhaustive. The fact is that I continue to find articles and
material dating from the early part of the century pertaining to psychologists' interest in the
law. For some more comprehensive reviews, see Brigham (1999), Cairns (1935), Fulero (in
press), Monahan and Loftus (1982), Tapp (1976), and Toch (1961).

[5]Many of the thoughts in the introduction of this paper are taken from Ogloff et al. (1996). I
am indebted to Alan Tomkins and Donald Bersoff for their insight into the development of
legal psychology.

to examine law, legal process, and legal decision-making (Kalman, 1986; Schlegel, 1979, 1980; Twining, 1973, 1985).

If the changes in the nature of legal education and legal scholarship provided the necessary background for the law and psychology movement, the work of early psychologists served to establish the field. Although Freud (1906), lectured judges in Vienna about the virtues of psychology for the law (Brigham, 1999; Tapp, 1976), Hugo Munsterberg generally is considered to be the father of law and psychology. Munsterberg, a student of Wilhelm Wundt's at the University of Leipzig, was the first director of Harvard's Psychological Laboratory. He is considered to be the founder of applied psychology (Boring, 1950; Hale, 1980; Moskowitz, 1977). Among other things, Munsterberg advocated applying psychology to the law, and criticized lawyers and judges for not embracing the research of psychologists that could be applied to law (Loh, 1981). In 1908, Munsterberg published *On the Witness Stand*, a book in which he reviewed a number of "psychology and law topics." He ended his introduction by writing that "my only purpose is to turn the attention of serious men to an absurdly neglected field which demands the full attention of the social community" (p. 12).

Unfortunately, rather than embracing psychology and psychological research, lawyers and scholars, including such luminaries as the renowned legal evidence scholar, John H. Wigmore (1909), chastised Munsterberg. Their criticisms were that Munsterberg's claims were exaggerated, and that psychology had not ascertained the data necessary to support Munsterberg's criticisms of the law. In a satire published in the *Illinois Law Review* (see also, Moore, 1907), Wigmore subjected Munsterberg's work to the scrutiny of cross-examination in a mock libel trial in which Munsterberg was accused of claiming more than his science could support or offer. Not surprisingly, Munsterberg was found guilty of exaggerating his claims (Ogloff et al., 1996).

Munsterberg not only was mocked by lawyers, his ideas about applying psychology to any field, let alone the law, were criticized by none other than Prof. Edward, Titchener of Cornell University (see Cairns, 1935). Titchener held firmly, as was the prevailing sense at the time, that psychology should remain pure and scientific, and should not be concerned with the application of its findings (Cairns, 1935). Interestingly, while Wigmore's (1909) criticism of Munsterberg (1908) is widely known and cited, the fact is that in his article, Wigmore pointed out that while psychology had little to offer the law at that time, the law would pay attention to relevant psychological findings when they became available. Ironically, then, the ideological concerns of Titchener—and those who shared his sentiments—likely did as much to hold back the application of psychology to the law as did the law's own reticence to open its arms to psychology. Cairns' words, written 65 years ago, ring as true today as they did when he wrote them:

> When a court lays down a rule of conduct which has a purely psychological content, it is no perversion of the method of science for the psychologist to determine whether or not the rule is psychologically valid. But the belief on the part of psychologists that it does constitute a perversion of scientific method, has been a real obstacle in the path of a synthesis of law and psychology at the points where they overlap (Cairns, 1935, p. 172).

In addition to Freud and Munsterberg, several psychologists writing in the first three decades of the 20th century either commented on the possible application of psychology to the law or actually conducted experiments on relevant topics. Some examples—including many who were prominent psychologists—are as follows: James McKeen Cattell (1895), a student of Wundt's who founded the first psychology laboratory at Columbia University in 1891, and an early APA president, had many interests, including the functional capacities of people in various institutions (Boring, 1950). Among his interests was the ability of people to accurately recall events, including the application of recall to the "court of justice" (Cattell, 1895, p. 761). John B. Watson (1913), the famed behaviorist, noted that judges could incorporate relevant work of psychologists into the law as that work was made available. Burtt (1925, 1931) and Paynter (1920) aided courts in trademark and trade name infringement cases by conducting experiments to determine whether the products in question led to confusion by the public. Moreover, Burtt (1925)—a psychologist—wrote a law review article on the topic! Hutchins and Slesinger (1928, 1929b) wrote a series of articles on the application of psychological findings to the law of evidence. Even the famous Russian psychologist, A. R. Luria (1932), investigated affect in newly arrested criminals, prior to their being questioned by police, in order to determine whether he could objectively differentiate those who were guilty from those who were innocent.

As early as 1926, M. Ralph Brown published a book called *Legal Psychology: Psychology Applied to the Trial of Cases, to Crime and Its Treatment, and to Mental States and Processes*. Hutchins and Slesinger (1929a) published an article called "Legal psychology." Another book published in 1929, entitled *Psychology for the Lawyer*, was written by McCarty (1929). Harold E. Burtt (1931) published a book with the title *Legal Psychology*. Finally, Cairns (1935) wrote a very informative and comprehensive book, *Law and the Social Sciences*. The book had a foreword by Roscoe Pound, who noted that "all the sciences which have to do with social control in any of its aspects have their bearing on jurisprudence ... It is evident, then, that a discussion of the relation of the several social sciences to law ... is timely and significant" (p. xiv). In his book Cairns (1935) reviewed five social sciences—anthropology, economics, sociology, psychology, political theory—and their application to the law. The book is insightful and, although written 65 years ago, the conceptual discussion concerning psychology and law is surprisingly contemporary.

Despite the chilling effect of Munsterberg's "trial," then, psychologists did continue to engage in research and writing about law and psychology well into the 1930s. In addition, movements such as sociological jurisprudence and legal realism led to the integration of social science, including psychology, into the law school curriculum. From the 1920s until the 1940s, several eminent law schools included social science material in their law courses. Even more surprising, perhaps, is that psychologist and other social scientists were hired as part of law faculties beginning in the late 1920s (Kalman, 1986; Loh, 1981; Schlegel, 1979, 1980; Stevens, 1983). This fact is surprising particularly because so few psychologists (without law degrees) are found on law faculties at the present time (Melton, Monahan, & Saks, 1987). Taken together, the "first step" in the law and psychology movement was much more far-reaching than is commonly thought or reported. With such a promising start, one must wonder what happened to the law and social science movement? Indeed, to the best of my knowledge, virtually no articles or books written by psychologists on the general topic of law and psychology appeared in the 1940s or 1950s.

## ONE STEP BACK—THE WILTING OF THE LAW AND PSYCHOLOGY MOVEMENT

It is impossible to determine definitively why the initial foray into law and psychology early in the 20th century was not sustained. Without getting into too much detail here, though, it appears that the early movement simply did not generate enough momentum to sustain itself. Other movements in law developed that overcame the initial force of the law and social science movement (e.g., law and economics).[6]

---

[6]Among the current movements is that of "law and economics." While economics is a social science, the methods and fields of enquiry differ sufficiently from psychology so as not to warrant discussion here. Interestingly, when Cairns (1935) reviewed social sciences and law 65 years ago, it was apparent that the law and economics movement was far less developed than was our own field. There is little doubt that the law and economics movement has had a much more significant impact on the law today than has law and psychology.

With the benefit of hindsight and speculation, a few factors emerge as possible reasons for the demise of the movement. The number of people researching and writing in the law remained small. Because there were no training programs for students, there were very few—if any—people to carry on the work of their academic parents. Researchers and writers in the field had no identified outlets for their work, and, given its applied nature, much of the work of legal psychologists was not in favor among those supporting the psychological status quo. There also was no formal organization of psychologists with interests in the law. It is doubtless, too, that the Great Depression and World War II had a detrimental effect on the growth of the field. While the postwar time was positive for the development of other areas of psychology (e.g., clinical psychology), law and psychology seemed to have been forgotten (Boring, 1950).

In addition to the forces within the discipline of psychology that prevented the continuing development of legal psychology after the 1930s, the fact is that there was a conservative backlash in law which limited the influence of the progressive scholars in the field (Friedman, 1985; Purcell, 1973; White, 1976). There is little doubt that the demise of legal realism had a chilling effect on legal psychology—as well as the application of the other social sciences to the law (Purcell, 1973). Indeed, the optimism and openness concerning the importance of the social sciences in law which marked the thinking of people like Oliver Wendell Holmes and Roscoe Pound diminished by the 1940s.

While the law and social science movement waned, it did not die and there are traces of work in psychology and law that was being done sporadically in the late 1940s and 1950s (Tapp, 1976); however, as we shall see below, it was not until the late 1960s that the law and psychology movement began to take the major step forward toward the current movement.

## THE SECOND STEP FORWARD—THE REBIRTH OF LAW AND PSYCHOLOGY IN THE 1960S

The contemporary history of law and psychology has been well documented (Brigham, 1999; Fulero, in press; Grisso, 1991; Monahan & Loftus, 1982; Ogloff et al., 1986; Tapp, 1976). If we contrast the scenario of the field 30 years ago as noted in the introduction, we can see a snapshot of the many changes that have occurred. Today there are too many journals in our field to name here—with our own journal *Law and Human Behavior* having been founded in 1977; in addition, APLS/Division 41 is a vital organization with approximately 3000 members (including some 500 student members), the 2000 meeting in New Orleans will be our 14th such meeting,[7] in 1998 there were at least 2500 articles published on topics in our field (because I restricted the search to terms the same as or similar to those used by Tapp, 1976, this is doubtless a gross underestimate), and there are now approximately 20 graduate programs in law and psychology, with at least 7 offering joint degrees in psychology and law. The growth of the field has also led to very strong research studies being published. Indeed, in 1999 the rejection rate of the society's flagship journal, *Law and Human Behavior*, was about 82%.[8]

In his presidential address in 1998, Brigham (1999) highlighted many of the important points of growth and development that have occurred since the 1950s. Among these were the introduction of the social science brief in *Brown v. Board of Education* in 1954, the founding of the American Psychology-Law Society in 1968–1969, the establishment of the Program in Law and Social Science at the National Science Foundation in 1971, the introduction of the first joint-degree Psychology-Law program at the University of Nebraska in 1974, the first review of psychology and law in the *Annual Review of Psychology* by Tapp (1976), the inception of the APLS journal *Law and Human Behavior* in 1977, the establishment of APA's Division 41 in 1980–1981, the APLS/Division 41 merger in 1984, the approval and publication of the Specialty Guidelines for Forensic Psychologists in 1991, and the introduction in 1995 of the APA journal *Psychology, Public Policy, and Law*.

The fact is that, without a doubt, law and psychology is "bigger and better" now than ever. Indeed, the momentum of the movement was rekindled in the 1960s and has gained considerable speed since that time (Ogloff et al., 1996). Although we have grown in number, in some tangible ways, the law and psychology movement appears to be approximately where it was in the 1920s with the sociological jurisprudence movement. Indeed, we have made relatively little inroads into the mainstream areas of law. As was the case in the 1920s, psychology has once again slowly made its way into case books and into the law school curriculum. Indeed, it was not until 1994 that law and psychology found its way into the *Annual Survey of American Law* (Satin, 1994). Some law schools even have opened up more doors to social scientists, bringing them once again into law schools as faculty (Grisso, Sales, & Bayless, 1982; Melton, 1990; Melton et al., 1987; Ogloff et al., 1996; Tapp, 1976; Wexler, 1990).

Despite its long history, though, the law and psychology movement has not caused any real waves in the law. Indeed, it is questionable

---

[7]Since this paper was presented, the 2000 biennial APLS meeting was held in New Orleans, and there were over 640 registrants with almost 400 paper presentations, symposia, or poster presentations.

[8]As conveyed by the current editor of the journal, Dr. Richard Wiener, at the business meeting of the APLS held at the biennial conference in New Orleans in March 2000.

whether much more than a few ripples have occurred. Support for these rather cynical statements can be found in countless legal decisions, statutes, and legal policy decisions. In fact, we still are at the stage in law and psychology where we celebrate those rare instances when the law does take heed of our work. For example, following an extensive review of the judiciary's use—or lack thereof—of child development research, Hafemeister and Melton (1987) concluded that

> the use of social science is still controversial and rather uncommon, especially in state courts. Courts appear unsure of whether and how to use social science to examine the policy questions that they have been asked to decide in recent decades. As a result ... reliance on social science is still largely a "liberal" practice of judges who have an expansive view of the judiciary's role in shaping legal doctrine and protecting disenfranchised groups (p. 55).[9]

In addition to our general failure to have had a significant impact on the law as a whole, contemporary writers have raised concerns, too, about the current direction—or lack thereof—of the field. In a recent article, Fox (1999) provides a critique of the law and psychology movement. In particular, he addresses the failure of psychology and law to promote social change that would produce social justice. Fox warns that "failing to challenge false assumptions about law inhibits efforts to bring about transformative change and makes the continued acceptance of injustice more likely" (pp. 11–12). Following a careful analysis, which emphasizes the extent to which psycholegal scholars have come to support a false consciousness about injustice, Fox advocates that we expose false consciousness and seek to end injustice. The article is thought-provoking and one can hope it will inspire some to return to the original roots of our field, which are reflected in the words of Saleem Shah, one of its founders: "Perhaps a basic challenge for psychology in its interactions with legal and social process is to bring relevant knowledge and skills to bear on major social inequities so that the policies and practices in our society can more truly comport with the deepest notions of what is fair and right and just' (Shah, 1978, p. 236).[10]

One can even question how effective the research has been in areas like juries and jury decision making—an area where much of the work in

---

[9]It must be noted that since their work more than a decade ago, the work of psychologists in the children and law area has seen some successes. Perhaps the best example is the United States Supreme Court's decision in *Maryland v. Craig*, 110 S.Ct. 3157 (1990). In *Craig*, the Court upheld a Maryland statute permitting the use of one-way closed circuit television to present the testimony of a child when the child would be likely to suffer significant emotional distress by being in the presence of the accused. The Court's decision tracks closely an *amicus curiae* brief that was presented in the case by the American Psychological Association.

[10]Shah is quoting Justice Felix Frankfurter in his dissenting opinion in *Solesbee v. Blakcom*, 339 U.S. 9, 16 (1950), where Justice Frankfurter was discussing the concept of "due process."

our field has been done (Bornstein, 1999; Diamond, 1997). For example, Bornstein (1999) analyzed the jury simulation research that has been published in *Law and Human Behavior* since its inception and found that—despite ongoing and longstanding calls for more externally valid methods—most studies still employ undergraduate students who are presented with written trial stimuli. Surprisingly, Bornstein found that rather than becoming more externally valid, the simulation studies have become less realistic over the life span of the journal.

One of the few areas in law and psychology which has been extensively studied and has had a significant impact on the law is that of eyewitness testimony (Wells et al., 1998). In that field, the success can be attributed to a careful, systematic line of research that has produced convergent findings. In addition, people in the field have presented their work in individual cases at the trial level, and more recently at the legislative and policy level.

Even in clinical forensic psychology where, arguably, most legal psychology activity occurs, commentators have noted the difficulty of the work of forensic psychologists given the unique legal and theoretical perspectives involved (Grisso, 1986; Melton, Petrila, Poythress, & Slobogin, 1997; Small, 1993).

## TOWARD A CONTINUED STRENGTHENING OF THE LAW AND PSYCHOLOGY MOVEMENT IN THE NEW MILLENNIUM

My almost cynical remarks about the lack of impact our field has had on the law—and on society—raise perhaps the most important question: Why has the law and psychology movement had so little an impact on the law (and, for that matter, on psychology)? Although many universities now offer courses at both the undergraduate and graduate levels in law and psychology, the courses are still considered to be outside the periphery of psychology. For example, law and psychology is rarely mentioned in detail introductory psychology textbooks. Failure to ponder—and find the answer to—this question may result in the demise of the movement, as happened in the mid-20th century.

In considering this question, I will present 12 points below that need to be addressed to ensure the continued growth and success of the field. It is all too easy—and too dangerous—to be complacent now that our field appears strong. By taking a critical perspective, then, it is my hope to cause us to become less apathetic and to continue to work hard to ensure the development and growth of the field of law and psychology. From a somewhat less morose perspective, in an attempt to ensure that history does not repeat itself, where possible I will make suggestions for addressing the concerns I raise. I should emphasize that the points listed and discussed below are not in any particular order of importance. Rather, they are the pressing issues that I have observed that must be addressed in our ongoing work.

## A ROSE BY ANY OTHER NAME? THE NAME AND DEFINITION OF THE FIELD

A seemingly trivial question, yet one which has caused much confusion and concern, is what to call the field of law and psychology. The obvious answer might be to call it "law and psychology"—as I just did—or "psychology and law." However, these terms are problematic because they imply that the field is merely some combination of law and of psychology. This simply is not true. The field of law and psychology has developed into its own discipline that, while borrowing heavily from both "law" and "psychology," combines elements of these disciplines in a unique manner—and adds considerably to the combination (Small, 1993). Furthermore, using the term "law and psychology" poses a question of what one calls those who work in the area. Surely, terms like "law and psychologists" or—as I'm embarrassed to admit a colleague and I suggested previously—"psychole-gologists" (Tomkins & Ogloff, 1990) are unnecessarily cumbersome. Also, other terms, like "forensic psychologist" or "criminal psychologist," as they have been interpreted and commonly used (see, e.g., Otto, Heilbrun, & Grisso, 1990), are too narrow to capture the breadth of the field.

One term that is broad enough to cover all areas of law about which psychology can be applied is "legal psychology." This term is by no means my own—nor by any means new. As noted above, Brown (1926) and Burtt (1931) both published books with the term "legal psychology" in the titles. Also, Toch's (1961) influential book *Legal and criminal psychology* uses the same term. Moreover, as previously noted, more than 70 years ago Hutchins and Slesinger (1929a) wrote a *Psychological Review* article entitled, simply, "Legal psychology."

For want of a better term, then, it would be appropriate to refer to our field as "legal psychology."[11] Legal psychology has a number of advantages over other names: First, it is sufficiently broad to cover all areas of

---

[11]In discussing this term with Bruce D. Sales, he correctly pointed out that this term might be limiting for programs offering joint psychology-law degrees (e.g., J.D./Ph.D.). Indeed, for persons with dual degrees in law and psychology, rather than being thought of as psychologists who specialize in legal studies, they may want to be identified, correctly, as having formal training in both fields.

work at the interface of psychology and law. Second, it signifies the independence—and uniqueness—of the "new" field that interfaces law and psychology (i.e., the new field is neither "psychology" nor "law," but a hybrid of both). Third, it has not been limited by any recent common usage.[12] Fourth, the term legal psychology parallels terms employed to describe other fields of psychology (e.g., biological psychology, clinical psychology, cognitive psychology, developmental psychology, etc). Fifth, and conceivably the best reason of all, people working in the area would have a common identity—they would be referred to as "legal psychologists."

It is possible that every person reading this paper has a different notion of what law and psychology is (hereinafter referred to as "legal psychology"). The reason is simple. There is no definition of the field that is generally acceptable. Curiously, even the few textbooks in the area fail to offer a definition of legal psychology. If one accepts that, conceptually at least, legal psychology can be as broad as is the law itself, then it is necessary to adopt a definition that is broad enough to include all potential realms of work done at the law and psychology interface. Furthermore, as the work in the area has demonstrated, legal psychology focuses on the law and its effects on individuals and society. Beyond that, of course, the law also is influenced by people and society. Thus, a suitably broad—yet parsimonious—definition might be as follows:

- Legal psychology is the scientific study of the effect of law on people; and the effect people have on the law. Legal psychology also includes the application of the study and practice of psychology to legal institutions and people who come into contact with the law.[13]

All laws are designed with one ultimate purpose in mind: to regulate human behavior. Contemporary definitions of psychology show that psychologists concern themselves with the study of behavior and mental processes. It follows that legal psychologists are interested in evaluating the assumptions that the law must make about human behavior, as well as studying the way in which the law responds to the changes in society that require changes in law.

---

[12]Just to emphasize the depth of the debate about what to call our field and our work, see Brigham (1999).

[13]Small (1993) offers a slightly different definition, that legal psychology is "the scientific study of human behavior relevant to laws and legal systems" (p. 687). Although this definition is useful, it may unnecessarily limit the focus of legal psychology on "human behavior" rather than on the impact or effect of law on behavior and mental processes. Similarly, legal psychology may extend beyond actual theories of human behavior. In fact, in his explanation of the definition, Small includes mental processes.

Adopting a uniform name for the field of "legal psychology," as well as a uniform definition, may help us overcome some of the confusion that surrounds the field. As trivial as it seems, this minor step may help to move those who work in the area in common directions, regardless of the specific topics on which they focus.

## THE IDENTITY OF THOSE WHO WORK IN THE FIELD OF LEGAL PSYCHOLOGY

Because of the potential breadth of topics included under the legal psychology umbrella, many people do legal psychology research or practice without realizing it. This relates to an additional concern: Because legal psychologists come from all areas of psychology, they may identify more with their traditional background in psychology than with legal psychology. For example, psychologists who work with children and families and conduct custody and access evaluations may be more likely to identify themselves as child psychologists than as legal psychologists. Although such self-characterizations may be appropriate, one would hope that psychologists who conduct at least part of their work in the legal realm would consider themselves at least "part-time" legal psychologists. By participating in professional associations of legal psychologists and completing ongoing continuing education in legal psychology, such psychologists could help ensure that they are developing the skills that enable them to carry out their work in a competent manner (see Ethical Standard 1.04, Boundaries of Competence, of the Ethical principles of psychologists and code of conduct, American Psychological Association, [APA], 1992).

Division 41 of the American Psychological Association (the American Psychology-Law Society) has approximately 3000 members currently, a greater than twofold increase from 1990, when there were approximately 1400 members. There is little doubt, however, that many APA members who are not members of Division 41 conduct some work in some area of psychology and law (e.g., assessments of legal competencies, custody and access evaluations, personal injury assessments). There is little, if any, empirical data to support my concern. However, all one need do to see my point is to review the topics of papers presented each year at the APA convention, and to notice how many papers beyond those sponsored by Division 41 could justifiably be considered legal psychology—at least as I have defined it here.

To continue to strengthen and develop, it is important that the field of legal psychology continue to attract more people—especially those who already work in the field, but who do not identify themselves, even secondarily, as legal psychologists. Therefore, steps must be taken to promote legal psychology, and to emphasize the need for applying psychological research and practice to the legal system. Division 41, in particular, has a responsibility to reach out to all people whose work falls within the broad areas of study and practice within legal psychology.

As a final indication of the degree to which the interests of people in the legal psychology community are divided, one need only consider the APA apportionment ballots and, in particular, the points allotted to Division 41. To determine the composition of council representatives for the APA Council, all members and fellows are allotted 10 points to direct to any division or state/provincial association. The results for the composition of the council representation for 1997 show that only 75 people allotted all 10 of their points to Division 41—with the majority of people allotting only 1 or 2 points to the division. The result of the apportionment is that Division 41 gets only 1 council representative for the division—out of 103 seats.[14]

## SECURING OUR PLACE IN PSYCHOLOGY

Legal psychology continues to be a secondary interest for most people who work in the area. To the extent that legal psychology is (or aspires to be) a true area of psychology, it is important to develop as a "primary" area. Although it may seem overly simplistic, one way for this to happen is to have a chapter—or a substantial portion of a chapter—in introductory psychology textbooks on legal psychology. Indeed, one commonly sees chapters or major sections of chapters in introductory psychology texts devoted to other emerging, and "newly emerged," fields such as health psychology and industrial organizational psychology. Including the field in introductory textbooks will expose all students in psychology to legal psychology, and all people teaching introductory psychology will become more familiar with the topic. As one who has taught several thousand students in introductory psychology courses, I recently have learned that textbook publishers are willing to pay close attention to the wishes of psychology instructors—especially those who can guarantee 1000 or 2000 textbooks sales annually. Thus, psychologists should lobby their textbook publishers to include chapters or major sections of introductory textbooks on legal psychology.

On a more positive note, in a recent review of education and training in legal psychology, Ogloff et al. (1996) reported that, in fact, some introductory psychology textbooks have provided some coverage of law and

[14]As of the 1998, Division 41 now has 2 council seats.

psychology (see, e.g., Lahey, 1992; Smith, 1993). Further, they note that "mainstream" textbooks in social psychology (see, e.g., Aaronson, Wilson, & Akert, 1994; Baron & Byrne, 1994; E. R. Smith & Mackie, 1995), abnormal psychology (see, e.g., D. S. Holmes, 1994; Nevid, Rathus, & Greene, 1994), and psychological assessment (see, e.g., Aiken, 1994) all provide extensive coverage of "legal" issues related to the subject. In addition to introductory psychology and mainstream psychology textbooks, Ogloff et al. also report that the number of textbooks in legal psychology per se have increased (see, e.g., Bartol & Bartol, 1994; Foley, 1993; Horowitz, Willging, & Bordens, 1998; Schuller & Ogloff, 2001; Swenson, 1993; Wrightsman, Nietzel & Fortune, 1997). These texts can serve as useful resources for psychologists and law professors who wish to introduce some coverage of legal psychology into their more mainstream courses.

Following along the "textbook exposure" line of thought, it also is useful for legal psychologists with interests in other specific areas of psychology (e.g., clinical or developmental) to encourage publishers of those textbooks to include chapters, or applications, concerning legal psychology in those areas. In all cases, though, it is important for legal psychologists to emphasize that, while their work may be discussed in relation to other areas of psychology, legal psychology is a distinct—yet highly integrated—area of psychology. Further, of course, it is important to continually emphasize that since the law is such a pervasive influence in society, for psychology to have an impact on society, it is effective for psychology to have an impact on the law.

## THE NEED TO FOCUS ON THE TRAINING AND CAREER OPTIONS OF OUR STUDENTS

There is absolutely no doubt that the future of legal psychology, whatever it holds, belongs to the students in training and those yet to come. Therefore, it is surprising and disconcerting that relatively little systematic attention has been paid to training and career issues. Melton (1987c) urged legal psychologists to "focus on 'thinking like a lawyer' and becoming a comfortable guest, if not an insider, in the legal community" (p. 293). What better way for social scientists to become comfortable in the legal community than to be trained in legal psychology, especially if the training provides structured information about the law and the legal system? A number of authors have considered the importance of training and education in psychology and law (see, e.g., Freeman & Roesch, 1992; Grisso et al., 1982; Hafemeister, Ogloff, & Small, 1990; Ogloff, 1990; Ogloff et al., 1996; Roesch, Grisso, & Poythress, 1986; Tomkins & Ogloff, 1990; Wexler, 1990).

Part of the concern for the lack of attention directed to training in legal psychology has been rectified with the National Invitational Conference on Education and Training in Law and Psychology that took place at Villanova Law School May 26–28, 1995. The Villanova Conference, as it has become to be known, was attended by approximately 60 invited people from across the field of legal psychology. The overarching purpose of the conference was to develop an agenda for legal psychology training into the 21st century, much the way the famous Boulder Conference of 1949 set the course for clinical psychology training for the remainder of the 20th century (Bersoff, et al., 1977).

The conference was broadly constituted and broadly focused, looking at education and training in legal psychology studies at all levels—undergraduate, graduate (including doctoral and dual-degree programs), practicum experiences, internship settings, postdoctoral programs, and continuing education opportunities. Although it is to soon for the products of the conference to be realized—or for its long-term impact on the field to be assessed—conference organizers and participants have written articles for the *American Psychologist* (Bersoff et al., 1997) as well as forwarded the possibility of an edited book to be published by the American Psychological Association. Further, other activities, such as the development of a series of videotapes about topics in law and psychology for use in courses, are underway. Finally, information from the conference has been presented at other meetings.

Apart from the Villanova Conference, the American Psychology Law Society's (Division 41 of the APA) Committee on Training and Careers has collected and distributed copies of course curriculum used in legal psychology courses and has developed a brochure describing the training programs available in legal psychology. The current syllabus collection, the third edition, includes almost 70 syllabi used in courses ranging from undergraduate to graduate in psychology, as well as some from law school courses on legal psychology topics.

While at long last some attention has been paid to the matter of education and training in legal psychology, little attention has been focused on career options and challenges for those who work in legal psychology. As the former Chair of the APLS/Division 41 Committee on Training and Careers from 1990 to 1994, I routinely fielded many questions from people seeking information about what kind of work is available for people with interests in legal psychology. As might be expected, most calls were from undergraduates just developing interests in the field, while other people had doctorate degrees in psychology or law degrees and were interested in developing their interests in the field. Addressing some of these needs, more recently, the Committee has developed an information booklet for students interested in pursuing a career in legal psychology.[15] Given the importance for the continued vitality of legal psychology of developing an awareness of the type of employment obtained by people in legal psychology as well as helping to carve out employment opportunities for those in the field, considerable additional attention needs to be devoted to this area in the future.

## LEGAL PSYCHOLOGISTS MUST BE SOPHISTICATED AND KNOWLEDGEABLE ABOUT THE LAW

Many people who work in the area of legal psychology lack sophisticated knowledge of the law. People have debated whether legal psychologists need to be trained formally in law (Grisso et al., 1982; Hafemeister et al., 1990; Ogloff et al., 1996; Tomkins & Ogloff, 1990). This debate has culminated in the consideration of joint-degree programs. Arguments against dual-degree training have emphasized the costs of such training and the fact that most people who work in legal psychology focus on one or two specific areas of law. Those who support dual-degree programs, by contrast, argue that while all legal psychologists do not require formal training in law, there are considerable advantages to pursuing formal training in law and psychology (Hafemeister et al., 1990). Foremost among these advantages is the ability of psychologists with law degrees to have a sophisticated understanding of the law. Indeed, many psychologists with little appreciation of law have "jumped into" legal psychology research only to produce work that is of questionable validity (see Hafemeister et al., 1990, for a discussion of this material; see also Pfeifer, 1992).

While it may not be essential for every legal psychologist to have extensive training in law, it is important that psychologists who work in the legal psychology area have an in-depth understanding of the law that pertains to their own areas of work. The most basic reason for this is that legal psychology research cannot be an effective catalyst in evaluating and changing the law if it lacks external validity and generalizability. Many years ago Konečni and Ebbeson (1979) emphasized this point in their review of the external validity of simulated jury research, writing that "Research in applied disciplines must be concerned with issues of external validity and generalizability to an unusually high degree ... What is surprising is the extent to which most studies in legal psychology have routinely ignored the external-validity problems, despite the obvious

---

[15]The syllabus collection and the careers booklet can be found on the APLS website at www.unl.edu/ap-ls

applied nature of legal psychology and the airing that the notion of external validity has received" (p. 40). Thus, having an appreciation of law and legal practice provides legal psychologists with the ability to examine the extent to which their research—and that done by others—may be externally valid.

A second reason for having a broad and in-depth understanding and appreciation of law is that is allows individuals the opportunity to identify interesting legal questions that are important for investigation by legal psychology (this point is expanded upon below).

A final reason for demanding that legal psychologists are knowledgeable about the law—especially that which is relevant to their own areas of work is that such a requirement is ethically appropriate. Ethical Standard 1.04 (Boundaries of Competence) of the "Ethical Principles of Psychologists and Code of Conduct" (APA, 1992) states that "psychologists provide services, teach, and conduct research only within the boundaries of their competence, based on their education, training, supervised experience, or appropriate professional experience." To be "competent" in work as a legal psychologist, then, one would need some expertise in law.

## WORK IN LEGAL PSYCHOLOGY MUST DEVELOP A THEORETICAL FOUNDATION

Just as some legal psychology research can be criticized for lacking legal sophistication, so, too, can it be criticized for lacking any theoretical foundation, especially from a psychological perspective. For science—including social science and, in this case, legal psychology—to develop and advance knowledge, we must develop an understanding of "why" some phenomenon in law exists. Thus, it is not enough to know *what* types of pretrial publicity affect jurors, for example, but *why* they react the way they do and *how* the media affects their decision making. Only when we develop and test theories that provide these causal explanations can we begin to fully understand the phenomenon. Furthermore, once we understand the cause of the phenomenon, we can begin to learn how the law can be revised, when necessary, to better reflect the reality of human behavior. Unfortunately, with rare exception (e.g., Wiener, 1993, 1995; Wiener & Hurt, 1997, in press; Wiener, Watts, Goldkamp, & Gasper, 1995), the vast majority of the research that has been done, and continues to be done, by legal psychologists only provides a description of "what" happens in the law, rather than providing any explanation of why or how the phenomenon exists.

Small (1993) provided a very useful analysis of the extent to which legal psychologists have failed to employ or develop psychological theories to explain the phenomena they study in the legal system. For the analysis, he considered regular articles in 28 issues of the journal *Law and Human Behavior* between 1986 and 1991. He chose that journal because it is the official journal of the American Psychology-Law Society (Division 41 of APA) and publishes work that is representative of the field. There were 150 articles, of which 105 were experimental. Small organized the 105 articles into three categories. The first (Stage I) include those articles in which "researchers simply attempt to define or describe a particular phenomenon ... usually some assumption the law makes about human behavior" (p. 690). Stage II articles were those in which "investigators construct descriptive theories that account for observed behavior" (p. 690). Finally, he defined Stage III as presenting "explanatory accounts ... to specify universal theory, independent of the domain specific mechanism" (p. 690). In terms of theory, then, articles in Small's Stage I could be termed "atheoretical," Stage II would be "partly theoretical," and Stage III would characterize articles that reflect theory (i.e., that explain causal relationships). An astounding 96 of 105 articles were merely descriptive in nature (atheoretical). A very few of the articles (9 of 105) were partly theoretical, posing descriptive theories to account for the phenomena observed. No articles were found to fall into Stage III.

There is little doubt that the work of legal psychologists has provided us with considerable information about the law, and the validity of the assumptions the law makes regarding human behavior. However, future researchers would do well to move beyond describing the law and merely testing legal assumptions. Only by applying psychological theory to the law in an attempt to explain causal relationships between the law and human behavior will we be able to advocate valid legal reforms, and to finally have a meaningful impact on the law.

As noted above, in a series of articles, Wiener and his colleagues (Wiener, 1993, 1995; Wiener & Hurt, 1997, in press; Wiener et al., 1995) have developed a model that they have termed "social analytic jurisprudence." Their model incorporates empirical psychological investigation with traditional legal analysis. The model is based on three assumptions concerning psychology's role in assisting with the development of public policy. First, the model assumes that the use of psychology as an empirical science can help study legal issues and provide useful information to courts and decision-makers. Second, legal psychologists should only participate in the debate of legal issues when they do so using results of psychological research. Finally, flowing from the first two assumptions, the model holds that the proper role of psychologists in public policy debates is as consultants and not as advocates. Although the focus of Wiener and colleagues' work has been on sexual harassment, the model can easily be applied to any number of areas of work in the field. While a review of this work is beyond the scope of the paper, I mention it here as an example of the direction our work ought to be following.

## THE NEED TO REMAIN OBJECTIVE—IN SCIENCE AND IN PRACTICE

In addition to ensuring to develop psychological theory in our work, we need conscientiously to remain objective both in our science and in our practice. As Wiener and Hurt (in press) emphasize, "The courts and legislatures are less likely to listen to the values of social scientists than to those scientists' empirical findings. It is only when psychology can offer empirically valid and reliable research findings that psychologists effectively block the court's ability to dismiss their arguments on political and ideological grounds." I am uncertain whether we are more likely to adopt dogmatic positions in our work than are others in psychology, but the fact is that there are many areas of research and practice where we have significant schisms in the field—whether it is the choice of tools for the assessment of risk for violence, the debate over recovered memories, or more mundane matters. While it is acceptable to have legitimate theoretical differences and disagreements about the interpretation of data, being dogmatic violates fundamental principles of science and does not help further our field.

In addition to the dogmatism that we see in our research (see Ogloff, 2001), a common criticism of those who testify as clinical forensic psychologists is that their opinions can be bought. While it is debatable whether and to what extent the practice of prostituting one's professional opinions occurs, the fact is that it would seem to exist in one form or another. There is inordinate pressure on forensic psychologists—particularly those in private practice—to conform their opinions to the side that retains their services. Of course, such behavior is unethical and it goes without saying that such behavior does a disservice to our profession and our credibility with the courts.

## THE FIELD OF LEGAL PSYCHOLOGY NEEDS TO EXPAND TO COVER ADDITIONAL AREAS OF LAW

Despite repeated warnings, topics covered by legal psychology remain narrow and obscure from a legal perspective. Ironically, considering the relative amount of research and writing being done, the work done early in the century, as highlighted above, showed more diversity than that which is generally being done to day. The last two editors of *Law and Human Behavior*, the official journal of the American Psychology-Law

Society (Division 41 of APA), have joined with other scholars to express their concern about the relatively narrow range of articles submitted for publication in their journal (Roesch, 1990; Saks, 1986; see also Tremper, 1987). Kagehiro and Laufer (1992), in the preface to their *Handbook of Psychology and Law*, provided a content analysis of articles published between 1966 and 1990 (depending on availability) in the most prominent journals in legal psychology. The results showed that, despite repeated concerns such as those mentioned above, the vast majority of articles published were in the areas of criminal law and criminal procedure, evidence-related concerns, jury issues, and mental health law topics.

In addition to the work of Kagehiro and Laufer (1992), Small (1993) also analyzed the areas of research of articles published in *Law and Human Behavior* between 1986 and 1991. As Small's results confirm, despite repeated calls for "broadening the discipline" (Ogloff, 1992), the majority of work in the field still falls into the areas of jury decision making and eyewitness testimony. Employing a different analysis, drawing on seven journals that publish empirical psychology and law research, Wiener, Watts, and Stolle (1993) also found that "jury decision making and eyewitness identification were the most commonly studied legal topics" (p. 88), accounting for some 60% of articles. In addition, "criminal law topics were studied far more frequently (67% ...) than civil law topics (45%)" (p. 88).

For psychology meaningfully to impact the law, legal psychologists must continue to broaden the focus of their work in the law. There really is no limit to the scope of inquiry available to legal psychologists. Indeed, to the extent the *every* law has as its purpose the control or regulation of human behavior, every law is ripe for psychological study (Ogloff, 1992). Perhaps as more psychologists now are more broadly knowledgeable about legal topics, and many have formal training in law, we can expect the areas of inquiry in legal psychology to more fully reflect the breadth of the law. Such movement in the field would, again, further help ensure its continued success.

## BECOMING LESS PAROCHIAL

As a Canadian, it is interesting for me to note how very parochial so much of the work is in the field of legal psychology (Ogloff, 2001). I suppose this is partly a function of the fact that by its very nature work in our field must be linked to laws—and laws vary among jurisdictions. Nonetheless, focusing exclusively on our legal systems prevents us from being as open as we might otherwise be to the various ways in which the law works in jurisdictions throughout the world. In addition, comparative research in our field can help determine the validity of some of the psychological principles we identify. Indeed, while the law may vary drastically across jurisdictions, we know that many principles of human behavior and mental processes are surprisingly similar.

The summer of 1999 saw the first joint meeting of the European Association of Psychology and Law (EAPL) and the APLS. The meeting was particularly well attended, with some 560 registrants from around the world. Perhaps the greatest success of the conference was to increase the awareness of registrants to the varying legal systems in the world, and to the shape of the legal psychology movement internationally. Recently, the EAPL and APLS agreed to organize another joint conference in 2003. This time, other national organizations of legal psychologists will be invited to join in to make it a truly international meeting.

## THE FIGHT AGAINST SEXISM AND ETHNOCENTRISM

In a recent chapter, Ogloff (2001), I note that for too long we have ignored sex/ethnic/cultural differences and gender roles in the phenomena we study. Without going into detail here, it is worth noting that these differences have either been ignored or blindly overlooked. Elsewhere I have written that,

> Such glaring oversight in the selection of populations and questions we consider is nothing short of shameful. Moreover, while there are obvious exceptions, the field of legal psychology has had difficulty attracting women and members of visible minorities. During my years as a member of the Executive Committee of the American Psychology-Law Society, we have engaged in many discussions of the need to increase the membership of these key groups in the society and in the leadership of the organization. We have largely failed on both counts. Only a fraction of our members are visible minorities, and women are under-represented both in the society and on the Executive Committee. (Ogloff, 2001, pp. 8–9)

As the above quotation points out, beyond considering sex/ethnic/cultural differences in the phenomena we study, it is important to have a broad representation of members of diverse groups not only working a legal psychologists, but taking on leadership roles in our societies. It is with regret that I say that it has been my experience that members of the very groups we seek to represent seem to be more likely than White males to turn down requests for service on committees or to stand for election in the society's executive committee. Doubtless this is because of the overcommitment that many of us endure, as well as a reticence to enter new arenas. Whatever the reason for the discrepancy that we see, it is something that simply must be corrected over time. The status quo is an ongoing embarrassment to us all, particularly in light of the huge diversity we see among forensic populations, particularly in North America (save for women offenders).

Finally, given that the populations with whom clinical forensic psychologists work are typically more diverse (at least ethnically and culturally so) than the mainstream populations in which we live, it is also essential that forensic psychologists be sensitive to issues arising from these diversities. At a basic level, we have a duty to ensure that our methods and practices are applicable and effective for all those populations with whom we work.

## WE MUST CONTINUE TO IDENTIFY AND SECURE FUNDING FOR THE RESEARCH AND PRACTICAL WORK IN OUR FIELD

It is easy to pay lip service to the breadth of the law and the wide range of possibilities of questions available for study by legal psychologists. Obtaining the funds necessary actually to conduct the research is considerably more difficult. This may be especially true in the realm of legal psychology where the work done does not fit neatly into either traditional psychological or legal scholarship. It has been the experience of many legal scholars that it is difficult to secure funding for their research from traditional psychology granting agencies. Likewise, agencies that fund legal scholarships have been found to be reluctant to fund social science research.

Despite the difficulty that researchers may encounter when attempting to secure funding for legal psychology research, some funding agencies have special programs for work in law and social science, mental health law, and related fields (e.g., National Institute of Justice, National Institute of Mental Health, and National Science Foundation). Furthermore, given the timeliness and importance of many topics in legal psychology, some special funding programs exist to further research in those areas (e.g., youth violence, child abuse, domestic violence). For example, the John D. and Catherine T. MacArthur Foundation has funded the large-scale Research Network on Mental Health and the Law (Appelbaum & Grisso, 1995; Grisso & Appelbaum, 1995; Grisso, Appelbaum, Mulvey, & Fletcher, 1995; Monahan & Steadman, 1996; Steadman et al., 1998; Winick, 1996). For the past 10 years, the Network has conducted comprehensive studies of legal competence, coercion, and risk assessment. In addition, the American Psychological Foundation has announced a grant funding program with the area of violence prevention as a target area for funding.

Although it is true that it may be difficult to obtain grants from traditional funding sources, many legal psychologists have found success in obtaining applied research contracts from government agencies and other bodies interested in funding applied research in the law. Such funding certainly has limitations, perticularly concerning the restriction on topics that may be studied by researchers. However, for the areas where there are funds available, applied research contracts provide a unique opportunity not only to do research, but to ensure that the research results will be seen by policymakers who have an interest in them. Indeed, it is most likely that the very party who contracts the research is interested in obtaining the results to evaluate some law or program related to the law. A definite shortcoming of contract research is that, frequently, such contracts provide that the products of the contract (e.g., research findings and reports) are owned by the party that funded the research. While this is understandable, of concern is a related clause that sometimes restricts the researcher's ability to publish or otherwise distribute the findings. Whenever possible, researchers should negotiate that such provisions be removed, as they can seriously limit the development of knowledge in a given area.

## THE NEED FOR INCREASED COMMUNICATION AND SUPPORT FOR THOSE WHO WORK IN LEGAL PSYCHOLOGY

Due to the relative recency—and obscurity—of the current legal psychology movement, there are relatively few places where more than one legal psychologist works. In academic settings, it is uncommon to have more than one person working in legal psychology in any given department. Further, it is a rare case when psychology departments, law schools, or other academic departments actively recruit legal psychologists. There is only a handful of joint-degree programs in legal psychology, and approximately 14 more that offer specialized graduate training in legal psychology (Ogloff et al., 1996). Thus, unless one works in such a program, it is unlikely that one will be exposed to a critical mass of people working in legal psychology. As a result, legal psychologists most often find themselves filling roles in departments that divide their attention from legal psychology. For example, a legal psychologist may be hired as a social psychologist and must teach social psychology courses and supervise graduate students in social psychology. Likewise legal psychologists on clinical psychology faculties often must teach clinical courses and supervise clinical graduate students in research and clinical work.

As a result of the relative isolation of legal psychologists in their work settings, opportunities for collaboration and sharing of ideas should be promoted to the extent possible by professional associations. Of course, professional meetings such as the annual APA convention and the biennial American Psychology-Law Society/Division 41 conference provide useful opportunities for those working in the field to gather, learn about one another's work, and spend time getting to know one another. In this day of the information highway and the World Wide Web, discussion lists and online services can, and have, facilitated this process. It would be beneficial for the field, though, if it were possible to arrange formal or informal visiting professor/scholar positions at those institutions with a critical mass of people working in legal psychology. Thus, scholars developing interests in legal psychology could associate with those already established in the field. Only with continued dialogue, collaboration, and collegiality can the field expand its focus and continue to grow.

## THE NEED TO INCREASE THE IMPACT OUR WORK HAS ON THE LEGAL SYSTEM

The law uses psychology like a drunk uses a lamp post—more for support than illumination. (Atributed to Loh, 1981)

Almost without a doubt, the greatest obstacle for legal psychology is that lawyers, judges, and policy makers typically have not embraced psychological findings, especially those findings that are critical of legal assumptions, unless the findings support their particular argument or position. Perhaps more disturbing is that more than 90 years ago Munsterberg (1908) stated exactly the same concern by noting that, while many fields adopted psychological findings, "The lawyer alone is obdurate. The lawyer and judge and the juryman are sure that they do not need the experimental psychologist. They do not wish to see that in this field preeminently applied experimental psychology has made strong strides ... They go on thinking that their legal instinct and their common sense supplies them with all that is needed and somewhat more ..." (p. 11).

There are two basic reasons that the law does not always make use of relevant psychological research in cases and legislation. First, lawyers, judges, and other legal policymakers may not be aware of the research that exists. Second, assuming they are aware of the relevant findings, 1they may choose not to rely upon them. When choosing not to rely on the findings, they may either question their validity, or decide that they will proceed with deliberate indifference to the findings. Thus, for psychology to have a maximum impact on the law, we must ensure that psychological findings relevant to the law find their way into the hands of lawyers, and that the findings we produce are valid and of high quality. Of course, those in the law still may ignore the findings, but the persistent development of valid findings that challenge the validity of laws or legal assumptions will be difficult to ignore over the long term. It is beyond the scope of this article to discuss research methodology, except to reiterate that legal psychology research must be externally valid to the law to be effective. The question arises, then, how best to ensure that relevant psychological research findings reach those in the legal system?

Melton (1987a) provided a useful discussion of how social science reaches the legal system and how best to "give psychology away" (pp. 493–494), and the reader is referred to Melton (1987a) to learn more about how social science finds its way into the legal system. Suffice it to say that lawyers, judges, and others in the legal system do not ready psychology journals—in my experience, they may not even know how to locate them if they had the desire. For example, in a survey of juvenile court judges and probation officers, Grisso and Melton (1987) found that they read *Psychology Today* more frequently than major law reviews, and that they were very unlikely to read any professional periodicals in psychology. Given that those in the legal system are unlikely to read articles where social scientists and mental health professionals are likely to publish, I will review Melton's suggestions for how to give psychology away. First, it is important to report relevant psychological research in sources that are accessible to those in the law. Such sources would include prestigious law reviews, practitioner journals, and the popular media. In addition, the Internet is becoming a popular medium for conveying information.

Aside from reporting research where those in the legal system will access it, psychologists would do well to use informal networks to diffuse information. Such networks could be informal or formal. Informal networks involve discussing relevant findings with people the psychologist knows in the legal system. Formal networks include professional organizations of lawyers who might be interested in a particular topic. They might also include relevant public interest groups.

The last point Melton (1987a) makes is that psychologists who attempt to have their findings make their way into the legal system must be willing to meet legal professionals on their own terms. As noted previously in this article, this requires having psychologists frame their work in legal terms and to ensure that it is legally relevant and valid.

Finally, in addition to concerns discussed above about training graduate students to become legal psychologists, it is advisable to devote considerable effort to teaching undergraduate courses in law and psychology and to teach courses in law schools that cover topics in law and psychology. Many undergraduates who take courses in law and psychology are interested in applying to law school—and many ultimately will go to law school. Of course, those already in law school will likely become lawyers. Thus, exposing future lawyers to research and practice in legal psychology may help ensure that they understand the research, and that psychological findings may make their way into the legal system.

## CONCLUSION

Although the legal psychology movement has experienced considerable growth and success in its second iteration is the 20th century, the concerns raised in the list presented here must be addressed to ensure that the movement does not wane—as it did in the first third of the century. In particular, those who work in the area of legal psychology must develop a common understanding of what, exactly, "law and psychology" or "legal psychology" is. Those in the field also should work to develop the area, and should help others whose work is relevant to the law realize the potential impact the work may have for the legal system.

In addition to "promoting" the field of legal psychology among psychologists, we must strive to ensure that the work is legally relevant and valid. To make meaningful changes to the law, though, and to promote our understanding of such phenomena in psychology, psychologists must take their work to the next plane—that which involves a theoretical conceptualization that will help explain such things as causal relationships.

For psychology to have a significant impact on the legal system, it is important that legal psychologists explore the rich questions that may be found across a broad spectrum of the law. By characterizing legal psychology questions as flowing from the law itself, rather than being a mere extension of some existing area of psychology, legal psychologists can help maximize the chance that their work will be relevant to the legal system, and may have some impact on it.

As the field develops, legal psychologists need to pay increased attention to funding sources for their work and to developing collaborations and professional networks of colleagues who share their interest. Finally, the field of legal psychology will only be able to sustain itself if the findings produced are recognized by those in the legal system and are used to influence the development of the law. Without making consistent and significant inroads into the legal system, the field will remain little more than an obscure collection of information that is disjointed and outside the realm of significance in the law. To the extent that psychology findings and the methods of psychological research may help to validate or refute the assumptions that the law makes about people and society, the findings will help further the causes of justice.

## REFERENCES

Aaronson, E., Wilson, T. D., & Akert, R. M. (1994). *Social psychology: The heart and the mind.* New York: Harper Collins.

Aiken, L. R. (1994). *Psychological testing and assessment* (8th ed.). Needham Heights, MA: Allyn & Bacon.

American Psychological Association. (1992). Ethical principles of psychologists and code of conduct. *American Psychologist, 47*, 1597–1611.

Appelbaum, P. S., & Grisso, T. (1995). The MacArthur Treatment Competence Study. I: Mental illness and competence to consent to treatment. *Law and Human Behavior, 19*, 105–126.

Baron, R. A., & Byrne, D. (1994). *Social psychology: Understanding human interaction.* Needham Heights, MA: Allyn & Bacon.

Bartol, C. R., & Bartol, A. M. (1994). *Psychology and law: Research and application.* Pacific Grove, CA: Brooks/Cole.

Bersoff, D. N., Goodman-Delahunty, J., Grisso, J. T., Hans, V. P., Poythress, N. G., Poythress, N. G., & Roesch, R. G. (1997). Training in law and psychology: Models from the Villanova Conference. *American Psychologist, 52*, 1301–1310.

Bornstein, B. H. (1999). The ecological validity of jury simulations. Is the jury still out? *Law and Human Behavior, 23*, 75–91.

Boring, E. G. (1950). *A history of experimental psychology* (2nd ed.). New York: Appleton-Century-Crofts.

Brigham, J. (1999). What is forensic psychology anyway? *Law and Human Behavior, 23*, 273–298.

Brown, M. R. (1926). *Legal psychology: Psychology applied to the trial of cases, to crime and its treatment, and to mental states and processes.* Indianapolis, IN: Bobbs-Merrill.

Burtt, H. E. (1925). Measurement of confusion between similar trade names. *Illinois Law Review, 19*, 320–342.

Burtt, H. E. (1931). *Legal psychology.* New York: Prentice-Hall.

Cairns, H. (1935). *Law and the social sciences.* London: Kegan Paul, Trench Trubner and Co.

Cattell J. M. (1895). Measurements of the accuracy of recollection. *Science, 2*, 761–766.

Diamond, S. S. (1997). Illuminations and shadows from jury simulations. *Law and Human Behavior, 21*, 561–572.

Foley, L. A. (1993). *A psychological view of the legal system.* Dubuque, IA: Wm. C. Brown.

Fox, D. R. (1999). Psycholegal scholarship's contribution to false consciousness about injustice. *Law and Human Behavior, 23*, 9–30.

Freeman, R. J., & Roesch, R. (1992). Psycholegal education: Training for forum and function. In D. K. Kagehiro, & W. S. Laufer (Eds.), *Handbook of psychology and law* (pp. 567–576). New York: Springer-Verlag.

Freud, S. (1906/1959). Psycho-analysis and the establishment of facts in legal proceedings. In J. Strachey (Ed.), *The standard edition of the complete works of Sigmund Freud, Volume 9* (pp. 103–114).

Friedman, L. M. (1985). *A history of American law* (2nd ed.). New York: Simon & Schuster.

Fulero, S. (1999). A history of Division 41 (American Psychology Law Society) A rock and roll odyssey. In D. Dewsbury (Ed.), *Unification through division: Histories of divisions of the American Psychological Association, Volume 4* (pp. 109–127). Washington, D.C.: American Psychological Association Press.

Grisso, T. (1986). *Evaluating competencies: Forensic assessments and instruments.* New York: Plenum.

Grisso, T. (1991). A developmental history of the American Psychology-Law Society. *Law and Human Behavior, 15*, 213–231.

Grisso, T., & Appelbaum, P. S. (1995). The MacArthur Treatment Competence Study. III: Abilities of patients to consent to psychiatric and medical treatments. *Law and Human Behavior, 19*, 149–174.

Grisso, T., Appelbaum, P. S., Mulvey, E. P., & Fletcher, K. (1995). The MacArthur Treatment Competence Study. II: Measures of abilities related to competence to treatment. *Law and Human Behavior, 19*, 127–148.

Grisso, T., & Melton, G. B. (1987). Getting child development research to legal practitioners: Which way to the trenches? In G. B. Melton (Ed.), *Reforming the law: Impact of child development research* (pp. 146–176). New York: Guilford.

Grisso, T., Sales, B. D., & Bayless, S. (1982). Law-related courses and programs in graduate psychology departments. *American Psychologist, 37*, 267–278.

Hafemeister, T., & Melton, G. B. (1987). The impact of social science research on the judiciary. In G. B. Melton (Ed.), *Reforming the law: Impact of child development research* (pp. 27–59). New York: Guilford.

Hafemeister, T., Ogloff, J. R. P., & Small, M. A. (1990). Training and careers in law and psychology: The perspectives of students and graduates of dual degree programs. *Behavioral Sciences and the Law, 8*, 263–283.

Hale, M. (1980). *Human science and social order: Hugo Munsterberg and origins of applied psychology*. Philadelphia: Temple University Press.

Holmes, D. S. (1994). *Abnormal psychology* (2nd ed.). New York: Harper Collins.

Holmes, O. W. (1881). *The common law*. Cambridge, MA: Harvard University Press.

Holmes, O. W. (1897). The path of the law. *Harvard Law Review, 10*, 457–478.

Horowitz, I. A., & Willging, T. E. (1984). *The psychology of law: Integrations and applications*. Toronto, Canada: Little Brown.

Horowitz, I. A., Willging, T. E., & Bordens, K. S. (1998). *Psychology and law: Integrations and applications* (2nd ed.). New York: Longman.

Hutchins, R. M., & Slesinger, D. (1928). Some observations on the law of evidence—Memory. *Harvard Law Review, 41*, 860–871.

Hutchins, R. M., & Slesinger, D. (1929a). Legal psychology. *Psychological Review, 36*, 13–26.

Hutchins, R. M., & Slesinger, D. (1929b). Some observations on the law of evidence—Consciousness of guilt. *University of Pennsylvania Law Review, 77*, 725–748.

Kagehiro, D. K., & Laufer, W. S. (1992). Preface. In D. K. Kagehiro & W. S. Laufer (Eds.), *Handbook of psychology and law* (pp. xi–xiii). New York: Springer-Verlag.

Kalman, L. (1986). *Legal realism at Yale, 1927–1960*. Chapel Hill, NC: University of North Carolina Press.

Konečni, V. J., & Ebbeson, E. B. (1979). External validity of research in legal psychology. *Law and Human Behavior, 3*, 39–70.

Lahey, B. B. (1992). *Psychology: An introduction* (4th ed.). Dubuque, IA: Wm. C. Brown.

Loh, W. D. (1981). Perspectives on psychology and Low. *Journal of Applied Social Psychology, 11*, 314–355.

Luria, A. R. (1932). *The nature of human conflicts*. W. Horsely Gantt (trans).

McCarty, D. G. (1929). *Psychology for the lawyer*. New York: Prentice-Hall.

Melton, G. B. (1987a). Bringing psychology to the legal system: Opportunities, obstacles, and efficacy. *American Psychologist, 42*, 488–495.

Melton, G. B. (Ed.). (1987b). *Reforming the law: Impact of child development research*. New York: Guilford.

Melton, G. B. (1987c). Training in psychology and law. In I. D. Weiner, & A. K. Hess (Eds.), *Handbook of forensic psychology* (pp. 681–697). New York: Wiley.

Melton, G. B. (1990). Realism in psychology and humanism in law: Psycholegal studies at Nebraska. *Nebraska Law Review, 69*, 251–277.

Melton, G. B., Monahan, J., & Saks, M. J. (1987). Psychologists as law professors. *American Psychologist, 42*, 502–509.

Melton, G. B., Petrila, J., Poythress, N. G., & Slobogin, C. (1997). *Psychological evaluations for the courts* (2nd ed.). New York: Guilford.

Monahan, J., & Loftus, E. F. (1982). The psychology of law. *Annual Review of Psychology, 33,* 441–475.

Monahan, J., & Steadman, H. J. (1996). Violent and violent people: How meterology can inform risk communication in mental health law. *American Psychologist, 51,* 931–938.

Moore, C. (1907). Yellow psychology. *Law Notes, 11,* 125–127.

Moskowitz, M. J. (1977). Hugo Munsterberg: A study in the history of applied psychology. *American Psychologist, 32,* 824–842.

Munsterberg, H. (1908). *On the witness stand: Essays on psychology and crime.* New York: Double-day, Page.

Nevid, J. S., Rathus, S. A., & Greene, B. (1994). *Abnormal psychology in a challenging world* (2nd ed.). Englewood Cliffs, NJ: Prentice-Hall.

Ogloff, J. R. P. (1990). Law and psychology in Canada: The need for training and research. *Canadian Psychology, 31,* 61–73.

Ogloff, J. R. P. (Ed.). (1992). *Law and psychology: The broadening of the discipline.* Durham, NC: Carolina Academic Press.

Ogloff, J. R. P. (1999). *Law and Human Behavior:* Reflecting back and looking forward. *Law and Human Behavior, 23,* 1–7.

Ogloff, J. R. P. (2001). Jingoism, dogmatism and other evils in legal psychology: Lessons learned in the 20th century. In R. Roesch, R. Corrado, & R. Dempster (Eds.), *Psychology in the courts: International advances in knowledge.* Amsterdam: Harwood Academic.

Ogloff, J. R. P., Tomkins, A. J., & Bersoff, D. N. (1996). Education and training in psychology and law/criminal justice: Historical foundations, present structures, and future developments. *Criminal Justice and Behavior, 23,* 200–235.

Otto, R. K., Heilbrun, K., & Grisso, T. (1990). Training and credentialing in forensic psychology. *Behavioral Sciences and the Law, 8,* 217–232.

Parker, L. C. (1980). *Legal psychology: Eyewitness testimony—Jury behavior.* Springfield, IL: Charles C. Thomas.

Paynter, H. (1920). A psychological study of trade-mark infringement. *Archives of Psychology, 42,* 8–22.

Pfeifer, J. E. (1992). Reviewing the empirical evidence on jury racism: Findings of discrimination or discriminatory findings? In J. R. P. Ogloff (Ed.), *Law and psychology: The broadening of the discipline* (pp. 331–351). Durham, NC: Carolina Academic Press.

Purcell, E. A., Jr. (1973). *The crisis of democratic theory: Scientific naturalism and the problem of value.* Louisville, KY: University Press of Kentucky.

Roesch, R. (1990). From the editor. *Law and Human Behavior, 14,* 1–3.

Roesch, R., Grisso, T., & Poythress, N. (1986). Training programs, courses, and workshops in psychology and law. In M. F. Kaplan (Ed.), *The impact of social psychology on procedural justice* (pp. 83–108). Springfield, IL: Thomas.

Roesch, R., Hart, S. D., & Ogloff, J. R. P. (1999). *Psychology and law: The state of the discipline.* New York: Kluwer Academic/Plenum.

Saks, M. (1986). The law does not live by eyewitness testimony alone. *Law and Human Behavior, 10,* 279–280.

Satin, M. I. (1994). Law and psychology: A movement whose time has come. *Annual Survey of American Law, 1994,* 581–630.

Schlegel, J. H. (1979). American legal realism and empirical social science: From the Yale experience. *Buffalo Law Review, 28,* 459–586.

Schlegel, J. H. (1980). American legal realism and empirical social science: The singular case of Underhill Moore. *Buffalo Law Review, 29,* 195–323.

Schuller, R., & Ogloff, J. R. P. (2001). *An introduction to law and psychology: Canadian perspectives.* Toronto: University of Toronto Press.

Shah, S. (1978). Dangerousness: A paradigm for exploring some issues in law and psychology. *American Psychologist, 33,* 224–238.

Small, M. A. (1993). Legal psychology and therapeutic jurisprudence. *Saint Louis University Law Journal, 37,* 675–713.

Smith, E. R., & Mackie, D. M. (1995). *Social psychology.* New York: Worth.

Smith, R. E. (1993). *Psychology.* St. Paul, MN: West.

Steadman, H. J., Mulvey, E., Monahan, J., & Robbins, P. C., Appelbaum, P. S., Grisso, T., Roth, L. H., & Silver, E. (1998). Violence by people discharged from acute psychiatric inpatient facilities and by others in the same neighborhoods. *Archives of General Psychiatry, 55,* 393–401.

Stevens, R. (1983). *Law school: Legal education in America from the 1850s to the 1890s.* Chapel Hill, NC: University of North Carolina Press.

Swenson, L. C. (1993). *Psychology and law for the helping professions.* Pacific Grove, CA: Brooks/Cole.

Tapp, J. L. (1976). Psychology and the law: An overview. *Annual Review of Psychology, 27,* 359–404.

Toch, H. (1961). *Legal and criminological psychology.* New York: Holt, Rinehart, & Winston.

Tomkins, A. J., & Ogloff, J. R. P. (1990). Training and career options in psychology and law. *Behavioral Sciences and the Law, 8,* 205–216.

Tomkins, A. J., & Oursland, K. (1991). Social and social scientific perspectives in judicial interpretations of the Constitution: A historical view and an overview. *Law and Human Behavior, 15,* 101–120.

Tremper, C. R. (1987). Sanguinity and disillusionment where law meets social science. *Law and Human Behavior, 11,* 267–276.

Twining, W. (1973). *Karl Llewellyn and the realist movement.* London: Weidenfeld and Nicolson.

Twining, W. (1985). Talk about realism. *New York University Law Review, 60,* 329–384.

Watson, J. B. (1913). Psychology as the behaviorist views it. *Psychological Review, 20,* 158–177.

Wells, G. L., Small, M., Penrod, S., Malpass, R. S., Fulero, S. M., & Brimacombe, C. A. E. (1998). Eyewitness identification procedures: Recommendations for lineups and photospreads. *Law and Human Behavior, 22,* 603–647.

Wexler, D. B. (1990). Training in law and behavioral sciences: Issues from a legal educator's perspective. *Behavioral Sciences and the Law, 8,* 197–204.

White, G. E. (1972). From sociological jurisprudence to realism: Jurisprudence and social change in early twentieth-century America. *Virginia Law Review, 58,* 999–1028.

White, G. E. (1976). *The American judicial tradition: Profiles of leading American judges.* New York: Oxford University Press.

Wiener, R. L. (1993). Social analytic jurisprudence and tort law: Social cognition goes to court. *Saint Louis University Law Journal, 37,* 503–551.

Wiener, R. L. (1995). Social analytic jurisprudence in sexual harassment litigation: The role of social framework and social fact. *Journal of Social Issues, 51,* 167–180.

Wiener, R. L. (1996). *AP/LS membership report.* Report presented to the APLS Executive Committee at the 1996 Biennial Conference in Hilton Head, South Carolina.

Wiener, R. L., & Hurt, L. E. (1997). Social sexual conduct at work: How do workers know when it is harassment and when it is not? *California Western Law Review, 34,* 53–97.

Wiener, R. L., & Hurt, L. E. (in press). An interdisciplinary approach to understanding social sexual conduct at work. *Psychology, Public Policy, and Law.*

Wiener, R. L., Watts, B. A., Goldkamp, K. H., & Gasper, C. (1995). Social analytic investigation of hostile workplace environments: A test of the reasonable woman standard. *Law and Human Behavior, 19,* 263–281.

Wiener, R. L., Watts, B. A., & Stolle, D. P. (1993). Psychological jurisprudence and the information processing paradigm. *Behavioral Sciences and the Law, 11,* 79–96.

Wigmore, J. H. (1909). Professor Munsterberg and the psychology of testimony: Being a report of the case of *Cokestone v. Munsterberg. Illinois Law Review, 3,* 399–445.

Winick, B. J. (1996). Foreword: A summary of the MacArthur Treatment Competence Study and an introduction to the special theme. *Psychology, Public Policy, and Law, 2,* 3–17.

Wrightsman, L. S., Nietzel, M. T., & Fortune, W. H. (1997). *Psychology and the legal system* (4th ed.). Pacific Grove, CA: Brooks/Cole.

# 2

# Psychological Jurisprudence

## Taking Psychology and Law into the Twenty-First Century

## JOHN DARLEY, SOL FULERO, CRAIG HANEY, AND TOM TYLER

The function of the law, of legal institutions, and of legal authorities is to regulate the behavior of citizens. If the law is to be effective in fulfilling its regulatory role, most citizens must obey most laws most of the time. While it is necessary to the effective functioning of society, public compliance with the law can by no means be taken for granted. Laws and the directives of legal authorities restrict the ability of citizens to behave as they wish. Consequently, people resist them and the acceptance of the dictates of the law is always problematic.

We want to argue that a central contribution that legal psychology can make to the field of law, which seeks to understand ways in which the rule of law can be effectively maintained, is to help to clarify how public compliance with the law can be facilitated. To foreshadow our argument, we will suggest that the current conventional wisdom, that seeks to produce compliance by imposing external controls on citizens largely through the threat of punishment, is failing. Instead, we need to turn to

JOHN DARLEY • Psychology Department, Princeton University, Princeton, New Jersey 08544-1010.    SOLOMON FULERO • Department of Psychology, Sinclair College, Dayton, Ohio 45402.    CRAIG HANEY • Department of Psychology, University of California—Santa Cruz, Santa Cruz, California 95064.    TOM TYLER • Department of Psychology, New York University, New York, New York 10003.

creating a society in which people willingly abide by the laws. The latter course involves the socialization of individuals into law-abidingness; it also involves creating a body of laws that people will willingly obey.

As this suggests, we believe that psychologists can expand the understanding of the motivations for human behavior that informs the thinking of legal authorities. The effort to do so reflects the development of a "psychological jurisprudence". Psychological jurisprudence involves the application of psychological knowledge to a core issue within the law. Of course, psychology has always been central to law, since "Laws embody theories of behavior. Legal rules, doctrines, and procedures necessarily reflect basic assumptions about human nature" (Haney, 1982, p. 191). Our goal is to make these assumptions consistent with modern psychological knowledge. Doing so is central to the goal of psychology to use psychological knowledge as the basis for legal change (Haney, 1980, 1993).

We believe that a better understanding of the psychology of human motivation is of great interest to legal authorities, to members if the legal profession, and to those working within legal institutions such as the courts, the police, and prisons. During the last several years all of these legal actors have expressed concern about their inability to effectively secure citizen compliance with the law.

Examples of the policy problems arising out of difficulties securing compliance abound. One set of problems relate to the difficulty of securing the acceptance of judicial decisions in matters as diverse as child support payments and dispute resolution decisions. Another set of problems involves difficulties gaining public compliance with laws ranging in scope from drug laws to income tax rules. Other problems stem from the inability to effectively change the future behavior of those who come before the law because of past illegal actions. Still others are linked to an inability to effectively manage the problems of the mentally ill through civil and criminal commitment. These many problems involved in implementing laws have led to widespread calls from legal authorities and law scholars for social science help in understanding how to secure the effective rule of law.

We view this call from legal authorities as an important opportunity for psychologists to put forward a new psychological perspective on people's relationship to society and to social rules—a "psychological" model of jurisprudence. The concerns being expressed by legal authorities suggest that the current models of the motivations that shape people's behavior are not providing legal authorities with an adequate basis for effective social regulation.

Our call for increased attention to psychological jurisprudence is linked to a more complete model of human motivation that is based upon a broader psychology of the person. Our efforts to develop such a model build upon the prior efforts of psychologists and other social scientists to speak to this same question of human motivation (see Cohn & White, 1990; Krislov et al, 1966; Melton, 1985; Tapp & Levine, 1977).

The idea of a complete "psychological" jurisprudence can potentially have many facets. Some are linked to an understanding of human motivation, others to an understanding of human cognition and decision-making. Our comments here will focus on issues of human motivation. However, we believe that the same core concept of psychological jurisprudence that we are applying to motivation in this analysis has implications for many other areas of law and psychology. In each area the law benefits from being guided by a complete and accurate model of the psychology of the person. Psychological jurisprudence is the application of such models to important areas of the law.

Psychological jurisprudence is also a distinctly empirical perspective on the problems presented by the law. It argues that our conception of the person should be based upon research about people's motivation, cognition, and decision-making. Like psychology more generally, the application of psychology to jurisprudence is an effort to define human nature through systematic and scientific methods of study. Our long-term goal is to establish a role for empirical findings in shaping the law. Like the proponents of the earlier legal realism movement, we argue that the roots of effective legal doctrine must lie in an accurate understanding of the nature of the social world. Psychological jurisprudence carries this basic premise further by taking advantage of the methodological skills of psychology.

## DETERRENCE: THE STANDARD APPROACH

When we consider possible motivations for people's law-related behavior, whether public or private, we can draw upon the extensive social psychological literature on the factors shaping people's behavior. Based upon the field theory model originally developed by Kurt Lewin, social psychologists usually think of behavior as being generated from two core motivations. The first is the set of forces exerted on the person by the external contingencies in the environment; while the second involves the motives and perceptions that the person brings to the situation. In Lewin's famous equation, behavior is viewed as a function of the person and the environment ($B=f(P,E)$).

Historically, it strikes us that those concerned with producing compliance with the law have been enthusiastic manipulators of the environment! That is, those concerned with producing compliant behavior have concerned themselves with shaping the environmental contingencies in a particular way, by moves that manipulate the impact of anticipated gains and/or anticipated losses. Calculation of each factor involves an assessment of the likelihood of potential gains and losses, as well as an evaluation of their expected utility (the amount to be gained or lost). This now is the classical subjective expected utility theory; taken together these calculations combine to tell people whether engaging in some action is likely to be beneficial to their personal self-interest.

The idea that people's behavior with respect to the law is shaped by calculations of expected gain and loss is the core premise of rational choice theory (Blumstein, Cohen, and Nagin, 1978). Within legal circles, the model is referred to as the "deterrence" or "social control" model of behavior and it seems to us that it is this model of the person that dominates law and public policy at this time. It is the model that comes naturally to mind to code drafters who are contemplating statutory drafting. To regulate behavior, the rational choice model focuses upon adjusting criminal sanctions to the needed level so that the expected losses associated with law breaking will lessen the likelihood that people will break the law. In the context of law, this model is referred to as the social control model of law-related behavior. This model suggests that the task of those drafting the law is to decide which acts should be prevented, and then to specify adequate penalties, generally fines or prison terms, so that the prohibited behavior is rarely enacted.

What if an unacceptable frequency of the prohibited behavior continues to be committed? There is an easy remedy within this model; if the observed rate of criminal behavior is thought to be high, the remedy is to increase the sentence for that criminal behavior, to increase the expected disutility of the prohibited actions so that people who would otherwise commit the behavior will be deterred. The task is to get the magnitude of the punishment adjusted to an appropriate level. As Bentham says: "If the apparent magnitude, or rather value of [the] pain be greater than the apparent magnitude or value of the pleasure or good he expects to be the consequence of the act, he [the average citizen] will be absolutely prevented from performing it" (Bentham, 1962, p. 396). Of course, the actual enactment of such an approach is more complex, and involves adjusting criminal justice system resources to change the likelihood of detection for committing a crime, the likelihood of conviction, and the severity of punishment.

The social control model is the primary model of human motivation that has guided the recent efforts of the American legal system to manage society. The application of this model of human motivation to the issue of social control has had dramatic effects on the nature of American society. Consider the case of the American prison population (Haney & Zimbardo, 1998). Because of the belief that crime is deterred by the threat and/or experience of punishment, a large number of American citizens have been convicted and sentenced to spend time in American prisons. Today the United States is a world leader in the proportion of its citizens it holds in prison.

Does a social control model work? Some research supports the suggestion that variations in the perceived certainty and severity of punishment do shape people's compliance with the law. In particular, people's behavior is often, although not always, found to be shaped by their estimate of the likelihood that, if they disobey the law, they will be caught and punished (see Nagin & Paternoster, 1991; Paternoster, 1987, 1989; Paternoster & Iovanni, 1986; Paternoster, Saltzman, Waldo, & Chiricos, 1983).

Although research supports the basic premise of the deterrence model, it also suggests that estimates of the likelihood of being caught and punished have, at best, a minor influence on people's behavior. For example, MacCoun (1993) estimates that about 5% of the variance in people's use of illegal drugs is explained by their estimates of the likelihood of being caught and punished for rule-breaking. In other words, research findings suggest that people's compliance with the law is not effectively explained by the measurement of the risks associated with law-breaking behavior (for a review examining what might be called "the mechanics of deterrence theory, see Robinson & Darley, 1997). As a result, social control strategies based primarily on a deterrence model of human behavior have had at best limited success (Ross, 1982; Tyler, 1997).

An observer can see a good deal of evidence that deterrence theory is being drawn on by legislatures in their desperate search for ways to control what they perceive to be an "out of control" crime problem. Increasing the severity of criminal sentences or passing "three strikes" laws are common examples of the effort to control crime (see Tyler & Boeckmann, 1997).

One approach to the problems of deterrence is to try to fix the deterrence model. Recently, such arguments have led to the idea of targeted deterrence strategies. One targeted strategy targets people. Ayres and Braithwaite (1992), for example, suggest that societies should first approach citizens by appealing to their moral values. They can, by doing so, isolate the small group of citizens unable to respond to such an appeal. Those people should subsequently be the focus of surveillance and social control. This allows authorities to concentrate their resources on those people likely to need social control. A second targeted strategy targets situations. Sherman (November, 1998) argues that the current deployment of police resources is more strongly shaped by political clout than it is by crime rates. As a consequence, police officers do not most heavily patrol the highest crime areas. He suggests that a greater effort is needed to put surveillance where the crime problem lies. Both of these strategies accept the basic deterrence argument and suggest that the issue is how to more effectively implement deterrence.

Thinking more broadly about situational influences on behavior. Another approach to the problem of social control is to try to encourage the legal system to think about the implications of the psychological model underlying deterrence theory. That model suggests that people are motivated by the situations in which they live. That is, it places the force of motivation within the situations that people live in, rather than in the characteristics of people. Because of this model, legal authorities believe that they can alter behavior by changing the nature of the immediate social environment. Put in more police officers, for example, and crime will decline.

As Haney points out, however, the psychological model used by the legal system seems curiously one-sided. While legal authorities believe that they can shape people's behaviors by manipulating the environment, they simultaneously believe that people's behavior is their own personal responsibility. When a person commits a crime the legal system places the responsibility for that crime on that person's psychological dispositions (Haney, 1982, 1999). The law, in other words, is based upon a theory of psychological individualism that views law-breaking as the result of personal dispositions. An alternative view, more consistent with the deterrence model, is to see law-breaking as the result of environmental pressures. If people live in environments that encourage crime, we might argue, they will commit crimes. The same person, put in an environment with different contingencies, will be a productive and law-following citizen.

Haney argues that psychologists should argue for more awareness of the "contextual" influences on human behavior (also see Haney & Zimbardo, 1998). This approach has the virtue of accepting the basic premises of the rational choice model, that people are influenced by the contingencies of the situation, but changing the social implications of that model. Instead of using that model of human motivation as a basis for a system of social control, the same model can be used as an explanation for human action.

Once we accept this broader contextual model of human behavior, our focus is naturally turned to the need for systematic efforts to eliminate poverty and substandard living conditions. If people are living in favorable social environments, in which they have economic opportunities and can live without the fear of violence, their behavior will be shaped by those contingencies away from engaging in criminal activity. Research supports this perspective by showing that the inability to find employment and the accompanying problem of poverty is one of the best predictors of engaging in criminal behavior.

## PSYCHOLOGICAL JURISPRUDENCE

Despite the efforts to improve the use of the deterrence model that we have outlined, we find signs that there is an increasing questioning about whether this model is, in fact, fundamentally flawed. If so, then we need to rethink the model of human motivation that we are applying to the law. To address the problems posed by the legal system, we need to develop a broader model of motivation. A psychological jurisprudence approach to this need can do so by expanding the scope of our conception of possible motivating factors to be more consistent with psychological models of the person.

Our expanded model of the person leads to an examination of a second type of factor that social psychologists view as central to the determination of people's behavior. That factor is the set of internal values that shape people's feelings about what is ethical or appropriate to do. We will focus on two such values: the belief that following the rules is the morally appropriate thing to do and the belief that rules are legitimate and ought to be obeyed.

## THE ROLE OF MORALITY AND LEGITIMACY IN PRODUCING LAW-ABIDINGNESS

Our argument is that the influence of these values on citizen behavior provides an alternative model upon which an effective legal system can be created and maintained. Further, we would argue that this model is a uniquely social psychological model. It builds upon the recognition by social psychologists that people develop internal values. These values are distinct from contemporaneous judgments of self-interest. Further, they exercise an important independent influence on people's behavior. Social values represent people's sense of what is ethically and morally appropriate behavior.

The concept of social values is nicely captured in Hoffman's comment on the development of moral values. He suggests that: "The legacy of both Sigmund Freud and Emile Durkheim is the agreement among social scientists that most people do not go through life viewing society's moral norms as external, coercively imposed pressures to which they must submit. Though the norms are initially external to the individual and often in conflict with his desires, the norms eventually become part of his internal motive system and guide his behavior even in the absence of external authority. Control by others is thus replaced by self-control" (Hoffman, 1977, pp. 85–86).

This quote articulates a central feature of social values—that their influence on people's behavior separates from the influence of factors in the external environment. Values become a part of the person and lead them to exercise self-regulation over their behavior. As a consequence, people do not so much comply with the law as they accept and consent to it, deferring to law and legal authority because they feel it is the right thing to do. In such a situation it is not necessary to shape people's behavior by threatening them with punishment for wrong-doing. People are taking the responsibility for following rules onto themselves. They do so if they feel that the law is reasonable and fair, so that they feel that it makes sense to them to be involved with legal authorities, to "sign on" to participation in society and acceptance of its rules. They then become willing to be governed by law and take on the responsibility for following laws and obeying the directives of legal authorities.

A recognition of the role of internal values is shaping law-related behavior suggests the possibility of a value-based perspective on people's behavior. That perspective emphasizes the importance of developing and sustaining a value climate, a "legal" or "civic" culture, in which people abide by the law because they feel it is the right thing to do.

This perspective importantly inverts the question that the legal system asks of psychology. Psychology is asked "how can the legal system bring people into compliance with the law?" The correct answer, we suggest, is threefold: (1) to create a set of laws that embody the moral intuitions of the citizens; (2) to create a legal authority that people trust, so that they accept its pronouncements as guides to morally proper behavior; and (3) to create a set of law enforcing procedures that give the citizens the respect that enables them to regard themselves as valued members of the community, even when legal decisions go against their interests.

Such a perspective represents an important program of action for legal psychologists to articulate and advocate within the legal community. It represents an important contribution that social and cognitive psychologists can make to our understanding of how society can effectively regulate citizen behavior, maintain social order, and promote an effective and efficient society.

As we have noted, there are two key social values central to a law-abidingness perspective. The first is the belief that it is morally right to follow the law. This judgment is linked to people's assessment that the behaviors prohibited by law are contrary to moral values. For example, murder is not simply illegal. Most people also believe that murder is morally wrong. Even if murder were suddenly made legal most people would not commit murders because murdering someone would still be contrary to their own sense of what is right and wrong.

The second key value is the belief that it is part of a person's duty as a citizen to accept legal rules and obey the directives of legal authorities. If citizens believe that legal authorities are legitimate, they regard them as entitled to be obeyed. In such a situation, they obey laws because they regard deferring to social authorities as part of the obligations associated with citizenship. As with morality, they view following rules issued by legitimate authorities as the appropriate social behavior. If, for example, a police officer tells a citizen to do something, for example, to pull to the side of the road or stop their car, the citizen typically accepts this directive. They regard it as appropriate for police officers to direct citizen behavior, and they follow these directives without requiring an explanation or justification. Further, they follow those directives without thinking about whether they will be punished for failure to comply.

These findings suggest that legal codes need to be in general accord with the shared conceptualization of right and wrong that exists among citizens (Darley & Zanna, 1982). In addition, legal authorities need to create and maintain their legitimacy in the eyes of the public. If citizens believe that legal authorities are legitimate and entitled to be obeyed, they obey laws because they regard deferring to social authorities as part of the obligations associated with citizenship. As with morality, they view following rules issued by legitimate authorities as the appropriate social behavior. In other words, it is not only important that citizens follow legal directives. It is also important that they do so without thinking about whether they will be punished for failure to comply.

Our argument is that, although the threat of punishment is always in the background when dealing with legal authorities, most people accept the decisions of those authorities not because they fear them, but because they view their actions as legitimate. Studies of Americans find that people's feelings of obligation to obey the police and the courts are generally quite high (Tyler, 1990), even in the face of widespread expressions of dissatisfaction with the law and with legal authorities (Tyler, 1997a; 1998, in press-c).

What could be said to a hard-headed deterrence theorist that might lead them to take these ideas seriously? What might demonstrate that these social values matter? We can examine this issue by testing their role in shaping compliance with the law. Tyler (1990) does so in a study of citizen's everyday acceptance of the law. He finds that both morality and legitimacy have an effect on compliance that is: (1) separate from the influence of risk assessments and (2) stronger than the impact of risk assessments. Other studies support this finding by demonstrating the important role of both moral values (Grasmick & Bursik, 1990; Grasmick & Green, 1980) and legitimacy (Beetham, 1991; Suchman, 1995) on reactions to law and legal authorities. These studies provide preliminary evidence that a law abidingness model can lead to a viable legal order (also see Tyler, 1997b; 1997c).

The law abidingness perspective directs our attention to two key issues: the socialization of moral values and feelings of obligation in individual citizens and the problems associated with sustaining a legal culture among adults. Put another way, we need to be concerned with creating citizens who respect the law, and legal authorities and laws that are capable of sustaining that respect. We will address these issues below.

## VALUE SOCIALIZATION

Developmental psychologists link to development of social values to the socialization experience of the child. Most children's basic orientation toward society and social institutions is most profoundly shaped during the early years of their lives, through their experiences with their families and school.

The study of moral value socialization suggests that a central factor shaping whether children take on key moral values is the relationship with their parents. Through mechanisms of identification and internalization, children develop a personal commitment to following moral rules, and link that commitment to their sense of themselves and their estimates of their self-worth. Thereafter the failure to follow moral rules leads to feelings of guilt, a negative emotional state that reflects a person's feeling that they have failed to act as they should. Of course, the form of moral values changes over time, and people can change their views about both what is morally right and why they should be concerned with following moral rules over the course of their lifetimes.

Research suggests that a second factor shaping the moral development of children and adolescents is peer interaction over issues of fairness, justice, sharing, and blame. This is particularly true if the moral discourse in these interactions is guided by a teacher or another adult. It is in these settings that the children learn the general moral rules involving harmful intents, responsibility for accidents, and other concepts relevant to the moral order. They also learn the conceptual structure linking these constructs into a unified system that determines which actions are moral, which immoral (Darley & Schultz, 1990).

The study of the development of views about the legitimacy of authorities leads to a focus on political socialization. Like the literature on moral socialization, the literature on political socialization suggests that basic orientations toward law and legal authorities develop early in life (Greenstein, 1965; Hess & Torney, 1967; Hyman, 1959; Merelman, 1986; Niemi, 1973). Children learn a sense of responsibility to obey rules and to accept the directives of legal authorities, authorities that they view themselves as obligated to obey. As with their moral values, people's feelings about obligation evolve throughout life (Tapp & Levine, 1966), however the basic feeling of obligation to authorities is rooted in childhood socialization.

Key to the success of a strategy of social regulation based upon law abidingness is the appropriate socialization of children. The childhood socialization process is the time during which basic social values develop and take on an independent role in shaping children's behavior. That role is evident as early as the teenage years, during which law abidingness is found to be linked to both moral values (Blasi, 1980) and to feelings of obligation toward legal authorities (Tyler, 1990).

Not all children learn social values. This is illustrated most clearly by the literature on moral socialization. That literature makes clear that at least some children are socialized in ways that minimize the development of moral values. Their socialization is characterized by inconsistent physical discipline (Blasi, 1980). It leads to a personality that is not guided by moral concerns, and to behavior that flows from instrumental judgments about the potential gains and costs associated with rule following and rule breaking. Similarly, children may not learn to respect and trust legal authorities. They may learn to fear those authorities and to regard them as adversaries and agents of external control.

A law abiding approach would not be possible with citizens who lack social values, since they do not have internal moral values or feelings of obligations that lead to law abidingness. Hence, the law-abiding society depends upon the successful socialization of most citizens. If this is accomplished legal authorities can then depend upon the voluntary deference of most citizens, most of the time. Such behavior allows society to function efficiently, with legal authorities directing their coercive resources at the small minority of citizens lacking in social values. If, however, that group becomes too large, it would rapidly overwhelm the ability of legal authorities to effectively implement social regulations.

## SUSTAINING A LEGAL CULTURE: THE MORALITY AND LEGITIMACY OF THE LEGAL SYSTEM

Irrespective of how they emerge from childhood, citizens live long adult lives. During those adult lives their social values continue to be shaped by the events of their society, as well as by their own personal and television-based experiences with the law. Those experiences can facilitate a continued respect for the law, or they can damage, shatter, or destroy citizen beliefs that the law and legal authorities embody values that citizens ought to support and obey. There are a number of requirements for a legal system to maintain the respect of citizens. First, to sustain its moral authority, the law must generally be consistent with people's shared sense of morality. If it is not, then people's desire to do what is morally right does not lead them to support legal authorities and obey the law. The laws must reflect the moral sensibilities of the citizenry.

## CRIMINAL CODES AND CITIZENS' MORALITY

Tyler (1990) finds that people generally view illegal behavior to also be immoral. However, in a more complex analysis Robinson and Darley (1995) demonstrate that there are many areas of law in which differences exist between law and public morality. These discrepancies suggest a potential problem for a law abidingness approach. They indicate areas in which law abidingness cannot be enhanced by appealing to moral values. We next illustrate some of the areas of conflict.

This model suggests the value of using an approach such as that of Robinson and Darley (1995) to identify areas in which the rule of law may be more shaky and problematic. These areas are likely to be those in which the public views law and divergent from their sense of moral correctness. Underlying such an analysis is an effort to examine the citizen's sense of morality and justice and to contrast it to the justice rules found in formal criminal codes. Psychologists have conducted a number of studies to understand the sense of morality. One such effort is that of Robinson and Darley (1995). Another is the work of Finkel (1995), who examines "commonsense" notions of law and justice among members of the public.

These efforts are consistent with the more general recent trend within law and social science to examine the "legal consciousness" of people within American Society (Ewick & Silbey, 1998; Flanagan & Longmire, 1996; Hamilton & Sanders, 1992; Haney, 1997; Merry, 1990). Further, such everyday notions of justice and morality need to be compared to both the actual law "on the books" and to the law that the public believes exists "on the books" (see Rossi & Berk, 1997).

The effort to understand people's views about the morality of formal laws involves studying two issues. The first is people's views about morality. The second are the formal laws governing behavior. Studies of the formal law in the United States have the problem that many criminal penalties are decided on a state by state basis. Consequently, there can be fifty different penalties for the same crime. So whether the citizen and the code's perception of right and wrong is in conflict with one another at first glance would need to be investigated on a state by state basis. Happily for our purposes a large majority of states have based their criminal code in whole or in part on the Model Penal Code, which was a modernized and unified code drafted by the influential American Law Institute in the 1960s.

It is useful to contrast citizens' intuitions with the Model Penal Code for two reasons: first because it is likely to be the code in force in most jurisdictions, and second because the code drafters settled some issues at the level of general principle and allowed those principles to dictate many sections of the code. We can therefore ask whether those principles, thought by the code drafters to be modern and rational, are in accordance with the direction of common sense.

## ATTEMPTED CRIMES

In one such study, psychologists (Darley, Sanderson, & LaMantha, 1996) examined the treatment of the concept of criminal attempt. The question at issue is this: When has a person come close enough toward committing a crime so that he has committed a criminal action, and what should the penalty for that action be? The model penal code (1962) holds that a person deserves punishment when the person has "formed a settled intent" to commit a crime, a subjectivist standard that focuses on the person's criminal intent. In keeping with the view that intent is what matters, the model penal code assigns the same penalty to attempt as it would to the completed offense. The model penal code, in other words, criminalizes quite early in the steps leading up to the crime and punishes the attempt quite severely. The older common law standard was vastly different: it did not criminalize attempt until the actor was in what was called "dangerous proximity" to the crime (the would-be burglar had broken into the store, for instance) and punished attempt to a lesser degree than the completed offense.

How do ordinary people think about attempt? Do they follow the subjectivist stance of the model penal code or do they hold the older common law view? Research findings suggest that people's intuitions are closest to the older common law formulation. They assign mild punishments to a situation in which a person communicates the intent to commit a crime, in which the person has decided to commit the crime and tells a friend that he will do it. They also assign mild punishments to a situation in which the person also goes to examine the premises that he/she plans to burgle. However, the punishments people assign for a "crime" show a sharp increase when the person finally reached the point of "dangerous proximity to the crime". Interestingly, even then the punishments they assign are nowhere near as severe as the penalties assigned to the completed offense. One way of summarizing this is to say that people do not accept the subjectivist perspective that regards the intent to do an action as the moral equivalent of doing the action.

## RAPE AND SEXUAL INTERCOURSE

In other studies psychologists have found areas in which changes in community standards may have created a discrepancy between the formal law and community opinion. The model penal code, drafted during the 1950s, assigns a very serious punishment to consensual intercourse with an underage partner. Citizens see this behavior as much less serious (Robinson & Darley, 1995). Further, the formal legal code mitigates the sentence for an offender if their underage partner has a history of promiscuity, and citizen respondents do not.

## OMISSIONS: FAILING TO HELP

In Anglo-American law, no penalty is imposed for failing to help a stranger, even if that stranger's life is at risk, and the help could be given at no risk to the helper. Studies of public views, however, suggest that people expect strangers to intervene to help when a person's life is in danger, and think that failure to do so is criminal and deserves a minor penalty.

This area of law also illustrates the problem of making generalizations about the relationship between public views and the formal law. While the discrepancy we have outlined exists when public views are compared to the model penal code, both Rhode Island and Wisconsin have rejected the model penal code recommendation of no liability in such cases, and imposed a duty to rescue on their citizens. The actions of those states may represent an effort to bring the formal law into line with public feelings about morality.

## THE CRIMINALIZATION OF EVERYTHING

As Coffee (1991, p. 193) points out, "the dominant development in substantive federal criminal law over the last decade has been the disappearance of any clearly definable line between civil and criminal law." This has occurred for a number of reasons, among them the convenience of the enforcing authorities. If, for instance, citizens provide false information on one of the thousands of forms they fill out for the federal government, then they may have committed a crime. This is true, irrespective of whether the errors were made with a criminal intent.

Coffee (1991) rather eloquently tells us why the blurring of the criminal law-civil law border is harmful. "This blurring of the border between tort and crime predictable will result in injustice, and ultimately will weaken the efficacy of the criminal law as a instrument of social control. ... To define the proper sphere of the criminal law, one must explain how its purposes and methods differ from those of tort law. Although it is easy to identify distinguishing characteristics of the criminal law- e.g. the greater role of intent in the criminal law, the relative unimportance of actual harm to the victim; the special character of incarceration as a sanction, and the criminal law's greater reliance on public enforcement- none of these is ultimately decisive. Rather, the factor that most distinguishes the criminal law is its operation as a system of moral education and socialization. The criminal law is obeyed not simply because there is a legal threat underlying it, but because the public perceives its norms to be legitimate and deserving of compliance.

We have outlined many examples of discrepancies between public views about particular types of wrongdoing and the formal law about such acts. It is also true that the public has more general views about the discrepancy between the formal law and their sense of right and wrong. A famous example of such a perceived divergence is the public's general belief that the courts are too easy on criminals. In other words, the public believes that people do not receive the morally appropriate punishment for many crimes. Instead, they receive too little punishment. So, again, legal code violations are punished in a way that citizens think is not appropriate.

## Code and Citizen Disconnects: Consequences and Cures

Part of our argument is that there is a dangerous problem created when the criminal codes and community standards conflict. To illustrate one aspect of the problem, consider an example of a recent area of law that has struggled with problems of the inconsistency of law with people's moral values: American drug policy. Although drug use is illegal, many citizens do not view the use of drugs as immoral. Consequently, there is no moral force leading those citizens to abide by the law.

The consequences of this initial disagreement with one law can generalize. As the law enforcement system spends more time eradicating marijuana in Western countries, the citizens become angered. Mines are planted and skirmishes take place between growers and sheriffs. As local citizens are tried and sent to jail for growing marijuana, the courts are increasingly seen as an instrument of oppression. Hence, the effort to enforce laws that the public does see as representing their moral code leads to a general radicalization of citizens and a rejection of the general law enforcement system. These problems remind us of the prohibition era of earlier days. Efforts to enforce the law against alcohol consumption led to widespread graft among "honest" citizens, to the development of entire "criminal" industries, and to the growth of gangs and gang violence.

How might legal authorities respond to a public belief that the law is inconsistent with citizen moral values? One approach is to seek to correct misconceptions. In the case of the courts being "too easy" on crime, studies suggest that in fact court sentences are very close to those that the public thinks are appropriate. In other words, there is no actual discrepancy, only a perceived one. The problem arises not from facts, but from misconceptions. Apparently, this misconception is generated, at least in part, by the way crime is reported in the mass media. Here education may be the best strategy.

Another approach to discrepancies between the formal law and public views is to seek to create a moral consensus in favor of the law. For example, after early efforts to diminish drug use by threats and long prison terms were unsuccessful greater effort was placed upon trying to create a feeling that drug use was morally wrong. Through campaigns such as "just say no to drugs" an effort was made to label drug use as morally wrong. In earlier campaigns against drug use lurid films were shown connecting the use of drugs to "junkies", "rape", "permissiveness", and "social ruin". If successful in developing beliefs among the public that drug use is morally wrong, those beliefs, once developed, provide a moral justification for law prohibiting the use of drugs. They also provide an additional motivation discouraging drug use.

Another recent example involves the effort to ban cigarette smoking in public indoor spaces. Citizens were quite ambivalent about whether cigarette smoking should be illegal when the evidence only suggested that smoking harmed the smoker. Given general American feelings that people are morally responsible for managing harm to themselves, it seemed wrong to make smoking illegal. When evidence of "second hand harm" from smoking developed, however, the case for laws restricting smoking became much stronger, since smoking was also a harm to other people. This evidence, however strong or weak it might be, supports the moral feeling that smoking should be prohibited when strangers are around.

## IRREDUCIBLE MORAL CONFLICTS

Sometimes legal authorities cannot rely on or create a moral consensus behind the law. This occurs within societies that are complex enough to contain communities that are in sharp moral disagreement with one another. In this situation, there can be no public consensus about what should be allowed and what should be illegal. In this country, when abortions were "illegal", many thought this law was morally wrong. Later, when abortions were declared by the Supreme Court to be a legal right, many others thought this policy was morally wrong.

When faced with such value differences, legal authorities cannot rely upon moral values as a basis for the acceptance of law. In this type of situation, the legitimacy of law and legal authorities becomes the key issue shaping public behavior.

### SUSTAINING A LEGAL CULTURE: THE LEGITIMACY OF LEGAL AUTHORITIES

As we have noted, sometimes legal authorities cannot rely upon or create a moral consensus behind the law. In such situations they rely upon the public view that they are legitimate authorities and ought to be obeyed. For example, when the Supreme Court declared abortion to be a legal right, it made a decision that many citizens thought was morally wrong. Yet, most citizens deferred to the decision. Why? Because they view the Supreme Court as a legitimate social institution whose decisions ought to be obeyed.

The belief that legal authorities are legitimate and entitled to be obeyed provides an alternative basis for the viability of law. As citizens the people within a society learn that they should obey legal and political authorities. They defer to those authorities because the authorities are entitled to make decisions about the appropriateness of behavior in particular situations (Kelman & Hamilton, 1989). For example, army officers are entitled to order soldiers into combat, just as political officials are entitled to direct citizens to join the army; to pay taxes, etc. Studies show that those citizens who view authorities as legitimate more willingly defer to their decisions (Tyler, 1990).

Legitimacy provides greater and more reliable authority to legal officials than does morality, since they have discretionary authority to decide what is appropriate. Within the scope of their prescribed roles, the police and courts make decisions and citizens believe that they ought to obey those decisions. Because legitimacy invests authorities with discretionary authority, it is a more flexible form of social value upon which to base the operation of the legal system. With morality, the discretion rests with citizens, who decide whether or not the law corresponds to their moral values.

The legitimacy of authorities is an especially promising basis for the rule of law because research suggests that it is not linked to agreement with the decisions made by legal authorities. If people viewed as legitimate those authorities who make decisions with which they agree, it would be difficult for legal authorities to maintain their legitimacy, since they are required to make unpopular decisions and deliver unfavorable outcomes.

Fortunately, from the perspective of legal authorities, studies suggest that legitimacy is linked to the fairness of the procedures used by authorities to make decisions (Lind and Tyler, 1975; Thibaut & Walker, 1975; Tyler, 1990, in press-a; Tyler, Boeckmann, Smith, & Huo, 1997; Tyler & Smith, 1997). They show that legal authorities can maintain their legitimacy by making decisions ethically (for some possible limits of this model, see Haney, 1991, and Tyler, in press-b).

The procedural justice model directs the study of legitimacy and obligation to the feelings, needs, and concerns of the people who deal with legal authorities. If those people believe that the legal authorities are exercising authority in fair ways, they are more likely to defer to those authorities. This is true for reactions to personal experiences with legal authorities (Tyler, 1990; Tyler, Casper, & Fisher, 1989). It is also true when people are evaluating national level political and legal authorities like the Supreme Court (Tyler, 1994; Tyler & Mitchell, 1994).

Perhaps most importantly, from the perspective of the legal system, a number of recent studies link judgments about procedural fairness to the willingness to both accept particular legal decisions (Kitzman & Emery, 1993; Lind, Kulik, Ambrose, & de Vera Park, 1993; Wissler, 1995) and to generally follow laws and legal rules (Kim & Mauborgne, 1993; Sparks, Bottoms, & Hay, 1996; Tyler, 1990). Procedural justice is found to play an especially important rule in securing compliance over time (Dillon & Emery, 1996; Paternoster, Brame, Bachman, & Sherman, 1997; Pruitt, Pierce, McGillicuddy, Welton, & Castrianno, 1993). It is clear that people's behavioral reactions to law and legal authorities are heavily influenced by their assessments of the fairness of legal procedures.

Further, studies of procedural justice judgments themselves indicate that when making them people are strongly influenced by the respect and dignity that they are accorded by authorities (Tyler & Lind, 1992). Since all citizens can, and should, be treated with dignity and respect by legal authorities, these findings suggest the viability of a procedural approach to managing social conflict.

## Law Abidingness as a Model for the Rule of Law

The key to understanding a psychological jurisprudence perspective is to recognize that the legal system relies upon the willingness of people to consent to the operation of legal authorities. Psychological jurisprudence emphasizes the importance of the active cooperation and willing acceptance of law and legal authorities by members of the public. That willing acceptance comes because people view the law as consistent with their moral values and/or because they view legal authorities as making their decisions justly. For psychological jurisprudence model to work, society needs to create and maintain supportive public values.

This model reflects an expanded model of human motivation. It recognizes that the roots of the effectiveness of regulatory authorities lie in the willingness of the public to be governed by the rules because they feel that their concerns and needs are being addressed by law and legal authorities. In a law abiding society most people will follow most laws most of the time because they think that this is the appropriate manner in which to behave. This self-regulation enhances the effectiveness of legal authorities by freeing them to pay attention to those problems or people that, for whatever reasons, are less amenable to self-regulation (Ayres & Braithwaite, 1992).

Psychological jurisprudence has implications for a wide variety of areas in law. In each area, legal authorities need to focus on the issue of creating and maintaining supportive public values. Consider an example from a recent study of citizen-police experiences. In this study researchers examined what transpired when the police were called to homes to deal with issues of domestic violence. The concern of the study was with subsequent compliance to the law on the part of the abusive men whose behavior led to the initial call. From a social control perspective we would expect that compliance to be increased by threats and/or punishments on the part of the police. From a psychological jurisprudence perspective we would argue for the value of police efforts to create and maintain respect for the law on the part of the abuser. The results support the value of a psychological jurisprudence perspective. If the police treat the abuser fairly during their encounter, that abuser is subsequently more likely to comply with the law. Fair treatment increases feelings of respect for the law, and leads abusers to be more willing to obey it in the future. This influence is greater than the impact of threatened or enacted punishments.

This study illustrates the core premise of the psychological jurisprudence perspective—that legal authorities should be concerned with developing the social values of citizens. This concern leads to a need to focus on the experience of those citizens, on their judgments about the practices and policies of legal authorities. Thus, psychological jurisprudence is a psychological perspective on the effective rule of law. It views the key to the successful rule of law as lying in an understanding of the social values of the citizenry, not in efforts to more effectively deploy coercive force.

## IMPLICATIONS FOR LAW

In our view the implications of this focus on creating and maintaining a law-abiding society are widespread and impact on many areas of the law. We outline some of the more important implications below.

### PERSONAL EXPERIENCES WITH LEGAL AUTHORITIES

People have a wide variety of types of personal experiences with legal authorities. Three types seem relevant to our discussion: seeking help, being regulated, and serving as a citizen. People seek help when they go to the police or courts for help in resolving some problem. They experience regulation when a police officer gives them a ticket, a judge levies a fine, or they are tried and punished for some crime. Finally, they act as citizens when they are jurors or witnesses.

The law abidingness perspective regards all of these types of personal contact with law and legal authorities as a socialization experience in which people refine their views about the law and legal authorities. The decisions made are evaluated via personal moral codes, and the authorities dealt with are evaluated through personal frameworks defining procedural justice. Viewed from this perspective, each personal experience represents an opportunity for legal authorities to strengthen the loyalty and support of members of the public. To do so, they must recognize the important role that people's sense of justice has in shaping their reactions to their experience.

Far from presenting a problem for police officers and judges, the centrality of justice to people's reactions to their experience actually provides authorities with the possibility of creating good will. If people acted based upon the favorability of their outcomes the loser to a dispute would automatically be unhappy, as would anyone who received a ticket. But, people do not. Instead, they evaluate their experience through a lens of justice. In the case of outcomes, authorities have the opportunity to frame and justify their decisions through reference to the moral values of those with whom they are dealing. In the case of procedures, they have the opportunity to treat everyone fairly.

A concrete example of the implications of these findings for strategies designed to build public respect for the law is shown by policing. If the police are to act as agents of socialization, they need to act in ways that people experience as respectful and fair. Efforts to gain public support for the police emphasize the need for respectful treatment of the public, as in the New York city police motto "Courtesy, Professionalism, Respect". Similarly, community policing initiatives are designed to increase personal interactions with police officers, interactions in which citizens will hopefully learn that the police are professional and fair (Friedmann, 1992; Rosenbaum, 1994; Skogan & Hartnett, 1997).

Consider an alternative problem central to law—responding to law breaking behavior. When a person is accused of breaking a law, there are several aspects of their experience with the legal system that are important from a psychological jurisprudence perspective. First, the procedure for determining guilt or innocence and for determining the punishment. This procedure has an important influence on the values of everyone involved, the offender, the victim, and others who personally experience the trial. All of these people react to the manner in which the legal system makes its decisions.

An important example of an approach to adjudication that emphasizes the importance of encouraging law abidingness among law-breakers is the restorative justice movement (Braithwaite, 1989). That movement has focused upon ways of reintegrating rule breakers into the community. The rule-breaking behavior is recognized and punished, but during the process of restorative justice conferences an effort is also made to encourage the rule-breaker to recognize that their behavior violates moral and social codes that are a part of their own self-image and, as a consequence, should be upsetting to them. In other words, an effort is made to use the rule-breaking as a way to encourage the rule-breaker to identify with social rules and commit themselves to not breaking those rules in the future.

Second, the decision about guilt, and the punishment itself. To everyone involved, the fairness of the outcome is also an important issue. First, both the victim's and the general public's views about law and the legal system are influenced by their assessments of the fairness of the verdict and sentence. Further, those fairness judgments also influence the feelings of the defendant. A sentence viewed as unjust encourages outrage, loss of respect for law, and further law-breaking behavior.

Finally, there is the experience of punishment. Studies consistently find that experiencing incarceration is not an effective way to encourage future law abidingness. This is hardly surprising, since there is nothing in the experience of spending time in jail or prison that encourages the development of moral values or leads to greater respect for law and legal authorities. As a consequence, when people leave the structured environment of incarceration, the internal values that might encourage law abidingness have not been strengthened.

For this reason efforts such as reintegrative justice, that are based upon trying to strengthen the importance of people's social values in shaping their law-related behavior try to avoid punishments such as jail or prison. They emphasize punishments such as acknowledgement of wrongdoing, apology, and restitution that connect people with the wrongness of their actions.

## THE ACCEPTANCE OF LAW AND LEGAL POLICY

People also react to law and legal authorities in a more symbolic way. Few have ever dealt with important legal authorities, such as the Supreme Court, who articulate legal doctrines that they are expected to accept and follow. As with personal experiences, people's responses to legal policies, decisions, and doctrines are shaped by their views about the fairness of Court decision-making. Legal institutions must be viewed as acting fairly if they are to receive public endorsements of their policies.

## MENTAL HEALTH LAW

The psychological jurisprudence model is already well developed within the field of mental health law through the pioneering work of Wexler on therapeutic jurisprudence (Wexler, 1990; Wexler & Winick, 1991). Therapeutic jurisprudence argues that when the legal system deals with potentially mentally disturbed people, whether through commitment hearings, commitments, or in other ways, a central concern of the authorities should be with the impact of their actions on the well being of the potentially disturbed person. That well being is, after all, central to mitigating the negative effects of whatever forms of mental illness initially brought the person into contact with the legal system. Like the treatment process itself, the legal system should be focused upon encouraging the mental health and well-being of the person. Of course, this benefits the legal system, since such individuals are more able to accept responsibility for following the law and are less likely to engage in inappropriate, illegal or violent acts.

## REFERENCES

Ayres, I., & Braithwaite, J. (1992). *Responsive regulation: Transcending the deregulation debate.* Oxford: Oxford University Press.

Beetham, D. (1991). *The legitimation of power.* Atlantic Highlands, N.J.: Humanities Press International.

Blasi, A. (1980). Bridging moral cognition and moral action: A critical review of the literature. *Psychological Bulletin, 88,* 1–45.

Blumstein, A., Cohen, J., & Nagin, D. (1978). *Deterrence and incapacitation.* Washington, D.C.: National Academy of Sciences.

Bowring, J. (Ed.) (1962). *The works of Jeremy Bentham (published under the superintendence of his executor.* London: Simpkin and Marshall.

Braithwaite, J. (1989). *Crime, shame, and reintegration.* Cambridge: Cambridge University Press.

Coffee, J. (1991). Does "unlawful" mean "criminal"? *Reflections on the Boston University Law Review disappearing tort/crime distinction in American law,* 193–246.

Cohn, E.S., & White, S.O. (1990). *Legal socialization. A study of norms and rules.* New York: Springer-Verlag.

Darley, J.M., Sanderson, C.A., & LaMantha, P.S. (1996). Community standards for defining attempt: Inconsistencies with the Model Penal Code. *American Behavioral Scientist, 39,* 405–420.

Darley, J.M., & Schultz, T.R. (1990). Moral rules: The content and acquisition. *Annual Review of Psychology, 41,* 525–556.

Darley, J.M., & Zanna, M.P. (1982). Making moral judgments. *American Scientist, 70,* 515–521.

Dillon, P.A., & Emery, R.E. (1996). Divorce mediation and resolution of child-custody disputes: Long-term effects. *American Journal of Orthopsychiatry, 66,* 131–140.

Ewick, P., & Silbey, S.S. (1998). *The common place of law.* Chicago: University of Chicago Press.

Finkel, N.J. (1995). *Commonsense justice: Jurors' notions of the law.* Cambridge: Harvard University Press.

Flanagan, T.J., & Longmire, D.R. (1996). *Americans view crime and justice.* Thousand Oaks: Sage.

Friedmann, R.R. (1992). *Community policing.* New York: Harvester Wheatsheaf.

Grasmick, H.G., & Bursik, R.J. (1990). Conscience, significant others, and rational choice. *Law and Society Review, 24,* 837–861.

Grasmick, H.G., & Green, D.E. (1980). Legal punishment, social disapproval, and internalization of inhibitors of illegal behavior. *Journal of Criminal Law and Criminology, 71,* 325–335.

Greenstein, F. (1965). *Children and politics.* New Haven: Yale.

Hamilton, V.L., & Sanders, J. (1992). *Everyday justice.* New Haven: Yale.

Haney, C. (1980). Psychology and legal change: On the limits of a factual jurisprudence. *Law and Human Behavior, 4,* 147–199.

Haney, C. (1982). Criminal justice and the nineteenth-century paradigm. *Law and Human Behavior, 6,* 191–235.

Haney, C. (1991). The fourteenth amendment and symbolic legality: Let them eat due process. *Law and Human Behavior, 15,* 183–204.

Haney, C. (1993). Psychology and legal change: The impact of a decade. *Law and Human Behavior, 17,* 371–398.

Haney, C. (1997). Commonsense justice and capital punishment. *Psychology, Public Policy, and Law, 3,* 303–337.

Haney, C. (1999). *Making law modern: Toward a social psychological model of justice.* Unpublished manuscript, University of California, Santa Cruz.

Haney, C., & Zimbardo, P. (1998). The past and future of U.S. prison policy: Twenty-five years after the Stanford prison experiment. *American Psychologist, 53,* 709–727.

Hess, R., & Torney, J. (1967). *The development of political attitudes in children.* New York: Aldine.

Hoffman, M. (1977). Moral internalization: Current theory and research. Advances in experimental social psychology (L. Berkowitz, Ed., Vol.10, pp. 85–133). New York: Academic.

Hyman, H. H. (1959). *Political socialization: A study in the psychology of political behavior.* New York: Free Press.

Kelman, H.C., & Hamilton, V.L. (1989). *Crime of obedience.* New Haven: Yale.

Kim, W.C., & Mauborgne, R.A. (1993). Procedural justice, attitudes, and subsidiary top management compliance with multinationals' corporate strategic decisions. *Academy of Management Journal, 36,* 502–526.

Kitzmann, K.M., & Emery, R.E. (1993). Procedural justice and parents' satisfaction in a field study of child custody dispute resolution. *Law and Human Behavior, 17,* 553–567.

Krislov, S., Boyum, K.O., Clark, J.N., Shaefer, R.C., & White, S.O. (1966). *Compliance and the law: A multi-disciplinary approach.* Beverly Hills: Sage.

Lind, E.A., Kulik, C.T., Ambrose, M., & de Vera Park, M. (1993). Individual and corporate dispute resolution. *Administrative Science Quarterly, 38,* 224–251.

Lind, E.A., & Tyler, T.R. (1988). *The social psychology of procedural justice.* New York: Plenum.

MacCoun, R.J. (1993). Drugs and the law: A psychological analysis of drug prohibition. *Psychological Bulletin, 113,* 497–512.

Merry, S.E. (1990). *Getting justice and getting even: Legal consciousness among working-class Americans.* Chicago: University of Chicago Press.

Melton, G.B. (1985). *The law as a behavioral instrument.* Nebraska Symposium on Motivation (Vol.33). Lincoln, NE: University of Nebraska Press.

Merelman, R.M. (1986). Revitalizing political socialization. In M. Hermann (Ed.), *Political psychology.* San Francisco: Jossey Bass.

Model Penal Code (1962). Washington, D.C.: American Law Institute.

Niemi, R.G. (1973). Political socialization. In J. Knutson (Ed.), *Handbook of political psychology.* San Francisco: Jossey Bass.

Nagin, D.S., & Paternoster, R. (1991). The preventive effects of the perceived risk of arrest. *Criminology, 29,* 561–585.

Paternoster, R. (1987). The deterrent effect of the perceived certainty and severity of punishment. *Justice Quarterly, 4,* 173–217.

Paternoster, R. (1989). Decisions to participate in and desist from four types of common delinquency. *Law and Society Review, 23,* 7–40.

Paternoster, R., Brame, R., Bachman, R., & Sherman, L.W. (1997). Do fair procedures matter? The effect of procedural justice on spouse assault. *Law and Society Review, 31,* 163–204.

Paternoster, R., & Iovanni, L. (1986). The deterrent effect of perceived severity. *Social Forces, 64,* 751–777.

Paternoster, R., Saltzman, L.E., Waldo, G.P., & Chiricos, T.G. (1983). Perceived risk and social control: Do sanctions really deter? *Law and Society Review, 17,* 457–479.

Paternoster, R., & Simpson, S. (1996). Sanction threat and appeals to morality. *Law and Society Review, 30,* 549–583.

Pruitt, D.G., Peirce, R.S., McGillicuddy, N.B., Welton, G.L., & Castrianno, L.M. (1993). Long term success in mediation. *Law and Human Behavior, 17,* 313–330.

Robinson, P.H., & Darley, J. (1997). *Justice, liability, and blame.* Boulder, CO: Westview.

Robinson, P.H., & Darley, J. (1997). The utility of desert. *Northwestern University Law Review, 91,* 453–499.

Rosenbaum, D.P. (1994). *The challenge of community policing.* Thousand Oaks, CA: Sage.

Ross, H.L. (1982). *Deterring the drinking driver.* Lexington, Mass.: Lexington.

Rossi, P.H., & Berk, R.A. (1997). *Just punishments: Federal guidelines and public views compared.* New York: Aldine.

Sherman, L. (1998, November). Alternative prevention strategies and the role of policing. Paper presented at a symposium on "Beyond incarceration: The economics of crime". Cambridge, Mass.: Harvard University.

Skogan, W.G., Hartnett, S.M. (1997). *Community policing, Chicago style*. Oxford: Oxford University Press.

Sparks, R., Bottoms, A., & Hay, W. (1996). *Prisons and the problem or order*. Oxford: Clarendon.

Suchman, M.C. (1995). Managing legitimacy: Strategic and institutional approaches. *Academy of Management Review, 20*, 571–610.

Tapp, J., & Levine, F. (1977). *Law, justice and the individual in society: Psychological and legal issues*. New York: Holt, Rinehart, and Winston.

Thibaut, J., & Walker, L. (1975). *Procedural justice*. Hillsdale, New Jersey: Erlbaum.

Tyler, T.R. (1990). *Why people obey the law*. New Haven: Yale.

Tyler, T.R. (1994). Governing amid diversity: Can fair decision-making procedures bridge competing public interests and values? *Law and Society Review, 28*, 701–722.

Tyler, T.R. (1997a). Citizen discontent with legal procedures. *American Journal of Comparative Law, 45*, 869–902.

Tyler, T.R. (1997b). Procedural fairness and compliance with the law. *Swiss Journal of Economics and Statistics, 133*, 219–240.

Tyler, T.R. (1997c). Compliance with intellectual property laws: A psychological perspective. *Journal of International Law and Politics, 28*, 101–115.

Tyler, T.R. (1998). Public mistrust of the law: A political perspective. *University of Cincinnati Law Review, 66*, 847–876.

Tyler, T.R. (in press-a). Social justice: Psychological contributions to international negotiations, conflict resolution, and world peace. *International Journal of Psychology*

Tyler, T.R. (in press-b). The psychology of legitimacy. In J. Jost, & B. Major (Eds.), *The psychology of legitimacy*. Cambridge: Cambridge University Press.

Tyler, T.R. (in press-c). The psychology of public dissatisfaction with government. In E. Theiss-Morse, & J. Hibbing (Eds.), *Trust in government*. University of Nebraska Press

Tyler, T.R., & Boeckmann, R.J. (1997). Three strikes and you are out, but why? The psychology of public support for punishing rule breakers. *Law and Society Review, 31*, 237–265.

Tyler, T.R., Boeckmann, R.J., Smith, H.J., & Huo, Y.J. (1997). *Social justice in a diverse society*. Boulder, CO: Westview.

Tyler, T.R., Casper, J., & Fisher, B. (1989). Maintaining allegiance toward political authorities. *American Journal of Political Science, 33*, 629–652.

Tyler, T.R., & Lind, E.A. (1992). A relational model of authority in groups. In M. Zanna (Ed.). *Advances in Experimental Social Psychology* (Vol.25, pp.115–191). NY: Academic Press.

Tyler, T.R., & Mitchell, G. (1994). Legitimacy and the empowerment of discretionary legal authority: The United States Supreme Court and abortion rights. *Duke Law Journal, 43*, 703–814.

Tyler, T.R., & Smith, H.J. (1997). Social justice and social movements. In D. Gilbert, S. Fiske, & G. Lindzey (Eds.), *Handbook of Social Psychology* (4th edition, Vol. 2, pp. 595–629). New York: McGraw-Hill.

Wexler, D.B. (1990). *Therapeutic jurisprudence: The law as a therapeutic agent*. Durham, NC: Carolina Academic Press.

Wissler, R.L. (1995). Mediation and adjudication in the small claims court. *Law and Society Review, 29*, 323–35

# Children, Psychology, and Law

*Reflections on Past and Future Contributions to Science and Policy*

## BETTE L. BOTTOMS, N. DICKON REPPUCCI, JENNIFER A. TWEED, AND KARI L. NYSSE-CARRIS[1]

The 1999 American Psychology-Law Society's Presidential Initiative has been the impetus for the field of Psychology and Law to examine itself carefully. The chapters within this volume reveal the products of that examination. For each subfield of Psychology and Law, scholars have reviewed noteworthy past accomplishments, evaluated the present state of knowledge, and identified future efforts needed to ensure that the subfield remains responsive to pressing societal questions. This chapter reflects our examination of the burgeoning subfield of Children, Psychology, and Law,

[1]*Authors' note*: We thank Tamara M. Haegerich, Deborah Connolly, Thomas Grisso, Gary Melton, Roger P. Weissberg, Carrie Fried, Mindy Schmidt, Lisa Trivits, Jill Antonishak, Brian Carreon and Maryfrances Porter for comments on earlier drafts of the manuscript.

BETTE L. BOTTOMS • Department of Psychology, University of Illinois at Chicago, Chicago, Illinois 60607-7137.    N. DICKON REPPUCCI • Department of Psychology, Gilmer Hall, University of Virginia, Charlottesville, Virginia 22904-4400.    JENNIFER A. TWEED • Department of Psychology, University of Virginia, Charlottesville, Virginia 22904-4400.    KARI L. NYSSE-CARRIS • Department of Psychology, University of Illinois at Chicago, Chicago, Illinois 60607-7137

which encompasses an exceptionally wide range of topics, including, but not limited to, juvenile justice and delinquency, custody and adoption, children's rights, child maltreatment, and children's eyewitness testimony. In fact, this subfield is so rich with knowledge directly relevant to law that Goodman, Emery, and Haugaard (1998) noted, "There are few other areas of law where the courts rely as heavily on social science data as they do for decisions about children's welfare" (p. 775). Not only do courts make use of the fruits of child/law research, but so do basic researchers, attorneys, policy makers, legislators, and mental health, social service, and police professionals. In keeping with the theme of this volume, we identify factors that led to the field's most notable past accomplishments and outline future challenges that must be met for the field to continue producing scientifically sound research that will have significant impact on law, policy, and practice relating to children.

## OUTSTANDING PAST ACCOMPLISHMENTS: WHAT CAN THEY TEACH US?

To understand what is needed to ensure future success for our field, it is first helpful to identify outstanding past achievements that illustrate how influential research is accomplished and how far-reaching its contributions can be. What constitutes an outstanding achievement in the field of Children, Psychology, and Law? Our answer: a program of research that advances psychological theory *and* results in concrete, beneficial changes in policies, laws, and/or practices relevant to children and child welfare. A clear route for accomplishing these results is for researchers to (a) identify a key assumption of the legal system (often a myth) that can be tested through psychological research, (b) test the assumption by using solid psychological theory and ecologically valid methods, and (c) disseminate the results to both scholars and policy and law makers. A particularly noteworthy example that can teach us much about the nature of conducting meaningful work is Thomas Grisso's program of research on adolescents' comprehension of Miranda warnings. Grisso's research specifically meets all of the requirements we have outlined, and, as a result, has had lasting impact.

Grisso (1980, 1981) examined the critical issue of children's understanding of their rights and their ability to comprehend the warnings offered by law enforcement when being taken into custody. Grisso's research design employed multiple measures to assess comprehension from appropriate samples of adolescent and adult offenders matched with non-offending participants. He found that juveniles younger than age 15 do not understand the meaning and importance of their Miranda rights as well as adults. Also, contrary to popular belief, level of comprehension is not strongly related to juveniles' prior experience with the legal system. Grisso concluded that young adolescents' comprehension of their rights is so poor that they should not be able to waive them without legal counsel. Although older adolescents of average intelligence evince cognitive comprehension of rights comparable to adults, Grisso cautioned that even they should not be treated as adults in all cases because comprehension does not ensure the ability to exercise rights.

Grisso's work is significant to developmental psychology because it is informative about adolescents' cognitive competence and decision-making abilities. It also has direct applications. Importantly, Grisso made significant efforts to inform policy and lawmakers about those applications. Specifically, to assess the impact social science literature was having in the court system, Grisso and Melton (1987) surveyed court personnel to determine what they read and how often. Similar to Saunders and Reppucci's (1977) findings with juvenile correctional facility superintendents, Grisso and Melton found that court personnel rarely read the scholarly journals in which psychologists typically publish their work. The study indicated that to reach justice system personnel, researchers need to target publications those professionals actually read (e.g., *Juvenile and Family Court Journal, Crime and Delinquency*) and need to use other means of dissemination (e.g., presentations and workshops at regional and national conferences, as we discuss later). Throughout his career, Grisso has done this. As a consequence, his targeted dissemination of the Miranda warnings research has had a direct impact in the field: By 1999, more than 25 appellate courts nationally had cited his findings (Grisso, personal communication, 2000).

Thus, Grisso's work is a model for research that contributes to psychology, policy, and law. Fortunately, there are several other examples in the field of Children, Psychology and Law, and we will use many of these examples throughout our chapter to illustrate various points. Next, we turn to several major substantive areas of child/law research, briefly reviewing past accomplishments and focusing on legal assumptions and myths that have received some empirical attention, but typically deserve more. We begin by introducing an overarching theme for much of this work: children's competencies.

## CENTRAL AREAS OF RESEARCH IN THE FIELD OF CHILDREN, PSYCHOLOGY, AND LAW

As mentioned above, influential child/law research often identifies a legal assumption that can be addressed by using psychological theory and methodology. Legal assumptions often concern children's competence (their capacities or abilities) in various domains. For this reason, competence is a psychological construct that, in some way, is involved in much research in the field of Children, Psychology and Law (e.g., Melton, 1984; Melton, Koocher, & Saks, 1983; Woolard, Reppucci, & Redding, 1996). For example, psychologists study children's capacities to provide informed consent in medical decision making situations, to provide custodial preference in contested custody cases, to understand and participate in their own legal proceedings, and to provide eyewitness testimony. Societal perceptions of children's competencies in various domains frequently drive policy; for example, the public's misguided overgeneralizations of juvenile offenders as "superpredators," a phrase coined by DiIulio (1995), has probably hastened the stiffening of penalties for youths charged with crimes as well as policies promoting transfers of juveniles to adult courts (Zimring, 1998). Children's actual competencies, however, may differ in important ways from perceived competencies, discrepancies that can be illuminated by psychological research. For example, if children are incompetent to understand the nature of their crimes or their rights in a courtroom context, then it would be misguided to remove them from juvenile court and subject them to adult procedures and penalties. Determining the nature of both actual and perceived competencies is the first step in assuring that children are guaranteed all rights commensurate with their competencies.

Another critical element in any discussion involving children and the law is acknowledging the precarious task of balancing the rights of children, families, and the state. When conducting research in this field, it is necessary to examine legal precedent and practice to appreciate the interplay of rights provided to each entity. Traditionally, the law entrusts parents with the right to make any and all decisions on their children's behalf, and parents must consent to any actions involving their child. Considered a fundamental right for centuries, parental autonomy to make decisions for their children was reinforced by several Supreme Court decisions early in the twentieth century (e.g., *Meyer v. Nebraska*, 1923; *Pierce v. Society of Sisters*, 1925). Legal support of parental autonomy is based on two assumptions: (a) that children under the age of 18 are incompetent to make certain decisions for themselves, and (b) that parents will make decisions in the best interest of their children. However, in some cases, such as child abuse and neglect, the state exercises its *parens patriae* authority, whereby the state is responsible for protecting members of society who cannot protect themselves, particularly children. In other instances, the rights of children may conflict with those of their parents, because, as initially pointed out by Justice Douglas's dissent in *Wisconsin v.*

*Yoder* (1972), parents and children may not always have the same interests. In situations where parental autonomy is challenged, conflicts
between the child, family, and state naturally arise. The notion of parental
autonomy has been challenged in a number of situations: (a) reproductive
health, including provision of contraception, treatment of sexually
transmitted diseases, and abortion; (b) termination or refusal of medical
treatment; (c) mental health commitment; (d) custody proceedings; and
(e) abuse and neglect situations, including discipline/corporal punishment practices. In many of these situations, the determination of competence may be of utmost importance.

Regarding the link between children's competence and their participation in decision making, it is worth noting that Melton (1999) recently
suggested a shift from understanding children's competence to restructuring intergenerational systems to accommodate decision making.
Melton argues that enabling children's graduated decision making will
give them a sense of dignity and foster maturity thereby providing a
foundation for adolescents to self-regulate their own risky behavior.
Although we agree that increasing children's participation in decisions
that concern their lives should be encouraged as a matter of values, little
empirical evidence exists to support this position per se. Rather than
abandoning the focus on maturity and competence, as Melton seems to
suggest, we advocate research on competence and its assessment and on
participation in decision making (e.g., Cauffman, Woolard, & Reppucci,
1999).

We now review several key areas of research in more detail (e.g.,
juvenile justice, medical decision making, divorce and custody, child maltreatment, children's eyewitness testimony), illustrating how child/law
research has addressed legal assumptions in each area, and in turn,
brought about improvements in law, policy, and practice. Throughout, we
highlight current knowledge and future challenges psychologists face in
each domain. It should be noted that this review, although covering much
material, is neither comprehensive nor exhaustive, as each of the topics
could have been chapters themselves.

## JUVENILE JUSTICE

Before 1899, any youth older than 7 years who committed a criminal
act was processed through the adult court system. At the turn of the century, many reformers made the assumption that juveniles lacked maturity
and judgment, and therefore, juveniles under age 14 should be treated
with a more tempered approach than the punitive focus of the criminal
justice system. This reform movement led to the creation of the first

juvenile court in Cook County, Illinois (Whitebread & Heilman, 1988). The juvenile court's philosophical underpinning was based on a rehabilitative ideal whereby children who came before the court would be provided individualized justice and treatment that would, in turn, result in community safety. Because the juvenile court was focused on treatment, reformers assumed that children would not need procedural safeguards, such as the due process rights afforded to adults processed through the criminal justice system. By the 1920's, most states had a juvenile court system that had original jurisdiction over youth under age 18, and the notion of developmental immaturity had been incorporated as a rationale for the separate juvenile justice system (Reppucci, 1999).

By the 1960s, however, it was widely believed that the juvenile court was not working. In the opinion of the U.S. Supreme Court, "the child receives the worst of both worlds: that he gets neither the protections accorded to adults nor the solicitous care and regenerative treatment postulated for children" (*Kent v. United States*, 1966). A historic Supreme Court case (*In re Gault*, 1967) dramatically transformed the juvenile court from an informal treatment arena to a due process, just desserts model. Consequently, along with societal perceptions of increased rates of juvenile violence, the due process revolution has led the juvenile court to become more punitive, thereby more closely approximating the adult criminal justice system. (For a history of the evolution of the juvenile court see Feld, 1998; 1999, and for an examination of relevant due process cases and their impact see Manfredi, 1998.) Furthermore, the recent trend toward legislating lower and lower ages of presumed competence and maturity questions the role of the juvenile court (e.g., most states have lowered the age at which juveniles can be transferred to the adult court system to 14 or younger, and some such as Michigan have no lower limit).

As a result of these changes, a debate is underway regarding whether the juvenile court should be maintained and rejuvenated or abolished all together (Feld, 1999; Scott & Grisso, 1997; Slobogin, Fondacaro, & Woolard, 1999). Proponents for abolition argue that the granting of some due process rights to juveniles, the upsurge in violent crimes, and the lack of demonstrated effectiveness of the juvenile court all indicate the need to establish one justice system overseeing both adult and juvenile offenders. Within this unified system, Feld (1998; 1999) argues that an automatic consideration of offender age as a mitigating factor will safeguard children from unduly strict punishment and streamline the court process. In contrast, Scott and Grisso (1997) argue that the fact that children and adults are developmentally different necessitates a separate juvenile court. Without such a court, they fear that the goal of rehabilitation will be entirely abandoned, something that will benefit neither juveniles nor society in general.

This important debate highlights the urgent need to determine children and adolescents' competence to understand legal concepts and to make decisions in legal contexts (Scott, Reppucci, & Woolard, 1995; Reppucci, 1999). Although psychological research has yielded a great deal of pertinent information (e.g., Grisso, 1980, 1981), psychologists in this field face the challenge of providing answers to a number of pressing questions that arise when juveniles enter our legal system. For example, more and more youth are being transferred to adult criminal court (Redding, 1997), an action that is predicated upon courts' assumption that adolescents can understand and participate in the law as well as adults can (Grisso & Schwartz, 2000). This assumption, however, is countered by the results of psychological research: In fact, juveniles younger than age 13 appear to lack the capacity to understand the law or their legal rights as adults do (Scott et al., 1995; Steinberg & Cauffman, 1996), and youth between the ages of 13 and 16 may need individualized assessment to ascertain their capacities (Steinberg & Cauffman, 1999). Much more research must be completed to understand the extent to which children understand their rights and how the court system might accommodate their levels of comprehension. In addition, more information is needed regarding children's adjudicative competence, including their ability to assist their own attorney when necessary (Cauffman et al., 1999) Also, within the context of a blame- and punishment-focused justice system, the construct of culpability becomes a pressing research issue (Cauffman et al., 1999; Fried & Reppucci, 2001; Grisso, 1996; Woolard, Fried, & Reppucci, 2001).

The goal of this research is both practical and theoretical. The practicality is directly focused on the nature of competence as a determinate of legal and public policy. To what degree should a youth be considered as responsible and thus as blameworthy as an adult for his or her illegal acts? Theoretically, the research has the potential to explicate the meaning of maturity and to seek understanding regarding the question "are children and adults different?" (Reppucci, 1999). Although the notion of a "bright line" separation based on age, as has been the case in law for decades, is clearly not applicable to everyone, developing probability ranges for youth's responsibility may be useful. For example, being able to state that the vast majority of youth below the age of 13 are not as responsible for their actions as adults whereas the vast majority above age 16 are as responsible, provides guidelines for applying the law (Steinberg & Cauffman, 1999), knowing full well that sometimes the younger child is indeed competent and the older person is not. This of course leaves children in the middle age group requiring individual assessment of their competencies and maturity. However, the question remains, what should be the components of that assessment? Currently, the components of assessment are all cognitive, e.g., knowing, understanding, and appreciating the facts, and voluntarily committing the action. Recent research is beginning to make a case for expanding the definition of competence by increasing the relevant components (e.g., psychosocial judgment factors, see Scott et al., 1995). It is in this realm that the research holds promise for our increased understanding of the nature of childhood versus adulthood.

Although adolescents 15 years and older may have cognitive capacities that are comparable to adults' (Grisso, 1980; Scott et al., 1995), psychological research has yet to determine whether adolescents at this age are as mature as adults on other psychosocial judgment factors such as temporal perspective, risk perception, responsibility, and peer influence (Scott et al., 1995; Steinberg & Cauffman, 1996). Some initial findings suggest that adolescents differ from adults on these judgment factors (Cauffman et al., 1999; Woolard et al., 2001). For example, one in-depth study of the adjudicative competence of several hundred male offenders age 15 and under, age 16 to 17, and age 18 to 35 has been completed and data are being analyzed (Woolard & Reppucci, in progress). Although preliminary results suggest no differences in cognitive measures of adjudicative competence, measures of legal judgement and psychosocial maturity do differ, e.g., younger juveniles were twice as likely to waive their rights to silence in response to a police interrogation vignette than were adults. These results have inspired a larger follow-up study of male and female offenders aged 11 to 24 (Grisso et al., 1999).

As juvenile crime, especially violent crime, escalated over the past 20 years, the measures and means by which the public is willing to punish these offenders has escalated as well. For instance, in the 1989 *Stanford* decision, the U.S. Supreme Court found it constitutional to execute youth who had committed a crime at age 16. Furthermore, the public's willingness to abandon rehabilitation as a goal is clear in the widespread support for various changes in legislation endorsing increased punishment for a wide range of crimes for very young juveniles. As an example of this trend, Crosby, Britner, Jodl, and Portwood (1995) found that nearly 60% of a sample of former jurors indicated they would be willing to sentence a juvenile as young as 10 years old to death. What data relevant to these issues can child/law researchers provide? A basic assumption behind harsher policies is that they deter juvenile crime. Yet researchers' initial examinations of the results of "get tough" punitive strategies of transfer and longer sentences challenge that assumption. Both short- and long-term recidivism rates are higher for adolescents tried in an adult criminal court than for juveniles processed within the juvenile justice system for the same type of crime (Bishop, Frazier, Lanza-Kanduce, & Winner, 1996; Winner, Lanza-Kanduce, Bishop, & Frazier, 1997). Policy evaluations of recently implemented waiver laws and blended sentencing (where a juvenile offender is initially committed to a youth facility and ordered to be transferred to an adult facility to complete the imposed sentence once he/she exceeds the maximum age of the juvenile center) are necessary to determine their impact. Moreover, there is some evidence that treatment alternatives are beneficial, particularly with serious offenders, further indicating that "get tough" policies may not be the most effective approach. For example, multisystemic therapy, an alternative to out-of-home placement that targets serious violent offenders, is an intensive intervention that accounts for the multiple contexts contributing to the problems young offenders experience. Treatment directed toward the offender, his or her family, friends, school, and the neighborhood environment has reduced recidivism rates (actual arrests and self-report) among serious juvenile offenders (Henggeler, Schoenwald, Bourdin, Rowland, & Cunningham, 1998).

There is a critical need to understand individual differences in background, offense, recidivism, and desistance. For example, some research indicates that the majority of male adolescents in their mid-teens engage in delinquent activity, and that those who do not have an early history of aggression, bullying, and other acting out behaviors are simply exercising their new found autonomy and will desist from their delinquent behaviors in a short period of time (Moffitt, 1993; Seidman, 1984). If this is the case, it may be reasonable to allow for a certain amount of jurisdictional leeway for making mistakes, similar to the "learner's permit" idea suggested by Zimring (1982, 1998). This is not to suggest a total lack of accountability for these youth, but rather that delinquent behavior by adolescent boys occurs so frequently that it may be described as normative. Empirical research indicates that the vast majority of adolescents commit some illegal acts (Elliot, 1994) and Moffitt (1993) has claimed that "it is statistically aberrant to refrain from crime during adolescence" (pp. 685–686). A challenge for psychology is to determine who are the desisters and who are the "life-persistent" adolescents who will probably become career criminals—the 6–16% of youth who are responsible for the bulk of all serious crimes committed by youth (Moffitt, 1993). Although this determination has received an increasing amount of attention in the past decade, relatively little is known about when and why adolescents cease delinquent behavior (Scott & Grisso, 1997).

Finally, gender differences deserve attention. Although official delinquency rates clearly indicate that adolescent males are responsible for the majority of offenses against persons and property, in recent years, adolescent female arrests for these crimes have increased dramatically and more rapidly than for males (Poe-Yamagata & Butts, 1996). For example, from 1985 to 1994, violent crime rates for males increased 67%, but for females 125% (Synder & Sickmund, 1995). Hoyt and Scherer (1998) reviewed such statistics and the current state of knowledge regarding female delinquency. They concluded that the standard practice of treating female delinquency as simply a subset or minor variation of male delinquency is unwarranted, and has led female delinquents "to encounter misguided justice and intervention" (p. 82). The empirical knowledge about female delinquency is sparse, and given the recent shifts in crime rates, this body of research should be expanded. To do this, Hoyt and Scherer argue that both same-sex and cross-gender studies of female delinquency are needed because substantial social and developmental gender differences change the etiology of delinquency. We argue that a major challenge for researchers is to develop comprehensive studies of female delinquency to enhance our understanding of the etiology of both female and male delinquents that can be used to create "efficient, impartial, and effective delinquency prevention and juvenile justice intervention efforts" (Hoyt & Scherer, p. 103).

## Future Challenges

Although researchers are starting to address the competencies of youth within the justice system, knowledge regarding the causes and precursors of juvenile delinquency and violence, especially among females, is greatly needed. A related topic receiving considerable attention is the prevalence of mental health disorders among the youth in the juvenile justice system. The challenge of assisting with prevention is perhaps the most exciting faced by psychologists. The prevention of delinquency before it emerges is arguably the best solution to the constellation of troubling issues surrounding juveniles' legal involvement. With the vast increase in knowledge regarding risk and protective factors (e.g., Gorman-Smith, Tolan, & Henry, 1999; Loeber & Farrington, 1998), prevention may be less "pie in the sky" than previously believed. Although mixed, preliminary findings from studies examining the impact of preventive efforts suggest that such efforts can be more effective than previously acknowledged (e.g., Fried & Reppucci, in press; Mulvey, Arthur, & Reppucci, 1993; Reppucci, Woolard, & Fried, 1999; Tate, Reppucci, & Mulvey, 1995; Tolan & McKay, 1996). Continued efforts at thorough program evaluation are likely to show that carefully designed interventions can have a positive impact on deterring juvenile violence. Such data would underscore the need to fund prevention initiatives.

## MEDICAL DECISION MAKING

Psychological researchers have contributed to understanding children's competence in medical decision making contexts, where questions of relevance to psychology and law abound. Children are generally not afforded the right to make medical decisions for themselves because they are considered incompetent to do so. As such, parents are trusted to make medical decisions for their children, whether deciding to administer or withhold treatment, because parents are expected to act in their child's best interest. Most states, however, authorize some minors to make their own medical decisions because of their special status, such as those who are married, or in the armed forces, or when the situation is deemed to be a public health interest as in the case of treatment for sexually transmitted diseases (English, 1999). Unfortunately, very little research has been conducted to determine children's and adolescents' competence to make these kinds of choices. Much more research is needed to begin to answer questions such as: At what age is a child able to participate in making medical decisions? Should teens be able to refuse medical treatment if terminally ill?

In one of the first empirical studies of legal assumptions about children's ability to make medical treatment decisions, Weithorn and Campbell (1982) compared young children and adolescents to adults in terms of their ability to choose between various medical decisions and the reasoning behind their choice. Results suggested few differences between 14-year-olds and adults in either reasoning or decisions. For younger children (age 9), the decisions were similar to adults, even though the reasoning was often not comparable. Subsequent research has tended to replicate Weithorn and Campbell's initial findings. A challenge faced by researchers in this domain is to remedy the fact that most of this research is based on middle-class, white populations in simulated laboratory situations rather than on samples of ethnically and socio-economically diverse youth in "real" situations. Interestingly, in one of the few studies using an appropriate sample of 13- to 21-year-old women facing a real life decision (they were in a clinic receiving results from a pregnancy test; Ambuel & Rappaport, 1992), all girls between 13 and 17 years old were found to be as competent as 18- to 21-year-old women regarding decision making about pregnancy, with one exception: 13- to 15-year-old girls who never considered abortion as an option were found to be significantly less legally competent than adult women and other adolescents who had considered abortion. (To assess competence, the researchers used three indices of cognitive competence and the perceived ability of the girl to make a voluntary, independent decision.)

Not surprisingly, the issue of adolescents making abortion decisions has been controversial. In two court cases (*Hartigan v. Zbaraz*, 1987; *Thornburg v. American College of Obstetricians*, 1986), the American Psychological Association (APA) submitted amicus curiae briefs strongly supporting an adolescent girl's competence (and right) to choose. Arguments were based on the medical decision-making literature in general. This stance provoked a heated debate about the role of values in the interpretation of scientific evidence (see Gardner, Scherer, & Tester, 1989; Melton, 1990; Scherer & Gardner, 1990). With the exception of the Ambuel and Rappaport (1992) investigation, little new research has been conducted on this topic, and ironically, the strong position taken by the APA (Interdivisional Committee on Adolescent Abortion, 1987) has precluded APA from taking an official stance regarding the possible lack of maturity of similarly aged juveniles regarding culpability for crimes because it would appear to be providing contradictory conclusions.

As we have noted, children are usually not able to make their own decisions about seeking treatment, except in specially delineated areas such as treatment for sexually transmitted diseases, which is viewed as being in the public good. Minors are generally not permitted to refuse treatment either, although this has been allowed in some instances (e.g., a 1994 Florida case resulted in a 15-year-old being allowed to refuse medication needed to sustain his life after two unsuccessful kidney transplants; Penkower, 1996). Parents are given the authority to seek and refuse needed medical treatment for their children because they are viewed as acting in the best interest of their children. A clear example of this reasoning is evident in *Parham v. J. R.* (1979), in which the Court upheld a parent's right, in conjunction with a doctor's concurrence, to admit his or her child to a mental hospital without a hearing, even against the child's wishes. Sometimes, even in life-threatening situations, medical treatment is refused by parents for religious reasons (Bottoms, Shaver, Goodman, & Qin, 1995). Although other countries such as England and Canada legally mandate medical care for children, all but a few states (e.g., South Dakota, Hawaii, Massachusetts, and Maryland) grant some form of religious exemption to child protection laws, allowing parents to escape legal consequences if failure to provide modern medical treatment results in harm to a child (Bullis, 1991). In such situations, balancing the rights between the child, family, and the state becomes quite complicated. In some cases where parents refuse obviously necessary treatment for their child, the state will use its *parens patriae* authority to temporarily terminate the parents' custody long enough to perform the necessary medical procedure. Parental custody is typically reinstated after the child receives treatment. Of course, this is only possible when the case reaches the attention of authorities.

## Future Challenges

What avenues should psychological researchers take in their future efforts to understand children's competencies in medical decision making contexts? As mentioned above, research using more appropriate samples in more realistic settings is needed. Further, we note that most extant research has primarily focused on and continues to be embedded within a cognitive framework. Thus, as it has been argued in reference to juvenile justice issues (Scott et al., 1995; Steinberg & Cauffman, 1996), it is imperative that future evaluations of adolescents' capacities in medical contexts include an examination of judgment factors such as peer and parental influence and temporal perspective. These factors are especially important given findings that parental influence may significantly impact an adolescent's treatment decision (Scherer, 1991; Scherer & Reppucci, 1988).

## DIVORCE, CUSTODY, AND TECHNOLOGY-ASSISTED FAMILY PLANNING

Conflicts between the rights of children, family, and the state are perhaps never more prominent than when children are involved in adjudication proceedings surrounding divorce, custody, and technology-assisted family planning. Psychological research has much to offer on a variety of issues that arise in these situations.

## Divorce

Much research has examined a question that has concerned our society for many years: What are the consequences of divorce on children? Our society's general assumption has been that the consequences are necessarily negative. Although psychological research has begun to delineate some of the effects of divorce, the extent to which and the ways in which divorce influences a child's welfare are still unclear. Research is needed to unravel the interaction of risk and protective factors that will likely provide the most useful model for determining the well-being of children from divorced and remarried families (Hetherington, Bridges, & Insabella, 1998). In general, researchers agree that children, adolescents, and adults from divorced and remarried families are at a higher risk for adjustment problems than children from stable marriages (Hetherington et al., 1998). Nevertheless, growing evidence suggests that many of the problems children from divorced families experience exist before the divorce occurred (Elliott & Richards, 1991; Hetherington et al., 1998). Similarly, researchers have found that the processes predicting marital dissolution sometimes lead children to develop long lasting, maladaptive behavior patterns (Katz & Gottman, 1995). In a meta-analysis of 92 studies of divorce, children from divorced families exhibited more behavior problems than children from non-divorced families; however, the effect size was moderate in general and even smaller for research with high methodological quality (Amato & Keith, 1991). Emery (1999b) notes that although divorce can increase the risk for psychological problems, the great majority of children do not require psychological treatment. Moreover, Kofkin and Reppucci (1991) found that parental divorce was the only major life crisis that people initially experienced as negative, but eventually considered it to be positive.

Another general assumption has been that unhappy parents should stay together for the sake of their children. In fact, psychological research finds that divorce is generally not in children's best interest. Even so, some studies reveal that divorce is not the worst outcome for children whose parents are involved in a highly acrimonious relationship (Emery, 1982; Maccoby, 1999). Other evidence suggests that for parents in a highly conflictual marriage relationship, a divorce may sometimes increase the hostility between the parents, further placing the child at risk (Hetherington, 1999). Goodman, Emery et al. (1998) contend that instead of focusing primarily on children's individual mental health status (as most existing research does), greater emphasis should be directed toward measuring well being more globally, by considering such factors as economic resources, which usually decline significantly for children after divorce (for a comprehensive review of issues related to divorce, foster care, and adoption, see Goodman, Emery et al., 1998). Psychological findings on the impact of risk and protective factors on child outcome over time could be useful in determining the extent to which marriage and divorce should be regulated by the state. For example, children's well being might be enhanced if the state enforced pre-commitment strategies (Scott, 1990) or required parent education classes for divorcing parents (Goodman, Emery et al., 1998).

## Custody Determinations

Society and the law have made a variety of assumptions in the domain of child custody determinations, assumptions that social science could address. Two central assumptions are that mothers are the best custodial parents, and that children, especially preadolescents, are not competent to participate in custody decision making. Are these assumptions correct? As fathers have become more involved with the daily tasks of child rearing and women have increased their participation in the workforce, determining custody arrangements has become a less automatic process than it was a few decades ago. Child custody decisions have generally been based on "the best interest of the child," a standard that has been criticized as indeterminant and speculative (Mnookin, 1978; Reppucci, 1984; Reppucci & Crosby, 1993). Yet in the absence of clear guidelines derived from research, judges in contested custody cases have no alternative but to apply the best interest standard, which means making custody determinations based essentially on value judgments formed from individual biases, court precedence, and various familial factors. Considerations are often given to the stability of the home environment, including the economic stability of each parent, and in some cases, more intimate details about the parents (e.g., sexual orientation, see below).

Some strongly advocate the awarding of custody solely to one parent as the least detrimental alternative for the child (Goldstein, Freud, & Solnit, 1973). Others, however, conclude that joint legal custody is preferable, and as a result, it is becoming the standard arrangement in most states (Goodman, Emery et al., 1998). Several strategies have been proposed for guiding judicial decisions: (a) the primary caretaker standard, which requires an accurate determination of who has served as the child's primary caretaker prior to the contested custody (Maccoby, 1999); (b) the approximation rule, whereby the decision is based on the child care arrangements prior to divorce or separation (Emery, 1999a; Scott, 1992); and (c) the "friendly parent" rule, whereby preference is given to the more cooperative parent (Folberg, 1991). Unfortunately, there is little if any empirical evidence to inform courts of the relative merits of each approach. This provides a future challenge for psychological researchers to meet.

Several reforms have been introduced to improve custody determination processes and outcomes. For example, in an effort to make contested custody cases less antagonistic, some jurisdictions have begun to use divorce mediation as an alternative to the traditionally adversarial litigation process. Although few studies have empirically assessed the presumed benefits of mediation, advocates contend that the experience of having directly participated in the decision-making process increases the parties' satisfaction with the outcome, increases the likelihood that the resulting arrangement will be upheld, and in turn, avoids future litigation (Dillon & Emery, 1996; Emery, 1994). Another reform movement challenges the assumption that children are not competent to participate in custody decisions. Specifically, reformers contend that allowing children to participate in custody decisions that directly affect their own welfare will lessen the presumed negative experience of a divorce and custody battle (e.g., Garrison, 1991; Melton, 1999). Even if future research supports this assumption, we believe it is prudent to remain sensitive to potential harm that could result from asking a child to articulate a preference for one parent over the other, especially if he or she does not have a clear preference and feels caught in the middle of parental conflict (Goodman, Emery et al., 1998). Further, the assumption that children should participate in custody decision making presumes that children are competent to participate, an assumption that may be valid for most adolescents, but which may be much less so for younger children. Thus, a psychological assessment of a pre-teen's maturity and competence to participate would seem in order. Several studies of children's involvement in custody decisions indicate that most judges assess children's wishes, and that, in general, children's degree of involvement in decisions is linearly related to their age, with most adolescents being involved in contested custody cases (e.g., Crosby-Currie, 1996; Garrison, 1991; Scott, Reppucci, & Aber, 1988). Research has not yet examined the consequences of expressing a preference on children's well-being.

As in the domains of juvenile justice and child abuse, highly publicized cases sway public opinion about custody issues. Several recent cases highlight interesting and controversial complexities involved in some custody situations, including political agendas, grandparents' visitation rights, and the rights of lesbian parents. For example, few events in 2000 received more media attention than the contested custody of Elian Gonzalez, a 6-year-old Cuban boy rescued off of the coast of Florida after his mother drowned while attempting to reach asylum in the United States. Legally, this case should have been straightforward; that is, the boy should have been returned to his father's custody in Cuba. The mother's vocal relatives in Miami, however, claimed custody by arguing that it would not be in the boy's best interests to be returned to a communist country. Because there was no evidence that the father was an unfit parent, psychological theory and research would weigh in on the side of the father being the parental choice. The father was, in fact, ultimately awarded custody, but only after protracted legal appeals in the U.S. court system fueled by political nationalism and emotion.

Grandparent rights have also received media attention. In the past 25 years, every state (but not the District of Columbia) has initiated statutes allowing grandparents and other adults to petition the court to secure legal child visitation rights. Recently, the Supreme Court agreed to examine the constitutionality of grandparent visitation statutes being implemented in the state of Washington (*Troxel v. Granville*, 2000). Although most observers agree that loving extended families can play a positive role in a child's life, no psychological research has examined the impact of situations involving continuing conflict between parents and grandparents. Analogous research on quarreling parents strongly suggests that contested custody and visitation disagreements can have a negative influence on the children involved. In June 2000, the Supreme Court ruled that the longstanding legal precedent that parents have a right to raise their children as they see fit (e.g., *Meyer v. Nebraska*, 1923; *Pierce v. Society of Sisters*, 1925), including the right to refuse grandparent visitation remains operational.

Another area of controversy in child custody focuses on gay and lesbian parents' rights to raise their own children. In the case of *Bottoms v. Bottoms* (1995), the mother of a lesbian woman petitioned the court to be awarded custody on the grounds that the daughter's lifestyle (i.e., her sexual orientation) rendered her an unfit parent. The court awarded custody to the grandmother and the Supreme Court of Virginia upheld the ruling. This ruling stands in direct contrast to research that discredits assumptions that lesbian and gay parents are unfit (Patterson, 1992; 1995; Patterson, Fulcher, & Wainright, in press). In short, Patterson and Redding (1996) assert that issues pertaining to the parents' sexual orientation should not be considered when making determinations of child custody, visitation, foster care, or adoption "unless and until the weight of the evidence can be shown to have shifted" (p. 29). This provides an excellent example of the legal system's rejection of social science research that is relevant to child law and policy.

## The Complications of New Reproductive Technologies

Finally, various advances in reproductive technologies have initiated a new domain in which children and law are brought together. Laws delineating parental rights have lagged behind the challenges posed by new reproductive technologies. Although technological breakthroughs are considered victories in the field of medicine, the advances in the use of artificial insemination and other assisted reproductive technologies (ART) have created havoc in the legal arena, and there is little research or legal precedent to inform or guide the law. Examples of questions created by these new techniques range from who has the legal right to the preserved sperm or eggs of deceased persons, to whether parents who used ART should tell their children of their origins and whether the children should be provided with records indicating the identity of their biological/genetic parents. These and other questions challenge some of the basic assumptions regarding parental rights and responsibilities for their children, while complicating the matters further by challenging social custom with biological breakthroughs.

Some of the dilemmas in determining legal parenthood can be illustrated by one of the most controversial reproductive techniques, surrogate motherhood. Although a few states such as Michigan developed laws more than a decade ago as a result of the much publicized case of Mary Beth Whitehead, a surrogate mother who decided that she wished to keep the child (note: after much time in the courts, the contractual parents maintained custody of the child Whitehead bore), most states have no laws in place regarding surrogacy (TASC, 1997). Accordingly, the lack of appropriate legislation regarding surrogacy and other assisted reproduction arrangements makes it extremely difficult for courts to delineate parental rights and responsibilities in these situations. For example, as in the widely publicized case of *Buzzanca v. Buzzanca* (1998), ART made it possible for five different people to be considered a parent of a child: two parents contracting for the baby, a sperm donor, an egg donor, and the surrogate mother. The legal conflict commenced not as result of a custody dispute between the surrogate and the intended parents, but when the intended mother, Luanne Buzzanca, filed for child support from the intended father, John Buzzanca, who had recently filed for divorce. Although the initial ruling in this case stated that the child had no legal parents, the California appellate court utilized an intent-based approach to declare Mr. and Mrs. Buzzanca the child's legal parents. The court reasoned that but for the actions of the Buzzancas to arrange for the surrogate mother to be impregnated with the donor embryo, the child would not have been created (Vorzimer & O'Hara, 1998). This ruling is significant in that it sets precedence for the enforceability of surrogacy contracts and was determined by the intent-based approach pioneered by the California court (*Johnson v. Calvert*, 1993).

To date, psychological research has offered little in the way of attempting to answer the questions posed by parenting facilitated by ART. Only a few studies have explored child well being and family relations in families where births resulted from artificial insemination (Golombok, Bhanji, Rutherford, & Winston, 1990; Golombok, Cook, Bish, & Murray, 1995), and there is very little research investigating the impact on families created by other assisted reproductive techniques. Even so, no evidence exists to suggest that new reproductive technologies pose a serious threat to child outcome or family relations.

## Future Challenges

In summary, psychological research is of direct relevance to law and policy regarding a child's place in changing and novel family circumstances. Researchers in this area face many future challenges. More research is clearly needed to understand how policy can ensure that children are accommodated in the best manner possible when their parents divorce. Research is also sorely needed on the factors that contribute to custody determinations that are truly in the best interests of children. That research needs to be responsive to myriad complex factors such as parental sexual orientation, child age, family relationships, and socioeconomic concerns. Finally, as scientific technology advances, producing increasingly complicated parenting situations, so too must psychological knowledge grow so that laws and policies can be informed and reflect the best interests of children and their families.

## CHILD MALTREATMENT

Balancing parental and child rights against each other and against the state's responsibility to protect children who are being maltreated is an exceptionally precarious undertaking (Portwood & Reppucci, 1997). Laws and policies related to child maltreatment and children's subsequent involvement in the legal system are often based on psychological assumptions that may have little empirical foundation. In this section, we consider policy and research related to efforts to define child maltreatment, prevent child abuse, and accommodate children's eyewitness testimony.

### Defining Abuse

According to national social service statistics, 13 of every 1,000 children in the U.S. were victims of some form of child maltreatment in 1998 (U.S. Department of Health and Human Services, 2000). As reported by Goodman, Emery et al. (1998), about half of child abuse claims received by social service agencies involve allegations of neglect, and the majority of the remainder involves reports of physical abuse (24%) or sexual abuse (13%). Estimates from retrospective victim surveys suggest that, before reaching adulthood, at least 25% of girls and 10% of boys will have an experience that many would define as sexual abuse (e.g., Elliot & Briere, 1995; Finkelhor, Hotaling, Lewis, & Smith, 1990), and more will experience other forms of child maltreatment including physical abuse and neglect (Goodman, Emery et al., 1998).

In light of these statistics, few would disagree that child maltreatment is a societal problem of great import, or that laws should protect children from maltreatment. Yet there is disagreement over the basic issue of what should be defined as child maltreatment (Reppucci & Fried, in press). Prevalence estimates such as those above depend on the definition of child maltreatment used by the information source. These definitions differ from researcher to researcher, as well as from discipline to discipline—in particular, from psychology to law. For example, Atteberry-Bennett (1987, as reported in Haugaard & Reppucci, 1988) found significant differences between legal and mental health professionals in what they considered instances of sexual abuse, with mental health professionals having a much broader definition. Can psychological research inform the law as it struggles to define child abuse in a meaningful way? Consider neglect: As mentioned above, the failure of parents to provide needed medical care to children is often recognized by the law as a punishable instance of neglect, but not if the medical care is withheld for religious reasons (Bottoms et al., 1995; Bullis, 1991). Is harm to children any different when medical neglect is brought about by indifferent or indigent parents as compared to parents driven by religious beliefs? Consider physical abuse: Many laws and social service policies specify that certain physical actions taken toward a child constitute physical abuse (e.g., a teacher slapping or hitting a child), yet those same actions may not be defined as abuse when they are applied by parents in the name of discipline. Is the psychological or physical impact of being hit mediated by the identity or ideological motivations of the perpetrator? In fact, research suggests that corporal punishment has many negative consequences (Straus, 1994, 1996; Straus & Stewart, 1999).

Consideration of definitional issues surrounding child sexual abuse provides several examples of assumptions made by laws that could be tested through research. For example, laws in most states hold that sexual abuse is constituted when persons younger than a certain age have sexual contact with adults. There are, of course, constraining elements that vary from jurisdiction to jurisdiction, such as the nature of the actions and the age of the adult, but age of the child is always a key defining element. This age differs across states; for example, in California, the age defining victims of sexual abuse is 14 (Goodman, Emery et al., 1998). In Illinois, one can be a child victim through the age of 16 (or 17 if the adult perpetrator holds a position of significant trust or authority relative to the victim). These laws are based on bright line developmental assumptions. One such assumption is that precisely at a certain age, adolescents gain competence in matters relevant to giving consent to sexual activity. Another underlying assumption is that all such sexual contact is harmful to children. Illinois' additional assumption appears to be that the crime is greater, perhaps more harmful and/or exploitative, when a perpetrator holds a position of power relative to the victim.

Are such assumptions correct? As we have illustrated already, psychological research has yet to understand fully children's competencies in a variety of domains, and that is certainly true in the domain of children's understanding of and ability to consent to sexual activity. Future psychological knowledge of this sort might be useful to courts in their task of defining the legal boundaries of sexual behavior (Oberman, 1994). Further, psychological research has already produced a great deal of information about the short- and long-term effects of various forms of adult/child sexual contact (for reviews, see Berliner & Elliott, 1996; Kendall-Tackett, Williams, & Finkelhor, 1993). Such findings may not, however, directly inform legal definitions of child sexual abuse, for at least two reasons. First, there is considerable variability in the way children respond to sexual abuse, with some children being remarkably resilient, and others severely harmed (Cicchetti & Rogosch, 1997; Kendall-Tackett et al., 1993). Psychology cannot yet offer enough specificity about the factors that determine various reactions to be of much practical use to law or policy makers. Second, in our society, child abuse is such an emotional topic that, as noted by Ondersma, Chaffin, Berliner, Cordon, Goodman, and Barnett (1999), "child maltreatment in all forms... is difficult to define, and may best be determined sociologically through consensus of a given society." In a 1998 *Psychological Bulletin* article, Rind, Tromovitch, and Bauserman meta-analytically examined studies of the effects of child sexual abuse and questioned the harmfulness of some forms of adult/child sexual contact. They even suggested that lawmakers should heed their conclusions. The ensuing controversy, which raged from within the research community (where experts debated the merits of the authors' methodology and interpretation) to U.S. Senators' offices and Dr. Laura's nationally syndicated radio talk show, suggests that society may not accept psychological research on the effects of adult/child sexual contact as relevant to the issue of what should and should not be defined by law as sexual abuse—at least research purporting to show non-negative effects of adult/child sexual contact. Ultimately, then, legal definitions may be based less on empirical demonstrations of harm than on societal norms and mores that view sexual contact between a child and an adult as morally reprehensible and exploitative under any condition (Ondersma et al., 1999).

## Preventing Child Sexual Maltreatment

Laws are designed not only to identify abuse and punish abusers, but also to prevent future child abuse. Psychological research is relevant to the assumptions underlying these laws, and in turn, relevant when considering the effectiveness of these laws. To start, basic laws criminalizing child abuse and punishing its perpetrators are, of course, based on the assumption that incarceration will prevent future abuse by making it less likely that those incarcerated will reoffend and by deterring potential offenders. Unfortunately, research reveals high recidivism rates for adult child sexual abusers in particular, casting doubt on at least part of this basic assumption (Winick & LaFond, 1998). As a result of particularly heinous and well publicized cases of reoffense, most notably the sexual assault and murder of 7-year-old Megan Kanka, politicians and legislatures have turned to increasingly severe policies. For example, the Jacob Wetterling Crimes Against Children Act, enacted by the United States Congress in 1994, required convicted sex offenders to register with their local law enforcement agency. In 1996, Megan's Law amended the Wetterling Act to require community notification about the presence of sex offenders. Notifications now range from registries available at local police stations to signs posted in offenders' front yards (Louisiana Criminal Code as cited in Winick, 1998). Note an implicit assumption of these laws: "stranger danger" (MacFarlane, Doueck, & Levine, 2000). That is, they assume that many children are abused by strangers and therefore, much child sexual abuse would be thwarted by notification that could allow parents to take protective measures. In fact, however, most child sexual abuse is not perpetrated by strangers; it is perpetrated by loved, trusted adults such as parents, parent's paramours, or other family members (e.g., U.S. Department of Health and Human Services, 1996). Consequently, these laws may have the unintended consequence of creating hardships for incest victims and their families. For example, in some cases it is deemed best for a family if the offending relative (e.g., father) remains with the family and receives treatment. In such cases, the offender will be subject to sex offender registration and community notification laws like any other offender (e.g., LaFond, 1998; Simon, 1998; Winick, 1998), bringing additional stigma and stress to the victim and the family. This becomes an especially problematic situation when it involves a juvenile sex offender because it obviates any possibility of normative rehabilitation for the youth. Moreover, existing data demonstrate that juvenile offenders recidivate at a much lower rate than adults (approximately 10% versus 40%, respectively), which suggests that the phenotypically similar behaviors of sex offending adults and youth may be genotypically very different (Trivits & Reppucci, 2000): a fact that should give pause to using the same intervention for both.

Of course, the main underlying assumption of registration and community notification laws is that they will curtail recidivism among convicted sex offenders. Schram and Milloy (1995) compared recidivism rates for 125 sex offenders in Washington State who were released before or after notification laws were enacted in the state. Offenders were matched in terms of number of sex offenses, victim type (child or adult), age, and race. After nearly 5 years in the community, offenders released after notification laws were enacted were statistically just as likely to be re-arrested for sex crimes (19% recidivism rate) as were offenders released before notification laws (22% recidivism rate). Notification did affect the timing of re-arrest, however: Offenders released with notification laws were re-arrested for new crimes sooner ($M = 2.5$ years) than offenders released without notification laws ($M = 5$ years). Thus, preliminary research is not supportive of the assumptions that drove these laws. Social scientists are challenged with continuing such informative studies, and with pursuing other avenues for prevention, such as developing effective treatment programs for perpetrators and designing community interventions to prevent child abuse by reaching both potential victims and potential offenders (see Wolfe, Reppucci, & Hart, 1995; for a review of child abuse prevention programs).

## Future Challenges

Our discussion illustrates that psychology has much to offer policy and lawmakers faced with the tasks of defining child maltreatment and designing policies to prevent it. Future research must strive for direct relevance to the issues at the forefront of consideration in each domain. For example, the struggle to define child maltreatment properly continues, as evidenced by the disparity among state child sexual abuse laws: In particular, laws in various states have differing lower age limits at which adolescents can consent to sexual activity. Here is a clear opportunity for psychological research to address the specific issue of sexual decision making competence among adolescents, and to inform the law of the findings. Psychology is also well positioned to join discussions about whether public policy is needed to address the recently recognized ills of psychological or emotional abuse. Psychology also needs to continue to test the assumptions behind laws and policies aimed at prevention. What will curtail recidivism among convicted sex offenders? Community notification? Involuntary civil commitment after time served? Or is there some other answer—perhaps to be suggested by informed researchers rather than by a fearful public and their political representatives who desperately want to prevent horrific murders like Megan Kanka's. Psychology needs to be proactive in suggesting novel and multidimensional prevention programs involving children, families, and the community.

## CHILDREN'S EYEWITNESS TESTIMONY

The societal recognition of child maltreatment, particularly child sexual abuse, is responsible for bringing increasing numbers of children into the courtroom as testifiers (Myers, 1998), and with them, a number of interesting legal and psychological issues. Children also provide forensic reports and eyewitness testimony in other types of cases. We now consider the basic and applied contributions of psychological research that has tested assumptions about children's actual and perceived competencies; first, in relation to understanding children's actual abilities to participate in forensic interviews and court proceedings as witnesses (usually victim/witnesses in child sexual abuse cases), and second, in relation to understanding the effects of courtroom accommodations for child witnesses on children's actual and perceived competence.

## Actual Competence

The accuracy of children's eyewitness testimony has been of concern in psychology and in society in general for over a century.[2] Initially, courts assumed that children were highly suggestible, inaccurate witnesses who were not competent to testify (Davis, 1998; Goodman, 1984). Laws that presumed children's incompetence virtually excluded child witnesses from the courtroom. In fact, the earliest psychological research testing this assumption supported these perceptions of incompetence (Whipple, 1911; for reviews, see Ceci & Bruck, 1993; Goodman, 1984). After years of inattention, there was a resurgence in children's testimony research in the early 1980s, mainly in response to the increased reporting of child abuse and after disastrous day care abuse cases highlighted children's potential

---

[2]Note that controversy has focused not only on children's eyewitness reports, but also on some adults', particularly on adults' reports of childhood abuse based on allegedly repressed, then recovered memories. Interestingly, initial legal reactions to such reports were far less skeptical than some reactions within the field of psychology itself. Very quickly after the first celebrated cases involving repressed memory testimony, states passed laws that extended normal statutes of limitations to accommodate testimony based on repressed memories of abuse. In some states, for example, victims may seek legal redress against their abusers long after normal statutes of limitations have elapsed, as long as they had no memory of the sexual abuse until shortly before filing suit (Brown, Scheflin, & Hammond, 1998). These laws are obviously based on very specific assumptions about the nature of memory for traumatic events—assumptions that are not shared by some psychological experts (Loftus, 1993; Lindsay & Read, 1995). Data from psychological research actually suggest that very few victims who say they experienced a period during which they forgot their abuse actually mean they forgot it so completely that they could meet such legal standards (Belli, Winkielman, Read, Schwarz, & Lynn, 1998; Epstein & Bottoms, 1999), casting doubt on the need for such delayed discovery exceptions. Even so, research has not produced evidence ruling out the possibility of delayed reports. In any case, these legal reactions are reminiscent of the tendency for some state legislatures in 1980s and 1990s to pass special laws designating child abuse committed in connection with satanic rituals a more serious offense than otherwise. Psychologists' (and the FBI's) best efforts failed to uncover evidence of the presumed epidemic of satanic ritual abuse cases which drove those laws (Bottoms, Shaver, & Goodman, 1996; Lanning, 1992).

suggestibility. At this time, assumptions of incompetence were tested again, with far more positive conclusions regarding children's testimonial competence.

For example, research reveals that children are not as suggestible as once thought, particularly when questioned about meaningful events under optimal reporting conditions (for reviews, see Goodman & Bottoms, 1993; McGough, 1994). Some of the first modern research on children's testimony revealed that children typically provide the most accurate information when they freely recall information in response to open-ended, non-leading questions (e.g., "What happened while you were in the house?"); however, they report very little information in response to such questions. The reality of legal investigations, however, is that more specific or focused questions (e.g., "Did you ride in Uncle Bill's car?") are often needed to determine what a child witnessed or whether a child experienced abuse. But, asking such questions raises the issue of suggestibility: Will children agree with an adult's or a parent's misleading (inaccurate) suggestion? This area of child/law research has been responsive to these applied questions, testing children's accuracy and resistance to suggestibility under conditions directly relevant to forensic situations. For example, research finds that younger children, particularly preschoolers, are generally more suggestible than older children and adults, and that their accuracy is particularly likely to suffer when interviewed by biased, coercive, or intimidating interviewers (Davis & Bottoms, in press; Garvin, Wood, Malpass, & Shaw, 1998; Lepore & Sesco, 1994; for a review, see Ceci & Bruck, 1995); when questioned with developmentally inappropriate language including "legalese" (Carter, Bottoms, & Levine, 1996; Perry et al., 1995); when questioned repeatedly with misleading questions (Leichtman & Ceci, 1995); when told falsehoods by a trusted adult (Haugaard, Reppucci, Laird, & Naufeld, 1991; Portwood & Reppucci, 1996); when interviewed after a long delay (Goodman, Batterman-Faunce, Schaaf, & Kenney, 2000); and when interviewed about events that were not central or meaningful or about events they did not directly experience (Pipe & Wilson, 1994; Rudy & Goodman, 1991). Note that such factors may or may not affect children's actual *memory*, rather, they may affect only children's *reports*. For example, like adults, children may be reluctant to report a well-remembered, embarrassing, or traumatic event or an event they are motivated to keep secret (Bottoms, Goodman, Schwartz-Kenney, & Thomas, 2000; Goodman & Schwartz-Kenney, 1992).

Because several researchers in this field heeded the call to conduct their research in ecologically valid manners, their findings have directly influenced policy. For example, the research has formed the basis for recommended guidelines for conducting optimal forensic interviews with alleged victims (Poole & Lamb 1998; Sorenson, Bottoms, & Perona, 1997). Over the past decade, forensic investigators have been responsive to these policy recommendations, and interviewing techniques have improved, ensuring more accurate reports from children. Even so, child interview protocols are still evolving, because there are still many unanswered questions about children's eyewitness abilities, questions that psychology should strive to answer.

## Perceived Competence

As we mentioned previously, perceptions of competence may differ from actual competence. A growing body of child testimony research has focused on adults' perceptions of children's accuracy. This research is driven by the fact that although children's actual accuracy may never be known in a legal context, children's testimony must be evaluated by forensic investigators, jurors, and judges, and justice may not be served if these perceptions are biased. This research finds that adults may not be very accurate in determining children's actual accuracy, and that their perceptions are influenced by a number of variables. These include case factors such as evidence strength and the presence of a corroborating child witness (Bottoms & Goodman, 1994); child witness factors such as age, race, child's level of pre-court preparation, and whether the child is a bystander- or victim-witness (Goodman, Golding, & Haith, 1984; Kovera & Borgida, 1996; Nightingale, 1993); and characteristics of the adults themselves such as gender, attitudes and biases, level of empathic concern, and personal history of abuse (Bottoms & Goodman, 1994; Gabora, Spanos, & Joab, 1993; Golding, Sanchez, & Sego, 1999; Haegerich & Bottoms, 2000; Isquith, Levine, & Scheiner, 1993). Although attorneys express interest in the latter findings to the extent that they want to use the findings during voir dire to identify the best jurors for their particular cases, the work has resulted in few policy or legal changes (e.g., education of juries or judges, modification of jury instructions).

Courts have, however, been very responsive to the results of some psychological research on children's testimony, and court reform based on research findings has been implemented in some jurisdictions. Perhaps the most important reforms include the development of special programs to prepare children for the task of testifying in court (Sas, Wolfe, & Gowdey, 1996), and innovations aimed at removing children from the potentially stressful courtroom altogether (e.g., replacing children's in-court testimony with testimony given via closed circuit television, in the form of hearsay testimony from another witness, or via videotaped pre-trial forensic interviews). Such accommodations have the potential to affect both the actual and the perceived credibility of child witnesses.

Do children need special accommodations when they enter a court of law? Two competing assumptions drive opposite answers to this question. On the one hand, there is a child advocacy based assumption that children need protections in the adult-designed courtroom, because testifying in court is a stressful and traumatic experience for children. On the other hand, the courts assume that face-to-face confrontation compels witnesses to tell the truth and promotes accurate fact-finding from jurors who will have many non-verbal cues to use to assess witness credibility (*Coy v. Iowa*, 1988). Both assumptions have been tested in research programs that have had impact on law governing children's evidence—such noteworthy impact that we highlight this work as another model (like Grisso's research on Miranda warnings) for researchers hoping to influence law through sound scientific research and effective dissemination efforts.

Goodman and colleagues (Goodman, Taub et al., 1992) tested the assumption that children are sometimes traumatized by testimony and could therefore benefit from accommodations. Their study of matched testifying and non-testifying child abuse victims in the Denver court system found that testifying was sometimes associated with emotional costs (though not always and perhaps not long-lasting costs), especially for children who had to testify multiple times and lacked maternal support. Children disclosed that their single greatest fear was facing the defendant in the courtroom, a fear that was associated with attenuated ability to answer prosecutors' questions. Other researchers have similarly found evidence of trauma to children who had to confront their accused abuser (Murray, 1995; Sas, 1991; Whitcomb, Shapiro, & Stellwagen, 1985). Goodman and others summarized these and other relevant psychological findings in an amicus brief submitted by the American Psychology-Law Society (APLS) and filed on behalf of the APA (see Goodman, Levine, Melton, & Ogden, 1991). The brief had significant impact on the Supreme Court's ruling in *Maryland v. Craig* (1990), which paved the way for the use of accommodating techniques in the courtroom.

Specifically, in the case at issue, alleged child sexual abuse victims testified via one-way closed circuit television (CCTV), where the defendant, judge, attorneys, and jury could see the testimony, but the children could not see them. Craig, the defendant, was convicted. The Maryland Court of Appeals reversed Craig's conviction, reasoning that the CCTV was used without proper showing of cause (i.e., that the children could not otherwise have communicated reasonably). The U.S. Supreme Court subsequently considered the case. In contrast to disappointing instances in which the Supreme Court ignored relevant social science findings in other domains (e.g., jury bias in death penalty cases, *Lockhart v. McCree*, 1986; see Bersoff, 1987; Thompson, 1989), the impact of this APA brief and the psychological findings it contained was remarkable. Justice O'Connor's majority opinion often paralleled the conclusions and even the language of the brief. The following quote from the majority opinion illustrates specific references to the APA brief and to Goodman's work (later published in 1992 as cited above): "Given the State's traditional and 'transcendent interest in protecting the welfare of children' ... and buttressed by the growing body of academic literature documenting the psychological trauma suffered by child abuse victims who must testify in court, see Brief for American Psychological Association as Amicus Curiae 7–13; G. Goodman et al., Emotional Effects of Criminal Court Testimony on Child Sexual Assault Victims, Final Report to the National Institute of Justice ..., we will not second-guess the considered judgment of the Maryland Legislature regarding the importance of its interest in protecting child abuse victims from the emotional trauma of testifying. Accordingly, we hold that, if the State makes an adequate showing of necessity, the state interest in protecting child witnesses from the trauma of testifying in a child abuse case is sufficiently important to justify the use of a special procedure that permits a child witness in such cases to testify at trial against a defendant in the absence of face-to-face confrontation with the defendant" (p. 16). As the authors of the brief themselves later noted, their effort in producing the brief "illustrates the need for psychological expertise on critical questions of social fact and the utility of the pro bono efforts of APLS members in bringing such knowledge to the legal system" (Goodman et al., 1991, p. 16).

We should note that the *Craig* decision did not end the debate over courtroom accommodations for children. Some state supreme courts (e.g., Pennsylvania) continue to rule that CCTV violates defendants' rights to state constitutional guarantees of face-to-face confrontation (Goodman, Tobey et al., 1998). Thus, psychological researchers continue to test assumptions surrounding courtroom accommodations for children with mock trial methodology designed to address how accommodations affect children's actual testimonial competence as well as jurors' perceptions of their competence (e.g., Davies & Noon, 1991; Goodman, Tobey et al., 1998; Ross et al., 1994; Swim, Borgida, & McCoy, 1993). Findings from this work are converging to indicate that although some children's actual accuracy may increase when they testify via alternative modes like CCTV, special accommodations may negatively influence jurors' perceptions of children's competence. Although special accommodations for children in the courtroom are not often requested by prosecutors (Gray, 1993) and in many cases, such alterations are not allowed, continued work investigating the impact of CCTV and other alternatives may directly influence future policy regarding courtroom accommodations of children's testimony.

## Future Challenges

We have shown that child witness research has had a noteworthy impact on law and policy. The research has also brought about significant theoretical advances across several subdisciplines of psychology (developmental, cognitive, and social). For example, research on children's eyewitness testimonial competence has yielded important basic knowledge about developmental changes in children's memory, and models for understanding the impact of stress and social influences on children's memory. Future researchers face the challenge of continuing this tradition while addressing formidable empirical issues, including the need to (a) identify forensic interview practices that maximize disclosures of real abuse while minimizing false reports, (b) understand psychological mechanisms underlying accurate and inaccurate reports of past events, especially when stress and trauma are involved, (c) determine how to distinguish true from false reports, and (d) identify individual differences (e.g., temperament, working memory capacity) that might affect children's testimony (a paramount question in the eyes of the court, which is concerned about the accuracy of specific children in specific cases). Continued attention to conducting scientifically sound research with ecologically valid techniques will ensure that future child witness research on these issues will yield generalizable results of importance to law and policy.

## OTHER LEGALLY RELEVANT DOMAINS OF CHILD/LAW RESEARCH

We have outlined the contributions of psychological research in illuminating the objective truth or falsehood of key legal assumptions in several major areas: legal decision making about juvenile justice, medical decision making, divorce and custody, child maltreatment, and children's eyewitness testimony. There are, of course, many other domains ripe for contributions from psychology viz a vis the models described above. For example, adoption, and other out-of-home placement policies and decisions are driven by assumptions about child development (Portwood & Reppucci, 1994). In particular, some groups, especially the National Association of Black Social Workers, argue that transracial adoptions may negatively affect a child's racial identity, and that courts should weigh child and parent race heavily when making adoption decisions, or prohibit transracial adoptions altogether (McRoy, 1989; Mini, 1994). In fact, however, psychological research finds no negative effects of transracial adoptions on children or families (e.g., Bagly, 1993; Simon, Altstein, & Melli, 1994). Furthermore, the Multiethnic Placement Act of 1994 prohibits an agency, or entity, that receives federal assistance and is involved in adoption or foster care programs from delaying or denying the placement of a child based on the child's or parent's race, color, or national origin. Unfounded assumptions about potential harm to birth parents or potential benefits for adoptees also drive laws and policies about sealing adoption records, yet very little empirical research has addressed these issues (Goodman, Emery et al., 1998).

Developmental assumptions also influence legal and political decisions regarding education, child labor, curfews, drinking age, and welfare reform. In particular, desires to curtail children's rights for the greater societal good and to protect children from harm drive policy decisions in these areas. It is important to note, however, that presumptions about competence that underlie policies in various domains are often blatantly discrepant. For example, nearly all states now sanction the legal drinking age as 21, yet adolescents can marry or be tried as an adult criminal at much younger ages in every state. More research on underlying competence issues and better dissemination of research findings could potentially bring about more rational laws and policies. Psychologists also have the potential to participate more actively in debates surrounding freedom of expression in schools, corporal punishment, and the right to receive special needs services. As we have noted throughout, societal perceptions of children's competencies in all these various domains currently drive policy and law, but children's actual competencies may differ in important ways from these perceptions. Such discrepancies can and should be illuminated by psychological research.

## RESEARCH, POLICY, AND LAW: TOWARD CLOSER FUTURE ALLIANCES

We now turn to an examination of critical issues that researchers must tackle if the field of Children, Psychology and Law is to move forward in a meaningful way. For us, forward movement is multidimensional, defined in terms of improving the basic scientific integrity of child/law research as well as its applicability to the policy and law that psychologists hope to affect. It also means significantly increasing the presence of psychological knowledge in critical debates about social issues involving children. In the next section, we suggest that the field will move forward if researchers are successful in (a) changing their orientation by becoming more proactive and less passive in affecting societal change, (b) improving their methodology in a variety of ways, (c) becoming more sensitive to the role that personal and societal ethics and values should and should not play in research, and (d) increasing their success in disseminating knowledge to the professionals who can actively use it.

## Moving Beyond Convention, Becoming More Proactive

We argue that it is time to be more innovative, creative, and generally proactive in using empirical findings to design concrete, specific programs and interventions to help children and families who are involved with legal issues. Psychologists are uniquely equipped to use psychological principles and social science findings to produce novel programs, procedures, and tools of use to courts and various professionals who deal directly with children. For example, during the past two decades, research to identify and delineate risk and protective factors and their interactions regarding violence, delinquency, teen pregnancy, school dropout, and other maladies of youth have provided legal, educational, and mental health professionals with information upon which to develop various preventive interventions (e.g., Gillock & Reyes, 1996; Walberg, Reyes, & Weissberg, 1997). The data suggest that along with reducing or alleviating risk factors, the most effective programs may need to enhance protective factors early in life (e.g., preschool programs targeted to urban, low-income children) to enhance cognitive and social development and, in turn, to reduce serious and chronic delinquency (Yoshikawa, 1993). Other examples focus on procedures and tools. Psychologists have taken an active role in designing optimal research-based forensic interview techniques that have been of great help to front-line professionals who interview suspected child abuse victims (e.g., Geiselman, Saywitz, & Bornstein, 1993; Sorenson et al., 1997; Poole & Lamb, 1998; Yuille, 1993). Others are currently using research to expand the definition of both culpability and adjudicative competence (Cauffman et al., 1999; Woolard et al., 2001), which should (a) result in improved assessment procedures for clinicians charged with making such determinations about juveniles charged with crimes and (b) aid in the development of guidelines regarding when a child should never be treated as mature as an adult (Steinberg & Cauffman, 1999). These proactive attempts to help social service and legal professionals conduct their investigations more effectively should benefit youth involved in child abuse and juvenile justice investigations. Note that the researchers involved in these efforts necessarily understood the legal and social service context of the psychological issues they studied. That is, the psychologists who designed interview protocols and developed the competence research first built collaborative relationships with social service and legal professionals to understand the exact nature of the problems they wanted to address. Collaboration between researchers and professionals in the legal system is essential for identifying opportunities for proactive intervention.

Psychological researchers are also in an excellent position to evaluate the success of innovative policies and programs that already exist. For example, laws requiring sexual offenders to register or to be committed to mental health treatment facilities after serving prison sentences were enacted in direct reaction to public sentiment and political agenda, not as a result of research findings. Are these programs achieving their goal of reducing sexual victimizations and criminal recidivism among sex offenders? And should the same guidelines apply for juvenile as for adult sex offenders given that recidivism rates for juveniles are significantly lower than for adults (Trivits & Reppucci, under review)? Some work is addressing this issue, but more is needed. A second example where psychologists could be helpful is in assessing programs derived from the restorative justice movement. Restorative justice is primarily concerned with addressing wrongs and establishing or restoring social equality in relationships (Llewellyn & Howse, 1999). A core element of most restorative justice programs is a direct encounter between the affected parties (i.e., victim, offender, and community) resulting in a plan for restoration; that is, an agreement of what the offender will do to restore relationships damaged by the offense. Restorative justice programs are gaining international support: A recent survey found that there are at least 1,000 such programs in North America and Europe (Umbreit & Greenwood, 1999). They have been pursued especially aggressively in Canada and reflect principles underlying alternative dispute resolution procedures common to the Maori of New Zealand (Levine, 2000). Psychologists are ideally suited to both evaluate current restorative justice programs and to facilitate expansion of such programs to new realms. Currently, youth participation in restorative justice programs is limited to juvenile offenders. Could the program work as effectively if the youth was a victim of crime? Could the victim-offender encounters be modified to accommodate child victims? Perhaps restorative justice is a particularly viable option in such cases if the victim and offender are related. These are just a few of the issues that will probably engage restorative justice researchers in the near future, and that should be informed by psychological theory.

Another excellent example of innovative policy is "teen court" or "youth court" programs, which have recently increased significantly in number. By 1998, there were between 400 and 500 teen courts in the United States, almost a tenfold increase since 1991 (Butts, Hoffman, & Buck, 1999). Although often under the administration of the local juvenile court or probation agency, teen courts serve primarily as a diversion alternative for first-time and young offenders charged with misdemeanors, such as traffic offenses, curfew violations, and truancy. Various models have been used to oversee youth courts, but a factor common to all the programs is the participation of community youth who serve in some capacity, either as judge, jury, or youth attorney. The most common model uses an adult as the presiding judge in the court and youth as the attorneys and other court personnel. The dispositions most often handed down by such courts, which are not given the authority to detain defendants, include community service and apology letters. Although preliminary observations suggest that teen juries often recommend tougher sentences than some judges, it is not yet clear what kind of impact teen courts have on recidivism rates or perceptions of the juvenile justice system. In response, the Office of Juvenile Justice and Delinquency Prevention (OJJDP) recently funded an evaluation of teen courts. The evaluation will provide process and outcome data on four representative youth court programs in the next few years (Butts, Hoffman, & Buck, 1999).

Alternative programs aimed at prevention of social problems for youth are also good examples of programs that could benefit from systematic evaluation and psychological knowledge. Programs like Teen Outreach, which emphasize adolescent volunteerism, seem to have various positive effects, including the reduction of teenage pregnancy and school dropout. Although some Teen Outreach programs have been carefully evaluated (Allen, Kuperminc, Philliber, & Herre, 1994), these kinds of programs are largely implemented on a local level, and careful examination of their implementation and comprehensive evaluation of their impact is generally lacking. Deterrence-type programs developed to scare children into behaving (e.g., Scared Straight) and boot camps gained popularity in the early 1990s and have proliferated with increasing public support of "get tough" policies. Initial investigations of the effects of these programs, however, reveal that most juveniles exposed to these interventions had comparable or even higher recidivism rates than did juveniles who were not exposed to these interventions (Lewis, 1983; MacKenzie & Brame, 1995). In the absence of methodologically sound evaluations, little is known about the efficacy of such programs, the reasons for their success or failure, and the types of children most amenable to their approaches. Even so, these types of programs continue to operate and to receive public support, further indicating the pressing need for program evaluations to determine their efficacy.

Many other preventive legal and social service initiatives are ripe for careful evaluation, or for the proactive involvement of psychologists armed with relevant data. Examples include (a) the establishment of children's advocacy centers nationwide to enhance the accuracy of information obtained from alleged child abuse victims and, in turn, to prevent child abuse by making prosecutions more effective (Sorenson et al., 1997); (b) the enforcement of curfews to prevent youth crime; (c) increasing the age at which teenagers may obtain driver's licenses as a way of addressing the high prevalence of serious car accidents involving inexperienced young drivers; and (d) holding parents responsible for their children's actions in an effort to increase accountability within families and prevent youth crime.

## METHODOLOGICAL ISSUES

The issues studied by researchers in the field of Children, Psychology, and Law are complex, and as a result, the research is very difficult to do well. Yet research can effectively influence law and policy only if it is performed in a scientifically sound manner using ecologically valid techniques. What are some of the methodological challenges psychologists face in meeting these requirements? How can researchers become better prepared to move the field forward in the meaningful ways we described earlier?

### Psychology and Law: Disciplinary Differences

On the one hand, the disciplines of Psychology and of Law are naturally complementary: The Law seeks to regulate human behavior; Psychology seeks to understand behavior. One of our major themes in this chapter is that psychology is uniquely suited to studying the assumptions about human behavior inherent in the law. On the other hand, the disciplines of Psychology and Law differ greatly in terms of perspective, method, language, and analogies (Goodman, Emery, et al., 1998; Haney, 1980; Ogloff & Finkelman, 1999). For example, one central difference is that psychology pursues truth—objective answers to specific questions under certain conditions. The law seeks justice—resolution of conflict through the provision of deserved outcomes to parties involved in legal cases. Justice determinations involve complex weightings of issues such as the common good vs. individual rights (Wrightsman, Nietzel, & Fortune, 1998). These differences must be understood and accommodated if psychologists are to design studies that will have an impact on law and policy.

The basic methods or processes of law and psychology differ greatly. Whereas psychologists use the scientific method to seek knowledge with the least possible influence from values or opinion, courts apply law through the study of precedence (what has been reasoned previously by other courts in individual cases) and courts seek resolution in individual cases through adversarial confrontation of two parties, from which justice is supposed to emerge. Laws are also subject to the influence of societal values and norms (Monahan & Walker, 1998). Thus, the foci of scientific and legal methods are quite different: Courts make decisions about individual cases (an ideographic, or case study approach), whereas psychologists usually study group trends (a nomothetic, or group level approach). This difference often leads to frustration when the two disciplines intersect. For example, in a child sexual abuse case in which the main evidence of a defendant's guilt is a child's testimony, a court may seek a specific opinion from an expert psychological witness about the accuracy and suggestibility of the particular child witness in that case. Yet the ethical research psychologist can offer only information about the accuracy of children tested in studies under circumstances approximating those in the case at hand. Although this fundamental difference will always exist to some degree, we believe the gulf can be narrowed. That is, for psychological research to be maximally useful for courts, psychologists must increase their attention to individual differences whenever possible. Researchers are beginning to do this in children's eyewitness testimony research (e.g., Bottoms, Davis, Nysse, Haegerich, & Conway, 2000; Bruck, Ceci, & Melnyk, 1997; Quas, Qin, Schaaf, & Goodman, 1997) and in various other child/law domains, as noted in previous examples. This should increase courts' receptiveness to psychological research.

## Ensuring the Generalizability of Research

Another issue that researchers must address if they are to have maximal effect on law, policy, and practice is to make their research generalizable beyond the laboratory and often specialized samples. That is, psychologists must ensure that their methods are ecologically valid. Unfortunately, this is often quite difficult. To attain ecological validity, it is first necessary for researchers to understand the law that is the context for the research. Some in the field of Psychology and Law have called for researchers to obtain increased training in legal studies (e.g., law school course work, Master of Legal Studies degrees) while in graduate school or as post-doctoral scholars (Bersoff et al., 1997). Perhaps a more realistic alternative for most researchers is to cultivate close collaborative relationships with legal scholars and other professionals who understand the law relevant to the psychologist's area of inquiry. As we have already noted, researchers must collaborate and communicate with legal professionals and policy makers. In fact, the current editor of *Law and Human Behavior* recently noted, "Psychologists interested in psychology and law need to have lawyers as collaborators so that we do not make errors in the questions we ask or the methods we employ" (Weiner, 1999). A similar argument has been forcefully presented for practitioners (Goldstein, Freud, Solnit, & Goldstein, 1986).

Practical issues such as time and money, as well as ethical issues, may constrain even the best attempts at ecological validity. It takes a great deal of funding to obtain the best samples and employ the best methods. To understand these challenges, consider mock jury research, which is often the target of concern with regard to ecological validity. Specifically, researchers interested in jurors' perceptions and decisions in cases involving child witnesses or juvenile offenders face the problem of not being allowed to study the deliberations of actual juries. Instead, they usually study mock jury decision making in the laboratory with undergraduate college students as jurors, a group of adults who are generally younger and more educated than many actual jurors. Moreover, mock jury studies cannot fully duplicate the experience of serving on a real jury (Diamond, 1997; Weiten & Diamond, 1979). The generalizability of some mock jury research is questioned not only because of the participants but also because it contains serious violations of realism (e.g., mock jurors are given incorrect verdict choices, inadmissible evidence is included in stimulus trials, artificial deliberation times are imposed). Other research, however, has attained noteworthy realism by including jury-eligible community members as mock jurors, jury instructions that would be given in an actual case, transcripts from actual trials or realistic trial simulations based on real case details. Some researchers have gone to exceptional lengths to attain ecological validity, such as Goodman, Tobey, and colleagues (1998) in the previously discussed study investigating jurors' reactions to courtroom accommodations of child testimony. In that study, children experienced an event, then were questioned individually about the event under direct- and cross-examination in an actual city courtroom. For each of more than 180 separate trial simulations, trained actors played key roles such as judge, attorneys, and bailiff, and over 1,200 jury-eligible community members filled the jury box. Closed-circuit television techniques were employed just as they might be in an actual case. Yet, even with generous funding for this research, ethical issues still necessarily limited this work: The "crime" in the case was a babysitter placing stickers on the children's exposed stomach rather than an actual instance of child sexual abuse.

It is important to note that although realism is sacrificed in the laboratory, experimental control is gained. Even if researchers had access to jury rooms, it would be difficult to draw cause and effect conclusions from the study of idiosyncratic groups of people considering cases that vary on multiple dimensions. Even the most artificial mock jury research, using college students as participants and written transcripts as stimuli, are very useful first steps in programs of research examining the effects of particular isolated variables on jury decision making. Convenience samples and written scenario methodology allows for the experimental control necessary to draw cause and effect conclusions about specific variables of interest, before moving on to more elaborately staged research to pursue provocative patterns of results (Diamond, 1997). Further, a recent meta-analysis by Bornstein (1999) reveals few differences in the judgments of undergraduate and community member jurors (see also Cutler, Penrod, & Dexter, 1990), and some research reveals few differences between mock jurors' decisions in studies using written scenarios versus more elaborate videotaped testimony (Goodman et al., 1987; Scheiner, 1988). Even so, such work is only the first step, and careful researchers need to replicate their findings with more elaborate, realistic studies to increase the probability that courts will take note of the findings.

Thus, laboratory studies have limitations, but excel in terms of experimental control. Ironically, one could argue that some areas of psychology and law research suffer from too much ecological validity and could benefit from some of the control gained through laboratory studies. That is, field studies are often confounded with a plethora of variables beyond the researcher's control, they sometimes lack control groups, and they often are limited by the impossibility of random assignment to alternate conditions. The challenge is to find compromises that will allow for experimental control as well as generalizability. It is possible that new technologies being developed outside of our field will help us as we attempt to improve the ecological validity of our studies. For example, could laboratory simulations be enhanced with virtual reality technology? Would this help psychologists circumvent practical and ethical problems, or would it create new ones? Clearly, new partnerships with professionals in disciplines such as computer science are necessary to understand how new technologies might be useful.

As noted previously, generalizability is not only dependent upon whether or not procedures are realistic, but also on the researcher's choice of subjects. Accessibility to the appropriate participant populations is often key to producing good research. For example, how generalizable are the findings from research wherein typical adolescent girls are asked to make decisions about hypothetical scenarios depicting themselves facing a decision about an unwanted pregnancy? Surely not as generalizable as research conducted with adolescents actually awaiting the results of their own pregnancy test in a clinic waiting room (Ambuel & Rappaport, 1992). Although we have been able to cite this and other examples of research that used appropriate samples (e.g., Crosby et al., 1995; Grisso, 1980), there is a clear need to continue efforts to conduct ecologically valid research. Although it is often convenient to use a sample of undergraduate students, or to have white middle class youth as participants in the appropriate age range respond to hypothetical vignettes, psychologists must move to participants of diverse socioeconomic backgrounds and ethnicities to evaluate the populations in question.

Finally, diversity should also be evident in the field of Children, Psychology, and Law—both in our participant samples and among the ranks of our researchers. Currently, for example, girls are typically underrepresented and minorities are overrepresented in much juvenile offender research (Hoyt & Scherer, 1998). Studies should be designed examining within-minority-group differences as well as between-group differences. The field also needs to make active efforts to attract and train researchers who are diverse in terms of gender and ethnicity. In particular, as in most professions today, minorities are very poorly represented. This is a particularly striking omission because some of the populations of interest are dominated by minority groups (e.g., African Americans are over-represented in the juvenile offender population and among the group of families likely to come to the attention of social service agencies).

## Ensuring Statistical Sophistication

The challenge of training researchers in the latest design strategies and statistical techniques is huge. It might be said that the field was founded on basic statistical models and methods, such as analysis of variance and Pearson's correlation coefficient. Today, however, researchers must be well versed in techniques such as structural equation modeling, meta-analysis, logistic regression, and cluster analysis in order to conduct complex experiments and quasi-experiments that improve the ecological validity of previous work. Particular attention needs to be paid to special statistical techniques such as logistic regression and logit analyses that can accommodate dichotomous independent and dependent variables, which exist in abundance in the real world (e.g., jury verdicts, presence or absence of victimization or criminal offense). Further, structural equation modeling could be very useful in examining complex relations between theoretical constructs (e.g., self-esteem, emotional regulation, and aggression in juvenile delinquents).

## Ethics and Values

A discussion of methodological challenges would not be complete without special attention to the complex ethical issues that arise in research with children (see Thompson, 1992, for a general discussion of ethics issues in child research). Such a discussion is timely, following a year in which the government entity responsible for oversight of human subjects research, the National Institute of Health's Office of Protection from Research Risks (OPRR), placed severe restrictions on research at a number of universities (e.g., Duke University, The University of Illinois at Chicago, Virginia Commonwealth University/Medical College of Virginia, the Uni-versity of Colorado at Boulder Health Sciences Center), effectively shutting down all human subjects research for months while policies and procedures for ensuring protections to human subjects were improved. These actions sent other institutions nationwide scrambling to examine carefully their own Institutional Review Board activities. Issues of informed consent figured centrally in the violations that sparked the OPRR's scrutiny of Institutional Review Board activity at major universities (Kaplan & Brownlee, 1999).

Issues of consent are central difficulties for child/law researchers. Gaining access to minors is quite different and more involved than working with adults. In most cases, parents must provide consent for their children to participate in a research project before the child is even informed of a study and asked to provide assent. It can be difficult, however, to contact some children's parents, especially the parents of detained juveniles or children in the foster care system. It may even be unethical to do so, as in cases where youth who have gone to a clinic to be tested for a sexually transmitted disease and do not want their parents notified. Several strategies have been employed to collect data in an ethical manner. With a detained population, parental notification and in some cases the use of a participant advocate associated with the facility has been deemed an appropriate solution because of the difficulties of locating parents. Written parental consent is still necessary, however, when conducting research with non-detained minors except in circumstances where the state has strong general welfare interests (e.g., interests such as treating communicable diseases, which would be jeopardized if youth did not seek treatment because parental consent was required).

In general, children have been identified as a vulnerable research population (Thompson, 1992). Rather than viewing children as becoming less vulnerable over time, however, researchers should work to elucidate the areas of cognitive, social, and personality development that are particularly sensitive for children at different ages. Thompson warns that assuming the risks of participating in a research project decrease or its benefits increase linearly with age may overlook developmental sensitivities that can emerge in different domains for children throughout childhood. For example, research exploring issues of self-concept, social comparison, or sexual knowledge may be more stressful or embarrassing for older than younger children. Therefore, researchers working with minors should adopt a framework that highlights these developmental sensitivities and considers the risks and benefits for child participants separately and independently for youth of different ages. Furthermore, it has been suggested that Institutional Review Boards' periodic reevaluations of longitudinal research involving children should continually review the methods and measures used, considering the impact such procedures may have on the participants at one time point versus another.

## The "Dilemma of Values" in Research

When embarking in areas of research that have the potential to influence important public policy issues such as juvenile detention procedures or custody determinations, psychologists must be diligent in maintaining objectivity when reporting research findings, including reporting findings that may not support the researchers' working theories or values. Judge Bazelon (1982), in an address to the American Psychological Association, urged psychologists to reveal the entire truth when publicly reporting their findings, primarily by disclosing the values underlying their work, and by acknowledging that there may be results that are contrary to their findings. He believes that the legal system needs empirical knowledge about human behavior. Empirical facts, however, should be entered along with their limitations into courtroom situations for public assimilation and action, rather than being entered as conclusive statements that may be based to some degree on values as well as data. Bazelon strongly advocates that the public (e.g., the jury) be left to integrate "the facts" with other information.

A case study of the role values can play in child/law research comes from the domain of child testimony research. In child abuse cases, two goals are paramount: guarding against false accusations of innocent adults, and detecting actual abuse and prosecuting offenders so that children can be protected from future risk. Modern child witness research has been framed in controversy, largely emanating from researchers' different degrees of attention to these goals as a function of different personal values about their importance (Davis, 1998). Today, however, a growing body of empirical evidence is beginning to bring consensus about factors that influence children's accuracy and suggestibility, and with consensus, the realization that these goals are compatible.

## DISSEMINATING PSYCHOLOGICAL RESEARCH RELEVANT TO POLICY AND LAW

Active dissemination of research findings is crucial to the future success of the field of Children, Psychology, and Law. As noted by Goodman,

Levine, and Melton (1992), "Psychology bears a social responsibility to provide the best available evidence on important questions of legal policy whenever it can do so (APA, 1991, Principal F). It should proceed with caution, but it should not be disabled by a requirement for perfect evidence" (p. 249). Psychological research can effectively influence social programs, policy, or law only to the extent that it comes to the attention of professionals "in the trenches": social workers, attorneys, judges, legislators, the public, and others (Grisso & Melton, 1987). No matter how good the research is, it can have an impact only if it is actively disseminated. When psychological knowledge reaches a stage where it indicates relatively specific directives for law or policy, psychologists have a duty to disseminate it to the professionals who can affect change (Reppucci, 1985). We now turn to a discussion of various opportunities psychologists have for disseminating their research, and the challenges sometimes encountered in the process. More than a decade ago, Grisso and Melton (1987) identified many avenues for and challenges to dissemination of psychological research. Most of their observations remain accurate today, and we refer the readers to chapters in that volume for more detail than we provide here.

## Reaching Legal Professionals and Practice Audiences

Some particularly promising dissemination routes include writing amicus briefs (Roesch, Golding, Hans, & Reppucci, 1991), publishing in venues likely to reach applied audiences (Grisso & Melton, 1987; Saunders & Reppucci, 1977), speaking about research at informal and formal gatherings of legal and social service professionals (Reppucci, 1985), providing expert testimony or consultation in legal cases (Loftus & Monahan, 1980; Reppucci, 1985), and educating professionals in the disciplines we hope to reach about psychological research.

Amicus briefs are excellent vehicles for psychologists to educate legal professionals, particularly trial court judges (Roesch et al., 1991). Amicus briefs are pointed research summaries written to influence pending court decisions. Although some amicus briefs are ignored or misinterpreted by courts (e.g., in *Williams v. Florida*, 1970, see Saks, 1977), others have been successful in carrying child research directly to lawmakers (e.g., in *Brown v. Board of Education*, 1954, and *Maryland v. Craig*, 1990). To capitalize on briefs as an opportunity to influence legal decision making, psychologists must overcome several challenges. First, psychologists must be aware of pending court rulings where psychological research could be particularly influential. At present, at least two newsletter columns alert psychologists to such cases: the "Judicial Notebook" column in the APA's *Monitor* (sponsored by the Society for the Psychological Study of Social Issues) and the "Case Notes" column in the newsletter of the Child Maltreatment Section of APA's Division 37. To identify cases of relevance to psychology, the authors of these columns often take advantage of *United States Law Week*, a publication reporting all cases granted a hearing (certiori) by the U.S. Supreme Court. Second, psychologists must find the time to write briefs when the opportunity presents itself. This is not always easy, because academics must squeeze such efforts into schedules already packed with normal research, teaching, and service responsibilities. Third, many psychologists are challenged by their lack of legal knowledge, thus they must involve legal scholars as co-authors on amicus briefs to address legal issues in cases correctly (Weiner, 1999).

Psychologists can also reach applied audiences by publishing articles about their research in discipline-relevant publications such as law reviews, state bar association and other professional newsletters, and various federal and state publications. For example, the official newsletter of the American Professional Society on the Abuse of Children, *The Advisor*, reaches hundreds of legal, mental health, and social service professionals who work within the field of child maltreatment. An article in *The Advisor* that describes research-based child interview techniques could reach many professionals who conduct child forensic interviews, and in turn, have a great impact on practice. An article published in the *Juvenile and Family Court Journal* is likely to reach an audience of juvenile justice professionals (Grisso & Melton, 1987). The potential impact of books may also be significant, as long as the books are marketed and indexed in manners that maximize the potential for reaching the intended audience.

Challenges for psychologists taking this approach, however, can be daunting. Psychologists who are employed at colleges and universities are generally rewarded for publications that appear in a rather narrowly defined set of outlets. That is, when promotion and tenure review committees examine faculty records, they usually look for peer-reviewed publications in top journals of the researcher's discipline such as *American Journal of Community Psychology, Child Development, Journal of Personality and Social Psychology*, and *Psychological Bulletin*, not law reviews or professional newsletters. Thus, researchers who wish to reach applied audiences face a difficult situation: articles in these journals will not reach applied audiences; but non peer-reviewed publications will not garner the researcher professional longevity. An obvious solution may be for academics to publish in both places, and Grisso and Melton (1987) give some concrete advice for such a strategy. In addition, outlets such as *Law and Human Behavior*, a well-respected journal for both applied and conceptual research, has a readership that includes both psychological and legal professionals. New cross-disciplinary journals that follow both law review and psychology journal formats are also providing prestigious peer-reviewed publication outlets. For example, *Psychology, Public Policy and Law* is published by the APA and is an accepted outlet for academic psychologists, but is also accessible to legal scholars because it is indexed in data bases used by both groups.

Oral presentations, lectures, seminars, and workshops allow psychologists to reach a large number of professionals in a relatively short period of time. For example, psychologists who attend the annual meeting of the American Professional Society on the Abuse of Children can disseminate research findings to and educate a wide variety of child protection professionals in a matter of days. Presentations at state and local meetings of prosecutors, judges, juvenile court and correctional personnel reach audiences who can use research, but who may use such conferences as their primary means for gaining new information (Saunders & Reppucci, 1977). These venues also facilitate professional networking, which may lead to future opportunities to influence programs, policies, and practices. There are a few obstacles to such a dissemination approach, but they are not formidable. Researchers must identify the appropriate meetings and develop the professional relationships that will lead to the necessary invitations to speak. Once a researcher has the opportunity to present research to an applied audience, the work must be described in a clear and understandable manner, free from psychological jargon, and free from assumptions that the audience has had training in social science methodology or statistics.

Expert testimony offers psychologists another means to disseminate research where it can have significant impact (Loftus & Monahan, 1980). The U.S. Supreme Court's ruling in *Daubert v. Merrell Dow Pharmaceuticals* (1993) stipulates that psychologists can offer expert testimony if the content of their testimony will assist the trier of fact and is relevant to the issue at bar (Faigman, Kaye, Saks, & Sanders, 1997). By offering expert testimony, psychologists can debunk common misconceptions jurors may harbor (e.g., that there is an identifiable pattern of symptoms that accurately indicates whether or not a child has suffered abuse, that youthful offenders always have an adult-like understanding of Miranda warnings), and by so doing, improve the outcomes of specific trials and educate presiding judges. Expert witnesses must, however, be careful to offer summaries of only solid, relevant psychological findings in a fair manner that does not arbitrarily favor the party who retained them. Value-influenced testimony and overstated opinions should be avoided, as well as ultimate issue testimony (e.g., whether a person is guilty or innocent), which may usurp the role of the jury (Bazelon, 1982).

Finally, the discipline of psychology should explore ways to reach applied audiences (e.g., future attorneys, judges, and practitioners) early in their careers. Many universities and colleges already offer courses in Psychology and Law that are gaining in popularity (Bersoff et al., 1997). Psychologists should make sure that such courses cover children's issues and that they are open to undergraduates from a wide range of majors. Psychologists should also explore opportunities to guest lecture in regular courses in various disciplines, or to teach or co-teach courses on social science methods and findings in law schools, and in social work, criminology, and criminal justice programs.

## Reaching Society at Large

Although reaching professionals in the trenches is perhaps the first dissemination issue that comes to mind, reaching society at large may be even more critical, inasmuch as many policies and laws are reflections of voter sentiments. The public obtains largely biased information about psychology via the media—popular press books, television, and movies. Unfortunately, the image of psychology and psychological research is largely distorted in these sources (Bottoms & Davis, 1996), a situation illustrated by a simple trip to the local bookstore. There one sees a "psychology" section filled with pop psychology—unscientific self-help books for every common malady from low self-esteem to relationship problems. If there is a Psychology and Law section, it is likely to be a collection of true crime stories or books about profiling serial killers. Psychologists should make efforts to build respect for research, for the science of psychology generally, and for the role psychology can play in advising the legal system. As noted, psychologists can begin educating the public by offering relevant undergraduate law and psychology courses, and including sections on children, psychology, and law in existing courses (e.g., introductory, developmental, community, and social psychology) or as independent courses (two of the authors, Reppucci and Bottoms, have taught a Children, Families, and Law course—Reppucci for the past two decades, and many of his former students now teach similar courses at their own universities). Also, psychologists can address community audiences when opportunities arise. For example, media interviews and university-sponsored lectures provide avenues for educating the general public about the role of psychology in law. Moreover, psychologists should make the effort to work with their institutions' public relations offices to arrange interviews with newspaper reporters about issues of relevance to children and law.

*Reaching Colleagues Within Our Own Discipline*

Finally, some of our dissemination efforts need to begin at home; that is, they should be aimed at the subdiscipline of Psychology and Law and the field of psychology generally. Journals such as *Law and Human Behavior*, *Criminal Justice and Behavior* and other psychology journals with developmental or applied emphases, or broadly defined audiences (e.g., *Child Development*, *Journal of Applied Psychology*, *Applied Developmental Science*, *American Psychologist*) could be lobbied to publish special issues devoted to children and law. Two such volumes appeared in *Law & Human Behavior* in 1993 and 1996, and another is underway. In 1984, Reppucci, Weithorn, Mulvey, and Monahan published the first edited book reviewing certain aspects of the field and such books continue to be important outlets (e.g., Bottoms, Kovera, & McAuliff, in press). Such efforts should increase as the field continues to grow. Finally, child/law researchers should maintain a high profile by arranging and participating in symposia and presenting papers at key conferences such as the American Psychological Association's national and regional meetings and the biennial meetings of the American Psychology-Law Society, the Society for Research in Child Development, the Society for Research on Adolescence, the Society for Community Research and Action, and the Society for the Psychological Study of Social Issues.

## CAUTIONARY NOTES AND CONCLUSIONS

We are optimistic about the potential for psychological knowledge to expand quickly in the new century, providing empirically derived information to difficult questions that arise when children, law, and social policy collide. Even so, we must acknowledge potential socio-political, legal, and professional obstacles that may hinder our progress. Although one of our ultimate goals is to influence law and policy, we must realize that the socio-political context may hinder our efforts. For example, more votes obviously exist in the general population than among psychological researchers. Consequently, societal opinion, not scientific evidence, usually drives legislative policy decisions. At times, policy makers may act in a manner that appears to be illogical and unscientific. For instance, Congress declares that researchers cannot survey adolescents about sexual behavior, unless in a treatment setting, yet they legislate regulations controlling it (Code of Federal Regulations, 1991). Further, although courts are less skeptical of social science evidence today than in the past, psychologists have a long way to go before they are offered a fully opened door to the courtroom. Some of this skepticism is a logical reaction to dubious experts who are too willing to parade unfounded opinions before the courts. Another source is legal professionals' failure to appreciate the scientific method, a fact that makes relevant law school courses particularly important. Finally, academics in traditional psychology departments may face obstacles within their own discipline. Although there have been great advancements in the recognition of the virtues of applied psychological research, some departments still value basic psychological research to a greater degree than theoretically driven, applied research. This can be an obstacle to junior scholars becoming involved in this research, which, by its very nature, is exceptionally time consuming when done right.

In closing, we have tried to underscore the fact that although research on some issues related to children and law (e.g., children's eyewitness testimony, child abuse and neglect, juvenile justice) has fortunately burgeoned over the last decade, there is still important work to be done in these areas, and many other pressing issues such as children's rights and adoption policies have not received as much attention as they deserve (Melton, Goodman, Kalichman, Levine, Saywitz, & Koocher, 1995; Schmidt & Reppucci, in press; Small & Limber, in press). We hope that our chapter has raised consciousness about a wide-ranging set of issues in great need of theoretical, empirical, and legislative attention, and that in turn, it will stimulate future scholarly activity on legally relevant issues currently faced by children and society at large. Importantly, we hope it will stimulate research yielding products applicable to society's struggle to accommodate children's concerns within our laws and policies.

## REFERENCES

Allen, J. P., Kuperminc, G., Philliber, S., & Herre, K. (1994). Programmatic prevention of adolescent problem behaviors: The role of autonomy, relatedness, and volunteer service in the Teen Outreach Program. *American Journal of Community Psychology, 22*, 617–638.

Amato, P. R., & Keith, B. (1991). Parental divorce and the well-being of children: A meta-analysis. *Psychological Bulletin, 110*, 26–46.

Ambuel, B., & Rappaport, J. (1992). Developmental trends in adolescents' psychological and legal competence to consent to abortion. *Law and Human Behavior, 16*, 129–154.

Bagly, C. (1993). Transracial adoption in Britain: A follow-up study, with policy considerations. *Child Welfare, 73*, 285–299.

Bazelon, D. L. (1982). Veils, values, and social responsibility. *American Psychologist, 37*, 115–121.

Belli, R. F., Winkielman, P., Read, J. D., Schwarz, N., & Lynn, S. J. (1998). Recalling more childhood events leads to judgments of poorer memory: Implications for the recovered/false memory debate. *Psychonomic Bulletin and Review, 5*, 318–323.

Berliner, L., & Elliott, D. (1996). Child sexual abuse. In J. Briere, L. Berliner, J. Bulkley, C. Jenny, & T. Reid (Eds.), *The APSAC handbook on child maltreatment* (pp. 51–71). Newbury Park, CA: Sage.

Bersoff, D. N. (1987). Social science data and the Supreme Court: *Lockhart* as a case in point. *American Psychologist, 42,* 52–58.

Bersoff, D. N., Goodman-Delahunty, J., Grisso, J. T., Hans, V. P., Poythress, N. G., Jr., & Roesch, R. G. (1997). Training in law and psychology: Models from the Villanova conference. *American Psychologist, 52,* 1301–1310.

Bishop, D. M., Frazier, C. E., Lanza-Kanduce, L., & Winner, L. (1996). The transfer of juveniles to criminal court: Does it make a difference? *Crime and Delinquency, 42,* 171–191.

Bornstein, B. H. (1999). The ecological validity of jury simulations: Is the jury still out? *Law and Human Behavior, 23,* 75–91.

Bottoms v. Bottoms, 249 VA 410 m 457 S. E. 2d 102 (1995).

Bottoms, B. L., & Davis, S. L. (1996). The creation of satanic ritual abuse. *Journal of Social and Clinical Psychology, 16,* 112–132.

Bottoms, B. L., Davis, S. L., Nysse, K. L., Haegerich, T. M., & Conway, A. R. A. (2000, March). Effects of social support and working memory capacity on children's eyewitness memory. In B. L. Bottoms & M. B. Kovera (Chairs), *Individual and contextual influences on adults' perceptions of children's reports.* Symposium conducted at the biennial meeting of the American Psychology/Law Society, New Orleans, LA.

Bottoms, B. L., & Goodman, G. S. (1994). Perceptions of children's credibility in sexual assault cases. *Journal of Applied Social Psychology, 24,* 702–732.

Bottoms, B. L., Goodman, G. S., Schwartz-Kenney, B. M., & Thomas, S. F. (2000). *Keeping secrets: Implications for children's eyewitness reports.* Manuscript submitted for publication.

Bottoms, B. L., Kovera, M. B., & McAuliff, B. D. (Eds.). (in press). *Children and the law: Social science and policy.* New York: Cambridge University Press.

Bottoms, B. L., Shaver, P. R., Goodman, G. S. (1996). An analysis of ritualistic and religion-related child abuse allegations. *Law and Human Behavior, 20,* 1–34.

Bottoms, B. L., Shaver, P. R., Goodman, G. S., & Qin, J. (1995). In the name of God: A profile of religion-related child abuse. *Journal of Social Issues, 51,* 85–111.

Brown v. Board of Education, 347 US 483 (1954).

Brown, D., Scheflin, A. W., & Hammond, D. C. (1998). *Memory, trauma treatment, and the law.* New York: Norton.

Bruck, M., Ceci, S. J., & Melnyk, L. (1997). External and internal sources of variation in the creation of false reports in children. *Learning and Individual Differences, 9,* 289–316.

Butts, J., Hoffman, D., & Buck, J. (1999). Teen courts in the United States: A profile of current programs. *Office of Juvenile Justice and Delinquency Prevention Fact Sheet, 118.*

Bullis, R. K. (1991). The spiritual healing "defense" in criminal prosecutions for crimes against children. *Child Welfare, 70,* 541–555.

Buzzanca v. Buzzanca, CA Sup. Ct. No. S069696 (1998).

Carter, C. A., Bottoms, B. L., & Levine, M. (1996). Linguistic and socioemotional influences on the accuracy of children's reports. *Law and Human Behavior, 20,* 335–358.

Cauffman, E., Woolard, J., & Reppucci, N. D. (1999). Justice for Juveniles: New perspectives on adolescents' competence and culpability. *Quinnipiac Law Review, 18,* 403–419.

Ceci, S. J., & Bruck, M. (1995). *Jeopardy in the courtroom: A scientific analysis of children's testimony.* Washington, DC: American Psychological Association.

Ceci, S. J., & Bruck, M. (1993). The suggestibility of the child witness: A historical review and synthesis. *Psychological Bulletin, 113,* 403–439.

Cicchetti, D., & Rogosch, F. A. (1997). The role of self-organization in the promotion of resilience in maltreated children. *Development and Psychopathology, 9,* 797–815.

Code of Federal Regulations (1991). Title 45, Public welfare. Part 46: Protection of human subjects. Department of Health & Human Services: National Institute of Health.

Coy v. Iowa, 487 U.S. 1012 (1988).

Crosby-Currie, C. A. (1996). Children's involvement in contested custody cases: Practices and experiences of legal and mental health professionals. *Law and Human Behavior, 20,* 289–311.

Crosby, C. A., Britner, P. A., Jodl, K. M., & Portwood, S. G. (1995). The juvenile death penalty and the Eighth Amendment: An empirical investigation of societal consensus and proportionality. *Law and Human Behavior, 19,* 245–261.

Cutler, B. L., Penrod, S. D., & Dexter, H. R. (1990). Juror sensitivity to eyewitness identification evidence. *Law and Human Behavior, 14,* 185–191.

Daubert v. Merrell-Dow Pharmaceuticals, 951 F.2d 1128 (9th Cir. 1991), vacated, 113 S. Ct. 2786 (1993).

Davies, G., & Noon, E. (1991). *An evaluation of live link for child witnesses.* London: Home Office.

Davis, S. L. (1998). Social and scientific influences on the study of children's suggestibility: A historical perspective. *Child Maltreatment, 3,* 186–194.

Davis, S. L., & Bottoms, B. L. (in press). The effects of social support on the accuracy of children's reports: Implications for the forensic interview. In M. L. Eisen, G. S. Goodman, & J. A. Quas (Eds.), *Memory and suggestibility in the forensic interview.* Hillsdale, NJ: Erlbaum.

Diamond, S. S. (1997). Illuminations and shadows from jury simulations. *Law and Human Behavior, 21,* 561–571.

DiIulio, J. (1995, November 27). The coming of the super-predators. *Weekly Standard,* p. 23.

Dillon, P. A., & Emery, R. E. (1996). Divorce mediation and resolution of child custody disputes: Long-term effects. *American Journal of Orthopsychiatry, 66,* 131–140.

Elliot, D. S. (1994). Serious violent offenders: Onset, developmental course, and termination. The American Society of Criminology Presidential Address. *Criminology, 32,* 1–21.

Elliott, B. J., & Richards, M. P. M. (1991). Children and divorce: Educational performance and behavior before and after parental separation. *International Journal of Law and the Family, 5,* 258–276.

Emery, R. E. (1982). Interparental conflict and the children of discord and divorce. *Psychological Bulletin, 92,* 31–330.

Emery, R. E. (1994). *Renegotiating family relationships: Divorce, child custody, and mediation.* New York: Guilford Press.

Emery, R. E. (1999a). Changing the rules for determining child custody in divorce cases. *Clinical Psychology Science and Practice, 6,* 323–327.

Emery, R. E. (1999b). *Marriage, divorce, and children's adjustment* (2nd ed.). Thousand Oaks, CA: Sage.

English, A. (1999). Case One: Consent and the limits of staff as "family". In J. Blustein & C. Levine (Eds.), *The adolescent alone: Decision making in health care in the United States* (pp. 183–190). New York: Cambridge University Press.

Epstein, M. A., & Bottoms, B. L. (1999). *Explaining the forgetting and recovery of traumatic memories: Is the construct of repression necessary?* Manuscript submitted for publication.

Faigman, D. L., Kaye, D. H., Saks, M. J., & Sanders, J. (1997). *Modern scientific evidence: The law and science of expert testimony.* St. Paul, MN: West.

Feld, B. C. (1998). The juvenile court. In M. H. Tonry (Ed.), *The handbook of crime and punishment* (pp. 509–541). New York: Oxford University Press.

Feld, B. C. (1999). *Bad kids: Race and the transformation of the juvenile court.* New York: Oxford University Press.

Finkelhor, D., Hotaling, G., Lewis, I. A., & Smith, C. (1990). Sexual abuse in a national survey of adult men and women: Prevalence, characteristics, and risk factors. *Child Abuse and Neglect, 14,* 19–28.

Folberg, J. (1991). *Joint custody and shared parenting.* New York: Guilford Press.

Fried, C. S., & Reppucci, N. D. (2001). Criminal decision making: The development of adolescent judgment, criminal responsibility and culpability. *Law and Human Behavior, 25,* 45–61.

Fried, C. S., & Reppucci, N. D. (in press). Youth violence: Correlates, interventions, and legal implications. In B. L. Bottoms, M. B. Kovera, & B. D. McAuliff (Eds.), *Children and the law: Social science and policy.* New York: Cambridge University Press.

Gabora, N. J., Spanos, N. P., & Joab, A. (1993). The effects of complainant age and expert psychological testimony in a simulated child sexual abuse trial. *Law and Human Behavior, 17,* 103–119.

Gardner, W., Scherer, D., & Tester, M. (1989). Asserting scientific authority: Cognitive development and adolescent legal rights. *American Psychologist, 44,* 895–902.

Garrison, E. G. (1991). Children's competence to participate in divorce custody decision making. *Journal of Clinical Child Psychology, 20,* 78–87.

Garvin, S., Wood, J. M., Malpass, R. S., & Shaw, J. S. (1998). More than suggestion: The effect of interviewing techniques from the McMartin Preschool case. *Journal of Applied Psychology, 83,* 347–359.

Geiselman, R. E., Saywitz, K. J., & Bornstein, G. K. (1993). Effects of cognitive questioning techniques on children's recall performance. In G. S. Goodman & B. L. Bottoms (Eds.), *Child victims, child witnesses: Understanding and improving testimony* (pp. 71–93). New York: Guilford.

Gillock, K. L., & Reyes, O. (1996). High school transition-related changes in urban minority students' academic performance and perceptions of self and school environment. *Journal of Community Psychology, 24,* 245–261.

Golding, J. M., Sanchez, R. P., & Sego, S. A. (1999). Brief research report: Age factors affecting the believability of repressed memories of child sexual assault. *Law and Human Behavior, 23,* 257–268.

Goldstein, J., Freud, A., & Solnit, A. (1973). *Beyond the best interests of the child.* New York: Free Press.

Goldstein, J., Freud, A., Solnit, A., & Goldstein, S. (1986). *In the best interests of the child.* New York, NY: Free Press.

Golombok, S., Bhanji, F., Rutherford, T., & Winston, R. (1990). Psychological development of children of the new reproductive technologies: Issues and a pilot study of children conceived by IVF. *Journal of Reproductive and Infant Psychology, 8,* 37–43.

Golombok, S., Cook, R., Bish, A., & Murray, C. (1995). Families created by the new reproductive technologies: Quality of parenting and social and emotional development of the children. *Child Development, 66,* 285–298.

Goodman, G. S. (Ed.) (1984). The child witness. *Journal of Social Issues, 40,* Whole Issue No. 2.

Goodman, G. S., Batterman-Faunce, J. M., Schaaf, J. M., & Kenney, R. (2000). Nearly 4 years after an event: Children's eyewitness testimony and adults' perceptions of children's accuracy. Manuscript submitted for publication.

Goodman, G. S., & Bottoms, B. L. (Eds.) (1993). *Child victims, child witnesses: Understanding and improving testimony.* New York: Guilford.

Goodman, G. S., Emery, R. E., & Haugaard, J. (1998). Developmental psychology and law: Divorce, child maltreatment, foster care, and adoption. In I. Siegel & A. Renninger (Eds.), *Child psychology in practice* (pp. 775–876). In W. Damon (Series Ed.), *Handbook of Child Psychology* (Vol. 4). New York: Wiley.

Goodman, G. S., Golding, J. M., & Haith, M. M. (1984). Jurors' reactions to child witnesses. *Journal of Social Issues, 40*, 139–156.

Goodman, G. S., Levine, M., & Melton, G. B. (1992). The best evidence produces the best law. *Law and Human Behavior, 16*, 244–251.

Goodman, G. S., Levine, M., Melton, G. B., & Ogden, D. (1991). Craig vs. Maryland. Amicus brief to the U.S. Supreme Court on behalf of the American Psychological Association. *Law and Human Behavior, 15*, 13–30.

Goodman, G. S., & Schwartz-Kenney, B. M. (1992). Why knowing a child's age is not enough: Influences of cognitive, social, and emotional factors on children's testimony. In H. Dent & R. Flin (Eds.), *Children as witnesses. Wiley series in the psychology of crime, policing and law* (pp. 15–32). Chichester, England UK: Wiley.

Goodman, G. S., Taub, E. P., Jones, D. P. H., England, P., Port, L., Rudy, L., & Prado, L. (1992). Testifying in criminal court: Emotional effects on child sexual assault victims. *Monographs of the Society for Research in Child Development, 57*(5, Serial No. 229).

Goodman, G. S., Tobey, A. E., Batterman-Faunce, J. M., Orcutt, H., Thomas, S., Shapiro, C., & Sachsenmaier, T. (1998). Face-to-face confrontation: Effects of closed-circuit technology on children's eyewitness testimony and jurors' decisions. *Law and Human Behavior, 22*, 165–203.

Gorman-Smith, D., Tolan, P. H., & Henry, D. (1999). The relation of community and family to risk among urban-poor adolescents. In P. Cohen, C. Slomkowski, & L. N. Robins (Eds.), *Historical and geographical influences on psychopathology* (pp. 349–367). Mahwah, NJ: Erlbaum.

Gray, E. (1993). *Unequal justice: The prosecution of child sexual abuse.* New York, NY: Free Press.

Grisso, T. (1980). Juveniles' capacities to waive *Miranda* rights: An empirical analysis. *California Law Review, 68*, 1134–1166.

Grisso, T. (1981). *Juveniles' waiver of rights: Legal and psychological competence.* New York: Plenum Press.

Grisso, T. (1996). Society's retributive response to juvenile violence: A developmental perspective. *Law and Human Behavior, 20*, 229–247.

Grisso, T., & Melton, G. B. (1987). Getting child development research to legal practitioners: Which way to the trenches? In G. B. Melton (Ed.), *Reforming the law: Impact of child development research* (pp. 146–176). New York: Guilford.

Grisso, T., Schwartz, R., Scott, E., Cauffman, E., Woolard, J., & Hollin, C. (1999, July). *Youth on trial: Developmental perspectives on youths' competence and culpability.* Symposium conducted at the international conference of the American Psychology/Law Society and the European Association of Psychology & Law, Dublin, Ireland.

Grisso, T., & Schwartz, R. (Eds.) (2000). *Youth on trial.* Chicago, IL: University of Chicago Press.

Haegerich, T. M., & Bottoms, B. L. (2000). Empathy and jurors' decisions in patricide cases involving child sexual assault allegations. *Law and Human Behavior, 24*, 421–448.

Haney, C. (1980). Psychology and legal change: On the limits of a factual jurisprudence. *Law and Human Behavior, 4*, 147–200.

Hartigan v. Zbaraz, 484 U.S. 171 (1987).

Haugaard, J., & Reppucci, N. D. (1988). *The sexual abuse of children: A comprehensive guide to current knowledge and intervention strategies.* San Francisco, CA: Jossey-Bass.

Haugaard, J., Reppucci, N. D., Laird, J., & Naufeld, T. (1991). Children's definitions of the truth and their competency as witnesses in legal proceedings. *Law & Human Behavior, 15*, 253–272.

Henggeler, S. W., Schoenwald, S. K., Bourdin, C. M., Rowland, M. D., & Cunningham, P. B. (1998). *Multisystemic treatment of antisocial behavior in children and adolescents.* New York: Guilford.

Hetherington, E. M. (1999). Should we stay together for the sake of the children? In E. M. Hetherington (Ed.), *Coping with divorce, single parenting, and remarriage: A risk and resiliency perspective* (pp. 93–116). Mahwah, NJ: Erlbaum.

Hetherington, E. M., Bridges, M., & Insabella, G. M. (1998). What matters? What does not? Five perspectives on the association between marital transitions and children's adjustment. *American Psychologist, 53,* 167–184.

Hoyt, S., & Scherer, D. G. (1998). Female juvenile delinquency: Misunderstood by the juvenile justice system, neglected by social science. *Law and Human Behavior, 22,* 81–107.

In re Gault, 387 US 1, 87 S Ct. 1428, 18 L. Ed. 2nd 527 (1967).

Interdivisional Committee on Adolescent Abortion (1987). Adolescent abortion: Psychological and legal issues. *American Psychologist, 42,* 73–78.

Isquith, P. K., Levine, M., & Scheiner, J. (1993). Blaming the child: Attribution of responsibility to victims of child sexual abuse. In G. S. Goodman & B. L. Bottoms (Eds.), *Child victims, child witnesses: Understanding and improving testimony* (pp. 203–228). New York: Guilford Press.

Jacob Wetterling Crimes Against Children and Sexually Violent Offender Registration Program, 42, U.S.C. § 14071.

Johnson v. Calvert, 851 P 2d 776, 61 U.S.L.W. 2721 (1993).

Kaplan, S., & Brownlee, S. (1999, October 11). Dying for a cure: Why cancer patients often turn to risky, experimental treatments—and wind up paying with their lives. *U.S. News and World Report, 127*(14), 34.

Katz, L. F., & Gottman, J. M. (1995). Marital interaction and child outcomes: A longitudinal study of mediating and moderating processes. In D. Cicchetti & S. L. Toth (Eds.), *Emotion, cognition, and representation. Rochester symposium on developmental psychopathology* (Vol. 6, pp. 301–342). Rochester, NY: University of Rochester Press.

Kendall-Tackett, K. A., Williams, L. M., & Finkelhor, D. (1993). Impact of sexual abuse on children: A review and synthesis of recent empirical studies. *Psychological Bulletin, 113,* 164–180.

Kent v. United States, 383 U.S. 541, 86 S.Ct. 1045, 16 L.Ed.2d 84 (1966).

Kofkin, J., & Reppucci, N. D. (1991). A reconceptualization of life events and its applications to divorce. *American Journal of Community Psychology, 19,* 227–250.

Kovera, M. B., & Borgida, E. (1996). Children on the witness stand: The use of expert testimony and other procedural innovations in U. S. child sexual abuse trials. In B. L. Bottoms & G. S. Goodman (Eds.), *International perspectives on child abuse and children's testimony: Psychological research and law* (pp. 201–220). Thousand Oaks, CA: Sage.

LaFond, J. Q. (1998). The costs of enacting a sexual predator law. *Psychology, Public Policy, and Law, 4,* 468–504.

Lanning, K. (1992). A law enforcement perspective on allegations of ritual abuse. In D. K. Sakheim & S. E. Devine (Eds.), *Out of darkness: Exploring satanism and ritual abuse* (pp. 109–146). New York: Lexington.

Llewellyn, J. J., & Howse, R. (1999). *Restorative justice: A conceptual framework.* Ottawa: Law Reform Commission of Canada.

Lepore, S. J., & Sesco, B. (1994). Distorting children's reports and interpretations of events through suggestion. *Journal of Applied Psychology, 79,* 108–120.

Levine, M. (2000). The New Zealand children, young persons, and their families act of 1989: Review and evaluation. *Behavioral Sciences and the Law, 18,* 517–556.

Lewis, R. V. (1983). Scared Straight—California Style: Evaluation of the San Quentin Squires program. *Criminal Justice & Behavior, 10,* 209–226.

Leichtman, M. D., & Ceci, S. J. (1995). The effects of stereotypes and suggestions on preschoolers' reports. *Developmental Psychology, 31,* 568–578.

Lindsay, D. S., & Read, J. D. (1995). "Memory work" and recovered memories of childhood sexual abuse: Scientific evidence and public, professional, and personal issues. *Psychology, Public Policy, and Law, 1,* 846–908.

Lockhart v. McCree, 106 S.Ct. 1758 (1986).

Loeber, R., & Farrington, D. P. (Eds.) (1998). *Serious and violent juvenile offenders: Risk factors and successful interventions.* Thousand Oaks, CA: Sage.

Loftus, E. F. (1993). The reality of repressed memories. *American Psychologist, 48,* 518–537.

Loftus, E. F., & Monahan, J. (1980). Trial by data: Psychological research as legal evidence. *American Psychologist, 35,* 270–283.

Maccoby, E. E. (1999). The custody of children of divorcing families: Weighing the alternatives. In R. A. Thompson & P. R. Amato (Eds.), *The postdivorce family: Children, parenting, and society* (pp. 51–70). Thousand Oaks, CA: Sage.

MacFarlane, M., Doueck, H., & Levine, M. (in press). Preventing child abuse and neglect. In B. L. Bottoms, M. B. Kovera, & B. D. McAuliff (Eds.), *Children and the law: Social science and policy.* New York: Cambridge University Press.

MacKenzie, D. L., & Brame, R. (1995). Shock incarceration and positive adjustment during community supervision. *Journal of Quantitative Criminology, 11,* 111–142.

Manfredi, C. P. (1998). *The Supreme Court and juvenile justice.* Lawrence, KS: University Press of Kansas.

Maryland v. Craig, 497 U.S. 836 (1990).

McGough, L. S. (1994). *Child witnesses: Fragile voices in the American legal system.* New Haven, CT: Yale University Press.

McRoy, R. G. (1989). An organizational dilemma: The case of transracial adoptions. *Journal of Applied Behavioral Science, 25,* 145–160.

Megan's Law, Public Law No: 104–145 (1996).

Melton, G. B. (1984). Developmental psychology and the law: The state of the art. *Journal of Family Law, 22,* 445–482.

Melton, G. B. (1990). Knowing what we do know: APA and adolescent abortion. *American Psychologist, 45,* 1171–1173.

Melton, G. B. (1999). Parents and children: Legal reform to facilitate children's participation. *American Psychologist, 54,* 935–944.

Melton, G. B., Goodman, G. S., Kalichman, S. C., Levine, M., Saywitz, K. J., & Koocher, G. P. (1995). Empirical research on child maltreatment and the law. *Journal of Clinical Child Psychology, 24,* 47–77.

Melton, G. B., Koocher, G. P., & Saks, M. J. (1983). *Children's competence to consent.* New York: Plenum.

Meyer v. Nebraska, 262 U.S. 390 (1923).

Mini, M. M. (1994). Breaking down the barriers to transracial adoption. *Hofstra Law Review, 22,* 897–968.

Mnookin, R. H. (1978). *Child, family, and state.* Boston: Little, Brown.

Moffitt, T. E. (1993). Adolescence-limited and life-course persistent antisocial behavior: A developmental taxonomy. *Psychological Review, 100,* 674–701.

Monahan, J., & Walker, L. (1998). *Social science in law: Cases and materials.* Westbury, NY: The Foundation Press.

Multiethnic Placement Act of 1994. (1995). 42 U.S.C. 5115a (Pub. L. No. 103–382, Title V, 553, 108 Stat. 4056).

Mulvey, E. P., Arthur, M. W., & Reppucci, N. D. (1993). The prevention and treatment of juvenile delinquency: A review of the research. *Clinical Psychology Review, 13,* 133–167.

Murray, K. (1995). *Live television link.* Edinburgh, Scotland: The Scottish Office.

Myers, J. E. B. (1998). *Legal issues in child abuse and neglect* (2nd ed.). Thousand Oaks, CA: Sage.

Nightingale, N. N. (1993). Juror reactions to child victim witnesses: Factors affecting trial outcome. *Law and Human Behavior, 17*, 679–694.

Oberman, M. (1994). Turning girls into women: Re-evaluating modern statutory rape law. *Journal of Criminal Law & Criminology, 85*, 15–79.

Ogloff, J. R. P., & Finkelman, D. (1999). Psychology and law: An overview. In J. R. P. Ogloff, R. Roesch, & S. D. Hart (Eds.), *Psychology and law: The state of the discipline* (pp. 1–20). New York: Kluwer/Plenum.

Ondersma, S. J., Chaffin, M., Berliner, L., Cordon, I., Goodman, G. S., Barnett, D. (1999). *Sex with children is abuse: Comments on the Rind et al. meta-analysis controversy.* Manuscript submitted for publication.

Parham v. J. R., 442 U.S. 584 (1979).

Patterson, C. J. (1992). Children of lesbian and gay parents. *Child Development, 63*, 1025–1042.

Patterson, C. J. (1995). Lesbian mothers, gay fathers, and their children. In A. R. D'Augelli & C. J. Patterson (Eds.), *Lesbian, gay, and bisexual identities over the lifespan: Psychological perspectives* (pp. 262–290). New York: Oxford University Press.

Patterson, C. J., Fulcher, M., & Wainwright, J. (in press). Children of lesbian and gay parents: Research, law, and policy. In B. L. Bottoms, M. B. Kovera, & B. D. McAuliff (Eds.), *Children and the law: Social science and policy.* New York: Cambridge University Press.

Patterson, C. J., & Redding, R. E. (1996). Lesbian and gay families with children: Implications of social science research for policy. *Journal of Social Issues, 52*, 29–50.

Penkower, J. A. (1996). The potential right of chronically ill adolescents to refuse life-saving medical treatment: Fatal misuse of the mature minor doctrine. *DePaul Law Review, 45*, 1165–1216.

Perry, N. W., McAuliff, B. D., Tam, P., Claycomb, L., Dostal, C., & Flanagan, C. (1995). When lawyers question children: Is justice served? *Law and Human Behavior, 19*, 609–629.

Pierce v. Society of Sisters, 268 U.S. 510 (1925).

Pipe, M. E., & Wilson, J. C. (1994). Cues and secrets: Influences on children's event reports. *Developmental Psychology, 30*, 515–525.

Poe-Yamagata, E., & Butts, J. A. (1996). *Female offenders in the juvenile justice system.* Washington, D.C.: Office of Juvenile Justice and Delinquency Prevention.

Poole, D. A., & Lamb, M. E. (1998). *Investigative interviews of children: A guide for helping professionals.* Washington, DC: American Psychological Association.

Portwood, S., & Reppucci, N. D. (1994). Intervention vs. interference: The role of the courts in child placement. In J. Blacher (Ed.), *When there's no place like home* (pp. 3–36). Baltimore, MD: Paul H. Brookes.

Portwood, S., & Reppucci, N. D. (1996). Adults' impact on the suggestibility of preschoolers recollections. *Applied Developmental Psychology, 17*, 175–198.

Portwood, S., & Reppucci, N. D. (1997). Balancing rights and responsibilities: Legal perspectives on child maltreatment. In J. R. Lutzker (Ed.), *Handbook of child abuse research and treatment.* New York, NY: Plenum.

Quas, J. A., Qin, J., Schaaf, J., & Goodman, G. S. (1997). Individual differences in children's and adults' suggestibility and false event memory. *Learning and Individual Differences, 9*, 359–390.

Redding, R. (1997). Juveniles transferred to criminal court: Legal reforms proposal based on social science research. *Utah Law Review, 3*, 709–763.

Redding, R. (1997). Juveniles transferred to criminal court: Legal reforms proposal based on social science research. *Utah Law Review, 3*, 709–763.

Reppucci, N. D. (1984). The wisdom of Solomon: Issues in child custody determinations. In N. D. Reppucci, L. A. Weithorn, E. P. Mulvey, & J. Monahan (Eds.), *Children, mental health, and the law* (pp. 59–78). Beverly Hills, CA: Sage.

Reppucci, N. D. (1985). Psychology in the public interest. In A. M. Rogers & C. J. Scheirer (Eds.), *The G. Stanley Hall Lecture Series* (Vol. 5). Washington, D.C.: American Psychological Association.

Reppucci, N. D. (1999). Adolescent development and juvenile justice. *American Journal of Community Psychology, 27,* 307–326.

Reppucci, N. D., & Crosby, C. (1993). Law, psychology, and children: Overarching issues. *Law & Human Behavior, 17,* 1–10.

Reppucci, N. D., Weithorn, L. A., Mulvey, E. P., & Monahan, J. (Eds.) (1984). *Children, mental health, and the law.* Beverly Hills, CA: Sage.

Reppucci, N. D., Woolard, J. L., & Fried, C. S. (1999). Social, community, and preventive interventions. *Annual Review of Psychology, 50,* 387–418.

Rind, B., Tromovitch, P., & Bauserman, R. (1998). A meta-analytic examination of assumed properties of child sexual abuse using college samples. *Psychological Bulletin, 124,* 22–53.

Roesch, R., Golding, S. L., Hans, V. P., & Reppucci, N. D. (1991). Social science and the courts: The role of amicus curiae briefs. *Law and Human Behavior, 15,* 1–11.

Ross, F., Hopkins, S., Hanson, E., Lindsay, R. C. L., Hazen, K., & Eslinger, T. (1994). The impact of protective shields and videotape testimony on conviction rates in a simulated trial of child sexual abuse. *Law and Human Behavior, 18,* 553–566.

Rudy, L., & Goodman, G. S. (1991). Effects of participation on children's reports: Implications for children's testimony. *Developmental Psychology, 27,* 1–26.

Saks, M. (1977). *Jury verdicts: The role of group size and social decision rule.* Lexington, MA: Lexington.

Sas, L. D. (1991). *Reducing the system-induced trauma for child sexual abuse victims through court preparation.* Ontario, Canada: London Family Court.

Sas, L. D., Wolfe, D. A., & Gowdey, K. (1996). Children and the courts in Canada. In B. L. Bottoms & G. S. Goodman (Eds.), *International perspectives on child abuse and children's testimony: Psychological research and law* (pp. 77–95). Thousand Oaks, CA: Sage.

Saunders, J. T., & Reppucci, N. D. (1977). Learning networks among administrators of human service institutions. *American Journal of Community Psychology, 5,* 269–276.

Scheiner, J. L. (1988, April). The use of the minimalist vignette as a method for assessing the generalizability of videotape trial simulation results. In M. Levine (Chair), *Simulated jury research on a child as a witness.* Symposium conducted at the meeting of the Eastern Psychological Association, Buffalo, NY.

Scherer, D. G. (1991). The capacities of minors to exercise voluntariness in medical treatment decisions. *Law and Human Behavior, 15,* 431–449.

Scherer, D., & Gardner, W. (1990). Reasserting the authority of science. *American Psychologist, 45,* 1173–1174.

Scherer, D., & Reppucci (1988). Adolescents' capacities to provide voluntary informed consent: The effects of parental influence and medical dilemmas. *Law and Human Behavior, 12,* 123–141.

Schmidt, M. G., & Reppucci, N. D. (in press). Children's rights and their capacities. In B. L. Bottoms, M. B. Kovera, & B. D. McAuliff (Eds.), *Children and the law: Social science and policy.* New York: Cambridge University Press.

Schram, D. D., & Milloy, C. D. (1995). Community notification: A study of offender characteristics and recidivism. Olympia, WA: Washington State Institute for Public Policy.

Scott, E. S. (1990). Rational decision-making about marriage and divorce. *Virginia Law Review, 76,* 9–94.

Scott, E. S. (1992). Pluralism, parental preference, and child custody. *California Law Review, 80,* 615–672.

Scott, E. S., & Grisso, T. (1997). The evolution of adolescence: A developmental perspective on juvenile justice reform. *Journal of Criminal Law and Criminology, 88,* 137–189.

Scott, E., Reppucci, N. D., & Aber, M. (1988). Children's preference in adjudicated custody decisions. *Georgia Law Review, 22,* 1035–1078.

Scott, E. S., Reppucci, N. D., & Woolard, J. L. (1995). Evaluating adolescent decision making in legal contexts. *Law and Human Behavior, 19,* 221–244.

Seidman (1984). The adolescent passage and entry into the juvenile justice system. In N. D. Reppucci, L. A. Weithorn, E. P. Mulvey, & J. Monahan (Eds.), *Children, mental health, and the law* (pp. 233–258). Beverly Hills, CA: Sage.

Simon, J. (1998). Managing the monstrous: Sex offenders and the new penology. *Psychology, Public Policy, and Law, 4,* 452–467.

Simon, R. J., Alstein, H., & Melli, M. S. (1994). *The case for transracial adoption.* Washington, DC: American University Press.

Slobogin, C., Fondacaro, M. R., & Woolard, J. (1999). A prevention model of juvenile justice: The promise of Kansas v. Hendricks for children. *Wisconsin Law Review, 2,* 185–226.

Small, M., & Limber, S. (in press). Advocacy for children's rights. In B. L. Bottoms, M. B. Kovera, & B. D. McAuliff (Eds.), *Children and the law: Social science and policy.* New York: Cambridge University Press.

Sorenson, F., Bottoms, B. L., & Peronä, A. (1997). *Intake and forensic interviewing in the children's advocacy center setting: A handbook.* Washington, D.C.: National Network of Children's Advocacy Centers.

Stanford v. Kentucky, 492 U.S. 361 (1989).

Steinberg, L., & Cauffman, E. (1996). Maturity of judgment in adolescence: Psychosocial factors in adolescent decision making. *Law and Human Behavior, 20,* 249–272.

Steinberg, L., & Cauffman, E. (1999). The elephant in the courtroom: A developmental perspective on the adjudication of youthful offenders. *The Virginia Journal of Social Policy & the Law, 6,* 389–417.

Strauss, M. A. (1994). *Beating the devil out of them: Corporal punishment in American families.* San Francisco: Jossey-Bass.

Strauss, M. A. (1996). Spanking and the making of violent society. *Pediatrics, 98,* 837–842.

Strauss, M. A., & Stewart, J. H. (1999). Corporal punishment by American parents: National data on prevalence, chronicity, severity, and duration, in relation to child and family characteristics. *Clinical Child and Family Psychology Review, 2,* 55–70.

Swim, J., Borgida, E., & McCoy, K. (1993). Videotaped versus in-court witness testimony: Does protecting the child witness jeopardize due process? *Journal of Applied Social Psychology, 23,* 603–631.

Synder, H. N., & Sickmund, M. (1995). *Juvenile offenders and victims: A national report.* Washington, D.C.: Office of Juvenile Justice and Delinquency Prevention.

TASC, The American Surrogacy Center, Inc. (1997). Legal overview of surrogacy laws by state. Available: *http://www.surrogacy.com/legals/map.html*

Tate, D. C., Reppucci, N. D., & Mulvey, E. P. (1995). Violent juvenile delinquents: Treatment effectiveness and implications for future action. *American Psychologist, 50,* 777–781.

Thompson, R. A. (1992). Developmental changes in research risk and benefit: A changing calculus of concerns. In B. Stanley and J. E. Sieber (Eds.), *Social research on children and adolescents* (pp. 31–64). Newbury Park, CA: Sage.

Thompson, W. C. (1989). Death qualification after *Wainwright v. Witt* and *Lockhart v. McCree. Law and Human Behavior, 13,* 185–215.

Thornburg v. American College of Obstetricians, 476 U.S. 747 (1986).

Tolan, P. H., & McKay, M. M. (1996). Preventing serious antisocial behavior in inner-city children: An empirically based family intervention program. *Family Relations: Journal of Applied Family and Child Studies, 45,* 148–155.

Trivits, L., & Reppucci, N. D. (2000). *In the best interests of the child? Developmental arguments against application of Megan's law to juveniles.* Manuscript submitted for publication.

Troxel v. Granville, 145 L. Ed. 2d 1068; 68 U.S.L.W. 3532 (2000).

Umbreit, M., & Greenwood, J. (1999). National survey of victim-offender mediation programs in the United States. *Mediation Quarterly, 6,* 235–251.

U.S. Department of Health and Human Services (2000). *HHS reports new child abuse and neglect statistics.* Available http://www.hhs.gov/news/press/2000pres/20000410.html.

U.S. Department of Health and Human Services (1996). *Child maltreatment 1994: Reports from the states to the national center on child abuse and neglect.* Washington, DC: U.S. Government Printing Office.

Vorzimer, A., & O'Hara, M. D. (1998). Buzzanca v Buzzanca: The ruling and ramifications. *TASC.* Available: *http://www.surrogacy.com/legals/jaycee/jayceesum.html*

Walberg, H. J., Reyes, O., & Weissberg, R. P. (Eds.). (1997). *Children and youth: Interdisciplinary perspectives.* Thousand Oaks, CA: Sage.

Weiner, R. (1999, June). *Law and Human Behavior Planning Project Report.* Presentation at the American Psychology-Law Society Presidential Initiative Conference, Vancouver, British Columbia.

Weiten, W., & Diamond, S. S. (1979). A critical review of the jury simulation paradigm: The case of defendant characteristics. *Law and Human Behavior, 3,* 71–93.

Weithorn, L. A., & Campbell, S. B. (1982). The competency of children and adolescents to make informed treatment decisions. *Child Development, 53,* 1589–1598.

Whipple, G. M. (1911). The psychology of testimony. *Psychological Bulletin, 8,* 307–309.

Whitcomb, D., Shapiro, E. R., & Stellwagen, L. D. (1985). When the victim is a child: Issues for judges and prosecutors. In *Issues and Practices in Criminal Justice.* Washington, DC: National Institute of Justice.

Whitebread, C., & Heilman, J. (1988). An overview of the law of juvenile delinquency. *Behavioral Sciences and the Law, 6,* 285–305.

Williams v. Florida, 399 US 78 (1970).

Winick, B. J. (1998). Sex offender law in the 1990s: A therapeutic jurisprudence analysis. *Psychology, Public Policy, and Law, 4,* 505–570.

Winick, B. J., & LaFond, J. Q. (Eds.) (1998). Sex offenders: Scientific, legal, and policy perspectives [Special Theme]. *Psychology, Public Policy, and Law, 4* (1–2).

Winner, L., Lanza-Kanduce, L., Bishop, D. M., & Frazier, C. E. (1997). The transfer of juveniles to criminal court: Reexamining recidivism over the long term. *Crime and Delinquency, 43,* 548–563.

Wisconsin v. Yoder, 406 U.S. 205 (1972).

Wolfe, D. A., Reppucci, N. D., & Hart, S. (1995). Child abuse prevention: Knowledge and priorities. *Journal of Clinical Child Psychology, 24* Supplement, 5–22.

Woolard, J. L., Fried, C. S., & Reppucci, N. D. (2001). Toward an expanded definition of adolescent competence in legal contexts. In R. Roesch, R. R. Corrado, & R. J. Dempster (Eds.), *Psychology in the courts: International advances in knowledge* (pp. 21–39). Amsterdam: Harwood Academic.

Woolard, J. L., & Reppucci, N. D. (in progress). *Juveniles' competence to stand trial.* New York: NY: Kluwer Academic/Plenum Press.

Woolard, J. L., Reppucci, N. D., & Redding, R. E. (1996). Theoretical and methodological issues in studying children's capacities in legal contexts. *Law and Human Behavior, 20,* 219–228.

Wrightsman, L. S., Nietzel, M. T., & Fortune, W. H. (1998). *Psychology and the legal system* (4th ed.). Pacific Grove, CA: Brooks/Cole.

Yuille, J. C. (1993). We must study forensic eyewitnesses to know about them. *American Psychologist, 48,* 572–573.

Yoshikawa, H. (1993). Prevention as cumulative protection: Effects of early family support and education on chronic delinquency and its risks. *Psychological Bulletin, 115,* 28–54.
Yoshikawa, H. (1993). Prevention as cumulative protection: Effects of early family support and education on chronic delinquency and its risks. *Psychological Bulletin, 115,* 28–54.
Zimring, F. E. (1982). *The changing legal world of adolescence.* New York: Free Press.
Zimring, F. E. (1998). *American youth violence.* New York: Oxford University Press.

# 4

# Forensic Assessment

## Current Status and Future Directions

## KIRK HEILBRUN, RICHARD ROGERS, AND RANDY K. OTTO

Forensic psychology and psychiatry have grown significantly and steadily during the last two decades. One important component of these specialty areas involves the assessment of those involved in criminal and civil litigation for the purpose of assisting legal decision-makers in making better-informed decisions about litigants, or helping attorneys more effectively advocate for their clients in the course of litigation. The achievement of either goal is facilitated by the assessment of litigants using reliable, valid techniques and measures, and the communication of these results in a concise, accurate fashion.

This chapter has several goals. First, we will provide a context for forensic assessment by reviewing its history and development since the 1960s. As we do so, it will become apparent that the number and sophistication of forensic assessment instruments and forensically relevant instruments[1] has increased significantly across these four decades. Since

---

[1] A forensic assessment instrument (FAI) is a tool used for the collection of information about a litigant's capacities that are directly relevant to a legal standard, such as "understanding"

KIRK HEILBRUN • Department of Clinical and Health Psychology, MCP Hahnemann University, Philadelphia, Pennsylvania 19102.    RICHARD ROGERS • Department of Psychology, University of North Texas, Denton, Texas 76203-3587    RANDY K. OTTO • Department of Mental Health Law and Policy, Louis de la Parte Florida Mental Health Center, University of South Florida, Tampa, Florida 33612-3899.

the authors of this chapter believe that the availability of relevant, theoretically sound, methodologically sophisticated forensic assessment tools
is strongly related to the value of the contributions that forensic clinicians
can make to the legal system, we have focused on the discussion of such
measures in this chapter.

Our second goal is to describe relevant influences on the development, validation, and use of forensic instruments. We will first provide a
typology of measures relevant to forensic assessment, and discuss the
implications for the development and use of forensic tools of each type.
Next, we will identify and discuss several important considerations, such
as developmental and cultural influences, population specificity, and the
extent to which forensic assessment should focus on answering ultimate
legal questions as well as measuring relevant capacities, and consider
how these issues affect the development and use of forensic assessment
instruments. Important sources of authority in the areas of law, ethics, and
standards of practice will also be identified; such authority is important in
the development and validation of forensic measures.

The material discussed in this chapter has important implications for
the use of forensic assessment instruments. Our third goal is to propose
an integrated set of guidelines for the forensic use of the various kinds of
assessment measures discussed in this chapter.

## HISTORY OF FORENSIC ASSESSMENT: A SUMMARY

The practice of forensic assessment has changed greatly over the past
40 years. Indeed, forensic evaluations conducted in the 1960s and 1970s
probably did not look much different from therapeutic evaluations conducted at that time (Grisso, 1987). Psychologists typically used
approaches and instruments that they employed in more traditional evaluations (i.e., clinical interviews and structured measures of intelligence,
academic achievement, personality, and psychopathology). Their evaluations were not structured around the legal question(s) with which the
court was concerned, but were focused on psychopathology, and their
consideration of legal issues was diagnostically, rather than functionally
or legally, based. For example, in a sample of 106 criminal defendants who

one's legal situation (as in competence to stand trial) or "knowing the wrongfulness" of certain behavior (as in criminal responsibility). A forensically relevant instrument measures
clinical constructs, such as malingering and psychopathy, which are often relevant to different legal standards. The terms "instrument," "measure," and "tool" will be used inter-
changeable throughout this chapter.

were evaluated for competence to proceed, McGarry (1965) reported that all defendants diagnosed as psychotic were considered by their examiners to be incompetent to stand trial ($N = 31$) and all defendants diagnosed as suffering from non-psychotic diagnoses were considered by the examiners to be competent to stand trial.

Beginning in the mid-1960s, however, forensic psychological assessment began to change as a function of interdisciplinary collaboration, the increasing legal sophistication of clinicians working in forensic settings, and increased professionalism of forensic psychology and forensic psychiatry more generally. In 1965 the first forensic assessment instrument was published· A Checklist of Criteria for Competency to Stand Trial (Robey, 1965). This checklist, developed by Ames Robey (a psychiatrist), simply directed the examining mental health professional to assess the degree to which intellectual limitations or symptoms of mental illness affected a defendant's ability to understand and participate in the legal process. The checklist ensured that the forensic examiner inquired and made judgments about the defendant's capacities in three main spheres: (1) understanding and comprehension of the legal process (including appreciation of the specific charges, allegations, and possible penalties), (2) capacity to work with one's attorney (including ability to provide case-relevant information and make case-relevant decisions), and (3) susceptibility to decompensation while awaiting trial. There were no scoring criteria or norms provided, and the reliability and validity of the instrument was not investigated. Although this instrument may seem unsophisticated by contemporary standards, it represented a major conceptual shift in the practice of forensic assessment. Robey's checklist made clear that forensic evaluators needed to examine and describe the relationship between clinical factors (e.g., intellectual functioning, psychopathology) and legally relevant behaviors (e.g., assisting counsel, understanding and participating in the legal system), rather than simply providing the court with a generic description of the examinee's clinical adjustment and functioning.

Following the introduction of Robey's Checklist, a number of other forensic assessment instruments were developed, most for assessment of criminal defendants. Lipsitt, Lelos, and McGarry (1971; McGarry, 1973) developed two measures for assessing trial competence (the Competence Screening Test [CST], an objectively scored, 22- item test focused on the defendant's knowledge of the legal system, and the Competency to Stand Trial Assessment Instrument [CAI], a semi-structured interview). Other criminal competence assessment instruments developed around this time include the Interdisciplinary Fitness Interview (Golding, Roesch, & Schreiber, 1984) and the Georgia Court Competency Test (Wildman et al.,

1979). Although this first generation of instruments represented an important step with respect to forensic evaluation, they also suffered from significant limitations: (a) information about the psychometric properties of these instruments was sometimes incomplete or absent, (b) manuals were not available, (c) the tests were not commercially published, making their distribution and use difficult, (d) some of the instruments appeared to be largely measures of knowledge rather than capacity or ability, (e) there was sometimes little correspondence between the law and the abilities assessed by some instruments, and (f) comparative norms were not available (Poythress, Nicholson, Otto, Edens, Bonnie, Monahan, & Hoge, 1999). As a result, these instruments did not become widely used, nor did they stimulate much research.

In the 1980s a number of other FAIs were developed for applications in juvenile and child custody contexts. Using a grant from the National Institute of Mental Health, Grisso (1981) developed four separate but related instruments to assess juvenile and adult defendants' understanding of the right to remain silent and avoid self incrimination. The psychometric properties of Grisso's instruments were clearly delineated in his book, which also served as a test manual. In addition, the instruments were grounded in the relevant legal test (*Miranda v. Arizona*, 1966), and were normed on juvenile and adult populations, both offenders and nonoffenders. Unfortunately, the stimulus materials were not published commercially until recently, and the tests did not see much use at the time.[2]

Around this time, Bricklin published two instruments designed for use in child custody evaluations: the Bricklin Perceptual Scales (BPS; Bricklin, 1984) and the Perception of Relationships Test (PORT; Bricklin, 1990a). The BPS and PORT were not directly tied to child custody laws, which vary from state to state, but they clearly were focused on factors relevant to child custody decision making (i.e., the BPS is designed to assess children's perceptions of their parents and their child care behaviors; the PORT is designed to measure children's perceptions of the nature and quality of their relationships with their parents). Although commercially published and distributed, the BPS and PORT have a number of limitations, including inadequate test manuals, incomplete information regarding their psychometric properties, lack of normative data, and limited validity data (for further discussion, see Melton, Petrila, Poythress, & Slobogin, 1997; Otto, Edens, & Barcus, in press).

Grisso (1987) identified both economic and legal influences that have discouraged research and innovation in the area of forensic assessment,

---

[2]A test manual and the instruments have recently been published and are commercially available (Grisso, 1998a, 1998b).

and warned of the negative consequences that could result without adequate research and development devoted to forensic tools. Indeed, Grisso described research-based knowledge and expertise as one important way in which forensic psychology could distinguish itself from other disciplines (e.g., psychiatrists and social workers) offering evaluation services to the courts, and provide a product that would address criticisms of forensic assessment practice such as ignorance of and irrelevance to the legal standard, intrusiveness into the court's decision-making, and insufficiency and lack of credibility of the information collected as part of the assessment (e.g., Grisso, 1986; 1987; Ziskin, 1996). Whatever the impact of Grisso's critique, it is noteworthy that in the following decade there was a dramatic increase in the number of commercially available forensic assessment instruments and psychological tests with clear forensic applications.

The 1990s has seen an explosion the number of assessment instruments developed and published specifically for application in forensic contexts (see Table 4.1 for a review).

Indeed, there have been more FAIs and forensically relevant instruments developed and published in the past 10 years than in the previous 40. The past decade has seen some important changes in how such instruments are developed, researched, and disseminated. First, commercial test publishers appear increasingly interested in this kind of assessment tool. One of us (RKO) has explained this by suggesting that as reimbursement for therapeutic assessment and testing has become more difficult due to financial constraints associated with managed care, test publishers faced with decreasing sales of standardized tests of intelligence, achievement, psychopathology, and personality may regard forensic assessment as an untapped resource and less vulnerable (at least presently)[3] to economic concerns related to managed care (Otto, 1999). The increase in the commercial publication of FAIs may also reflect increasing economic sophistication and motivation on the part of those involved in the development of such instruments.

In addition, the process by which forensic instruments are developed and published has changed over time. Two approaches are typically seen. First, a number of FAIs have been commercially published and distributed only after an extended period during which their design was reviewed and refined, their reliability and validity were researched and subjected to peer review, and normative data were collected. It is this methodical and scientific approach that Grisso (1987) called for in his discussion of the

---

[3]But there are some indications that managed care is entering into the forensic arena, too. For further discussion, see Petrila (1999).

TABLE 4.1. FORENSIC ASSESSMENT INSTRUMENTS: 1960–1999

| 1960s | 1970s | 1980s | 1990s |
|---|---|---|---|
| A Checklist of Criteria for Competency to Stand Trial (Robey, 1965) | Competency Screening Test (McGarry, 1971) | Interdisciplinary Fitness Interview (Roesch & Golding, 1980) | Competency Assessment for Standing Trial for Defendants with Mental Retardation (Everington & Luckasson, 1992) |
| | Competency Assessment Instrument (McGarry, 1971) | Instruments for Assessing Understanding and Appreciation of Miranda Rights (Grisso, 1981) | MacArthur Competence Adjudication Tool-Criminal Adjudication (Poythress et al., 1999) |
| | Georgia Court Competency Test (Wildman et al., 1989) | Rogers Criminal Responsibility Assessment Scales (Rogers, 1984) | Validity Indicator Profile (Frederick, 1997) |
| | | M Test (Beabor et al., 1985) | Victoria Symptom Validity Test (Slick et al., 1997) |
| | | Bricklin Perceptual Scales (1984) | Test of Memory Malingering (Tombaugh, 1996) |
| | | Custody Quotient (Gordon & Peek, 1989) | Computerized Assessment of Response Bias (Allen et al., 1992) |
| | | | Malingering Probability Scale (Silverton & Gruber, 1998) |
| | | | Malingering Scale (Schretlen & Arkowitz, 1990) |

Structured Interview of
Reported Symptoms
(Rogers et al., 1991)
Structured Inventory of
Malingered Symptoms
(Smith, 1992)
Paulhus Deception Scales
(Paulhus, 1998)
Psychopathy Checklist-Revised
(Hare, 1991)
Level of Service Inventory-Revised
(Bonta & Andrews,
2000)
Rapid Risk Assessment for
Sex Offender Recidivism
(Hanson, 1998)
Minnesota Sex Offender
Screening Test (Epperson,
Kaul, & Hesselton, 1998)
Sex Offender Risk
Appraisal Guide (Quinsey
et al., 1998)
Sexual Violence
Recidivism-20 (Boer et al.,
1997)
Static-99 (Hanson &
Thornton, 2000)
Violence Prediction Scheme
(Webster et al., 1994)
Violence Risk Appraisal
Guide (Quinsey et al., 1998)

TABLE 4.1. CONTINUED

| 1960s | 1970s | 1980s | 1990s |
|-------|-------|-------|-------|
|       |       |       | HCR-20 (Webster et al., 1994) |
|       |       |       | Spousal Assault Risk Assessment (Kropp et al., 1995) |
|       |       |       | MacArthur Competence Adjudication Tool-Treatment (Grisso & Appelbaum, 1998) |
|       |       |       | Independent Living Scales (Loeb, 1996) |
|       |       |       | Parent Awareness Skills Survey (Bricklin, 1990) |
|       |       |       | Perception-of-Relationships Test (Bricklin, 1990) |
|       |       |       | Parent Perception of Child Profile (Bricklin & Elliott, 1991) |
|       |       |       | Uniform Child Custody Evaluation System (1994) |
|       |       |       | Ackerman-Schoendorf Parent Evaluation of Custody Test (Ackerman & Schoendorf, 1992) |
|       |       |       | Parent Perception of Child Profile (Bricklin & Elliott, 1991) |
|       |       |       | Child Abuse Potential Inventory (Milner, 1994) |

economic and scientific future of forensic psychology. It is encouraging that a number of FAIs and forensically relevant instruments developed in this way are now available for application in various forensic evaluation contexts: competence to proceed (the MacArthur Competence Assessment Tool-Criminal Adjudication; Poythress, Monahan, Bonnie, & Hoge, 1999), competence to consent to treatment (the MacArthur Competence Assessment Tool-Treatment; Grisso & Appelbaum, 1998), assessment of malingered psychopathology (the Structured Interview of Reported Symptoms; Rogers, Bagby, & Dickens, 1991), assessment of malingered cognitive impairment (the Validity Indicator Profile, Frederick, 1997), assessment of malingered memory deficits (the Test of Memory Malingering, Tombaugh, 1996; the Victoria Symptom Validity Indicator, Slick et al., 1997), assessment of risk for violence and reoffending (the HCR-20, Webster, Douglas, Eaves, & Hart, 1997; the Level of Service Inventory-Revised, Andrews, & Bonta, 1997; the VRAG, Harris, Rice, & Quinsey, 1993) and assessment of psychopathy (the Psychopathy Checklist-Revised; Hare, 1991).

By contrast, a number of instruments have been developed and made available for use (some through commercial publication) with only limited research and development (see Otto, Edens, & Barcus, in press, and Otto, Borum, & Hart, in preparation, for further discussion). For example, some instruments are apparently used by forensic examiners with no available test manual (e.g., the Rapid Risk Assessment for Sexual Offending; Hanson, 1997). Others may be used despite limited knowledge about their basic psychometric properties (e.g., the Sex Offender Risk Appraisal Guide, Quinsey et al., 1997; the Parent Awareness Skills Survey, Bricklin, 1990; the Parent Perception of Child Profile, Bricklin, & Elliott, 1991). Yet other tools are published and used without adequate validation and cross validation research (e.g., the Minnesota Sex Offender Screening Tool-Revised; Epperson, Kaul, & Hesselton, 1998; Minnesota Department of Corrections, undated), and some are commercially published prior to peer review, and with limited research available to support their intended use (e.g., the Parent Awareness Skills Survey, Bricklin, 1990; the Parent Perception of Child Profile, Bricklin & Elliott, 1991; the Malingering Probability Scale, Silverton & Gruber, 1998).

## FORENSIC ASSESSMENT INSTRUMENTS: A TYPOLOGY

Rogers (1987) postulated an inverse relationship in forensic evaluations between clinical certainty based on empirical validation, and legal relevance. He theorized that the best-validated clinical measures (e.g., the

WAIS-III) would have only marginal relevance to most forensic cases. Conversely, psycholegal measures, with their obvious relevance to forensic assessment, are often constrained in the extent to which their users can express clinical certainty based on empirical validation. Such validation is limited by the inherent ambiguity of legal standards, continued evolution in case law, and the judicial consideration of idiographic issues. The inverse relationship between certainty and relevance creates an implicit tension for the practice of forensic psychology. In acknowledging this tension, forensic psychology is best served through use of a range of psychological measures that capitalize on their respective strengths of empirical validation and legal relevance. We have already identified forensic assessment instruments (FAIs) and forensically relevant instruments (FRIs) as important categories of measures that can be used in forensic assessment. In this section, we will also discuss a third category: clinical instruments.

## FORENSIC ASSESSMENT INSTRUMENTS

A forensic assessment instrument is a measure that is directly relevant to a specific legal standard and its included capacities that are needed for the individual being evaluated to meet that legal standard. Grisso (1986) provided a valuable template for the validation of forensic assessment instruments. He proposed that the critical first step is a deconstruction of a particular legal standard into specific functional abilities. Because legal standards are open-textured, they are not reducible to a formal operationalization of explicit criteria. In the absence of operationalized criteria, a primary purpose of forensic assessment instruments is the reliable appraisal of specific abilities as they relate directly to a particular legal standard. Whether the user should then apply these data to draw a conclusion regarding the ultimate legal issue has been debated vigorously; this debate is discussed later in this chapter. However, the application of FAI data toward this end certainly represents a better-informed choice than applying less relevant or valid data toward answering the ultimate legal question.

For purposes of illustration, we focus on competence to stand trial, a psycholegal issue that has been subjected to extensive research in an effort to standardize its assessment through forensic measures. Following Grisso (1986), the first step in validating these competency measures is deconstruction of competence to stand trial into functional abilities. In this respect, forensic clinicians appear to have two major advantages. First, the standard appears relatively straightforward: Athe test must be whether he has sufficient present ability to consult with his lawyer with a reasonable degree of rational understanding B and whether he has a rational as well as factual understanding of the proceedings against him" (*Dusky v. United States*, 1960, p. 789, hereinafter *Dusky*). Second, the United States Supreme Court has consistently upheld the *Dusky* decision. Despite these advantages, the deconstruction of competence to stand trial has proved problematic. As observed by Rogers and Grandjean (2000), scholars have disparate views on competence to stand trial as a legal standard, describing it as: (a) two conjunctive prongs, based on *Dusky*, that address the capacity to consult with counsel, and the rational and factual understanding of the proceedings (Melton, Petrila, Poythress, & Slobogin, 1997; Shuman, 1996), (b) three conjunctive prongs, based on *Dusky* and *Drope v. Missouri* (1975; hereinafter *Drope*), that add Aotherwise assist with [their] defense@ as a third prong (ABA Criminal Justice Mental Health Standards, 1989; see also Freckelton, 1996; Slovenko, 1995), or (c) two broad dimensions, based on *Dusky* and *Drope*, that consist of competence to assist counsel and decisional competence (Bonnie, 1992).

Differences in the conceptualization of competence to stand trial are reflected in different forensic assessment instruments. Cruise and Rogers (1998) found that several forensic measures emphasized factual understanding more than rational understanding of the proceedings, and the ability to consult with counsel was sometimes assessed in a limited fashion (e.g., using the Georgia Court Competence Test; Wildman et al., 1979). Moreover, attempts to establish convergent validity using measures of psychological impairment have often yielded mixed or modest results (Nicholson, Briggs, & Robertson, 1988; Otto et al., 1998; Ustad, Rogers, Sewell, & Guarnaccia, 1996).

Important advances have been made in the assessment of competence to stand trial and other psycholegal issues through the use of forensic assessment instruments. Because the development of forensic assessment instruments is linked to the translation of the legal standard into relevant capacities, however, the limits on the clarity of the legal standard itself only magnify the standard challenges in developing any assessment instrument. Our discussion has illustrated this with a legal standard B competence to stand trial B that is relatively clear and well-defined. The challenges in developing a forensic measure for a less well-defined legal standard may be easily imagined. This overview also addresses the limits on empirically validated clinical certainty. Because of the inherent constraints on their validity, forensic assessment instruments must be augmented by forensically relevant instruments and clinical measures.

## FORENSICALLY RELEVANT INSTRUMENTS

Forensically relevant measures are a critical step removed from forensic measures. While forensic measures focus on specific legal standards and their included functional capacities, forensically relevant measures address clinical constructs that are sometimes pertinent to legal standards. Because their constructs are clinical in nature, forensically relevant measures can minimize problems with definitional ambiguity and idiographic influences. Two examples of important issues addressed by forensically relevant measures are psychopathy and malingering.

Psychopathy is an important consideration in forensic assessment, particularly that relevant to the assessment of violence and criminal recidivism risk in contexts such as criminal sentencing, parole decision-making, and Not Guilty by Reason of Insanity release decision-making. The clinical construct of psychopathy is not rigidly demarcated by statute or case law. Current formulations of psychopathy are informed by theory (Cleckley, 1976; Millon, Simonsen, & Birket-Smith, 1997) and operationalized into specialized measures. When measured by an instrument such as the Psychopathy Checklist-Revised (PCL-R; Hare, 1991), psychopathy can be reliably assessed with extensive construct and criterion-related validity. Measures such as the PCL-R and the PCL-Screening Version (Hart, Hare, & Forth, 1992) appear to make valuable contributions to the broader assessment of violence and recidivism risk, although some caution may need to be exercised in applying these results to specific settings (Hemphill, Templeman, Wong, & Hare, 1998; Salekin, Rogers, & Sewell, 1996; but cf. Quinsey et al., 1998).

Malingering is a core issue in both criminal and civil forensic evaluations. Malingering is suspected in a minority of forensic cases, based on the adversarial nature of the legal proceedings and the potential benefits of appearing mentally of physically disordered. Rogers, Salekin, Sewell, Goldstein, and Leonard (1998), in a prototypical analysis of forensic psychologists, suggested a prevalence rate of malingering of 17.4% among individuals feigning mental disorders, cognitive impairment, and/or medical syndromes.

Clinical methods for the classification of feigning have focused on feigned psychopathology and cognitive impairment. This research is informed by a systematic appraisal of detection strategies, designed specifically for malingered mental disorders and feigned cognitive impairment (Rogers, 1997; Rogers & Shuman, 2000). More than a dozen forensically relevant measures were developed during the last decade to assess malingering (see Table 4.1). These malingering measures vary widely in their types of validation, use of detection strategies, and accuracy of classification.

Well-validated, forensically relevant measures provide a good balance between clinical certainty and legal relevance. Their clinical constructs can be rigorously tested with sophisticated research designs. Their applicability to forensic cases can be formally assessed as well.

## CLINICAL MEASURES

This broad category refers to standard psychological tests that were developed for use in diagnosis, symptom and deficit description, and intervention-planning with clinical populations. Some such instruments have been carefully validated, with established national norms and meticulous attention to external validity. A good example of psychometric rigor may be seen in the Wechsler Adult Intelligence Scale B Third Edition (WAIS-III; Wechsler, 1997).

Some established psychological tests have been criticized for their clinical utility (e.g., the MCMI-III; Millon, 1994; 1997; for a critique, see Rogers & Salekin, 1999) or ecological validity (e.g., the Halstead-Reitan Neuropsychological Battery; Reitan & Wolfson, 1993; for commentary, see Henrichs, 1990), so forensic clinicians should be aware of potential problems with established instruments that they use in forensic contexts. For purposes of illustration, we consider the usefulness of the Minnesota Multiphasic Personality Inventory-2 (MMPI-2; Butcher, Dahlstrom, Graham, Tellegen, & Kaemmer, 1989) for application to insanity evaluations. A recent survey (Borum & Grisso, 1995) indicated that the MMPI/MMPI-2 are used at some time by nearly all forensic psychologists conducting insanity evaluations. Given such popularity, forensic clinicians may assume that an extensive body of research describes its clinical applicability to criminal responsibility. However, relatively few MMPI and MMPI-2 studies have addressed insanity evaluations; those that do not suggest any reliable profile or scale differences between individuals adjudicated as sane and those adjudicated Not Guilty be Reason of Insanity (Rogers & Shuman, 2000). For example, Rogers and McKee (1995) reported counterintuitive results in a large descriptive study of insanity evaluations. For the MMPI-2 psychotic tetrad (Scales 6, 7, 8, and 9), sane defendants with major mental disorders had marked elevations ($M_{psychotic\ tetrad}$= 78.5) as contrasted to insane (M = 67.8) or Guilty But Mentally Ill (M = 70.5) defendants.

Clinical instruments can provide valuable data about level of impairment and functioning. For the best-validated measures, findings may be presented with a high degree of clinical certainty. However, the applicability of such findings to specific legal standards and included constructs is not straightforward. Evaluators cannot conclude that a specific finding on a clinical measure is necessarily or directly relevant to a legal question or relevant legal construct, as illustrated with the example of the MMPI/MMPI-2.

## DEVELOPMENT AND USE OF FORENSIC ASSESSMENT INSTRUMENTS: IMPORTANT CONSIDERATIONS

There are several particular considerations in the development and use of forensic assessment instruments and forensically relevant tools. We will discuss four such considerations in this section: developmental, population specificity, cultural, and the question of capacity versus ultimate issue focus.

### DEVELOPMENTAL INFLUENCES

Those involved in criminal and civil litigation range in age across the entire lifespan. Although age is only a rough marker for developmental maturity, it will be considered as an important indicator for the sake of this discussion. There are two broad reasons why age is particularly important in the development and application of forensic assessment instruments. First, there are important differences between children, adolescents, and adults in capacities for understanding, reasoning, autonomy, communication, and psychosocial judgment (Nottelmann, 1987; Steinberg, 1990; Steinberg & Cauffman, 1996). Second, the law's demands on litigants vary by age, particularly for children and adolescents versus adults (Melton et al., 1997), and even between younger and older adolescents (Heilbrun, Leheny, Thomas, & Huneycutt, 1997). As a consequence, assessment of relevant forensic capacities must take into account the effects of age (Scott, Reppucci, & Woolard, 1995; Woolard, Reppucci, & Redding, 1996), and researchers are increasingly inclined toward developing forensic assessment instruments and forensically relevant instruments that are specific to age.

Two examples are helpful. On the legal question of competence to stand trial, the development and validation of the MacArthur Competence Assessment Tool-Criminal Adjudication (Poythress, Monahan et al., 1999) represents a significant advance that allows the forensic clinician to compare a defendant's capacities to understand, reason, and appreciate areas relevant to participating in the criminal process to those of other defendants (with and without mental disorder). This same tool, however, could not be used in a straightforward fashion to assess juveniles' capacities relevant to competence to stand trial in juvenile court. Important differences between juvenile court and criminal court include the expectation for autonomous decision-making, rules of evidence, the right to a jury trial, and the consequences of a criminal conviction versus a delinquency adjudication. Given these differences, it would be most appropriate to develop a tool specific to juveniles and juvenile court, using similar derivation and validation procedures as the MacCAT-CA but yielding a final version that differed from the MacCAT-CA in substance if not structure.

A second example involves a forensically relevant instrument, the Psychopathy Checklist-Revised (Hare, 1991) that may also be useful in the assessment of developing psychopathy in adolescence. Again, the straightforward application of the adult version of the PCL-R would not be indicated. In contrast to the example in the previous paragraph, there is attention to the law's demands in this example. Psychopathy as a construct is relevant to capacities associated with various legal questions, but the construct itself is not informed by these legal questions or included capacities. However, there is an important question about whether psychopathy as a disorder is meaningful when applied to adolescents. Since this is partly an empirical question, meaningful answers will come from the investigation of psychopathic characteristics in adolescents, and the persistence or desistence of associated behaviors into adulthood. The practical objection to using the PCL-R with adolescents that some of the adult criteria (e.g., multiple marital relationships) are not meaningful with juveniles. Since this problem has been addressed by the development of a tool to measure psychopathy specifically in adolescence (the Psychopathy Checklist – Youth Version; Forth, Kosson, & Hare, 1996), the practical problems have been diminished, and the answers to the empirical questions can be addressed in research using the PCL-YV. When research has helped the field understand if and how psychopathy does apply to adolescents, then the PCL-YV may be applicable to certain legal questions concerning juveniles and other adolescents.

## POPULATION-SPECIFIC INFLUENCES

Any kind of psychological test, diagnostic instrument, or decision-making heuristic works best when it is applied to individuals within or similar to the population on which the tool was developed and validated. Indeed, when there is no empirical evidence about the applicability and interpretation of results in a different population, it is usually preferable to avoid using that instrument to evaluate someone from a different population. In a forensic context, we would propose that "population" incorporate at least age, clinical status, and legal status. The influences of age were discussed in the immediately previous section. "Clinical status" includes the extent to which broad categories of disorder (e.g., major mental disorders such as schizophrenia and affective disorders with psychotic features; substance abuse; non-psychotic affective disorders, anxiety disorders, personality disorders, conduct disorders, learning disorders, and cognitive deficits). Legal status would mean, at a minimum, that an instrument used in an evaluation of a criminal defendant have associated validation research with criminal defendants; likewise, an evaluation of a defendant or plaintiff in a civil context should employ instruments supported by some research application to individuals involved in civil litigation.

FAIs carry an additional requirement not applied to FRIs: they must demonstrate applicability to a specific legal status. "Legal status" is defined by three parameters: (1) the nature of the litigation (e.g., civil versus criminal), (2) the specific legal question(s) associated with this litigation (e.g., competence to stand trial, fitness to parent, competence to make a will), and (3) the nature of the functional capacities associated with the particular legal standard. Population specificity is addressed through the validation process. To the extent that forensic assessment instruments are developed and validated on samples comparable in age, legal status, and clinical status to the population with whom they are subsequently used, the fit between the FAI and the individual is better and the FAI more directly applicable.

## CULTURAL INFLUENCES

Cultural influences are another aspect of population specificity, but merit additional comment. It is important, of course, that a forensic assessment instrument include appropriate racial and ethnic diversity in its validation samples if that FAI is to be applied to individuals in minority groups. It is important to avoid mistaken assumptions about ethnicity. First, ethnicity is considered more than a simple designation; the individual's ethnic identity must be observed. Second, broad ethnic categories (e.g., Hispanic American) are often misleading because they overlook important within-minority differences in language and culture (Puente, 1990). Forensic psychologists may be forced to choose between well-validated measures that have unknown generalizability to a specific minority group, versus idiosyncratic methods that can be tailored to a specific group but are not as well-validated.

The importance of cultural issues is highlighted in family law. For example, the development of FAIs for child custody evaluation must take into account a broad range of cultural and religious influences that can have a significant impact on what would be considered "good" or even "acceptable" parenting practices. It seems unlikely that any measure, no matter how well validated, could incorporate the full range of such culturally diverse influences in an area like child custody, particularly in culturally heterogeneous countries such as the United States. Rather than expect a forensic measure to provide such relevant cultural information, particularly in unusual circumstances that are not likely to be reflected in a validation sample, it is preferable to obtain information about that specific culture and the associated expectations regarding childrearing practices, and integrate this information with the findings obtained from other sources regarding parenting capacities and fitness.

## CAPACITIES VERSUS ULTIMATE LEGAL ISSUE FOCUS

For over 20 years, there has been a vigorous debate within the field regarding whether forensic clinicians should answer the "ultimate legal issue"—the question which the court must ultimately decide—or limit the conclusions expressed in reports and in testimony to descriptive and empirical data relevant to a litigant's capacities that are included within and relevant to the ultimate legal issue (Bonnie & Slobogin, 1980; Grisso, 1986; Melton et al., 1997; Morse, 1978a; 1978b; 1982; Poythress, 1982; Rogers & Ewing, 1989; Slobogin, 1989). The complex debate remains ongoing, and appears unlikely to be resolved through consensus in the field. It will not be discussed further in the present chapter. However, it is important to note that this debate has implications for how forensic assessment instruments are developed and validated.

When an FAI is developed to both measure capacities *and* combine these capacities to answer the ultimate legal question, then one research strategy might include the validation of such a tool using a "known groups" design. That is, individuals who have been adjudicated as incompetent to stand trial might constitute one group, those with identified mental health problems but not adjudicated incompetent for trial might be a second, and incarcerated jail inmates not selected for mental health problems a third. The problem with using legal status as the sole identifier of the "known group" is that such adjudications are potentially confounded with a number of influences, including court, jurisdiction, seriousness of charges, availability of forensic beds, and clinical-forensic findings. This led Roesch and Golding (1980) to propose that a "blue ribbon panel" composed of individuals knowledgeable about relevant law and forensic procedures independently review cases and assign them into groups. Such a procedure would increase the internal validity of this process, although perhaps at the expense of generalizability, and would also involve significantly more expense. It seems reasonable to conclude that both strategies could be used in the larger process of validating an FAI for competence to stand trial.

To some extent, a similar research strategy can be employed in developing FAIs that focus on capacities only. For example, the MacCAT-CA (Poythress et al., 1999) was developed to measure relevant capacities for competency to stand trial. Both defendants who were incompetent to stand trial and those who were not adjudicated as incompetent were included in the validation research. However, the manual makes it clear that MacCAT-CA is designed to measure capacities, not the ultimate legal question of trial competence. Even with the MacCAT-CA, individual capacities are organized under the legal prongs of *Dusky*. Validation research strategies may be comparable between the two approaches, then, but there remain important differences in whether (and how) the measured capacities are combined in an attempt to answer the larger legal issue before the court.

## Sources of Authority and Their Relevance to Forensic Assessment

When considering whether a particular test is appropriate for use in the context of a forensic evaluation, there are different sources of authority that provide some direction to the psychologist. These sources, which are briefly discussed in the following sections, are generally consistent and primarily differ with respect to their level of specificity.

### RELEVANT LAW

Legal standards are an important source of authority in the conceptualization and development of forensic measures. A review of relevant case law and statutes across jurisdictions can inform researchers whether (a) the legal standards for a particular question are well defined and broadly accepted, (b) diverse standards and definitions exist, or (c) an area is relatively poorly conceptualized and defined. The most straightforward translation of legal standards and included capacities can occur under the first circumstance. As previously noted for competence to stand trial, however, even well defined and broadly accepted standards pose a rigorous challenge in their operationalization and validation. When different standards exist (e.g., M'Naghten versus ALI for insanity), then an FAI must either be developed to provide data relevant to the broadest question, and tailored for use in jurisdictions using the narrower standard, or specifically limited to use in jurisdictions with that particular standard. Systematic comparisons of statutes, administrative codes, and case law from different jurisdictions can help to provide detail when FAI developers are first operationalizing relevant capacities.

Having discussed law among the sources of authority relevant to forensic assessment, we will now turn to professional standards. These will include standards for psychological testing, as well as ethical standards.

## STANDARDS FOR EDUCATIONAL AND PSYCHOLOGICAL TESTING

The *Standards for Education and Psychological Testing* (AERA/APA, 1999; hereinafter *Test Standards*) are a set of standards, jointly authored by the American Educational Research Association, the American Psychological Association, and the National Council on Measurement in Education "to provide criteria for the evaluations of tests, testing practices, and the effects of test use" (p. 2). These standards support the availability of technical information on assessment techniques. Such technical information would allow test users to evaluate the appropriateness and determine the technical adequacy of a test, and assess the propriety of its application and interpretation in a particular case. The standards included are flexible, so that different types of assessment instruments can be evaluated using the most appropriate criteria.

These *Test Standards* contain three parts. Part I focuses on test construction, evaluation, and documentation (i.e., standards for validity, reliability, measurement error, test construction and norming, scoring, and communication of results). Part II deals with fairness in testing (i.e., issues of fairness and bias in testing, rights and responsibilities of test takers, and assessment of persons with disabilities and from diverse backgrounds). Part III pertains to testing applications (i.e., responsibilities of test users, testing in education and employment settings, testing and public policy, and testing and program evaluation). Instruments used by psychologists in forensic contexts should meet the relevant criteria established in the *Test Standards*, unless there is some justification that can be clearly articulated for not meeting these standards.

## ETHICAL PRINCIPLES OF PSYCHOLOGISTS AND CODE OF CONDUCT

Section 2 of the Ethical Principles of Psychologists and Code of Conduct (American Psychological Association, 1992) directs professional practice with respect to psychological evaluation and assessment, and arguably applies to all psychologists. Standard 2.02(a) requires that psychologists use assessment techniques in ways that are appropriate in light of research or other evidence. Standard 2.04(a) emphasizes that psychologists should be familiar with the reliability, validation, and related standardization or outcome studies of the techniques they use. Standard 2.04(e) directs that psychologists be aware of cases in which particular assessment techniques or norms may not be applicable or may require adjustment in administration or interpretation. Standard 2.08(b) and (c) require that psychologists take responsibility for the validity and interpretation of tests, including those yielding automated reports. Such automated reports based on proprietary information pose a particular obstacle to addressing this standard in a satisfactory way.

## SPECIALTY GUIDELINES FOR FORENSIC PSYCHOLOGISTS

The Specialty Guidelines for Forensic Psychologists (Committee on Ethical Guidelines for Forensic Psychologists, 1991) contain a number of sections that are relevant to forensic assessment and the use of tools in the process of such assessment. Under Section VI(A), such assessment should reflect "current knowledge of scientific, professional and legal developments" within the specific area of assessment (1991, p. 661).

The nature of the documentation should be more detailed and extensive than in non-forensic measures, as it should be anticipated that the results will be subjected to "reasonable judicial scrutiny" (Section VI(B), 1991, p. 661). The importance of testing alternative hypotheses is underscored. Specifically, forensic psychologists are asked to examine "the issue at hand from all reasonable perspectives, actively seeking information that will differentially test plausible rival hypotheses" (Section VI(C), 1991, p. 661). In addition, relevance is particularly important; any assessment measure should "bear directly upon the legal purpose" of the evaluation and provide "support for their product, evidence, or testimony" (Section VI(F)(2), 1991, p. 662). Finally, the forensic assessment process should facilitate communication that will "promote understanding and avoid deception" (Section VII(A), 1991, p. 663).

## STANDARD OF PRACTICE LITERATURE

A number of scholars have discussed the various ways in which forensic assessment instruments can be applied (e.g., Grisso, 1986; Melton et al., 1997; Rogers & Shuman, 2000). A specific analysis of the role of psychological testing in forensic assessment, with suggested guidelines for test selection, has been provided by Heilbrun (1992) and Rogers and Shuman (2000). Therefore, the present discussion will focus on FRIs and the clinical measures that are described in this chapter. Heilbrun (1992) suggested that in order for a test to be used in a forensic context, it should first be commercially available and accompanied by a manual describing its development, psychometric properties, and administration procedure. He also recommended that the instrument be listed or reviewed in a readily available source. All parties to a legal proceeding should have reasonable access to information regarding the test and its utility, allowing preparation for direct and cross-examination.

Because test reliability limits test validity, Heilbrun recommended that examiners exercise caution when using instruments with relevant reliability coefficients of less than .80. It should be added that this is a stringent standard with which reasonable professionals might disagree, but the purpose of this recommendation was to focus attention on the test's reliability—and to require justification when using tests the lower levels of reliability. Heilbrun also suggested that the test should be relevant to the legal issue and that, when possible, this should be established by validation research published in refereed journals. In order to ensure generalizability from the testing situation, Heilbrun noted that instruments should be administered in a standardized manner. Heilbrun cautioned that differences between the examinee and the population on which a test was developed, or differences between the purposes for which a test was developed and how it is being used should be considered by the examiner, with any differences being noted and reflected in cautions that the examiner offers regarding the validity of the findings. Heilbrun also noted that, where appropriate, response styles and their impact on test results should be considered by the examiner.

## CHECKLIST FOR USE OF FORENSIC ASSESSMENT INSTRUMENTS, FORENSICALLY RELEVANT MEASURES, AND PSYCHOLOGICAL TESTS IN FORENSIC CONTEXTS

In this section, we will synthesize our discussion and offer integrated recommendations to guide psychologists as they consider the appropriateness of using a particular test in a forensic evaluation. We emphasize that these are general guidelines, and the significance of any one may depend on a number of factors. Psychologists should always use their professional judgment, but those using tests that do not meet the guidelines set out below should bear the burden of justification.

## COMMERCIAL PUBLICATION OF THE TEST

Ideally, tests used by psychologists in forensic evaluations will be commercially published and distributed. This ensures a reasonable level of availability and uniformity of test stimulus materials and protocols. Non-commercial publication and distribution of a test would appear to be acceptable providing that there is relevant information regarding the test (described under "test manual," next) that can be provided to test users and others.

## AVAILABLE TEST MANUAL

Test manuals are a primary and authoritative resource that describe the user qualifications, and the development, standardization, administration, scoring, and psychometric properties of the instrument (including its reliability and validity). As noted above, there are a number of instruments currently used in forensic evaluations that do not have test manuals. This shortcoming increases the possibility of inappropriate application, administration, scoring, and interpretation.

## DEMONSTRATED LEVELS OF RELIABILITY

Test reliability limits test validity. Psychologists should only use instruments with known and adequate levels of reliability. The particular type of reliability that is most important may vary across tests and situations, but psychologists should consider factors such as internal consistency, inter-rater reliability, test-retest reliability, and reliability of parallel forms. In most circumstances, reliability should be demonstrated in more than one of these forms.

## DEMONSTRATED LEVELS OF VALIDITY

In addition to demonstrated levels of reliability, tests used by psychologists in forensic evaluations should also have established validity. In the abstract, the validity of a test can be considered in a variety of ways (e.g., discriminant validity, predictive validity, concurrent validity, construct validity, face validity), and must be demonstrated (preferably through more than one form, and across multiple studies) before a psychologist considers using such a test in a forensic evaluation.

But test validity in not best considered in the abstract; a test should be valid *for the purpose for which it will be used*. The most appropriate analysis of a test's validity considers whether that test is valid for a particular application, when used in a particular way, and with a particular population. For example, although the WAIS-III provides valid estimates of intellectual functioning, few would argue that cognitive abilities on the WAIS-III can be directly related to a criminal defendant's appreciation of the index offense in an insanity case. This analysis of purpose is especially important when forensic psychologists employ clinical measures that evaluate constructs not directly related to the legal issue.

Forensic psychologists must also consider whether a test that is of proven validity for a specific purpose is valid with the particular examinee. Issues of ethnicity, race, setting, and age may affect test results and test validity. To address these important issues, psychologists using tests must review the norms and standardization so that informed decisions can be rendered about their applicability to a particular case.

### SUCCESSFUL PEER REVIEW

The importance and value of the peer review process cannot be overestimated. Generally, tests used in forensic evaluations will have been subjected to peer review. Reliability and validity studies should be published in refereed journals, allowing the most objective examination of the test and its properties. Psychologists should be skeptical of tests that have not undergone the peer review process, and whose properties have only been investigated by the authors.

### DECISION MAKING FORMULAS ARE KNOWN TO THE EXAMINERS

Forensic examiners are obligated by law, ethics, and standards of practice to fully reveal the information forming the basis for their opinions. Forensic psychologists should not employ tests that offer scores, opinions, or predictions based on formulae that are unknown to the examiner. Although test publishers may offer concerns about proprietary interests and test security, legal and practice guidelines would appear to outweigh these interests.

## CONCLUSION

Forensic assessment has grown and advanced significantly during the last twenty years in particular. The present chapter has reviewed and critically analyzed conceptual and empirical developments, as well as the addition of a variety of FAIs and FRIs that are relevant to the legal decision-making process. Despite the important advances that we have described in this chapter, however, there is currently a significant problem with the use of forensic assessment tools that have not been developed and validated through a rigorous process involving empirical investigation and critical peer review. An insistence on strong scientific support guiding the process of forensic assessment and shaping the tools that it employs will allow the mental health professions to provide legal decision-makers with the best-informed basis for legal decisions involving the behavioral sciences.

# REFERENCES

Ackerman, M., & Schoendorf, K. (1992). *The Ackerman-Schoendorf Parent Evaluation of Custody Tests (ASPECT)*. Los Angeles: Western Psychological Services.

Allen, L.A., Conder, R.L., Green, P., & Cox, D.R. (1992, 1999). *Manual for the Computerized Assessment of Response Bias*. Durham, NC: Cognisyst.

American Bar Association (1989). *Criminal justice mental health standards*. Washington, D.C.: Author.

American Educational Research Association, American Psychological Association, National Council on Measurement in Education (1999). *Standards for educational and psychological testing* (Third ed.). Washington, DC: American Educational Research Association.

American Psychological Association (1992). Ethical principles of psychologists and code of conduct. *American Psychologist, 47*, 1597–1611.

Andrews, D. A., & Bonta, J. (1997). *Manual for the Level of Service Inventory-Revised*. North Tonawanda, NY: Multi-Health Systems.

Boer, D. P., Hart, S. D., Kropp, P. R., & Webster, C. D. (1997). *Manual for the Sexual Violence Risk-20*. Burnaby, BC: Mental Health, Law, & Policy Institute, Simon Fraser University.

Bonnie, R. (1992). The competence of criminal defendants: A theoretical reformulation. *Behavioral Sciences & the Law, 10*, 291–316.

Bonnie, R., & Slobogin, C. (1980). The role of mental health professionals in the criminal process: The case for informed speculation. *Virginia Law Review, 66*, 427–522.

Bonta, J., & Andrews, J. (2000). *Manual for the Level of Service Inventory-Revised*. Tonawanda, NY: Multi-Health Systems.

Borum, R., & Grisso, T. (1995). Psychological test use in criminal forensic evaluations. *Professional Psychology: Research and Practice, 26*, 465–473.

Borum, R., & Grisso, T. (1996). Establishing standards for criminal forensic reports: An empirical analysis. *Bulletin of the American Academy of Psychiatry and the Law, 24*, 297–317.

Bricklin, B. (1990a). *Perceptions-of Relationships-Test Manual*. Furlong, PA: Village Publishing.

Bricklin, B. (1990b). *Parent Awareness Skills Survey Manual*. Furlong, PA: Village Publishing.

Bricklin, B. (1984). *Bricklin Perceptual Scales Manual*. Furlong, PA: Village Publishing.

Bricklin, B., & Elliott, G. (1991). *Parent Perception of Child Profile Manual*. Furlong, PA: Village Publishing.

Butcher, J. N., Williams, C. L.., Graham, J. R., Tellegen, A., & Kaemmer, B. (1989). *MMPI-2: Manual for administration and scoring*. Minneapolis: University of Minnesota Press.

Cleckley, H. (1976). *The mask of sanity* (4th ed.). St. Louis, MO: Mosby.

Committee on Ethical Guidelines for Forensic Psychologists (1991). Specialty guidelines for forensic psychologists. *Law and Human Behavior, 15*, 655–665.

Cruise, K. R., & Rogers, R. (1998). An analysis of competency to stand trial: An integration of case law and clinical knowledge. *Behavioral Sciences and the Law, 16*, 35–50.

Drope v. Missouri, 420 U.S. 162 (1974).

Dusky v. United States, 362 U.S. 402 (1960).

Epperson, D. L., Kaul, J. D., & Hesselton, D. (1998, September). *Final report on the development of the Minnesota Sex Offender Screening Tool-Revised (MnSOST-R)*. Presented at the annual meeting of the Association for the Treatment of Sexual Abusers, Vancouver, BC, Canada.

Everington, C., & Luckasson, R. (1992). *Manual for Competence Assessment for Standing Trial for Defendants with Mental Retardation: CAST-MR*. Worthington, OH: IDS Publishing.

Forth, A., Kosson, D., & Hare, R. (1996). *Psychopathy Checklist: Youth Version*. Ottawa, Ontario: Carleton University.

Freckelton, I. (1996). Rationality and flexibility in assessment of fitness to stand trial. *International Journal of Law and Psychiatry, 19*, 39–59.

Frederick, R. (1997). *Manual for the Validity Indicator Profile*. Minnetonka, MN: National Computer Services.

Golding, S. L., Roesch, R., & Schreiber, J. (1984). Assessment and conceptualization of competency to stand trial: Preliminary data on the Interdisciplinary Fitness Interview. *Law and Human Behavior, 8*, 321–334.

Gordon, R., & Peek, L. (1989). *The Custody Quotient. Research manual*. Dallas, TX: Wilmington Institute.

Grisso, T. (1981). *Juveniles' waiver of rights: Legal and psychological competence*. New York: Plenum.

Grisso, T. (1986). *Evaluating competencies: Forensic assessments and instruments*. New York: Plenum Press.

Grisso, T. (1987). The economic and scientific future of forensic psychological assessment. *American Psychologist, 42*, 831–839.

Grisso, T. (1998a). *Instruments for assessing understanding and appreciation of Miranda rights*. Sarasota, FL: Professional Resource Press.

Grisso, T. (1998b). *Instruments for assessing understanding and appreciation of Miranda rights-Manual*. Sarasota, FL: Professional Resource Press.

Grisso, T., & Appelbaum, P. (1998). *MacArthur Competence Assessment Tool-Treatment (MacCAT-T)*. Sarasota, FL: Professional Resource Press.

Hanson, R. K. (1997). *The development of a brief actuarial risk scale for sexual offense recidivism* (User Report No. 1997-04). Ottawa, Ontario, Canada: Department of the Solicitor General of Canada.

Hanson, K., & Thornton, D. (2000). Improving risk assessments for sex offenders: A comparison of three actuarial scales. *Law and Human Behavior, 24*, 119–136.

Hare, R. (1991). *Manual for the Hare Psychopathy Checklist-Revised*. North Tonawanda, NY: Multi-Health Systems.

Harris, G. T., Rice, M. E., & Quinsey, V. L. (1993). Violent recidivism of mentally disordered offenders: The development of a statistical prediction instrument. *Criminal Justice and Behavior, 20*, 315–335.

Hart, S. D., Cox, D. N., & Hare, R. D. (1996). *Manual for the Screening Version of Psychopathy Checklist Revised (PCL:SV)*. Toronto: Multi-Health Systems.

Heilbrun, K. (1992). The role of psychological testing in forensic assessment. *Law and Human Behavior, 16*, 257–272.

Heilbrun, K., Leheny, C., Thomas, L., & Huneycutt, D. (1997). A national survey of U.S. statutes on juvenile transfer: Implications for policy and practice. *Behavioral Sciences & the Law, 15*, 125–149.

Hemphill, J. F., Templeman, R., Wong, S., & Hare, R. D. (1998). Psychopathy and crime: Recidivism and criminal careers. In D. Cooke, A, Forth, & R. Hare (Eds.), *Psychopathy: Theory, research, and implications for society* (pp. 375–398). Dordrecht, Netherlands: Kluwer Academic.

Henrichs, R. W. (1990). Current and emergent applications of neuropsychological assessment: Problems of validity and utility. *Professional Psychology: Research and Practice, 21*, 171–176.

Kropp, P. R., Hart, S. D., Webster, C. D., & Eaves, D. (1995). *Manual for the Spousal Assault Risk Assessment Guide*. Vancouver, BC: British Columbia Institute on Family Violence.

Lipsitt, P., Lelos, D., & McGarry, A. (1971). Competency for trial: A screening instrument. *American Journal of Psychiatry, 128*, 105–109.

Loeb, P. (1996). *Manual for the Independent Living Scales*. San Antonio, TX: Psychological Corporation.

McGarry, A. L. (1965). Competence for trial and due process via the State hospital. *American Journal of Psychiatry, 122*, 623–630.

McGarry, A. (1971). *Competency to stand trial and mental illness*. Rockville, MD: Department of Health, Education and Welfare.

Melton, G. B., Petrila, J., Poythress, N., & Slobogin, C. (1997). *Psychological evaluations for the courts: A handbook for attorneys and mental health professionals* (2nd edition). New York: Guilford.

Millon, T. (1994). *The Millon Clinical Multiaxial Inventory-III manual*. Minneapolis: National Computer Systems.

Millon, T. (1997). *The Millon Clinical Multiaxial Inventory-III manual (2nd edition)*. Minneapolis: National Computer Systems.

Millon, T., Simonsen, E., Birket-Smith, M., & Davis, R. D. (Eds.), *Psychopathy: Antisocial, criminal and violent behaviors*. New York: Guilford.

Milner, J. (1994). Assessing physical child abuse risk: The Child Abuse Potential Inventory. *Clinical Psychology Review, 14*, 547–557.

Minnesota Department of Corrections (undated). *Minnesota Sex Offender Screening Tool revised (MnSOST-R)*. St. Paul, MN: Author.

*Miranda v. Arizona*, 384 U.S. 436 (1966).

Morse, S. (1978a). Crazy behavior, morals, and science: An analysis of mental health law. *Southern California Law Review, 51*, 527–654.

Morse, S. (1978b). Law and mental health professionals: The limits of expertise. *Professional Psychology, 9*, 389–399.

Morse, S. (1982). Reforming expert testimony: An open response from the tower (and the trenches). *Law and Human Behavior, 6*, 45–47.

Nicholson, R. A., Briggs, S. R., & Robertson, H. C. (1988). Instruments for assessing competency to stand trial: How do they work? *Professional Psychology: Research and Practice, 19*, 383–394.

Nottelmann, E. (1987). Competence and self-esteem during transition from childhood to adolescence. *Developmental Psychology, 23*, 441–450.

Otto, R. K. (1999, February). *The future of forensic psychology: A view towards the future in light of the past*. Paper presented at Sam Houston State University, Department of Psychology and College of Criminal Justice.

Otto, R. K., Edens, J. F., & Barcus, E. (in press). The use of psychological testing in child custody evaluations. *Family and Conciliation Courts Review*.

Otto, R.K., Poythress, N.G., Nicholson, R., Edens, J., Monahan, J., Bonnie, R., Hoge, S., & Eisenberg, M. (1998). Psychometric properties of the MacArthur Competence Assessment Tool—Criminal Adjudication (MacCAT-CA). *Psychological Assessment: A Journal of Consulting and Clinical Psychology, 10*, 435–443.

Petrila, J. (1999, October). *Emerging issues in managed care and delivery of forensic services*. Paper presented at the Annual Meeting of the National Association of State Mental Health Program Directors-Forensic Division, Tarrytown, New York.

Poythress, N.G. (1982). Concerning reform in expert testimony: An open letter from a practicing psychologist. *Law and Human Behavior, 6*, 39–43.

Poythress, N., Monahan, J., Bonnie, R., & Hoge, S. K. (1999). *MacArthur Competence Assessment Tool-Criminal Adjudication*. Odessa, FL: Psychological Assessment Resources 1999.

Poythress, N., G., Nicholson, R., Otto, R. K., Edens, J. F., Bonnie, R. J., Monahan, J., & Hoge, S. K. (1999). *Professional manual for the MacArthur Competence Assessment Tool-Criminal Adjudication*. Odessa, FL: Psychological Assessment Resources.

Puente, A. E. (1990). Psychological assessment with minority group members. In G. Goldstein & M. Hersen (Eds.), *Handbook of psychological assessment* 2nd ed., pp. 505–520). New York: Pergamon Press.

Quinsey, V. L., Harris, G. T., Rice, M. E., & Cormier, C. A. (1998). *Violent offenders: Appraising and managing risk*. Washington, DC: American Psychological Association.

Reitan, R. M., & Wolfson, D. (1993). *The Halstead-Reitan Neuropsychological Test Battery: Theory and clinical interpretation*. Tucson, AZ: Neuropsychological Press.

Robey, A. (1965). Criteria for competency to stand trial: A checklist for psychiatrists. *American Journal of Psychiatry, 122*, 616–622.

Roesch, R., & Golding, S. L. (1980). *Competency to stand trial*. Urbana-Champaign, IL: University of Illinois Press.

Rogers, R. (1984). *Manual for the Rogers Criminal Responsibility Assessment Scales*. Odessa, FL: Psychological Assessment Resources.

Rogers, R. (1987). Ethical dilemmas in forensic evaluations. *Behavioral Sciences and the Law, 5*, 149–160.

Rogers, R. (Ed.) (1997). *Clinical assessment of malingering and deception* (2nd ed.). New York: Guilford.

Rogers, R., & Ewing, C.P. (1989). Ultimate opinion proscriptions: A cosmetic fix and a plea for empiricism. *Law and Human Behavior, 13*, 357–374.

Rogers, R., & McKee, G. R. (1995). Use of the MMPI-2 in the assessment of criminal responsibility. In Y. S. Ben-Porath, J. R. Graham, G. C. N. Hall, R. D. Hirschman, & M. S. Zaragoza (Eds.), *Forensic applications of the MMPI-2* (pp.103–126). Newbury Park, CA: Sage.

Rogers, R. & Grandjean, N. (2000, March). *Competency measures and the Dusky standard: A conceptual mismatch?* Paper presented at the Biennial Conference of the American Psychology-Law Society/APA Division 41, New Orleans.

Rogers, R., & Sewell, K. W. (1999). The R CRAS and insanity evaluations: A re-examination of construct validity. *Behavioral Sciences and the Law, 17*, 181–194.

Rogers, R., & Shuman, D. W. (2000). *Conducting insanity evaluations*. New York: Guilford Publications.

Rogers, R., & Shuman, D. W. (in press). The "Mental Status at the Time of the Offense" measure: Its validation and admissibility under *Daubert. Journal of the American Academy of Psychiatry and Law.*

Rogers, R., Bagby, M., & Dickens, S. (1992). *Manual for the Structured Interview of Reported Symptoms*. Odessa, FL: Psychological Assessment Resources.

Rogers, R. Salekin, R. T., & Sewell, K. W. (1999). Validation of the Millon Multiaxial Inventory for Axis II disorders: Does it meet the *Daubert* standard? *Law and Human Behavior, 23*, 425–443.

Rogers, R., Salekin, R., Sewell, K., Goldstein, A., & Leonard, K. (1998). A comparison of forensic and nonforensic malingerers: A prototypical analysis of explanatory models. *Law and Human Behavior, 22*, 353–367.

Salekin, R., Rogers, R., & Sewell, K. (1996). A review and meta-analysis of the Psychopathy Checklist and the Psychopathy Checklist-Revised: Predictive validity of dangerousness. *Clinical Psychology: Science and Practice, 3*, 203–215.

Scott, E., Reppucci, N. D., & Woolard, J. (1995). Evaluating adolescent decision making in legal contexts. *Law and Human Behavior, 19*, 221–244.

Shuman, D. W. (1996). *Psychiatric and psychological evidence* (2nd ed.). Colorado Springs: Shepherds/McGraw-Hill.

Silverton, L., & Gruber, C. (1998). *Manual for the Malingering Probability Scale*. Los Angeles, CA: Western Psychological Services.

Slobogin, C. (1989). The ultimate issue issue. *Behavioral Sciences & the Law, 7*, 259–268.

Slobogin, C., Melton, G. B., & Showalter, C. R. (1984). The feasibility of a brief evaluation of mental state at the time of the offense. *Law and Human Behavior, 8*, 305–320.

Slick, D., Hopp, G., Strauss, E., & Thompson, G. B. (1997). *Professional manual for the Victoria Symptom Validity Test*. Odessa, FL: Psychological Assessment Resources.

Slovenko, R. (1995). Assessing competency to stand trial. *Psychiatric Annals, 25*, 392–397.

Steinberg, L. (1990). Autonomy, conflict, and harmony in the family relationship. In S. Feldman & G. Elliott (Eds.), *At the threshold: The developing adolescent* (pp. 255–276). Cambridge: Harvard University Press.

Steinberg, L., & Cauffman, E. (1996). Maturity of judgment in adolescence: Psychosocial factors in adolescent decision-making. *Law and Human Behavior, 20*, 249–272.

Tombaugh, T. (1996). *Manual for the Test of Memory Malingering*. North Tonawanda, NY: Multi-Health Systems.

Ustad, K., Rogers, R., Sewell, K., & Guarnaccia, C. (1996). Restoration of competency to stand trial: Assessment with the GCCT-MSH and the CST. *Law and Human Behavior, 20*, 131–146.

Webster, C. D., Douglas, K. S., Eaves, D., & Hart, S. D. (1997). *Manual for the HCR-20: Assessing risk for violence (Version 2)*. Burnaby, BC: Mental Health, Law, & Policy Institute, Simon Fraser University.

Webster, C. D., Harris, G. T., Rice, M. E., Cormier, C., & Quinsey, V. L. (1994). *The Violence Prediction Scheme: Assessing dangerousness in high risk men*. Toronto: Centre of Criminology, University of Toronto.

Weschler, D. (1997). *Wechsler Adult Intelligence Scale—Third edition*. San Antonio: Psychological Corporation.

Wildman, R., Batchelor, E., Thompson, L., Nelson, F., Moore, J., Patteson, M,, & deLaosa, M. (1979). *The Georgia Court Competency Test*. Unpublished manuscript, Forensic Services Division, Central State Hospital, Milledgeville, GA.

Ziskin, J. (1996). *Coping with psychiatric and psychological testimony*. Los Angeles, CA: Law and Psychology Press.

# 5

# Risk Assessment

## DALE E. MCNIEL, RANDY BORUM, KEVIN S. DOUGLAS, STEPHEN D. HART, DAVID R. LYON, LYNNE E. SULLIVAN, AND JAMES F. HEMPHILL

Risk assessment is, most generally, the process of understanding hazards to minimize their negative consequences. Although there are many areas at the interface of psychology and law where risk assessment is involved, this chapter will focus on assessment of risk for *violence*, in view of its important place in the field and the considerable level of research activity in this domain. We will focus much of our comments on assessment of the risk of violence among people with mental disorders, given the frequency with which this group is the subject of clinical and research attention in psychology and law. The chapter is organized into three major areas: recent advances, current issues, and recommendations for the future.

DALE E. MCNIEL • Department of Psychiatry, School of Medicine, University of California, San Francisco, California 94143-0984    RANDY BORUM • Department of Mental Health Law & Policy, Florida Mental Health Institute, University of South Florida, Tampa, Florida 33612    KEVIN S. DOUGLAS • Department of Mental Health Law and Policy, Florida Mental Health Institute, University of South Florida, Tampa, Florida 3361 STEPHEN D. HART • Department of Psychology, Simon Fraser University, Burnaby, British Columbia, Canada V5A 1S6    DAVID R. LYON • Department of Psychology, Simon Fraser University, Burnaby, British Columbia, Canada V5A 1S6    LYNNE E. SULLIVAN • Child Study and Treatment Center and University of Washington, Tacoma, Washington 98498    JAMES F. HEMPHILL • Department of Psychology, Simon Fraser University, Burnaby, British Columbia, Canada V5A 1S6.

## RECENT ADVANCES

### Shift in Models from Dangerousness to Risk Assessment

In the 1960s and 1970s, the prediction of violence became a widely accepted framework for research and practice regarding forecasting future violence. This model was focused on evaluating whether an individual was "dangerous". The concept of dangerousness was included as an element in many civil commitment statutes, court decisions, and criminal statutes (Brooks, 1978; Shah, 1978). The model fell into disfavor, however, due in part to its confounding of the variables on which the prediction is based, the type of event being predicted, and the likelihood of the event being predicted. In the late 1980s and 1990s, the violence prediction approach, which was derived from legal conceptions of violent and dangerous offenders, was largely replaced by a model of violence assessment influenced by public health (Mercy & O'Carrol, 1988; Rosenberg & Fenley, 1991). This model viewed violence not simply as a crime like forgery or burglary, but also as a health problem like heart disease or cancer. This led to a focus on *risk*, which included explicit disaggregation of risk factors (predictor variables), harm (the seriousness of the violence), and risk level (the probability that violence will occur) (Monahan & Steadman, 1994a). The model implied that assessments would need to be made on an ongoing basis rather than only a one time prediction (or classification of someone as a "dangerous" person). In view of the public health goal of preventing and reducing harm, the model implied that risk management as well as risk assessment was an important objective of the evaluation. This approach has been referred to as risk assessment.

This change in the prevailing professional view of violence potential involved decreased emphasis on the evaluation task as violence prediction per se. To view the task of assessing violence potential as pure prediction assumes that dangerousness is a dichotomous variable that either is or is not present within a given individual. Implicitly, the degree of danger is assumed to be static and not subject to change. In contrast to this approach, the risk assessment paradigm does not view violence potential as a static, dichotomous, dispositional construct; rather it is seen as being contextual (dependent on situations and circumstances), dynamic (subject to change), and continuous (varying along a continuum of probability) (Borum, Fein, Vossekuil, & Berglund, 1999; National Research Council, 1989).

In our view, the field has largely accepted the task as being one in which the clinician assesses the nature and degree of risk that a given individual may pose for certain kinds of behaviors, in light of anticipated conditions and contexts, and considers the types of interventions that might reduce the violence potential (Heilbrun, 1997; Steadman, in press).

## ESTABLISHMENT OF ASSOCIATION BETWEEN VIOLENCE AND MENTAL DISORDER

Since the 1960s there has been a significant change in the prevailing view within scientific and professional psychology regarding the relationship between violence and mental disorder. Research and conventional wisdom in social science from the 1960s through the 1980s argued that people with mental disorders were not more violent, and were potentially less violent, than people without a disorder. It was posited that there was no statistically significant relationship between violence and mental illness, once factors such as drug abuse, poverty, gender, age, and previous institutionalization were taken into account (Monahan, 1981; Monahan & Steadman, 1983). In support of this position, researchers pointed to studies showing that discharged psychiatric patients were rarely convicted of violent crimes.

In the 1990s, studies using epidemiological methods reached different conclusions. These new studies used representative samples of the population, rather than studying persons already identified by hospitals and courts as being violent and mentally disordered. This approach permitted conclusions about the relationship between mental illness and violence that were not confounded by the selection bias associated with attempting to generalize about the relationship between mental disorder and violence from the subgroup of mentally ill patients identified as in need of treatment or containment. American epidemiological studies showed that rates of violence among people with a major mental disorder (e.g., schizophrenia, bipolar disorder, and major depression) are three to five times higher than for people without a disorder; and, conversely, that rates of mental disorder among people who are violent are approximately three to four times higher than for people who are not violent (Link, Andrews, & Cullen, 1992; Monahan, 1992; Swanson, Holzer, Ganju, & Jono, 1990). European epidemiological studies similarly found a positive association between the presence of major mental disorders and rates of violence (Eronen, Tiihonen, & Hakola, 1996; Hodgins, Mednick, Brennan, Schulsinger, & Engberg, 1996). Additional research concerning the relationship between violence and mental illness suggested that much of the difference in rates of violence between patient and non-patient groups could be accounted for by the presence of substance abuse disorders, although major mental illness also made an independent contribution to violence risk (Swanson, 1994). In addition, there were indications that another important factor accounting for differences in rates of violence between patient and non-patient groups was presence of active psychotic symptoms, rather than diagnosis or patient status *per se* (Link, Andrews, & Cullen, 1992).

In our opinion, the current prevailing view in psychology is that there is a statistically significant relationship between violence and mental illness, but that the size of the association is modest. Moreover, the presence of comorbid substance abuse and/or active psychotic symptoms appear to be more salient risk factors than the mere presence of a diagnosable disorder (Link, Monahan, Steuve, & Cullen, 1999; Swanson, Borum, Swartz, & Monahan, 1996; Steadman et al., 1998).

## RECOGNITION THAT THE BASE RATES OF VIOLENCE ARE HIGHER THAN ONCE THOUGHT

In the 1970s through the 1980s, there was pessimism that reasonable rates of predictive accuracy could ever be achieved because violence in general—and among people with mental illness—was a very rare event. Infrequent (low base rate) events are inherently difficult to predict on a statistical basis. For example, early studies estimated that less than 5% of discharged psychiatric patients were violent over a one year follow-up period (Monahan & Steadman, 1983). Such studies, however, tended to rely on arrest for a violent crime as the criterion of violence. Hypothesizing that some violence occurs that would escape official detection or at least not result in arrest, researchers in the late 1980s and 1990s used multiple sources of information—such as self-report, reports of collateral sources such as family and friends, and hospital records—to detect violent events. Results from these studies showed rates of violence among psychiatric patients that were much higher than previous estimates. These methods have yielded estimates that during the few weeks preceding hospitalization about 10–20% of patients engage in physically assaultive behavior and another 20–30% show milder forms of aggression such as threats and property damage (McNiel & Binder, 1986; Rossi et al., 1986; Tardiff & Sweillam, 1980). During short-term hospitalization, about 15% of civilly committed patients engage in physically assaultive behavior, and another 30–35% engage in fear-inducing behavior (McNiel, Greenfield, & Binder, 1988; Otto, 1992). During the first several months following discharge from civil hospitals to the community, about 25–30% of patients engage in violence severe enough to injure their victims, and another 20–25% of patients show milder forms of aggression (Borum, 1996; Klassen & O'Connor, 1988; Steadman et al., 1998). The precise rates vary somewhat according to the study group, criterion for violence, and follow-up interval. However, they are certainly not infrequent enough to be considered rare events.

## RECOGNITION THAT CLINICIANS HAVE SOME DEGREE OF PREDICTIVE ACCURACY

Throughout the latter 1970s and much of the 1980s, the professional and scientific communities were pessimistic about the ability of mental health professionals to forecast violence with any degree of accuracy. In 1981, a comprehensive review of the few existing studies of predictive accuracy concluded that *"psychiatrists and psychologists are accurate in no more than one out of three predictions of violent behavior over a several-year period among institutionalized populations that had both committed violence in the past (and thus had a high base rate for it) and who were diagnosed as mentally ill"* (Monahan, 1981, pp. 77, emphasis in original).

Notwithstanding scientific and professional reticence, the law continued to demand opinions from mental health professionals when making determinations about dangerousness. Research in the 1980s and 1990s has produced more optimistic conclusions about the worthiness of that activity. A review of existing research, fairly read, suggests that mental health professionals do have a modest ability to predict violence, at least in some situations, and that their predictions are significantly more accurate than chance (Lidz, Mulvey, & Gardner, 1993; Litwack & Schlesinger, 1999; McNiel & Binder, 1991; Mossman, 1994; Otto, 1992).

## DEVELOPMENT OF NEW INFORMATION ABOUT SPECIFIC RISK FACTORS

A large amount of productive research has been conducted in the late 1980s and 1990s on what cues or factors have a predictive association with later risk of violence. These may be broadly categorized as demographic/ personal history, dispositional, clinical, and contextual domains. Although a review of these variables will not be undertaken here, a few examples will be illustrative (for reviews of these variables, see Douglas & Webster, 1999; McNiel, 1998; Melton, Petrila, Poythress, & Slobogin, 1997; Monahan & Steadman, 1994b; Otto, in press; Tardiff, 1996). Among demographic/ personal history factors, a history of violence consistently emerges as a strong predictor of future violence (McNiel, 1998). Among dispositional variables, an extensive series of studies has supported the construct of psychopathy as an indicator of violence in adult male criminal populations, which has recently been extended to various other groups such as women, adolescents, and civil psychiatric patients (Hare, 1991, 1996; Hemphill, Hare, & Wong, 1998). Among clinical variables, psychiatric diagnosis remains controversial as to its role as a risk factor for violence. Increased attention has been given recently to more specific aspects of psychopathology such as particular psychotic symptoms (Link, Cullen, & Andrews, 1992; Swanson, Borum, Swartz, & Monahan, 1996) and problems with anger management (Novaco, 1994). A modest amount of research has been undertaken about contextual risk factors, such as aspects of the interpersonal environment (Estroff, Zimmer, Lachicotte, & Benoit, 1994; Straznickas, McNiel, & Binder, 1993) and neighborhood in which the individual resides (Silver, Mulvey, & Monahan, 1999).

## DEVELOPMENT OF NEW ASSESSMENT APPROACHES

Early assessments for the prediction of dangerousness relied heavily on clinical interviews and traditional evaluation techniques such as psychological testing. However, discouraging conclusions from such studies led the field to consider alternative approaches.

One such approach is the purely *actuarial* method. For over 50 years, there has been considerable debate in clinical psychology about the relative merits of clinical judgment versus actuarial approaches, in which the items on the risk scale are weighted and combined according to a fixed and explicit alogrithm (Meehl, 1954). In the general psychology literature, many studies show that such statistical formulas generally perform as well or better than clinical judgments (Borum, Otto, & Golding, 1993; Grove & Meehl, 1996; Grove, Zald, Lebow, Snitz, & Nelson, 2000). In the 1990s, several researchers developed actuarial tools for estimating the risk of violence among psychiatric patients or offenders (e.g., Borum, 1996; Gardner, Lidz, Mulvey, & Shaw, 1996; Hanson & Thornton, 2000; Harris, Rice, & Quinsey, 1993; McNiel & Binder, 1994; Steadman et al., 2000; Webster, Harris, Rice, Cormier, & Quinsey, 1994). A quantitative review conducted in 1994 concluded that, in predicting violent behavior, statistical equations seemed to reliably outperform unaided clinical judgments only in studies with long term (more than one year) follow-up periods (Mossman, 1994). In addition, in the area of violence risk assessment, few studies have directly compared the predictive accuracy of clinical judgements and actuarial procedures using the same information to arrive at assessments of risk within the same samples. Although it is more conventional to envision the actuarial measures as tools that can support or assist in decision making, some researchers have advocated that statistical equations should replace, not augment, clinical judgment for appraising the likelihood of future violence (Faust & Ziskin, 1988; Quinsey, Harris, Rice, & Cormier, 1998).

Arising from the polemic between unaided clinical judgment and pure actuarial formulas, an innovative trend in risk assessment technology has emerged: the use of *structured or guided clinical assessment* (Boer, Hart, Kropp, & Webster, 1997; Borum, in press; Kropp, Hart, Webster, & Eaves, 1999; Webster, Douglas, Eaves, & Hart, 1997). Although used in other areas of clinical-forensic practice—notably the assessment of competency to stand trial—structured guidelines are new in the area of violence risk assessment. In this approach, the clinician's inquiry is guided by a preestablished list of risk (and potentially protective) factors that are selected from the existing research and professional literature. Typically, these instruments have structured scoring schemes for each item, although they are not generally intended to be used as formal tests. The objective of these tools is to focus clinicians on relevant data to gather during interviews and review of records, so that the final judgment, although not statistical, is informed by available research. Recent empirical studies indicate that appraisals of violence risk based on guided clinical assessments perform as well or better than some actuarial predictions (Douglas, Ogloff, Nicholls, & Grant, 1999; Kropp & Hart, 2000).

## CURRENT ISSUES

Despite the significant advances that have occurred in recent years, the field of violence risk assessment continues to grapple with several basic and applied issues. These will be summarized next.

### INADEQUATE CONCEPTUALIZATION OF VIOLENCE

Violence is a complex behavior with multiple determinants, manifestations, and outcomes. The ambiguities of this state of affairs interfere with advancement of knowledge about the topic. For example, operational definitions used in studies of violence vary widely, limiting consensus about whether what is being studied represents a unitary construct. Similarly, the relative merits of conceptualizing violence as a *broad-band unitary construct* as opposed to a more *situation-specific* issue (e.g., spousal violence, sexual violence, severe versus mild, threatened versus actual, instrumental versus reactive, community versus institutional, family versus stranger-directed, etc.) remain to be elucidated. It seems highly likely that some risk factors will be associated with specific forms of violence (e.g., a history of sexual offenses may be an important risk factor for future sexual violence, but probably is not for future bank robbery; or reactive violence may be associated with low intelligence, but instrumental violence may be associated with high intelligence).

A related issue concerns limitations of defining violence simply as the presence/absence of some act during some follow-up interval, i.e., the likelihood of occurrence in a fixed time period. Restricting the focus in this way may lead to ignoring risk factors that may be associated with the nature, severity, frequency, and imminence of violence.

## INSUFFICIENT THEORY, ESPECIALLY ABOUT THE CAUSES OF VIOLENCE

Much of the current research efforts concerning violence risk assessment are primarily directed toward achieving the 'best' prediction, i.e., the highest correlation between the prediction and the outcome. Variables initially may be selected based on some theoretical considerations, but the emphasis is often empirical and data-driven. A limitation of this approach is that it does not reveal *why* certain variables are linked to violence risk. Useful theories should help identify putative risk factors for further study. Moreover, understanding of possible mechanisms by which variables may link to violent outcomes could have relevance to development of interventions designed to reduce that risk.

## OVEREMPHASIS ON STATIC, HISTORICAL, AND DISPOSITIONAL RISK FACTORS AND INATTENTION TO CONTEXTUAL, DYNAMIC, AND PROTECTIVE FACTORS

Various static, historical, and dispositional risk factors (e.g., history of violence, history of prior arrests, psychopathy, etc.) have shown excellent predictive utility over the long term. However, many clinical decisions at the interface of psychology and law require evaluating short-term risk of violence, such as decisions about involuntary civil commitment, discharge from short-term hospitals, duty to protect third parties from patients who make serious threats of violence, etc. Conceptually, even "high risk" individuals are actually violent for only a small proportion of the time; presumably the timing of their violence is influenced by situational factors. In our view, increased attention to situational precipitants and state-dependent features holds promise for short-term risk assessment. An additional potential benefit of this area of study is that dynamic and situational risk factors are often more amenable to change than dispositional factors.

In addition, the topic of resilience and protective factors (Glantz & Johnson, 1999; Rutter, 1990) has received little attention in the area of violence risk assessment. Understanding of these positive attributes could help explain why some individuals with many risk factors do not become violent. Understanding of protective factors may provide clues to development of new methods of risk management and prevention.

## LACK OF INTEGRATION OF SCIENCE AND PRACTICE

Despite the impressive achievements that have been made in refinement of methods for violence risk assessment (e.g., actuarial tools, structured clinical assessment tools), these have not achieved widespread acceptance among practitioners. In our opinion, understanding of the issues of implementation and translation of research findings to practice represents a current problem. An additional problem is that different assessment procedures may be required depending on the context. For example, in many situations in which psychologists are required to make risk assessments, there are no actuarial tools and minimal base rate information is available. The extent to which the usefulness of actuarial tools can be extrapolated from the setting in which the assessment tool was originally developed to new settings represents an ongoing challenge in integrating science into practice. For example, how relevant is a risk assessment tool developed on a criminal population to a noncriminal population? How relevant is a tool developed on a sample that gave informed consent to be in a research project concerning violence risk assessment to a general population containing many uncooperative individuals who might differ from the reference group in ways pertinent to their violence potential? More generally, violence risk assessment tools have largely been developed on people who were considered at low enough risk to be allowed to be in less restrictive settings which permitted the opportunity to become violent. How can these tools be generalized to the clinical situation in which one is confronted with someone who does not share these features?

An additional issue in translating science into practice concerns risk communication. No matter how accurate a risk assessment is, if the results are communicated in an ineffective manner, the results will be suboptimal. Recent conceptual work (Monahan & Steadman, 1996) and some empirical data (Heilbrun, O'Neill, Strohman, Bowman, & Philipson, 2000) suggest promising directions for improving communication about risk.

## INSUFFICIENT PSYCHOLEGAL ANALYSIS

Since violence risk assessment, either explicitly or implicitly, is done within a legal context, there is a need for articulation of its specific meaning for that context. An approach to this problem is psycholegal content analysis. Because this approach may be less widely known than the other matters discussed so far, we will devote more space to explaining it.

What is *psycholegal content analysis*? In essence, this approach is a multi-step process that integrates the traditions of legal and social scientific research, literature review, analysis, and writing. The essential aim of this process is to provide a *legally-informed scientist-practitioner approach* to violence risk assessment. Although the basic concepts underlying this approach has been previously articulated as generally relevant to clinical-forensic assessment (Grisso, 1986; Monahan & Walker, 1988), it has had limited application in the area of violence risk assessment. We outline the steps in the process in the numbered points that follow:

1. *Analysis of Law and Distillation of Legal Principles.* The legal authority—typically a statute—is identified, and aspects that relate to the psychological question (here, violence risk assessment) are isolated. Then, the case law (or equivalent, such as administrative tribunal decisions) that provides the interpretation of this authority is analyzed for the purpose of extracting principles of law. As many readers will recognize, this essentially is preparing a memorandum of law. There are literally dozens of risk-relevant legal areas that could be the subject of analysis, and hundreds if geographic jurisdiction (i.e., country, state, province) is factored in. Each requires thorough statutory (if applicable) and case law analysis in order to abstract important risk-relevant principles, both in terms of substance and process.

2. *Application of Social Scientific Knowledge to Legal Principles.* This step itself involves several main tasks. First, existing social scientific knowledge can be applied to the legal principles. That is, what research exists that bears directly upon the legal principle or standard? Second, if there is no research directly on point, theory or indirectly related research that suggests a plausible answer can be forwarded to address the legal principle. Third, legal principles for which there is no relevant research may be addressed though novel social scientific inquiry; that is the legal principles can form the basis of research questions in subsequent scientific studies. We do not wish to forward the position that scientific inquiry should be constrained to limits or parameters set by law, only that some proportion of forensic scientific study is devoted to evaluating the assumptions and principles of the law.

3. *Application of Clinical Practice to Legal Principles.* This aspect of the model promotes clinical practice that, through being informed by the legal principles identified in Step 1, as well as the scientific knowledge in Step 2, can optimally inform legal decision-makers and statutory and

common law mandates. As with Step 2, clinical practice should not be constrained by the limits of the law, but clinical practice that transpires within legal arena must, at a minimum, address legal principles in an optimal manner. Without knowledge of legal principles stemming from statute and case law, this is unlikely to occur.

4. *Interplay between Science and Practice*. Essentially, this feature of the model involves the "regular" scientist-practitioner approach, although couched in a legal infrastructure. We do not wish to oversimplify the scientist-practitioner model; it has been the subject of considerable professional discourse, and disagreement, since the Boulder conference in 1949. Nonetheless, there has been increasing professional discussion of the benefits of a scientist-practitioner approach to risk assessment (Borum, 1996; Douglas, Cox, & Webster, 1999).

5. *Effect of Science and Practice on Law*. Although the main focus of this model is the extent to which risk assessment science and practice are able to respond to legal principles and standards, it is important also that good quality science and practice affect the law. This may occur on a case-by-case basis, for instance where legal decisions such as discharge from civil commitment are informed by state-of-the-discipline scientific and clinical knowledge. It also may occur on an appellate case level, through the adoption by courts of general social scientific principles. Monahan and Walker (1998; see also Monahan & Walker, 1988) have proposed a comprehensive system where social science research can be adopted by trial- and appellate-level courts either to assist in the determination of fact, or to help in shaping policy and common law (through integrating social science into appellate decisions, it essentially takes on a precedential character). Further, risk-relevant legislation could be informed by forensic psychological knowledge.

## IMPACT OF LEGAL MECHANISMS RELEVANT TO VIOLENCE RISK ASSESSMENT

In addition to carrying out the psycholegal content analysis described above, there is also a need to evaluate those legal mechanisms designed to direct or facilitate the risk assessment process. That is, there is a need to empirically evaluate the legal assumptions that underpin the laws surrounding the prediction and management of violence risk, to in Haney's (1980) words, close "the gap between psychological fact and legal fiction" (p. 154). This idea is not new, and much of the research described throughout this book reflects attempts to understand and assess the law from a psychological perspective. In fact, some of the early work, or "first generation" research (e.g., Cocozza & Steadman, 1976; Kozol, Boucher, & Garofalo, 1972; Steadman, 1977; Steadman & Cocozza, 1974; Thornberry & Jacoby, 1979) in the risk assessment field was used to evaluate one of the most basic legal assumptions in this area—that mental health professionals could accurately forecast violence. Although, the issues have changed since the first generation research was conducted, the need to empirically evaluate such laws still remains.

The importance of psycholegal evaluations in the risk assessment area has become more pressing in recent years due to the rapid expansion of laws relating to risk management and risk prediction. During the past decade there has been a proliferation of laws pertaining to sexual (psychopath) predators, sex offender registration and community notification, stalking, and psychotherapists' duty to protect victims of threatened violence, to list a few. All of these laws are integrally connected to the risk assessment process. In some capacity or other, they serve as tools for risk management because their purpose is to reduce the risk of future violence (Hart, 1998; Heilbrun, 1997). Additionally, most of these laws explicitly or implicitly mandate risk assessment because the type or level of intervention usually reflects the risk posed.

Unfortunately, few hard data are currently available at present to provide an understanding of the impact of many of these laws. Indeed, it is not known whether these laws diminish the risk of future violence, increase the risk of future violence, or whether they have no appreciable impact on future violence at all. Methodologically, these are difficult issues to study because random assignment is often practically and ethically impossible to employ; however, considering the prevalence of these risk-related laws and the seriousness of their implications, it is important that their efficacy be examined. In the discussion that follows many of these issues are highlighted using the example of community notification or Megan's laws.

Prior to 1990 no jurisdiction in the United States had any form of community notification law. However, faced with the choice of implementing community notification laws or the loss of some federal funding, 47 states had enacted such laws by 1997 (Matson & Lieb, 1997). The basic premise behind these laws is that by notifying members of the public about the release of high risk sex offenders, they will be able to take preventative steps to avoid being victimized. Matson and Lieb (1997) distinguished three general approaches to the process of notification: broad notification where the information is widely disseminated; limited notification to specific individuals or groups perceived to be at risk; and public access to registration information about sex offenders in their community.

A number of states also utilize formal risk assessment instruments or committees to designate an offender as low, medium, or high risk and then adjust the scope of notification according to the level of risk posed (Matson & Lieb, 1997). Information about low risk offenders for instance, is typically shared only among law enforcement agencies whereas information about high risk offenders is widely broadcast to the community at large.

From this brief description of community notification laws, a number of legal assumptions and the empirical questions that flow from these assumptions are readily apparent. For example: Do the risk assessment procedures employed distinguish offenders into meaningful levels of risk? Do notification procedures actually alert the intended recipients? Are some notification procedures more effective than others? Are there meaningful measures the public can take to reduce their risk of being victimized? Do these measures reduce the rate of re-offense? If so, does the public respond to notification by implementing such measures? Will notification lead to sex offenders traveling outside of their community to perpetrate offenses? These are only some of the issues associated with notification laws, but they illustrate the importance of obtaining empirical data, especially in view of the debate over the merit of these laws. To illustrate, advocates maintain the laws have an important role to play in safeguarding the public from potential sex offenders (Lieb, 1996). On the other side, detractors suggest the laws may actually increase the rate of re-offense by increasing an offender's level of stress (Berliner, 1996; Prentky, 1996). To date there has been little empirical investigation of these laws. A study in Washington State comparing matched groups of sex offenders either subject to community notification or not, reported that the two groups recidivated sexually at approximately the same rate, and that there was a trend for the community notification group to be re-arrested for any new offense at a higher and faster rate than the no-notification group. Clearly, more research will be needed before the influence of community notification on safeguarding the public is fully known.

Although the example of community notification is important, the general point is that the field of psychology and law can fulfill a useful role in evaluating risk-related laws. This information is important because ineffective legal interventions do justice to no-one: they do not provide the protection victims deserve; they needlessly infringe the rights of offenders and impede sincere efforts to integrate successfully back into society; and they divert society's attention and resources from exploring other, possibly more effective, intervention strategies. Ultimately, the most successful empirical efforts in this area will be those that do not simply determine which laws work, but which laws work best and why.

# RECOMMENDATIONS FOR THE FUTURE

We suggest several promising avenues to advance the field of violence risk assessment.

## INCREASED RELIANCE ON THEORY

In our view, future work in the area of violence risk assessment would benefit from increased reliance on theory. Development and articulation of theoretical approaches could facilitate understanding as well as prediction of violence. Theoretically-based research could suggest ways to identify new risk factors which could guide intervention. Finally, theoretical models could provide a basis for interpretation of current research which has identified empirical associations between various variables and violent behavior.

## CONCEPTUAL ANALYSIS OF VIOLENCE

Further work on defining violence could have benefits in terms of increased specificity and clarity of research efforts. Development of a taxonomy of risk factors could be undertaken. In addition to articulation of dispositional, situational, and clinical risk factors, work directed toward explication of protective factors that predict resilience in spite of the presence of risk factors for violence would be useful. Explicit consideration of the role of treatment and other interventions (e.g., medications, level of care, outpatient commitment, level of supervision, etc.) in reducing risk could fruitfully be incorporated in future work on violence risk assessment. In addition, further research could profitably explore *interactions* among risk factors, as research to date has largely been limited to study of main effects.

## STUDY OF CLINICAL DECISION MAKING ABOUT VIOLENCE RISK

Improvements in violence risk assessment may be facilitated not only by research on what variables are correlated with violence, but also by study of what cue utilization strategies by clinicians lead to accurate and inaccurate evaluations of violence potential. The small amount of research on this topic to date suggests that clinicians are prone to systematic errors that may lead to over- or under-estimating the risk of violence in individual patients (e.g., Lidz, Mulvey, & Gardner, 1993; McNiel & Binder, 1995; McNiel, Lam, & Binder, in press). For example, clinicians appear more prone to error in their assessments of risk by females than by males. Moreover, research suggests that it may be possible to identify situations in which risk assessments are likely to have more predictive validity (McNiel, Sandberg, & Binder, 1998; Mulvey & Lidz, 1995), such as when they are made contingent on the presence of certain risk factors being present (e.g., substance abuse). Another related topic that warrants attention concerns the extent to which the variables identified in research studies as predictive of violent behavior are actually available to clinicians who are expected to evaluate individuals' risk of violence (Elbogen, Calkins, Tomkins, & Scalora, 1999).

At a broader level, research on violence risk assessment could profit from investigation of *effectiveness* of risk assessment methods as well as their *efficacy*. Of course, it is important to establish the validity of risk assessment methods in controlled research (efficacy research). It is also important to demonstrate how use of these tools in applied settings improves outcomes (effectiveness research). Does the use of scientifically based risk assessment methods result in better decisions about potentially violent situations?

## Use of Interdisciplinary Approaches

Because of the complex and multidimensional nature of violence, in our opinion multidisciplinary approaches have much to offer to psychology and law. The disciplines most traditionally associated with research on violence include psychology, sociology, criminology, and psychiatry. In addition to collaborating with members of other disciplines, psychologists may benefit from application of conceptual approaches derived in other intellectual traditions. A few examples include:

### Epidemiology

The application of epidemiological methods has yielded substantial benefits in the last decade in establishing a scientific basis for the widely held belief of an association between mental disorder and violence. In our opinion, this approach could yield further useful information by describing the levels of risk of violence in given settings by people with certain risk factors. In other words, base rate information is not currently available for many situations in which risk assessments are needed; descriptive, epidemiological studies are needed to provide this information.

### Psychometrics

With the adoption of a revised set of Standards for Educational πand Psychological Testing (American Psychological Association, 1999) psychologists developing tools for assessment of violence potential will need to consider how their measures comport with the new expectations. Additionally, psychologists developing risk assessment methods may benefit from application of contemporary psychometric methods such as item response theory (e.g., Cooke, Michie, Hart, & Hare, 1999) to their tools. Those developing risk assessment methods need to attend to issues of diversity in their selection of study groups, e.g., in terms of gender, race, ethnicity, culture, etc., to document the groups to whom their results can be generalized. Of course, practitioners using the new tools are responsible for basic understanding of the reliability and validity data concerning the measures.

## Neuroscience

Several studies have found an association between repetitive impulsive aggression and low concentrations of the major serotonin metabolite 5-hydroxyindoleacetic acid (5-HIAA) in the cerebrospinal fluid (Linnoila & Virkkunen, 1992). Incorporation of variables such as this in future work could identify risk factors for violence that are potentially treatable with appropriate medications (Volavka, 1995).

Similarly, structural damage to the orbitofrontal lobes of the brain has long been associated with behavioral aberrations including aggression, disinhibition, irritability, poor judgment, and shallow affect. Recent neuroimaging research has suggested correlations between orbitofrontal size and psychopathic traits in individuals without structural lesions (Raine, Lencz, Bihrle, LaCasse, & Coletti, 2000). Neurobehavioral research offers the potential for useful new leads violence risk assessment (Tardiff, 1996).

## Family violence

Maladaptive interaction sequences can lead to violence in intimate relationships. The literature on family violence has included various approaches to understanding relevant system dynamics (Strauss, Hamby, Boney-McCoy, & Sugarman, 1996). Incorporation of such approaches could enhance development of approaches to violence risk assessment.

## Sociobiology

The subarea of sociobiology bases predictions of human behavior on concepts from evolutionary theory. For example, Daly and Wilson (1990) proposed that victim selection in homicide is substantially affected by the implications of that choice for reproduction of the genetic line of the perpetrator. This represents an example among various theoretically-based perspectives that may provide new understanding of violence which would bear on risk assessment.

## DISSEMINATION

Need for practice guidelines. Although the topic of practice guidelines has not been without controversy, we feel that further consideration of this issue is warranted in the area of violence risk assessment. The general trend for evidence-based health care has led to development of practice guidelines in many fields, based on reviews of pertinent scientific studies. Moreover, the American Psychological Association has already undertaken development of practice guidelines in other areas of clinical-forensic work, notably the conduct of child custody evaluations in divorce proceedings (American Psychological Association, 1994). Development of practice guidelines concerning the assessment of violence risk would potentially yield a distillation of what the available scientific research best supports for clinical practice in this area.

### DEVELOPMENT OF TRAINING AND EDUCATIONAL MATERIALS

For the field to benefit from the developments that have accrued over the last 15 years in violence risk assessment, targeting various stakeholder groups warrants consideration.

### Clinical practitioners

Although much research effort is being directed toward developing violence risk assessment tools, their widespread adoption in clinical practice has yet to occur. Work is needed to understand the obstacles to adoption of new approaches in order to potentially impact the practice of risk assessment. Some possible methods of dissemination to practitioners include presentation of continuing education to professional groups as well as publication in psychology and law journals.

### Attorneys and Judges

Through mechanisms such as trial testimony and submission of amicus briefs, members of the court may be educated about the extent to which testimony about violence risk assessment has a sound scientific basis.

## Policy Makers

Psychologists may be of assistance in education of policy makers about the current state of the science relative to violence risk assessment. For example, as relevant legislative and policy reforms are undertaken, psychologists may help in wording of statutes and policies in ways that are consistent with the current state of the field.

## Paraprofessionals

Given that the occupation of many people (e.g., police officers; staff of jails, prisons, and psychiatric hospitals; workers in domestic violence shelters, etc.) involves contact with potentially violent people, paraprofessional training in the risk factors for violence may have value in improving the safety of many such individuals. As relevant educational programs are developed, education about basic skills in the evaluation and management of violence risk could be incorporated in annual staff education, in a manner analogous to annual training in cardiopulmonary resuscitation (CPR).

## Potential Victims

A little explored area for further work has to do with educating potential victims about the risk factors for violence. This could be applied to high risk groups, such as women in battered women's shelters and support groups; family caregivers of mentally ill and demented relatives, etc. Potentially, this type of community education could help such groups be better able to anticipate and avoid violent situations.

### ETHICAL ISSUES

Given the high stakes and multiple competing priorities associated with violence risk assessment, ongoing attention to ethical aspects of research and practice in this area will be needed. From a research perspective, we offer caution against the tendency that can occur to assume that psychologists who do not share one's own beliefs must be unethical. As it stands now, the field includes various approaches that can all claim some scientific basis. We would argue, however, that ethical practice in either research or clinical domains requires keeping up with scientific developments. In clinical work we would argue that having one's risk assessments based in objective risk factors with empirical support in peer reviewed journals is desirable. In addition, the practitioner needs to attend to the complex array of professional obligations associated with violence risk assessment, which are generally articulated in the APA's Ethical Principles of Psychologists (American Psychological Association, 1992) and the Specialty Guidelines for Forensic Psychologists (Committee on Ethical Guidelines for Forensic Psychologists, 1991).

## SUMMARY

In conclusion, we have attempted to illustrate how the area of risk assessment has made significant advances in the last 15 years. As the field moved from an emphasis on the prediction of violence and identification of "dangerous" persons to a risk assessment model, application of new research approaches led to optimism that improvements in evaluation of violence potential were possible. A substantial re-invigoration of research and clinical interest in the topic has ensued, which has resulted in much productive research determining the evidence for many risk factors for violence, as well as innovative ways to utilize that information to improve the risk assessment process. Our hope in making recommendations for the future is that the findings of the science of violence risk assessment can facilitate evidenced-based practice in this area, and that the science may be advanced through incorporation of theoretical perspectives to help understand as well as predict violence. Optimally, future work in this area will improve not only the quality of the risk assessment enterprise, but will do so in a way that will facilitate improved management of that risk.

## REFERENCES

American Psychological Association. (1992). Ethical principles of psychologists and code of conduct. *American Psychologist, 47*, 1597–1611.

American Psychological Association. (1994). Guidelines for child custody evaluations in divorce proceedings. *American Psychologist, 49*, 677–680.

American Psychological Association (1999). *Standards for educational and psychological testing.* Washington, D.C.: American Psychological Association.

Berliner, L. (1996). Community notification of sex offenders: A new tool or a false promise? *Journal of Interpersonal Violence, 11*, 294–295.

Boer, D., Hart, S., Kropp, R., & Webster, C. (1997). *Manual for the Sexual Violence Risk—20.* Vancouver, British Columbia: The British Columbia Institute Against Family Violence.

Borum, R. (1996). Improving the clinical practice of violence risk assessment. *American Psychologist, 51*, 945–956.

Borum, R. (in press). Assessing violence risk among youth. *Journal of Clinical Psychology.*

Borum, R., Fein, R., Vossekuil, & Berglund, J. (1999). Threat assessment: Defining an approach for evaluating risk of targeted violence. *Behavioral Sciences and the Law, 17*, 323–337.

Borum, R., Otto, R., & Golding, S. L. (1993). Improving clinical judgment and decision making in forensic evaluation. *Journal of Psychiatry and Law, 21*, 35–76.

Brooks, A. (1978). Notes on defining the dangerousness of the mentally ill. In C. Frederick (Ed.), *Dangerous behavior: A problem in law and mental health*. Washington, D.C.: U.S. Government Printing Office.

Cocozza, J., & Steadman, H. (1976). The failure of psychiatric predictions of dangerousness: Clear and convincing evidence. *Rutgers Law Review, 29*, 1084–1101.

Committee on Ethical Guidelines for Forensic Psychologists. (1991). Specialty guidelines for forensic psychologists. *Law and Human Behavior, 15*, 655–665.

Cooke, D. J., Michie, C., Hart, S. D., & Hare, R. D. (1999). Evaluating the Screening Version of the Hare Psychopathy Checklist—Revised (PCL-SV): An item response theory analysis. *Psychological Assessment, 11*, 3–13.

Daly, M., & Wilson, M. (1988). Evolutionary social psychology and family homicide. *Science, 242*, 519–524.

Douglas, K. S., Cox, D., & Webster, C. D. (1999). Violence risk assessment: science and practice. *Legal and Criminological Psychology, 4*, 149–184.

Douglas, K. S., Ogloff, J. P., Nicholls, T. L., & Grant, I. (1999). Assessing risk for violence among psychiatric patients: The HCR-20 violence risk assessment scheme and the Psychopathy Checklist: Screening Version. *Journal of Consulting and Clinical Psychology, 67*, 917–930.

Douglas, K. S., & Webster, C. D. (1999). Predicting violence in mentally and personality disordered individuals. In R. Roesch, S.D. Hart, & Ogloff, J.P. (Eds.), *Psychology and the law: The state of the discipline* (pp. 175–239). New York: Kluwer Academic/Plenum.

Elbogen, E. B., Calkins, C., Tomkins, A. J., & Scalora, M .J. (1999, July). *Clinical practice and violence risk assessment: Availability of MacArthur risk factors across psychiatric settings*. Paper presented at the Psychology and Law International Conference, Dublin, Ireland.

Eronen, M., Hakola, P., & Tiihonen, J. (1996). Mental disorders and homicidal behavior in Finland. *Archives of General Psychiatry, 53*, 497–591.

Estroff, S. E., Zimmer, C., & Lachicotte, W. S., & Benoit, J. (1994). The influence of social networks and social support on violence by persons with serious mental illness. *Hospital and Community Psychiatry, 45*, 669–679.

Faust, D., & Ziskin, J. (1988). The expert witness in psychiatry and psychology. *Science, 241*, 31–35.

Gardner, W., Lidz, C. W., Mulvey, E. P., & Shaw, E. C. (1996). A comparison of actuarial methods for identifying repetitively violent patients with mental illnesses. *Law and Human Behavior, 20*, 35–46.

Glantz, M. D., & Johnson, J. L. (Eds.). (1999). *Resilience and development: Positive life adaptations*. New York: Plenum.

Grisso, T. (1986). Evaluating *competencies: Forensic assessments and instruments*. New York: Plenum.

Grove, W. M., & Meehl, P. E. (1996). Comparative efficiency of informal (subjective, impressionistic) and formal (mechanical, alogrithmic) prediction procedures: The clinical-statistical controversy. *Psychology, Public Policy, and Law, 2*, 293–323.

Grove, W. M., Zald, D. H., Lebow, B. S., Snitz, B. F., & Nelson, C. (2000). Clinical versus mechanical prediction: A meta-analysis. *Psychological Assessment, 12*, 19–30.

Haney, C. (1980). Psychology and legal change: On the limits of a factual jurisprudence. *Law and Human Behavior, 17*, 371–398.

Hanson, R. K., & Thornton, D. (2000). Improving risk assessments for sex offenders: A comparison of three actuarial scales. *Law and Human Behavior, 24*, 119–136.

Hare, R. D. (1991). *Manual for the Hare Psychopathy Checklist—Revised*. Toronto, Ontario: Multi-Health Systems.

Hare, R. D. (1996). Psychopathy: A clinical construct whose time has come. *Criminal Justice and Behavior, 23*, 25–54.

Harris, G. T., Rice, M. E., & Quinsey, V. L. (1993). Violent recidivism of mentally disordered offenders: The development of a statistical prediction instrument. *Criminal Justice and Behavior, 20*, 315–335.

Hart, S. D. (1998). The role of psychopathy in assessing risk for violence: Conceptual and methodological issues. *Legal and Criminological Psychology, 3*, 121–137.

Heilbrun, K., (1997). Prediction versus management models relevant to risk assessment: The importance of legal decision-making context. *Law and Human Behavior, 21*, 347–359.

Heilbrun, K., O'Neill, M. L., Strohman, L. K., Bownam, Q., & Philipson, J. (2000). Expert approaches to communicating about violence risk. *Law and Human Behavior, 24*, 137–148.

Hemphill, J. F., Hare, R. D., & Wong, S. (1998). Psychopathy and recidivism: A review. *Legal and Criminological Psychology, 3*, 139–170.

Hodgins, S., Mednick, S. A., Brennan, P. A., Schulsinger, F., & Engberg, M. (1996). Mental disorder and crime: Evidence from a birth cohort. *Archives of General Psychiatry, 53*, 189–496.

Klassen, D., & O'Connor, W. A. (1989). Assessing the risk of violence in released mental patients: A cross-validation study. *Psychological Assessment: A Journal of Consulting and Clinical Psychology, 1*, 75–81.

Kozol, H. R., Boucher, R., & Garofalo, R. (1972). The diagnosis and treatment of dangerousness. *Crime and Delinquency, 18*, 371–392.

Kropp, P. R., & Hart, S. D. (2000). The Spousal Assault Risk Assessment (SARA) Guide: Reliability and validity. *Law and Human Behavior, 24*, 101–118.

Kropp, P. R., Hart, S., Webster, C., & Eaves, D. (1999). *Manual for the Spousal Assault Risk Assessment Guide* (3rd ed.). Toronto: Multi-Health Systems.

Lidz, C. W., Mulvey, E. P., & Gardner, W. (1993). The accuracy of predictions of violence to others. *Journal of the American Medical Association, 269*, 1007–1011.

Lieb, R. (1996). Community notification laws: "A step toward more effective solutions." *Journal of Interpersonal Violence, 11*, 298–300.

Link, B. G., Andrews, H. A., & Cullen, F. T. (1992). The violent and illegal behavior of mental patients reconsidered. *American Sociological Review, 57*, 275–292.

Link, B. G., Monahan, J., Steuve, A., & Cullen, R. T. (1999). Real in their consequences: A sociological approach to understanding the association between psychotic symptoms and violence. *American Sociological Review, 64*, 316–332.

Link, B. G., & Steuve, A. (1994). Psychotic symptoms and the violent/illegal behavior of mental patients compared to community controls. In J. Monahan, & H. J. Steadman (Eds.), *Violence and mental disorder: Developments in risk assessment* (pp. 137–159). Chicago: University of Chicago Press.

Linnoila, V. M. I., & Virkkunen, M. (1992). Aggression, suicidality, and serotonin. *Journal of Clinical Psychiatry, 53 (supplement)*, 46–51.

Litwack, T. R., & Schlesinger, L. B. (1999). Dangerousness risk assessments: Research, legal, and clinical considerations. In A. K. Hess & I. B. Weiner (Eds.), *The handbook of forensic psychology* (2nd ed., pp. 171–217). New York: Wiley.

Matson, S., & Lieb, R. (1997). *Megan's Law: A review of state and federal legislation*. Olympia, Washington: Washington State Institute for Public Policy.

McNiel, D. E. (1998). Empirically-based clinical evaluation and management of the potentially violent patient. In P.K. Kleespies (Ed.), *Emergencies in mental health practice: Evaluation and management*. (pp.182–202). New York: Guilford.

McNiel, D. E., & Binder, R. L. (1986). Violence, civil commitment, and hospitalization. *Journal of Nervous and Mental Disease, 174*, 107–111.

McNiel, D. E., & Binder, R. L. (1991). Clinical assessment of the risk of violence among psychiatric inpatients. *American Journal of Psychiatry, 148*, 1317–1312.

McNiel, D. E., & Binder, R. L. (1994). Screening for risk of inpatient violence: Validation of an actuarial tool. *Law and Human Behavior, 18*, 579–586.

McNiel, D. E., & Binder, R. L. (1995).Correlates of accuracy in the assessment of psychiatric inpatients' risk of violence. *American Journal of Psychiatry, 152*, 901–906.

McNiel, D. E., Greenfield, T. K., & Binder, R. L (1988). Predictors of violence in civilly committed acute psychiatric patients. *American Journal of Psychiatry, 145*, 965–970.

McNiel, D. E., Lam, J. N., & Binder, R. L. (in press). Relevance of inter-rater agreement to violence risk assessment. *Journal of Consulting and Clinical Psychology*.

Meehl, P. E. (1954). *Clinical vs. statistical prediction*. Minneapolis: University of Minnesota Press.

Melton, G. B., Petrila, J., Poythress, N. G., & Slobogin, C. (1997). *Psychological evaluations for the courts* (2nd ed.). New York: Guilford.

Mercy, J. A., & O'Carroll. (1988). New directions in violence prediction: The public health arena. *Violence and Victims, 3*, 285–301.

Monahan, J. (1981). Predicting *violent behavior: An assessment of clinical techniques*. Beverly Hills, CA: Sage.

Monahan, J. (1992). Mental disorder and violent behavior: Perceptions and evidence. *American Psychologist, 47*, 511–521.

Monahan, J., & Steadman, H. J. (1983). Crime and mental disorder: An epidemiological approach. In N. Morris and N. Tonry (Eds). *Crime and justice: An annual review of research*. Chicago: University of Chicago Press.

Monahan, J., & Steadman, H. J. (1994a). Toward a rejuvenation of risk assessment research. In J. Monahan & H. J. Steadman (Eds.), *Violence and mental disorder: Developments in risk assessment* (pp. 1–17). Chicago: University of Chicago Press.

Monahan, J., & Steadman, H. J. (Eds.).(1994b). *Violence and mental disorder: Developments in risk assessment*. Chicago: University of Chicago Press.

Monahan, J., & Steadman, H. J. (1996). Violent storms and violent people: How meteorology can inform risk communication in mental health law. *American Psychologist, 51*, 931–938.

Monahan, J., & Walker, L. (1988). Social science research in law: A new paradigm. *American Psychologist, 43*, 465–472.

Monahan, J., & Walker, L. (1998). *Social science in law: Cases and materials* (4th ed.). Westbury, New York: Foundation Press.

Mossman, D. (1994). Assessing predictions of violence: Being accurate about accuracy. *Journal of Consulting and Clinical Psychology, 62*, 783–792.

Mulvey, E. P., & Lidz, C. W. (1995). Conditional prediction: A model for research on dangerousness to others in a new era. *International Journal of Law and Psychiatry, 18*, 129–143.

National Research Council. (1989). *Improving risk communication*. Washington, D.C.: National Academy Press.

Novaco, R. (1994).Anger as a risk factor for violence among the mentally disordered. In J. Monahan and H. J. Steadman (Eds.), *Violence and mental disorder: Developments in risk assessment* (pp. 21–59). Chicago: University of Chicago Press.

Otto, R. (1992). The prediction of dangerous behavior: A review and analysis of "second generation" research. *Forensic Reports, 5*, 103–134.

Otto, R. (in press). Assessing and managing violence risk in outpatient settings. *Journal of Clinical Psychology*.

Prentky, R. A. (1996). Community notification and constructive risk reduction. *Journal of Interpersonal Violence, 11*, 295–298.

Quinsey, V. L., Harris, G.T., Rice, M. E., & Cormier, C. A. (1998). *Violent offenders: Appraising and managing risk.* Washington, D.C.: American Psychological Association.

Raine, A., Todd, L., Bihrle, S., LaCasse, L., & Colleti, P. (2000). Reduced prefrontal gray matter volume and reduced autonomic activity in antisocial personality disorder. *Archives of General Psychiatry, 57,* 119–127.

Rosenberg, M., & Fienley, M. (Eds.). (1991). *Violence in America: A public health approach.* New York: Oxford University Press.

Rossi, A. M., Jacobs, M., Monteleone, J., Olsen, R., Surber, R. W., Winkler, E. L., & Womack, A. (1986). Characteristics of psychiatric patients who engage in assaultive or other fear-inducing behaviors. *Journal of Nervous and Mental Disease, 174,* 154–160.

Rutter, M. (1990). Psychosocial resilience and protective mechanisms. In J. Rolf, A. S. Masten, D. Ciccchetti, K. H. Nuechterlein, & S. Weintraub (Eds.), *Risk and protective factors in the development of psychopathology* (pp. 181–214). New Your: Cambridge University Press.

Schram, D. D., & Milloy, C. D. (1995). *Community notification: A study of offender characteristics and recidivism.* Olympia, Washington: Washington State Institute for Public Policy.

Shah, S. (1978). Dangerousness: Some definitional, conceptual, and public policy dilemmas. In C. Frederick (Ed.), *Dangerous behavior. A problem in law and mental health* (pp.153–191). Washington D.C.: US Government Printing Office.

Silver, E., Mulvey, E.P., & Monahan, J. (1999). Assessing violence risk among discharged psychiatric patients: Toward and ecological approach. *Law and Human Behavior, 23,* 237–255.

Steadman, H. J. (1977). A new look at recidivism among Patuxent inmates. *Bulletin of the American Academy of Psychiatry and the Law, 5,* 200–209.

Steadman, H. J. (in press). From dangerousness to risk assessment of community violence: Taking stock at the turn of the century. *Journal of the American Academy of Psychiatry and the Law.*

Steadman, H. J., & Cocozza, J. (1974). *Careers of the criminally insane.* Lexington, Mass.: Lexington, Books.

Steadman, H. J., Mulvey, E.P., Monahan, J., Robbins, P. C., Appelbaum, P. S., Grisso, T., Roth, L. H., & Silver, E. (1998). Violence by people discharged from acute psychiatric inpatient facilities and by others in the same neighborhoods. *Archives of General Psychiatry, 55,* 393–401.

Steadman, H. J., Silver, E., Monahan, J, Appelbaum, P. S., Robbins, P. C., Mulvey, E. P., Grisso, T., Roth, L. H., & Banks, S. (2000). A classification tree approach to the development of actuarial violence risk assessment tools. *Law and Human Behavior, 24,* 83–100.

Straus, M. A., Hamby, S. L., Boney-McCoy, S., & Sugarman, D. B. (1996). The revised Conflict Tactics Scales (CTS2): Development and preliminary psychometric data. *Journal of Family Issues, 17,* 283–316.

Straznickas, K. A., McNiel, D. E., & Binder, R. L. (1993). Violence toward family caregivers of the mentally ill. *Hospital and Community Psychiatry, 44,* 385–387.

Swanson, J. W. (1994). Mental disorder, substance abuse, and community violence: An epidemiological approach. In J. Monahan & H. J. Steadman (Eds.), *Violence and mental disorder: Developments in risk assessment* (pp. 101–137). Chicago: University of Chicago Press.

Swanson, J. W., Borum, R., Swartz, M. S., & Monahan, J. (1996). Psychotic symptoms and disorders and the risk of violent behavior in the community. *Criminal Behavior and Mental Health, 6,* 317–338.

Swanson, J. W., Holzer, C., Ganju, V., & Jono, R. (1990). Violence and psychiatric disorder in the community: Evidence from the Epidemiologic Catchment Area Surveys. *Hospital and Community Psychiatry, 41,* 761–770.

Tardiff, K. (1996). *Concise guide to assessment and management of violent patients* (2nd ed.). Washington, D.C.: American Psychiatric Press.

Tardiff, K., & Sweillam, A. (1980). Assault, suicide, and mental illness. *Archives of General Psychiatry, 37*, 164–169.

Thornberry, T., & Jacoby, J. (1979). *The criminally insane: A community follow-up of mentally ill offenders.* Chicago: University of Chicago Press.

Volavka, J. (1995). *Neurobiology of violence.* Washington, D.C.: American Psychiatric Press.

Webster, C. D., Douglas, K., Eaves, D., & Hart, S. D. (1997). *HCR-20: Assessing risk for violence (version 2).* Burnaby, British Columbia: Mental Health, Law, and Policy Institute, Simon Fraser University.

Webster, C. D., Harris, G. T., Rice, M. E., Cormier, C., & Quinsey, V. L. (1994). *The Violence Prediction Scheme: Assessing dangerousness in high risk men.* Toronto: University of Toronto.

# 6

# Competency

*Past, Present, and Future*

## PATRICIA A. ZAPF, JODI L. VILJOEN, KAREN E. WHITTEMORE, NORMAN G. POYTHRESS, AND RONALD ROESCH

This chapter presents a review of the field of competency to the end of the 20th century, a commentary on the present state of the field, and speculation about the directions that the field will take in the future.[1] We have chosen to limit our discussion to one specific type of competency—competency to stand trial—as this has been the area to receive the most attention in terms of both research and commentary. We strongly advocate using the work that has been done with respect to competency to stand trial as a blueprint for developing the research and methodology in other areas of competency. This would allow for quicker advancement in other areas of competency research by navigating researchers and practitioners

[1]We have attempted to accurately represent current thinking in this area by allowing individuals who were not part of the competency work group to meet with us and share their ideas at the APA convention in Boston in 1999.

PATRICIA A. ZAPF • Department of Psychology, University of Alabama, Tuscaloosa, Alabama, 35401-0348.    JODI L. VILJOEN • Department of Psychology, Simon Fraser University, Burnaby, Birtish Columbia, Canada V5A 1S6.    KAREN E. WHITTEMORE • Forensic Psychiatric Services Commission, Surrey, British Columbia, Canada V3V 4B8. NORMAN G. POYTHRESS • Department of Mental Health Law & Policy, University of South Florida, Tampa, Florida 33612-3899.    RONALD ROESCH • Mental Health, Law, and Policy Institute, Simon Fraser University, Burnaby, British Columbia, Canada V5A 1S6.

through the early developmental stages and thus allowing them to bypass those steps that may be less effective in advancing the field while focusing on others that are more effective.

We begin with a review of the field of competency to stand trial, including the development and refinement of criteria for competency, the tools and techniques developed for assessing competency to stand trial, and the methods used to treat individuals found incompetent to stand trial. We then comment on the current state of the field, including outstanding advancements in the field, obstacles that have been overcome, and those that still remain to be addressed. In addition, we comment on how the field has applied psychological research and knowledge to legal issues, how the field has investigated psycholegal phenomena, as well as how the field has studied and evaluated the law. Finally, we will speculate about where the field needs to go in the future and how it will get there.

## PAST: REVIEW OF THE FIELD

A cursory review of the literature on competency to stand trial published within the past few decades indicates changing foci within this area. In the early years, much of the research conducted and commentary written focused on developing and defining the criteria for competency to stand trial. Once psycholegal criteria were identified, the focus then shifted to the development of instruments to assess competency to stand trial and each of the different psycholegal criteria. The research and literature then moved toward a focus on determining the psychometric properties of these newly developed competency assessment instruments and then towards refining these instruments and the further development of more sophisticated tools for the assessment of competency. Currently, it appears that there is a move toward the idea of linking different types of competencies (i.e., competency to stand trial, competency to plead guilty, competency to waive counsel) and toward the application of knowledge, research, and practice in one area to other areas within the field of competence (i.e., competency to stand trial, competency to consent to treatment).

We now turn to a more detailed review of the literature on competency to stand trial. As discussed above, the vast majority of the research in the field of competency has focused on the area of competency to stand trial whereas other areas of competency tend to be less well defined and have traditionally been less well researched. We hope that by focusing on competency to stand trial we can learn from the advancements as well as the setbacks that have occurred with regard to this area of competency and can inform our knowledge and future research in other less well-researched areas of competency such as competency to consent to research, competency to be executed, and competency to consent to voluntary hospitalization.

## CRITERIA

It has been a generally accepted legal principle in Western jurisprudence that incompetent individuals should not be allowed to proceed with a trial (*Blackstone*, 1783; *Frith's Case*, 1790). The notion that an individual must be competent to proceed in the criminal justice system originated in English common law and has been traced to the 17th century (Winick, 1983). Its roots are found in the common law prohibition on trials in absentia and in the difficulties encountered by the courts when the defendant remained mute[2] and failed to plead to the charges (Winick, 1983).

The legal principle of being required to be competent to proceed with criminal proceedings evolved at a time when defendants were expected to represent themselves in most criminal matters (and, in fact, representation by counsel was prohibited in certain types of cases). Despite the fact that representation by counsel is now guaranteed by the Sixth Amendment to the *U. S. Constitution* as well as the *Canadian Charter of Rights and Freedoms*, competency to proceed remains an important legal principle. Modern justification for the incompetency doctrine includes: safeguarding the accuracy of any criminal adjudication (Bonnie, 1993; GAP Report, 1974; Winick, 1985); guaranteeing a fair trial (GAP Report, 1974); preserving the dignity and integrity of the legal process (Bonnie, 1992, 1993; GAP Report, 1974; Winick, 1983, 1985, 1996); ensuring that any defendant who is found guilty knows why he or she is being punished (GAP Report, 1974); and preserving the notion of individual autonomy (Bonnie, 1993; Winick, 1992).

Within the United States, the issue of competency extends as far back as the early 1800s. In 1835, the defendant in *United States v. Lawrence* was found unfit to stand trial after his failed attempt to assassinate President Jackson. Some 60 years later, the appellate court in *Youtsey v. United States* (1899) held that "it is not 'due process of law' to subject an insane person to trial upon an indictment involving liberty or life" (p. 941). Since that time, various courts in the United States have essentially ruled that the

---

[2]Two categories were identified: "mute by visitation of God" and "mute of malice". Winick (1983, 1996) details the consequences of each of these two categories wherein individuals determined to be in the former category were spared a torturous ritual and individuals determined to be in the latter were not. The former category initially included the "deaf and dumb" but was gradually expanded to include "lunatics" (see Winick, 1983, 1996).

issue of competency is "fundamental to an adversary system of justice" (*Drope v. Missouri*, 1975, p. 172; see also *Dusky v. United States*, 1960; *Godinez v. Moran*, 1993).

The modern standard in U.S. law was established in *Dusky v. United States* (1960). Although the exact wording varies, all states use a variant of the *Dusky* standard to define competency (Favole, 1983). In *Dusky*, the Supreme Court held that:

> It is not enough for the district judge to find that 'the defendant is oriented to time and place and has some recollection of events', but that the test must be whether he has sufficient present ability to consult with his lawyer with a reasonable degree of rational understanding—and whether he has a rational as well as factual understanding of the proceedings against him. (p. 402)

Although the concept of competency to stand trial has been long established in law, its definition, as exemplified by the ambiguities of *Dusky*, has never been explicit. The Group for the Advancement of Psychiatry (1974) wrote a report on competency to stand trial that documented some of the competency-related questioning conducted by the trial judge in Milton Richard Dusky's first trial on the issue of competency. From the trial judge's questions, it appears that some of the necessary elements to be considered competent to stand trial included that the defendant: be oriented to time, place, and person; know who his or her attorney is; know what he or she has been charged with; and know (to some extent) or express a knowledge of some of the incidents leading up to the commission of the offense that he or she was alleged to have committed. In addition, from this report it appears that, prior to the U.S. Supreme Court's prevailing decision regarding competency to stand trial (i.e., *Dusky v. United States*, 1960), the court was operating under the assumption that to be considered competent to stand trial an individual "must possess sufficient capacity to comprehend the nature and object of the proceedings and his [or her] own position in relation to those proceedings; and to be able to advise counsel rationally in the preparation and implementation of his [or her] own defense" (GAP Report, 1974, p. 916). The standard for competency that was subsequently decided upon by the U. S. Supreme Court in Milton Richard Dusky's case appears to be slightly more vague than the standard that was operated on by the trial judge in his case. Nevertheless, it is the standard that was set out by the U. S. Supreme Court in 1960 that is the current standard adapted by every jurisdiction today.

Canada's incompetency doctrine has a somewhat shorter history than that of the United States but has been interpreted through English common law as meaning that individuals charges with a criminal offence must be able to understand the nature of the proceedings and assist counsel in order to participate in their own defence and to have a fair trial (see *Regina v. Pritchard*, 1836: *The Queen v. Berry*, 1876).

The modern standard for competency (fitness)[3] to stand trial in Canada was recently codified in 1992. Prior to this time, the criteria that were used were taken from case law. Specifically, the English common law case of *Regina v. Pritchard* (1836) was the case that was most often used. *Pritchard* identified three issues to be examined in determining whether an individual was competent to stand trial:

> First, whether the prisoner is mute of malice or not; secondly, whether he can plead to the indictment or not; thirdly, whether he is of sufficient intellect to comprehend the course of the proceedings on the trial, so as to make a proper defence—to know that he might challenge any of you to whom he may object—and to comprehend the details of the evidence which in a case of this nature must constitute a minute investigation. (p. 304)

In the 1970s the Law Reform Commission of Canada wrote a report on mental disorder in the criminal process in which a number of recommendations were outlined with respect to competency. In this report, three criteria for a finding of incompetency were delineated: an inability to understand the nature or object of the proceedings, an inability to understand the personal importance of the proceedings, or an inability to communicate with counsel (LRCC Report, 1976; see also Lindsay, 1977). In 1992, the *Criminal Code of Canada* was amended and changes were made to the legal procedures related to the determination of competency. Explicit guidelines were set out in Section 2, which include a definition as well as standards for the determination of competency to stand trial. *Unfit to stand trial* is a legal term that is currently defined as follows:

> Unable on account of mental disorder to conduct a defence at any stage of the proceedings before a verdict is rendered or to instruct counsel to do so, and, in particular, unable on account of mental disorder to (a) understand the nature or object of the proceedings, (b) understand the possible consequences of the proceedings, or (c) communicate with counsel. (C. C. C., §. 2, 1992)

Since 1992 there have been finer distinctions made in case law with respect to the recently codified standards. In *Regina v. Taylor* (1992), the Ontario Court of Appeal decided "the test to be applied in determining the accused's ability to communicate with counsel is one of limited cognitive capacity" (p. 553). This means that it is not necessary that accused individuals be able to act in their own best interests, but rather, must only be able to recount the necessary facts pertaining to the offence to counsel so that counsel can present a proper defence. The appellate judges in

---

[3]Fitness to stand trial is a term that is equivalent to competency to stand trial and is used in Canada and other countries (e.g., England).

*Taylor* decided that the " 'limited cognitive capacity' test strikes an effective balance between the objective of the fitness rules and the constitutional right of the accused to choose his own defence and to have a fair trial within a reasonable time" (p. 567).

## ASSESSMENT

Competency to stand trial evaluations is the most common type of pretrial evaluations (Nicholson, 1999). It has been estimated that approximately 25,000 to 39,000 competency evaluations are conducted annually in the United States (Hoge et al., 1997; Steadman & Hartstone, 1983). Webster, Menzies, and Jackson (1982) estimated that more than 5000 fitness evaluations are conducted annually in Canada, while recent estimates show an increase in the number of fitness evaluations conducted each year in Canada (see Ohayon, Crocker, St-Onge, & Caulet, 1998; Roesch et al., 1997). The courts rely heavily upon mental health professionals to evaluate competency. Although, historically, medical practitioners were called upon to conduct competency evaluations, the qualifications of psychologists and social workers have been increasingly recognized (Melton et al., 1997). Since competency is a legal rather than a clinical issue, the final determination regarding competency rests with the court. Research, however, indicates that judges very rarely disagree with evaluator decisions (Hart & Hare, 1992; Reich & Tookey, 1986). Some argue that this high rate of agreement might suggest that courts are too ready to "abdicate their role as decision-maker" (Melton et al., 1997, p. 129).

Although mental health professionals appear to have established a secure niche in the assessment of competency, their involvement has not gone unquestioned. Slovenko (1995) argues that mental health professionals are no more qualified to assess competence than lawyers or judges, and that the practice of involving mental health professionals is antiquated, stemming from a time when competency evaluations were commonly misused. Also, Bonnie (1992) argues that defense attorneys should be more involved in decisions regarding competency, with referrals to mental health professionals made only as a last resort.

Competency evaluations were, in the past, conducted almost exclusively in inpatient facilities. There has, however, been a clear shift towards outpatient evaluations over the last few decades (Cooper & Grisso, 1997; Grisso, 1992; Grisso, Cocozza, Steadman, Fisher, & Greer, 1994). One of the most significant benefits of outpatient evaluations is reduced cost. Winick (1985, 1996) asserted that whereas in the past $185 million was spent annually on inpatient competency evaluations, this figure has drastically decreased in recent years with the transition to outpatient evaluations.

Another benefit of outpatient evaluations is that they provide defendants with increased legal protection since they are quicker, consistent with constitutional rights to a speedy trial, and less restrictive.

This trend towards outpatient evaluations has been slower to take place in Canada. Recent revisions to the *Criminal Code of Canada* direct that competency assessments should be conducted out of custody, unless the prosecutor convinces the court that an inpatient evaluation is necessary (s. 672.16). Despite this, research conducted in the province of British Columbia found that the majority of competency assessments continue to be conducted in in-patient forensic facilities (Roesch et al., 1997). The continued use of inpatient evaluations may be due to concern regarding whether community-based assessments sufficiently protect the public (Davis, 1994), as well as a lack of appropriate outpatient facilities (Roesch et al., 1997).

Although considerable variability exists in rates of incompetence among defendants referred for evaluations, research has generally indicated that only a small proportion of these defendants are found incompetent (Roesch & Golding, 1980). The low rate of incompetence, which is estimated as 20% of referred defendants, suggests that a number of referrals may be inappropriate (Roesch et al., 1999). Inappropriate referrals may be unintentional, due simply to poor understanding of the competency standard by attorneys (Roesch & Golding, 1980), or an intentional attempt to delay the trial, investigate the feasibility of an insanity plea, or discover new information about the defendant (Ogloff, 1991; Roesch & Golding, 1980; Verdun-Jones, 1981). In addition, competency evaluations may be used as an expedient means of acquiring treatment for mentally ill defendants (Dickey, 1980; Grisso & Seigel, 1986; Melton et al., 1997; Roesch & Golding, 1980; Zapf & Roesch, 1998).

Recently enacted limits on the lengths of competency commitments appear to have led to a decrease in inappropriate referrals (Slovenko, 1995). However, the use of competency screening instruments, which screen out individuals who are clearly competent to stand trial, hold further promise in deterring inappropriate referrals (Roesch et al., 1999).

In the past, general psychological assessment instruments, including intelligence and personality tests, were used in competency evaluations, if assessment instruments were used at all. Since such assessment instruments measure constructs that are only indirectly related to competency and fail to consider the legal aspects of competency, their use was widely criticized (Grisso, 1986; Roesch & Golding, 1980). In response, specialized competency assessment instruments were developed.

Robey (1965) is credited with the development of the first formalized measure of competency, which was devised as a checklist. Following this,

the Competency Screening Test (CST; Lipsett, Lelos, & McGarry, 1971) and
the Competency Assessment Instrument (CAI; Laboratory of Community
Psychiatry, 1974) were developed in the early 1970s as part of a research
project funded by the National Institute of Mental Health. The CST is a 22-
item sentence completion test, which is used as a screening instrument.
The CAI, in contrast, is a longer and more thorough structured interview,
which assesses 13 functional areas including the defendant's appraisal of
legal defenses, knowledge of courtroom procedure, and relationship with
his or her attorney.

In the late 1970s and early 1980s a number of additional instruments
were developed. These included the Georgia Court Competency Test
(GCCT; Wildman et al., 1978; Johnson & Mullet, 1987), the Interdisciplinary Fitness Interview (IFI; Golding, Roesch, & Schreiber, 1984; Golding,
1993), and the Fitness Interview Test (FIT; Roesch, Webster, & Eaves, 1984;
Roesch, Zapf, Eaves, & Webster, 1998). All of these instruments have since
been revised and are currently being used in both research and practice
today.

The Computer-Assisted Competence Assessment Tool (CADCOMP;
Barnard et al., 1991) is a lengthier assessment instrument that consists of
272 questions that tap into a broad set of areas. Whereas most of the previously mentioned instruments take approximately 30 to 45 minutes to
administer, the CADCOMP takes approximately 1 to $1\frac{1}{2}$ hours. In addition, several instruments have been developed for use with specific populations. The Competence Assessment for Standing Trial for Defendants
with Mental Retardation (CAST-MR; Everington & Luckasson, 1992) was
developed for use with mentally retarded defendants. Based on the recognition that expressive language skills are likely to be impaired in this population, the CAST-MR utilizes a multiple-choice format. In addition, the
GCCT was revised in order to make it appropriate for use with young
offenders. This new version is called the Georgia Court Competency Test-
Juvenile Revision (GCCT-JR; Cooper, 1997).

The instrument that has elicited the most attention in recent years is
the MacArthur Competency Assessment Tool—Criminal Adjudication
(MacCAT-CA; Hoge, Bonnie, Poythress, & Monahan, 1999). The MacCAT-
CA has been referred to as a "new generation" instrument, as it addresses
many of the criticisms leveled at previous instruments (Melton et al., 1997,
p. 149). One of the criticisms has been that many of the previously developed instruments are too narrow, placing too much emphasis on legal
knowledge factors, such as the roles of courtroom personnel, and failing
to assess broader considerations, such as whether a defendant is competent to plead guilty (Melton et al., 1997; Nicholson, 1999). Another criticism is that while the legal construct of competency to stand trial relates

to the defendants' *capacity* rather than current *ability*, it is not clear whether current instruments measure capacity (Melton et al., 1997). Finally, it has been noted that, in general, competency instruments are not clearly tied to legal theory (Nicholson, 1999).

In contrast to other instruments, the MacCAT-CA assesses the broader construct of competence to proceed to adjudication rather than competence to stand trial. Following the theoretical model of competence proposed by Bonnie (1992), it measures competence to assist counsel as well as decisional competence. Also, the MacCAT-CA explicitly evaluates defendant capacities by providing defendants with information that they are retested on rather than requiring the defendant to come up with the correct information in one attempt.

The relative predictive power of competency assessment instruments is significantly higher than that of traditional assessment instruments (Nicholson & Kugler, 1991) and judges appear to value data from these competency assessment instruments in evaluation reports (Terhune, 1990). In addition, research generally indicates that competency assessment instruments have strong reliability and potentially high validity (Melton et al., 1997).

Since judges generally concur with evaluator opinions, one of the challenges in establishing the validity of competency assessment instruments is the lack of independent criteria with which to compare the instruments. Although this criterion problem is acknowledged as serious (Golding, Roesch, & Screiber, 1984), it can be mitigated by the use of multiple competency criteria in research (Nicholson & Kugler, 1991).

Despite generally favorable findings, mental health professionals appear reluctant to adopt competency assessment instruments as a routine part of competency evaluations (Borum & Grisso, 1995; Skeem, Golding, Cohen, & Berge, 1998). In a survey conducted by Borum and Grisso (1995), one-third of respondents reported that they used forensic assessment instruments regularly. In contrast, most respondents reported use of general psychological instruments such as the WAIS-R. In light of the described advances in assessment, this practice seems inadequate (Golding, 1990; Nicholson, 1999).

## TREATMENT

If an individual is found incompetent to stand trial, the issue then becomes one of treatment to restore competence. Traditionally, incompetent defendants were hospitalized for an indeterminate length of time. In 1972, the United States Supreme Court held that incompetent defendants could not be held "more than the reasonable period of time necessary to determine whether there is a substantial probability that he will obtain that capacity in the foreseeable future" (*Jackson v. Indiana*, p. 738). Additionally, the ruling held that continued hospitalization is justified only by progress toward the goal of restoration. The *Jackson* decision requires that incompetent defendants, who are not likely to become competent, be civilly committed if they meet state criteria or released. This ruling, however, left two major issues unresolved, namely, the length of confinement that might be considered reasonable, and those factors that might be considered when determining whether a defendant would likely benefit from treatment (Roesch & Golding, 1979).

Following the *Jackson* decision, the treatment of incompetent defendants has received greater attention (Roesch, Ogloff, & Golding, 1993). As a result of the decision, mental health professionals assessing the issue of competence must also determine the likelihood that the incompetent individual will be restored to competence in the foreseeable future. Cuneo and Brelje (1984) found an accuracy rate of 78% for mental health professional's predictions of competency restoration; however, this accuracy rate must be examined in the context of the base rate for competency restoration, which was 74%. Indeed, restoration to competence has been found to be successful for most individuals (Cuneo & Brelje, 1984; Nicholson, Barnard, Robbins, & Hankins, 1994; Nicholson & McNulty, 1992). This research, however, did not examine how predictions of competency restoration are made, and Cuneo and Brelje (1984) called for future research to examine this issue.

Carbonell, Heilbrun, and Friedman (1992), attempted to predict trial competency using demographic, criminal history, and clinical predictors in a discriminant analysis. Nine variables predicted restoration of competency in 72.2% of the cases. These variables included the following: perceptual motor dysfunction as measured by the Bender Gestalt (competent group showing less impaired performance on Bender base score and Bender class score), verbal IQ (competent group having higher mean verbal IQ score), performance IQ (competent group having higher mean performance IQ score), Block Design score from the WAIS-R (competent group having higher mean score), diagnosis of affective disorder (competent group having higher likelihood), diagnosis of psychotic disorder other than schizophrenia, affective disorder, or organic mental disorder with psychotic features (competent group less likely to be so diagnosed), presence of organic mental disorder (competent group more likely to receive this diagnosis), and diagnosis of antisocial personality disorder (competent group less likely to receive this diagnosis). While these results appeared promising, when they attempted a cross-validation, the accuracy of prediction dropped to 59.5%, just over chance prediction. The authors concluded that caution should be used in predicting competency, however, they suggested that future research focus on more functional, legal abilities.

This is precisely what Nicholson and his colleagues (Nicholson et al., 1994) attempted to do. Results suggested that demographic variables were unrelated to two outcome measures: competency restoration and length of stay in hospital. Alternatively, greater impairment in psycholegal ability, severe psychotic symptoms, and aggression directed toward others since the arrest, were associated with negative outcome (were less likely to be restored to competency and had a longer stay in hospital). Alternatively, a history of criminality and alcohol use around the time of the offence were associated with more positive outcomes. The researchers qualify their findings by stating that the results are consistent with previous research suggesting the need for caution when attempting to predict competency restoration. The low base rate for failure to restore competency increases the difficulty of accurately predicting competency restoration.

The *Jackson* decision also lead to an increased need to determine what treatment regime is most effective for incompetent defendants. The traditional approach to the treatment of incompetent individuals has been medication (Siegel & Elwork, 1990; Roesch, Hart, & Zapf, 1996). It is assumed that once the mental disorder is under control, the individual will be restored to competence. This approach ignores the functional abilities required for competence. That is, a person may be mentally ill and still able to perform the legal tasks required for competence. In the United States there has been a move toward offering problem-oriented treatment that focuses on the functional abilities of incompetence (Davis, 1985; Pendleton, 1980).

Davis (1985) and Pendleton (1980) described different approaches for the treatment of individuals found incompetent to stand trial. Davis (1985) recommends an individualized treatment, suggesting that treatment planning should follow the assessment process to address the specific reasons the individual was found incompetent. As such, treatment should focus on functional behavior that addresses the individual's ability to understand the nature and object of the proceedings, understand the possible consequences of the proceedings, and/or rationally communicate with counsel and participate in his or her own defense. After an understanding of the area of deficiency is noted, individuals may be grouped according to the bases of their deficiency such as low intellectual functioning, or psychotic-confused which is designed to further enhance the focus on the special needs of each group.

The approach taken by Pendleton (1980) focuses on eliminating or reducing those symptoms that interfere with the defendant's ability to stand trial, such as delusional beliefs about the offense or the attorney.

While traditional forms of treatment such as medication are used, specialized treatment is offered to assist an individual's understanding of the court process and proceedings, and develop rational skills essential for the accused to communicate and cooperate with his or her attorney. This treatment approach also requires patient participation in a mock trial, in which the patient is exposed to a simulated courtroom situation tailored to his or her own case.

Research comparing the effectiveness of functional approaches to treatment with medication suggests that a problem-solving approach that specifically addresses those functional capacities required for competence, in addition to traditional forms of treatment such as medication, are more effective than the traditional treatment of medication alone (Siegel & Elwork, 1990).

Overall, the treatment of incompetent individuals continues to be an important, but undeveloped area of research. Some experts in the field have offered a proposal for change in the procedures for dealing with incompetent defendants, arguing for the treatment of these defendants on an outpatient basis (Roesch, Ogloff, & Golding, 1993); and allowing a provisional trial for incompetent defendants (Burt & Morris, 1972; Roesch & Golding, 1979, 1987; Winick, 1995). The implementation of such practices would step beyond the current treatment regime for incompetent defendants.

## PRESENT: COMMENTARY ON THE FIELD

It is always prudent to take a step back from an area of research and to have a look at its history, its current state, and the direction that it might (or should) be headed in the future. The previous review of the literature on competency to stand trial has revealed those areas within the field that have been subject to much research and commentary. It has also alluded to those areas that have been under-researched and that need to be further developed in the future (a topic to which we will return in the final section of this paper). We now offer a comment on the current state of the field, including advancements that have been made and obstacles that have been overcome, how the field has applied psychological research and knowledge to legal issues and how the field has investigated psycholegal phenomena, as well as how the field has studied and evaluated the law.

### ADVANCEMENTS AND OBSTACLES

One of the major outstanding advancements in the field of competency has been the development and refinement of a number of competency assessment instruments. The advancement has occurred simultaneously within a couple of different areas of the field, competency to stand trial and competency to consent to treatment; however, this advancement has, arguably, had more of an impact within the area of competency to stand trial than it has in other areas.

As was previously illustrated in the above literature review, much research within the area of competency to stand trial has focused on the development and refinement of instruments designed to assist in the evaluation of competency. These instruments began as rather crude checklists and have evolved into sophisticated and psychometrically sound empirically-derived assessment tools. The MacArthur Foundation Research Network on Mental Health and the Law has funded the research and development of two assessment tools that are currently considered to be the best in the field. These two instruments—the MacArthur Competence Assessment Tool-Criminal Adjudication (MacCAT-CA; Hoge, Bonnie, Poythress, & Monahan, 1999) and the MacArthur Competence Assessment Tool-Treatment (MacCAT-T; Grisso & Appelbaum, 1998a)— each measure three psycholegal abilities (capacity to understand, appreciation, and reasoning) within their respective legal contexts. These assessment instruments were empirically derived and are based on Bonnie's (1992, 1993) conceptualization of competency

Another outstanding advancement in the field has been the expansion of research on competency issues to include a focus on two previously neglected populations—children and adolescents. The relatively recent shift in attention of several researchers toward these two segments of the population can be considered a major advancement in the field. Issues of competency in children and juvenile defendants are becoming increasingly important and must be considered in light of cognitive maturity and developmental factors. Research and commentary has begun to address these issues within the area of competency to stand trial (e.g., Cooper, 1997; Cowden & McKee, 1995; Grisso, 1997, 1998; Heilbrun, Hawk, & Tate, 1996; McKee, 1998; Savitsky & Karras, 1984) as well as other areas within the field of competency (e.g., Grisso, 1980, 1981, 1998; Flin & Spencer, 1995; Scott, 1992; Scott, Reppucci, & Woolard, 1995).

There are several obstacles within the larger field of competency research that have been overcome and a few that still remain to be addressed. Remedies for those obstacles that have been overcome include better definitions of competence to consent to treatment, competency to stand trial, and other criminal competencies, in addition to well-developed assessment instruments for the evaluation of competencies in both criminal and civil domains. Obstacles that still need to be addressed include a relative lack of empirical research on competency to consent to treatment, competency to be executed, competency to consent to voluntary hospitalization, and competency to consent to research, as well as the restoration of competency. In addition, there still exists a need to better disseminate knowledge gained through research and to educate professionals and practitioners working in the field. In the field of competency, research needs to be disseminated not only to those professionals and practitioners who conduct competency assessments and work with individuals found incompetent, but also to legal professionals, including defense attorneys, prosecutors, and judges.

There also exists, within the field of competency, other potential obstacles that are political in nature. It is important to be aware of these possible obstacles and to think about their impact on the field as well as possible remedies for them. An example of such an obstacle would be the (possible) resistance by medical researchers and drug companies to the suggestion that stricter standards of competence to consent should be used in research or treatment. In addition, some have argued that consent should be a continuous process throughout the duration of a research project rather than just at the beginning of the project (Expert Panel Report to the National Institutes of Health, 1998; National Bioethics Advisory Commission, 1998). It is easy to see how the promotion or implementation of these types of suggestions or research findings may run up against political resistance. Currently, it often appears to be the case that, when considering issues of voluntary hospitalization, an individual is allowed to give his or her "informed assent" rather than informed consent when agreeing to undergo psychiatric hospitalization and it is possible that some physicians/psychiatrists may be resistant to the suggestion of using stricter standards than those currently being used in this situation.

## Psycholegal Applications

The law moves very slowly and it is often difficult to make changes in the law or in the way that laws are applied. Additionally, it also takes a long time for changes in the law to make an impact on practice. With respect to the field of competency, it appears that individual legal cases impact upon the law and drive change with respect to competency more than do the results of research on competency. This, however, does not mean that research on competency has nothing to offer the law. As researchers in this field, we need to be making more attempts to educate practitioners and legal professionals about what psychology and psychological research in the field of competency has to offer. Competency is a field where psychology is relatively heavily relied upon by the law and where psychology has the opportunity to make an impact and to inform changes in the law. The key is to make the research in this area accessible for the courts and legal professionals.

With respect to decision making in the law, within the field of competency there are different decision makers regarding the issue of competence depending upon the specific area of focus. For example, the principal investigator in the case of competency to consent to research, the admitting physician in the case of competency to consent to voluntary hospitalization, or the treating physician in the case of competency to consent to treatment is the ultimate decision maker, whereas the court is the ultimate decision maker in the case of competency to stand trial and other criminal competencies. The decision of the principal investigator, admitting physician, or treating physician is usually considered to be final and is often acted upon without any formal legal proceeding. How are these final decisions or the processes involved in coming to these final decisions, which are legal decisions but are not made by legal decision makers, different from or similar to the processes and the final decisions made by legal decision makers? In order to better understand legal decision making with respect to competency it may be necessary to investigate how the legal process of decision-making compares to the everyday process that occurs in different contexts all the time.

In addition to decision-making in the law, noncompliance with the law is an important consideration with respect to the application of the law within the field of competency. In terms of non-compliance with the law, the degree to which physicians or researchers have considered anything beyond informed consent when treating someone or having someone participate in research falls into this category. Whenever other considerations come into play, such as the fact that an assenting patient could medically benefit from a treatment even though he or she may be unable to give true informed consent, decisions to proceed with treatment are technically considered to be in non-compliance with the law regarding informed consent. Sometimes it may be the case that these other considerations are given more weight than the inability of the assenting individual to give informed consent. This occurs whenever an "incompetent" individual is allowed to voluntarily admit him or herself to the hospital for treatment. In order to further understand issues of competence and the application of the law, it may be necessary to examine instances of technical non-compliance with the law.

To better understand our own legal system with respect to issues of competency, it is useful to investigate the ways that other countries deal with these same (or equivalent) issues. One example of this is with regard to the basic nature of the criminal justice system. The United States,

Canada, and England use an adversarial system whereas other European countries use an inquisitorial system. How does the notion of an individual's ability to assist counsel differ with respect to these two types of systems? What happens with respect to the different types of criminal competencies in countries such as France and Switzerland (to name but a few) that have an inquisitorial system? It may be necessary to look toward countries such as these to investigate issues of competency so as to gain a better understanding of the role that these issues play within our own criminal justice system.

A similar argument could be made for the close investigation of issues of criminal competency with respect to female defendants and those defendants from minority groups or underrepresented segments of the population. Are issues of competency defined any differently for groups such as these and, if so, how and why? The research to date seems to suggest that less women are referred for inpatient evaluations of competency to stand trial and that more women appear to be evaluated on an outpatient (as opposed to an inpatient) basis. Similarly, the research appears to suggest that a greater proportion of ethnic minorities are referred for evaluations of competency to stand trial and that a greater proportion of those who are referred are found incompetent (see Nicholson & Kugler, 1991; Roesch & Golding, 1980). Why is this the case? Perhaps part of the explanation includes language deficits or barriers. If this is the case, however, it seems as if the field may need to come up with ways around this in order to adhere to the law and to be fair to those individuals who do not have a good command of the English language.

## PSYCHOLEGAL INVESTIGATION OF LEGAL PHENOMENA

The law has made a number of behavioral assumptions with respect to the issue of competence, which, until relatively recently, psychology has more or less accepted blindly and without reservation. A simple example of this is illustrated by the fact that in the not too distant past, psychosis and incompetence were essentially considered to be one in the same. Legal professionals (defense attorneys, prosecutors, judges) and jail personnel made the assumption that if an accused individual displayed certain types of behaviors (i.e., such as those symptomatic of psychosis) he or she was unable to perform the necessary psycholegal abilities to be considered competent. This was further reinforced by psychologists and other mental health professionals who, more or less, accepted this assumption until research began to indicate otherwise. Research on competent and incompetent individuals has indicated that this relationship isn't nearly as clear-cut as one might assume. That is, psychotic symptoms are not necessarily indicative of an individual's compromised ability to perform certain required psycholegal abilities. There continues to be a large number of individuals referred for evaluations of competency to stand trial; however, only a minority of these individuals are found incompetent. This may, in part, be due to the advanced understanding of the relationship between symptoms and performance as well as a focus on assessing the functional abilities of defendants referred for competency evaluations.

Similarly, the law has made the implicit assumption that certain cognitive or psycholegal abilities are distinct and separable from each other. For example, the law, with respect to competence, has identified three abilities that are necessary for an individual to be considered competent— understanding, appreciation, and reasoning. Only recently, however, have we begun to question whether these three abilities are actually distinct from one another (e.g., Zapf, 1998; Zapf & Roesch, in press).

Psychology has shown the tendency to accept the behavioral assumptions inherent in the law without question. Another example can be seen within the context of the Canadian law regarding competency (fitness) to stand trial. The *Criminal Code of Canada* has set out three abilities that an individual must possess to be considered fit to stand trial. Psychological assessment instruments have been developed by researchers to assess these three abilities (i.e., Roesch, Webster, & Eaves, 1984; Roesch, Zapf, Eaves, & Webster, 1998). Factor analyses of the items contained in these instruments, however, reveal two factors rather than three (Bagby, Nicholson, Rogers, & Nussbaum, 1992). Interpreters of these results have assumed that there was a problem with the construction of the instrument developed to assess the three legal abilities rather than that the three legal abilities may only represent two psychological abilities. Recently, however, we have begun to question the law and its assumptions rather than only question the results of psychological research that do not parallel what the law has set out.

A further example of behavioral assumptions that the law has made with respect to competence is illustrated in the issue of whether competence is a global or a discreet construct. That is, is competence context-specific or is it a general characteristic? Psychology has always asserted that competence is context-specific and that it varies with time and with specific abilities. Psychology has also assumed that the law viewed competence in the same manner—until recently. In the 1990s, in both the United States and Canada, the courts have made decisions that appear to go against this longstanding view of competence held by psychology. In *Godinez v. Moran* (1993) and *Regina v. Whittle* (1994) the Supreme Courts of the United States and Canada respectively have held that there is to be only one standard for competence regardless of the context. The consequence of these decisions is that psychology is now questioning the assumptions of the law and is attempting to study these issues in an empirical manner (see Perlin, 1996; Zapf, 1998).

There is research being conducted within the realm of juvenile competence that looks at expanding the predicates for incompetency to include developmental considerations rather than simply mental retardation and mental disorder (see Cowden & McKee, 1995; Grisso, 1997, 1998). This is an area that has been overlooked by the law and in which psychology has not simply blindly accepted the assumptions of the law, but rather, has taken a proactive step in attempting to conduct research and to further inform the law. As a discipline, we need to do more of this.

Bonnie (1992, 1993) has written about the justification for competency law. He has discussed three justifications for the ban on allowing an incompetent individual to proceed with trial—dignity, reliability, and autonomy. These are justifications that the law has made, however, it would be interesting to test these assumptions and attempt to determine if these three principles are in fact compromised by allowing incompetent individuals to proceed to trial with the assistance of counsel. This is just one example of assumptions that the law has made that have not yet been addressed by psychology.

The methods that have been used for competence research in the past have involved relatively simple methodologies and statistical analyses. Recently, however, the methodologies and statistical analyses have become more complex and have led to advances in the field. An examination of the relationship between different types of competencies has been made possible by using more sophisticated statistical analyses and the use of meta-analysis and other statistical techniques has enabled researchers to better determine relationships and characteristics relevant to competence.

One of the difficulties in conducting empirical research on competency is the fact that, given the low base rate of incompetence, it is difficult to gather a large group of incompetent individuals. As a result, much of the research that has been conducted has used large groups of competent individuals and relatively small groups of incompetent individuals. Future research endeavors need to include large groups of incompetent individuals as it is this group that will serve to elucidate our understanding of incompetence. It is logical to assume that more about incompetence can be learned by studying incompetent individuals than by studying competent individuals.

With respect to the competence assessment instruments that have been and are continuing to be developed, it may be necessary to consider issues of item difficulty more than has been done in the past. This appears to be an under-researched area that may need to be elaborated on in the future. In addition to item difficulty, issues to be addressed in the future might include the idea that cut-off scores are inappropriate for assessing competency (for anything other than a research-directed goal) and the notion that more normative-type data may be necessary in some areas of competence research.

## PSYCHOLOGICAL EVALUATION OF LAW

If psychology is to have an impact and inform the law then it is necessary to evaluate the law in order to make changes to the law or legal procedures. A few examples of the empirical analysis of the effects of law include research on the effects of *Charter* amendments and Bill C-30 on competency and insanity remands in Canada (see Roesch et al., 1997), research on (in)voluntary hospitalization and competence to consent to treatment (Appelbaum, Mirkin, & Bateman, 1981; Grisso & Appelbaum, 1998b), and research comparing the standards for competency to stand trial between countries and across jurisdictions (see Zapf & Roesch, in press).

In terms of the application of principles from general psychology to questions of law concerning competence, it would be interesting to attempt to apply general psychological research concerning vicarious versus real interactions to issues of participation in legal proceedings. Is there a difference between vicarious participation and real participation in terms of the abilities required of an individual to be competent to stand trial? What about other types of competencies in both the criminal and civil justice systems?

There are a few points of debate between psychology and the law with respect to the area of competence. First, the aforementioned question about whether competence is context-specific or global in nature appears to be an issue that has recently arisen and that has caused a lot of debate within the field (see Perlin, 1996). Second, the issue of consent versus assent and which of these should be considered to be the standard that is used when determining competence in specific contexts appears to be a point of debate for some researchers and commentators in the field (see Grisso & Appelbaum, 1998b). Third, the issues surrounding competency to be executed have engendered a lot of debate among professionals and scholars alike (see Brodsky, Zapf, & Boccaccini, in press for a review). This debate appears to be more ethical in nature but it reflects a difference between what the law mandates professionals to do and what many of their own professional ethics bodies suggest they not do. These are not the only areas of debate in psychology and law with respect to issues of competence and this chapter is by no means meant to reflect a comprehensive consideration of the issues discussed. Rather, the point is to examine where we have been and where we have yet to go in the 21st century.

## THE PHENOMENOLOGY OF LAW

The general public often gains an impression of the law through the media and the political coverage of issues. Often these impressions are incorrect or exaggerated. The general public tends to overestimate the base rate of incompetency and related constructs because the media picks up on the relatively rare high profile case and blows it out of proportion. With the exception of those individuals who take courses or learn about the law through more formal means, the media and possibly the Internet are responsible for much of the information people gain about the law.

It is important for professionals and scholars involved in the interface between psychology and the law to do what they can to inform the public about the true nature of certain psychological disorders or concepts. For example, with respect to competency issues, it would be important for psychologists to make sure that they educate the public, whenever possible, about the true base rate of incompetency and related issues such as the distinction between competency and insanity. Obviously, this is a large task and one that may be unrealistic to fulfill in a complete way; however, as psychologists and mental health professionals, we need to be aware of the public's perceptions of the law and do what we can to ensure that these are accurate to the extent possible.

It is also important to remember that it may not just be the general public that has misperceptions about psychology and its role in the legal system. Legal professionals or individuals who are serving as jurors may also hold misperceptions. Psychologists and other mental health professionals should take care to clarify accurately the advances that have occurred in research and practice with respect to certain legal and psychological issues as well as attempt to target the appropriate resources to educate the lay public and legal professionals about the psychological impact of laws and legal issues as well as psychological issues that pertain to the law. This education of the public and of legal professionals can occur through presentations at interdisciplinary conferences as well as through collaboration between legal professionals and mental health professionals. It is important that these collaborations are two-way in that psychologists educate legal professionals about the psychological issues related to competency or other legal issues and legal professionals educate psychologists about the complexities of a specific defendant's trial and the abilities that are expected of a particular individual in a particular case. In addition to all of this, it is most important for psychologists and other mental health professionals to clarify and clear up any misperceptions held by others that they may become aware of through their work.

## FUTURE: BRIDGE TO THE FUTURE

There are many factors that have lead to success in the field of competency. Included among these are well-developed forensic assessment instruments, a well-developed understanding of some types of competency (i.e., competency to stand trial), good training and education (in some states and provinces) of those professionals and practitioners involved in competency assessments regarding the issues involved in the evaluation of competency, and a move toward outpatient assessments that has been successful in terms of economics as well as the increased liberty of clients and patients. In order to continue to make progress in the field of competency, we propose certain factors that will lead to success, including methodologies to be used, domains in which research results should be presented, and substantive areas upon which to focus.

### METHODS LIKELY TO BE SUCCESSFUL IN THE FUTURE

Methods that are likely to be successful in elucidating issues of competency in the future include sophisticated statistical analyses such as item response theory, structural equation modeling, and meta-analyses to name but a few. The challenge will lie in presenting the results of these analyses in a manner that can be understood by practitioners and legal professionals who may not be trained in these techniques. It will be up to the researchers in the field to ensure that their results are accessible and interpretable by those individuals who will use the results.

It will be important to use large groups of incompetent defendants or individuals (depending upon the specific type of competency being examined) to better understand incompetence and the restoration of competence. It may also become important to attempt to determine if there are different classes or categories of incompetence. This would be important in terms of determining the most appropriate assessment and treatment techniques for different types of incompetent individuals.

The focus to the present has been mainly on quantitative methods and this has produced some very respectable research and has allowed a number of advances in the field of competence. In the future, however, our understanding of competence may also become illuminated through the use of high quality (and proven, possibly in other areas of investigation) qualitative techniques and methodologies. In addition to the aforementioned methods, we also need to remain open to exploring methodologies that may be tested and proven in other fields but which could be modified or adapted for use in investigating issues of competence.

## Areas of Application for Emerging Issues to be Addressed

There are a number of domains in which emerging issues can be addressed so as to ensure that the knowledge generated through research impacts upon the law and the legal process. The first of these would be to publish manuscripts in legally accessible journals. That is, journals or newsletters that are specifically targeted towards legal professionals. This would involve publishing these articles in a format that is familiar to these professionals and in a manner that educates with regard to psychological concepts and terminology as well as to the results of the research. In addition to publishing in legally accessible sources, workshops, conferences, or meetings between mental health professionals and legal professionals could be organized. The objective is to actively target the intended audience rather than to publish only in psychological journals and then question why the legal community is unfamiliar with the work being done in the field. With respect to the field of competency specifically, it might be educational for both mental health and legal professionals to conduct certain types of competency evaluations together, so that both professionals could learn from and assist each other.

## SUBSTANTIVE AREAS UPON WHICH TO FOCUS

There are certain areas within the field of competency that need to be further addressed through empirical research and scholarly commentary in order to expand upon the ideas and advancements that have already been gained. These include: continued refinement of instruments and development of additional instruments in the under-researched areas of competency; further distinction between consent and assent; expansion of the idea that competence should be continually assessed; recognition of possible political resistance and ways to counter that resistance; and publication of research results in sources that will reach lawyers, judges, and other legal professionals as well as in sources that will reach practitioners in the field. In addition to these areas, it will be important to the future of the field of competency that we learn from the research that has already been conducted in certain segments of this field (i.e., competency to stand trial) and apply this knowledge to other areas of the field and other types of competencies. Rather than start from ground zero in each specific context, we need to learn to apply knowledge from other areas to the new area so as to conserve resources and make better use of our research time.

There are a few substantive areas that, we believe, need to be focused on in the future for the research in the area of competence to really make an impact upon legal conceptualizations and procedures. One of the first steps will be to link the research on more than one type of competence. Traditionally, competency research has focused on one type of competence or another. Only recently have some researchers begun to link the research on more than one type of competence. For example, Winick (1987) was the first to link the literature on treatment decision-making to the literature on criminal competence. Bonnie (1993) has expanded this theoretical discussion to include tests of criminal competence that parallel those from the treatment decision-making literature. Zapf (1998) has built upon the conceptual foundation laid by Winick and Bonnie to establish an empirical link between these two types of competencies. Linking research on different types of competencies will serve to illuminate the distinctions and similarities that may be crucial to our conceptualizations of and the procedures related to different types of competencies.

Competency research has traditionally focused mainly on the assessment of competence rather than on the treatment and restoration of competence. At the present time, issues of treatment and restoration do not apply to competence to consent to research at all. If someone is unable to give their informed consent to participate in research, we simply do not allow them to participate rather than attempt to restore them to competence. The treatment programs that do exist focus mainly on issues of competence to stand trial and tend to target education about the legal system rather than the underlying cognitive deficits that may contribute to incompetence. It is generally agreed upon that incompetence is more than merely a lack of knowledge. Rather, there appears to be some underlying cognitive deficit(s) that account for incompetence. Future research needs to focus more specifically on what these underlying cognitive deficits are and how we can use this knowledge to develop treatment programs that will be effective at targeting the underlying cause of incompetence.

It will also be important to further investigate issues of competency with minority populations and other understudied populations, such as children, adolescents, and older adults. One specific area that needs to be specifically addressed is the contribution of language differences as a barrier to findings of competence or incompetence. Additionally, more cross-cultural research will be necessary to further our understanding of our own as well as other cultures in terms of how competency is conceptualized, assessed, and restored within different contexts.

*Top Five Topics to be Addressed in the Future of Competency Research*

The top five topics that we believe need to be addressed in the future include:

(1) Develop and expand the research on under-researched areas of competency (e.g., competency for execution, competency to consent to research, competency to consent to voluntary hospitalization). This includes using the literature on competency to stand trial as a blueprint for building the research in other areas of competency.

(2) Focus on children, adolescents, and the elderly. A developmental, lifespan approach to the study of competence is necessary to gain a better understanding of competence, incompetence, and the restoration of competence.

(3) Focus on the underlying cognitive abilities or deficits that are implicated in different (or all) types of incompetence.

(4) Focus on the treatment and restoration of incompetence.

(5) Focus on research that links two or more different types of competencies and that examines relevant similarities and differences.

## REFERENCES

Appelbaum, P. S., Mirkin, S. A., & Bateman, A. L. (1981). Empirical assessment of competency to consent to psychiatric hospitalization. *American Journal of Psychiatry, 138,* 1170–1176.

Bagby, R. M., Nicholson, R. A., Rogers, R., & Nussbaum, D. (1992). Domains of competency to stand trial: A factor analytic study. *Law and Human Behavior, 16,* 491–507.

Blackstone, W. (1783). *Commentaries on the laws of England* (9th ed.). London: W. Strahan.

Barnard, G. W., Thompson, J. W., Freeman, W. C., Robbins, L., Gies, D., & Hankins, G. C. (1991). Competency to stand trial: Description and initial evaluations of a new computer-assisted assessment tool (CADCOMP). *Bulletin of the American Academy of Psychiatry and Law, 19,* 367–381.

Bonnie, R. J. (1992). The competence of criminal defendants: A theoretical reformulation. *Behavioral Sciences and the Law, 10,* 291–316.

Bonnie, R. J. (1993). The competence of criminal defendants: Beyond *Dusky* and *Drope. University of Miami Law Review, 47,* 539–601.

Borum, R. & Grisso, T. (1992). Psychological test use in criminal forensic evaluations. *Professionals Psychology, Research and Practice, 26,* 465–473.

Brodsky, S. L., Zapf, P. A., & Boccaccini, M. (in press). The last competency: An examination of legal, ethical, and professional ambiguities regarding evaluations of competence for execution. *Journal of Forensic Psychology Practice*.

Burt, R. A., & Morris, N. (1972). A proposal for the abolition of the incompetency plea. *The University of Chicago Law Review, 40*, 66–95.

Carbonell, J. L., Heilbrun, K., & Friedman, F. L. (1992). Predicting who will regain trial competency: Initial promise unfulfilled. *Forensic Reports, 5*, 67–76.

Cooper, D. K. (1997). Juveniles' understanding of trial-related information: Are they competent defendants? *Behavioral Sciences and the Law, 15*, 167–180.

Cooper, D. & Grisso, T. (1997). Five year research update (1991–1995): Evaluations for competence to stand trial. *Behavioral Sciences and the Law, 15*, 347–364.

Cowden, V., & McKee, G. (1995). Competency to stand trial in juvenile delinquency proceedings: Cognitive maturity and the attorney-client relationship. *Journal of Family Law, 33*, 629–660.

Criminal Code of Canada, R. S. C., C-46 (1985).

Cuneo, D. J., & Brelje, T. B. (1984). Predicting probability of attaining fitness to stand trial. *Psychological Reports, 55*, 35–39.

Davis, D. (1985). Treatment planning for the patient who is incompetent to stand trial. *Hospital and Community Psychiatry, 36*(3), 268–271.

Davis, S. (1994). Fitness to stand trial in Canada in light of the recent Criminal Code amendments. *International Journal of Law and Psychiatry, 17*, 319–329.

Dickey, W. (1980). Incompetency and the nondangerous mentally ill. *Criminal Law Bulletin, 16*, 22–40.

Drope v. Missouri, 420 U. S. 162 (1975).

Dusky v. United States, 362 U. S. 402 (1960).

Everington, C. T., & Luckasson, R. (1992). *Competence Assessment for Standing Trial for Defendants with Mental Retardation (CAST-MR)*. Columbus, OH: International Diagnostic Systems, Inc.

Expert Panel Report to the National Institutes of Health (June, 1998). *Research involving individuals with questionable capacity to consent*. Presented at the 76th Meeting of the Advisory Committee to the Director National Institutes of Health. Bethesda, MD.

Favole, R. J. (1983). Mental disability in the American criminal process: A four issue survey In J. Monahan, & H. J. Steadman (Eds.), *Mentally disordered offenders: Perspectives from law and social science* (pp. 247–295). New York: Plenum.

Flin, R., & Spencer, J. R. (1995). Children as witnesses: Legal and psychological perspectives. *Journal of Child Psychology and Psychiatry and Allied Disciplines, 36*, 171–189.

Frith's Case, 22 How. St. Tr. 307 (1790).

Godinez v. Moran, 509 U. S. 389 (1993).

Golding, S. L. (1990). Mental health professionals and the courts: The ethics of expertise. *International Journal of Law and Psychiatry, 13*, 281–307.

Golding, S. L. (1993). *Interdisciplinary Fitness Interview-Revised: A training manual*. State of Utah Division of Mental Health.

Golding, S. L., Roesch, R., & Screiber, J. (1984). Assessment and conceptualization of competency to stand trial: Preliminary data on the Interdisciplinary Fitness Interview. *Law and Human Behavior, 8*, 321–334.

Grisso, T. (1980). Juveniles' capacities to waive Miranda rights: An empirical analysis. *California Law Review, 68*, 1134–1166.

Grisso, T. (1981). *Juveniles' waiver of rights: Legal and psychological competence*. New York: Plenum.

Grisso, T. (1986). *Evaluating competencies: Forensic assessments and instruments*. New York: Plenum Press.

Grisso, T. (1992). Five-year research update (1986–1990): Evaluations for competence to stand trial. *Behavioral Sciences and the Law, 10*, 353–369.

Grisso, T. (1997). The competence of adolescents as trial defendants. *Psychology, Public Policy, and Law, 3*, 3–32.

Grisso, T. (1998). *Forensic evaluation of juveniles*. Sarasota, FL: Professional Resource Press.

Grisso, T., & Appelbaum, P. S. (1998a). *MacArthur Competence Assessment Tool for Treatment (MacCAT-T)*. Sarasota, FL: Professional Resource Press.

Grisso, T., & Appelbaum, P. S. (1998b). *Assessing competence to consent to treatment: A guide for physicians and other health professionals*. New York: Oxford University Press.

Grisso, T., Cocozza, J., Steadman, H., Fisher, W., & Greer, A. (1994). The organization of pretrial forensic evaluation services. *Law and Human Behavior, 18*, 377–393.

Grisso, T. & Seigel, S. K. (1986). Assessment of competency to stand criminal trial. In W. J. Curran, A. L. McGarry, et al. (Eds.), *Forensic psychiatry and psychology: Perspectives and standards for interdisciplinary practice* (pp. 145–165). Philadelphia: F. A. Davis.

Group for the Advancement of Psychiatry. (1974). *Misuse of psychiatry in the criminal courts: Competency to stand trial* (89). New York: Author.

Hart, S D., & Hare, R. D. (1992). Predicting fitness to stand trial: The relative power of demographic, criminal, and clinical variables. *Forensic Reports, 5*, 53–65.

Heilbrun, K., Hawk, G., & Tate, D. C. (1996). Juvenile competence to stand trial: Research issues in practice. *Law and Human Behavior, 20*, 573–578.

Hoge, S. K., Bonnie, R. J., Poythress, N., & Monahan, J. (1999). *The MacArthur Competence Assessment Tool-Criminal Adjudication (MacCAT-CA)*. Odessa, FL: Psychological Assessment Resources.

Hoge, S. K., Bonnie, B. J., Poythress, N., Monahan, J., Eisenberg, M., & Feucht-Haviar, T. (1997). The MacArthur Adjudicative Competence Study: Development and validation of a research instrument. *Law and Human Behavior, 21*, 141–179.

Jackson v. Indiana, 405 U.S. 715 (1972).

Johnson, W. G., & Mullet, N. (1987). Georgia Court Competency Test-R. In M. Hersen & A. S. Bellack (Eds.), *Dictionary of behavioral assessment techniques*. New York: Pergamon.

Laboratory of Community Psychiatry (1974). *Competency to stand trial and mental illness*. New York: Aronson.

Law Reform Commission of Canada (1976). A report to parliament on mental disorder in the criminal process. Ottawa, Ontario: Author.

Lindsay, P. S. (1977). Fitness to stand trial: An overview in light of the recommendations of the Law Reform Commission of Canada. *Criminal Law Quarterly, 19*, 303–348

Lipsett, P. D., Lelos, D., & McGarry (1971). Competency for trial: A screening instrument. *American Journal of Psychiatry, 128*, 105–109.

McKee, G. R. (1998). Competency to stand trial in preadjudicatory juveniles and adults. *Journal of the American Academy of Psychiatry and the Law, 26*, 89–99.

Melton, G. B., Petrila, J., Poythress, N. G., & Slogobin, C. (1997). *Psychological evaluations for the courts: A handbook for mental health professionals and lawyers* (2nd ed.). New York: Guilford.

National Bioethics Advisory Commission, (1998). *Research involving persons with mental disorders that may affect decision making capacity*. Washington DC: Author.

Nicholson, R. A. (1999). Forensic treatment: A review of programs and research. In R. Roesch, S. Hart, & J. Ogloff (Eds.), *Psychology and law: The state of the discipline* (pp. 122–173). New York: Kluwer Academic/Plenum Publishers.

Nicholson, R. A., Barnard, G. W., Robbins, L., & Hankins, G. (1994). Predicting treatment outcomes for incompetent defendants. *Bulletin of the American Academy of Psychiatry and Law, 22*(3), 367–377.

Nicholson, R. A., & Kugler, K. E. (1991). Competent and incompetent criminal defendants: A quantitative review of comparative research. *Psychological Bulletin, 109*, 355–370.

Nicholson, R. A., & McNulty, J. L. (1992). Outcome of hospitalization for defendants found incompetent to stand trial. *Behavioral Sciences and the Law, 10*, 371–383.

Ohayon, M. M., Crocker, A., St-Onge, B., & Caulet, M. (1998). Fitness, responsibility, and judicially ordered assessments. *Canadian Journal of Psychiatry, 43*, 491–495.

Ogloff, J. (1991). *The use of the insanity defence in British Columbia: A qualitative and quantitative analysis.* Technical Report, Dept. of Justice Canada.

Pendleton, L. (1980). Treatment of persons found incompetent to stand trial. *American Journal of Psychiatry, 137*, 1098–1100.

Perlin, M. L. (1996). "Dignity was the first to leave": Godinez v. Moran, Colin Ferguson, and the trial of mentally disabled criminal defendants. *Behavioral Sciences and the Law, 14*, 61–81.

Regina v. Pritchard, 7 Can. & P. 304, 173 E. R. 135 (1836).

Regina v. Taylor, 77 C. C. C. (3d) 551 (Ont. C. A. 1992).

Regina v. Whittle, 2 S. C. R. 914 (1994).

Reich, J. H., & Tookey, L. (1986). Disagreements between court and psychiatrist on competency to stand trial. *Journal of Clinical Psychiatry, 47*, 29–30.

Robey, A. (1965). Criteria for competency to stand trial: A checklist for psychiatrists. *American Journal of Psychiatry, 122*, 616–623.

Roesch, R., & Golding, S. L. (1979). Treatment and disposition of defendants found incompetent to stand trial: A review and a proposal. *International Journal of Law and Psychiatry, 2*, 349–370.

Roesch, R., & Golding, S. L. (1980). *Competency to stand trial.* Urbana, IL: University of Illinois Press.

Roesch, R., & Golding, S. L. (1987). Defining and assessing competency to stand trial. In I. B. Weiner & A. K. Hess (Eds.), *Handbook of forensic psychology.* New York: Wiley.

Roesch, R., Hart, S. D., & Zapf, P. A. (1996). Conceptualizing and assessing competency to stand trial: Implications and applications of the MacArthur Treatment Competence Model. *Psychology, Public Policy, and Law, 2*(1), 96–113.

Roesch, R., Ogloff, J. R. P., & Golding, S. L. (1993). Competency to stand trial: Legal and clinical issues. *Applied and Preventive Psychology, 2*, 43–51.

Roesch, R., Ogloff, J. R. P., Hart, S. D., Dempster, R. J., Zapf, P. A., & Whittemore, K. E. (1997). The impact of Canadian Criminal Code changes on remands and assessments of fitness to stand trial and criminal responsibility in British Columbia. *Canadian Journal of Psychiatry, 42*, 509–514.

Roesch, R., Webster, C. D., & Eaves, D. (1984). *The Fitness Interview Test: A method for examining fitness to stand trial.* Toronto: University of Toronto Centre of Criminology.

Roesch, R., Zapf, P. A., Eaves, D., & Webster, C. D. (1998). *Fitness Interview Test* (Rev. ed.). Burnaby, BC: Mental Health, Law and Policy Institute, Simon Fraser University.

Roesch, R., Zapf, P. A., Golding, S. L., & Skeem, J. L. (1999). Defining and assessing competency to stand trial. In A. K. Hess, I. B. Weiner (Eds.), *The handbook of forensic psychology* (2nd ed., pp. 327–349). New York: Wiley.

Savitsky, J. C., & Karras, D. (1984). Competency to stand trial among adolescents. *Adolescence, 19*, 349–358.

Scott, E. (1992). Judgment and reasoning in adolescent decision making. *Villanova Law Review, 37*, 1607–1669.

Scott, E., Reppucci, N. D., & Woolard, J. (1995). Evaluating adolescent decision making in legal contexts. *Law and Human Behavior, 19*, 221–244.

Siegel, A. & Elwork, A. (1990). Treating incompetence to stand trial. *Law and Human Behavior, 14*, 57–65.

Skeem, J. L., Golding, S. L., Cohen, N. B., & Berge, G. (1998). Logic and reliability of evaluations of competence to stand trial. *Law and Human Behavior, 22,* 519–547.

Slovenko, R. (1995). Assessing competency to stand trial. *Psychiatric Annals, 25,* 392–393, 397.

Steadman, H. J. & Hartstone, E. (1983). Defendants incompetent to stand trial. In J. Monahan, & H. J. Steadman (Eds.), *Mentally disordered offenders: Perspectives from law and social science* (pp. 39–62). New York: Plenum Press.

Terhune, S. (1990). Forensic vs. standard assessment instruments: Preference of judges in a competency to stand trial case. *Dissertation Abstracts International, 51*(2-B), 1007.

The Queen v. Berry, 1 Q. B. D. 447 (1876).

United States v. Lawrence, 26 F. Cas. 887 (D. C. Cir. 1835).

Verdun-Jones, S. N. (1981). The doctrine of fitness to stand trial in Canada: The forked tongue of social control. *International Journal of Law and Psychiatry, 4,* 363–389.

Webster, C. D., Menzies, R. J., & Jackson, M. A. (1982). *Clinical assessment before trial.* Toronto: Butterworths.

Winick, B. J. (1983). Incompetency to stand trial: Developments in the law. In J. Monahan, & H. J. Steadman (Eds.), *Mentally disordered offenders: Perspectives from law and social science* (pp. 3–38). New York: Plenum.

Winick, B. J. (1985). Restructuring competency to stand trial. *UCLA Law Review, 32,* 921–985.

Winick, B. J. (1987). Incompetency to stand trial: An assessment of costs and benefits, and a proposal for reform. *Rutgers Law Review, 39,* 243–287.

Winick, B. J. (1992). On autonomy: Legal and psychological perspectives. *Villanova Law Review, 37,* 1705–1777.

Winick, B. J. (1995). Reforming incompetency to stand trial and plead guilty: A restated proposal and a response to Professor Bonnie. *The Journal of Criminal Law and Criminology, 85,* 571–624.

Winick, B. J. (1996). Incompetency to proceed in the criminal process: Past, present, and future. In D. B. Wexler & B. J. Winick (Eds.), *Law in a therapeutic key: Developments in therapeutic jurisprudence.* Durham, NC: Carolina Academic Press.

Wildman, R. W., II, Batchelor, E. S., Thompson, L. Nelson, F. R., Moore, J. T., Patterson, M. E., & DeLaosa, M. (1978). *The Georgia Court Competency Test: An attempt to develop a rapid quantitative measure of fitness for trial.* Unpublished manuscript, Forensic Services Division, Central State Hosptial, Miledgeville, GA.

Youtsey v. United States, 97 F. 937 (6th Cir. 1899).

Zapf, P. A. (1998). *An investigation of the construct of competence in a criminal and civil context: A comparison of the FIT, the MacCAT-CA, and the MacCAT-T.* Unpublished doctoral dissertation, Simon Fraser University, Burnaby, British Columbia, Canada.

Zapf, P. A. & Roesch, R. (1998). Fitness to stand trial: Characteristics of remands since the 1992 Criminal Code Amendments. *Canadian Journal of Psychiatry, 43,* 287–293.

Zapf, P. A., & Roesch, R. (in press). A comparison of the MacCAT-CA and the FIT for making determinations of competency to stand trial. *International Journal of Law and Psychiatry.*

# 7

# Eyewitness Research

## R. C. L. LINDSAY, JOHN C. BRIGHAM, C. A. ELIZABETH BRIMACOMBE, AND GARY L. WELLS

"I remember really feeling confident that was the man...I was just positive he did it" —Jennifer Thompson, after learning that the man she identified as her attacker was innocent.

Errors by eyewitnesses can have profound negative consequences. The most obvious of these negative consequences is for the mistakenly identified. Ronald Cotton, for instance, served nearly 11 years in prison before DNA proved that Jennifer Thompson's actual attacker was Bobby Poole. The negative consequences of eyewitness mistakes are not confined to the innocent suspect, however. Eyewitness mistakes can also contribute to further victimization. For example, while Cotton went to prison Poole remained free and went on to commit several other violent offences before he was finally caught. The eyewitness often suffers as well. For example, although Thompson learned in 1995 that her identification of Cotton was mistaken, five years later she still reports feelings of self-guilt for her mistaken identification.

RODERICK C. LINDSAY • Department of Psychology, Queen's University, Kingston, Ontario, Canada K7L 3N6. JOHN C. BRIGHAM • Department of Psychology, Florida State University, Tallahassee, Florida 32306. C. A. ELIZABETH BRIMACOMBE • Department of Psychology, University of Victoria, Victoria, British Columbia, Canada V8W 3P5. GARY L. WELLS • Psychology Department, Iowa State University, Ames, Iowa 50011.

Research on eyewitness testimony the reasons for errors in eyewitness memory, some of which have led to wrongful imprisonment. The research has spawned recommendations on how these errors can be minimized. The eyewitness literature is now widely read (e.g., most introductory social psychology texts have chapters on psychology and law and virtually all of these chapters discuss eyewitness issues) and broadcast via popular media (e.g., Oprah; Good Morning America). It is a literature filled with counterintuitive findings that are of clear applied value to the police and justice system and may lead to a reduction in the risk of mistaken identification.

Applications to the legal system have included: Expert testimony in hearings and at trial; consultation with attorneys and law enforcement; workshop presentations, addresses, and written articles directed toward attorneys, judges, and law enforcement; and working with the administrative branch of government to develop improved policies and procedures. Indeed, the findings of eyewitness identification research form the foundation of *Eyewitness Evidence: A Guide for Law Enforcement* recently developed by the Department of Justice (for a full discussion of the development of the DOJ guide, see Wells et al., 2000). In this chapter we trace the evolution of the current interest in this topic, trace the impact of the eyewitness literature, and provide a vision for future research.

## REVIEW OF THE FIELD

Early in the 20th Century, psychologists recognized the value of empirical studies of human memory for understanding the nature of error in eyewitnesses' recollections of the details of crimes (e.g., Binet, 1905; Munsterberg, 1908; Stern, 1910; Whipple, 1911). The early work established that eyewitnesses are prone to error and suggestion, but provided little in the way of recommendations for improvement However, little further work in the area occurred until the revival of interest in eyewitness issues in the 1970s. During the past three decades, research dedicated to the study of eyewitnesses has flourished, yielding a wealth of findings of clear applied value.

There are a number of ongoing debates about psychological principles/questions in the eyewitness area. The suggestibility of children has been a hot topic for two decades with some researchers claiming that children are easily influenced while others assert that children rarely lie (e.g., Leippe, Romanczyk, & Manion, 1991). Assessing the truthfulness or accuracy of testimony of children and adults remains a contentious issue. Methods used to assess the accuracy of eyewitness statements will continue to generate interest. For example, the Criteria-Based Content Analysis (CBCA) technique has been put forth as a way to determine the truth of a child's allegation of sexual abuse by analyzing an interview transcript (e.g., see Raskin & Esplin, 1991). However, a research review (Ruby & Brigham, 1997) indicated that there are many ambiguities and unanswered questions surrounding the CBCA technique. Perhaps the hottest controversy has been the debate about the validity of "recovered" memories and repression, with the vigorous debate often generating more heat than light (e.g., see Poole, Lindsay, Memon, & Bull, 1995).

The impact of high stress or arousal on identification accuracy remains a topic of interest. Progress in this area is clearly hampered by the ethical limitations imposed on experimenters by the topic. This is particularly true as the most arousing eyewitness conditions are likely to be those where the perpetrator has a weapon, causing "weapon focus" on the part of witnesses (Steblay, 1992). The interaction between the race of the witness and the perpetrator is another area of considerable research interest. A recent meta-analysis of 39 face recognition studies involving almost 5,000 participants found that the *own-race bias*, the tendency for people to recognize faces of their own race more accurately than faces of another race, accounted for about 15% of the variability in performance (Meissner & Brigham, in press-a). This research issue is lively enough to have spawned a special issue of the journal, *Psychology, Public Policy, and the Law* on the topic (Goodman-Delahunty, in press).

## FACTORS LEADING TO SUCCESS

We see five factors as being especially important in accounting for the success of eyewitness research. First, unlike some areas in the interface of psychology and law, eyewitness research lends itself readily to the use of the experimental method. As a result, eyewitness researchers are able to isolate cause-effect relations. Second, there is a long history of research in psychology on human memory, thereby providing a foundation for some of the basic cognitive processes involved in the acquisition, storage, and retrieval of memories. Third, unlike some areas in the interface of psychology and law, the criterion variable in eyewitness research (accuracy of recall and recognition) is well defined, readily operationalized, and intuitively understood as the important criterion variable for real-world application. Because eyewitness researchers create the witnessed events (e.g., staged crimes), there is no debate about what constitutes a desirable response from the eyewitness (i.e., correct or accurate recall and recognition). Fourth, eyewitness researchers have been publishing their work in some of the most visible and rigorous journals in scientific psychology (such as the *Journal of Applied Psychology, the Journal of Personality and Social Psychology, Journal of Experimental Psychology: Applied, Journal of Experimental Psychology: Learning, Memory, and Cognition, American Psychologist, and Psychological Bulletin*). This has earned eyewitness research a measure of respect and visibility in traditional scientific psychology that some other areas of the interface of psychology and law do not yet have. Finally, we think that the success of eyewitness research owes at least in part to the fact that there is a demonstrable and serious problem to address. Recent examinations of actual cases of wrongful conviction, for instance, have shown that eyewitness identification error accounts for more convictions of innocent persons than all other causes combined (see Wells, Small, Penrod, Malpass, Fulero, & Brimacombe, 1998).

## NOTABLE SUCCESSES

We believe that the eyewitness area has been marked by six particularly outstanding achievements:

### *Illustrating the Malleability of Memory*

The pioneering work of Elizabeth Loftus (e.g., Loftus, 1979; Powers, Andriks, & Loftus, 1979) illustrated that eyewitness memory could change in response to various sources of influence, such as post-event misinformation and bias in the phrasing of questions. This work replicated some earlier findings that witness memory was fallible, but added two important aspects. First, Loftus and her colleagues showed that testimony is affected not just by what happens prior to and during a witnessed event, but also what happens after the event. Second, more than her predecessors, Loftus added strong theoretical components to the discussion of eyewitness memory. Loftus' findings intrigued and sparked the research activity of many psychologists who sought to understand the malleability of eyewitness memory and eyewitnesses' insight into the accuracy of their crime recollections. Loftus' work also stimulated considerable debate about the mechanisms responsible for these effects (e.g., Bekerian & Bowers, 1983; Bowers & Bekerian, 1984; Lindsay, 1994; McCloskey & Zaragoza, 1985).

### *System and Estimator Variables*

Wells (1978) distinguished between variables that are, at least in principle, controllable by the criminal justice system: *system variables*, such as interviewing techniques and police lineup procedures, and *estimator variables*, those which are not controllable, such as race and degree of arousal of the witness. This distinction served to clearly delineate the explanatory power and prescriptive value of variables studied by eyewitness researchers. Research devoted to estimator variables is useful in determining how eyewitness memory can be affected by aspects of the crime situation e.g., presence of a weapon, (Maass & Kohnken, 1989) and characteristics of the witness such as age, gender, and race (e.g., Leippe, Romanczyk, & Manion, 1991; Ng & Lindsay, 1994; Pozzulo & Lindsay, 1998; Slone, Brigham, & Meissner, 2000). In contrast, system variable research does more than explain *why* eyewitness errors occur. These findings, by virtue of focussing on crime investigation procedures such as the timing of obtaining witnesses' estimates of confidence in their lineup identification decisions, also explain how eyewitness errors can be minimized or prevented (Wells, 1993). System variable research has thus been a powerful force in fuelling eyewitness researchers' recommendations and guidelines for police procedures and legal policy. For example, the American Psychology-Law Society recently produced a "white paper" on the topic of eyewitness identification procedures in an attempt to move the U.S. closer to adopting policies based on system variable research (Wells et al., 1998).

## New Interviewing Methods

Based in part on research demonstrating the malleability of eyewitness memory as well as basic cognitive and social processes, psychologists developed improved interviewing techniques designed to yield more accurate reports (e.g., the cognitive interview, Geiselman, Fisher, MacKinnon, & Holland, 1985, 1986). These techniques increased the amount of correct information that could be obtained from eyewitnesses with minimal or no increases in false reports. Again, this work led to considerable additional research and debate about exactly which aspects of the procedures were critical to the improved performance (Koehnken, Milne, Memon, & Bull, 1999). The results of this research provide concrete suggestions for changes in police interrogation procedures that could reduce the problems of memory malleability.

## Documentation of Lineup Biases

Work throughout the 1970s and 80s documented potentially high levels of false positive identification as a result of biased identification procedures (e.g., Buckhout, Alper, Chern, Silverberg, & Slomovits, 1974; Buckhout, Figueroa, & Hoff, 1975; Lindsay & Wells, 1980; Lindsay, Wallbridge, & Drennan, 1987; Malpass & Devine, 1981). These procedural biases include structural lineup bias (e.g., the suspect fits the eyewitness' description of the culprit whereas the others in the lineup do not) as well as instructional bias (e.g., failing to warn eyewitnesses that the actual culprit might not be in the lineup) and administration bias (such as cues from the lineup administrator as to which person is the suspect; e.g., having only the suspect wearing clothing similar to that worn by the criminal during the crime). These system variable studies provided compelling evidence that wrongful convictions were likely to result from the use of poor identification procedures.

## New Identification Procedures

Although it was clear that lineup biases presented a problem, unbiased lineups produced relatively high rates of false positive identification as well. New identification procedures were designed to yield more accurate identification decisions, first focusing on reductions in false positive choices. For example, the idea of blank lineups was introduced and tested (Wells, 1984). A blank lineup is one in which, unbeknownst to the eyewitness, there are no suspects. Eyewitnesses who select someone from a blank lineup can be discounted whereas those who resist selecting someone from a blank lineup can then be shown a lineup in which there is a suspect. Perhaps the most successful of the new identification procedures is the sequential lineup. In a sequential lineup, the eyewitness views only one person at a time rather than viewing all lineup members at once (Lindsay & Wells, 1985). The ability of these new procedures to reduce the chances of mistaken identification of suspects while maintaining the ability of eyewitnesses to identify the actual culprit is a major contribution to improving the reliability of eyewitness identification evidence. This work continues with new procedures developed to improve the performance of child eyewitnesses (Pozzulo & Lindsay, 1999). Children were shown to make as many correct identifications as adults but more likely than adults to falsely identify innocent people (Pozzulo & Lindsay, 1998). Pozzulo and Lindsay (1999) asked children to first eliminate all lineup members but one by indicating either which lineup member looked most like the person they had seen or by removing lineup members least like the person seen until only one lineup member remained. Once the lineup was reduced to a single person, the children were reinforced for having made useful decisions, instructed to be very careful because choosing a wrong person was a serious error, and then asked if the "surviving" lineup member was the person they had seen. Correct and false positive identification rates using this procedure were at adult levels for children as young as eight years of age. In addition to research on how to reduce mistaken identifications without reducing correct identifications, recent work has focused on increasing correct identification rates without increasing mistaken identification rates (Luus & Wells, 1991; Wells, Rydell, & Selau, 1993). Other work has focused on ways to measure lineup bias and the development of absolute standards to differentiate biased from unbiased lineups (Brigham, Meissner, & Wasserman, 1999; Brigham & Pfeifer, 1994).

## Impact on Policy

The early research produced some suggestions for police and the courts (Munsterberg, 1908) but these attempts to influence policy were rebuffed by the legal community (Wigmore, 1909). The more recent work in the area has had a dramatic impact on policy. The Law Reform Commission of Canada consulted with researchers in the eyewitness area and based many of its final recommendations on the eyewitness literature available at the time (Brooks, 1983). The British Home Office developed guidelines for police based on the eyewitness literature (Home Office, 1976; 1978). Recently, the U.S. Department of Justice consulted with eyewitness researchers in preparing the first American national guide for law enforcement officials to follow when collecting eyewitness evidence. The resulting document, entitled Eyewitness Evidence: A Guide for Law Enforcement (Technical Working Group for Eyewitness Evidence, 1999), draws on psychological research to support its directives for interviewing eyewitnesses in criminal cases and for conducting identification procedures.

## OBSTACLES TO SUCCESS: PAST AND PRESENT

From a methodological perspective, studying eyewitness issues is a difficult task. The major obstacle faced by researchers is achieving a high level of ecological validity. From a practical stance, eyewitness researchers have not had an easy time of influencing police procedures and judicial policy. Some examples of the challenges faced by eyewitness researchers follow.

## Ecological Validity

The normal operating procedure for eyewitness researchers is to stage crimes (usually thefts) for unsuspecting research participants and subsequently ask those participant-witnesses to try to identify the perpetrator from a photo lineup. Achieving a good level of ecological validity is difficult as some aspects of crimes are difficult to simulate due to ethical or other practical constraints (e.g., victimization, weapon focus, sexual abuse of children). Thus the eyewitness literature focuses almost exclusively on bystanders rather than victims of non-violent thefts. Although it is possible to simulate relevant aspects of crimes such as long delays between the event and testing of witness memory or time-unlimited jury deliberation, few studies exist that examine these issues because of the logistical and resource issues involved.

The eyewitness literature has evolved considerably from early investigations that studied list learning and then generalized to eyewitness memory. However, most current research deals with small numbers of independent variables, leaving open the possibility that complex interactions among relevant variables remain hidden. This issue can be addressed by designing more complex studies, but resource issues will always play a part in researchers' decisions. Possible interactions and other concerns leave doubts about the generalizability of the results of eyewitness research and many lawyers use the specter of low ecological validity to discredit psychological research.

On the other hand the types of phenomena that eyewitness researchers commonly study may depend less on ecological validity than on internal validity. Establishing that the sequential lineup produces fewer mistaken identifications than does the simultaneous lineup, for instance, tells us a great deal about the causes of mistaken identification. The ability to generalize this phenomenon to actual cases probably depends more on the internal validity of the cause-effect relation than it does on the ecological characteristics of the crime that was simulated.

Data from actual crimes can sometimes be compared to data from simulated crimes to examine similarities and differences. For instance, Sporer's (1996) analysis of the descriptions of culprits given by 100 actual eyewitnesses shows remarkable similarity to the descriptions that staged-crime eyewitnesses give (Wells, Rydell, & Seelau, 1993). Rates at which actual eyewitnesses identify fillers (known innocents) from lineups are similar to the rates obtained in simulated crime studies (Wright & McDaid, 1996). Meta-analyses comparing laboratory and field studies have shown few differences in the patterning of results, except that laboratory studies generally produce higher levels of accuracy overall than do field studies (Cutler, Penrod, & Martens, 1987). Studies in which the subject-witnesses know that the crime event is not real have not produced appreciably different results from studies in which the subject-witnesses think that the event was a real crime (Murray & Wells, 1983). Analyses of actual cases of mistaken identification that were proven by forensic DNA tests tend to confirm what staged-crime studies have shown regarding dissociations between the confidence of an eyewitness and the accuracy of an eyewitness (Wells et al., 1998).

One of the problems with generalizing from eyewitness experiments to actual cases is that eyewitness experiments use fixed-effect designs that control for other factors that could be naturally correlated with each other in actual cases. For instance, controlled experiments might show that high arousal interferes with memory, but arousal can correlate with how close the witness is to the offender. As a result, the most aroused witnesses might be better witnesses in actual cases because they had a better view of the culprit (Yuille & Cutshall, 1986; also see Tollestrup, Turtle, & Yuille, 1994).

## Resistance from the Legal System

Historically, the legal system has failed to collect any empirical data on its own. Legal scholars were, and to a great extent still are, trained to treat eyewitness issues in the law as doctrinal rather than empirical. Case law and legislation are used to argue cases, and the actual behavior of people other than those directly involved in the case at hand is often ignored. At least since Wigmore (1909), the legal system has resisted psychological concepts and empirical research data as a source of legal thinking and policy in the eyewitness area. Thus, while they have generally not collected data themselves, lawyers also have rejected the data collected by social scientists. As a result, legal thinking has been driven by assumptions, rather than knowledge of human behavior (Melton, 1992?).

## Implementation of Recommendations

Even when criminal justice systems accept the role of psychology as a source of pertinent information, the implementation of recommendations is not a trivial matter, at least in North America (Lindsay, 1999; Wells, Malpass, Lindsay, Fisher, Turtle, & Fulero, 2000). Direct avenues of communication between researchers and policy makers are not commonplace. Police and courts are at best ambivalent about accepting advice from psychologists. A mechanism is needed for implementing widespread change. The recent Technical Working Group for Eyewitness Evidence illustrates that researchers, lawyers, and law enforcement officers can discuss eyewitness issues and come to some level of agreement about preferred police procedures. What is needed is a forum for such interactions to continue periodically so that police and the justice system can benefit from our ever increasing knowledge of eyewitness psychology.

## Resistance to Scientific Expert Testimony

The one mechanism that is *potentially* available to inform the justice system about eyewitness issues, at least in principle, is expert testimony. Although psychologists have testified in many cases about eyewitness research in many jurisdictions expert, testimony on eyewitness issues is often not permitted by courts, and the right of trial judges to reject such testimony has generally been upheld in higher courts (Brigham, Wasserman, & Meissner, 1999). To the extent that experts are barred from the courtroom, juries and judges may be deprived of relevant, empirically-based information that could be useful in evaluating the probative value of eyewitness evidence (see Leippe, 1995).

## UNIQUE ISSUES PERTAINING TO WOMEN AND MINORITY POPULATIONS

The authors of every chapter in this book have endeavoured to speak to unique issues pertaining to women and minority populations. Within the eyewitness area, little research has focused on gender, but a good deal of research has looked at race, most often at Whites and Blacks in the U.S. Because gender and minority issues fall within the realm of estimator variable research, as topics of inquiry they are interesting to researchers, although their study may not yield the practical value that comes with the study of system variables. What eyewitness research is relevant to women and minorities?

### Own-race Bias

As noted earlier, the own-race bias in facial recognition has been extensively studied and the relevance of the phenomenon to eyewitness identification discussed. It is generally more difficult to recognize faces of another race than faces of one's own race (Meissner & Brigham, in press-a; Slone, Brigham, & Meissner, 2000).

### Race of Lineup Constructor

In addition, race has been shown to influence the way that people construct lineups, such that people use a looser criterion (i.e., more faces are seen as similar to each other) when constructing lineups of other-race faces than when constructing own-race lineups (Brigham & Ready, 1985).

### Own-sex Bias

There is also some evidence of an "own-sex bias" in identifications, although it does not appear to be as strong or as consistent as the own-race bias (Slone et al., 2000). It appears to be caused largely by women recognizing women better than they recognize men. At present it is unknown whether the race effects found regarding lineup construction and measuring lineup fairness (see below) could apply to sex as well.

## Race of Mock Witness

The race of mock witnesses used to measure lineup fairness has recently been shown to be important (Lindsay, Ross, Smith, & Flanigan, 1999). Mock witnesses are people who researchers involve in a "behind the scene" analysis of their eyewitness identification experiments. These individuals never view the crime but instead they are provided with the eyewitness' description of the culprit and then shown the lineup and asked to choose the person they believe to be the suspect. To the extent that the mock witnesses can correctly identify the suspect without ever having viewed the culprit, researchers discount their lineup as an effective test of eyewitness memory. Data from mock witnesses are used to generate a numerical index of the degree to which the lineup can be considered "fair". For a discussion of issues surrounding the measurement of lineup fairness, see Brigham, Meissner, and Wasserman (1999), Brigham and Pfeifer (1994), and Malpass and Lindsay (1999). Although the pattern of results is complicated, it is clear that same-race and other-race mock witnesses can differ substantially in their choices of lineup members, and that the pattern of choices interacts with the race of witness providing the description as well.

## THE EXPERIENCE OF LAW:
## THE PHENOMENOLOGY OF LAW

### UNDERSTANDING THE LAW

The understanding of eyewitness issues by the general public has been explored in studies of children's understanding of legal procedures (REFS) and surveys of common knowledge about memory and eyewitness evidence (Brigham & Bothwell, 1983; Deffenbacher & Loftus, 1982; Lindsay, 1994; Yarmey & Jones, 1983). However, these studies do not tell us how the public comes to have these understandings. The impact of media such as talk shows, news shows, PBS reports, and high-profile cases probably account for some knowledge. However, entertainment such as police programs (e.g., NYPD Blue) likely account for at least as much of public opinion on legal issues as the non-fiction sources.

### WHAT DO LAY PEOPLE UNDERSTAND ABOUT THE LAW?

#### "Common Knowledge" Surveys

Various populations such as undergraduates, members of the general public, and lawyers have been surveyed about their knowledge of eyewitness issues. It is common to find significant misunderstandings of many effects demonstrated in the eyewitness literature (e.g., Brigham & WolfsKeil, 1983; Rahaim & Brodsky, 1982; Shaw, Garcia, & McClure, 1999). For example, Shaw et al. (1999) questioned lay people about their beliefs concerning the factors that affect eyewitness testimony accuracy and found that respondents generally failed to note system variables such as police interrogation procedures as a source of error in eyewitness accounts.

## Perceptions of Jury Effectiveness

Research on the perceived role of juries indicates that many misconceptions exist. People generally do not understand how difficult it is for the jury to discriminate between accurate and inaccurate eyewitness testimony (Lindsay, Wells, & O'Connor, 1989; Lindsay, Wells, & Rumpel, 1981; Wells, Lindsay, & Ferguson, 1979).

## Personal Experiences

Personal experiences with the justice system in the roles of victim, witness, juror, and occasionally defendant, provide many people with their most dramatic sources of information about the law and the justice system.

## ROLE OF PSYCHOLOGY IN EDUCATING PEOPLE ABOUT LAW

## General Public

The general public learns about eyewitness issues via the mass media, university courses for some, and direct experience in the criminal justice system. Media accounts have improved dramatically in recent years as print and electronic media have begun to recognize that there is a scientific literature and have relied increasingly on eyewitness experts to describe findings. Nevertheless, such cannot be relied upon to adequately prepare people for the role of juror in cases involving eyewitness evidence.

## Jurors

Psychologists can play an important role in educating jurors about eyewitness issues via expert testimony. Obviously, one limitation of this educational effort is the tendency for courts in *many* jurisdictions routinely to exclude testimony by eyewitness experts. Moreover, courts in all jurisdictions conduct the majority of eyewitness cases without benefit of an eyewitness expert.

## Defense Attorneys

Consultation, workshops, presentations at meetings, and articles in attorney-oriented publications (hopefully using a minimum of psychological jargon) all help to dispense knowledge about eyewitness memory to attorneys. As with jurors, only a small fraction of attorneys will be exposed to eyewitness issues via these sources.

## Prosecutors

Prosecutors represent an important group in the justice system that could benefit greatly from exposure to eyewitness expertise. Some positive exposure does occur via workshops and published papers. However, prosecutors often have a negative response to eyewitness experts because their expertise is almost always offered by the defense to refute the evidence of prosecution witnesses (Brigham & WolfsKeil, 1983) and because they fear that giving credibility to eyewitness research findings will hinder their abilities to win cases (Wells et al., 2000). This trend could be reduced or reversed by a greater emphasis on conditions favorable to the prosecution. For example, recent arguments that better lineup procedures will make the evidence more reliable and convincing to jurors could lead prosecutors to be more interested in eyewitness identification research (Wells et al., 2000). Also, recent findings indicating that very fast identification decisions are likely to be correct (Sporer, 1994; Smith, Lindsay, & Pryke, in press) was considered of great interest to Canadian prosecutors who reported that some Canadian judges were dismissing cases because they felt that fast decisions indicated that the witness had not taken the identification task seriously (Lindsay, 2000).

## Judges

Workshops and articles in judge-oriented publications (again avoiding psychological jargon) as well as expert testimony help to inform the judiciary. Unfortunately, many judges have minimal exposure to eyewitness issues despite these sources. Obviously this problem is exacerbated when the judges choose to exclude eyewitness expertise from the courtroom.

## Law Enforcement

Law enforcement officers also are exposed to eyewitness research via consultation, workshops, presentations at meetings, and articles in law enforcement-oriented publications. As the 'front line' users of many system variables, it is critical that law enforcement be aware of the implications of using various interviewing and identification procedures. The proportion of officers exposed to the research is likely to be very small and one important task is to find ways of increasing such exposure. In a very positive development along these lines, the recent publication by the U.S. Department of Justice of guidelines on the collection and preservation of eyewitness evidence (Technical Working Group for Eyewitness Evidence, 1999) cites several research articles on eyewitness evidence and the guide is widely distributed to law enforcement in the U.S.

## BRIDGE TO THE FUTURE

### IDENTIFYING BEHAVIORAL ASSUMPTIONS IN THE LAW

Identifying behavioral assumptions in the law has been a constant source of research ideas in the eyewitness area throughout its history and particularly over the past 25 years. Researchers have tested the U.S. Supreme Court's assumptions as stated in the *Neil v. Biggers* (1972) and *Manson v. Brathwaite* (1977) cases (e.g., Wells & Murray, 1983). Surveys of assumptions and opinions of law enforcement, attorneys, and judges about identification and other eyewitness issues have demonstrated serious discrepancies between empirical research results and the expectations of various groups representing the legal system (e.g., Brigham & Wolfskeil, 1983). The following assumptions have been addressed and found to be partially or totally in error.

### Memory is Like a Videotape

Memory for events is not like a videotape. Witnesses can rarely remember all details of a person or event they have seen. Thinking back on events is not like replaying the original scene. The 'recording' can be edited after the event such that some eyewitness reports will contain information that was not part of the original event.

### Eyewitnesses Recall Accurately the Source of their Memories

Eyewitnesses frequently and systematically confuse the source of information such that an object, face, or action seen in one context may be mistakenly recalled as having been seen in a different context (D. Lindsay, 1994).

## Showups are Effective if Conducted Quickly

A showup is an identification procedure in which the eyewitness views only the suspect rather than an entire lineup. The assumption in law has been that showups are suggestive procedures, but they are reliable if the witnessed event was very recent owing to the freshness of the witness' memory. Although one early study seemed to support this assumption (Gonzalez, Ellsworth, & Pembroke, 1994), other research has shown that showups produce higher rates of mistaken identification of suspects than do properly conducted lineups even when the witnessed event was very recent (see Dekle, Beale, Elliot, Huneycutt, 1996; Lindsay, Pozzulo, Craig, Lee, & Corber, 1997; Wogalter, Marwitz, & Leonard, 1992; Yarmey, Yarmey, & Yarmey, 1996).

## Multiple Identification Procedures are Independent

Biased procedures for a mugshot search or live and photo lineup or showup can affect responses to subsequent identification procedures (e.g., live or photographic lineup; see Gorenstein & Ellsworth, 1980). Accordingly, in-court identifications might be virtually meaningless as tests of memory for the crime; instead the witness is likely to rely on the memory of the more recent lineup identification.

## Witnesses can Ignore Bias

Witnesses are not able to ignore or skip over biased interviewing or identification procedures to retrieve their original memory of the event. Biased interviewing and identification procedures routinely reduce the accuracy of witness reports and decisions. Of particular concern, biases often induce false positive reports (see Loftus 1979 for a summary of numerous studies demonstrating this problem). Similarly, biased lineups produce erroneous identifications (Lindsay, Wallbridge, & Drennan, 1987; Lindsay & Wells, 1980; Malpass & Devine, 1981).

## Defense Attorneys can Prevent Lineup Biases

Having a defense attorney present at a live or photo lineup, or videotaping the procedure, is not always helpful because lawyers do not routinely perceive and report on biases. In part, this is a result of inadequate knowledge on the part of attorneys, such that many do not recognize the sources of error present in the situation (see Cutler & Penrod, 1995).

## Cross-examination is Effective

Cross-examination may not be very effective for detecting truthfulness versus lying and is entirely ineffective for discriminating accurate from inaccurate identifications (e.g., see Lindsay, Wells, & O'Connor, 1989; Lindsay, Wells, & Rumpel, 1981; Wells, Lindsay, & Ferguson, 1979).

## Prosecutors will Minimize Bias

Prosecutors frequently fail to handle identification and non-identification evidence in an even-handed, fair manner. Even in the presence of clear evidence to the contrary, some prosecutors will pursue cases based entirely on weak, even biased identification evidence (Connors, Lundregan, Miller, & McEwan, 1996).

## Jurors understand Eyewitness Issues

Jurors lack adequate knowledge about the factors that affect eyewitness accuracy to permit informed decisions in many cases. In the absence of expert testimony, jurors will frequently decide eyewitness cases based on inaccurate expectations of eyewitness abilities and no understanding of the nature and impact of biased procedures on eyewitness reports (see Chapter 12 of Cutler & Penrod, 1995, for a review of this work).

## Non-identifications are not Informative

Witnesses frequently choose no one from a lineup because the perpetrator is not in the lineup. Witnesses choose foils from lineups much more often when the perpetrator is not in the lineup than when the perpetrator is in the lineup. Thus, the failure of a witness to identify a suspect (either by making no choice or by choosing a foil) is evidence of innocence just as identification of suspects is evidence of guilt (Lindsay, Lim, Marando, & Cully, 1986; Wells & Lindsay, 1980; Wells & Olson, 2000).

### SUGGESTIONS FOR FURTHER RESEARCH

Further research is essential in all facets of eyewitness psychology. Both system and estimator variables need to be studied in the context of event memory, finding suspects, identifying suspects, and the impact and interpretation of eyewitness evidence in court. Many principles of psychology will continue to be applied in the eyewitness area. General memory models and principles clearly must play a central role in understanding eyewitness issues. This connection can only become clearer and stronger as more research on *episodic memory* is incorporated into the mainstream of memory research. Similarly, principles of *social influence* are critical to research on witness suggestibility and juror persuasion. *Demand characteristics* appear to be as relevant to the eyewitness situation as they are to the laboratory (Wells & Luus, 1990). Our specific suggestions for issues deserving of future research are as follows:

## Nature of Events

To date the majority of evidence collected has used brief thefts as the model. How important is duration and nature of the crime to subsequent memory of the event? How much information is retained from complex versus simple crimes? Is the amount of information retained constant as the amount available increases, or do witnesses remember more as more happens?

## Better Descriptions

It would be particularly useful to develop procedures for obtaining better (more complete and accurate) descriptions of people. Descriptions are critical to the early stages of an investigation and can determine whether a case will be resolved quickly, or in some cases if the case ever will be resolved. Are descriptions of some features more likely to be accurate than descriptions of other features? If so, which features are described most/least accurately? Is the accuracy of memory for actions related to the accuracy of memory for people? Research on *verbal overshadowing* (e.g., Fallshore & Schooler, 1995; Finger & Pezdek, 1999) indicates that urging eyewitnesses to provide a full description of the perpetrator may interfere with their ability to identify him later. Future research should clarify the precise conditions under which this phenomenon occurs (see Meissner & Brigham, in press-b, for a meta-analysis).

## Eyewitness Testimony of Victims versus Bystanders

For ethical reasons it is not easy to conduct staged empirical studies where eyewitnesses are victims of crimes. As a result, the eyewitness literature speaks almost exclusively to the eyewitness testimony of bystanders to crimes (see, however, Hosch, & Cooper, 1982; Hosch, Leippe, Marchioni, & Cooper 1984). How do victims perceive, remember, and recount their eyewitness experiences? Can creative, ethically-sound methods be developed to compare victims with bystanders?

## Sources of Errors

Additional work on the sources of eyewitness errors is essential. What processes lead to eyewitness errors (e.g., source monitoring, demand characteristics, suggestion)? Under what conditions is each most likely to produce errors? What impact do drugs have on witness memory for events and people? How important are viewing conditions such as lighting and distance as determinants of witness accuracy?

## Composites

Despite some research on composite faces, many questions remain to be answered. Can people recognize targets from composites in everyday situations (i.e., when they are not explicitly looking for them)? Are witnesses who provide more detailed open-ended descriptions better at producing composites? Are witnesses who produce better composites better at identification from lineups? Do people remember these pictures if they are not in front of them?

## Wanted Posters

How effective are "wanted" posters? As with composites, do people remember these pictures if they are not in front of them? The ability to view a photo of a person's face, retain that image, and then recognize that individual in person at a later time has, to our knowledge, never been investigated empirically. Yet, this is precisely the task we are asking people to do in missing persons cases when we display posters.

## Mugshots

How difficult is it for witnesses to recognize faces seen in mug shots? Are there cross-race effects in mugshot searches? What is the impact of age of photo on the success of mugshot searches? What are the effects of viewing mugshots on subsequent performance in identification tasks? Are all mugshot sorting techniques equally effective? If not, which techniques are superior and why do they work better?

## Identifications "in-situ"

In situ identification procedures are those in which the eyewitness is taken to a location in which a suspect has been placed among people in that location (e.g., a bar, restaurant, concert). The witness is asked to walk through the location and point out the criminal if present. Are *in situ* identification procedures inherently biased? What instructions should be used with such procedures and what kinds of records (e.g., video) can be used to establish the fairness of a given in situ procedure? Are all settings equally acceptable or unacceptable for such procedures (e.g., restaurants, coffee shops, libraries, etc)?

## Showups

For various reasons related to policy considerations, showups are likely to continue to be a tool used in identifying criminal suspects (see Wells et al., 2000). Are there ways to reduce the inherent suggestiveness of such procedures? Could carefully worded instructions to the eyewitness prior to the showup reduce the risk to innocent suspects? Because similarity of clothing is commonly a factor in detaining a suspect for a showup, what role does clothing play in the showup identification process?

## Blind Identification Procedures

What is the impact of keeping the officer presenting the lineup 'blind' to the identity of the suspect? Is the impact the same for all identification procedures? How can we persuade police to adopt blind testing?

## Base Rates

Can we determine real world base-rates of target-present and target-absent lineups?

## Alternative Identification Procedures

Can useful information be obtained from identification procedures that include voice, body, and motion cues? Is it better to attempt to identify such cues from a single (live or videotaped) lineup or independently from separate lineups? Are there better ways of presenting lineups to special populations such as children or the elderly? Can we develop a better procedure for use in cases involving multiple perpetrators?

## Post-identification Procedures

Can we 'undo' procedural errors? What 'postdictors' are the most valid indicators of eyewitness accuracy (e.g., witness confidence, response latency, etc)? Are these criteria externally valid? How does the presence of other witnesses and knowledge of their decisions influence witness post-dictors such as confidence, memory for quality of the viewing conditions, perceived difficulty of the identification task, etc (co-witness effects)?

## Testimony of Eyewitnesses in Court

Are jurors' perceptions of witness credibility entirely predicted from confidence? What other factors may influence perceived credibility?

## Alibis

A credible alibi is often the only defense that an innocent person has against a mistaken identification. How difficult is it to recall where you were at a specific but arbitrary date and time? What factors influence the perceived credibility of an alibi? What impact do various forms of alibis (e.g., from family versus friends versus strangers) have on perceptions of guilt?

## Jurors' Knowledge of System Variables

We know very little about jurors' understanding of system variables as the surveys to date have concentrated mostly on estimator variable effects.

## Methods for Eyewitness Research

We view experimental studies as the best method for advancing psychological knowledge about eyewitness issues. However, a continued emphasis on ecologically valid methods is required both to enhance generalizability and to increase the impact of the research on the legal community. A balance must be maintained between experimental control and ecological validity. In addition to continued use of experimental methods, we also need field studies and research on real eyewitnesses to provide other points of comparison.

## Police Setting the Agenda

An approach that has rarely been taken so far but could lead to future success is to work with the law enforcement community on what they perceive as problems. Most research to date has been driven by researchers' (and granting agencies') agendas. As researchers' interactions with police increase, *they* are exposed to *law enforcement's* concerns about eyewitness memory. It would be a very positive step for researchers to develop and test procedures designed to resolve such concerns (e.g., procedures that will improve the quality of person descriptions or increase hit rates without increasing false alarms). Although some research has been reactive to specific police procedures (e.g., Lindsay & Bellinger, 1999), generally the topics selected for study seem to be based on the belief that police were performing poorly.

## CONCLUSION

Although it may seem a cliché, nothing succeeds like success. The prior successes of the eyewitness area produced a number of highly productive research programs. Those programs generated a literature that is now widely read within psychology and increasingly relied on by those in the criminal justice system. Student interest in the area is high, which leads to graduate applications and new generations of researchers who, instead of having to be convinced to change their research interests to include eyewitness issues, were trained in the area to start. Eyewitness researchers have achieved tremendous success in advancing knowledge of eyewitnesses and making their theory and research findings available to the legal system. Yet, the area remains ripe with avenues for investigation.

## REFERENCES

Bekerian, D., & Bowers, J. (1983). Eyewitness testimony: Were we misled? *Journal of Experimental Psychology: Learning, Memory, and Cognition, 19*, 139–145.

Bowers, J., & Bekerian, D. (1984). When will postevent information distort eyewitness testimony? *Journal of Applied Psychology, 69*, 466–472.

Binet, A. (1905). La science du termoignage. *L'Annee Psychologique, 11*, 128–137.

Brigham, J. C., & Bothwell, R.K. (1983). The ability of prospective jurors to estimate the accuracy of eyewitness identifications. *Law and Human Behavior, 7*, 19–30.

Brigham, J. C., Meissner, C. A., & Wasserman, A. W. (1999). Applied issues in the construction and expert assessment of photo lineups. *Applied Cognitive Psychology, 13*, S73–S92.

Brigham, J. C., & Pfeifer, J. E. (1994). Evaluating the fairness of lineups. In D. F. Ross, J. D. Read, & M. P. Toglia (Eds.), *Adult eyewitness testimony: Current trends and developments* (pp. 201–222). Cambridge: Cambridge University Press.

Brigham, J. C., & Ready, D. J. (1985). Own-race bias in lineup construction. *Law and Human Behavior, 9*, 415–424.

Brigham, J. C., Wasserman, A. W., & Meissner, C. A. (1999). Disputed eyewitness evidence: Important legal and scientific issues. *Court Review, 36*(2), 12–25.

Brigham, J. C., & WolfsKeil, M. P. (1983). Opinions of attorneys and law enforcement personnel on the accuracy of eyewitness identifications. *Law and Human Behavior, 7*, 337–349.

Brooks, N. (1983). *Pretrial eyewitness identification procedures: Police guidelines*. Ottawa: Law Reform Commission of Canada.

Buckhout, R., Alper, A., Chern, S., Silverberg, G., & Slomovits, M. (1974). Determinants of eyewitness performance on a lineup. *Bulletin of the Psychonomic Society, 4*, 191–192.

Buckhout, R., Figueroa, D., & Hoff, E. (1975). Eyewitness identification: Effects of suggestion & bias in identification from photographs. *Bulletin of the Psychonomic Society, 6*, 71–74.

Connors, E., Lundregan, T., Miller, N., & McEwan, T. (1996). Convicted by juries, exonerated by science: Case studies in the use of DNA evidence to establish innocence after trial. Alexandria, VA: National Institute of Justice.

Cutler, B. L., & Penrod, S. D. (1995). *Mistaken identification: The eyewitness, psychology, and the law*. New York: Cambridge University Press.

Cutler, B. L., Penrod, S. D., & Martens, T. K. (1987). The reliability of eyewitness identification: The role of system and estimator variables. *Law and Human Behavior, 11*, 233–258.

Deffenbacher, K. A., & Loftus, E. F. (1982). Do jurors share a common understanding concerning eyewitness behavior? *Law & Human Behavior, 6*, 15–30.

Dekle, D. J., Beale, C. R., Elliot, R., & Huneycutt, D. (1996). Children as witnesses: A comparison of lineup versus showup identification methods. *Applied Cognitive Psychology, 10*, 1–12.

Fallshore, M., & Schooler, J. W. (1995). The verbal vulnerability of perceptual expertise. *Journal of Experimental Psychology: Learning, Memory, & Cognition, 21*, 1608–1623.

Finger, K., & Pezdek, K. (1999). The effect of cognitive interview on face identification: Release from verbal overshadowing. *Journal of Applied Psychology, 84*, 340–348.

Geiselman, R. E., Fisher, R. P., MacKinnon, D., & Holland, H. (1985). Eyewitness memory enhancement in the police interview: Cognitive retrieval mnemonics versus hypnosis. *Journal of Applied Psychology, 70*, 401–412.

Geiselman, R. E., Fisher, R. P., MacKinnon, D., & Holland, H. (1986). Enhancement of eyewitness memory with the cognitive interview. *American Journal of Psychology, 99*, 385–401.

Gonzalez, R., Ellsworth, P. C., & Pembroke, M. (1994). Misidentifications and failures to identify in lineups and showups. *Journal of Personality and Social Psychology*.

Gorenstein, G. W., & Ellsworth, P. C. (1980). Effect of choosing an incorrect photograph on a later identification by an eyewitness. *Journal of Applied Psychology, 65*, 616–622.

Goodman-Delahunty, J. (in press). Cross-race face identification by eyewitnesses. *Psychology, Public Policy, and Law*.

Grisso, T., & Saks, M. J. (1991). Psychology's influence on constitutional interpretation: A comment on how to succeed. *Law & Human Behavior, 15*, 205–211.

Hosch, H. M., & Cooper, D. S. (1982). Victimization as a determinant of eyewitness accuracy. *Journal of Applied Psychology, 67*, 649–652.

Hosch, H. M., Leippe, M. R., Marchioni, P. M., & Cooper, D. S. (1984). Victimization, self-monitoring, and eyewitness identification. *Journal of Applied Psychology, 69*, 280–288.

Koehnken, G., Milne, R., Memon, A., & Bull, R. (1999). The cognitive interview: A meta-analysis. *Psychology, Crime, & Law, 5*, 3–27.

Leippe, M. R. (1995). The case for expert testimony about eyewitness memory. *Psychology, Public Policy, and Law, 1*, 909–959.

Leippe, M. R., Romanczyk, A., & Manion, A.P. (1991). Eyewitness memory for a touching experience: Accuracy differences between child and adult witnesses. *Journal of Applied Psychology, 76*, 367–379.

Lindsay, D. S. (1994). Memory source monitoring and eyewitness testimony. In D. F. Ross, J. D. Read, & M. P. Toglia (Eds.), *Adult eyewitness testimony: Current trends and developments* (pp.27–55). New York: Cambridge University Press.

Lindsay, R. C. L. (1994). Expectations of eyewitness performance: Jurors' verdicts do not follow from their beliefs. In D. F. Ross, J. D. Read, & M. P. Toglia (Eds), *Adult eyewitness testimony*. Cambridge University Press: New York.

Lindsay, R. C. L. (1999). Applying applied research: Selling the sequential lineup. *Applied Cognitive Psychology, 13*, 219–225.

Lindsay, R. C. L. (2000, July). Eyewitness evidence. Workshop presented at the Ontario Crown Attorney's Office Annual Retreat, London, Ontario.

Lindsay, R. C. L., & Bellinger, K. (1999). Alternatives to the sequential lineup: The importance of controlling the pictures. *Journal of Applied Psychology, 84*, 315–321.

Lindsay, R.C.L., Lim, R., Marando, L., & Cully, D. (1986). Mock-juror evaluations of eyewitness testimony: A test of metamemory hypotheses. *Journal of Applied Social Psychology, 16*, 447–459.

Lindsay, R. C. L., Pozzulo, J., Craig, W., Lee, K., & Corber, S. (1997). Simultaneous lineups, sequential lineups, and showups: Eyewitness identification decisions of adults and children. *Law and Human Behavior, 21*, 391–404.

Lindsay, R. C. L., Ross, D. F., Smith, S. M., & Flanigan, S. (1999). Does race influence measures of lineup fairness? *Applied Cognitive Psychology, 13*(SI), S109–S119.

Lindsay, R. C. L., Wallbridge, H., & Drennan, D. (1987). Do the clothes make the man? *Canadian Journal of Behavioural Science, 19*, 463–478.

Lindsay, R. C. L., & Wells, G. L. (1980). What price justice? Exploring the relationship of lineup fairness to identification accuracy. *Law & Human Behavior, 4*, 303–313.

Lindsay, R. C. L., & Wells, G. L. (1985). Improving eyewitness identification from lineups: Simultaneous versus sequential lineup presentation. *Journal of Applied Psychology, 70*, 556–564.

Lindsay, R. C. L., Wells, G. L., & O'Connor, F.J. (1989). Mock-juror belief of accurate and inaccurate eyewitnesses: A replication and extension. *Law and Human Behavior, 13*, 333–339.

Lindsay, R. C. L., Wells, G. L., & Rumpel, C.M. (1981). Can people detect eyewitness identification accuracy within and across situations? *Journal of Applied Psychology, 66*, 79–89.

Loftus, E. F. (1979). *Eyewitness testimony*. Cambridge, MA: Harvard University Press.

Luus, C. A. E., & Wells, G. L. (1991). Eyewitness identification and the selection of distracters for lineups. *Law and Human Behavior, 15*, 43–57.

Maass, A., & Kohnken, G. (1989). Eyewitness identification. Simulating the "weapon effect". *Law and Human Behavior, 13*, 397–408.

Malpass, R. S., & Devine, P. G. (1981). Eyewitness identification: Lineup instructions and the absence of the offender. *Journal of Applied Psychology, 66*, 482–489.

Malpass, R. S., & Lindsay, R. C. L. (1999). Measuring lineup fairness. *Applied Cognitive Psychology, 13*(SI), S1–S7.

Manson v. Brathwaite, 432 U.S. 98, 112, 97 S. Ct. 2243, 2252, 53 L. Ed. 2d 140 (1977).

McCloskey, M., & Zaragoza, M. (1985). Misleading postevent information and memory for events: Arguments and evidence against memory impairment hypotheses. *Journal of Experimental Psychology: General, 114*, 1–16.

Meissner, C. A., & Brigham, J. C. (in press a). Thirty years of investigating the own-race bias in memory for faces: A meta-analytic review. *Psychology, Public Policy, and Law*.

Meissner, C. A., & Brigham, J. C. (in press b). A meta-analysis of the verbal overshadowing effect in face identification. *Applied Cognitive Psychology*.

Melton, G. B. (1992). The law is a good thing (psychology is, too): Human rights in psychological jurisprudence. *Law & Human Behavior, 16*, 381–398.

Munsterberg, H. (1908). *On the witness stand: Essays on psychology and crime*. New York: Clark Boardman.

Murray, D., & Wells, G. L. (1982). Does knowledge that a crime was staged affect eyewitness performance? *Journal of Applied Social Psychology, 12*, 42–53.

Neil v. Biggers, 409 U.S. 188, 93 S. Ct. 375; 34 L. Ed. 2d 401 (1972).

Ng, W. J., & Lindsay, R. C. L. (1994). Cross-race facial recognition: Failure of the contact hypothesis. *Journal of Cross-Cultural Psychology, 25*, 217–232.

Poole, D. A., Lindsay, D. S., Memon, A., & Bull, R. (1995). Psychotherapy and the recovery of memories of childhood sexual abuse: U.S. and British practitioners' opinions, practices, and experiences. *Journal of Consulting and Clinical Psychology, 63*, 426–437.

Powers, P., Andriks, J., & Loftus, E. (1979). Eyewitness accounts of females and males. *Journal of Applied Psychology, 64*, 339–347.

Pozzulo, J. D., & Lindsay, R. C. L. (1998). Identification accuracy of children versus adults: A meta-analysis. *Law and Human Behavior, 22*, 549–570.

Pozzulo, J. D., & Lindsay, R. C. L. (1999). Eliminating the innocent: Enhancing the accuracy and credibility of child witnesses. *Journal of Applied Psychology. 84*, 167–176.

Rahaim, G. L., & Brodsky, S. L. (1982). Empirical evidence versus common sense: Juror and lawyer knowledge of eyewitness accuracy. *Law & Psychology Review, 7*, 1–15.

Raskin, D. C., & Esplin, P. W. (1991). Assessment of children's statements of sexual abuse. In J. Doris (Ed.), *The suggestibility of children's recollections* (pp. 153–164). Washington, D.C.: American Psychological Association.

Ruby, C. L., & Brigham, J. C. (1997). The usefulness of the Criteria-Based Content Analysis technique in distinguishing between truthful and fabricated allegations: A critical review. *Psychology, Public Policy, and Law, 3*, 705–737.

Shaw, J. S. III, Garcia, L. A., & McClure, K. A. (1999). A lay perspective on the accuracy of eyewitness testimony. *Journal of Applied Social Psychology, 29*, 52–71.

Slone, A. E., Brigham, J. C., & Meissner, C. A. (2000). Social and cognitive factors affecting the own-race bias in Whites. *Basic and Applied Social Psychology, 22*, 71–84.

Smith, S. M., Lindsay, R. C. L., & Pryke, S. (in press). Postdictors of eyewitness errors: Can false identifications be diagnosed? *Journal of Applied Psychology.*

Sporer, S. L. (1994). Decision times and eyewitness identification accuracy in simultaneous and sequential lineups. In D. F. Ross, J. D. Reid, & M. P. Tolia (Eds.), *Adult eyewitness testimony* (pp. 300–327). New York: Cambridge University Press.

Sporer, S. L. (1996). Psychological aspects of person descriptions. In S. L. Sporer, R. S. Malpass, & G. Koehnken (Eds.), *Psychological issues in person identification* (pp. 53–86). Mahwah, NJ, USA: Erlbaum.

Sporer, S. L. (1996). Describing others: Psychological issues. In S. L. Sporer, R. S. Malpass, & G. Koehnken (Eds.), *Psychological issues in person identification* (pp. 53–86). Mahwah, NJ: Erlbaum.

Steblay, N. M. (1992). A meta-analytic review of the weapon focus effect. *Law and Human Behavior, 16*, 413–424.

Stern, L. W. (1910). Abstracts of lectures on the psychology of testimony. *American Journal of Psychology, 21*, 273–282.

Technical Working Group for Eyewitness Evidence (1999). *Eyewitness evidence: A guide for law enforcement.* Washington, DC: United States Department of Justice, Office of Justice Programs.

Tollestrup, P. A., Turtle, J. W., & Yuille, J. C. (1994). Actual victims and witnesses to robbery and fraud: An archival analysis. In D. F. Ross, J. D. Read, & M. P. Toglia (Eds.), *Adult eyewitness testimony.* Cambridge: Cambridge University Press.

Wells, G. L. (1978). Applied eyewitness testimony research: System variables and estimator variables. *Journal of Personality and Social Psychology, 36*, 1546–1557.

Wells, G. L. (1984). The psychology of lineup identifications. *Journal of Applied Social Psychology, 14*, 89–103.

Wells, G. L. (1993). What do we know about eyewitness identification? *American Psychologist, 48*, 553–571.

Wells, G. L., & Lindsay, R. C. L. (1980). On estimating the diagnosticity of eyewitness non-identifications. *Psychological Bulletin, 88*, 776–784.

Wells, G. L., Lindsay, R. C. L., & Ferguson, T. J. (1979). Accuracy, confidence, and juror perceptions in eyewitness identification. *Journal of Applied Psychology, 64*, 440–448.

Wells, G. L., & Luus, E. (1990). Police lineups as experiments: Social methodology as a framework for properly-conducted lineups. *Personality and Social Psychology Bulletin, 16*, 106–117.

Wells, G. L., Malpass, R. S., Lindsay, R. C. L., Fisher, R. P., Turtle, J. W., & Fulero, S. (2000). Eyewitness research: The long road to National guidelines. *American Psychologist, 55*, 581–598.

Wells, G. L., & Murray, D. M. (1983). What can psychology say about the *Neil v. Biggers* criteria for judging eyewitness accuracy? *Journal of Applied Psychology, 68*, 347–362.

Wells, G. L., & Olson, E. A. (2000). The informational value of eyewitness responses to lineups: Incriminating versus exonerating evidence. Manuscript under editorial review.

Wells, G. L., Rydell, S. M., & Selau, E. P. (1993). The selection of distractors for eyewitness lineups. *Journal of Applied Psychology, 78*, 835–844.

Wells, G. L., Small, M., Penrod, S., Malpass, R. S., Fulero, S. M. & Brimacombe, C. A. E. (1998) Eyewitness identification procedures: Recommendations for lineups and photospreads, *Law and Human Behavior, 22*, 603–647.

Whipple, G.M. (1911). The psychology of testimony. *Psychological Bulletin, 8*, 307–309.

Wigmore, J. H. (1909). Professor Munsterberg and the psychology of evidence. *Illinois Law Review, 3*, 399–345.

Wogalter, M. S., Marwitz, D. B., & Leonard, D. C. (1992). Suggestiveness in photospread lineups: Similarity induces distinctiveness. *Applied Cognitive Psychology, 6*, 443–453.

Wright, D. B., & McDaid, A. T. (1996). Comparing system and estimator variables using data from real lineups. *Applied Cognitive Psychology, 10*, 75–84.

Yarmey, A. D., & Jones, H. P. T. (1983). Is the psychology of eyewitness identification a matter of common sense? In S. Lloyd-Bostock & B. R. Clifford (Eds.), *Evaluating witness evidence: Recent psychological research and new perspectives* (pp. 13–40). Chichester, England: Wiley.

Yarmey, A. D., Yarmey, M. J., & Yarmey, A. L. (1996). Accuracy of eyewitness identifications in showups and lineups. *Law and Human Behavior, 20*, 459–477.

Yuille, J., & Cutshall, J. (1986). A case study of eyewitnesses' memory of a crime. *Journal of Applied Psychology, 71*, 291–301.

# 8

# Jurors and Juries

## A Review of the Field

### EDITH GREENE, SONIA R. CHOPRA,
### MARGARET BULL KOVERA,
### STEVEN D. PENROD, V. GORDON ROSE,
### REGINA SCHULLER, AND
### CHRISTINA A. STUDEBAKER

JURORS AND JURIES: A REVIEW OF THE FIELD

Angel Maturino Resendiz, a rail-riding Mexican drifter, confessed to killing nine people and pleaded not guilty by reason of insanity but a Texas jury convicted Resendiz of capital murder and sentenced him to death. Former Louisiana governor Edwin Edwards was also tried by a jury and convicted of extorting nearly $3 million from companies that

EDITH GREENE • Department of Psychology, University of Colorado, Colorado Springs, Columbia 80933    SONIA R. CHOPRA • Department of Psychology, Simon Fraser University, Burnaby, British Columbia, Canada V5A 1S6.    MARGARET BULL KOVERA • Florida International University, North Miami, Florida 33181.    STEVEN D. PENROD • Department of Psychology, John Jay College of Criminal Justice, The City University of New York, New York, New York 10019-1199.    V. GORDON ROSE • Program in Law and Forensic Psychology, Simon Fraser University, Burnaby, British Columbia, Canada V5A 1S6.    REGINA SCHULLER • Department of Psychology, York University, Toronto, Ontario, Canada M3J 1P3.    CHRISTINA ANN STUDEBAKER • Research Division, Federal Judicial Center, Washington, DC 20002.

applied for riverboat-casino licenses. An Australian judge aborted a murder retrial because he feared that jurors in that case would be prejudiced by information about the defendant's previous trial available on a popular and controversial internet site. Finally, a Miami jury determined that cigarettes caused the diseases of three Florida smokers and awarded $6.9 million to two of the smokers. This constituted the first time a jury found on behalf of smokers in a class action lawsuit.

In each of these well-watched trials and in hundreds of thousands of other cases decided out of the glare of the limelight each year, common people become jurors and pass judgment on their fellow citizens. It is an experience unlike any other; requiring a roomful of strangers to process complex, confusing, and contradictory evidence, understand and apply the appropriate law, and collectively reach resolution about the issues being contended. It is also an experience that is ideal for scholarly inquiry: How do jurors evaluate evidence? On what basis are their decisions made? How do the formal proceedings of a trial enhance or impair their decision making capabilities? How do individuals reason collectively and reach consensus on these weighty and complicated issues? In what ways, if any, should the system be reformed to increase the likelihood of reasonable and defensible verdicts?

Although only a small proportion of legal disputes are ultimately resolved by jury trial, still thousands of such cases are decided by juries each year and predictions about how juries would decide cases influence decisions to settle civil lawsuits and to accept plea-bargains in criminal cases. Thus, jury trials assume a role of central importance in the law. As such, they have captured the attention of cognitive and social psychologists who, through the application of psychological theory and research methods, are able to lend an empirical perspective to our understanding of what jurors and juries do. In the phraseology of one commentator, such scholarly inquiry can "open the black box" of the deliberation room to reveal the complex cognitive and social processes at work in this setting (MacCoun, 1993). The psycholegal analysis of juror and jury decision making has the dual capability of testing and refining psychological theory as it applies to the real-world context of a courtroom and simultaneously, of providing a scientific look at the assumptions the law makes about the behavior of jurors and juries.

In this chapter, we provide both retrospective and prospective looks at the field of juror and jury research. We review the literature as it pertains to jury selection, the influence of evidence, judicial instructions, and deliberations on jurors' decisions. We describe various models of juror and jury decision making. We comment on the early history of work in this field and concerns about its legal relevance, and provide a close look at several important methodological issues. Finally, casting our eyes to the future, we discuss the move to reform aspects of jury trials to enhance the experience for jurors, describe emerging and novel areas of research, and voice lingering concerns about our ability to communicate these findings to the legal system.

This review is necessarily selective; in the course of its preparation we were struck by the quantity and diversity of jury-related research, particularly work that has been completed in recent years. Thus, a number of important and well-crafted studies have no doubt been omitted. But it was not our intention to be exhaustive. Rather, we hope that this overview will highlight important milestones, findings, trends, and lingering issues in this exciting and burgeoning field.

## A REVIEW OF WHAT WE KNOW

### JURY SELECTION

At the beginning of each trial, attorneys, judges, or both question potential jurors in an attempt to reveal whether they have any biases that will hamper their ability to render a fair decision. *Voir dire* is the process by which jurors are excused from jury service. Attorneys may challenge a juror for cause if during questioning, the juror exhibits a bias that will prevent him or her from hearing the case fairly. Attorneys must state an explicit reason for this type of challenge and for a juror to be excused using this method, the judge must approve the challenge. Attorneys may also use a limited number of peremptory challenges to eliminate jurors whom they believe to be unfavorable without providing a justification for the challenge.[1] The underlying premises of *voir dire* are that jurors have identifiable characteristics that will influence their decision in a case, that attorneys know which juror characteristics will predict their verdicts, and that the removal of jurors with these characteristics will result in higher quality jury deliberations and verdicts. Below, we review the empirical research addressing the underlying premises of voir dire.

### ARE JUROR CHARACTERISTICS RELATED TO VERDICT?

Researchers have found few demographic characteristics that consistently predict juror verdicts. In one of the earliest investigations of this topic, Simon (1967) found that juror occupation, gender, income, religion,

---

[1]There are certain limitations to peremptory challenges; a juror may not be excused solely because of his or her race (*Batson v. Kentucky*, 1986; *Edmonson v. Leesville Concrete Co.*, 1991; *Georgia v. McCollum*, 1992, *Powers v. Ohio*, 1991) or gender (*J.E.B. v. Alabama, ex rel T.B.*, 1994). Attorneys may be asked to explain their justification for exercising a peremptory challenge if the judge suspects they are excusing jurors based on their race or gender.

and age did not significantly predict verdicts across two different cases. However, the ability of juror gender to predict verdict appears to be case-specific. For example, Simon (1967) found that women were more likely to convict a defendant of incest than were men. Other research supports the finding that women may be more likely to convict in cases involving sexual crimes against women and children (e.g., Bottoms & Goodman, 1994; Brekke & Borgida, 1988; Kovera, Levy, Borgida, & Penrod, 1994; Kovera, Gresham, Borgida, Gray, & Regan, 1997). Researchers have also shown that the effects of juror race tend to depend on the particulars of the case being tried (Brigham & Wasserman, 1999; Nietzel & Dillehay, 1986; Simon, 1967). One of the few demographic variables that has been shown to be a significant predictor of verdict is juror education, in part because it is related to antilibertarian attitudes (Moran, Cutler, & Loftus, 1990).

Are jurors' personality characteristics any more predictive of verdict than are their demographic characteristics? A meta-analysis of the literature correlating authoritarian personality with verdict suggests that authoritarian jurors are significantly more likely to convict than jurors who are less authoritarian (Narby, Cutler, & Moran, 1993). If one considers a specific type of authoritarian personality, legal authoritarianism, the relationship between this personality characteristic and verdict is even stronger (Narby et al., 1993). Researchers have also demonstrated that the personality characteristic of "belief in a just world" (Lerner, 1970) predicts verdict, although it can lead jurors to either derogate crime victims or harshly punish defendants (Gerbasi, Zuckerman, & Reis, 1977; Moran & Comfort, 1982).

Juror attitudes have been a somewhat more fruitful method of predicting verdicts. For example, Moran, Cutler, and DeLisa (1994) demonstrated that juror attitudes toward tort reform predicted verdicts in three different criminal cases. Attitudes appear to be especially good predictors of juror verdicts when the attitudes are related to the specific issues involved in a case. Researchers have shown that attitudes toward women predict verdicts in rape cases (Weir & Wrightsman, 1990), attitudes toward psychiatrists and the insanity defense predict verdicts when the defendant claims insanity as a defense (Cutler, Moran, & Narby, 1992), and attitudes toward drugs predict verdicts in a controlled substance trial (Moran et al., 1990). A recent meta-analysis of the death qualification literature suggests that there is a small but reliable correlation between attitudes toward the death penalty and verdict (Nietzel, McCarthy, & Kern, 1999). Moreover, researchers have demonstrated this relationship in both trial simulations (Cowan, Thompson, & Ellsworth, 1984) and actual cases (Moran & Comfort, 1986). In a rare exception, attitudes toward eyewitnesses did not predict verdicts in a case involving eyewitness evidence (Narby & Cutler, 1994).

Of course, outside events may influence jurors' case-specific attitudes prior to trial. Specifically, media coverage of the crime, the defendant, or the impending trial may influence jurors' attitudes about the guilt or innocence of a particular defendant. In two surveys of potential jurors in real cases, Moran and Cutler (1991) demonstrated that jurors' knowledge of pretrial publicity was positively correlated with perceptions of defendant guilt. As jurors' knowledge of the media coverage surrounding the case increased, so did their beliefs that the defendants had committed the crimes with which they had been charged. Moreover, knowledgeable jurors were unaware of their bias. Trial simulation studies have also demonstrated that jurors who have been exposed to pretrial publicity are more likely to find the defendant guilty at trial (Dexter, Cutler, & Moran, 1992; Kramer, Kerr, & Carroll, 1990; Ogloff & Vidmar, 1994; Otto, Penrod, & Dexter, 1994)

## DOES JURY SELECTION IDENTIFY BIASED JURORS?

Research suggests that attorneys may not be particularly skilled at identifying jurors who might be biased against their client. Olczak, Kaplan, & Penrod (1991) provided attorneys with demographic information about jurors who had previously participated in a trial simulation. Therefore, the researchers had information about their verdict choice in a particular case. A sample of attorneys was asked to play the role of the defense attorney in that case. After they read the facts of the case and the demographic information for each of 36 possible jurors, the attorneys indicated 12 jurors who would be acceptable for a jury and 12 whom they would exclude. The attorneys were more likely to make incorrect decisions (i.e., reject jurors who had acquitted the defendant and accept jurors who had convicted the defendant) than correct decisions based on the available demographic information. In a more ecologically valid simulation in which attorneys watched videotapes of a voir dire, attorneys were still unable to reliably predict which jurors would be biased against them (Kerr, Kramer, Carroll, & Alfini, 1991).

Research on voir dire in actual trials has presented a more optimistic view of attorneys' abilities to exclude biased jurors. Diamond and Zeisel (1974) arranged for 10 criminal cases to be tried in the presence of three juries: a jury chosen at random from the jury pool, a jury consisting of jurors who had been challenged and excused in that case, and the actual jury seated in the trial. The real juries were more likely to acquit than the other juries. This difference may have been caused by the real juries' knowledge that their decision would result in a real defendant going to prison rather than the attorneys' success in identifying jurors who would treat the defendant fairly. Analysis of the jurors' predeliberation ballots, however, did reveal that defense attorneys were successful in eliminating more jurors who would have convicted their client than those who would have acquitted their client. Prosecuting attorneys were also relatively successful in their identification of jurors who would acquit the defendant.

Analysis of voir dire in four felony trials also suggests that attorneys excuse jurors who are most biased against their side (Johnson & Haney, 1994). As indicated by jurors' scores on a legal authoritarianism measure, defense attorneys use their peremptory challenges to excuse jurors who are the most biased against the defendant. Similarly, prosecutors use their peremptory challenges to excuse the most defense-oriented jurors. The overall authoritarianism score of the jurors who were seated in these cases, however, did not significantly differ from the overall score of the first 12 jurors called for jury duty or from a randomly chosen group of 12 jurors. So although attorneys can identify jurors who will be biased against their side (Diamond & Zeisel, 1974; Johnson & Haney, 1994), excusing these people from jury service may not produce a jury that has noticeably different attitudes than a jury chosen through more expedient means (Johnson & Haney, 1994).

All of these studies of voir dire effectiveness have examined the ability of attorneys to identify biased jurors. Does the use of social science methods increase the probability that biased jurors will be excused from jury duty? Research comparing traditional jury selection methods based on attorneys' intuitions and implicit personality theories to scientific jury selection suggests that neither method is superior in all cases (Horowitz, 1980). A more extended voir dire may increase the predictive validity of scientific jury selection (Moran et al., 1994).

## DOES THE JURY SELECTION PROCESS PRODUCE BETTER JUROR DECISIONS?

Very few studies have examined whether the jury selection process actually results in better jury decisions. Once can infer from the results of the Johnson and Haney (1994) study of felony voir dire that the jury selection process will not improve juror decisions. If the jury is just as biased after jury selection as it would have been without this process, how can the voir dire process improve juror decisions? Perhaps voir dire could improve juror decisions without altering the composition of the jury. Some have argued that a nondirective voir dire could be used to persuade jurors to follow the laws of due process (Middendorf & Luginbuhl, 1995).

Is it possible that mere exposure to the voir dire process itself could improve juror decisions? In one study (Dexter et al., 1992), researchers manipulated whether jurors went through an extended voir dire in which the defense attorney reminded the jurors to be objective and to ignore pretrial publicity or a minimal voir dire. In addition, some jurors were exposed to pretrial publicity whereas others were not. Although the extended voir dire did cause jurors to find the defendant less culpable, the extended voir dire did not eliminate the biasing effect of pretrial publicity on juror verdicts (Dexter et al., 1992). There is also some evidence that voir dire can increase juror bias in certain types of cases. Specifically, jurors who watched a voir dire in which jurors were questioned about their attitudes toward the death penalty were more likely to convict a defendant and were more likely to render a death sentence than were jurors who did not view a death qualification procedure (Haney, 1984). Thus, there is little evidence to support the proposition that jury selection improves juror decision making and there is some evidence that it may even harm the quality of their decisions.

## The Influence of Evidence on Juror Decisions

Research regarding the influence of evidence on juror decisions has generally taken the following developmental path. First, researchers design studies that examine whether a particular type of evidence influences juror decisions. Second, researchers investigate whether jurors can differentiate between good evidence and poor evidence. Finally, if the research demonstrates that jurors are unable to make decisions that appropriately weight the evidence under consideration, researchers begin to explore whether there are legal remedies available to help jurors make better decisions. Below, we provide some examples of more mature research areas (e.g., research on eyewitness and expert testimony) in which data from all three research phases exist and an area of research that is in earlier stages (e.g., research on hearsay evidence).

## EYEWITNESS TESTIMONY

Eyewitness identifications clearly influence juror decisions. Early research demonstrated that jurors are more likely to convict a defendant if an eyewitness identifies him as the perpetrator than if there is only circumstantial evidence to implicate him in the crime (Loftus, 1974). Moreover, the eyewitness identification increased convictions even when jurors learned that the witness had been discredited, for instance when jurors heard that the eyewitness had very poor eyesight and was not wearing glasses at the time of the crime.

Not only do eyewitness identifications influence juror decisions; they influence juror decisions irrespective of the witnessing conditions. Cutler and his colleagues (Cutler, Penrod, & Dexter, 1990; Cutler, Penrod, & Stuve, 1988) conducted several trial simulations in which they manipulated the conditions under which the eyewitness viewed the perpetrator and identified the suspect. Jurors' perceptions of defendant culpability and identification accuracy were not influenced by a variety of factors that influence the accuracy of eyewitness identifications, including weapon focus, a disguised perpetrator, and the violence involved in the crime. Jurors were also insensitive to the effects of improper lineup instructions, mugshot searches, and biased choice of lineup foils on identification accuracy. Indeed, despite the extremely small relationship between eyewitness accuracy and confidence, witness confidence was the only variable that reliably influenced juror judgments.

Are there methods we could use to sensitize jurors to the factors that influence the reliability of eyewitness identifications? Research suggests that an expert witness for the defense who testifies about the factors influencing eyewitness identifications increases juror sensitivity to those factors (Cutler, Dexter, & Penrod, 1989; Cutler, Penrod, & Dexter, 1989). Specifically, jurors who hear this testimony find the defendant more culpable when the eyewitness identification is made under good witnessing conditions than when the identification is made under poor conditions. Moreover, these jurors' judgments of defendant culpability are not influenced by witness confidence. The benefits of this type of adversarial expert testimony seem to be eliminated if the prosecution offers their own expert to rebut the testimony of the defense expert. In at least one study, opposing expert testimony caused jurors to become skeptical about all eyewitness identifications, even those made under good witnessing conditions (Cutler & Penrod, 1995). The expert testimony of a nonadversarial expert witness also appears to be ineffective at sensitizing jurors to the factors they should consider when evaluating the reliability of eyewitness evidence. Instead, it causes jurors to be skeptical of all identifications (Cutler, Dexter, & Penrod, 1990). Finally, two studies have demonstrated that judicial instruction on the factors associated with reliable eyewitness identifications neither sensitizes jurors to these factors nor causes them to be skeptical of all eyewitnesses (Cutler, Dexter, & Penrod, 1990; Greene, 1988).

## EXPERT EVIDENCE

Numerous empirical studies have shown that expert evidence influences jury decisions. Jurors provided with expert evidence on the factors that increase the likelihood of false identifications viewed eyewitness identifications with more skepticism than did jurors who did not hear expert testimony (Fox & Walters, 1986). Mock jurors who heard expert evidence on battered woman syndrome were less likely to convict a woman who has killed her abusive partner than were jurors who did not hear this evidence (Schuller, 1992; Schuller & Cripps, 1998; Schuller & Hastings, 1996). Expert evidence can also increase conviction rates. Jurors who hear expert evidence on rape trauma syndrome are more likely to convict a defendant of rape (Brekke & Borgida, 1988), and jurors who hear expert testimony about child sexual abuse are more likely to convict a defendant accused of child molestation (Kovera et al., 1994). The effects of expert testimony are stronger when the testimony provides an explicit link between the research described in the expert testimony and the case facts (concrete or specific testimony; Brekke & Borgida, 1988; Fox & Walters, 1986; Schuller, 1992) and when it is presented earlier in the trial (Brekke & Borgida, 1988; Schuller & Cripps, 1998). In addition to influencing juror verdicts, concrete expert testimony appears to sensitize jurors to important factors to consider when considering the reliability of other evidence (Cutler, Dexter, & Penrod, 1989; Cutler, Penrod, & Dexter, 1989; Kovera et al., 1997).

Thus, research demonstrates that expert testimony has a small but reliable effect on juror decisions (Nietzel et al., 1999). Although the expert psychological evidence in the above studies was generally based on valid research (cf., Kovera et al., 1994), it is probable that unreliable expert testimony is admitted in court (Kovera & McAuliff, in press). Can jurors discriminate between valid research presented by experts and junk science? Results of two studies suggest that jurors will have difficulty making these distinctions. In a trial simulation that utilized a videotaped trial, variations in the construct validity of the expert's research did not influence undergraduate participants' judgments of witness credibility or their verdict (Kovera, McAuliff, & Hebert, 1999). Further research with actual jurors demonstrated that expert testimony describing studies containing a confound, missing a control group, or having the potential for experimenter cueing effects is just as influential as valid research (McAuliff & Kovera, 1999a, 1999b). Only jurors who were dispositionally predisposed to enjoy thinking (i.e., were high in Need for Cognition) adjusted their evaluations of the expert testimony and other trial participants when the expert's research failed to include the appropriate control group. But even these highly motivated jurors did not notice the other flaws.

The Supreme Court has suggested that cross-examination, the presentation of contradictory information, and judicial instruction on the burden of proof will help jurors recognize flawed scientific evidence if it is mistakenly admitted in court (*Daubert v. Merrell Dow Pharmaceuticals, Inc.*, 1993). Research is just beginning to examine whether procedural safeguards such as these can help jurors recognize flawed expert evidence when they confront it. Early efforts suggest that cross-examination does not make jurors more skeptical of expert evidence (Kovera et al., 1994; 1999). However, at least one study suggests that it also does not help jurors become more sensitive to variations in the methodological quality of research presented by an expert (Kovera et al., 1999). Schuller and Paglia (1999) report more encouraging results from their study of the effects of expert testimony on juror decisions in a homicide trial. They found that jurors were less likely to rely on an expert opinion based on hearsay evidence that was not corroborated by other evidence at trial than on expert opinion based on hearsay that was corroborated.

## HEARSAY EVIDENCE

Hearsay evidence is a statement made by one person (the witness) about a statement made by another person (the declarant) outside of court (Federal Rules of Evidence, 1984). Because the declarant is generally not available for cross-examination, the courts are concerned that the witness's report of the declarant's statement may be deliberately or unintentionally inaccurate and that jurors' decisions will be unduly influenced by this unreliable information. Therefore, this type of evidence regularly is excluded from trial (Park, 1987). However, there are many exceptions to the routine exclusion of hearsay, including spontaneous utterances and deathbed statements (Federal Rules of Evidence, 1984). Some evidence scholars have argued that because jurors regularly evaluate the credibility of secondhand information in their everyday lives, they are capable of judging the reliability of hearsay evidence; therefore, this type of evidence should be admitted at trial (Park, 1987).

Empirical research suggests that concerns about the influence of hearsay evidence on juror judgments may be unnecessary. Trial simulation studies using written transcripts (Landsman & Rakos, 1991; Rakos & Landsman, 1992) or audiotaped trial stimuli (Paglia & Schuller, 1998) suggests that hearsay evidence does not influence juror verdicts. In the most realistic study examining the effect of hearsay evidence on juror judgments, participants witnessed a simulated theft of a computer (Miene, Park, & Borgida, 1992). Witnesses were interviewed in the presence of another person who became a hearsay witness. Miene and colleagues created four different versions of a criminal trial in which they manipulated the presence of hearsay testimony and the presence of eyewitness testimony. Consistent with the findings of earlier research, the presence of hearsay evidence did not increase the likelihood that jurors would convict the defendant. Studies that have manipulated the presence of cautionary instructions that routinely accompany the presentation of hearsay evidence at trial find that jurors are not influenced by hearsay evidence, irrespective of the presence of these instructions (Paglia & Schuller, 1998; Rakos & Landsman, 1992). Only one study has found any effect of hearsay evidence on juror judgments (Schuller, 1995). It is possible that these findings differ from previous research because in this study, an expert witness rather than a lay witness presented the hearsay evidence.

Because they question the reliability of hearsay evidence, some evidence scholars may be reassured by the findings that hearsay has little to no impact on juror decisions. However, it should be even more desirable for jurors to be able to differentiate between reliable and unreliable hearsay evidence. Preliminary evidence suggests that jurors may be up to this task. Kovera, Park, and Penrod (1992) created a hearsay simulation in which eyewitnesses first viewed a videotaped event and then, after varying delays, responded to questions during a videotaped interview. Hearsay witnesses viewed one of these eyewitness interviews and then responded to questions during a videotaped interview conducted either one day or one week after they had viewed the eyewitness interview. Both types of witnesses were more accurate if there were shorter delays between witnessing the event and the subsequent interview. Confirming the results of earlier research (Cutler, Penrod, & Stuve, 1990), mock jurors who viewed these interviews were unable to distinguish between accurate and inaccurate eyewitnesses. However, jurors found the testimony of good hearsay witnesses to be more accurate, more useful and of higher quality the testimony of poor hearsay witnesses. It is unclear from this study how jurors made these distinctions and whether their evaluations of the hearsay witness would have influenced their verdicts at trial because these data were not collected. Further research is needed to determine under what conditions jurors can discriminate between good and poor quality hearsay evidence and whether any legal procedures are necessary to assist jurors in making these distinctions.

## JUDICIAL INSTRUCTIONS

One issue that seems to have been resolved to the general satisfaction of researchers, if not of the courts, is the difficulty that jurors have understanding and using legal instructions. Research from as early as 1935 suggested that juries often fail to follow instructions because they fail to understand them (see Elwork & Sales, 1985). Empirical research suggests that jurors may not comprehend a significant portion of the information presented in judicial instructions (Charrow & Charrow, 1979; Elwork, Sales & Alfini, 1982; Hastie, Penrod, & Pennington, 1983; Kerr & Bray, 1982; Ogloff, 1998; Rose & Ogloff, 1998; Severance & Loftus, 1982; Steele & Thornburg, 1988). Comprehension is often as low as 50% for the pattern instructions in use in various American states (Elwork & Sales, 1985). Strawn and Buchanan (1976) showed participants a 25-minute video of pattern jury instructions in a burglary case. Only 57% of the participants believed that circumstantial evidence was "legal" or sufficient for a conviction, whereas 23% felt that, when confronted with two equally reasonable scenarios (one suggesting guilt and the other innocence), the accused should be convicted. Only half of participants understood that the accused had no onus to disprove guilt, and only a quarter of them believed that they must disregard out-of-court statements by an accused.

Examination of actual jury trials does little to dispel the notion that jurors do not typically understand jury instructions. Severance and Loftus (1982) found that nearly one quarter of the 405 jurors they sampled had asked for clarification of their instructions, on issues of "intent" and "reasonable doubt." Steele and Thornburg (1988), interviewing former jurors, found that "about a third or more of the juries disagree about the meaning of the instructions, but most of those come to accommodation among themselves about the meaning of those instructions before reaching a verdict" (p. 98). Similarly, a study of Michigan citizens called for jury duty suggests that actual jurors instructed in real cases understood fewer than 50% of the instructions they received (Reifman, Gusick, & Ellsworth, 1992).

Comprehension of jury instructions is particularly problematic in capital cases in which juries are charged with the important duty of determining whether a defendant should be sentenced to death. Penalty phase instructions in many states instruct jurors to consider mitigating and aggravating factors associated with the commission of the crime when deciding whether to sentence a defendant to death (Diamond, 1993). However, research suggests that even after hearing penalty phase instructions, jurors cannot provide reasonable definitions of the terms "aggravating" and "mitigating" nor can they correctly classify circumstances as mitigating or aggravating (Haney & Lynch, 1994, 1997). Perhaps even more troubling is the finding that jurors have more difficulty understanding the concept of a mitigating factor (i.e., a circumstance that would suggest the death penalty should not be imposed) than the concept of an aggravating factor (Haney & Lynch, 1994, 1997). Attempts to improve juror comprehension of penalty phase instructions by rewriting them in non-technical language have met with mixed success (Wiener, Pritchard, & Weston, 1995). Moreover, a failure to understand penalty phase instructions is correlated with a willingness to impose the death penalty (Wiener et al., 1995).

Some authors have argued that jury instructions are fundamentally flawed because they fail to recognize that jurors are active processors of information (Diamond, 1993; Wiener et al., 1995). Jurors have preconceptions about the law before they enter the courtroom and these preconceptions influence how they view trial evidence (Smith, 1991, 1993). Because jury instructions do not address these sometimes mistaken preconceptions, jurors may be doomed to make decisions that are at odds with the law.

One of the methodological criticisms of simulation research on the effectiveness of jury instructions is that the experimental unit in such studies is typically the juror, not the jury. Critics argue that the group deliberation process improves comprehension. Hastie et al. (1983) found that group comprehension of criminal jury instructions was about 80%, as compared to about 30% for individuals, and Greene and Johns (in press) showed that deliberation can also enhance jurors' understanding of civil negligence instructions. On the other hand, some researchers maintain that deliberation does not eliminate legal misunderstanding, and even the best numbers show that group comprehension is far from perfect (Elwork & Sales, 1985; Reifman et al., 1992). Some research has gone beyond a simple numerical comparison of individuals and groups. Hartwick, Sheppard, and Davis (1982) demonstrated that relative to individuals, groups do not tend to make fewer errors of omission but do make more errors of commission.

One issue that researchers still dispute is the appropriate way to measure comprehension of instructions. Many researchers have used a "paraphrase" test (e.g., Charrow & Charrow, 1979; Steele & Thornburg, 1988), in which subjects restate the law as they understand it and researchers score the statements for accuracy (Charrow & Charrow, 1979). This approach suffers from many problems. For instance, Steele & Thornburg (1988) found that the most common response on their paraphrase test was "no response." Thus, the paraphrase test fails to distinguish between a lack of ability to recall the instruction and a lack of understanding. Severance and Loftus (1982) have argued for an "application test" that measures a juror's ability to *apply* the law as instructed to a fact pattern. This test measures something more closely approximating what real jurors are required to do and can easily provide information about the specific aspects of instructions that are or are not well understood by participants (Rose & Ogloff, 1998).

Although some authorities suggest rewriting instruction to improve comprehension (Elwork, Sales, & Alfini, 1977; Kagehiro, 1990; Kerr & Bray, 1982; Severance & Loftus, 1982), others claim that rewording instructions results in little, if any, improvement (Charrow & Charrow, 1979; Steele & Thornburg, 1988). Tanford's (1992) review of the literature suggests that even on rewritten instructions, error rates on comprehension tasks remain as high as 75%. He argues that if the law itself is incomprehensible, as often seems to be the case, rewriting will never render the instructions on the law understandable. Other strategies suggested to improve juror performance include providing jurors with written copies of the instructions and repeated instruction to the jury over the course of the trial (e.g., Sales et al., 1977; Greene & Johns, in press), jury note-taking, and so on. The literature does not offer unequivocal support for any of these remedies, however, and generally suggests that none of them produce much of an improvement (e.g., Charrow & Charrow, 1979; Heuer & Penrod, 1988, 1989; Ogloff, 1998).

## Jury Deliberations

On the basis of Kalven and Zeisel's now classic study (1966), as well as numerous jury simulations (e.g., see Davis, 1980; MacCoun & Kerr, 1988; Stasser, Kerr, & Bray, 1982; Zeisel & Diamond, 1978), we know that the initial verdict preferences among the jurors are highly predictive of the final jury verdict. The tendency of individuals to become more extreme in their initial positions following group discussion, a phenomenon first identified by social psychologists in the 1970s, seems to well capture the jury's task, as long as we make a slight modification. For criminal trials, the simple "majority" decision rule must be modified to incorporate what has been referred to as the leniency bias (MacCoun & Kerr, 1988; Kerr, MacCoun, & Kramer, 1996). That is, although the majority tends to prevail, the standard of guilt beyond a reasonable doubt in criminal trials results in a bias that favors the accused: proacquittal factions appear more influential than proconviction factions, and when a clear majority does not prevail, verdicts are more likely to result in acquittals than in convictions.

As the verdict is a group product, however, it is clear that the nature and quality of the deliberations that takes place among the jurors are likely to play a significant role in the outcome of the decision. These more subtle influences and pressures that are operative at this group level are less well understood. Moreover, some recent evidence tends to suggest that the preferences expressed by the jurors in their first ballot are not necessarily equivalent to the jurors' predeliberation opinions. By interviewing actual jurors, Sandys and Dillehay (1995) found that in the majority of cases, considerable discussion had occurred among the jurors before their first verdict poll was ever taken.

At a very general level of analysis, Hastie et al. (1983) identified two broad styles that juries tend to adopt when confronting their task.

Although some juries, referred to as verdict driven juries, begin their deliberations with an initial verdict poll, others, referred to as evidence driven, begin their deliberations with a focus on the evidence. In this latter style of deliberation, the emphasis is on story construction and polls or the expression of verdict preferences do not occur until much later into the deliberations. Experimental studies have demonstrated that such discussion can alter the actual outcome of the initial verdict distribution (e.g., Davis, Kameda, Parks, Stasson, & Zimmerman, 1989). Thus, although it is fair to say that the verdict distribution of the group on the first ballot is a good predictor of the final verdict, the distribution of votes on the first ballot is not necessarily veridical with predeliberation preferences (Sandys & Dillehay, 1995).

The study of jury behavior, like small group research more generally, has focused to some extent on two group processes; normative and informational influence. Although both forms of influence are used to reach unanimity, they produce very different outcomes. Informational influence produces private acceptance (i.e., conversion) whereas normative influence elicits public agreement (i.e., compliance) (e.g., see Smith & Kassin, 1993). It is useful to consider these two sources of social influence when we consider how variations in the structure of the jury task can influence the jury's decision making process.

Research on jury size (e.g., 6 vs. 10 or 12) and decision rule (unanimity vs. majority) is a case in point. During the 1970s, the U.S. Supreme Court addressed both the issue of jury size (*Williams v. Florida*, 1970; *Ballew v. Georgia*, 1978) and decision rule (*Johnson v. Louisana*, 1972; *Apodaca et al. v. Oregon*, 1972), ruling in both instances that modifications to the jury (i.e., reduction in size, nonanimous decisions) would not adversely affect the decision making process. These rulings spurred a flurry of research activity. Not surprisingly, both of these structural aspects of the jury's task have been found to affect the deliberation process in a number of important ways.

Taken in their entirety, studies examining the effects of jury size demonstrate that six member juries—in contrast to 12 member juries—tend to be less representative of the community, recall fewer aspects of the evidence, spend less time deliberating, and are less likely to declare themselves hung (Kerr & MacCoun, 1985; Nemeth, 1981; Saks, 1977; Zeisel, 1971; for a review see Saks & Marti, 1997). Thus, although smaller juries may arrive at quicker decisions, they are less likely to represent minority positions than are 12 member juries. And, in addition to the decreased variability in the perspectives, evidence suggests that the smaller the group, the greater the pressure on a dissenting member to conform (Saks & Marti, 1997).

Similarly, a number of differences in the nature and quality of the jurors' deliberations have been found as a function of the decision rule assigned to the jury, with juries assigned to a majority, as opposed to a unanimous, decision rule, discussing both the evidence and the law less thoroughly, and taking less time to arrive at a decision (Hastie et al., 1983). Moreover, members of small factions in the majority decision rule juries are less likely to express themselves and less satisfied with the jury verdict, compared to members of small factions in unanimous juries. Thus, similar to the concerns associated with 6-member juries, majority decision rules result in quicker decision.

Although we are aware of some of the general group processes that are operative in the jury, in terms of theoretical models of *jury* behavior (as opposed to *juror* behavior), the field is far less developed. In 1977, Gerbasi et al., in their review of the field, noted the limited attention that the "jury as a group" had received. Since this early review of jury research, others have similarly lamented this limitation (e.g., Diamond, 1997), and it was again recently echoed in a meta-analysis that examined the state of the field (Nietzel et al., 1999). Yet, it is the group—not the individual—that renders the final verdict, and the question of how the jury as a group decision making body performs its function is crucial. The complex relationship between the jurors' predeliberation verdict preferences and the final group verdict highlights the importance of studying the jury as a group and the need for further theoretical developments in this area (e.g., see Kerr et al., 1996).

## DECISIONS ABOUT DAMAGES

Much of what we know about juries comes from studies of criminal cases. Fortunately, the results of these studies (e.g., on comprehension of jury instructions, the effects of jury size, jurors' use of extra-evidentiary information) often generalize to civil juries (MacCoun, 1993). Increasingly, though, psychologists have turned their attention to decision making by jurors and juries in civil cases and to the issues unique to those lawsuits. In this section, we review the research on how jurors make decisions about damages, an issue that is uniquely "civil".

Unlike criminal juries, civil juries determine penalties for wrongdoing in the form of damage awards.[2] Critics have been quick to blame juries for

---

[2]Damage awards are generally of two types. Compensatory damage awards are intended to compensate for both economic (e.g., lost wages, medical costs) and noneconomic (e.g., pain and suffering) losses. Punitive damage awards, assessed much less frequently, are intended to punish the defendant and deter the defendant and others from similar conduct in the future.

a host of perceived ills in the civil justice system, including a general trend toward verdicts in favor of highly sympathetic plaintiffs and damage awards of astronomical sizes (for a review of these criticisms, see Daniels & Martin, 1995; Vidmar, 1995). In fact, there is no evidence of an increase in the frequency of plaintiffs' verdicts (Hans, 1996; Vidmar, 1998) and although a small number of large damage awards have increased the mean awards for some types of cases, median compensatory damage awards have not increased (Gross & Syverud, 1996). Nonetheless, the media are quick to inform us about cases that result in lavish damage awards (Bailis & MacCoun, 1996), such as the $81 million awarded to the family of a retired school janitor who died of lung cancer after smoking cigarettes for forty years. (The jury reasoned that both the janitor, Jesse Williams, and the defendant, Phillip Morris Company, were at fault.) Partly as a result of this attention by the media, critics have questioned jurors' abilities to reason competently when assessing damages. What do we really know about jurors' and juries' capabilities in this realm?

Many recent studies have focused on factors influencing the size and variability of damage awards (Anderson & MacCoun, 1999; Cather, Greene, & Durham, 1996; Diamond & Casper, 1992; Feigenson, Park, & Salovey, 1997; Hastie, Schkade, & Payne, 1999; Raitz, Greene, Goodman, & Loftus, 1990; Robbennolt & Sobus, 1997; Robbennolt & Studebaker, 1999; Saks, Hollinger, Wissler, Evans, & Hart, 1997; Wissler, Evans, Hart, Morry, & Saks, 1997; Zickafoose & Bornstein, 1999) since this topic has received much attention in the legal field, including cases before the U.S. Supreme Court (*BMW of North America v. Gore*, 1996; *TXO Production Corp. v. Alliance Resources Corp.*, 1993). What have we learned from this work?

The severity of the plaintiff's injury is a consistent predictor of compensatory damage awards (Feigenson et al., 1997; Vidmar, 1995; Wissler et al., 1997). The finding that people with smaller losses receive less compensation and those with greater losses receive more compensation is termed "vertical equity" (Wissler et al., 1997). This is good news; the bad news is the existence of "horizontal *in*equity": there are large differences in awards for seemingly similar injuries. Wissler and her colleagues asked whether these inequalities reflect differences in the perceptions of harm associated with the injuries, differing monetary valuations on similarly-perceived harms, or the use of improper considerations (e.g., nature of case, characteristics of litigants) by jurors assessing damages for pain and suffering. The results of their jury simulation study showed that awards were far from random, rather, they were strongly affected by the perceived severity and duration of the harm suffered by the plaintiff. Moreover, jurors and judges evaluate injuries in remarkably similar ways (Wissler, Hart, & Saks, 1999). For both groups, the extent of perceived disability and mental suffering were the strongest predictors of overall severity judgments and awards. This finding calls into question the assertion that jurors lack the ability to intelligently evaluate injuries and assess compensation. On both tasks, jurors were nearly indistinguishable from judges (Wissler et al., 1999).

Although outcome severity is the only legally relevant factor in damages assessments, some recent work suggests that awards may also be influenced by the perceived fault of the litigants. Contrary to the law's intentions, jurors sometimes conflate judgments of damages with those of responsibility (Robbennolt, in press). For example, Greene, Johns, & Smith (in press) varied the conduct of the *defendant* in a simulated automobile negligence case and found that conduct evidence influenced jurors' and juries' awards. In post-trial interviews with actual jurors, Vidmar (1995) found that jurors discussed defendants' admissions of liability in their deliberations on damages.

Others (Feigenson et al., 1997; Wissler, Kuehn, & Saks, in press; Zickafoose & Bornstein, 1999) have shown that the conduct of the *plaintiff* also matters. This research demonstrates the phenomenon of "double discounting": jurors tend to discount their awards to reflect their sentiments about the plaintiff's role in causing an accident and the judge then further reduces the award to account for the plaintiff's responsibility.

On occasion, damage awards are influenced by the perceived status of the defendant, although not, apparently, by perceptions the defendant's wealth (the so-called "deep pockets effect"). Corporate defendants are made to pay more than individual defendants because jurors apparently find it easier to impose sanctions against an impersonal entity and hold corporations to higher standards of conduct than individuals (Hans & Ermann, 1989; MacCoun, 1996).

Concerns about excessive and unpredictable damage awards have produced a variety of proposed and enacted reforms in the ways that jurors' decisions are structured. The reforms include imposing a statutory cap or ceiling on non-economic and punitive damages, raising the burden of proof related to damages, and limiting the evidence to which jurors are exposed when they determine damage awards. In recent years, psychologists have begun to empirically examine the effects of these reforms.

In their evaluation of the effects of caps on noneconomic damages, Saks et al. (1997) found that, rather than reducing the variability in awards, caps actually increased award variability in cases that involved low- and medium-severity injuries. In the realm of punitive damages, Robbennolt and Studebaker (1999) have shown that when the cap on punitive damages was relatively high, mock jurors made larger and *more* variable punitive damage awards than did jurors whose awards were not capped. Restricting punitive awards apparently has other unintended consequences: mock jurors in two studies inflated their compensatory awards when they had no option to award punitive damages (Anderson & MacCoun, 1999; Greene, Coon, & Bornstein, 2000). Taken together, these studies suggest that caps may not be the solution to large and variable damage awards.

Some commentators (e.g., Ghiardi & Kircher, 1995) had suggested that evidence regarding the defendant's reckless or malicious conduct and his financial status may prejudice jurors' thinking about compensatory damages owed to the plaintiff and further, that compensatory evidence (e.g., the severity of the plaintiff's injury) can inappropriately influence punitive judgments. According to these arguments, bifurcation is necessary to avoid prejudice. Data are mixed on whether bifurcation is effective. Although one recent study (Greene, Woody, & Winter, 2000) showed that mock jurors did not improperly consider punitive damages evidence in their decisions about compensation, another study (Robbennolt & Studebaker, 1999) showed that bifurcation reduced the impact of compensatory evidence on punitive damage awards.

More generally, these findings offer little support to the critics who decry jurors' judgments about damages. Jurors are apparently not swayed by sympathy for injured plaintiffs or against deep pocket defendants. Jurors appropriately attend to evidence about outcome severity although they also factor considerations related to responsibility into their calculations of damages. Jurors apparently do not use punitive damages evidence inappropriately. Finally, because of the opportunity to deliberate as a group, jurors may have an important advantage over the alternative decision maker—the judge (Vidmar, 1998). The combined judgment of jurors, enhanced through the process of deliberation, may render verdicts that are far more rational and predictable than the media and some legislators would lead us to expect.

## DECISION MAKING IN COMPLEX CIVIL CASES

Psychologists have also begun to evaluate claims that some cases, primarily complex civil cases, may be too complicated for laypersons to decide due to the length of trial, the highly technical nature of some evidence, and the sometimes arcane questions of law that are involved. Studies of decision making in complex civil cases have involved both simulation methodology and interviews.

The picture that emerges from a series of analogue studies conducted by Horowitz and his colleagues is of a jury whose abilities and verdicts are significantly impacted by nuances in trial procedure. They have shown, for example, that preinstructed jurors made more appropriate distinctions among multiple plaintiffs with differing degrees of injury than did jurors who were instructed after the evidence (ForsterLee, Horowitz, & Bourgeois, 1993); that access to a trial transcript focused jurors' attention on relevant evidence (Bourgeois, Horowitz, & ForsterLee, 1993); and that complex language influenced jurors' abilities to appropriately compensate plaintiffs who suffered injuries of varying severities (Horowitz, ForsterLee, & Brolly, 1996).

In their interviews of jurors in four complex cases and their analysis of the deliberations of "research juries" (jurors who sat through the trial and deliberated on videotape at the trial's conclusion), a committee of the ABA Litigation Section (1990) concluded that although jurors sometimes felt confused, bored, and alienated during the trial, their deliberations resulted in defensible verdicts. Finally, Lempert (1993) systematically examined the reports of twelve complex trials including those studied by the ABA Committee and concluded that on balance, jurors' verdicts were justified.

None of these findings suggest that jurors are inherently unable to decide complex cases. Rather, they suggest that judges need to structure complex trials in ways that are conducive to jurors' understanding. More broadly, they underscore Ellsworth's (1999) contention that before assuming that jurors are governed by their hearts, we should consider the possibility that the justice system does little to encourage the intelligent use of their minds.

## MODELS OF JUROR AND JURY DECISION MAKING

The question of how jurors and juries evaluate and integrate the complex and contradictory array of evidence presented at trial in order to arrive at a verdict has been of considerable theoretical interest to psychologists for some time (Ellsworth & Mauro, 1998). Indeed, since the 1970s, several models of juror decision making have been proposed and, with varying success, empirically tested. A comprehensive review of these models can be found in a collection of chapters edited by Hastie (1993a).

These models fall into one of two camps—the mathematical and the explanation-based approaches. In terms of the mathematical approaches, Hastie (1993b) outlines three types of models: 1) probability theory approaches (e.g., Schum & Martin, 1993), 2) algebraic approaches (e.g., Anderson, 1981; see Hastie, 1993b), and 3) stochastic process model approaches (e.g., Kerr, 1993). Within each of these approaches, jurors are conceptualized as performing a series of "mental" calculations in which the relevance and implications of the various pieces of evidence are translated into an assessment of guilt (e.g., a probability estimate). Although the models differ with respect to the manner in which the evidence is tracked, combined, and weighted by the juror (e.g., weighted averaging, sequential averaging) the outcome of these calculations is a judgment about guilt or innocence, or as Hastie has characterized it, a reading on a "mental meter" that represents the jurors' state of belief regarding the guilt or innocence of the defendant. The outcome of this calculation or "reading" on the meter is then compared to a decision criterion for a determination of guilt. Although these models are quite sophisticated, their ability to generate specific predictions has been limited because of the underlying assumption that pieces of evidence can be conceptualized as unitary and discrete entities with inherent value (Ellsworth & Mauro, 1998; Hastie 1993b). As the more recent conceptualizations of juror decision making clearly suggest, this assumption is not supported.

In contrast to the mathematical modeling approaches, explanation-based conceptualizations of the jurors' task have emphasized the jurors' cognitive organization or representation of the evidence (Bennett & Feldman, 1981; Pennington & Hastie, 1986). The most theoretically advanced of the explanation-based approaches is the Story Model developed by Pennington and Hastie (1986). Within this approach, the jurors' mental representation of the evidence is conceptualized in terms of a "narrative" structure in which the causal and intentional relations between the various pieces of evidence presented at trial are organized into a coherent whole or story (Pennington & Hastie, 1986; 1988). After the judge provides jurors with the legal instructions explaining the relevant law (e.g., what the prosecution must prove for the accused to be found guilty) and the verdict options (e.g., second degree murder, manslaughter) the decision process then involves the jurors' attempts to find the best fit or match between the story constructed and one of the verdict categories provided by the judge (e.g., murder, manslaughter, not guilty).

What is perhaps most noteworthy in this approach and others that adopt an explanation-based type of approach (e.g., see Diamond & Casper, 1992; Ellsworth, 1993) is the emphasis on the juror as an active participant in the evaluation and interpretation of the trial information. Rather than viewing the juror as a passive recipient who merely records the information presented at trial for later analysis, the juror, in his or her attempt to understand the meaning of the evidence, is engaged in an "active, constructive comprehensive process in which evidence is organized, elaborated, and interpreted" (Pennington & Hastie, 1993, p. 194). As such, the Story Model elucidates quite eloquently why particular interpretations may be derived from the evidence presented at trial and also why different individuals exposed to the same trial information and format may arrive at different verdict decisions. For instance, with respect to the former, alterations in the context and structure of the task itself may result in different verdict decisions.

Along these lines, Pennington and Hastie (1988) conducted a study in which they manipulated the ease with which a particular story could be abstracted from the trial testimony by altering the presentational format of the evidence presentation. They found that the easier it was for an individual to construct a particular story from the trial evidence (i.e., because it closely followed the chronological order of the alleged events), the more likely it was that a verdict consistent with that story was rendered. In short, pieces of evidence derived their meaning from the context in which they were embedded—the other evidence. This overarching conceptualization of juror decision making has strong intuitive appeal and has been extremely useful for understanding how jurors perform their task. For instance, predictions about the effects of joinder on criminal charges, limiting instructions, expert testimony, and variations in the timing of testimony and instructions (to name but few variables that jury researchers have studied, see generally, Nietzel et al., 1999) can readily be generated and tested within this approach.

Also noteworthy in the explanation-based approaches is the recognition that jurors do not arrive at the courthouse as blank slates but rather, with a host of beliefs, attitudes, and experiences that they draw upon to interpret the meaning of the evidence. Since jurors are not all in agreement when they enter their deliberations after hearing the same trial evidence, individual differences can clearly play a role as well. Why, on the basis of the evidence does one juror see a story consistent with guilt, while another sees a story consistent with innocence? Jurors' story interpretations are derived not only from the trial evidence, but also from their factual and social knowledge of the world—beliefs, attitudes, and experiences that they bring with them into the courtroom.

## HOW WE KNOW WHAT WE KNOW

Research examining juror and jury decision making has evolved in many ways over the past forty years. The legal relevance of the questions has been significantly enhanced and, although generally similar methods have been used over the years (Bornstein, 1999), there has been a shift towards stronger research methods. The field has advanced in both breadth and depth as growing numbers of researchers have contributed to the growing volume of completed studies. Not only have new research areas been addressed (e.g., the recent emergence of studies of civil juries) but we now have programmatic research on several issues (e.g., jury instructions, pretrial publicity) and are witnessing increased use of meta-analytic summaries of research—something that is only possible when a sufficient number of inter-related studies is available.

## EARLY HISTORY OF JURY RESEARCH

The earliest systematic and inter-related set of studies on the jury can be traced to the University of Chicago Jury Project of the 1950s and 1960s headed by Harry Kalven and Hans Zeisel (Broeder, 1958). This law-sociology collaboration produced a number of early empirical studies which undoubtedly inspired many aspiring researchers (e.g., Broeder, 1958; James, 1958; Strodtbeck, James, & Hawkins, 1957; Strodtbeck & Mann 1956) and the project yielded Kalven and Zeisel's important and enduring volume on *The American Jury* (1966).

Despite this impressive groundbreaking work that could serve as a strong foundation for future research, the field of juror and jury research has suffered from an identity crisis over the years. Is it a subset of social psychology, a subset of cognitive psychology, or a separate area of psychology that stands on its own? Is it basic research or applied research? Should it be conducted within a controlled laboratory or in the field? Is its purpose and focus to advance psychological theory or legal theory or to simply aid the courts? Although an appropriate response may be "all of the above," it is a rare individual study that is able to address all of these issues. More importantly, it is not clear that individual studies should address every issue. Rather, each study should be evaluated in terms of the question(s) being addressed and the fit between the research question and the approach to addressing that question. Jury research as a whole benefits from a variety of approaches.

The roots of the juror/jury research identity crisis can be easily understood once the history of the research is examined. Although the American legal system and jury trials predate the formal study of psychological processes by hundreds of years (and the related British common law and jury systems are several hundred years older), the empirical examination of juror and jury behavior was not recognized as an independent area of psychological research until relatively recently (i.e., the 1970s). Consequently, early research was often forced to fit into the established areas of cognitive psychology and social psychology. This was not difficult because the encoding and processing of trial evidence and other information such as pretrial publicity and judge's instructions by individual jurors is undeniably a cognitive task, and jury deliberation is undeniably a group process involving social interaction among jury members.

However, the forced fit did cause problems. Because traditional psychology places a high premium on basic research designed to test and advance theories and less value on research that applies theories (or merely applies psychological research methods to real-world contexts), early researchers in the field likely were rewarded (at least in the form of journal publication and other common scholarly rewards) for examining, or at least emphasizing, theoretical issues.

As psychologists began to enter the jury research arena in the 1970s, their research largely reflected topics of contemporary research interests in social and cognitive psychology—particularly, attitudes, stereotyping, information processing and group processes. (For detailed reviews of early jury research see Davis, Bray, & Holt, 1977; Erlanger, 1977; Gerbasi et al., 1977 and the volume edited by Kerr and Bray, 1982.) For example, several studies examined the influence of juror attitudes, personality characteristics or demographics on guilt judgments (e.g., Mitchell & Byrne, 1973; Reed, 1965, Reed & Reed, 1977; Wolfgang & Reidel, 1973). Race and attractiveness of victims and defendants were also common topics of early research (e.g., Landy & Aronson, 1969; Nemeth & Sosis, 1973; Sigall & Ostrove, 1975). In addition, group processes of jury deliberation received substantial attention—as reflected in the research conducted by Strodtbeck and his colleagues which examined the influence of juror status on participation during deliberation as well as fellow jurors' receptivity to arguments (James, 1959; Hawkins, 1961; Strodtbeck et al., 1957; Strodtbeck & Mann, 1956).

Given that the majority of this research was published in psychology journals, it can be assumed that it was judged to be relevant to the field of psychology. The legal relevance of that psychological research, however, was low. Not only did the questions generally lack importance to the legal field, but the methods that were used significantly limited the generalizability of research findings to the practice of law. Some researchers may have dismissed the importance of legal relevance at the time, arguing that the purpose of their research was theory testing rather than application. But, as Weiten and Diamond pointed out in their review of early jury simulation studies, researchers "have generally not been very timid about discussing practical implications" despite typically "provid[ing] some caveat that their findings are merely suggestive regarding the practical realities of jury functioning" (1977, p. 75).

## BRINGING ATTENTION TO LEGAL RELEVANCE

Low legal relevance of early studies is not surprising when one considers that most of the researchers were trained and working in the social sciences rather than the law. In addition, it is unlikely that their peers, who were responsible for evaluating and reviewing the research, had any legal training either. But the ability to explain the low legal relevance of early research does not serve as an excuse for continued oversight or ignorance of that aspect in future work. Jury researchers recognized this fact and began learning more about the legal system—specifically, examining jury processes as they operate in the real world—and then began integrating that knowledge into their research. By the late 1970s and early 1980s, collaborative work involving psychologists (or sociologists) and lawyers and individuals with dual training was increasing noticeably (e.g., Buchanan, Pryor, Taylor, & Strawn, 1978; Elwork et al., 1977; Kairyo, Schulman, & Harring, 1975; Padawer-Singer & Barton, 1975; Penrod & Hastie, 1979; Sales, Elwork, & Alfini, 1977; Suggs, & Sales, 1978; Thompson, Cowan, Ellsworth, & Harrington, 1984). It was during this era that dual training programs in psychology and law originated.

An important step in educating individuals about legal relevance as it applied to research questions and the methods used to study those questions was the 1979 publication of a special issue of *Law and Human Behavior* devoted to the topic of simulation and the law. The issue contained extensive critiques of jury simulation research, including discussion of inadequate sampling of jury-eligible community members as participants, inadequate trial simulations (e.g., the presentation of brief written trial summaries rather than videotaped mock trials, the lack of any procedure resembling voir dire), inappropriate dependent measures (e.g., measures of recommended punishment rather than guilt, the omission of dichotomous judgments of guilt), lack of jury deliberations, and participants' awareness that their decisions had no real-world consequences (Bray & Kerr, 1979; Weiten & Diamond, 1979).

For several reasons, these critiques were instrumental in raising consciousness about factors that might influence the quality of jury research. First, they were authored by psychologists doing active research in the field, not lawyers or legal academics whose criticisms could have been dismissed or discounted by arguing that "they don't understand how empirical research is conducted." Second, they appeared as part of a special issue, thereby emphasizing the importance of addressing these problems. And third, they appeared in *Law and Human Behavior*, which had been established just two years earlier as a journal devoted to research integrating issues of psychology and law. Equal importance was attributed to conducting quality research and being able to apply it to real-world legal contexts. If jury researchers wanted their work to be taken seriously in the legal field, they could no longer ignore these criticisms.

## Psychology and Law Becomes Its Own Field

With the initiation of its own journal in 1977 and its own division within APA in 1981 the field of psychology and law (and consequently juror and jury research) began establishing its own standards for research. Applied research was just as important as basic research, aiding and informing the courts was as worthy a goal as advancing psychological theory, and external and ecological validity concerns could not be minimized. With these new standards, the look of jury and juror research began to change.

### Areas of Research

Of course, some studies examining topics such as juror attitudes and personality characteristics and defendant attractiveness still appeared after the 1979 special issue of *Law and Human Behavior*, but they gradually became less common. Increasing attention was given to topics that were squarely rooted in the law. For example, from the mid-1970s to the mid-1980s questions about the impact of jury size and decision rules on jury decisions were addressed by a number of researchers, as described above. Other topics beginning to receive attention were juror decision making in capital cases and the effects of excluding jurors who opposed the death penalty from the guilt phase of the proceedings (Bronson, 1970; Cowan et al., 1984; Haney, 1984; Jurow, 1971; Luginbuhl & Middendorf, 1989; Neises & Dillehay, 1987), models of juror and jury decision making (Kaplan, 1983; Tanford & Penrod, 1983; Pennington & Hastie, 1981, 1986, 1988; Penrod & Hastie, 1979, 1980), jurors' understanding of standards of proof (Dane, 1985; Kagehiro & Stanton, 1985; MacCoun, 1984), the influence of opening statements on juror verdicts (Pyszczynski, Greenberg, Mack, & Wrightsman, 1981), the influence of different insanity standards on verdict decisions (Blunt & Stock, 1985; Finkel, Shaw, Bercaw, & Koch, 1985), and factors influencing juror evaluation of eyewitness testimony (Deffenbacher, 1980; Wells & Leippe, 1981; Wells, Lindsay, & Ferguson, 1979).

The breadth of jury research obviously increased after psychology and law became its own field, but the growth and diversification occurred mainly in the area of criminal law. Although some of the earliest studies involved civil jury issues (Broeder, 1959; Eakin, 1975; Nemeth, 1977; Strodtbeck et al., 1957; Thomas & Hogue, 1976; Zeisel & Callahan, 1963), systematic research in the civil arena did not begin until the 1990s. Currently, as described above, civil jury research is experiencing an increase in breadth and depth similar to that observed in criminal jury research in the 1980s.

Although legal relevance has become an important criterion by which juror and jury research is evaluated, the application of psychological theories to legal contexts still occurs. For example, psycholinguistic principles have been applied in revisions to jury instructions to examine the effect on juror comprehension of the instructions (Elwork et al., 1977; Severance & Loftus, 1982), Bayes' theorem has been applied as an educational tool to help jurors evaluate statistical evidence (Faigman & Baglioni, 1988), persuasion theory has been used as a framework to predict jurors' responses to expert testimony (Kovera et al., 1999), and manipulations based on the principles of anchoring and hindsight bias have been included in several recent studies concerning the determination of civil damage awards (Casper, Benedict, & Perry, 1989; Greene et al., in press; Hastie et al., 1999; Robbennolt & Studebaker, 1999).

MEDIATIONAL PROCESSES. Once the occurrence of a phenomenon has been reliably demonstrated, advances are made by attempting to understand why it occurs and whether there are any limitations to the conditions under which it occurs. This information can play a crucial role in guiding proposed changes to the legal system and directions for future research. For example, the negative effects of pretrial publicity on guilt judgments about a defendant have been well demonstrated (see Studebaker & Penrod, 1997 for a review), but data concerning mediating mechanisms such as attributions about a defendant's credibility and trustworthiness (Greene & Dodge, 1995; Otto, Penrod, & Dexter, 1994) or evaluations of evidence are just beginning to be examined. Other research on mediational processes has shown that evidence (as compared to extralegal factors) strongly influences juror decision making (Visher, 1987) and that the articulation of multiple interpretations of evidence during jury deliberations impedes the reaching of a unanimous verdict (Holstein, 1985). To more fully understand juror and jury decision making, more attention needs to be given to mediational processes.

META-ANALYSIS. In addition to applied research and more traditional theory-driven research, meta-analytic research on juror and jury topics has also begun to emerge. To date, meta-analyses of research examining jury size (Saks & Marti, 1997), the influence of juror death penalty attitudes on verdicts (Allen, Mabry, & McKelton, 1998; Nietzel et al., 1999), and the influence of pretrial publicity on guilt judgments about a defendant (Steblay, Besirevic, Fulero, & Jimenez-Lorente, 1999) have been published. Nietzel et al. (1999) also recently used meta-analysis to examine general characteristics of jury research published between 1977 and 1994 as well as the more specific issues of the effects of judicial instructions on juror comprehension and jury behavior, the influence of expert psychological testimony on jury decision making, and the influence of joinder of criminal charges on jury decision making.

Because meta-analysis is a technique that statistically integrates prior empirical research, meta-analyses naturally lag behind the appearance of the original research. The information about general effect sizes that meta-analysis provides, however, is superior to that provided by traditional literature reviews that are limited in their ability to resolve different findings across studies. Furthermore, meta-analyses can integrate information on moderators, mediators, and interactions, given that relevant studies providing data on such relationships have been completed. For this reason, continued research on these types of questions are likely to be necessary even after an initial meta-analysis on a topic has been published. The advantages of meta-analysis over traditional literature reviews are likely to prove quite valuable when presenting summaries of research to the courts.

## A Closer Look at Research Methods

Strong criticisms of jury research methods appeared over twenty years ago in the 1979 special issue of *Law and Human Behavior*. Have research methods changed since that time? Examining 72 simulation studies published in various sources before 1979, Bray and Kerr (1982) reported that students served as participants in 67% of the studies. Bornstein (1999) recently updated this research and found that of the 113 jury simulation studies that appeared in *Law and Human Behavior* between 1977 and 1996, 65% had students as participants. The percentages actually hovered around 40% in the years during and immediately after the publication of the spate of articles and chapters raising questions about the use of students (late 1970s and early 1980s) but jumped to a higher level (70–;80%) by the mid-1990s.

In addition to the use of student participants, early jury research was criticized for using inadequate trial simulations—in particular, the common use of brief, written summaries. Bray and Kerr (1982) reported that 54% of the studies they examined involved the presentation of written materials, and 89% of those used an abbreviated fact summary. Almost 17% of the studies involved live or videotaped presentations and the remaining 29% presented stimulus materials via audiotape. By comparison, Bornstein (1999) reports that 55% of the 113 jury simulations he examined used written trial materials. He noted a downward trend in the use of videotaped trial materials despite the lowered costs and increased availability of recording equipment.

## ARE THERE METHOD FACTOR MAIN EFFECTS OR INTERACTIONS WITH OTHER VARIABLES?

Are these trends deplorable or worrisome? One very telling way to answer that question is to ask whether differences in research methods produce differences in research results. These differences can take two forms. First, there might be a "main-effect" difference in the rates at which, to take one example, student jurors and non-student jurors convict defendants or find civil defendants liable. As a practical and theoretical matter, differences such as these are far less important than the second type of difference. That is, there might be "interactive" differences in the way that students versus non-students (to stay with that example) respond to experimental manipulations such as manipulations of presentations of statistical evidence.

The second difference is more worrisome than the first because it suggests that factors associated with the methods used may limit the generalizability of research findings based on experimental manipulations of variables. It is one thing to know that students may be better at handling the statistics that accompany DNA evidence, but it is another matter to know that non-student jurors (perhaps because they are less accustomed to handling statistics or learning new information about statistics) are more easily misled by specious arguments about the implications of DNA evidence than are students. In this situation we would be wrong to conclude, on the basis of student-based simulation research, that "real jurors" are unaffected by specious arguments about statistical evidence. If we stopped our research and never ran "real jurors" we would fail to discover that, in fact, real jurors are seriously misled by specious arguments. (Remember, this is merely an example.) These main-effect and interaction questions are essentially empirical ones, and we are beginning to gain some insights into both as a result of recent meta-analytic research. We focus on two issues: students versus non-students and trial presentation methods.

*STUDENT VERSUS NON-STUDENT JURORS.*   Bornstein (1999) reports that only 5 of 26 studies using both students and non-students reported main-effect differences and if there was a pattern, it tended to be that students were more lenient to criminal defendants (3 studies with one reversal) and civil plaintiffs (1 study). Only 2 of 26 studies reported interactions between student/non-student status and independent variables. Cutler, Penrod and Dexter (1990) found that students were more sensitive to one of nine manipulations of eyewitness evidence (a search of mugshots versus no search), and Bornstein and Rajki (1994) found interactions between factors such as student/non-student status and juror race. But the overall story is that both main-effect and interaction differences are rather rare. Bornstein (1999) reached the same conclusion based on a review of several instances in which it was possible to compare studies that used different samples (student and non-student jurors).

Nietzel et al. (1999) took a slightly different approach to these questions. They looked for interactions between methods factors and other variables by comparing the effect sizes produced by a manipulated variable when it was, for example, presented to students versus non-students. They did this in several different jury research domains. In the death penalty arena they found that death penalty attitudes were more strongly related to jury decisions among non-students ($r = .19$) than among students ($r = .10$). With respect to the effect of judicial instructions on juror decisions they found no clear pattern—standard instructions (as compared to no instructions) had a slightly larger effect on students' decisions than non-students, but enhanced instructions had stronger effects on non-students' decisions than the presentation of no instructions. Two other comparisons of instructions yielded similar results. Students proved slightly more affected by expert testimony ($r = .17$) than non-students ($r = .14$) and the effects of joinder of criminal charges against a defendant yielded identical effect sizes for both groups ($r = .26$). The one consistent finding was that death penalty attitudes were more strongly related to judgments among non-students than among students—perhaps a reflection of more stable and well-elaborated attitudes among the (typically) older non-student group.

METHODS OF TRIAL PRESENTATION. Bornstein (1999) reported that 3 of 11 studies comparing methods of trial presentation yielded significant main effect differences in criminal conviction rates but the differences did not display a consistent pattern. Only one of the 11 studies yielded an interaction with another variable: Borgida (1979) found that a manipulation of the number of character witnesses in a trial influenced verdicts when the trial was presented in video format but not when the trial transcript was read to jurors.

Nietzel et al. (1999) also compared effect sizes across presentation methods and found some noteworthy differences. With respect to death penalty attitudes, it appears that more realistic forms of presentation may dampen the relationship between attitudes and juror judgments. Thus, the effects sizes for real trials and written transcripts ($r = .10$) were both smaller than for videotaped presentations, which we presume to be abbreviated ($r = .16$), audiotaped ($r = .34$) and questionnaire ($r = .16$) presentations. With respect to the studies of instruction effects, for the two categories of presentation method most commonly used, videotaped presentations yielded larger effects than transcripts in 3 of 4 comparisons. For studies of expert testimony there was no consistent pattern. Written and audiotaped presentations yielded larger effect sizes (both $r = .21$) than videotaped presentations ($r = .13$), with live simulations falling in between ($r = .17$). The most promising generalization may be that more complex stimulus materials mute the relationship between death penalty attitudes and juror judgments.

Although the findings discussed above shed some light on the question of whether differences in research methods produce differences in results, more research will help to clarify the relationship. Furthermore, examination of additional methods factors such as the inclusion of jury deliberation and the inclusion of voir dire like procedures would provide a more complete picture of the ways in which research methods may or may not limit the generalizability of research findings.

## GROWTH AND IMPACT OF JURY RESEARCH

The number of topics examined by jury researchers has grown considerably over the years. One reason for this growth is the publication outlet provided by the establishment of *Law and Human Behavior*. How much jury research has appeared in the journal since its inception? Is the publication of jury research limited to *Law and Human Behavior*? In their survey of jury research published in 10 leading journals in the years 1977 through 1994, Nietzel et al. (1999) located 265 studies "in which investigators described, predicted, manipulated, or measured juror behavior, jury decision making, or jury process." Of these studies, 40% were published in *Law and Human Behavior*.

In an effort to more broadly survey published jury research we conducted a search within the APA PSYCHINFO database. PSYCHINFO currently covers over 1500 psychology and related journals and the database reaches back to 1887 (though, obviously, the number of journals covered declines as one looks farther back into time and does not include the first two volumes [1977 and 1978] of *Law and Human Behavior*). We searched titles and abstracts for the presence of the words "juror" or "jury" or "juries." This yielded 1427 articles from 1887 through 1999. Of this number (which includes a modest percentage of irrelevant materials not culled from the totals), 595 were published in the 1990s (134 in *Law and Human Behavior*), 494 in the 1980s (68 in *Law and Human Behavior*), 224 in the 1970s, and 40 prior to 1970. It is evident that the sheer volume of jury-related research grew dramatically in the 1970s and 1980s with somewhat slower growth in the 1990s. There was a significant growth in publications in *Law and Human Behavior* in the late 1990s—no doubt partially fueled by its expansion from four to six issues per year in 1990.

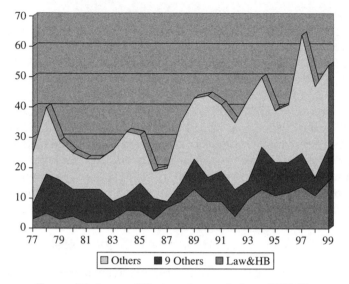

FIGURE 8.1. Jury publicatons in psychology 1977–99.

Figure 8.1 displays publication data for the period 1977 through 1999. The figure includes the 1977–1994 data reported by Neitzel et al. for *Law and Human Behavior*—with new data added through 1999 and data for the nine other journals previously examined by Nietzel et al. for 1977–1994, with new data added for later years. In addition to these analyses, data are presented on other journals containing jury research for 1976–1999. The general trend is upward—with some inexplicable peaks and troughs.

Another index of the state of the science of jury studies concerns the number of individuals contributing to the body of research. A count of the most-published authors in the full PSYCHINFO search reveals that no one individual has contributed more than 2% of the 1427 articles published since 1887. A list of the top 15 producers from this database (Table 8.1) suggests that the research enterprise is widely distributed across a large number of researchers.[3] Although the total count for these 15 individuals appears to account for about one-sixth of all publications, several of these individuals have collaborated on research and thus the number of unique articles published by this group is probably in the neighborhood of 200.

It is one matter to generate a body of research and it is another matter for that research to have an impact on policy or, at least, thinking about

---

[3]In addition, the work of research-psychologists who have tended to publish jury-related studies in law reviews (e.g., Valerie Hans, Neil Vidmar) would not be included in a search of psychology journals.

TABLE 8.1. TOP 15 PRODUCERS OF JUROR AND JURY RESEARCH

| Researcher | Authorships | TP-All Cites |
|---|---|---|
| Steven Penrod | 31 | 148 |
| Brian Cutler | 25 | 55 |
| Edith Greene | 25 | 53 |
| Saul Kassin | 23 | 112 |
| Elizabeth Loftus | 22 | 99 |
| Irwin Horowitz | 20 | 60 |
| Norbert Kerr | 19 | 66 |
| Norman Finkel | 16 | 50 |
| Martin Kaplan | 15 | 56 |
| James Davis | 14 | 22 |
| Reid Hastie | 13 | 210 |
| Eugene Borgida | 11 | 30 |
| Shari Diamond | 10 | 101 |
| Rob MacCoun | 10 | 37 |
| Gary Wells | 10 | 42 |
| TOTAL | 264 | |

policy. Much of the jury research generated by psychologists is intended to shed light on policy issues, legal practices and legal theory. One way to gauge whether the research is having an impact is to look at citations to jury research in the law.[4] The strategy in conducting this search was to use Westlaw's TP-ALL database to identify citations to jury-related articles published by the top fifteen authors identified in the PSYCHINFO search.[5]

The results of this search are shown in Table 2. Two important points should be made about these results. First, these are counts of articles in which authors have been cited and the totals do not tally citations to

---

[4]Citation counts within the law are not uncommon—indeed, a recent article by Shapiro (2000) reports the results of a study of the most-cited legal books published [by law professors] since 1978. Residing at the 30th position is *Inside the Jury*, a report of empirical work by three psychologists, Hastie, Penrod & Pennington (1983)—which apparently made the list due to Penrod's position as a law-faculty member. Psychologists also fared well in Shapiro's study of most-cited non-legal books, with volumes by Gilligan (1982) at the top spot, Loftus (1979, 1996) at position 15 and Nisbett (1980) at 18.

[5]Westlaw's TP-ALL database covers almost all law reviews and trial practice materials (the materials most commonly available to lawyers in law libraries) but only a few interdisciplinary journals. In addition, the database is full-text which makes the contents highly accessible to users. Because some of the authors publish in other areas, the search term emphasized variants on the term "jury"—and, in an effort to avoid selection of non-psychologist authors with the same last name members of the top 15, the search required the presence of a variation on the word psychology or psychologist [psych!] within 200 words of the authors name. Thus, a typical search term was: "HASTIE W/10 (JURY OR JURIES OR JUROR OR JURORS) W/200 PSYCH.

multiple research publications by an author in a single article—the maximum count is one citation per law article. Second, these results probably underestimate actual number of law articles/citations by about 50%—mostly due to the limitation imposed by the search term.[6]

What the results indicate is that jury research is visible to and being cited by writers in the legal community. In some respects the impact might be considered relatively minor—there are, after all, nearly 200 law reviews producing multiple volumes and large numbers of articles each year. In other respects the impact may be fairly substantial—at least when compared to the citation rates for competing forms of research and writing.[7]

## A LOOK TO THE FUTURE

As we move into the next century, it is important that we preserve the scholarly methods for analysis of the jury that have proven successful in the past and that we extend our work into new domains, both methodologically and substantively. To increase our impact on the legal system, we should continue to examine proposed and enacted jury reforms and innovations as well as the assumptions underlying them. We should also expand our efforts to include new domains of research and emerging areas of litigation, and, perhaps most importantly, amplify our efforts to make this work known outside of academic circles. In this section, we discuss the current climate of justice system reform and describe how researchers can and should capitalize on lawmakers' and the public's considerable interest in reforming the process of jury trials.

## THE JURY REFORM MOVEMENT

The jury reform movement gained considerable momentum in the 1990s as a result of a series of notorious cases in the U.S. (Blum, 1996;

[6]This point is illustrated by the count obtained if one searches, without the "PSYCH!" limitation for less common names such as Borgida, Kassin or MacCoun—whose counts would jump to 45, 147 and 70 respectively. The count for Davis soars to more than 1200—hence the need for the qualifying term.

[7]As the results in Table 2 demonstrate, citations to authors of research articles who are not also authors of jury books, are a small fraction of citations to books. These results are undoubtedly partly the product of two factors. First, books are far more likely to be found on the shelves of law libraries than are social science journals. In addition, many legal researchers are accustomed to dealing with online reference materials, and it is only a slight exaggeration to say that every legal thought that has ever found its way to ink in the past twenty years is and has been available in full-text format through Westlaw and/or LEXIS for some time. With the recent exception of *Psychology, Public Policy and Law*, psychology

Cripe, 1999; Marder, 1999; Penrod & Heuer, 1997). In the criminal realm, we learned intimate details about Rodney King, the Menendez brothers, O. J. Simpson, and Timothy McVeigh. On the civil side, we had to the $2.9 million McDonald's coffee verdict, $11.1 billion Texaco-Pennzoil verdict, as well as tobacco, silicone breast implant, and gun-related litigation. Media coverage of these extraordinary trials has led the public to decry the jury system and proclaim the need for reform (Blum, 1996; Chappelear, 1999; Cripe, 1999; Hans, Hannaford, & Munsterman, 1999; Marder, 1999). Although these cases are clearly not representative of most litigation in the United States or the rest of the world, they have generated increased discussion amongst legal scholars, legislators, judges, and attorneys regarding the workings of the jury system.

The reform movement has spawned the formation of task forces that propose and institute changes in the way that jury trials are conducted (e.g., Dann & Logan, 1996, discussing changes in Arizona; Kelso, 1996, describing California reforms; McMahon & Kornblau, 1995, reporting on the New York Jury Project; Uebelein, 1999, detailing Hawaii's reform efforts). Among the recommendations are these: preinstructing jurors before they hear any evidence so they understand what issues are being contended, allowing jurors to ask questions of the witnesses, providing juror notebooks with a list of the witnesses and perhaps a summary of their testimony, allowing mini-summations during the course of a lengthy trial, providing written copies of all the instructions for jurors to use during deliberations, and allowing jurors to discuss the case before deliberation, provided that they do not reach a conclusion prior to the end of the trial. These reforms encourage juror participation and increase the quality of information jurors are provided—changes that will serve justice by facilitating informed, rational decisions, while simultaneously increasing juror satisfaction with the process (Dann, 1993; Ellsworth, 1999).

This reform zeitgeist has provided a prime opportunity for jury researchers to work with judges, lawyers, and legislators to test the efficacy of these proposed reforms and others. Ten years ago, Tanford (1991) examined the use of social science evidence on jury instructions by appellate courts, legislatures, and rule-making commissions. His findings suggest that commissions were most likely to incorporate social science research into their decisions, perhaps due to the commissioners' perceived roles as information gatherers. An examination of jury reform

journals are not available full-text to lawyers nor are more than a handful indexed by citation in legal indexes. (We describe this concern in more detail below.) In short, despite the apparent interest in empirical jury research, lack of access to psychology research articles by legal professionals is clearly a major impediment to wider use of jury research.

commission members listed in recently published reports reveals, however, that social scientists were not among those consulted (see Kelso, 1996; McMahon & Kornblau, 1995). Proactively seeking involvement with law reform commissions may be the most profitable means of generating changes that reflect social scientific research, and our presence can provide a mechanism for empirically evaluating these proposed reforms.

The good news is that this type of collaboration has begun. The University of Michigan Journal of Law Reform recently held a symposium entitled Jury Reform: Making Juries Work, designed to bring together judges, lawyers, legal academics, social scientists, and jurors to share ideas, discuss problems, and develop solutions (see Ellsworth, 1999). Ellsworth (1999) reported "astonishing" agreement amongst the various symposium attendees that criticisms of jurors and juries were largely unwarranted, and, consistent with the long-held beliefs of many social scientists, that the system *itself* is in need of a fix:

> There is little support for the popular notion that bad jury decisions are caused by bad jurors. Social scientists therefore reject the "Bad Juror" theory as a general explanation for questionable verdicts, and prefer a "Bad System" theory, arguing that the decision making task is presented to the jury in ways that make it unnecessarily difficult to reach a well-informed, accurate decision. (p. 223)

Another hopeful sign comes from the collaboration of the National Center for State Courts and the Arizona judiciary to conduct a field study of the Arizona reform that allow jurors to discuss the evidence among themselves during the trial (Hannaford, Hans, & Munsterman, 2000). (Arizona courts have been at the forefront of the reform movement in the U.S. and have sought input from experts in the fields of communication, educational psychology and jury decision making to evaluate their proposed reforms.) Empirical analysis of this procedure shows that mid-trial discussions allow jurors to resolve confusion about the evidence but apparently do not translate into observable differences in how jurors report using the evidence or the law. They also do not affect the likelihood that the judge will agree with the jury's verdict (Hannaford et al., 2000).

The Michigan and Arizona examples represent the best of the jury reform movement. Unfortunately, many proposed reforms are based on "common knowledge" assumptions, anecdotal accounts, or personal experiences (Finkel, 1997; Saks, 1992; Tanford, 1991). Consider, for example, the jury nullification "problem" that has become popularized by the press, Marder (1999) points to the misconception that jury nullification occurs when emotion, irrational thought, in-group bias, or ignorance leads to a verdict divergent from what the evidence suggests. She argues that claims of widespread jury nullification are largely inaccurate. And yet, proposals calling for a change to the unanimous verdict requirement are likely based, in part, on this alleged nullification crisis (King, 1999; Marder, 1999). Judicial, legislative, and public responses calling for non-unanimous verdicts represent an uninformed reaction to a perceived, non-existent problem. Although non-unanimous juries may reduce the number of deadlocked juries, they will also likely result in less thorough discussion, and less juror satisfaction and confidence (Hastie et al., 1983). In fact, there is no empirical support for the assumption that nullification rates vary as a function of jury decision rule. Marder suggests that the way to reduce claims of jury nullification is to strive for diversity on jury panels, thereby reducing opportunities for commentators to declare in-group bias as the basis for verdicts. Increasing the diversity of jury panels, which should be an inherent goal of the legal system, may be the most effective way to restore confidence in verdicts without compromising the breadth and quality of deliberation.

The lesson here is that when evaluating and generating proposed reforms, we must look carefully at what the perceived problems actually are, determine if they are indeed detrimental to the efficient and fair resolution of disputes, and generate or disseminate data on possible solutions. In the process, we should continue to reject the bad juror presumption, focus on systemic changes, and work in tandem judges, lawyers, legal commentators, and other social scientists to focus on appropriate remedies.

In evaluating reform procedures, we should consider both the obvious goals of enhancing jurors' abilities to decide cases fairly, and the less obvious by-products of properly conducted trials, such as enhancing the experience for jurors. Consider, for example, the possibility of juror note-taking and the provision of written judicial instructions. Although these procedures apparently do not significantly improve comprehension of judicial instructions, they may make jurors feel more satisfied with the process and confident in their verdicts (Heuer & Penrod, 1988, 1989, 1994a). For these reasons alone, their use should be encouraged.

In addition to participating in reform task forces, we must continue our efforts to rebut erroneous assumptions about jurors that remain entrenched in the system. For example, as previously noted, many researchers have demonstrated that juror comprehension of judicial instructions is poor. Yet, there is evidence that real jurors may be making incorrect decisions based on confusing instructions. In 2000, the U.S. Supreme Court ruled that the judge presiding over a death penalty case is not obligated to do more than refer to the instructions when confronted with a jury's question about a crucial sentencing instruction (*Weeks v. Angelone*, 2000). At trial, the Virginia jury asked the judge to clarify

whether the death penalty was mandatory if the jurors found that the
State had proven either of two aggravating circumstances. Rather than
answering "no" (the correct response), the trial judge told jurors to reread
the instruction (Garvey, Johnson, & Marcus, 2000). Two hours later the
jury returned a death sentence—although most of the jurors were in tears
when polled about that decision.

A study published in the Cornell Law Review shortly after the *Weeks*
case was decided tested the ability of mock jurors to understand the
instructions that had been given in the original trial (Garvey et al., 2000).
Garvey et al. found that 41% of mock jurors given this instruction
assumed, incorrectly, that they were required to impose a death sentence
if they found that Weeks' conduct was heinous, vile or depraved (the
aggravating factor agreed upon by the actual jury). With regard to the second aggravator, future dangerousness, 38% of mock jurors believed that a
death sentence was mandatory if the aggravating circumstance was
proven. Directing jurors to reread the instructions actually resulted in an
*increase* in the percentage of individuals who believed they were required
to impose death. Clarifying instructions, on the other hand, significantly
reduced the percentage of jurors who believed death was mandatory if
aggravating factors were proven beyond a reasonable doubt. So, although
it may be clear to researchers that jurors have difficulty understanding
and applying their instructions, the legal system continues to ignore the
available research or find reasons to discount its conclusions.

Work on instruction comprehension is by no means the only body of
empirical data that judges have opted to dismiss or misapply. For example, in *Lockhart v. McCree* (1986) the United States Supreme Court rejected
the well documented pro-prosecution biasing effects of death qualification (see Cowan et al., 1984; Fitzgerald & Ellsworth, 1984; Goodman-
Delahunty, Greene, & Hsiao, 1998; Haney, 1984; Thompson, 1989;
Thompson et al., 1984). The U.S. Supreme Court decisions reducing the
required jury size (*Williams v. Florida*, 1970) and eliminating the unanimity requirement for jury decisions (*Johnson v. Louisiana*, 1972) were made
contrary to, or in the absence of, social scientific research data. Current
calls for reformation of the jury decision rule at the state court level (see
Kelso, 1996) are based on assumptions about jury nullification and hung
juries derived from faulty logic. After reviewing judicial, legislative, and
law commission usage of social scientific evidence, Tanford (1991) concluded that the courts not only ignore empirical data, but also make decisions contrary to what social scientific research would suggest.

How can we facilitate the proper use of our research by the judiciary?
There is no easy answer to that question. Simplification and replication
may improve our chances, but we will likely always be forced to contend

with questions about our methodology (Diamond, 1997) and concerns about inconsistencies in the literature (Ellsworth, 1991; Faigman, 1989). Meta-analytic techniques, described above, speak to some of these concerns. For meta-analyses to be possible, however, there must be a core body of research in a given area. Unfortunately, we tend to shy away from replication because of the value publishers place on novel ideas. Replication need not be considered an unrewarding chore yielding non-publishable results. Rather, we should both replicate and augment findings by examining the efficacy of proposed alternatives (e.g., by testing comprehension levels among law students, lawyers, and those with advanced degrees) as well as testing proposed solutions (e.g., revision, written instructions, pre-instruction). This programmatic work has been modeled nicely in the area of pre-trial publicity effects. Researchers have not only shown that pre-trial publicity has a biasing influence on jurors, but also that judicially proposed remedies to eliminate bias are largely ineffective (see Studebaker & Penrod, 1997 for a review).

## EMERGING AND NOVEL AREAS OF RESEARCH

The topics amenable to jury research are virtually limitless. Many traditional areas of trial law have not yet been systematically addressed and the future will likely bring entirely new types of litigation, replete with unanswered questions about how jurors will interpret evidence, assimilate facts, and reach decisions. Obviously, the best way to develop research questions is to research the law itself. Read about civil and criminal procedure, read evidence textbooks, gather information about cases described in the newspaper, talk to attorneys and judges, get online reports of cases, and watch for appellate court decisions. Collaborating with area trial consultants can result in another source of ideas and data. In the course of their work, trial consultants may encounter cases containing broad-based research questions that have not yet been addressed and for which they lack resources for further study. Consulting firms that specialize in certain types of cases may also have large databases of pretrial juror questionnaires, mock jury questionnaires, or juror exit-interviews for a number of similar cases. Additionally, consulting firms often have contact with large numbers of community members. Fostering an amiable relationship with a consultant may allow a psychologist to distribute various questionnaires to a diverse sample of participants across a variety of cases, thereby increasing the convergent validity of research results. By being immersed in the law through reading, teaching, awareness of current decisions, and contacts with those in the legal system, questions and methods for carrying out research may emerge naturally.

## Juror-Centered Research

Identification and study of procedural variables is one way to examine the workings of the jury system but empirical study of the perceptions and experiences of jurors themselves is also valuable. Jurors' satisfaction with their service is integral to the well being of the jury system. If jurors are made to feel unappreciated, frustrated, or angry about their experience, they will be less willing to serve in the future, and they may vent their anger to the media, thereby increasing public reluctance to serve. The result may be less representative jury panels.

Questions posed to jurors can identify potential areas for study (e.g., What aspects of your jury service did you find frustrating? What parts of jury duty were rewarding? What questions remained in your mind at the conclusion of your jury service?). More focused questioning can supplement laboratory-based research (e.g., findings on comprehension of judicial instructions) or clarify and document anecdotal accounts (e.g., stress levels after jury service). Data from exit-interviews and post-trial surveys may be more persuasive to judges and policy-makers than other types of data, as they eliminate some of the external validity criticisms leveled at simulation research (see Diamond, 1997).

Until recently, little was known about the stressors associated with jury duty. A handful of mostly anecdotal studies had reported that some jurors undergo extreme levels of stress, complete with physical and mental symptoms, as a result of jury service (e.g., Dabbs, 1992; Feldmann & Bell, 1991; Hafemeister & Ventis, 1994; Kaplan & Winget, 1992; Kelley, 1994). A large-scale study conducted by the National Center for State Courts (NCSC, 1998) surveyed judges across the country and collected data from jurors and potential jurors in six jurisdictions in order to assess sources of juror stress, remedies employed by judges, and suggestions from both jurors and the judiciary on how to make jury service more satisfying. Nearly all of the judges surveyed (97%) agreed that "courts have a responsibility to prevent, address, or minimize juror stress" (p. 76) and 78% indicated that they employed stress-reduction methods in their courtrooms. These findings indicate a willingness amongst judges to alleviate stress felt by potential and actual jurors. The jurors themselves indicated a range of stress responses, most of which were mild, with more severe responses occurring in longer trials and capital cases. The survey identified a number of factors perceived as stressful, many of them involved procedural aspects of the trial, voir dire, and assembly/waiting periods. Interestingly, some of the people who were called for jury duty but did not serve also experienced stress, likely a result of the interruption to their daily lives, waiting to be called, and a lack of closure or feeling of accomplishment. Exit interviews with venire members not seated on a trial could be informative regarding procedural changes in the pre-trial process.

Strier (1997) conducted a statewide survey of California trial and appellate judges regarding proposed jury system reforms. A majority of judges believed that improving juror orientation could and should improve juror competence (Strier, 1997). This suggests another area into which jury researchers can expand their efforts—the development and testing of jury orientation materials and programs. What information do jurors want to know? In what areas do they feel orientation leaves them uninformed? How beneficial are current orientation materials?

One of the rationales for utilizing citizen jurors is that jury service provides an education about the workings of the legal system (Law Reform Commission of Canada, 1979; Marder, 1997; Quinlan, 1993). However, if jurors are leaving the courtroom as uninformed as they were on arrival, this goal is not being met. As psychologists with knowledge of how information is most effectively processed, the types of stimuli most conducive to retention, and the human tendency to rely on heuristic shortcuts and pre-existing knowledge when presented with vague or ambiguous information (see, e.g., Baron, 1994; Elwork et al., 1982; Fiske & Taylor, 1991; Tulving, 1983), we could serve both the individual juror and the legal system as a whole by working to improve jurors' orientations. Informed jurors will make better decisions and feel better about their service. Increased public and judicial confidence in juror competency may be the result.

## CROSS-CULTURAL STUDIES

There have been few cross-cultural comparisons of jury systems throughout the world. Although the American jury has been the focus of most empirical research, this system has obvious similarities to jury procedures in Canada, the U.K., Australia, and other Commonwealth countries. Russia and Spain have revived their jury systems and various Caribbean countries employ juries as well (Vidmar, 1999a). Cross-cultural study is informative to research on contemporary jury issues, particularly in light of the fact that legal commentators and some courts refer to other systems in support of their arguments and decisions (Vidmar, 1999a; see e.g., Hoffman, 1997; R. v. Levogiannis, 1993). Although the legislative, judicial, and public concerns about jury procedures are similar across cultures, the proposed solutions may vary (Vidmar, 1999a).

Procedural differences are conducive to empirical evaluation. For example, in Canada, the impartiality of jurors is deemed a question of fact, not a question of law, and as such, the determination of whether a prospective juror is partial is made by triers selected from the pool of potential jurors and not by the judge (Criminal Code, 1985). In contrast, courts in the U.S. restrict this decision to the trial judge (LaFave & Israel, 1985). There are advantages to both systems In Canada, potential jurors have more involvement in the process, and the task of assessing impartiality not only in oneself, but also in other potential jurors, becomes a salient issue to all members of the venire (see generally, Vidmar, 1999b). The Canadian system avoids the possibility of judicial favoritism toward one side or the other, as the judge has no input in which prospective jurors are dismissed for cause. On the other hand, the triers themselves might be partial, and may be less cognizant of their partiality than an experienced trial judge.[8] The triers may also be less able to recognize partiality in others than a judge, or may feel they are unqualified to make such a decision. Which system is most effective at identifying biased jurors? Does involvement of the potential jurors increase their awareness of potential bias and increase their perceived control over the situation, or does it make them and other panel members feel uncomfortable?

Media coverage of the American legal system might also affect public perception of the Canadian judicial system. In Canada, only a small percentage of citizens serve as jurors (Law Reform Commission of Canada, 1979). Yet the majority of the population has access to American television, and watch shows like Law and Order, The Practice, and NYPD Blue, and news coverage of the many "trials of the century." Do Canadians understand the differences between the American and Canadian judicial systems? If not, their expectations of effective justice, trial procedures, and proper jury verdicts may be unreasonable, and those who do serve on jury trials may have incorrect assumptions about the results of their decisions.

These are but a few of the myriad examples of potential research questions. *Law and Contemporary Problems* devoted an entire issue (Spring, 1999) to jury systems around the world that provides an excellent starting point for those interested in cross-cultural jury research.

## GRAND JURY PROCEDURES AND REFORMS

Although the procedural aspects of grand juries are under fire in a variety of jurisdictions (Feser, 1999; Hafetz & Pellettieri, 1999; National

---

[8]Once an impartial juror is seated, that juror replaces one of the original triers, and the process continues until another juror is seated, who then replaces the second original trier, and so on. Thus, the potential for bias in the triers would not likely affect the composition of the panel too significantly.

Association of Criminal Defense Lawyers, 1998) and public awareness of these proceedings has increased as a result of President Clinton's legal troubles, grand juries are largely ignored by academic researchers. But, as one law professor put it, "Grand juries, petit jurics, and civil juries do differ from each other, but they are all juries of sorts. Adjectives should not obscure nouns" (Amar, 1995, p. 1176).

Grand jury reform proposals are slowly gaining attention at both the state and federal levels (see Hafetz & Pellettieri, 1999), and, as is the case with the petit and civil jury reform movements discussed above, some of these proposals are conducive to social scientific investigation. Although the secrecy of grand jury proceedings may serve as a barrier to field studies and juror interviews, simulation methods or archival research could still profitably be used to evaluate this system. Additionally, in some jurisdictions (e.g., California) information on grand jury proceedings in civil matters is being made available to the public (Feser, 1999).

## TECHNOLOGY IN THE COURTROOM

Although few people are strangers to computers or computer technology, the courts have been slower to enter the electronic age (Lederer, 1999b). This situation is changing, though. As Lederer (1997, 1999a) reports, eight state facilities and approximately 30 federal facilities in the United States as well as perhaps 50 courtrooms worldwide are currently considered "high technology courtrooms" (Lederer, 1997). Courts are beginning to admit documents and pictures as electronic evidence in the form of digital photographs, electronically scanned documents, and computer generated animations or simulations (Lederer, 1999a).

Novel evidence presents new challenges to current evidentiary rules (see Carbine & McLain, 1999; Lederer, 1999a). One of the most contentious issues concerns the use of computer simulations; these are controversial because they take the known facts, and in concert with the principles of physics, render a moving image of what *might have* happened (see Bennett, Leibman, & Fetter, 1999; Berkoff, 1994). Those who question the use of realistic in-court computer simulations raise concerns that a jury will afford the simulation more weight than is warranted (for reviews see Bennett et al., 1999; Berkoff, 1994; Carbine & McLain, 1999; Lederer, 1999a). In fact, Bennett et al. (1999) failed to find differences in assignment of blame and verdict award between mock juries that viewed computer simulations in conjunction with expert testimony as compared to those who received expert testimony alone. Further research is warranted on the impact of computer animation and computer simulations as demonstrative evidence. The increasing use of technology in the courtroom could be beneficial to the trial process, expediting the proceedings, creating a break in the monotony of testimony, and perhaps improving juror comprehension (Cate & Minnow, 1993; Lederer, 1997; 1999a).

Another technological advance that could impact jury-decision making is the presentation of remote witness testimony via videoconferencing (Lederer, 1999a). The use of videotaped testimony raises questions regarding the value of demeanor evidence, the rights of the litigants (especially in criminal trials) to confront witnesses, and the importance of physical presence in determining the truthfulness of testimony (Lederer, 1999a).[9] Lederer (1999a) reports that although empirical research conducted by the Courtroom 21 Project[10] suggests that jurors are seemingly ambivalent regarding remote testimony, judging it no better or worse than live testimony, many questions regarding credibility and truthfulness await further empirical testing. If remote testimony proves successful, we may be entering an age where "virtual trials" take place, whereby all of the evidence, arguments and instructions are presented electronically (Lederer, 1999b, p. 801). Clearly this proposition will require intensive empirical scrutiny at many levels, not the least of which will be the impact upon the triers of fact.

## THE INTERNET

An estimated 200 million people use the Internet worldwide and the number is growing rapidly (Nua, Ltd., 1999, 2000). With an increase in Internet-based commerce, the proliferation of online pornographic material, the increased savvy of computer hackers, concerns about the privacy of employees' computer activities, and the admissibility of email as evidence of harassment or negligence, entirely new areas of law are developing. Cases involving these issues are beginning to reach the courthouse (for reviews, see "Communities," 1999; Dixon, 1999; Kaplan, 1998; Lewis, 1999; Morgan, 1999). As Internet cases go to trial, jurors' attitudes, beliefs, and experiences with cyberspace will be of paramount importance to the outcomes. This is a prime time for social scientists to develop new

---

[9]These are the same issues that arise when children testify by closed-circuit television (see Goodman et al., 1998; Ross et al., 1994; Tobey, Goodman, Batterman-Faunce, Orcutt, & Sachsenmaier, 1995), but research in this area is far from conclusive as to the ability of jurors to evaluate the veracity of the testimony, and there are likely important differences in credibility judgments and attributions made about child as opposed to adult witnesses who are not physically present in the courtroom.

[10]A project of the William & Mary Law School and the National Center for State Courts involving implementation of technology into the courtroom. More information on the project is available at http://www.courtroom21.net.

programs of research on these issues that will be informative to lawmakers, the judiciary, attorneys, and jurors alike.

One area of Internet law that has already received considerable attention involves the applicability of free speech protections and the assessment of community standards with regard to sexual obscenity and pornography distributed online (see Communications Decency Act, 1996; Kaplan, 1998; Lewis, 1999; *Reno v. American Civil Liberties Union*, 1997). In *Miller v. California* (1973), the U.S. Supreme Court held that a national standard for assessing obscenity was "unascertainable" and suggested instead that statewide standards, or even more desirably, the standards of a single city, be used. This reasoning sets the stage for analysis of jurors' sentiments on the issue. Variants of this issue emerge in cases involving online distribution of pornographic material that is unsolicited or that is linked to relatively benign, non-descriptive, or misleading domain names (e.g. *www.whitehouse.com*) which may inadvertently be accessed by individuals who are offended by the material.

The privacy of Internet communications and online activity is relevant to a number of criminal and civil trial issues. For example, should employees expect their email messages to be private? Or, should they reasonably foresee that their communications at work are subject to interception by their employers, law enforcement agencies, and the government? Should employers be held responsible for promoting a hostile work environment in sexual harassment cases when employees are accessing pornography at work or passing sexist jokes via email? Can an employee be fired for visiting non-work related web sites while using company equipment? Are email communications between an attorney and her client protected under attorney/client privilege? Will jurors perceive harassing emails as evidence of stalking behavior? In addition to providing novel research topics, increased public Internet usage factors into traditional areas of psycholegal research, such as the spread of pre-trial publicity, and also generates new perspectives on old issues—such as the possibility of Internet publication of jury damage awards and verdict rationales as a condition of punitive damages in civil litigation (see Curcio, 1998). Finally, the Internet offers the opportunity to conduct research in a novel way—by collecting data online (see Azar, 2000a, 2000c; Beans, 2000).

## ONLINE RESEARCH

The American Psychological Association's April 2000 issue of *Monitor on Psychology* was devoted to psychology and the Internet and gave examples of research currently being conducted on the world wide web, information about creating a web-based study, and discussion of the benefits, costs, and ethical considerations of online research (Azar 2000a, 2000b, 2000c, 2000d; Beans, 2000). Both experimental and survey jury research are now being conducted online (see Azar, 2000c; O'Neil, 2000) and as more individuals become web-savvy and connections become faster and more powerful, it is likely that on-line jury simulations will also soon become reality. Despite concerns about the representativeness of web-based samples, researchers can compare Internet results with those generated from traditional laboratory techniques. If findings converge, greater confidence can be had about the results (see Azar, 2000a). In this manner, web-based research can provide a way to conduct replication studies (the importance of which was previously discussed) without the expenditure of excessive time or money.

## COMMUNICATING WITH THE LEGAL SYSTEM

Consider the statement of Chief Justice Lamer in *Dagenais v. Canadian Broadcast Corp.* (1994) on the topic of pre-trial publicity (1994): "I doubt that jurors are always adversely influenced by publications. There is no data available on this issue" (p. 884). Perhaps the single most important issue that we need to address in the future is an old issue: how do we make our research known to those in the legal system, and even more critically, how do we get them to actually *use* it? The easy answer is that we need to increase publication efforts in law journals, judicial newsletters, and bar association materials. We know that judges and attorneys do not turn to psychology journals when they conduct research. Rather, they use legal databases and cite other legal scholars, not social scientists. Additional remedies include publishing in journals that are available on-line and revising, simplifying, and summarizing previously-published scholarly work for a law-related journal.

Other remedies may be able to generate change. Education of key players in the legal system likely works best when human contact is a factor. By getting involved in law reform commissions and volunteering to participate at Inns of Court, judicial conferences, and bar association, paralegal association, law clerk organization and law student meetings, psychologists contribute more to the knowledge base of the attendees in a few hours than a lengthy curriculum vitae ever could. Finally, we should make it a goal of our organizations (e.g., American Psychology-Law Society) to generate and implement ongoing education programs for those outside of our discipline. Similarly, our conference planners should strive to recruit and involve more diverse participants—lawyers, judges, clerks, and law students—so that they may share their view of the law with psychologists.

This is an exciting time for jury researchers, with emerging areas of law, innovative reforms, sophisticated methodologies, increased communication capabilities, and technological advances all playing a role in shaping the field for the next several years. The apparent judicial indifference (or lack of knowledge about) our work should serve to underscore the importance of conducting well-crafted, relevant research studies and of communicating their findings to the legal system. Both psychology and the law will profit.

## REFERENCES

Allen, M., Mabry, E., & McKelton, D. (1998). Impact of juror attitudes about the death penalty on juror evaluations of guilt and punishment: A meta-analysis. *Law and Human Behavior, 22*, 715–731.

Amar, A. R. (1995). Reinventing juries: Ten suggested reforms. *U. C. Davis Law Review, 28*, 1169–1194.

American Bar Association (1990). Jury comprehension in complex cases. Washington, D.C.

Anderson, M.C., & MacCoun, R.J. (1999). Goal conflict in juror assessments of compensatory and punitive damages. *Law and Human Behavior, 23*, 313–330.

Anderson, N. H. (1981). *Foundations of information integration theory.* New York: Academic Press.

Azar, B. (2000a). A Web of research. *Monitor on Psychology 31*(4), 42 45.

Azar, B. (2000b). Resources for creating Web-based experiments. *Monitor on Psychology, 31*(4), 43.

Azar, B. (2000c). A Web experiment sampler. *Monitor on Psychology, 1*(4), 16 17.

Azar, B. (2000d). Online experiments: Ethically fair or foul? *Monitor on Psychology, 31*(4), 48 52.

Bailis, D. S., & MacCoun, R. J. (1996). Estimating liability risks with the media as your guide: A content analysis of media coverage of tort litigation. *Law and Human Behavior, 20*(4), 419–429.

Baldwin, J., & McConville, M. (1979). Trial by jury: Some empirical evidence on contested criminal cases in England. *Law and Society Review, 13*, 861–890.

Baron, J. (1994). *Thinking and deciding* (2nd ed.). New York: Cambridge University Press.

*Batson v. Kentucky*, 476 U.S. 79 (1986).

Beans, B. E. (2000). Free of charge, open all hours. *Monitor on Psychology, 31*(4), 48–49.

Becker, T. L., Hildum, D. C., & Bateman, K. (1965). The influence of jurors' values on their verdicts: A courts and politics experiment. *Southwestern Social Science Quarterly, 45*, 130–140.

Bennett, R. B., Leibman, J. H., & Fetter, R. E. (1999). Seeing is believing; or is it? An empirical study of computer simulations as evidence. *Wake Forest Law Review, 34*, 257–294.

Bennett, W. L. & Feldman, M. S. (1981). *Reconstructing reality in the courtroom: Justice and judgement in American culture.* New Brunswick, NJ: Rutgers University Press.

Berk, R. A., Hennessy, M., & Swan, J. (1977). The vagaries and vulgarities of scientific jury selection: A methodological evaluation. *Evaluation Quarterly, 1*, 143–158.

Berkoff, A. T. (1994). Computer simulations in litigation: Are television generation jurors being misled? *Marquette Law Review, 77*, 829–855.

Bermant, G., & Coppock, R. (1972–1973). Outcomes of six- and twelve-member jury trials: An analysis of 128 civil cases in the state of Washington. *Washington Law Review, 48*, 593–596.

Bermant, G., McGuire, M., McKinley, W., & Salo, C. (1974). The logic of simulation in jury research. *Criminal Justice and Behavior, 1*, 224–233.

Bevan, W., Albert, R. S., Loiseaux, P. R., Mayfield, P. N., & Wright, G. (1958). Jury behavior as a function of the prestige of the foreman and the nature of his leadership. *Journal of Public Law, 7*, 419–449.

Blauner, R. (1975). The sociology of jury selection. In A. F. Ginger (Ed.), *Jury selection in criminal trials*. Tiburon, CA: Law Press.

Blum, A. (1996, January 22). Jury system undergoes patchwork remodeling. *The National Law Journal*, p. A I.

Blunt, L. W., & Stock, H. V. (1985). Guilty but mentally ill: An alternative verdict. *Behavioral Sciences and the Law, 3*, 49–67.

BMW of North America, Inc. v. Gore, 517 U. S. 559 (1996).

Boehm, V. (1968). Mr. Prejudice, Miss Sympathy and the authoritarian personality: An application of psychological measuring to the problem of jury bias. *Wisconsin Law Review*, 734–750.

Bornstein, B. H. (1999). The ecological validity of jury simulations: Is the jury still out? *Law and Human Behavior, 23*, 75–91.

Bornstein, B. H., & Rajki, M. (1994). Extra-legal factors and product liability: The influence of mock jurors' demographic characteristics and intuitions about the cause of an injury. *Behavioral Sciences and the Law, 12*, 127–147.

Bottoms, B. L., & Goodman, G. S. (1994). Perceptions of children's credibility in sexual assault cases. *Journal of Applied Social Psychology, 24*, 702–732.

Bourgeois, M.J., Horowitz, I.A., & ForsterLee, L. (1993). Effects of technicality and access to trial transcripts on verdicts and information processing in a civil trial. *Personality and Social Psychology Bulletin, 19*, 220–227.

Bray, R. M., & Kerr N. L. (1982). Methodological considerations in the study of the psychology of the courtroom. In N. L. Kerr & R. M. Bray (Eds.), *The psychology of the courtroom*. New York: Academic Press.

Bray, R. M., & Kerr, N. L. (1979). Use of the simulation method in the study of jury behavior. *Law and Human Behavior, 3*, 107–119.

Brekke, N., & Borgida, E. (1988). Expert psychological testimony in rape trials: A social-cognitive analysis. *Journal of Personality and Social Psychology, 55*, 372–386.

Brigham, J. C., & Wasserman, A. W. (1999). The impact of race, racial attitude, and gender on reactions to the criminal trial of O. J. Simpson. *Journal of Applied Social Psychology, 29*, 1333–1370.

Brody, A. (1957). Selecting a jury—Art or blind-man's buff? *Criminal Law Review, 4*, 67–78.

Broeder, D. W. (1958). The University of Chicago Jury Project. *Nebraska Law Review, 38*, 744–761.

Bronson, E. J. (1970). On the conviction proneness and representativeness of the death-qualified jury: An empirical study of Colorado veniremen. *University of Colorado Law Review, 42*, 1–32.

Buchanan, R. W., Pryor, B., Taylor, K. P., & Strawn, D. V. (1978). Legal communication: An investigation of juror comprehension of pattern jury instructions. *Communication Quarterly, 26*, 31–35.

Buckhout, R., Weg, S., Reilly, V., & Frohboese, R. (1977). Jury verdicts: Comparison of 6- vs. 12-person juries and unanimous vs. majority decision rule in a murder trial. *Bulletin of the Psychonomic Society, 10*, 175–178.

Buckhout, R. (1977). *Jury verdicts: Comparison of six vs. twelve person juries and unanimous vs. majority decision rule in a murder trial (CR-12)*. Brooklyn, New York: Center for Responsive Psychology.

Carbine, J. E., & McLain, L. (1999). Proposed model rules governing the admissibility of computer-generated evidence. *Computer and High Technology Law Journal, 15*, 1–72.

Casper, J. D., Benedict, K., & Perry, J. L. (1989). Juror decision making, attitudes, and the hindsight bias. *Law and Human Behavior, 13*, 291–310.

Cate, F. II., & Minnow, N. N. (1993). Communicating with juries. *Indiana Law Journal, 68*, 1101–1118.

Cather, C., Greene, E., & Durham, R. (1996). Plaintiff injury and defendant reprehensibility: Implications for compensatory and punitive damage awards. *Law and Human Behavior, 20*, 189–205.

Chappelear, S. E. (1999). Jury trials in the heartland. *University of Michigan Journal of Law Reform, 32*, 241–277.

Charrow, R. P., & Charrow, V. R. (1979). Making legal language understandable: A psycholinguistic study of jury instructions. *Columbia Law Review, 79*, 1306–1374.

Christie, R. (1977). Probability v. precedence: The social psychology of jury selection. In G. Bermant, C. Nemeth, & N. Vidmar (Eds.), *Psychology and the law*. Lexington, Massachusetts: Lexington Books (D. C. Heath & Co.), 265–281.

Communications Decency Act, 47 U. S. C. S. § 223 (1996).

Communities virtual and real: Social and political dynamics of law in cyberspace. (1999). *Harvard Law Review, 112*, 1586–1609.

Cowan, C. L., Thompson, W. C., & Ellsworth, P. C. (1984). The effects of death qualification on jurors' predisposition to convict and on the quality of deliberation. *Law and Human Behavior, 8*, 53–79.

Cox, M., & Tanford, S. (1989). Effects of evidence and instructions in civil trials: An experimental investigation of rules of admissibility. *Social Behaviour, 4*, 31–55.

Criminal Code. R S C. 1985, c. C 46.

Cripe, K. T. (1999). Empowering the audience: Television's role in the diminishing respect for the American judicial system. *UCLA Entertainment Law Review, 6*, 235–282.

Curcio, A. A. (1998). Breaking the silence: Using a notification penalty and other notification measures in punitive damages cases. *Wisconsin Law Review, 1998*, 343–385.

Cutler, B. L., Dexter, H. R., & Penrod, S. D. (1989). Expert testimony and jury decision making: An empirical analysis. *Behavioral Sciences and the Law, 7*, 215–225.

Cutler, B. L., Dexter, H. R., & Penrod, S. D. (1990). Nonadversarial methods for sensitizing jurors to eyewitness evidence. *Journal of Applied Social Psychology, 20*, 1197–1207.

Cutler, B. L., Moran, G., & Narby, D. J. (1992). Jury selection in insanity defense cases. *Journal of Research in Personality, 26*, 165–182.

Cutler, B. L. & Penrod, S. D. (1995). *Mistaken identification: The eyewitness, psychology, and the law*. Cambridge: Cambridge University Press.

Cutler, B. L., Penrod, S. D., & Dexter, H. R. (1989). The eyewitness, the expert psychologist, and the jury. *Law and Human Behavior, 13*, 311–322.

Cutler, B. L., Penrod, S. D., & Dexter, H. R. (1990). Juror sensitivity to eyewitness identification evidence. *Law and Human Behavior, 14*, 185–191.

Cutler, B. L., Penrod, S. D., & Stuve, T. E. (1988). Juror decision making in eyewitness identification cases. *Law and Human Behavior, 12*, 41–55.

Dabbs, M. O. (1992). Jury traumatization in high profile criminal trials: A case for crisis debriefing? *Law and Psychology Review, 16*, 201–216.

*Dagenais v. Canadian Broadcast Corp.*, 3 S. C. R. 835 (1994).

Dane, F. C. (1985). In search of reasonable doubt: A systematic examination of selected quantification approaches. *Law and Human Behavior, 9*, 141–158.

Daniels, S., & Martin, J. (1995). *Civil juries and the politics of reform*. Evanston, IL: Northwestern University Press.

Dann, B. M. (1993) "Learning lessons" and "speaking rights": Creating educated and democratic juries. *Indiana Law Journal, 68*, 1229–1279.

Dann, B. M., & Logan, G., III. (1996). Jury reform: The Arizona experience. *Judicature, 79*, 280–286.

*Daubert v. Merrell Dow Pharmaceuticals, Inc.*, 113 S.Ct. 2786 (1993).

Davis, J. H. (1980). Group decision and procedural justice. In M. L. Fishbein (Ed.), *Progress in social psychology* (vol. 1, pp. 157–229). Hillsdale, NJ: Erlbaum.

Davis, J. H., Bray, R. M., & Holt, R. (1977). The empirical study of decision processes in juries: A critical review. In J. L. Tapp, & F. J. Levine (Eds.) *Law, justice, and the individual in society: Psychological and legal issues*. New York: Holt, Rinehart, and Winston.

Davis, J. H., Kameda, T., Parks, C., Stasson, M., & Zimmerman, S. (1989). Some social mechanics of group decision making: The distribution of opinion, polling sequence, and implications of consensus. *Journal of Personality and Social Psychology, 57*, 1000–1012.

Deffenbacher, K. A. (1980). Eyewitness accuracy and confidence: Can we infer anything about their relationship? *Law and Human Behavior, 4*, 243–260.

Diamond, S. S. (1993). Instructing on death: Psychologists, juries, and judges. *American Psychologist, 48*, 423–434.

Diamond, S. S. (1997). Illuminations and shadows from jury simulations. *Law and Human Behavior, 21*, 561–571.

Diamond, S. S., & Casper, J. D. (1992). Blindfolding the jury to verdict consequences: Damages, experts, and the civil jury. *Law and Society Review, 26*, 513–563.

Diamond, S. S., & Zeisel, H. (1974). A courtroom experiment on juror selection and decision-making. *Personality and Social Psychology Bulletin, 1*, 276–277.

Dixon, R. (1999). With nowhere to hide: Workers are scrambling for privacy in the digital age. *Journal of Technology Law and Policy, 4*, 1–60.

Eakin, B. A. (1975). An empirical study of the effect of leadership influence on decision outcomes in different sized jury panels. *Kansas Journal of Sociology, 11*, 109–126.

*Edmonson v. Leesville Concrete Co.*, 500 U.S. 614 (1991).

Ellsworth, P. C. (1991). To tell what we know or wait for Godot? *Law and Human Behavior, 15*, 77–90.

Ellsworth, P. C. (1999). Jury reform at the end of the century: Real agreement, real changes. *University of Michigan Journal of Law Reform, 32*, 213–225.

Ellsworth, P. C., & Mauro, R. (1998). Psychology and law. In D. T. Gilbert, S. T. Fiske, & G. Lindzey. *The handbook of social psychology* (pp. 684–732). New York: Aronson.

Elwork, A., Alfini, J. J., & Sales, B. D. (1982). Towards understandable jury instructions. *Judicature, 65*, 432–443.

Elwork, A., & Sales, B. D. (1985). Jury instructions. In S. Kassin & L. Wrightsman (Eds.), *The psychology of evidence and trial procedure* (pp. 280–297). Beverly Hills, CA: Sage.

Elwork, A., Sales, B. D., & Alfini, J. J. (1977). Juridic decisions: In ignorance of the law or in light of it? *Law and Human Behavior, 1*, 163–189.

Elwork, A., Sales, B. D., & Alfini, J. J. (1982). *Making jury instructions understandable*. Charlottesville, VA: Michie.

Erlanger, J. (1977). Jury research in America: Its past and future. *Law and Society Review, 4*, 345–370.

Faigman, D. L. (1989). To have and have not: Assessing the value of social science to the law as science and policy. *Emory Law Journal, 38*, 1005–1095.

Faigman, D. L., & Baglioni, A. J. (1988). Bayes' theorem in the trial process: Instructing jurors on the value of statistical evidence. *Law and Human Behavior, 12*, 1–17.

*Federal Rules of Evidence*. (1984). St. Paul, MN: West.

Feigenson, N., Park, J., & Salovey, P. (1997). Effect of blameworthiness and outcome severity on attributions of responsibility and damage awards in comparative negligence cases. *Law and Human Behavior, 21*, 597–617.

Feldmann, T. B., & Bell, R. A. (1991). Crisis debriefing of a jury after a murder trial. *Hospital and Community Psychiatry, 42*, 79–81.

Feser, J.M., Jr. (1999). The California civil grand jury: From watchdogs to watched dogs. *McGeorge Law Review, 30*, 748–758.

Finkel, N. J. (1997). Commonsense justice, psychology and the law: Prototypes that are common, senseful, and not. *Psychology, Public Policy, and Law, 3*, 461–489.

Finkel, N. J., Shaw, R., Bercaw, S., & Koch, J. (1985). Insanity defenses: From the jurors' perspective. *Law and Psychology Review, 9*, 77–92.

Fiske, S. T., & Taylor, S. E. (1991). *Social cognition* (2nd ed.). New York: McGraw Hill

Fitzgerald, R., & Ellsworth, P. C. (1984). Due process vs. crime control. *Law and Human Behavior, 8*, 31–51.

Forsterlee, L., & Horowitz, I. A. (1997). Enhancing juror competence in a complex trial. *Applied Cognitive Psychology, 11*, 305–319.

ForsterLee, L., Horowitz, I. A., Bourgeois, M. J. (1993). Juror competence in civil trials: Effects of preinstruction and evidence technicality. *Journal of Applied Psychology, 78*(1), 14–21.

Fox, S. G., & Walters, H. A. (1986). The impact of general versus specific expert testimony and eyewitness confidence upon mock juror judgment. *Law and Human Behavior, 10*, 215–228.

Garvey, S. P., Johnson, S. L., & Marcus, P. (2000). Correcting deadly confusion: Responding to jury inquiries in capital cases. *Cornell Law Review, 85*, 627–655.

Georgia v. McCollum, 505 U.S. 42 (1992).

Gerbasi, K. C., Zuckerman, M., & Reis, H. T. (1977). Justice needs a new blindfold: A review of mock jury research. *Psychological Bulletin, 84*, 323–345.

Ghiardi, J., & Kircher, J. (1995). *Punitive damages law and practice.* Deerfield, IL: Clark, Boardman, and Callaghan.

Goodman, G. S., Tobey, A. E., Batterman-Faunce, J. M., Orcutt, H. K., Thomas, S., Shapiro, C., & Sachsenmaier, T. (1998). Face-to-face confrontation: Effects of closed circuit technology on children's eyewitness testimony and jurors' decisions. *Law and Human Behavior, 22*, 165–201.

Goodman-Delahunty, J., Greene, E., & Hsiao, W. (1998). Construing motive in videotaped killings: The role of jurors' attitudes toward the death penalty. *Law and Human Behavior, 22*, 257–271.

Greene, E. (1988). Judge's instruction on eyewitness testimony: Evaluation and revision. *Journal of Applied Social Psychology, 18*, 252–276.

Greene, E., Coon, D., & Bornstein, B. (2000). *The effects of limiting punitive damage awards.* Unpublished manuscript, University of Colorado.

Greene, E., & Dodge, M. (1995). The influence of prior record evidence on juror decision making. *Law and Human Behavior, 19*, 67–78.

Greene, E., & Johns, M. (in press). Jurors' use of instructions on negligence. *Journal of Applied Social Psychology.*

Greene, E., Johns, M., & Smith, A. (in press). The effects of defendant conduct on jury damage awards. *Journal of Applied Psychology.*

Greene, E., Woody, W.D., & Winter, R. (2000). Compensating plaintiffs and punishing defendants: Is bifurcation necessary? *Law and Human Behavior, 24*, 187–205.

Gross, S. R., & Syverud, K.D. (1996). Don't try: Civil jury verdicts in a system geared to settlement. *UCLA Law Review, 44*, 1 + (Retrieved from Lexis-Nexis database on the World Wide Web).

Hafemeister, T. L., & Ventis, W. L. (1994). Juror stress: Sources and implications. *Trial, 30*(10), 68–71.

Hafetz, F. P. (1999). Time to reform the grand jury. *Champion, 23*, 12–16, 63–65.

Haney, C. (1984). On the selection of capital juries: The biasing effects of the death qualification process. *Law and Human Behavior, 8*, 121–132.

Haney, C., & Lynch, M. (1994). Comprehending life and death matters: A preliminary study of California's capital penalty instructions. *Law and Human Behavior, 18*, 411–436.

Haney, C., & Lynch, M. (1997). Clarifying life and death matters: An analysis of instructional comprehension and penalty phase closing arguments. *Law and Human Behavior, 21*, 575–595.

Hannaford, P.J., Hans, V. P., & Munsterman, G.T. (2000). Permitting jury discussions during trial: Impact of the Arizona Reform. *Law and Human Behavior, 24*, 359–382.

Hans, V.P. (1996). The contested role of the civil jury in business litigation. *Judicature, 79*, 242–248.

Hans, V.P., Hannaford, P.L., & Munsterman, G.T. (1999). The Arizona jury reform permitting civil jury trial discussions: The views of trial participants, judges, and jurors. *University of Michigan Journal of Law Reform, 32*, 349–377.

Hans, V., & Ermann, M.D. (1989). Responses to corporate versus individual wrongdoing. *Law and Human Behavior, 13*, 151–166.

Harris, R.J., (1978). The effect of jury size and judge's instructions on memory for pragmatic implications from courtroom testimony. *Bulletin for Psychonomic Society, 11*, 129–132.

Hartwick, J., Sheppard, B.H., & Davis, J.H. (1982) Group remembering: Research and implications. In R. Guzzo (Ed.), *Improving group decision making in organizations: Working from theory* (pp. 41–72). New York: Academic Press.

Hastie, R. (1993a) (Ed.), *Inside the juror: The psychology of juror decision making*. New York: Cambridge University Press.

Hastie, R. (1993b) Introduction. In R. Hastie (Ed.), *Inside the juror: The psychology of juror decision making* (pp. 3–41). New York: Cambridge University Press.

Hastie, R., & Pennington, N. (1993). The story model for juror decision making. In R. Hastie (Ed.), *Inside the juro*. (pp. 192–221). New York: Cambridge University Press.

Hastie, R., Penrod, S.D., & Pennington, N. (1983). *Inside the jury*. Cambridge, MA: Harvard University Press.

Hastie, R., Schkade, D.A., & Payne, J.W. (1999). Juror judgments in civil cases: Hindsight effects on judgments of liability for punitive damages. *Law and Human Behavior, 23*, 597–614.

Hawkins, C. (1961). *Interaction and coalition realignments in consensus-seeking groups: a study of experimental jury deliberations*. Unpublished doctoral dissertation, University of Chicago.

Heuer, L., & Penrod, S. D. (1988). Increasing jurors' participation in trials: A field experiment with jury notetaking and question asking. *Law and Human Behavior, 12*, 231–261.

Heuer, L., & Penrod, S. D. (1989). Instructing jurors: A field experiment with written and preliminary instructions. *Law and Human Behavior, 13*, 409–430.

Heuer, L., & Penrod, S. D. (1994). Juror notetaking and question asking during trials: A national field experiment. *Law and Human Behavior, 18*, 121–150.

Hinkle, A. L. (1979). *The effect of expert witness and jury size on jury verdicts: A simulation study*. Unpublished doctoral dissertation, Auburn University.

Hoffman, M. B. (1997). Peremptory challenges should be abolished: A trial judge's perspective. *University of Chicago Law Review, 64*, 809–871.

Holstein, J. A. (1985). Jurors' interpretations and jury decision making. *Law and Human Behavior, 9*, 83–100.

Horowitz, I. A. (1980). Juror selection: A comparison of two methods in several criminal cases. *Journal of Applied Social Psychology, 19,* 86–99.

Horowitz, I. A., & Bordens, K. S. (1990). An experimental investigation of procedural issues in complex tort trials. *Law and Human Behavior, 14,* 269–285.

Horowitz, I. A., ForsterLee, L., & Brolly, I. (1996). Effects of trial complexity on decision making. *Journal of Applied Psychology, 81,* 757–768.

Horowitz, I. A. & Willging, T. E. (1984). *The psychology of law: Integrations and applications.* Boston: Little, Brown.

*J.E.B. v. Alabama, ex rel. T.B.,* 511 U.S. 127 (1994).

James, R. (1958). *Jurors' reactions to alternative definitions of legal insanity.* Unpublished doctoral dissertation, University of Chicago.

James, R. (1959). Status and competence of jurors. *American Journal of Sociology, 64,* 563–570.

*Johnson v. Louisiana,* 406 U.S. 356 (1972).

Johnson, C., & Haney, C. (1994). Felony voir dire: An exploratory study of its content and effect. *Law and Human Behavior, 18,* 487–506.

Jurow, G. (1971). New data on the effect of a death qualified jury on the guilt determination process. *Harvard Law Review, 84,* 567–611.

Kagehiro, D. K. (1990). Defining the standard of proof injury instructions. *Psychological Science, 1,* 194–200.

Kagehiro, D. K., & Stanton, W. C. (1985). Legal vs. quantified definitions of standards of proof. *Law and Human Behavior, 9,* 159–178.

Kairys, D., Schulman, J., & Harring, S. (1975) (Eds.). *The jury system: New methods for reducing prejudice.* Philadelphia: National Jury Project and National Lawyers Guild.

Kalven, H. Jr., & Zeisel, H. (1966). *The American jury.* Boston: Little, Brown.

Kaplan, M. F. (1983). A model of information integration injury deliberation. *Academic Psychology Bulletin, 5,* 91–96.

Kaplan, R. D. (1998). Cyber-smut: Regulating obscenity on the Internet: This new "internet" community, without any true geographic boundaries, does not fit within the current framework for analysis of community standards and regulation of interstate "distribution" of obscenity. *Stanford Law and Policy Review, 9,* 189–200.

Kaplan, S. M., & Winget, C. (1992). Occupational hazards of jury duty. *Bulletin of the American Academy of Psychiatry and the Law, 20,* 325–332.

Kelley, J. E. (1994). Addressing juror stress: A trial judge's perspective. *Drake Law Review, 43,* 97–125.

Kelso, J. C. (1996). Final report of the blue ribbon commission on jury system improvement. *Hastings Law Journal, 47,* 1433–1518.

Kerr, N. L. (1993). Stochastic models of juror decision making. In R. Hastie (Ed.), *Inside the juror.* (pp. 116–135). New York: Cambridge University Press.

Kerr, N. L., & Bray, R. M. (1982). *The psychology of the courtroom.* New York: Academic Press.

Kerr, N. L., & MacCoun, R. J. (1985). The effects of jury size and polling method on the process and product of jury deliberation. *Journal of Personality and Social Psychology, 48,* 349–363.

Kerr, N., MacCoun, R., & Kramer, G. (1996). Bias in judgment: Comparing individuals and groups. *Psychological Review, 103,* 687–719.

Kessler, J. B. (1973). An empirical study of six- and twelve-member jury decisionmaking processes. *University of Michigan Journal of Law Reform, 6,* 712–734.

King, N. J. (1999). The American criminal jury. *Law and Contemporary Problems, 62,* 41–67.

Kovera, M. B., Gresham, A. W., Borgida, E., Gray, E., & Regan, P. C. (1997). Does expert testimony inform or influence juror decision-making? A social cognitive analysis. *Journal of Applied Psychology, 82,* 178–191.

Kovera, M. B., Levy, R. J., Borgida, E., & Penrod, S. D. (1994). Expert testimony in child sexual abuse cases: Effects of expert evidence type and cross-examination. *Law and Human Behavior, 18,* 653–674.

Kovera, M. B., & McAuliff. B. D. (in press). The effects of peer review and evidence quality on judge evaluations of psychological science: Are judges effective gatekeepers? *Journal of Applied Psychology.*

Kovera, M. B., McAuliff, B. D., & Hebert, K. S. (1999). Reasoning about scientific evidence: Effects of juror gender and evidence quality on juror decisions in a hostile work environment case. *Journal of Applied Psychology, 84,* 362–375.

Kovera, M. B., Park, R. C., & Penrod, S. (1992). Jurors' perceptions of eyewitness and hearsay evidence. *Minnesota Law Review, 76,* 703–722.

Kramer, G. P., Kerr, N. L., & Carroll, J. S. (1990). Pretrial publicity, judicial remedies, and jury bias. *Law and Human Behavior, 14,* 409–437.

LaFave, W. R., & Isreal, J. H. (1985). *Criminal procedure* (Hombook Series, student ed.). St. Paul, MN: West.

Landsman, S., & Rakos, R. F. (1991). A research essay: A preliminary empirical enquiry concerning the prohibition of hearsay evidence in American courts. *Law and Psychology Review, 15,* 65–85.

Landy, D., & Aronson, E. (1969). The influence of the character of the criminal and his victim on the decision of simulated jurors. *Journal of Experimental Social Psychology, 5,* 141–152.

Law Reform Commission of Canada. (1979). *Studies on the jury.* Ottawa, ON: Author.

Lederer, F. I. (1997). *The courtroom as a stop on the information superhighway* [Online]. Available: http):///www.courtroom2l.net/AUSTLREF.HTML

Lederer, F. I. (1999a). The new courtroom: The intersection of evidence and technology: Some thoughts on the evidentiary aspects of technologically presented or produced evidence. *Southwestern University Law Review, 28,* 389–403.

Lederer, F. I. (1999b). Trial advocacy: The road to the virtual courtroom? A consideration of today's-and tomorrow's-high-technology courtrooms. *South Carolina Law Review, 50,* 799–844.

Lempert, R. (1993). Civil juries and complex cases: Taking stock after twelve years. In R. Litan, (Ed.), *Verdict: Assessing the civil jury.* Washington, D.C.: Brookings Institution.

Lerner, M.J. (1970). The desire for justice and reactions to victims. In J. Macaulay & L. Berkowitz (Eds.), *Altruism and helping behavior* (pp. 205–229). Orlando, FL: Academic Press

Lewis, P. E. (1999). A brief comment on the application of the "contemporary community standard" to the Internet. *Campbell Law Review, 22,* 143–166.

*Lockhart v. McCree,* 476 U.S. 162 (1986).

Loh, W. D. (1984). *Social research in the judicial process: Cases, readings, and text.* New York: Sage.

Luginbuhl, J., & Middendorf, K. (1988). Death penalty beliefs and jurors' responses to aggravating and mitigating circumstances in capital trials. *Law and Human Behavior, 12,* 263–281.

MacCoun, R. J. (1984). *Modeling the impact of extralegal bias and defined standards of proof on the decisions of mock jurors and juries.* Unpublished doctoral dissertation, Michigan State University.

MacCoun, R. (1993). Getting inside the black box: What empirical research tells us about civil jury behavior. In R. Litan (Ed.) *Verdict: Assessing the civil jury.* Washington, D.C.: Brookings Institution.

MacCoun, R. (1996). Differential treatment of corporate defendants by juries: An examination of the "deep pockets" hypothesis. *Law and Society Review, 30,* 121–161.

MacCoun, R. J., & Kerr, N. L. (1988). Asymmetric influence in mock deliberation: Jurors' bias for leniency. *Journal of Personality and Social Psychology, 54*, 21–33.

Marder, N. S. (1997). Deliberations and disclosures: A study of post-verdict interviews of jurors. *Iowa Law Review, 82*, 465–546.

Marder, N. S. (1999). The interplay of race and false claims of jury nullification. *University of Michigan Journal of Law Reform, 32*, 285–321.

McAuliff, B. D., & Kovera, M. B. (1999a, August). *Can jurors detect methodological flaws in scientific evidence?* Paper presented at the 107th Annual Convention of the American Psychological Association, Boston, MA.

McAuliff, B. D., & Kovera, M. B. (1999b, July). *Juror sensitivity to methodological flaws in expert evidence.* Paper presented at the meeting of the European Association for Psychology and Law, Dublin, Ireland.

McMahon, C., & Kornblau, D. L. (1995). Chief Judge Judith S. Kaye's program of jury selection reform in New York. *St. John's Journal of Legal Commentary, 10*, 263–289.

Middendorf, K., & Luginbuhl, J. (1995). The value of a nondirective voir dire style in jury selection. *Criminal Justice and Behavior, 22*, 129–151.

Miene, P., Park, R. C., & Borgida, E. (1992). Juror decision making and the evaluation of hearsay evidence. *Minnesota Law Review, 76*, 51–94.

Miller v. California, 413 U. S. 15 (1973).

Mills, L. R. (1973). Six- and twelve-member juries: An empirical study of trial results. *University of Michigan Journal of Law Reform, 6*, 671–711.

Mitchell, H. E., & Byrne, D. (1973). The defendant's dilemma: Effects of jurors' attitudes and authoritarianism on judicial decisions. *Journal of Personality and Social Psychology, 25*, 123–129.

Moran, G., & Comfort, J. C. (1982). Scientific juror selection: Sex as moderator of demographic and personality predictors of impaneled felony juror behavior. *Journal of Personality and Social Psychology, 43*, 1052–1063.

Moran, G., & Comfort, J. C. (1986). Neither "tentative" nor "fragmentary": Verdict preference of impaneled felony jurors as a function of attitude toward capital punishment. *Journal of Applied Psychology, 71*, 146–155.

Moran, G., & Cutler, B. L. (1991). The prejudicial impact of pretrial publicity. *Journal of Applied Social Psychology, 21*, 345–367.

Moran, G., Cutler, B. L., & DeLisa, A. (1994). Attitudes toward tort reform, scientific jury selection, and juror bias: Verdict inclination in criminal and civil trials. *Law and Psychology Review, 18*, 309–328.

Moran, G., Cutler, B. L., & Loftus, E. F. (1990). Jury selection in major controlled substance trials: The need for extended voir dire. *Forensic Reports, 3*, 331–348.

Morgan, C. (1999). Employer monitoring of employee electronic mail and Internet use. *McGill Law Journal, 44*, 849–902.

Narby, D. J., & Cutler, B. L. (1994). Effectiveness of voir dire as a safeguard in eyewitness cases. *Journal of Applied Psychology, 79*, 729–734.

Narby, D. J., Cutler, B. L., & Moran, G. (1993). A meta-analysis of the association between authoritarianism and jurors' perceptions of defendant culpability. *Journal of Applied Psychology, 78*, 34–42.

National Association of Criminal Defense Lawyers, Inc. (1998). Grand jury reform: High time for a bill of rights for the grand jury. *Champion, 22*, 5, 12, 34.

National Center for State Courts (1998). Through the eyes of the juror: A manual for addressing juror stress. (NCSC Publication No. R-209). Williamsburg, VA: Author.

Neises, M. L., & Dillehay, R. C. (1987). Death qualification and conviction proneness: Witt and Witherspoon compared. *Behavioral Sciences and the Law, 5*, 479–494.

Nemeth, C. (1977). Interactions between jurors as a function of majority vs. unanimity decision rules. *Journal of Applied Social Psychology, 7*, 38–56.

Nemeth, C. (1981). Jury trials: Psychology and the law. *Advances in Experimental Social Psychology, 14*, 309–367.

Nemeth, C., & Sosis, R. H. (1973). A simulated jury study: Characteristics of the defendant and the jurors. *Journal of Social Psychology, 90*, 221–229.

Nietzel, M. T., & Dillehay, R. C. (1986). *Psychological consultation in the courtroom.* New York: Pergamon Press.

Nietzel, M. T., McCarthy, D. M., & Kern, M. J. (1999). Juries: The current state of the empirical literature. In R. Roesch, S. D. Hart, & J. R. P. Ogloff (Eds.), *Psychology and law: The state of the discipline* (pp. 23–52). New York: Kluwer Academic/Plenum Publishers.

Nua, Ltd. (1999) How many online? [On-line] Available: *http://www.nua.ie/surveys/how_many_online/world.html.*

Nua, Ltd. (2000) How many online? [On-line] Available: *http://www.nua.ie/surveys/how_many_online/index.html.*

O'Neil, K. (2000). A guide to running surveys and experiments on the World-Wide Web. [On-line]. Available: http://psych.unl.edu/psychlaw/guide/guide.asp.

Ogloff, J. R. P. (1998). *Judicial instructions and the jury: A comparison of alternative strategies.* Paper prepared for the British Columbia Law Foundation.

Ogloff, J. R. P., & Vidmar, N. (1994). The impact of pretrial publicity on jurors: A study to compare the relative effects of television and print media in a child sexual abuse case. *Law and Human Behavior, 18*, 507–525.

Olczak, P. V., Kaplan, M. F., & Penrod, S. (1991). Attorneys' lay psychology and its effectiveness in selecting jurors: Three empirical studies. *Journal of Social Behavior and Personality, 6*, 431–452.

Otto, A. L., Penrod, S. D., & Dexter, H. D. (1994). The biasing impact of pretrial publicity on juror judgments. *Law and Human Behavior, 18*, 453–470.

Padawer-Singer, A. M., & Barton, A. H. (1975). The impact of pretrial publicity on jurors' verdicts. In R. J. Simon (Ed.), *The jury system in America: A critical overview.* Beverly Hills, CA: Sage.

Padawer-Singer, A. M., Singer, A. N., & Singer, R. L. (1977). An experimental study of twelve vs. six member juries under unanimous vs. nonunanimous decisions. In B. D. Sales (Ed.), *Psychology in the legal process.* New York: Spectrum.

Paglia, A., & Schuller, R. A. (1998). Jurors' use of hearsay evidence: The effects of type and timing of instructions. *Law and Human Behavior, 22*, 501–518.

Park, R. (1987). A subject approach to hearsay reform. *Michigan Law Review, 86*, 51–94.

Pennington, N., & Hastie, R. (1981). Juror decision-making models: The generalization gap. *Psychological Bulletin, 89*, 246–287.

Pennington, N., & Hastie, R. (1986). Evidence evaluation in complex decision making. *Journal of Personality and Social Psychology, 51*, 242–258.

Pennington, N., & Hastie, R. (1988). Explanation-based decision making: Effects of memory structure on judgment. *Journal of Experimental Psychology: Learning, Memory, and Cognition, 14*, 521–533.

Pennington, N., & Hastie, R. (1993). Reasoning in explanation-based decision making. *Cognition, 49*, 123–163.

Penrod, S., & Hastie, R. (1979). Models of jury decision-making: A critical review. *Psychological Bulletin, 86*, 462–492.

Penrod, S., & Hastie, R. (1980). A computer simulation of jury decision making. *Psychological Review, 87*, 133–159.

Penrod, S. D., & Heuer, L. (1997). Tweaking commonsense: Assessing aids to jury decision-making. *Psychology, Public Policy, and Law, 3*, 259–284.

*Powers v. Ohio*, 499 U.S. 400 (1991).

Pyszczynski, T. A., Greenberg, J., Mack, D., & Wrightsman, L. S. (1981). Opening statements in a jury trial: The effect of promising more than the evidence can show. *Journal of Applied Social Psychology, 11*, 434–444.

Quinlan, P. (1993). Secrecy of jury deliberations-Is the cost too high? *Criminal Reports, 22*, 127–165.

R. v. Levogiannis, 4 Can. S. C. R. 475 (1993).

Raitz, A., Greene, E., Goodman, J., & Loftus, E. F. (1990). Determining damages: The influence of expert testimony on jurors' decision making. *Law and Human Behavior, 14*, 385–395.

Rakos, R. F., & Landsman, S. (1992). Researching the hearsay rule: Emerging findings, general issues, and future directions. *Minnesota Law Review, 76*, 655–681.

Redmount, R. S. (1957). Psychological tests for selecting jurors. *Kansas Law Review, 5*, 391–403.

Reed, J. P. (1965). Jury deliberations, voting and verdict trends. *Southwest Social Science Quarterly, 45*, 361–370.

Reed, J. P., & Reed, R. S. (1977). Liberalism-conservatism as an indicator of jury product and process. *Law and Human Behavior, 1*, 81–86.

Reifman, A., Gusick, S. M., & Ellsworth, P. C. (1992). Real jurors' understanding of the law in real cases. *Law and Human Behavior, 16*, 539–554.

*Reno v. American Civil Liberties Union*, 521 U. S. 844 (1997).

Robbennolt, J. K. (in press). Outcome severity and judgments of responsibility: A meta analytic review. *Journal of Applied Social Psychology*.

Robbennolt, J. K., & Sobus, M. S. (1997). An integration of hindsight bias and counterfactual thinking: Decision-making and drug courier profiles. *Law and Human Behavior, 21*, 539–560.

Robbennolt, J. K., & Studebaker, C. A. (1999). Anchoring in the courtroom: The effects of caps on punitive damages. *Law and Human Behavior, 23*, 353–373.

Rose, V. G., & Ogloff, J. R. P. (1998, March). *A method of assessing the comprehensibility of jury instructions*. Paper presented at the Biennial Meeting of the American Psychology-Law Society, Redondo Beach, CA.

Ross, D. F., Hopkins, S., Hanson, E., Lindsay, R. C. L., Hazen, K., & Eslinger, T. (1994). The impact of protective shields and videotape testimony on conviction rates in a simulated trial of child sexual abuse. *Law and Human Behavior, 18*, 553–566.

Roth v. United States, 354 U.S. 476 (1957).

Saks, M. J. (1977). *Jury verdicts: The role of group size and social decision rule*. Lexington, MA: Lexington Books (D.C. Heath).

Saks, M. J. (1992). Do we really know anything about the behavior of the tort litigation system- and why not? *University of Pennsylvania Law Review, 140*, 1147–1287.

Saks, M. J., Hollinger, L. A., Wissler, R. L., Evans, D. L., & Hart, A. J. (1997). Reducing variability in civil jury awards. *Law and Human Behavior, 21*, 243–256.

Saks, M. J. & Marti, M. W. (1997). A meta-analysis of the effects of jury size. *Law and Human Behavior, 21*, 451–467.

Sales, B. D., Elwork, A., & Alfini, J. J. (1977). Improving comprehension for jury instructions. In B. D. Sales (Ed.), *The criminal justice system* (pp. 23–90). New York: Plenum.

Sandys, M., & Dillehay, R. C. (1995). First-ballot votes, predeliberation dispositions, and final verdicts in jury trials. *Law and Human Behavior, 19*, 175–195.

Schuller, R. A. (1992). The impact of battered woman syndrome evidence on jury decision processes. *Law and Human Behavior, 16*, 597–620.

Schuller, R. A. (1995). Expert evidence and hearsay: The influence of "secondhand" information on jurors' decisions. *Law and Human Behavior, 19*, 345–362.

Schuller, R. A., & Cripps, J. (1998). Expert evidence pertaining to battered women: The impact of gender of expert and timing of testimony. *Law and Human Behavior, 22*, 17–31.

Schuller, R. A., & Hastings, P. A. (1996). Trials of battered women who kill: The impact of alternative forms of expert evidence. *Law and Human Behavior, 20*, 167–187.

Schuller, R. A., & Paglia, A. (1999). An empirical study: Juror sensitivity to variations in hearsay conveyed via expert evidence. *Law and Psychology Review, 23*, 131–152.

Schulman, J., Shaver, P., Colman, R., Emrich, B., & Christie, R. (1973, May). Recipe for a jury. *Psychology Today*, pp. 37–83.

Schum, D. A., & Martin, A. W. (1993). Formal and empirical research on cascaded inference in jurisprudence. In R. Hastie (Ed.) *Inside the juror: The psychology of juror decision making.* New York, NY: Cambridge University Press.

Sealy, A. P., & Cornish, W. R. (1973b, April). Juries and the rules of evidence. *Criminal Law Review*, pp. 208–223.

Severance, L. J., & Loftus, E. F. (1982). Improving the ability of jurors to comprehend and apply criminal jury instructions. *Law and Society Review, 17*, 153–197.

Shapiro, F. R. (2000). The most-cited legal books published since 1978. *The Journal of Legal Studies, 29*, 397–407.

Sigall, H., & Ostrove, N. (1975). Beautiful but dangerous: Effects of offender attractiveness and nature of crime on juridic judgment. *Journal of Personality and Social Psychology, 88*, 149–150.

Simon, R. J. (1967). *The jury and the defense of insanity.* Boston: Little, Brown.

Simon, R. J. (1968). The effects of newspapers on the verdicts of potential jurors. In R. J. Simon (Ed.), *The sociology of law.* San Francisco: Chandler.

Smith, V. L. (1991). Prototypes in the courtroom: Lay representations of legal concepts. *Journal of Personality and Social Psychology, 61*, 857–872.

Smith, V. L. (1993). When prior knowledge and law collide: Helping jurors to use the law. *Law and Human Behavior, 17*, 507–536.

Smith, V. L., & Kassin, S. (1993). Effects of the dynamite charge on the deliberations of deadlocked mock juries. *Law and Human Behavior, 17*, 625–643.

Sorensen, R. (1954). *The role of public sentiment and personal prejudice in jury trials of criminal cases.* Unpublished doctoral dissertation, University of Chicago.

Stasser, G., Kerr, N. L., & Bray, R. M. (1982). The social psychology of jury deliberations: Structure, process, and product. In N. L. Kerr & R. Bray (Eds.), *The psychology of the courtroom* (pp. 221–256). New York: Academic Press.

Steblay, N. M., Besirevic, J., Fulero, S. M., & Jimenez-Lorente, B. (1999). The effects of pretrial publicity on juror verdicts: A meta-analytic review. *Law and Human Behavior, 23*, 219–235.

Steele, W. W., & Thornburg, E. G. (1988–89). Jury instructions: A persistent failure to communicate. *North Carolina Law Review, 67*, 77–119.

Strawn, D. J., & Buchanan, R. W. (1976). Jury confusion: A threat to justice. *Judicature, 59*, 478–483.

Strier, F. (1997). The road to reform: Judges on juries and attorneys. *Loyola of Las Angeles Law Review, 30*, 1249–1275.

Strodtbeck, F., James, R., & Hawkins, C. (1957). Social status injury deliberations. *American Sociological Review, 22*, 713–718.

Strodtbeck, F., & Mann, R. (1956). Sex role differentiation injury deliberations. *Sociometry, 19*, 3–11.

Studebaker, C. A., & Penrod, S. D. (1997). Pretrial publicity: The media, the law, and commonsense. *Psychology, Public Policy, and Law, 3*, 428–460.

Suggs, D., & Sales, B. D. (1978). Using communication cues to evaluate prospective jurors in the voir dire. *Arizona Law Review, 20*, 629–642.

Tanford, J. A. (1991). Law reform by courts, legislatures, and commissions following empirical research on jury instructions. *Law & Society Review, 25*, 155–175.

Tanford, J. A. (1992). The law and psychology of jury instructions. In J. R. P. Ogloff (Ed.), *Law and psychology: The broadening of the discipline* (pp. 305–329). Durham, NC: Carolina Academic Press.

Tanford, S., & Penrod, S. (1983). Computer modeling of influence in the jury: The role of the consistent juror. *Social Psychology Quarterly, 46,* 200–212.

Thomas, E. A., & Hogue, A. (1976). Apparent weight of evidence, decision criteria, and confidence ratings in juror decision making. *Psychological Review, 83,* 442–465.

Thompson, W. C. (1989). Death qualification after Wainwright v. Witt and Lockhart v. McCree. *Law and Human Behavior, 13,* 185–215.

Thompson, W. C., Cowan, C. L., Ellsworth, P. C., & Harrington, J. C. (1984). Death penalty attitudes and conviction proneness: The translation of attitudes into verdicts. *Law and Human Behavior, 8,* 95–113.

Tobey, A. E., Goodman, G. S., Batterman-Faunce, J. M., Orcutt, H. K., & Sachsenmaier, T. (1995). Balancing the rights of children and defendants: Effects of closed circuit television on children's accuracy and jurors perceptions. In M. S. Zaragoza et al. (Eds.), *Memory and testimony in the child witness* (pp. 214–239). Thousand Oaks, CA: Sage.

Tulving, E. (1983). *Elements of episodic memory.* Oxford: Clarendon Press.

TXO Production Corp. v. Alliance Resources Corp., 509 U.S. 443 (1993).

Uebelein, C. (1999). Jury innovations in the 21st century. *Hawaii Bar Journal, 3,* 6.

Valenti, A., & Downing, L. (1974–1975). Six versus twelve member juries: An experimental test of the Supreme Court assumption of functional equivalence. *Personality and Social Psychology Bulletin, 1,* 273–275.

Vidmar, N. (1979). The other issues in jury simulation research: A commentary with particular reference to defendant character studies. *Law and Human Behavior, 3,* 95–106.

Vidmar, N. (1995). *Medical malpractice and the American jury: Confronting the myths about jury incompetence, deep pockets, and outrageous damage awards.* Ann Arbor, Michigan: The University of Michigan Press.

Vidmar, N. (1998). The performance of the American civil jury: An empirical perspective. *Arizona Law Review, 40,* 849–899.

Vidmar, N. (1999a). Forward. *Law and Contemporary Problems, 62,* 1–6.

Vidmar, N. (1999b). The Canadian criminal jury: Searching for a middle ground. *Law and Contemporary Problems, 62,* 141–172.

Vidmar, N., & Rice, J. J. (1993). Assessments of noneconomic damage awards in medical negligence: A comparison of jurors with legal professionals. *Iowa Law Review, 78,* 883–911.

Visher, C. A. (1987). Juror decision making: The importance of evidence. *Law and Human Behavior, 11,* 117.

Warren, M. (chair) (2000, March). *An examination of scholarly publishing in psychology and law: Why do we publish what we publish? How do we select it? Is peer review fair to authors? What do people in the real world want from our literature?* Symposium presented at the biennial conference of the American Psychology-Law Society, New Orleans, LA.

Weeks v. Angelone, 120 S. Ct. 727 (2000).

Weir, J. A., & Wrightsman, L. S. (1990). The determinants of mock jurors' verdicts in a rape case. *Journal of Applied Social Psychology, 20,* 901–919.

Weiten, W., & Diamond, S. S. (1979). A critical review of the jury simulation paradigm. *Law and Human Behavior, 3,* 71–93.

Wells, G. L, & Leippe, M. R. (1981). How do triers of fact infer the accuracy of eyewitness identifications? Using memory for peripheral detail can be misleading. *Journal of Applied Psychology, 66,* 682–687.

Wells, G. L., Lindsay, R. C., & Ferguson, T. J. (1979). Accuracy, confidence, and juror perceptions in eyewitness identification. *Journal of Applied Psychology, 64,* 440–448.

Wiener, R. L., Pritchard, C. C., & Weston, M. (1995). Comprehensibility of approved jury instructions in capital murder cases. *Journal of Applied Psychology, 80,* 455–467.

Williams v. Florida, 399 U.S. 78 (1970).

Wissler, R. L., Evans, D. L., Hart, A. J., Morry, M. M., & Saks, M. J. (1997). Explaining "pain and suffering" awards: The role of injury characteristics and fault attributions. *Law and Human Behavior, 21,* 181–207.

Wissler, R. L., Hart, A. J., & Saks, M. J. (1999). Decision-making about general damages: A comparison of jurors, judges, and lawyers. *Michigan Law Review, 98,* 751–826.

Wissler, R. L., Kuehn, P., & Saks, M. J. (in press). Instructing jurors on general damages. *Psychology, Public Policy, and Law.*

Wolfgang, M., & Reidel, M. (1973). Race and the death penalty. *Annals of the Academy of Political and Social Science, 407,* 119–133.

Zeisel, H. (1971). And then there were none: The diminution of the federal jury. *University of Chicago Law Review, 38,* 710–724.

Zeisel, H., & Callahan, T. (1963). Split trials and time saving: A statistical analysis. *Harvard Law Review, 76,* 1606–1625.

Zeisel, H., & Diamond, S. (1976). The jury selection in the Mitchell-Stans conspiracy trial. *American Bar Foundation Research Journal, 1,* 151–174.

Zeisel, H., & Diamond, S. S. (1978). The effect of peremptory challenges on jury verdict: An experiment in a federal district court. *Stanford Law Review, 30,* 491–531.

Zickafoose, D. J., & Bornstein, B. H. (1999). Double discounting: The effects of comparative negligence on mock juror decision making. *Law and Human Behavior, 23,* 577–596.

# 9

# The Monetary Worth of Psychological Injury

## What Are Litigants Suing For?

## JOTI SAMRA AND WILLIAM J. KOCH

There exist public perceptions that a "litigation crisis" or "litigation explosion" exists, and that this crisis is wreaking havoc on our civil court system (Endelman, Abraham, & Erlanger, 1992; Galanter, 1986; Saks, 1992). This public perception of a litigation crisis appears to be the result of media attention given to very large damage awards (Bailis & MacCoun, 1996; Lind, 1997; see Greene et al., this book, for illustrative examples). However, the existence of this "explosion" of litigation has been seriously questioned by legal scholars. Michael Saks refers to the tort litigation system as a "mouse with an otherworldly roar" (1992, p. 1287), and emphasizes that we lack proper longitudinal base rates to make any claims about alleged increases in litigiousness. Regardless, the media, policymakers, politicians, and other professionals apparently believe that litigation runs amok, and the public appears to accept these commentators' perceptions as factual. Given these widely-held beliefs, it behooves civil forensic psychology researchers to investigate the factors that influence individuals'

JOTI SAMRA • Program in Law and Forensic Psychology, Simon Fraser University and Clinical Psychology Resident, Department of Psychiatry & Behavioral Sciences, University of Washington School of Medicine, Seattle, Washington 98195. WILLIAM J. KOCH • Psychology Residency Training, Health Psychology Clinic, University of British Columbia Psychiatry, University of British Columbia Hospital, Vancouver, British Columbia, Canada V6T 2B5.

decisions to claim and litigate. An understanding of the factors driving people to proceed with civil litigation is intimately related to the question of what losses litigants are attempting to redress.

Undoubtedly, one of the oldest known motivations for human behavior is financial incentive. When litigating, plaintiffs are apparently seeking both justice and economic compensation (see Wayte, Samra, Robbennolt, Heuer, & Koch, this book). Therefore, it seems that legal scholars and the courts need greater knowledge of the magnitude and nature of economic loss associated with different types of tortious events and mental health conditions. Economic theories of litigation, as addressed in our previous chapter, suggest that the magnitude of loss should be associated with decisions to litigate and the outcome of litigation. In fact, injury severity (a legally relevant factor) has been demonstrated to be a reliable predictor of damage awards (see Greene et al. chapter, this book). One class of loss of particular interest to psychologists is the loss associated with deficits in mental health.

In this chapter, we review the known literature on direct and indirect losses associated with different mental health conditions, and tortious events commonly resulting in mental health conditions, which may be litigated in civil proceedings. We then discuss the conundrum of litigation – that is, the extent to which litigation or compensation systems are thought to exacerbate the losses of plaintiffs and thus complicate judgments of liability and damages. We conclude with a discussion of promising areas for future research.

## THE ECONOMICS OF MENTAL INJURIES

In this section, we will review: (a) the mechanisms through which reimbursement for psychological injuries may be obtained; (b) approaches to estimating mental health costs; and (c) the economic costs and other losses associated with specific mental health conditions and tortious events.

### MECHANISMS FOR OBTAINING REDRESS FOR PSYCHOLOGICAL INJURIES

The compensability of psychological injuries is increasingly being recognized (Douglas, Huss, Murdoch, Washington, & Koch, in press; Melton, Petrila, Poythress, & Slobogin, 1997), although there still exist restrictions in both Canada and the United States on the degree and types of compensation that may be received for psychological injuries (Douglas et al., in press; Goodman-Delahunty & Foote, 1995). There are two primary mechanisms through which restitution for psychological injuries may be obtained: civil tort systems, and workers' compensation systems (Melton et al., 1997). A tort is a civil wrong for which the law provides compensation (Linden, 1997). The purpose of tort litigation is to provide monetary compensation to injured parties in order to return those parties to their original, pre-injury position (Douglas & Koch, 2001; Waddams, 1997). Very generally, this compensation may be for direct economic losses associated with the injury (e.g., medical expenses), non-quantifiable damages (e.g., pain and suffering), and future damages (e.g., future loss of earnings; see Douglas et al., in press, for a detailed review of the types of tort damages that are compensable in both American and Canadian jurisprudence).

Although both workers' compensation and civil tort systems may provide monetary compensation for psychological injuries, these systems differ in several fundamental ways (Melton et al., 1997; Roberts & Young, 1997). First, workers' compensation systems developed as no-fault insurance systems originally instituted to replace tort redress for work-related injuries and disability. Thus, the adoption of workers' compensation systems in North America resulted in employers having to give up the rights and defenses they previously held under the civil tort system, and employees having to give up the compensation available under tort law. A second related difference is that workers' compensation systems provide restitution to injured parties only for medical or rehabilitation costs, and for costs related to loss of earning capacity; in contrast, injured parties who pursue litigation through civil torts may also be compensated for pain and suffering. Finally, the guidelines for redress under workers' compensation systems are delineated in provincial or state legislature, whereas torts are adjudicated by the civil judicial system. As a result, the degree of compensation available under workers' compensation systems is well defined and circumscribed, whereas it is much more variable under civil tort litigation.

## APPROACHES TO ESTIMATING MENTAL HEALTH COSTS

Prior to reviewing the magnitude of costs associated with various mental conditions, we will describe the two main approaches used to estimate the costs of mental disorders.

### Human Capital Approach

The Human Capital approach "considers the productive contributions a person makes to society and argues that, in a competitive labor market, the value of these productive contributions is best measured by the market wage" (Greenberg, Stiglin, Finkelstein, & Berndt, 1993, p. 406;

see also Gottlieb, 1988). Within this approach, both the direct and indirect costs of mental health conditions are estimated. *Direct costs* are relatively easy to calculate, and include all health and mental health treatment costs, including costs related to professional medical/psychiatric services, rehabilitation, counseling, and medication (Booth, Zhang, Rost, Clardy, Smith, & Smith, 1997; Eckett, 1995; Greenberg et al., 1993; Hammerman & Maikowski, 1983). In contrast, *indirect/hidden costs* are more difficult to quantify. Indirect/hidden costs include costs related to lost wages, lost productivity (e.g., foregone potential employment), caregivers' costs/ burden, and early mortality (Booth et al., 1997; Eckett, 1995; McCrone & Weich, 1996).

## Willingness to Pay Approach

The second approach taken to estimate mental health costs is the Willingness to Pay approach, which incorporates "the adverse effects of pain and suffering, or other quality-of-life issues, as well as the possible willingness of sufferers to pay more than their expected earnings loss if they could avoid an illness" (Greenberg et al., 1993, p. 406; see also Gottlieb, 1988). In contrast to the Human Capital approach, this approach utilizes the individual (and not the society) as the starting point for analysis, and considers individuals' estimations of the benefits and costs of an injury or disorder, and their consequent willingness to pay to avoid same (Haase, 1992). One of the principal difficulties with this approach is that predictions of the duration and course of an illness are required, as are estimates of the future costs and impact of the illness upon workplace activity (Greenberg et al., 1993). This leads one to ask to what extent mental health conditions remit and relapse, and the average episode duration of various mental health conditions. A second fundamental limitation is that although the Willingness to Pay approach theoretically espouses consideration of factors such as quality of life in estimating costs, these types of factors are not easily quantifiable.

> It is very hard to describe in economic costs what happens to a mother with [panic attacks] with five children who suddenly finds herself housebound and unable to drive. She must still take care of the family while walking around with terrifying attacks of anxiety that cause her to think she is going to die. Although it is extremely difficult to translate matters related to quality of life into monetary values, it cannot be denied that these social and psychological costs are substantial. (Edlund & Swann, 1987, p. 1279)

Although there is little debate that many mental health conditions compromise an individual's quality of life, data on the mental health costs associated with pain and suffering are notably lacking (Rice & Miller, 1998). There is, however a considerable body of literature that has examined the direct and indirect costs of mental disorders.

## Direct and Indirect Costs of Mental Health Conditions

In 1999, the U.S. Department of Health and Human Services released the first Surgeon General's Report on Mental Health – *Mental Health: A Report of the Surgeon General* – a comprehensive document which highlights the psychosocial and economic magnitude of mental health and mental illness. Two major themes underlie the Surgeon General's Report: (1) the position that mental health is fundamental to health in general; and (2) the assertion that mental disorders constitute legitimate health conditions. In line with the position of this report, particularly in the last decade the economic, social, and personal magnitude of mental health conditions has begun to be recognized.

In 1990, the World Health Organization (WHO) estimated that, in developing regions (where four-fifths of the world population resides), mental disease accounted for 11% of the total disease burden and 1% of mortality rates (Murray & Lopez, 1996). In fact, five of the ten leading causes of disability world-wide were psychological conditions (i.e., depression, alcohol use, bipolar affective disorder, schizophrenia, and obsessive-compulsive disorder). Future projections are that mental illness will account for 15% of the world-wide disease burden by 2020, with major depression becoming one of the 3 leading causes of this burden (Murray & Lopez, 1996). Despite these startling figures, *The Global Burden of Disease* report concluded the impact of mental disorders on health and productivity is grossly unrecognized by public health care systems and policymakers (Murray & Lopez, 1996).

The direct and indirect costs of mental health conditions have been most extensively studied in the United States. In 1990, the total economic cost of mental illness in the US was estimated to be $147.8 billion, with the breakdown of costs by disorder being as follows: anxiety disorders—$46.6 billion; schizophrenic disorders—$32.5 billion; affective disorders—$30.4 billion; and, other disorders—$38.4 billion (Rice & Miller, 1998). Not surprisingly to some readers, the indirect costs of mental illness ($79 billion) were estimated to be higher than the direct costs ($69 billion), with the bulk of the indirect costs being attributable to loss of productivity in usual activities (Rice & Miller, 1998).

### Costs of Specific Mental Health Conditions

There are three primary types of situations from which psychological injuries may arise: (1) workplace injuries; (2) motor vehicle accidents (MVAs); and, (3) criminal victimization. Redress for psychological injuries resulting from workplace injuries will, in most cases, be obtained via adjudication through a workers' compensation system. Although workers' compensation systems are no-fault systems which have contractual obligations to cover workers' medical, rehabilitation, and income-replacement costs, as many as 20% of workers' compensation claims are contested (Roberts & Young, 1997). The most common workplace-related injuries that psychologists may encounter are soft tissue injuries, posttraumatic stress disorder (PTSD), and traumatic brain injury (TBI; Bennett & Raymond, 1997; Crook, Moldofsky, & Shannon, 1998). Overall however, claims for mental/psychological injury under workers' compensation systems represent only a small proportion of total claims (Lippel, 1990).

Civil litigation for psychological injuries is more likely to arise from MVAs or other tortious events (e.g., crime-related experiences). In virtually all cases, compensation for psychological injuries resulting from MVAs and crime is obtained via civil tort litigation (although there are exceptions; for example, injury from an MVA which occurs during hours of employment may more appropriately be compensated by a workers' compensation board). In the case of MVAs, psychological injuries for which compensation may be sought are also most likely to be soft tissue injuries, PTSD, or TBI (Bennett & Raymond, 1997; Ehlers, Mayou, & Bryant, 1998; Green, McFarlane, Hunter, & Griggs, 1993; Miller, 1998; Vingilis, Larkin, Stoduto, Parkinson-Heyes, & McLellan, 1996). Crime- related psychological injuries (e.g., from sexual harassment; sexual assault) are commonly PTSD and anxiety/depression (Bisson & Shepherd, 1995; Resnick, Kilpatrick, & Lipovsky, 1991; Sorenson & Golding, 1990; Steketee & Foa, 1987). Within employment litigation contexts, anxiety disorders, PTSD, depression, and somatoform disorders are common (Goodman-Delahunty & Foote, 1995).

We will first review the costs associated with specific diagnostic categories (e.g., depression). This will be followed by a discussion of costs associated with specific types of tortious events (e.g., sexual harassment). As depression and anxiety disorders account for the largest proportion of mental health costs in the US (Rice & Miller, 1998), and as these two disorders have high co-morbidity among workplace injured (Ash & Goldstein, 1995; Burton, Polatin, & Gatchel, 1997), MVA-injured (see Taylor & Koch, 1995), and criminally victimized individuals (Boudreaux, Kilpatrick, Resnick, Best, & Saunders, 1998; Riggs, Dancu, Gershuny, Greenberg, & Foa, 1992), the bulk of the discussion will focus on the costs associated with depression and anxiety disorders.

## Depression

Depression has been the most frequently studied disorder with respect to economic costs. Estimates of the lifetime prevalence of Major

Depressive Disorder (MDD) range from 10 to 25 percent for women and between 5 and 12 percent for men (APA, 1994). The total annual costs of depression in the US have been estimated to be upwards of $43 billion (Greenberg et al., 1993). Over half of this figure (55%, or $23.8 billion) has been estimated to be attributable to morbidity costs (e.g., absenteeism from work; reduction in productive capacity), 28% of the total costs ($12.4 billion) are attributable to direct costs, and the remaining 17% ($7.5 billion) relate to mortality costs. Other estimates suggest that the direct costs of depression range from $12.4 to $19.2 billion per annum in the US, and constitute less than 10% of the total costs for depression (see Booth et al., 1997). Extrapolating from these more liberal figures, the total annual costs of depression in the US may be well over $100 billion. Prospective examinations of health care costs in the US reveal that costs per person were almost fives times as high for depressed or anxious patients ($3,320 per 6-month period) than costs for non-distressed patients ($749; Simon, Ormel, VonKorff, & Barlow, 1995).

High rates of general, work, social, and economic disability are found among those with affective disorders (see Kouzis & Eaton, 1994; Parikh, Wasylenki, Goering, & Wong, 1996). However, the above estimates of the costs of depression are conservative ones, as they do not account for factors such as declines in quality of life (Greenberg et al., 1993), despite evidence that depression impacts individuals' capacities for social functioning, negatively impacts family and marital relationships, and impacts perceived quality of life (Lane & McDonald, 1994; Ramirez & Cervera, 1999). The physical and emotional effects of depression have been found to be comparable to the effects of chronic medical conditions such as diabetes, arthritis, back, lung, or gastrointestinal disorders (see Candilis & Pollack, 1997).

Clearly, the costs of depression will increase with longer or repeated episode durations. The course of untreated episodes of major depression is variable, but any one episode may last for 6 months or longer (American Psychiatric Association [APA], 1994). In 20–30% of afflicted individuals, depressive symptoms may persist for months or years, and continue to be associated with disability or subjective distress; in 5–10% of cases, the depression may continue to significantly impair functioning for 2 years or greater (APA, 1994). These duration figures should be alarming to readers given the prevalence of depression and the fact that only about one-third of individuals with depression receive treatment (Rupp, 1995).

SUB-THRESHOLD DEPRESSION.    As with Major Depression, the presence of sub-threshold depression is correlated with higher rates of disability and lost work days, increased usage of mental health services, poorer self-ratings of emotional health, and increased likelihood of suicide attempts (see Judd, Paulus, Wells, & Rapaport, 1996). Elevated rates of financial strain and chronic limitations in physical/job functioning are reported both by those with major and sub-threshold depression (Judd et al., 1996). Thus, it is clear that depressive affect, whether of diagnostic severity or just sub-threshold intensity, has substantial economic effects on sufferers. This has major implications for disability insurers and auto insurers, and other third-party payers who are faced with high rates of depression-related claims. To the extent that claimants experience depressive affect of even sub-clinical intensity but itself or in combination with other health problems, their direct and indirect economic losses will increase.

## Anxiety Disorders

The total cost of anxiety disorders in the US in 1990 has been estimated as being $46.6 billion (Rice & Miller, 1998). The bulk of these costs appear to relate to increased health care utilization. In an investigation from the National Institute of Mental Health Epidemiological Catchment Area study (NIMH-ECA), men and women with anxiety disorders (i.e., panic disorder, obsessive compulsive disorder [OCD], or phobias) were more likely than those without such disorders to be seeking assistance from the health or social services systems (Leon, Portera, & Weissman, 1995). Anxiety-disordered patients also demonstrate a high prevalence of unexplained physical complaints that may result in increased usage of expensive medical services. For example, approximately one-half of patients with generalized anxiety disorder (GAD) seek symptom relief via general medicine, with high rates of presentation to emergency rooms, high rates of bowel complaints, and multiple expensive physical investigations such as exercise tests, arteriograms, and endoscopy (Roy-Byrne, 1996).

PANIC DISORDER. Panic Disorder (PD) is an anxiety disorder with a lifetime prevalence rate estimated as being between 1.5 and 3.5 percent of adults (APA, 1994). Individuals with PD consume higher rates of medical care resources than do individuals without PD (Siegel, Jones, & Wilson, 1990). Physical functioning, bodily pain, and general health scores for panic disorder patients are similar to scores obtained from patients with chronic medical conditions (Candilis & Pollack, 1997). As most individuals with PD do not seek treatment, the bulk of the economic costs relate to indirect costs (Edlund & Swann, 1987). The health and social impairment rates (e.g., social, marital functioning, financial dependency) among patients with PD have been found to be comparable to rates for depressed patients, with individuals with PD being overrepresented in disability and welfare populations (Candilis & Pollack, 1997). PD patients score lower on measures of quality of life in comparison to control groups, and also are more likely to be unemployed with lower incomes (Katerndahl & Realini, 1997). There is also evidence that individuals with PD have higher rates of work disability than do non-afflicted individuals (see Siegel et al., 1990). Therefore, a diagnosis of PD places a claimant at higher risk for greater direct costs of both mental and physical health treatment, and greater indirect costs via lost wages and caregiver time.

GENERALIZED ANXIETY DISORDER. Generalized Anxiety Disorder (GAD) is an anxiety disorder with lifetime prevalence of approximately 5 percent (APA, 1994). High rates of mental health and medical comorbidity are found among individuals with GAD. To illustrate, Soue'tre et al. (1994) found that among GAD patients, the most frequent comorbid mental health concerns were depression (28%) and alcohol abuse/dependence (25%), and the highest medical comorbidity was for gastroenterologic and gynecologic symptoms (10%). The average health care cost per three months for comorbid GAD patients was $1,269, whereas the cost for GAD patients without comorbid complaints was $667. Interestingly, Soue'tre et al. (1994) found that three of the four variables that best predicted health care costs in GAD patients were comorbidity, past history of anxiety, and severity of anxiety symptoms (age was the fourth predictive variable). Thus, while GAD has substantial direct costs on its own, it is instructive that the presence of comorbid mental or physical health complaints markedly increases direct costs for GAD sufferers.

POSTTRAUMATIC STRESS DISORDER. Posttraumatic Stress Disorder (PTSD) is an anxiety disorder with widely varying estimates of prevalence. In general population surveys, lifetime prevalence of PTSD has been estimated at between 1 and 14 percent of respondents. However, targeted samples of trauma victims have been shown to have much higher rates of PTSD (see e.g., review by Taylor & Koch, 1995). Population-based data on the utilization of health services for individuals with posttraumatic stress disorder is lacking (Amaya-Jackson et al., 1999), and at the present time there are no studies which speak directly to the general health care costs of traumatically induced mental health problems (i.e., PTSD; Koch & Fairbrother, 1999). However, there are several indirect, yet converging lines of evidence which suggest that trauma exposure and/or PTSD is associated with negative personal, economic, and vocational costs. As PTSD is a common consequence of MVAs, sexual harassment, and sexual assault (Douglas & Koch, 2001; Koch & Fairbrother, 1999, Taylor & Koch, 1995) – all being events for which restitution for psychological injuries may occur – examination of the costs of PTSD is essential.

Posttraumatic stress in general has been found to be associated with impairment in social, financial, physical, and psychological functioning (Amaya-Jackson et al., 1999). Individuals who report posttraumatic stress symptoms (PTSS) are more likely to report impaired subjective social support, to report that their income poorly meets their needs, to have spent more than 7 days in bed in the preceding 3 months, to report suicidal thoughts, to report increased general medical and mental health outpatient visits, and to use psychotropic drugs (Amaya-Jackson et al., 1999). Individuals who meet diagnostic criteria for PTSD are more functionally impaired than are those who meet sub-threshold levels of PTSS (Amaya-Jackson et al., 1999). Additionally, individuals with PTSD are more likely than those without PTSD to have other co-morbid psychiatric disorders (Sautter, Brailey, Uddo, Hamilton, Beard, & Borges, 1999; Solomon & Davidson, 1997). For example, it has been reported that 40–50%, or more, of PTSD patients have comorbid depression (Blanchard & Hickling, 1996; Kessler, Sonnega, Bromet, Hughes, & Nelson, 1995). This, of course, places PTSD claimants with comorbid depression at greater risk for the economic losses associated with depression, a double whammy if one believes these different disorders have independent negative effects on economic functioning.

The negative impact of PTSD upon employment has been relatively well established. In their review of the labor force participation research for individuals who have suffered traumatic exposure (i.e., to combat, childhood abuse, concentration camp experiences, and refugee status), Fairbank, Ebert, and Zarkin (1999) found a consistent pattern whereby exposure to traumatic stress is associated with reduced labor market outcomes. Among male monozygotic twin pairs of American Vietnam veterans, a diagnosis of PTSD was found to be associated with a higher likelihood of being unemployed at follow-up, even controlling for genetic factors (McCarren, James, Goldberg, Eisen, True, & Henderson, 1995). Male Vietnam veterans with PTSD have been found to be five times as likely to be unemployed, in comparison to veterans without PTSD (Kulka et al., 1990). Even after statistically adjusting for the economic effects of variables such as demographic factors, depression, alcohol abuse/dependence, chronic medical conditions, and panic disorder, women veterans with PTSD have been found to be ten times more likely than women veterans without PTSD to be unemployed, and male veterans with PTSD are three times more likely to be unemployed, in comparison to their veteran counterparts without PTSD (Zatzick et al., 1997). Middle-aged Cambodian refugees who live in the US and have PTSD have lower annual incomes and are more likely to be receiving public financial assistance than similar refugee adults without a mental health diagnosis (Sack,

Clarke, Kinney, Belestos, Chanrithy, & Seeley, 1995). Finally, symptomatic status has been directly related to economic variables. Vietnam veterans with higher PTSD symptom scores have been found to have significantly lower incomes, lower educational attainment, and greater unemployment than those with lower symptom scores, independent of degree of combat exposure and service unit (Vincent, Long, & Chamberlain, 1994). In conclusion then, PTSD is associated with markedly reduced employment and thus claimants with this diagnosis are at risk for lost wages, an indirect cost.

## Tortious Events Associated with Economic Loss

In the following section, the costs associated with specific tortious events which commonly arise in civil litigation will be summarized. The following will constitute the focus of this section: traumatic brain injury[1]; sexual harassment; and, other crime-related injuries.

TRAUMATIC BRAIN INJURY.    As workplace injuries and MVAs are the primary causes of traumatic brain injuries (Bennett & Raymond, 1997), the costs associated with TBI are important to examine. According to North American estimates, TBIs result in 200–300 hospital admissions per 100,000 per annum; the incidence of severe TBI, which is a primary cause of persistent disability, has been estimated at 14 per 100,000 per annum (Annoni, Beer, & Kesselring, 1992). The annual costs relating to TBI patients in the US have been estimated to range from $9–$12.5 billion annually (Bennett, Jacobs, & Schwartz, 1989). On a per-patient basis, the rehabilitation costs alone over one TBI patient's lifetime have been estimated at $500,000, if that patient is maintained in the community (Barry & Schafer, 1993). Estimates for the total cost of care have been as high as $9 million over a severe TBI patient's lifetime (Papastrat, 1992). Over the past several decades, increases in the numbers of head injuries have occurred concurrently with decreases in the numbers of deaths from TBIs; thus, many more TBI patients are surviving than before (see McMordie, Barker, & Paolo, 1990). Even severely impaired patients have only a 5-year life expectancy reduction over the 20 years post-TBI, compared to the general non-injured population (Stambrook, Moore, & Peters, 1990).

As with depression, the bulk of the costs of TBI relate to indirect costs (i.e., direct costs for TBI care account for only 12% of total TBI costs; McGregor & Pentland, 1997). TBI patients are most often young to middle-aged adults, and consequently have many potentially employable years

---

[1]For our purposes, traumatic brain injury is conceptualized as a tortious event (as opposed to a mental health condition), as it as an event which results in multi-factorial consequences and deficits which include, but are not limited to, cognitive and mental health sequelae.

remaining—thus, the financial costs to society are high in particular due to the loss in productive years of employment. Rates of return to work (RTW) following TBI range from a dismal 10% to an optimistic 70% (see Cifu et al., 1997), and are impacted by various factors relating primarily to the patients' pre-injury demographics, and characteristics of the brain injury (Samra, 1999). For example, among severe head injury patients, a significant majority has been found to be working pre-injury (85%), but only a minority (29%) are not working post-injury (Brooks, McKinlay, Symington, Beattie, & Campsie, 1987).

In addition to the negative economic implications of a failure to RTW, unemployment can be conceptualized as a negative life event that has detrimental effects upon an individual's well-being (Lubusko, Moore, Stambrook, & Gill, 1994). Unemployment negatively impacts an individual's physical, psychological, and social health and well-being (Cook, 1983; Guirguis, 1999; Julkunen & Saarinen, 1994; Turner, 1995). Reactions to unemployment include anger, hostility, and even abuse upon spouses and children (Perrucci, 1994). Increased rates of depression for both the unemployed individual and his or her spouse occur (Shelton, 1985). In addition to the lost productivity of an unemployed individual, the social costs of unemployment are more far-reaching, and include the costs of providing other types of social services which are required to address the psychological problems (e.g., increased mortality rates, suicides, rates of imprisonment) associated with unemployment (Shelton, 1985). For these reasons, it easy to see how the negative sequelae of a workplace or MVA injury may be much more far-reaching than simply a loss of income.

In addition to the negative economic and subjective impact of unemployment, other residual impairments that impact upon quality of life often persist. Even following TBI rehabilitation, 40% of patients have persistent motor disabilities, 50% have continuing cognitive impairments, and 60% suffer from psychoaffective changes (Mazaux & Richer, 1998). The quality of family and social life is often significantly impacted (Mazaux & Richer, 1998); for example, TBI typically results in a decrease in the family income; and, as a result of economic strain, families may have to borrow money, lose their possessions, or declare bankruptcy (McMordie & Barker, 1988).

SEXUAL HARASSMENT.    In both the US and Canada, sexual harassment victims may initiate legal actions in civil proceedings (Aggarwal, 1987). Sexual harassment cases are most frequently litigated in civil court as common-law torts (e.g., assault and battery, intentional infliction of emotional distress, negligence; Benedek, 1996). Sexual harassment has significant economic costs for both employers and victims, with the annual costs of sexual harassment for Fortune 500 companies having been estimated at

$6.7 million per annum (Stamato, 1992). For victims, the tangible losses associated with sexual harassment may include the loss of employment, seniority, or promotion (Simon, 1996). The costs of non-tangible, psychological effects are less easily quantified. The US Merit Systems Protection Board (USMSPB, 1988) estimated the cost of vacation and sick leave resulting from sexual harassment between May 1985 and May 1987 to be in excess of $250 million.

A discussion of the common sequelae of sexual harassment may serve to illustrate the indirect and personal costs associated with sexual harassment victimization. Sexual harassment has been found to be associated with anxiety, depression, PTSD, alcohol misuse, somatic complaints, poorer health habits, and increased health care utilization among victims (see Murdoch & McGovern, 1998 for a review). Sexual harassment is also associated with lower job satisfaction/morale, increased job turnover, and lower productivity (Stohr & Beck, 1994). Additional sequelae of sexual harassment include feelings of disgust, anger, decreased job motivation, distraction, dread of work, and a sense of stress, loss, and victimization (Terpstra, 1986; Woody & Perry, 1993). In some cases, sexual harassment does result in diagnosable disorders, with Adjustment Disorder being the most common; other commonly diagnosed disorders are Dysthymia, Major Depression, Anxiety Disorders, and PTSD (Simon, 1996). Although specific figures on the direct and indirect costs of sexual harassment are unavailable, the costs associated with specific diagnostic disorders (i.e., affective and anxiety disorders) do exist, and may be extrapolated to gain an understanding of the economic costs associated with sexual harassment. Findings that only 12% of sexual harassment victims seek professional help for their problems (Crull, 1982), and only one percent pursue any type of legal action (Terpstra & Baker, 1992) serve to strengthen the conjecture that the indirect costs of sexual harassment are underrecognized, and likely exceed the direct costs of victimization.

CRIME. The direct, tangible costs of personal crime have been estimated at being $105 billion per annum in the United States (Miller, Cohen, & Wiersema, 1996). When the intangible costs of crime are accounted for (e.g., pain, suffering, and reduced quality of life) via estimations from willingness to pay and jury-awards methods, the estimates of the total costs of crime jump to $450 billion annually. Violent crime, including drunk driving and arson, accounts for the bulk of these costs ($425 billion), with costs related to property crime accounting for the remaining amount. The cost of mental health expenditures alone for victims of crime has been estimated as being between $5.8 and $7.2 billion annually; however, there is generally little research in this area (Cohen & Miller, 1998; Miller, Cohen, & Rossman, 1993). As much as 20% of all mental health care expenditures in the United States may be the result of violent crime, with the bulk of the costs being for victims who are treated for victimization experiences (Miller et al., 1996).

The costs associated with specific criminal events have been less well-studied. In particular, there is little research on the mental health costs for victims of specific crimes (Miller et al., 1993). However, as with sexual harassment, in both the US and Canada, individuals are able to initiate civil proceedings to obtain compensation for psychological injuries resulting from criminal events, which may or may not have simultaneously been adjudicated in criminal court. The bulk of the existing literature on sequelae of crime stems from research on sexual assault victims (Riggs et al., 1992). Sexual victimization is one of the most commonly encountered criminal events encountered by psychologists (Douglas & Koch, in press), and the non-tangible costs associated with sexual victimization have been relatively well-studied. Increased health care utilization is observed among sexually assaulted women (Douglas & Koch, 2001). Byrne, Resnick, Kilpatrick, Best, and Saunders (1999) examined the effects of physical and sexual assault on employment, poverty status, and education, and found that for women with a previous history of any assault who were employed at the first interview, their employment and income at year three was significantly less if they had suffered any assault in the intervening two years. Thus, assault alone has negative economic repercussions, but this effect appears most reliable for women who have had a pre-existing trauma (reviewed by Koch & Fairbrother, 1999). Paralleling the literature on sexual harassment, diagnoses of depression, PTSD, and other anxiety disorders are frequently observed among sexually assaulted individuals (Douglas & Koch, 2001). Estimates suggest that up to half, or more of rape victims, and one-quarter of non-sexual assault victims have meet diagnostic criteria for PTSD post-injury (see Resnick et al., 1991; Rothbaum, Foa, Murdock, Riggs, & Walsh, 1991, as cited in Riggs et al., 1992).

Although the research on the effects of non-sexual crimes is sparse (Resick, 1987), there is growing evidence that criminal victimization results in negative sequelae such as anxiety, depression, intrusive thoughts/images, and sleep disturbances (Resick, 1987; Riggs et al., 1992). Again, although exact figures on the direct and indirect costs of specific types of criminal events are unavailable, knowledge of the psychological sequelae of these events may allow one to indirectly extrapolate the costs that may be associated with these tortious events. In conclusion, victims of crime (particularly sexual victimization) are more likely to experience direct costs of increased health care utilization and indirect costs associated with lost wages, not to mention the intangible costs of pain and suffering.

## THE LITIGATION CONUNDRUM

The data on the costs associated with specific mental health conditions and tortious events were reviewed to better understand what specific losses litigants may be seeking to redress via civil litigation. However, there is an implicit assumption in this statement: that there is a linear relationship between the occurrence of a tortious event, a subsequent psychological injury (and associated psychological sequelae), and an ensuing decision to litigate for monetary compensation (see Figure 9.1).

Unfortunately, there is a dearth of literature that speaks specifically to the accuracy of this supposition. Furthermore, (as will be reviewed below) there are methodological limitations with the literature that does exist. This is problematic as the probability that an individual will engage in formal civil litigation appears to depend on a complex interplay of separate, yet interdependent events. First, an individual must experience a potentially tortious event. Second, that individual must cognitively appraise that event as causing an injury or loss. Third, the individual must initiate a claim. Finally, the claimant must be sufficiently dissatisfied with the response of the defendant to proceed to court. Each of these stages is necessary for a torts action to reach a court of law. More importantly, the individual must make decisions at each stage of this process, and these decisions may be influenced by a host of mediating variables. As Figure 2 illustrates, there are many individual, systemic, and procedural variables that may influence whether an event is appraised as a tortious event, whether psychological losses will be perceived to have resulted from that event, and whether the claimant will litigate.

We know that the decision to litigate is not static, but rather a fluid decision process that is influenced by multiple factors at different decision points over time. For example, various individual difference factors (see Waite et al., this book, chapter 10) may serve to influence whether an injury is indeed experienced (e.g., there may be sex differences in the likelihood of experiencing a particular tortious event, such as sexual harassment). In a more specific example, ruminative coping styles may not only increase the probability of PTSD following an MVA (Ehlers, Mayou, & Bryant, 1998), but may also influence the claimant's perception of justice,

FIGURE 9.1. Linear Relationship Between Injury, Losses, and the Decision to Litigate.

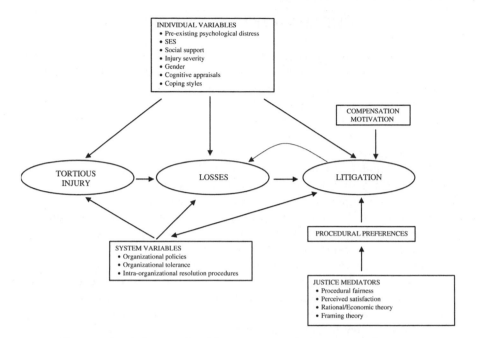

FIGURE 9.2. Mediating Variables Impacting the Decision to Litigate.

thus decreasing his or her likelihood of early, pre-trial settlement. Additionally, individual difference variables such as socioeconomic status (SES) may determine whether formal litigation is a viable option (e.g., a potential litigant may possess inadequate funds to hire legal representation). As a final example, there is likely a person-occupation interaction that mediates the extent of loss associated with given tortious events. Thus, while a manual laborer who suffers chronic lower back pain in a MVA may suffer a substantial indirect loss secondary to subsequent lost wages, a university professor who suffers the same back pain from an MVA may suffer relatively little wage loss because of the different physical requirements of their employment.

Our model described in Figure 9.2 assumes that some individual difference variables (e.g., pre-existing psychological distress, gender, risk-taking) will increase the risk of suffering a tortious injury, while some individual difference variables will mediate between the tortious injury and the severity of loss (e.g., cognitive appraisals, coping styles, injury-occupation interaction). The model also suggests that some individual difference variables will directly influence litigation (e.g., trait anger, anti-defendant attitudes), and that litigation itself will have some effect on the individual (e.g., increasing psychological distress). Further, systemic variables (e.g., intra-organizational policies and resolution procedures) may lessen or increase the likelihood of a tortious event occurring, may mediate between the tortious injury and the severity of ensuing losses, and may influence the likelihood of initiating formal litigation. It is also plausible that the frequency of litigation within a particular organization may serve to shape the adoption or development of specific intra-organizational policies and resolution procedures. Finally, justice mediators (e.g., perceived satisfaction; perceived procedural fairness) may impact individuals' procedural preferences, hence directly impacting the probability of litigation (see Wayte et al., this book, chapter 10).

It is important to recognize the existence of such mediating variables, as these serve to complicate our understanding of the relationship between various tortious events and the subsequent occurrence of psychological injuries, as well as the degree of loss suffered. In civil litigation contexts, this is directly relevant because the determination of losses (and the attributions for the source of those losses) directly impact damage awards and, arguably, decisions to litigate. The remainder of this section will focus more specifically on two mediating factors: the influence of litigation upon experienced psychological losses, and the impact of compensation motivation on the likelihood of formal litigation. We will conclude with a brief discussion of some of the caveats in determining causation in litigation contexts.

## DOES LITIGATION EXACERBATE PSYCHOLOGICAL LOSSES?

An important mediating variable which needs to be considered in understanding the relationship between tortious injuries, associated losses, and decisions to litigate is the impact of the litigation process itself. One alternative explanation to the simple model presented in Figure 1 (i.e., that injury leads to losses, which results in litigation) is that the process of litigation itself may be associated with further losses (e.g., new or exacerbated symptomatology; see Figure 2). Lees-Haley (1988) defines the Litigation Response Syndrome (LRS) as a "stress response associated with the process of litigation" (p. 3), comprising a constellation of symptoms which are, by definition, presumed to be the sole result of involvement in litigation (as opposed to stemming from the original injury precipitating the litigation). Implicit in the definition of this syndrome is that observed LRS-related symptoms should be transient, and should resolve with the litigation process or lawsuit.

Although the concept of LRS is an interesting one, at the present time there is little empirical support for this hypothesis. Further, there is the inherent difficulty of distinguishing LRS-related symptoms from symptoms resulting directly from tortious events. For example, if hypothetically we know that that litigating MVA-PTSD claimants have trait anger (Spielberger, 1996) scores at the 90th percentile of normal controls, and non-litigating MVA-PTSD claimants have scores at the 60th percentile, does this difference reflect (a) the untoward effects of litigation, per se, (b) the greater psychological distress initially suffered by the (subsequent) litigants that explains their decision to litigate, or (c) a pre-existing personality difference that differentially amplifies the psychological loss subsequent to the MVA? While there is substantial evidence that anger proneness exacerbates PTSD (see review by Douglas & Koch, 2001), there are no existing data which clearly demonstrate that otherwise well-matched litigants and non-litigants differ in anger proneness, much less that anger proneness increases within litigants during the course of litigation. Clearly, such data are required before claims about the impact of litigation on symptomatology can be made.

Litigation may also serve to exacerbate/lead to new symptomatology in more complicated ways. It has been hypothesized that PTSD symptoms are influenced by the process of litigation via re-traumatization (e.g., where the victim is required to confront his/her history repeatedly to lawyers and consultants; Pitman, Sparr, Saunders, & McFarlane, 1996). Further, the adversarial legal system may exacerbate victims' sense of vulnerability and victimization via placing them "on trial" (Pitman et al., 1996), asking them to prove their illness (Bellamy, 1997), and removing their sense of control (Strasburger, 1999). In a similar vein, it has been suggested that situational stressors resulting from protracted litigation may interact with the effects of trauma and pre-existing personality traits to result in exaggerated symptom presentation, or "false imputation" of symptoms (Weissman, 1990).

For illustrative purposes, we have focused on the impact of litigation on PTSD symptomatology. However, the above suppositions are similarly applicable to other mental health conditions and tortious events. For example, in the arena of sexual harassment, it has been suggested that the process of litigation itself may result in adverse emotional effects upon victims, and hence it may be difficult to tease apart the effects of the harassment from the effects of retaliation following the complaint (e.g., a more hostile work environment; Simon, 1996).

In sum, it is clear that more research investigating the causal/exacerbating impact of litigation upon psychological symptomatology is desperately needed before conclusive statements refuting or supporting the concept of LRS are made. Although the LRS model has difficulty explaining why not all researchers have found more extreme psychological symptoms among litigating groups (see Pitman et al., 1996), it appears premature to assume no ill effect of litigation on the psychological status of claimants.

## DOES COMPENSATION MOTIVATION INFLUENCE PSYCHOLOGICAL SYMPTOMS OF LITIGANTS?

A second alternative to the simple model of litigation presented in Figure 1 is that motivation for compensation may lead to exaggerated symptom presentation. Compensation may serve to reinforce and maintain injury behavior (e.g., chronic pain) in the same way that all human behavior is reinforced (Fordyce, 1985, as discussed by Rohling et al., 1995). The concept of "secondary gain" has been used to explain the motivating incentive of compensation in reinforcing the presentation and/or exaggeration of psychological symptomatology (Pitman et al., 1996).

Compensation seeking appears to result in greater endorsement of psychopathology among combat-related PTSD samples (e.g., Frueh, Smith, & Barker, 1996; Frueh, Gold, & de Arellano, 1997) and among head-injured samples (e.g., Youngjohn, Davis, & Wolfe, 1997). As well, there is some support that individuals seeking, or receiving, compensation for personal injuries demonstrate compromised behavioral outcomes (e.g., return to work rates) in comparison to those not receiving compensation. Compensation for physical injury is associated with delayed recovery from low back pain, with financially compensated back injury patients reporting higher degrees of pain, disability, psychological disturbance, unemployment, and length of time off work (Greenough & Fraser, 1989). Chronic pain patients receiving compensation are less likely to report a return to full activity post-treatment (Carron, DeGood, & Tait, 1985). Individuals who receive workers' compensation payments receive more treatment, over a longer time period, in comparison to their non-compensated counterparts (Simmonds & Kumar, 1996). Further, individuals whose injuries occurred at work (and hence warranted compensation) remained off work for longer periods of time than those not injured at work, regardless of the severity of the injury (Sander & Meyers, 1986). Further, physically injured workers who received higher monthly payments from a worker's compensation insurance company have been found to be less likely to complete vocational rehabilitation programs and RTW (Gardner, 1991). Among patients with minor head injury, duration of absence from work has been found to be significantly longer for patients who had ongoing claims for compensation (88 days) compared to those with no such claims (24 days; Cook, 1972).

Meta-analyses have also supported the negative impact of financial compensation. A meta-analytic review of the association between financial compensation and chronic pain demonstrated that receipt of financial compensation (e.g., workers compensation, disability payments) is associated with greater pain experiences, and decreased treatment efficacy (Rohling, Binder, & Langhinrichsen-Rohling, 1995). Similarly, another meta-analytic review demonstrated that closed head injury patients with financial incentives demonstrated more disability and compromised neuropsychological scores, despite having less severe injuries (Binder & Rohling, 1996).

However, other researchers have failed to obtain confirmation of the hypothesis that compensation results in exaggerated symptom presentation. Financial compensation has not consistently been found to be associated with an incentive to remain off work (Barnes, Smith, Gatchel, & Mayer, 1989; Blanchard et al., 1998; Cornes, 1992; Talo, Hendler, & Brodie, 1989). Additionally, patients who are receiving compensation benefits have been found to not differ from those not receiving compensation in terms of non-organic and organic signs of pain or psychological distress; similarly, chronic pain patients with pending litigation have been found to not differ in terms of non-organic pain signs, psychological distress, and various descriptions/indicators of pain (see Dworkin, Handlin, Richlin, Brand, & Vannucci, 1985). Dworkin and colleagues (1985) examined the moderating impact of employment status upon treatment responsiveness, and found that employment status (working vs. not working) was predictive of treatment responsivity, whereas compensation or litigation status was not. Smith and Frueh (1996) found that among Vietnam combat veterans with PTSD, compensation-seeking status did not distinguish between valid versus exaggerated symptom responding, whereas comorbidity with depression did distinguish response style. One should note, however, that subsequent studies by Frueh (Frueh, et al., 1996; 1997) found that compensation-seeking among veterans with PTSD was associated with symptom overendorsement.

In conclusion, it appears clear that compensation-seeking and the receipt of compensation for subjective health problems has some impact on individuals' endorsement of symptoms and on their return to work. Nonetheless, there are many contrary findings. Despite these contrary findings, there appears to be a common perception that compensation motivation is a primary explanatory variable for health complaints in litigants (Evans, 1994).

## CAVEATS IN DETERMINING CAUSATION IN LITIGATION CONTEXTS

There are several difficulties that arise in making determinations of the relationship between psychological injury and ensuing symptomatology.

First, the litigation environment is unique insofar as there appear to be different base rates of symptoms than are seen in traditional assessment contexts (Lees-Haley & Brown, 1993). For example, on a neuropsychological screening measure for cognitive dysfunction (Symbol Digit Modalities Test; Smith, 1982) a significant proportion (10 out of 20) of personal injury litigants without a reported history of brain injury demonstrated impaired scores (Lees-Haley, 1988). Personal injury claimants with no history of brain injury or neuropsychological impairment similarly self-report high levels of neuropsychological-related complaints (Lees-Haley, 1992; Lees-Haley & Brown, 1993). Explanations for these elevated rates of psychological complaints are varied, and include litigation-related stress, emotional distress stemming from the precipitating injury (or related, non-neuropsychological injuries), interactions with pre-existing psychological conditions, and malingering (Lees-Haley & Brown, 1993). Nonetheless, whatever the cause, it appears that the emotional and cognitive functioning of personal injury litigants may be compromised even in the absence of objective neurological damage. However, at present, the normative database on cognitive and emotional test measures using litigating samples is limited, and requires further research attention. Examination of the impact of affective status and other non-cognitive emotional factors on litigants' cognitive functioning is also needed in order to elucidate the reasons for litigants' observed, compromised performance on neuropsychological measures.

Second, in addition to the problems associated with inadequate normative data, there are several limitations associated with applying the findings of research on the relationship between compensation and symptomatology to litigation contexts. One problem with the debate on this matter is the muddy definition of compensation status. Conceptually, *seeking compensation* for health-related problems is different than already *receiving compensation* for health-related disability. Theoretically, the incentive for either consciously exaggerating symptoms or unconsciously over-attending to non-pathological subjective experiences should be different in these two circumstances, unless one assumes that individuals who are receiving continuing compensation payments are fearful of losing same in the event of improvement. The studies reviewed in the preceding section have examined the impact of compensation status and compensation-seeking, but not litigation per se, upon symptomatology. Although litigation and compensation frequently go hand-in-hand, they are not equivalent concepts. Attempts to generalize findings on the relationship between compensation and symptomatology to litigation contexts is problematic for several reasons. The process of litigation does not imply that compensation is or will necessarily be received. Further, the psychological sequelae that may be associated with litigation may differ starkly from simple, clear-cut compensation cases (e.g., the adversarial environment of a personal injury litigation suit differs in some fundamental ways from a non-adversarial, no-fault workers compensation system). Thus, research needs to examine the similarities and differences in simple compensation versus litigation contexts. Additionally, it is plausible that individuals with more symptoms are the justifiably more likely to litigate. For example, Blanchard et al. (1998) found that individuals who initiated litigation post-MVA had higher levels of posttraumatic stress symptoms, higher levels of subjective distress, more severe physical injuries, and more impaired social functioning than did non-litigating MVA victims. Of course, it is difficult to rule out the possibility that those who initiated litigation may have been motivated to portray themselves more negatively and more symptomatically than they actually were; however, Blanchard et al. found that even at 12-month follow-up, litigants who had settled remained more distressed than injured parties who never initiated litigation. Others have similarly found that injury disability and emotional distress does not necessarily resolve following the cessation of litigation (Guest & Drummond, 1992; see Hadjistavropoulos, 1999).

Further, if one believes that reinforcement contingencies control symptom endorsement, the ultimate evidence for such a hypothesis is symptomatic change when the contingency changes or symptom stability over time under the same contingency. A positive reinforcement contingency is present for individuals considering, intending, or pursuing compensation for their injuries because there is an *anticipated* reward for symptom over-endorsement. In torts litigation cases, once an individual has won a damage suit, there is no more incentive for symptom overendorsement because such individuals receive lump sum payments and, barring appeals, their case is not reopened. Ergo, if this reinforcement contingency contributed significantly to litigants' symptom endorsement, they should show a substantial diminution of symptoms once litigation is settled. Because of the paucity of long term follow-up data on litigants, we know little about the validity of this hypothesis. In a study from the UK, Mayou, Tindel, and Bryant (1997) found, however, that MVA litigants with resolved litigation did not appear to show substantial recovery up to five years post-MVA if they had not done so prior to the end of litigation.

Similarly, if this positive reinforcement contingency plays a large role in symptom overendorsement, one would expect marked interference with both spontaneous remission of symptoms and with treatment-related remission. Over a one-year follow-up in New York, Blanchard et al. (1998) found that litigating MVA survivors and non-litigating MVA survivors did not show different rates of spontaneous remission of PTSD symptoms. In other words, litigants showed as much relative improvement as non-litigants despite being under different reinforcement contingencies for symptom endorsement. In an open trial of cognitive behavioral therapy for MVA-PTSD conducted in British Columbia, Canada, Taylor, Fedoroff, Koch, and Thoradarson (in preparation) found that litigation status did not predict response to treatment. Therefore, MVA-PTSD patients in litigation were just as likely to show symptomatic improvement during and after short term treatment than did MVA-PTSD patients not in litigation. These findings from three different countries are not easily explained by a strict financial incentive model of symptom endorsement in litigants.

Unfortunately, at present the mixed findings that exist in the literature in this area preclude definitive conclusions from being made. Differences between litigating and non-litigating patients are not consistently found (Kolbison, Epstein, & Burgess, 1996). Methodological limitations with conducting research in this area also make it difficult to know whether litigation itself leads to increased symptom reporting, or vice-versa. Large scale prospective, longitudinal designs would be required to compare the pre- and post-injury characteristics of individuals who do, versus do not engage in litigation.

## FUTURE DIRECTIONS IN CIVIL FORENSIC PSYCHOLOGY

In this chapter, we have attempted to amalgamate the literature pertaining to the monetary worth of psychological injury, as well as describe problems in determining relationships among injuries, psychological sequelae, and decisions to litigate. However, this arena of civil forensic psychology is a growing field, with numerous research possibilities. In this final section, we suggest some relevant avenues for future research.

### ECONOMICS OF PSYCHOLOGICAL INJURIES

While it is believed that most personal injury cases are settled out of court, it would be of interest both to scholars and to the insurance and legal communities to know what case characteristics predict damage awards in cases that do proceed to formal litigation. A content analysis of judgments across various personal injury cases and their relationship to specific monetary awards may be a first step in this process (e.g., to examine the case, litigant, judge, and defendant characteristics that are predictors of the amount awarded). Of course, there are inherent limitations to this type of research. First, there is the issue of whether reasons for judgments actually provide enough information to enable such content analyses (i.e., this assumes that judges accurately describe their reasons for awarding damages). Second, in both Canada and the United States, reasons for judgments are provided only in non-jury trials, thus precluding an accurate sample of jurors' reasons for awarding damages. Third, only a small proportion of cases actually go to trial. The latter two issues limit the generality of any conclusions based on judges' reasons for damage awards. Finally, obtaining court records for content analysis may be an expensive and onerous task. An indirect manner of obtaining this type of information would be to conduct research where case characteristics (e.g., demographic variables) are correlated with outcomes (i.e., amount of damages); alternatively, personal injury vignettes may be used as analogue stimuli for judges (as subjects) and potential jurors to respond to.

A glaring hole in the literature pertaining to the economics of psychological injuries is the absence of literature speaking to the pain and suffering related costs of psychological injuries and tortious events. An indirect manner of examining the monetary value judges and juries place upon the subjective, pain and suffering costs of injury (rather than direct and indirect costs) would be to calculate the average compensation amount for various types of injuries, and subtract from those the average estimated direct/indirect costs (to examine if there does exist a discrepancy and, if so, how large that discrepancy is). Of course, a potential outcome of such an analysis may be that the population-determined direct and indirect costs of specific mental disorders may be larger than the average compensation provided. Scaling injury severity studies that are similar in methodology to Rodriguez and Bogett's (1989) study, but with a focus on mental (rather than physical) injuries would be helpful. Specifically, utilization of a weighting scale for different types of injuries could be of assistance in providing an index of the measurable value laypersons ascribe to various types of mental injuries, and their related sequelae (including associated pain and suffering).

To better understand the subjective losses associated with mental health conditions, we need to have a coherent general strategy for measuring quality of life across types of injuries or disorders. It is obvious that the types of injuries/disorders that are represented in civil litigation are so varied that it is difficult to compare worth across the disorders. Booth et al. (1997) recommend the use of the Medical Outcomes Study SF-36 (Ware & Sherbourne, 1992) which assesses a wide range of health and quality-of-life functioning variables. Related to the question above, we need to have an index of the normative quality of life so that we can contrast the relative impacts of different injuries on quality of life.

It would also be of interest to know what the average community member would be willing to pay to avoid specific negative mental health outcomes. This is probably a much more complex question than it sounds because such community members' willingness to pay will likely be related to a host of variables, including, for example, experience with affected family members, education, culture, and personality. For example, it may be that a sample of respondents with little familial experience of mental disorders will place little or no value on the absence of mental disorders. Related to this question, how do we define the "average community member"? Would this be similar to the "reasonable person" standard used in different types of legal proceedings, or would it be something different, e.g., those "psychologically-minded" individuals who may have greater awareness of the relation between psychological well-being and daily functioning?

## Specific Areas Warranting Investigation

Our review of the costs of mental health conditions revealed that, overall, there is a substantial amount of literature which addresses the direct and indirect costs of certain conditions (e.g., depression; anxiety disorders), but that data on the pain and suffering costs of these injuries are virtually absent. Furthermore, there exists virtually no literature on certain mental health conditions and tortious events that may be litigated in civil proceedings. For example, although there exists a significant body of literature addressing the losses associated with sexual victimization experiences, there is presently little data that directly speaks to the monetary worth and losses associated with non-sexual criminal victimization. Research in this area is greatly needed. Also, the economic, social, and personal costs of MVAs extend beyond those associated exclusively with psychiatric diagnoses (Jeavons, Greenwood, & Horne, 1996), and warrant more research attention (Di Gallo & Parry-Jones, 1996). Although there exists a significant body of research examining PTSD sequelae of MVAs, the research on other sub-clinical effects is lacking. A longitudinal examination of individuals who have been injured in MVAs may be useful in providing data on the average claim type and average associated sequelae of MVAs (e.g., by following up injured patients on outcome variables such as average days of work loss, and physical and mental health care service utilization patterns). Given that MVAs are likely the single largest cause of PTSD in the Western world (Norris, 1992), it seems peculiar that we know so little about the economic losses directly accruing from MVA-PTSD. Related to this, it may be useful to examine the economic impact of sub-clinical conditions and other tortious mental health complaints.

## LITIGATION AS A CONFOUNDING VARIABLE

As reviewed earlier, research demonstrates that overall, engagement in litigation is associated with higher levels of distress, not all of which is accounted for by factors such as injury severity. Studies that more systematically examine the impact of litigation on psychological symptoms are required. This could be conducted by comparing samples of litigants versus non-litigants, matched on factors such as injury severity and demographics. Koch, Shercliffe, Fedoroff, Iverson, and Taylor's (2000) survey of psychologists (primarily forensic psychologists) and personal injury lawyers revealed that psychologists are more likely than lawyers to view secondary gain and iatrogenic factors (i.e., litigation stress) as at least moderately impacting plaintiff's symptoms. It would be interesting to know the reasons for these inter-professional differences. Examining the observations of psychologists who work with litigants would appear to be a first step in this process.

Related to the above, it may be interesting to examine reasons for the public's perception that a "litigation explosion" exists. At present, there is little research on this area. Conducting surveys of randomly selected laypersons on issues such as the perceived ease and success rates of fraudulently obtaining money via insurance claims may shed light on the public perception of this issue. Matching respondents on demographics, and examining the predictive value of personal injury and litigation history on attitudes toward the litigation system may help elucidate the variables that account for the widespread negative public attitudes toward the civil litigation system. Surveys with actual litigants may be useful to determine what factors impacted their decisions to litigate. It would be prudent to concurrently examine litigants' perceptions of fairness/justice, their perceptions of worsened/improved symptomatology during the process of litigation, their perceptions of resource loss (and their strategies for recouping resources), as well as the cost-benefit appraisals they made which are associated with litigation. We would recommend a contrasted-group design using actual litigants (who proceeded forth to trial) and non-litigants (i.e., those who engaged in pre-trial settlement) who are matched on demographic and injury factors.

It may also be useful to examine patient subtypes that are differentially impacted by compensation and litigation-related factors (see Hadjistavropoulos, 1999). For example, does internal coping style or pre-injury economic status influence litigation and/or the severity of symptom presentation?

In terms of conducting assessments with personal injury patients, normative data on injured populations who are and are not in litigation (e.g., depressed litigants vs. depressed non-litigants) who are matched on important variables (e.g., depression severity) are desperately needed. Ostensibly, there is the inherent difficulty of matching litigants and non-litigants on relevant variables (i.e., so that they differ only on litigant status). However, this difficulty should be dissuade researchers from attempting to obtain such data, but rather should encourage innovation.

Finally, empirical studies that examine factors potentially mediating decisions to litigate (as presented in Figure 2) are needed. For example, MVA litigants could be tracked longitudinally on measures such as general distress, trait anger, and their perceptions of the fairness of the insurance system. Specific hypotheses could then be put forth and tested for example, it may be that individuals with higher trait anger at Time A would be more distressed at both Time A and Time B; also, individuals with low fairness perceptions at Time A may be more likely to continue forth to trial.

## CONCLUSION

The study of litigants and, in particular, the study of economic costs and judicial decision-making during torts litigation is an exciting, and growing field of research. A central research question within civil forensic psychology relates to attempting to understand the factors predicting litigation, and the nature of losses litigants are attempting to redress. Our understanding of the monetary worth of psychological conditions is still crude but suggests that psychological injuries have profound economic impacts on MVA survivors, as well as individuals who have suffered workplace injuries and criminal victimization. To date, explanations of the relationship between psychological distress and litigation have been limited to simple linear models. In this chapter, we have described a more complex model that better illustrates the complex interplay between individual difference factors, systemic factors, procedural variables, and the litigation process. It is hoped that this model provides some concrete hypotheses for future empirical evaluation.

An enhanced knowledge of the prevalence and costs of psychological injuries offers psycho-legal scholars a unique opportunity to better understand why some injured parties litigate while others settle. Understanding that the process of litigation itself may contribute to deficits in a litigant's daily functioning and thus compound his/her loss is an important point for researchers and clinicians in this area. Unfortunately, existing data do not allow us to conclusively comment on the role of litigation on symptom presentation and claimants' ultimate decisions to litigate. A great deal of interesting research remains to be done in this area, although many complications unique to the insurance and legal context will challenge researchers' creativity. We must emphasize the difficulties involved in conducting research with insurance companies, given their understandable reluctance to encourage additional claims and the restricted access to confidential information that is often a given in insurance and torts litigation settings. Despite this, civil forensic researchers are encouraged to utilize innovative ways of examining injured persons decisions to litigate.

# REFERENCES

Allen, J. P., Kuperminc, G., Philliber, S., & Herre, K. (1994). Programmatic prevention of adolescent problem behaviors: The role of autonomy, relatedness, and volunteer service in the Teen Outreach Program. *American Journal of Community Psychology, 22,* 617–638.

Amato, P. R., & Keith, B. (1991). Parental divorce and the well-being of children: A meta-analysis. *Psychological Bulletin, 110,* 26–46.

Ambuel, B., & Rappaport, J. (1992). Developmental trends in adolescents' psychological and legal competence to consent to abortion. *Law and Human Behavior, 16,* 129–154.

Bagly, C. (1993). Transracial adoption in Britain: A follow-up study, with policy considerations. *Child Welfare, 73,* 285–299.

Bazelon, D. L. (1982). Veils, values, and social responsibility. *American Psychologist, 37,* 115–121.

Belli, R. F., Winkielman, P., Read, J. D., Schwarz, N., & Lynn, S. J. (1998). Recalling more childhood events leads to judgments of poorer memory: Implications for the recovered/false memory debate. *Psychonomic Bulletin and Review, 5,* 318–323.

Berliner, L., & Elliott, D. (1996). Child sexual abuse. In J. Briere, L. Berliner, J. Bulkley, C. Jenny, & T. Reid (Eds.), *The APSAC handbook on child maltreatment* (pp. 51–71). Newbury Park, CA: Sage.

Bersoff, D. N. (1987). Social science data and the Supreme Court: *Lockhart* as a case in point. *American Psychologist, 42,* 52–58.

Bersoff, D. N., Goodman-Delahunty, J., Grisso, J. T., Hans, V. P., Poythress, N. G., Jr., & Roesch, R. G. (1997). Training in law and psychology: Models from the Villanova conference. *American Psychologist, 52,* 1301–1310.

Bishop, D. M., Frazier, C. E., Lanza-Kanduce, L., & Winner, L. (1996). The transfer of juveniles to criminal court: Does it make a difference? *Crime and Delinquency, 42,* 171–191.

Bornstein, B. H. (1999). The ecological validity of jury simulations: Is the jury still out? *Law and Human Behavior, 23,* 75–91.

Bottoms v. Bottoms, 249 VA 410m 457 S. E. 2d 102 (1995).

Bottoms, B. L., & Davis, S. L. (1996). The creation of satanic ritual abuse. *Journal of Social and Clinical Psychology, 16,* 112–132.

Bottoms, B. L., Davis, S. L., Nysse, K. L., Haegerich, T. M., & Conway, A. R. A. (2000, March). Effects of social support and working memory capacity on children's eyewitness memory. In B. L. Bottoms, & M. B. Kovera (Chairs), *Individual and contextual influences on adults' perceptions of children's reports.* Symposium conducted at the biennial meeting of the American Psychology/Law Society, New Orleans, LA.

Bottoms, B. L., & Goodman, G. S. (1994). Perceptions of children's credibility in sexual assault cases. *Journal of Applied Social Psychology, 24*, 702–732.

Bottoms, B. L., Goodman, G. S., Schwartz-Kenney, B. M., & Thomas, S. F. (2000). *Keeping secrets: Implications for children's eyewitness reports.* Manuscript submitted for publication.

Bottoms, B. L., Kovera, M. B., & McAuliff, B. D. (Eds.). (in press). *Children and the law: Social science and policy.* New York: Cambridge University Press.

Bottoms, B. L., Shaver, P. R., Goodman, G. S. (1996). An analysis of ritualistic and religion-related child abuse allegations. *Law and Human Behavior, 20*, 1–34.

Bottoms, B. L., Shaver, P. R., Goodman, G. S., & Qin, J. (1995). In the name of God: A profile of religion-related child abuse. *Journal of Social Issues, 51*, 85–111.

Brown v. Board of Education, 347 US 483 (1954).

Brown, D., Scheflin, A. W., & Hammond, D. C. (1998). *Memory, trauma treatment, and the law.* New York: Norton.

Bruck, M., Ceci, S. J., & Melnyk, L. (1997). External and internal sources of variation in the creation of false reports in children. *Learning and Individual Differences, 9*, 289–316.

Butts, J., Hoffman, D., & Buck, J. (1999). Teen courts in the United States: A profile of current programs. *Office of Juvenile Justice and Delinquency Prevention Fact Sheet, 118.*

Bullis, R. K. (1991). The spiritual healing "defense" in criminal prosecutions for crimes against children. *Child Welfare, 70*, 541–555.

Buzzanca v. Buzzanca, CA Sup. Ct. No. S069696 (1998).

Carter, C. A., Bottoms, B. L., & Levine, M. (1996). Linguistic and socioemotional influences on the accuracy of children's reports. *Law and Human Behavior, 20*, 335–358.

Cauffman, E., Woolard, J., & Reppucci, N. D. (1999). Justice for Juveniles: New perspectives on adolescents' competence and culpability. *Quinnipiac Law Review, 18*, 403–419.

Ceci, S. J., & Bruck, M. (1995). *Jeopardy in the courtroom: A scientific analysis of children's testimony.* Washington, DC: American Psychological Association.

Ceci, S. J., & Bruck, M. (1993). The suggestibility of the child witness: A historical review and synthesis. *Psychological Bulletin, 113*, 403–439.

Cicchetti, D., & Rogosch, F. A. (1997). The role of self-organization in the promotion of resilience in maltreated children. *Development and Psychopathology, 9*, 797–815.

Code of Federal Regulations (1991). Title 45, Public welfare. Part 46: Protection of human subjects. Department of Health & Human Services: National Institute of Health.

Coy v. Iowa, 487 U.S. 1012 (1988).

Crosby-Currie, C. A. (1996). Children's involvement in contested custody cases: Practices and experiences of legal and mental health professionals. *Law and Human Behavior, 20*, 289–311.

Crosby, C. A., Britner, P. A., Jodl, K. M., & Portwood, S. G. (1995). The juvenile death penalty and the Eighth Amendment: An empirical investigation of societal consensus and proportionality. *Law and Human Behavior, 19*, 245–261.

Cutler, B. L., Penrod, S. D., & Dexter, H. R. (1990). Juror sensitivity to eyewitness identification evidence. *Law and Human Behavior, 14*, 185–191.

Daubert v. Merrell-Dow Pharmaceuticals, 951 F.2d 1128 (9th Cir. 1991), vacated, 113 S. Ct. 2786 (1993).

Davies, G. & Noon, E. (1991). *An evaluation of live link for child witnesses.* London: Home Office.

Davis, S. L. (1998). Social and scientific influences on the study of children's suggestibility: A historical perspective. *Child Maltreatment, 3*, 186–194.

Davis, S. L., & Bottoms, B. L. (in press). The effects of social support on the accuracy of children's reports: Implications for the forensic interview. In M. L. Eisen, G. S. Goodman, & J. A. Quas (Eds.), *Memory and suggestibility in the forensic interview.* Hillsdale, NJ: Erlbaum.

Diamond, S. S. (1997). Illuminations and shadows from jury simulations. *Law and Human Behavior, 21,* 561–571.

DiIulio, J. (1995, November 27). The coming of the super-predators. *Weekly Standard,* p.23.

Dillon, P. A., & Emery, R. E. (1996). Divorce mediation and resolution of child custody disputes: Long-term effects. *American Journal of Orthopsychiatry, 66,* 131–140.

Elliot, D. S. (1994). Serious violent offenders: Onset, developmental course, and termination. The American Society of Criminology Presidential Address. *Criminology, 32,* 1–21.

Elliott, B. J., & Richards, M. P. M. (1991). Children and divorce: Educational performance and behavior before and after parental separation. *International Journal of Law and the Family, 5,* 258–276.

Emery, R. E. (1982). Interparental conflict and the children of discord and divorce. *Psychological Bulletin, 92,* 31–330.

Emery, R. E. (1994). *Renegotiating family relationships: Divorce, child custody, and mediation.* New York: Guilford Press.

Emery, R. E. (1999a). Changing the rules for determining child custody in divorce cases. *Clinical Psychology Science and Practice, 6,* 323–327.

Emery, R. E. (1999b). *Marriage, divorce, and children's adjustment* (2nd ed.). Thousand Oaks, CA: Sage.

English, A. (1999). Case One: Consent and the limits of staff as "family". In J. Blustein & C. Levine (Eds.), *The adolescent alone: Decision making in health care in the United States* (pp. 183–190). New York: Cambridge University Press.

Epstein, M. A., & Bottoms, B. L. (1999). *Explaining the forgetting and recovery of traumatic memories: Is the construct of repression necessary?* Manuscript submitted for publication.

Faigman, D. L., Kaye, D. H., Saks, M. J., & Sanders, J. (1997). *Modern scientific evidence: The law and science of expert testimony.* St. Paul, MN: West.

Feld, B. C. (1998). The juvenile court. In M. H. Tonry (Ed), *The handbook of crime and punishment* (pp. 509–541). New York: Oxford University Press.

Feld, B. C. (1999). *Bad kids: Race and the transformation of the juvenile court.* New York: Oxford University Press.

Finkelhor, D., Hotaling, G., Lewis, I. A., & Smith, C. (1990). Sexual abuse in a national survey of adult men and women: Prevalence, characteristics, and risk factors. *Child Abuse and Neglect, 14,* 19–28.

Folberg, J. (1991). *Joint custody and shared parenting.* New York: Guilford Press.

Fried, C. S., & Reppucci, N. D. (2001). Criminal decision making: The development of adolescent judgment, criminal responsibility and culpability. *Law and Human Behavior, 25,* 45–61.

Fried, C. S., & Reppucci, N. D. (in press). Youth violence: Correlates, interventions, and legal implications. In B. L. Bottoms, M. B. Kovera, & B. D. McAuliff (Eds.), *Children and the law: Social science and policy.* New York: Cambridge University Press.

Gabora, N. J., Spanos, N. P., & Joab, A. (1993). The effects of complainant age and expert psychological testimony in a simulated child sexual abuse trial. *Law and Human Behavior, 17,* 103–119.

Gardner, W., Scherer, D., & Tester, M. (1989). Asserting scientific authority: Cognitive development and adolescent legal rights. *American Psychologist, 44,* 895–902.

Garrison, E. G. (1991). Children's competence to participate in divorce custody decision making. *Journal of Clinical Child Psychology, 20,* 78–87.

Garvin, S., Wood, J. M., Malpass, R. S., & Shaw, J. S. (1998). More than suggestion: The effect of interviewing techniques from the McMartin Preschool case. *Journal of Applied Psychology, 83,* 347–359.

Geiselman, R. E., Saywitz, K. J., & Bornstein, G. K. (1993). Effects of cognitive questioning techniques on children's recall performance. In G. S. Goodman, & B. L. Bottoms (Eds.),

*Child victims, child witnesses: Understanding and improving testimony* (pp. 71–93). New York: Guilford.

Gillock, K. L., & Reyes, O. (1996). High school transition-related changes in urban minority students' academic performance and perceptions of self and school environment. *Journal of Community Psychology, 24,* 245–261.

Golding, J. M., Sanchez, R. P., & Sego, S. A. (1999). Brief research report: Age factors affecting the believability of repressed memories of child sexual assault. *Law and Human Behavior, 23,* 257–268.

Goldstein, J., Freud, A., & Solnit, A. (1973). *Beyond the best interests of the child.* New York: Free Press.

Goldstein, J., Freud, A., Solnit, A., & Goldstein, S. (1986). *In the best interests of the child.* New York, NY: Free Press.

Golombok, S., Bhanji, F., Rutherford, T., & Winston, R. (1990). Psychological development of children of the new reproductive technologies: Issues and a pilot study of children conceived by IVF. *Journal of Reproductive and Infant Psychology, 8,* 37–43.

Golombok, S., Cook, R., Bish, A., & Murray, C. (1995). Families created by the new reproductive technologies: Quality of parenting and social and emotional development of the children *Child Development, 66,* 285–298.

Goodman, G. S. (Ed.). (1984). The child witness. *Journal of Social Issues, 40, Whole Issue No. 2.*

Goodman, G. S., Batterman-Faunce, J. M., Schaaf, J. M., & Kenney, R. (2000). *Nearly 4 years after an event: Children's eyewitness testimony and adults' perceptions of children's accuracy.* Manuscript submitted for publication.

Goodman, G. S., & Bottoms, B. L. (Eds.) (1993). *Child victims, child witnesses: Understanding and improving testimony.* New York: Guilford.

Goodman, G. S., Emery, R. E., & Haugaard, J. (1998). Developmental psychology and law: Divorce, child maltreatment, foster care, and adoption. In I. Siegel, & A. Renninger (Eds.), *Child psychology in practice* (pp. 775–876). In W. Damon (Series Ed.), *Handbook of Child Psychology* (Vol. 4). New York: Wiley.

Goodman, G. S., Golding, J. M., & Haith, M. M. (1984). Jurors' reactions to child witnesses. *Journal of Social Issues, 40,* 139–156.

Goodman, G. S., Levine, M., & Melton, G. B. (1992). The best evidence produces the best law. *Law and Human Behavior, 16,* 244–251.

Goodman, G. S., Levine, M., Melton, G. B., & Ogden, D. (1991). Craig vs. Maryland. Amicus brief to the U.S. Supreme Court on behalf of the American Psychological Association. *Law and Human Behavior, 15,* 13–30.

Goodman, G. S., & Schwartz-Kenney, B. M. (1992). Why knowing a child's age is not enough: Influences of cognitive, social, and emotional factors on children's testimony. In H. Dent, & R. Flin (Eds.), *Children as witnesses. Wiley series in the psychology of crime, policing and law* (pp. 15–32). Chichester, England UK: Wiley.

Goodman, G. S., Taub, E. P., Jones, D. P. H., England, P., Port, L., Rudy, L., & Prado, L. (1992). Testifying in criminal court: Emotional effects on child sexual assault victims. *Monographs of the Society for Research in Child Development, 57*(5, Serial No. 229).

Goodman, G. S., Tobey, A. E., Batterman-Faunce, J. M., Orcutt, H., Thomas, S., Shapiro, C., & Sachsenmaier, T. (1998). Face-to-face confrontation: Effects of closed-circuit technology on children's eyewitness testimony and jurors' decisions. *Law and Human Behavior, 22,* 165–203.

Gorman-Smith, D., Tolan, P. H., & Henry, D. (1999). The relation of community and family to risk among urban-poor adolescents. In P. Cohen, C. Slomkowski, & L. N. Robins (Eds.), *Historical and geographical influences on psychopathology* (pp. 349–367). Mahwah, NJ: Erlbaum.

Gray, E. (1993). *Unequal justice: The prosecution of child sexual abuse.* New York, NY: Free Press.

Grisso, T. (1980). Juveniles' capacities to waive *Miranda* rights: An empirical analysis. *California Law Review, 68*, 1134–1166.

Grisso, T. (1981). *Juveniles' waiver of rights: Legal and psychological competence.* New York: Plenum Press.

Grisso, T. (1996). Society's retributive response to juvenile violence: A developmental perspective. *Law and Human Behavior, 20*, 229–247.

Grisso, T., & Melton, G. B. (1987). Getting child development research to legal practitioners: Which way to the trenches? In G. B. Melton (Ed.) *Reforming the law: Impact of child development research* (pp. 146–176). New York: Guilford.

Grisso, T., Schwartz, R., Scott, E., Cauffman, E., Woolard, J., & Hollin, C. (1999, July). *Youth on trial: Developmental perspectives on youths' competence and culpability.* Symposium conducted at the international conference of the American Psychology/Law Society and the European Association of Psychology & Law, Dublin, Ireland.

Grisso, T., & Schwartz, R. (Eds.) (2000). *Youth on trial.* Chicago, IL: University of Chicago Press.

Haegerich, T. M., & Bottoms, B. L. (2000). Empathy and jurors' decisions in patricide cases involving child sexual assault allegations. *Law and Human Behavior, 24*, 421–448.

Haney, C. (1980). Psychology and legal change: On the limits of a factual jurisprudence. *Law and Human Behavior, 4*, 147–200.

Hartigan v. Zbaraz, 484 U.S. 171 (1987).

Haugaard, J., & Reppucci, N. D. (1988). *The sexual abuse of children: A comprehensive guide to current knowledge and intervention strategies.* San Francisco, CA: Jossey-Bass.

Haugaard, J., Reppucci, N. D., Laird, J., & Naufeld, T. (1991). Children's definitions of the truth and their competency as witnesses in legal proceedings. *Law & Human Behavior, 15*, 253–272.

Henggeler, S. W., Schoenwald, S. K., Bourdin, C. M., Rowland, M. D., & Cunningham, P. B. (1998). *Multisystemic treatment of antisocial behavior in children and adolescents.* New York: Guilford.

Hetherington, E. M., (1999). Should we stay together for the sake of the children? In E. M. Hetherington (Ed), *Coping with divorce, single parenting, and remarriage: A risk and resiliency perspective* (pp. 93–116). Mahwah, NJ: Erlbaum.

Hetherington, E. M., Bridges, M., & Insabella, G. M. (1998). What matters? What does not? Five perspectives on the association between marital transitions and children's adjustment. *American Psychologist, 53*, 167–184.

Hoyt, S., & Scherer, D. G. (1998). Female juvenile delinquency: Misunderstood by the juvenile justice system, neglected by social science. *Law and Human Behavior, 22*, 81–107.

In re Gault, 387 US 1, 87 S Ct. 1428, 18 L. Ed. 2nd 527 (1967).

Interdivisional Committee on Adolescent Abortion (1987). Adolescent abortion: Psychological and legal issues. *American Psychologist, 42*, 73–78.

Isquith, P. K., Levine, M., & Scheiner, J. (1993). Blaming the child: Attribution of responsibility to victims of child sexual abuse. In G. S. Goodman, & B. L. Bottoms (Eds.), *Child victims, child witnesses: Understanding and improving testimony* (pp. 203–228). New York: Guilford Press.

Jacob Wetterling Crimes Against Children and Sexually Violent Offender Registration Program, 42, U.S.C. § 14071.

Johnson v. Calvert, 851 P 2d 776, 61 U.S.L.W. 2721 (1993).

Kaplan, S., & Brownlee, S. (1999, October 11). Dying for a cure: Why cancer patients often turn to risky, experimental treatments—and wind up paying with their lives. *U.S. News and World Report, 127*(14), 34.

Katz, L. F., & Gottman, J. M. (1995). Marital interaction and child outcomes: A longitudinal study of mediating and moderating processes. In D. Cicchetti, & S. L. Toth (Eds.),

*Emotion, cognition, and representation. Rochester symposium on developmental psychopathology* (Vol. 6, pp. 301–342). Rochester, NY: University of Rochester Press.

Kendall-Tackett, K. A., Williams, L. M., & Finkelhor, D. (1993). Impact of sexual abuse on children: A review and synthesis of recent empirical studies. *Psychological Bulletin, 113*, 164–180.

Kent v. United States, 383 U.S. 541, 86 S.Ct. 1045, 16 L.Ed.2d 84 (1966).

Kofkin, J., & Reppucci, N. D. (1991). A reconceptualization of life events and its applications to divorce. *American Journal of Community Psychology, 19*, 227–250.

Kovera, M. B., & Borgida, E. (1996). Children on the witness stand: The use of expert testimony and other procedural innovations in U. S. child sexual abuse trials. In B. L. Bottoms, & G. S. Goodman (Eds.), *International perspectives on child abuse and children's testimony: Psychological research and law* (pp. 201–220). Thousand Oaks, CA: Sage.

LaFond, J. Q. (1998). The costs of enacting a sexual predator law. *Psychology, Public Policy, and Law, 1*, 160 504.

Lanning, K. (1992). A law enforcement perspective on allegations of ritual abuse. In D. K. Sakheim, & S. E. Devine (Eds.), *Out of darkness: Exploring satanism and ritual abuse* (pp. 109–146). New York: Lexington.

Llewellyn, J. J., & Howse, R. (1999). *Restorative justice: A conceptual framework.* Ottawa: Law Reform Commission of Canada.

Lepore, S. J., & Sesco, B. (1994). Distorting children's reports and interpretations of events through suggestion. *Journal of Applied Psychology, 79*, 108–120.

Levine, M. (2000). The New Zealand children, young persons, and their families act of 1989: Review and evaluation. *Behavioral Sciences and the Law, 18*, 517–556.

Lewis, R. V. (1983). Scared Straight—California Style: Evaluation of the San Quentin Squires program. *Criminal Justice & Behavior, 10*, 209–226.

Leichtman, M. D., & Ceci, S. J. (1995). The effects of stereotypes and suggestions on preschoolers' reports. *Developmental Psychology, 31*, 568–578.

Lindsay, D. S., & Read, J. D. (1995). "Memory work" and recovered memories of childhood sexual abuse: Scientific evidence and public, professional, and personal issues. *Psychology, Public Policy, and Law, 1*, 846–908.

Lockhart v. McCree, 106 S.Ct. 1758 (1986).

Loeber, R., & Farrington, D. P. (Eds.). (1998). *Serious and violent juvenile offenders: Risk factors and successful interventions.* Thousand Oaks, CA: Sage.

Loftus, E. F. (1993). The reality of repressed memories. *American Psychologist, 48*, 518–537.

Loftus, E. F., & Monahan, J. (1980). Trial by data: Psychological research as legal evidence. *American Psychologist, 35*, 270–283.

Maccoby, E. E. (1999). The custody of children of divorcing families: Weighing the alternatives. In R. A. Thompson, & P. R. Amato (Eds.), *The postdivorce family: Children, parenting, and society* (pp. 51–70). Thousand Oaks, CA: Sage.

MacFarlane, M., Doueck, H., & Levine, M. (in press). Preventing child abuse and neglect. In B. L. Bottoms, M. B. Kovera, & B. D. McAuliff (Eds.), *Children and the law: Social science and policy.* New York: Cambridge University Press.

MacKenzie, D. L., & Brame, R. (1995). Shock incarceration and positive adjustment during community supervision. *Journal of Quantitative Criminology, 11*, 111–142.

Manfredi, C. P. (1998). *The Supreme Court and juvenile justice.* Lawrence, KS: University Press of Kansas.

Maryland v. Craig, 497 U.S. 836 (1990).

McGough, L. S. (1994). *Child witnesses: Fragile voices in the American legal system.* New Haven, CT: Yale University Press.

McRoy, R. G. (1989). An organizational dilemma: The case of transracial adoptions. *Journal of Applied Behavioral Science, 25*, 145–160.

Megan's Law, Public Law No: 104–145 (1996).

Melton, G. B. (1984). Developmental psychology and the law: The state of the art. *Journal of Family Law, 22*, 445–482.

Melton, G. B. (1990). Knowing what we do know: APA and adolescent abortion. *American Psychologist, 45*, 1171–1173.

Melton, G. B. (1999). Parents and children: Legal reform to facilitate children's participation. *American Psychologist, 54*, 935–944.

Melton, G. B., Goodman, G. S., Kalichman, S. C., Levine, M., Saywitz, K. J., & Koocher, G. P. (1995). Empirical research on child maltreatment and the law. *Journal of Clinical Child Psychology, 24*, 47–77.

Melton, G. B., & Koocher, G. P., & Saks, M. J. (1983). *Children's competence to consent.* New York: Plenum.

Meyer v. Nebraska, 262 U.S. 390 (1923).

Mini, M. M. (1994). Breaking down the barriers to transracial adoption. *Hofstra Law Review, 22*, 897–968.

Mnookin, R. H. (1978). *Child, family, and state.* Boston: Little, Brown.

Moffitt, T. E. (1993). Adolescence-limited and life-course persistent antisocial behavior: A developmental taxonomy. *Psychological Review, 100*, 674–701.

Monahan, J., & Walker, L. (1998). *Social science in law: Cases and materials.* Westbury, NY: The Foundation Press.

Multiethnic Placement Act of 1994. (1995). 42 U.S.C. 5115a (Pub. L. No. 103–382, Title V, 553, 108 Stat. 4056).

Mulvey, E. P., Arthur, M. W., & Reppucci, N. D. (1993). The prevention and treatment of juvenile delinquency: A review of the research. *Clinical Psychology Review, 13*, 133–167.

Murray, K. (1995). *Live television link.* Edinburgh, Scotland: The Scottish Office.

Myers, J. E. B. (1998). *Legal issues in child abuse and neglect* (2nd ed.). Thousand Oaks, CA: Sage.

Nightingale, N. N. (1993). Juror reactions to child victim witnesses: Factors affecting trial outcome. *Law and Human Behavior, 17*, 679–694.

Oberman, M. (1994). Turning girls into women: Re-evaluating modern statutory rape law. *Journal of Criminal Law & Criminology, 85*, 15–79.

Ogloff, J. R. P., & Finkelman, D. (1999). Psychology and law: An overview. In J. R. P. Ogloff, R. Roesch, & S. D. Hart (Eds.) *Psychology and law: The state of the discipline* (pp. 1–20). New York: Kluwer/Plenum.

Ondersma, S. J., Chaffin, M., Berliner, L., Cordon, I., Goodman, G. S., Barnett, D. (1999). *Sex with children is abuse: Comments on the Rind et al., meta-analysis controversy.* Manuscript submitted for publication.

Parham v. J. R., 442 U.S. 584 (1979).

Patterson, C. J. (1992). Children of lesbian and gay parents. *Child Development, 63*, 1025–1042.

Patterson, C. J. (1995). Lesbian mothers, gay fathers, and their children. In A. R. D'Augelli & C. J. Patterson (Eds.), *Lesbian, gay, and bisexual identities over the lifespan: Psychological perspectives* (pp. 262–290). New York: Oxford University Press.

Patterson, C. J., Fulcher, M., & Wainwright, J. (in press). Children of lesbian and gay parents: Research, law, and policy. In B. L. Bottoms, M. B. Kovera, & B. D. McAuliff (Eds.), *Children and the law: Social science and policy.* New York: Cambridge University Press.

Patterson, C. J., & Redding, R. E. (1996). Lesbian and gay families with children: Implications of social science research for policy. *Journal of Social Issues, 52*, 29–50.

Penkower, J. A. (1996). The potential right of chronically ill adolescents to refuse life-saving medical treatment: Fatal misuse of the mature minor doctrine. *DePaul Law Review, 45*, 1165–1216.

Perry, N. W., McAuliff, B. D., Tam, P., Claycomb, L., Dostal, C., & Flanagan, C. (1995). When lawyers question children: Is justice served? *Law and Human Behavior, 19,* 609–629.

Pierce v. Society of Sisters, 268 U.S. 510 (1925).

Pipe, M. E., & Wilson, J. C. (1994). Cues and secrets: Influences on children's event reports. *Developmental Psychology, 30,* 515–525.

Poe-Yamagata, E., & Butts, J. A. (1996). *Female offenders in the juvenile justice system.* Washington, D.C.: Office of Juvenile Justice and Delinquency Prevention.

Poole, D. A., & Lamb, M. E. (1998). *Investigative interviews of children: A guide for helping professionals.* Washington, DC: American Psychological Association.

Portwood, S., & Reppucci, N. D. (1994). Intervention vs. interference: The role of the courts in child placement. In J. Blacher (Ed.), *When there's no place like home* (pp. 3–36). Baltimore, MD: Paul H. Brookes.

Portwood, S., & Reppucci, N. D. (1996). Adults' impact on the suggestibility of preschoolers recollections. *Applied Developmental Psychology, 17,* 175–198.

Portwood, S., & Reppucci, N. D. (1997). Balancing rights and responsibilities: Legal perspectives on child maltreatment. In J. R. Lutzker (Ed.), *Handbook of child abuse research and treatment.* New York, NY: Plenum.

Quas, J. A., Qin, J., Schaaf, J., & Goodman, G. S. (1997). Individual differences in children's and adults' suggestibility and false event memory. *Learning and Individual Differences, 9,* 359–390.

Redding, R. (1997). Juveniles transferred to criminal court: Legal reforms proposal based on social science research. *Utah Law Review, 3,* 709–763.

Redding, R. (1997). Juveniles transferred to criminal court: Legal reforms proposal based on social science research. *Utah Law Review, 3,* 709–763.

Reppucci, N. D. (1984). The wisdom of Solomon: Issues in child custody determinations. In N. D. Reppucci, L. A. Weithorn, E. P. Mulvey, & J. Monahan (Eds.), *Children, mental health, and the law* (pp. 59–78). Beverly Hills, CA: Sage.

Reppucci, N. D. (1985). Psychology in the public interest. In A. M. Rogers & C. J. Scheirer (Eds.), *The G. Stanley Hall Lecture Series* (Vol. 5). Washington, D.C.: American Psychological Association.

Reppucci, N. D. (1999). Adolescent development and juvenile justice. *American Journal of Community Psychology, 27,* 307–326.

Reppucci, N. D., & Crosby, C. (1993). Law, psychology, and children: Overarching issues. *Law & Human Behavior, 17,* 1–10.

Reppucci, N. D., Weithorn, L. A., Mulvey, E. P., & J. Monahan (Eds.). (1984). *Children, mental health, and the law.* Beverly Hills, CA: Sage.

Reppucci, N. D., Woolard, J. L., & Fried, C. S. (1999). Social, community, and preventive interventions. *Annual Review of Psychology, 50,* 387–418.

Rind, B., Tromovitch, P., & Bauserman, R. (1998). A meta-analytic examination of assumed properties of child sexual abuse using college samples. *Psychological Bulletin, 124,* 22–53.

Roesch, R., Golding, S. L., Hans, V. P., & Reppucci, N. D. (1991). Social science and the courts: The role of amicus curiae briefs. *Law and Human Behavior, 15,* 1–11.

Ross, F., Hopkins, S., Hanson, E., Lindsay, R. C. L., Hazen, K., & Eslinger, T. (1994). The impact of protective shields and videotape testimony on conviction rates in a simulated trial of child sexual abuse. *Law and Human Behavior, 18,* 553–566.

Rudy, L., & Goodman, G. S. (1991). Effects of participation on children's reports: Implications for children's testimony. *Developmental Psychology, 27,* 1–26.

Saks, M. (1977). *Jury verdicts: The role of group size and social decision rule.* Lexington, MA: Lexington.

Sas, L. D. (1991). *Reducing the system-induced trauma for child sexual abuse victims through court preparation.* Ontario, Canada: London Family Court.

Sas, L. D., Wolfe, D. A., & Gowdey, K. (1996). Children and the courts in Canada. In B. L. Bottoms & G. S. Goodman (Eds.), *International perspectives on child abuse and children's testimony: Psychological research and law* (pp. 77–95). Thousand Oaks, CA: Sage.

Saunders, J. T., & Reppucci, N. D. (1977). Learning networks among administrators of human service institutions. *American Journal of Community Psychology, 5,* 269–276.

Scheiner, J. L. (1988, April). The use of the minimalist vignette as a method for assessing the generalizability of videotape trial simulation results. In M. Levine (Chair), *Simulated jury research on a child as a witness.* Symposium conducted at the meeting of the Eastern Psychological Association, Buffalo, NY.

Scherer, D. G. (1991). The capacities of minors to exercise voluntariness in medical treatment decisions. *Law and Human Behavior, 15,* 431–449.

Scherer, D., & Gardner, W. (1990). Reasserting the authority of science. *American Psychologist, 45,* 1173–1174.

Scherer, D., & Reppucci (1988). Adolescents' capacities to provide voluntary informed consent: The effects of parental influence and medical dilemmas. *Law and Human Behavior, 12,* 123–141.

Schmidt, M. G., & Reppucci, N. D. (in press). Children's rights and their capacities. In B. L. Bottoms, M. B. Kovera, & B. D. McAuliff (Eds.), *Children and the law: Social science and policy.* New York: Cambridge University Press.

Schram, D. D., & Milloy, C. D. (1995). Community notification: A study of offender characteristics and recidivism. Olympia, WA: Washington State Institute for Public Policy.

Scott, E. S., (1990). Rational decision-making about marriage and divorce. *Virginia Law Review, 76,* 9–94.

Scott, E. S. (1992). Pluralism, parental preference, and child custody. *California Law Review, 80,* 615–672.

Scott, E. S., & Grisso, T. (1997). The evolution of adolescence: A developmental perspective on juvenile justice reform. *Journal of Criminal Law and Criminology, 88,* 137–189.

Scott, E., Reppucci, N.D., & Aber, M. (1988). Children's preference in adjudicated custody decisions. *Georgia Law Review, 22,* 1035–1078.

Scott, E. S., Reppucci, N. D., & Woolard, J. L. (1995). Evaluating adolescent decision making in legal contexts. *Law and Human Behavior, 19,* 221–244.

Seidman (1984). The adolescent passage and entry into the juvenile justice system. In N. D. Reppucci, L.A. Weithorn, E. P. Mulvey, & J. Monahan (Eds.), *Children, mental health, and the law* (pp. 233–258). Beverly Hills, CA: Sage.

Simon, J. (1998). Managing the monstrous: Sex offenders and the new penology. *Psychology, Public Policy, and Law, 4,* 452–467.

Simon, R. J., Alstein, H., & Melli, M. S. (1994). *The case for transracial adoption.* Washington, DC: American University Press.

Slobogin, C., Fondacaro, M. R., & Woolard, J. (1999). A prevention model of juvenile justice: The promise of Kansas v. Hendricks for children. *Wisconsin Law Review, 2,* 185–226.

Small, M., & Limber, S. (in press). Advocacy for children's rights. In B. L. Bottoms, M. B. Kovera, & B. D. McAuliff (Eds.), *Children and the law: Social science and policy.* New York: Cambridge University Press.

Sorenson, E., Bottoms, B. L., & Perona, A. (1997). *Intake and forensic interviewing in the children's advocacy center setting: A handbook.* Washington, D.C.: National Network of Children's Advocacy Centers.

Stanford v. Kentucky, 492 U.S. 361 (1989).

Steinberg, L., & Cauffman, E. (1996). Maturity of judgment in adolescence: Psychosocial factors in adolescent decision making. *Law and Human Behavior, 20,* 249–272.

Steinberg, L., & Cauffman, E. (1999). The elephant in the courtroom: A developmental perspective on the adjudication of youthful offenders. *The Virginia Journal of Social Policy & the Law, 6*, 389–417.

Strauss, M. A. (1994). *Beating the devil out of them: Corporal punishment in American families.* San Francisco: Jossey-Bass.

Strauss, M. A. (1996). Spanking and the making of violent society. *Pediatrics, 98*, 837–842.

Strauss, M. A., & Stewart, J. H. (1999). Corporal punishment by American parents: National data on prevalence, chronicity, severity, and duration, in relation to child and family characteristics. *Clinical Child and Family Psychology Review, 2*, 55–70.

Swim, J., Borgida, E., & McCoy, K. (1993). Videotaped versus in-court witness testimony: Does protecting the child witness jeopardize due process? *Journal of Applied Social Psychology, 23*, 603–631.

Synder, H. N., & Sickmund, M. (1995). *Juvenile offenders and victims: A national report.* Washington, D.C.: Office of Juvenile Justice and Delinquency Prevention.

TASC, The American Surrogacy Center, Inc. (1997). Legal overview of surrogacy laws by state. Available: *http://www.surrogacy.com/legals/map.html*

Tate, D. C., Reppucci, N. D., & Mulvey, E. P. (1995). Violent juvenile delinquents: Treatment effectiveness and implications for future action. *American Psychologist, 50*, 777–781.

Thompson, R. A. (1992). Developmental changes in research risk and benefit: A changing calculus of concerns. In B. Stanley, J. & E. Sieber (Eds.), *Social research on children and adolescents* (pp. 31–64). Newbury Park, CA: Sage.

Thompson, W. C. (1989). Death qualification after *Wainwright v. Witt* and *Lockhart v. McCree. Law and Human Behavior, 13*, 185–215.

Thornburg v. American College of Obstetricians, 476 U.S. 747 (1986).

Tolan, P. H., & McKay, M. M. (1996). Preventing serious antisocial behavior in inner-city children: An empirically based family intervention program. *Family Relations. Journal of Applied Family and Child Studies, 45*, 148–155.

Trivits, L., & Reppucci, N. D. (2000). *In the best interests of the child? Developmental arguments against application of Megan's law to juveniles.* Manuscript submitted for publication.

Troxel v. Granville, 145 L. Ed. 2d 1068; 68 U.S.L.W. 3532 (2000).

Umbreit, M., & Greenwood, J. (1999). National survey of victim-offender mediation programs in the United States. *Mediation Quarterly, 6*, 235–251.

U.S. Department of Health and Human Services (2000). *HHS reports new child abuse and neglect statistics.* Available http://www.hhs.gov/news/press/2000pres/20000410.html.

U.S. Department of Health and Human Services (1996). *Child maltreatment 1994: Reports from the states to the national center on child abuse and neglect.* Washington, DC: U.S. Government Printing Office.

Vorzimer, A., & O'Hara, M. D. (1998). Buzzanca v Buzzanca: The ruling and ramifications. *TASC.* Available: *http://www.surrogacy.com/legals/jaycee/jayceesum.html*

Walberg, H. J., Reyes, O., & Weissberg, R. P. (Eds). (1997). *Children and youth: Interdisciplinary perspectives.* Thousand Oaks, CA: Sage.

Weiner, R. (1999, June). *Law and Human Behavior Planning Project Report.* Presentation at the American Psychology-Law Society Presidential Initiative Conference, Vancouver, British Columbia.

Weiten, W., & Diamond, S. S. (1979). A critical review of the jury simulation paradigm: The case of defendant characteristics. *Law and Human Behavior, 3*, 71–93.

Weithorn, L. A., & Campbell, S. B. (1982). The competency of children and adolescents to make informed treatment decisions. *Child Development, 53*, 1589–1598.

Whipple, G. M. (1911). The psychology of testimony. *Psychological Bulletin, 8*, 307–309.

Whitcomb, D., Shapiro, E. R., & Stellwagen, L. D. (1985). When the victim is a child: Issues for judges and prosecutors. In *Issues and Practices in Criminal Justice*. Washington, DC: National Institute of Justice.

Whitebread, C., & Heilman, J. (1988). An overview of the law of juvenile delinquency. *Behavioral Sciences and the Law, 6*, 285–305.

Williams v. Florida, 399 US 78 (1970).

Winick, B. J. (1998). Sex offender law in the 1990s: A therapeutic jurisprudence analysis. *Psychology, Public Policy, and Law, 4*, 505–570.

Winick, B. J., & LaFond, J. Q. (Eds.). (1998). Sex offenders: Scientific, legal, and policy perspectives [Special Theme]. *Psychology, Public Policy, and Law, 4* (1–2).

Winner, L., Lanza-Kanduce, L., Bishop, D. M., & Frazier, C. E. (1997). The transfer of juveniles to criminal court: Reexamining recidivism over the long term. *Crime and Delinquency, 43*, 548–563.

Wisconsin v. Yoder, 406 U.S. 205 (1972).

Wolfe, D. A, Reppucci, N. D., & Hart, S. (1995). Child abuse prevention: Knowledge and priorities. *Journal of Clinical Child Psychology, 24* Supplement, 5–22.

Woolard, J. L., Fried, C. S., & Reppucci, N. D. (2001). Toward an expanded definition of adolescent competence in legal contexts. In R. Roesch, R. R. Corrado, & R. J. Dempster (Eds.), *Psychology in the courts: International advances in knowledge* (pp. 21–39). Amsterdam: Harwood Academic.

Woolard J. L., & Reppucci, N. D. (in progress). *Juveniles' competence to stand trial*. New York: NY: Kluwer Academic/Plenum Press.

Woolard, J. L., Reppucci, N. D., & Redding, R. E. (1996). Theoretical and methodological issues in studying children's capacities in legal contexts. *Law and Human Behavior, 20*, 219–228.

Wrightsman, L. S., Nietzel, M. T., & Fortune, W. H. (1998). *Psychology and the legal system* (4th ed). Pacific Grove, CA: Brooks/Cole.

Yuille, J. C. (1993).We must study forensic eyewitnesses to know about them. *American Psychologist, 48*, 572–573.

Yoshikawa, H. (1993). Prevention as cumulative protection: Effects of early family support and education on chronic delinquency and its risks. *Psychological Bulletin, 115*, 28–54.

Yoshikawa, H. (1993). Prevention as cumulative protection: Effects of early family support and education on chronic delinquency and its risks. *Psychological Bulletin, 115*, 28–54.

Zimring, F. E. (1982). *The changing legal world of adolescence*. New York: Free Press.

Zimring, F. E. (1998). *American youth violence*. New York: Oxford University Press.

# 10

# Psychological Issues in Civil Law

## TRISTIN WAYTE, JOTI SAMRA, JENNIFER K. ROBBENNOLT, LARRY HEUER, AND WILLIAM J. KOCH

The interaction between psychology and civil law issues is a relatively new, but growing area of research. That only two of the chapters in this book are devoted to civil law issues speaks to the current state of psychological knowledge in this area. This being the case, we have chosen a broad focus, with three primary goals; (a) reviewing theory and research in individuals' sense of justice, which may explain why individuals resort to litigation, (b) research relating to decisionmaking in civil law, and (c) providing a brief discussion on the burgeoning area of psycholegal research in contract and property law. While this review is inevitably cursory and not comprehensive, we believe it will highlight pertinent

TRISTIN WAYTE • Department of Psychology, Simon Fraser University, Burnaby, British Columbia, Canada V5A 1S6.    JOTI SAMRA • Program in Law and Forensic Psychology, Simon Fraser University and Clinical Psychology Resident, Department of Psychiatry & Behavioral Sciences, University of Washington School of Medicine, Seattle, Washington 98195.    JENNIFER K. ROBBENNOLT • Faculty of Law, University of Missouri-Columbia, School of Law, Columbia, Missouri 65211.    LARRY HEUER • Department of Psychology, Barnard College, Columbia University, New York, New York 10027. WILLIAM J. KOCH • Health Psychology Clinic, University of British Columbia Psychiatry, University of British Columbia Hospital, Vancouver, British Columbia, Canada V6T 2B5.

areas of study and serve to stimulate new research into various civil law issues.

The probability that an individual will engage in formal civil litigation depends on a complex interplay of separate, yet interdependent events. Once an injury or grievous act has occurred, each step in the process of seeking redress for the wrong (initial response, complaint or claim, and litigation) may provide unique contributions to the probability of formal litigation. An understanding of the factors driving people to litigate is informed by several research areas, including (a) distributive and procedural justice, (b) individual and procedural factors related to litigation settlement, and (c) consumer satisfaction with alternative dispute resolution.

Several salient research questions that emerge when looking at individuals' sense of justice. What procedures facilitate settlement and perceived fairness? What factors enhance satisfaction with outcomes? Are there notable individual differences in perceived fairness and litigiousness? We begin by reviewing theoretical models that have been used to explain whether disputes will be settled prior to engagement in formal litigation. After reviewing a series of models, a relational justice model (Lind & Tyler 1988; Tyler, 1989; Tyler & Lind, 1992) will be used to frame the discussion on procedural fairness, the role of satisfaction in fairness ratings, and potential individual differences in likelihood of litigation. We then review the factors that enhance satisfaction and perceived fairness with formal and alternative dispute resolution procedures. Subsequently, we discuss the limited research about those attributes of individuals that may facilitate settlement or predict litigation.

The ability of decision-makers in the civil arena to make legally relevant decisions is a central concern of those in the field. Legal decision-makers are called upon to sort through a complex array of information to determine liability and assess damage awards, while not allowing extra-legal artifacts such as sympathy or attitudes about the role and nature of the civil system to contaminate those decisions. Some important questions that emerge in relation to civil decisionmaking are: How are decisions about liability and damages made? What extra-legal factors come to play in juror decisionmaking and how do these affect the decision process? These questions will be briefly entertained in the second section of this chapter.

Psycholegal research in the areas of contracts and property law is a very new and promising area of study that deserves more attention. Issues relating to contracts are an integral part of everyday life, and the manner in which individuals conceptualize their rights and obligations under contracts may affect bargaining and enforcement of terms.

Research questions that emerge include: How do contract schemas impact juror decisionmaking? What is the role of "psychological contracts" in employee–employer relations? How does the language of contracts impact perceived fairness, as well as contractual acceptance and enforcement? Psychological research issues in property law include the developmental course of individual's conception of property rights, how rights protections impact property conceptions, and individuals' preferences regarding the right to dispose property.

Finally, we conclude with a discussion of promising future directions in civil law and psychology. After suggestions are made relating to the topics covered in this chapter, we discuss promising directions in psyc holegal research in commercial and business arenas. While our space limits the depth of coverage, we hope this chapter provides the reader with an overview of pertinent areas of civil law that have received considerable interest in the psycholegal literature, as well as some areas that show promise for future growth and understanding.

## PERCEPTIONS OF JUSTICE

### ATTRIBUTES AFFECTING THE LIKELIHOOD OF PRETRIAL SETTLEMENT

Understanding the factors that influence a litigant's decision to settle prior to trial or to proceed to formal litigation is important to psychologists interested in basic questions about human behavior, legal scholars interested in developing models of legal behavior, and reformers pursuing amendments intended to influence legal behavior. For example, in the 1st session of the 104th Congress in 1995, the U.S. House of Representatives proposed a "Contract with America", which, among other things, included a bill entitled "The common sense legal reforms act of 1995" that proposed "loser pays" laws, limits on punitive damages, and reform of product liability laws intended to stem the "endless tide" of litigation. A proposal such as this assumes a "litigation crisis" exists in the American civil system, and that the proposed reforms will be successful in curbing the problem. As will be discussed in greater detail below, reform efforts designed to reduce litigation must make assumptions about human behavior, legal processes and potentially complex psycholegal interactions. Unfortunately, much of what is required to understand what reforms are needed and what kind of amendments will alter legal behavior requires information about tort law and litigation behavior that does not yet exist (see Daniels & Martin, 1997; Saks, 1992). Understanding behavior within the civil system and factors affecting litigation requires attention to the various decision points at which a person may settle a dispute informally or appeal it to more formal avenues of resolution. Additionally, we need to consider variables in the environment where the dispute first arose, such as the efficacy of available avenues for settling the problem. We will begin our discussion on models that explore factors affecting whether disputes will be settled informally or advanced to formal litigation.

A variety of models have been employed by researchers to explain dispute settlement. Among the models reviewed below are rational decisionmaking process (i.e., economic theories), versus those that assume an irrational decisionmaking process (i.e., cognitive/prospect theories) to account for what leads individuals to accept pre-trial settlement or proceed to formal litigation (i.e., trial). We then describe how the larger body of work on procedural justice and satisfaction may inform the question of why people litigate.

## RATIONAL MODELS OF DECISION MAKING

Rational (economic) models of decisionmaking (e.g., subjective expected utility models), dominated early efforts to explain litigants' choices of settlement versus trial. The underlying assumption of rational models of litigation behavior is that individuals make rational choices to settle or litigate calculated on maximization of economic utility. From this perspective, a defendant considering settlement versus trial would settle for (or set their reservation price) an amount equal to or less than the monetary cost of an adverse trial decision multiplied by the probability of that decision, plus trial costs, minus settlement costs. Legal scholars espousing such models assume that the parties to civil litigation are risk-neutral (e.g., they would be indifferent between a certain $10,000 settlement or a 10% chance of a $100,000 damage award) when deciding between settlement and trial (e.g., Danzon & Lillard, 1983; Posner, 1973; Priest, 1985; Priest & Klein, 1984; Wittman, 1985).

Because of the high cost of pursuing a civil claim to trial, most commentators have suggested that trials represent negotiation failures (e.g., Gross & Syverud, 1991; Trubek et al., 1983). Rational decisionmaking models offer several explanations for such failures. One explanation is that the parties miscalculated their chances of prevailing at trial. Another explanation is that the parties might realize the potential for joint-gain that a settlement offers, but be unable to agree on how to allocate it (e.g., Cooter, Marks, & Mnookin, 1982). Alternatively, trials result when one or both parties employ distributive bargaining tactics that interfere with their ability to discover the overlap between their true reservation points

(Raiffa, 1982). A fourth explanation is offered by asymmetric cost models (e.g., Bebchuk, 1996; Rosenberg & Shavell, 1985) which assume that plaintiffs pursue frivolous litigation in order to exploit the defendants' willingness to settle in order to avoid the costs of litigation. Finally, asymmetric information models (e.g., Bebchuk, 1988; Katz, 1990; Polinsky & Rubinfeld, 1993) propose that plaintiffs can capitalize on privately held information about the validity of their claim to exact offers from defendants who must make probabilistic judgments about the merits of the plaintiff's claim.

While generally acknowledging the value of rational decisionmaking models as a starting point for understanding litigant preferences for settlement versus trial, critics point to a growing body of research showing that plaintiffs (a) are not risk-neutral in their assessment of their options, and (b) deviate from rationality in systematic ways. Thus, the support for economic models of litigant behavior has been decreasing, whereas the support for cognitive (also called "irrational" theories) has been growing. These latter theories take into consideration the cognitive processes that interfere with perfect rationality in human decisionmaking. One of the most influential approaches to understanding deviations from rationality is prospect theory (Kahneman & Tversky, 1979), which is considered below.

## COGNITIVE THEORIES

Psychologists have demonstrated that human decisionmaking in many situations does not conform to the predictions of economic models. One area in which economic models have been faulted is decisionmaking under conditions of uncertainty, such as those involving the risky choices available to litigants who are considering whether to settle for a certain outcome, or pursue a more attractive but uncertain outcome at trial. According to economic decisionmaking models, a litigant would be expected to be indifferent to the choice between a 60% chance of obtaining a $100,000 award at trial and a certain $60,000 settlement offer. However, research on prospect theory by Kahneman and Tversky [1979 (hereinafter Kahneman & Tversky, Prospect Theory), 1981 (hereinafter Tversky & Kahneman, The Psychology of Choice), 1984, 1986 (hereinafter Tversky & Kahneman, Rational Choice)] has demonstrated that decisionmakers are not indifferent, and that the nature of their preferences is affected by how such risky choices are framed: When framed as gains, people are risk-averse, but when framed as losses people are risk-seeking. So, for example, when participants in one study were asked to choose between a certain $240 gain versus a 25% chance of a $1000 gain, 84%

opted for the gain, despite the fact that the expected value of the chance option was higher. On the other hand, participants offered a choice between a sure $750 loss versus a 75% chance of a $1000 loss, 87% of them preferred the risky alternative, despite the fact that the expected value of the options was identical (Tversky & Kahneman, 1986).

These findings have direct implications for plaintiff and defendant preferences for settlement versus trial. The same settlement offer is more attractive when viewed as a potential gain (as it is likely to be viewed by a plaintiff) than when it is viewed as a potential loss (as it is likely to be viewed by a defendant). Thus, prospect theory (Tversky & Kahneman, 1991; Kahneman & Tversky, 1979) predicts a systematic divergence in approaches to risk between defendants and plaintiffs in civil litigation. In fact, numerous studies of actual settlement negotiations reveal lower settlements than would be predicted by economic models (Rachlinski, 1996). Gross and Syverud (1991) compared final settlement offers and results at trial in cases involving personal injury, vehicular negligence, medical malpractice, commercial transactions, employment, and real estate. In every type of case, the final offer from defendants was lower than the final award. This result is consistent with framing theory in that defendants (facing losses) are risk-seeking, evidenced by their conservative offers leading them to the risky trial. However, economic, utility-maximization models do not explain these findings. Of course, such data, by virtue of the lack of control for extraneous variables, permit alternative explanations that are consistent with economic models. Rachlinski (1996) notes that such a finding could be reconciled with economic models if the plaintiffs were less wealthy than the defendants. However, some experiments (Korobkin & Guthrie, 1994; van Koppen, 1990) with appropriate controls, support a framing model of litigant preferences for settlement versus trial in civil cases.

In one of the earliest studies of the implications of prospect theory for civil negotiations, van Koppen (1990) conducted four experiments employing an imaginary vignette among undergraduates and law students testing the hypotheses that (1) when deciding between settlement or trial, defendants are risk-seeking and plaintiffs are risk-averse; and, (2) that parties expecting to lose at trial will be risk-seeking, while those expecting to win at trial would be risk-averse. The findings supported the hypothesis that litigants expecting to lose were relatively more risk-seeking (although the litigants who expected to win were also risk-seeking). Hypothesis 1 was supported only for the undergraduate participants. van Koppen's results showed a considerable effect of the win versus lose frame manipulation, despite the fact that the differences in expectations were not particularly large. van Koppen suggested that the difference might be explained by laypersons' focus on gains versus losses as a function of their role as plaintiffs, while the law students may be more inclined to focus on the rights and duties raised by the case materials, and are therefore less affected by the gain-loss frame expected to result from the role assignment. van Koppen concluded that such findings in an analogue study might explain the tendency for plaintiffs to win in court (McEwen & Maiman, 1986; Yngvesson & Hennessey, 1975), as the disputes ending in trial will be over represented by risk—averse plaintiffs and risk-seeking defendants.

Korobkin and Guthrie (1994) provided additional support for framing effects in civil litigation. These researchers had undergraduates read one of several fictitious cases describing disputes pertaining to vehicular negligence, easements, or visitation rights. The information provided to participants was varied so that a settlement offer was framed as a gain or a loss (participants who read the vehicular negligence case were told that their insurance company had offered them a settlement of $21,000 while the outcome at trial would be either a $10,000 award or a $28,000 award; for half of the subjects this settlement offer would cover $10,000 more than their loss, while for the other half this settlement would cover $10,000 less than their loss). In each of the disputes, the participants were more likely to accept the offer when it was framed as a gain than as a loss. Unfortunately, the framing manipulation employed in each case is arguably confounded with whether the settlement offer is equitable, leaving some ambiguity as to the causal mechanism driving these effects.

In a recent article, Guthrie (2000) addresses an aspect of prospect theory that has received little attention from legal scholars, noting that Tversky and Kahneman's (1992) framework of risk attitudes reflects a four-fold structure of moderate versus low risk and gain versus loss. Most of the research testing the implications of prospect theory for decisionmaking in civil cases (including that described above) has focused on the theory's predictions in settings involving moderate- to high-probability risk. This research has shown participants to be risk-seeking for moderate- to high-probability losses and risk-averse for moderate- to high-probability gains. However, the theory makes the opposite prediction for individuals facing low-probability risks. Under such conditions, individuals are expected to be risk-seeking for gains and risk-avoidant for losses. So, for example, Tversky and Kahneman (1992) found individuals to exhibit a preference for a 1% chance of gaining $400 over a certain $4 gain (risk-seeking for low-probability gains), but a preference for paying a certain $4 fine over a 1% chance of a $400 fine (risk-avoidant for low-probability losses). Guthrie (2000) summarizes other studies that show a greater tendency for risk-seeking than risk-aversion in low-probability gain-frames and a greater tendency for risk-aversion than risk-seeking under low-probability loss-frames. Guthrie's research tested the low-probability framing predictions among first—year law students who read a fictitious case from the perspective of either the plaintiff or the defendant. In a series of analogue studies using law students, Guthrie showed that plaintiffs were risk-seeking (with the majority preferring trial) while defendants were risk-averse (the majority preferred settlement) when presented with the choice between a settlement versus trial with identical expected values. So, for example, plaintiffs given a choice between a certain $50 settlement offer or a trial with an expected value of $50 (1% chance of a $5,000 award) tended to prefer trial, while defendants given a choice between a settlement offer of $50 versus a trial with a 1% chance of a $5,000 payment preferred settlement.

Guthrie (2000) points out that while the findings of previous experimental work on civil decisionmaking under risk is consistent with the behavior of litigants in ordinary litigation, it is unlikely to be descriptive in "frivolous litigation—the quintessential example of low-probability litigation" (p. 168). Thus, in frivolous litigation, contrary to van Koppen's predictions examined above, plaintiffs are expected to be risk-seeking while defendants are risk-averse. Guthrie notes that this exception gives plaintiffs an advantage in settlement negotiations. Assuming there is an overlap between the plaintiffs' and the defendants' offers, the disputants will likely settle for an amount that is greater than the expected value of the litigation. Guthrie suggests that a test of the predictions of prospect theory for frivolous litigation is in order.

Recent research has moved away from the assumptions of rationality among litigants choosing between settlement and trial. While few of these researchers are likely to quarrel with the assertion that subjective expected utilities play a role in litigants' decisions about how to pursue their claims, their empirical work has relied more on theories that attempt to explain deviations from such normative models. Thus, the research described above demonstrates how the framing of options in terms of potential losses (a likely perspective of defendants) versus potential gains (a likely perspective of plaintiffs) can influence preferences for trial versus settlement, in a manner consistent with the predictions of prospect theory.

Below, we discuss briefly another line of work with direct implications for procedural preferences, which, like prospect theory, goes beyond the economic prediction of rational self-interested behavior.

## PROCEDURAL JUSTICE THEORY

Thibaut and Walker (1975, 1978) proposed their theory of procedural justice at a time when social psychologists were relying heavily on distributive justice models to understand individuals' responses to social conflict. While the underlying assumption of distributive justice (DJ) models was that fair *outcomes* were the key to understanding disputants' satisfaction with the resolution of conflict, Thibaut and Walker's observation of defendants in criminal cases led them to speculate that, while DJ theories were surely correct, there was more to the story. According to Thibaut and Walker, procedural preferences were importantly determined by disputant perceptions of fairness regarding *procedures*. A central component to this theory is that if individuals view procedures as fair (e.g., perception of due process), then outcomes will be viewed as just, even if the outcome is not personally favourable. This prediction has been strongly supported in numerous laboratory studies (e.g., Houlden, 1980; Houlden, LaTour, Walker, and Thibaut, 1978; Kurtz & Houlden, 1981; Lind, Erickson, Friedland, & Dickenberger, 1978; Thibaut, Walker, LaTour, & Houlden, 1974; Sheppard, 1985).

Many of the early procedural justice studies examined preferences for bargaining (e.g., plea) versus a procedure that included a third-party decision-maker who permitted both disputants to present evidence on their behalf and who then issued a binding decision. Thibaut, Walker and their colleagues referred to this latter procedure as an "adversarial procedure", because it has the essential characteristics of a trial in the U.S. civil justice system. The consistent finding in these studies was a preference for an adversarial rather than a bargaining procedure (e.g., Houlden et al., 1978; LaTour, 1978; LaTour, Houlden, Walker, & Thibaut, 1976; Walker, LaTour, Lind, & Thibaut, 1974). As will be discussed in greater detail below, research in procedural justice perceptions explains this preference for adversarial procedures. Of course, this preference structure does not fit neatly with the oft-reported finding that the vast majority of civil disputes are settled in pre-trial negotiations. For example, depending on the U.S. jurisdiction 12–68% of medical malpractice claims are settled without trial, and as many as 90% of other types of claims (such as personal injury) are settled through mediation or informal negotiation (e.g., Daniels & Martin 1997; Danzon & Lillard, 1983; Gifford & Nye, 1987; Gross & Syverud, 1996; Ross, 1980; Trubek et al., 1983). One study that explicitly addressed this disparity between the findings of the justice studies and the overwhelming popularity of negotiated settlements in actual disputes led the researchers to suggest that much of the justice research engaged the participants in winner-take-all conflicts that were not amenable to negotiated settlements (Heuer & Penrod, 1986). When these authors modified the procedures employed by earlier justice studies to permit compromise settlements, or multi-issue integrative settlements (e.g., efficient trade-offs among multiple issues of differing priorities to the negotiators), these negotiated settlements were more popular. At the same time, this study replicated the finding that procedural fairness was the best predictor of procedural preferences. This finding fits nicely with that of Houlden (1980) who surveyed undergraduates and inmates about their preferences for a variety of plea bargaining procedures. Houlden found that the best predictors of preference for the procedures were opportunity to have one's say and procedural fairness. More recent support is found in divorce mediation research; the protection of rights in the process of mediation versus litigation accounted for variability in individual's ratings of the two types of procedures (Kelly, 1996). In fact, in their field study of those involved in child custody disputes, Kitzmann and Emery (1993) found that fairness perceptions in the process (litigation versus mediation), determined individual's satisfaction with those procedures over the structure of the proceedings.

In addition to the proposition that procedural fairness would be an important predictor of procedural preferences, Thibaut and Walker's theory of procedural justice also specified which procedural criteria were important for fairness perceptions. Thibaut and Walker shared the assumption of DJ theorists that disputants were motivated to obtain fair and desirable outcomes. Therefore, they postulated that the determinants of fair procedure were disputants' opportunities to tell their side of the story ("process control"), and the degree of participant influence on dispute outcome ("decision control"). Many studies have supported this hypothesis that process and decision control were central to definitions of procedural fairness (e.g., Tyler, 1987; Tyler, Rasinski, & Spodick, 1985).

## SATISFACTION AND PERCEIVED FAIRNESS

### Satisfaction with Outcomes, Courts, and Judges

Other justice research has investigated the consequences of fair treatment on disputant satisfaction with procedures, outcomes, leaders, and institutions. We review such literature primarily because it suggests that fairness is important in these models, just as it was in the models of preferences summarized above. Further, this work sheds additional light on the meaning of fairness. Perhaps most litigation is the result of disputants' dissatisfaction with earlier efforts to solve conflict. It is possible that lack of procedural fairness in these earlier efforts leads disputants to seek binding decisions from the courts, but to our knowledge this has not been tested explicitly.

Tyler and his colleagues have conducted two particularly informative investigations of the role of fairness among participants in the legal process. Tyler (1984) surveyed defendants in traffic and misdemeanor court about their satisfaction after their case was completed. Participants answered a series of questions about case outcome; including absolute outcome and outcome relative to their expectations and relative to others, as well as both procedural and distributive fairness. Tyler found that the fairness variables accounted for considerably more of the defendants' satisfaction with their outcome, the judge, and the court, than did the absolute and relative outcome measures. He also found that procedural fairness was a better predictor than distributive fairness of satisfaction with the court procedures while distributive fairness was a better predictor of outcome satisfaction. The two fairness variables were about equally predictive of satisfaction with the judge. Although this study was limited to misdemeanor cases, a subsequent study by Casper, Tyler, and Fisher (1988) surveyed over 400 convicted felony defendants and replicated the finding that procedural and distributive fairness were important predictors of outcome satisfaction. This finding is further supported by a study of over 600 felony defendants by Landis and Goodstein (1986). This study again found procedural fairness to be an important predictor of the defendants' evaluations of their case. It is particularly noteworthy that in neither the Casper, Tyler, and Fisher (1988) study nor the Landis and Goodstein (1986) study was the role of fairness on satisfaction qualified by the outcome of the case.

Before we delve further into specific criteria of resolution procedures that facilitate procedural preferences and fairness, we will turn briefly to the use of alternative dispute resolution and the effect on justice considerations.

## Alternative Dispute Resolution Procedures

Alternative dispute resolution (ADR) procedures are advocated and employed by the civil court system and organizations to minimize. A wide variety of ADR mechanisms have been developed for different types of disputes, such as mediation, settlement conferences, summary jury trials, and early neutral evaluations. The purposes of such alternative procedures are to (a) streamline disputes and (b) decrease the financial costs of litigation by circumventing adversarial proceedings. For example, divorce mediation is frequently used in place of adversarial divorce procedures, and is assumed to be more cost-effective, less conflicted, and in general more satisfactory for the couple (Kelly, 1996, 1989). As will be discussed below, these claims have not been fully supported by research (Twaite, Keiser, & Luchow, 1998; Vidmar, 1992), but such alternative procedures are still advocated by many scholars in a civil system that places a premium on timely settlements. We first review research comparing different resolution procedures in the civil system, then we review aspects of resolution

procedures that facilitate perceived fairness and settlement in organizations. A theme in this research is that procedural fairness and justice appear
to predict participant satisfaction in disputes more than the type of adjudication employed to resolve the problem (Lind et al., 1990; Vidmar, 1992).

Lind and colleagues (1990) asked individuals involved with personal
injury litigation for their evaluation of procedural fairness and outcome
satisfaction of three third-party procedures (traditional trial and two alternative third-party procedures—arbitration and judicial settlement) versus
bilateral settlement. A bilateral settlement is a contract or agreement in
which both parties are bound to fulfill obligations reciprocally towards
each other. In this context, both parties agree upon their own and the
other party's rights and obligations, rather than having a third party (i.e.,
a judge) unilaterally impose obligations. The results showed that participating in third-party procedures was not as negative as bilateral settle-
ment-proponents often assume. Those involved in traditional trials and
arbitration rated these higher for procedural fairness compared to those
involved in bilateral settlement. Participants did not feel alienated by the
traditional trial setting, in fact, the trial enhanced their sense of dignity.
Arbitration had slightly higher ratings for dignity over bilateral settlements. The authors contend the courtroom solemnity provided the participants' issues with a level of importance not seen in bilateral settlement.
This enhanced the level of dignity among litigants, which increased their
satisfaction. The results for judicial settlements showed a different pattern, in that participants rated the outcome as less satisfying than bilateral
settlement, and led people to feel less comfortable with the procedures.
Lind and colleagues (1990) findings generally do not support the tenets of
ADR, and calls for replication of the results and further examination of
fairness perceptions across different types of resolution procedures. If
civil claims resolved through ADR are viewed as less fair and disputants
see their outcomes as less satisfying, these alternatives have the potential
to erode public confidence in the civil system for handling problems.

Although alternative dispute procedures have not been shown to be
the panacea for tort reform, this type of resolution is still being advocated
as a sound alternative to court-based procedures in a number of contexts.
One context is divorce mediation, which takes place in a less formal
atmosphere and involves a neutral third party (mediator) who works
with disputants to develop a mutually agreeable resolution to their problem (Donohue, 1991; Donohue, Drake & Roberto, 1994). While some
authors (Kelly, 1996, 1989) claim 60–85% of divorcing couple who go
through mediation are satisfied with the procedures, research comparing
mediation and litigation is not as flattering to the former. In a review of
the literature comparing litigation versus mediation, Vidmar (1992) found

no consistent relationship between satisfaction and type of adjudication. In fact, his review of actual cases of divorce mediation showed that mediation in this context is often viewed as inflexible, and couples in court-mandated mediation may resent being involved with their own decisions. This resentment may be even higher among couples whose marriage and separation are highly conflicted, compared to couples whose separation is relatively amicable. If the dispute involves legal rights, couples actually prefer third-party control (Vidmar, 1992). Also, there is mixed support for the contention that mediation improves post-divorce relationships between spouses (Twaite et al., 1998). In these authors' review of 7 long-term studies on post-divorce relationship, 4 studies found improved post-divorce relationships after mediation when compared to litigation, while 3 separate studies showed minimal differences. Twaite and colleagues (1998) suggest that any new research in this area should take into account the scope of issues the couple is handling through mediation, and the time to complete the process.

The application of procedural justice theory to child custody disputes is limited (Kitzmann & Emery, 1993). Child custody disputes should be considered unique insofar as the disputants know each other quite well, and often have ongoing contact, even following resolution of the dispute. The limited findings available suggest that mothers report equal satisfaction with mediation and litigation. In contrast, fathers report more control in mediation, and reported more fairness and satisfaction with mediation (see Kitzmann & Emery, 1993 for a discussion). In these studies, sole physical custody was almost always awarded to the mother; thus, differences in fathers' satisfaction can be attributed to differences in perceived procedural (and not distributive) justice. In the case of positive outcomes, disputants tend to be satisfied regardless of the procedure used. However, in the case of poor outcomes, procedural fairness perceptions are more important in determining satisfaction (Lind & Tyler, 1988). Kitzmann and Emery (1993) found that both dispute and disputant characteristics were influential in determining the relative importance outcome favorability and procedural fairness had upon satisfaction. Procedural factors (respect and decision control) were most important for individuals in litigation (versus mediation), individuals who were at a disadvantage (i.e., fathers), and individuals who reported having lost what they wanted.

## An Expanding Conception of the Meaning of Fairness

Much of the fairness research summarized above was conducted with a general view that important procedural criteria for fairness evaluations were process control (or "voice") and decision control. However, other research has identified additional procedural criteria. While Thibaut and Walker's (1975, 1978) focus on disputants' motives to obtain fair and beneficial outcomes led them to identify the procedural criteria of process and decision control (largely due to their view that disputants valued control for its role in permitting them to influence the outcomes of their disputes), numerous studies revealed findings inconsistent with Thibaut and Walker's assumption. For example, Lind, Lissak, and Conlon (1983) reported that variations in decision control had no influence on procedural justice judgments, while variations in process control had a substantial effect. Other studies have reported both process and decision control effects on fairness judgments, but have found process control effects to be considerably larger (e.g., Tyler, 1987). In a more direct challenge to the importance of control in instrumental theory of procedural justice theory, Tyler, Rasinski, and Spodick (1985) reported several studies showing benefits of voice for procedural fairness judgments beyond what could be explained by disputant perceptions of outcome control. These authors argued that such voice effects support a value-expressive role of voice in addition to the rational, instrumental effects of voice described by Thibaut and Walker. More recently, this non-instrumental, voice enhancement of procedural fairness judgments has been reported in an experimental design (Lind, Kanfer, & Earley, 1990).

## Relational Justice Model

Lind and Tyler (1988; Tyler, 1989; Tyler & Lind, 1992) proposed a Group Value Theory of procedural justice. This relational model emphasizes individuals' concerns about their relationships with social groups and the authorities representing those groups. The model assumes that group identification and group membership is psychologically rewarding, and that individuals are motivated to establish and maintain group bonds. Membership in a social group is considered an integral part of a person's identity, and the quality of the relationship between the individual and an organization is hypothesized to mediate claiming behavior. If this relationship is negative or adversarial, the model predicts that individuals will feel exploited and be more likely to litigate. If a positive relationship exists between the individuals and the organization, individuals are more likely to perceive outcomes as fair, even when they involve a personally adverse outcome (Lind, 1997; Tyler & Lind, 1992). According to this theory, when individuals are focused on their long-term relationships with groups, they evaluate the fairness of procedures according to a different set of criteria than the control variables proposed by Thibaut and Walker. Lind and Tyler proposed that under such circumstances procedures are evaluated according to three criteria: the *trustworthiness* of the authorities enacting the procedures; the *neutrality* of those authorities; and information emanating from the procedure about the individual's *standing* in the group.

There is substantial indirect support for this suggestion that individuals are sensitive to issues such as polite or respectful treatment (e.g., Bies & Moag, 1986; Bies & Shapiro, 1987; Tyler & Bies, 1990; Tyler & Folger, 1980) or information about their standing in the group (Huo, Smith, Tyler, & Lind, 1996; MacCoun, et al., 1988; Tyler & DeGoey, 1995). One particularly impressive demonstration of the role of the relational variables for disputant satisfaction in a legal setting is Tyler's (1989) survey of Chicago residents. Tyler asked his respondents to answer a series of questions about a recent encounter with a legal authority (e.g., a peace officer or a judge). Questions involved personal opportunities for process and decision control during their encounter and the perceived trustworthiness, neutrality, and respectfulness of the authority. Tyler found that when the control variables and the relational variables were entered simultaneously as predictors of procedural fairness, only the relational variables contributed virtually all of the unique variance. A similar finding was reported in a subsequent study by Tyler (1989) that surveyed individuals in both a legal and an organizational context.

At least two recent articles have suggested a role for apologies in promoting the settlement of civil litigation prior to trial. For example, Levi (1997) notes that plaintiff lawyers often ignore the role of apologies for dispute settlement, despite consistent reports of their value in obtaining settlement (e.g., Goldberg, Green, & Sander, 1985; Goldberg, Sander & Rogers, 1992; Wagatsuma & Rosett, 1986). Similarly, Shuman (2000) notes that a sincere apology is often identified by plaintiffs as the factor that might have averted civil litigation. Although neither Levi (1997) nor Shuman (2000) refer to the justice literature summarized here, it seems likely that the role of apologies, clearly a symbolic factor, taps psychological mechanisms (e.g., respectfulness) similar to those identified by the justice research.

Overall, we think the justice research identifies an extremely potent set of factors determining litigant decisions about litigation. Regardless of whether the dispute is resolved in pre-trial settlement discussions or at trial, disputant perceptions of procedures is a rich variable affecting satisfaction with dispute resolution.

## Reducing Litigation

According to the relational justice model, efforts to reduce litigious behavior should focus on the relationship between the employee and the employer. Lind (1997) contends that the likelihood of someone suing an organization goes beyond simple procedural justice perceptions. The perceived relationship between employee and employer appears to be an important predictor of claiming behavior. As noted in the previous section, if this relationship is negative, the employee may feel exploited and self-interested behavior may increase. When a positive relationship exists, the employee is more likely to trust the organization and believe that decisions are made in a fair manner. Thus, perceptions of injustice may lead to litigation. Finally, if people feel they have received some kind of restitution (whether financial, moral, or emotional) for their concerns, they are more likely to abandon their claims (Lind, 1997; Lind et al., 1990). Employees who view organizational policies as fair, who feel that procedures were neutral (unbiased), and who trust the organization are less hostile subsequent to dismissal actions and promotion decisions, and are less likely to consider litigation (Bies & Tripp, 1993; Youngblood, Klebe, & Favia, 1992).

Other factors considered important in enhancing fairness and reducing the likelihood of litigation include (a) status recognition of the employee and (b) control (Bies & Tyler, 1993). First, consistent with relational theories of justice, if the employee feels their status in the organization is accounted for and recognized during procedures, this facilitates perceived fairness. Second, consistent with Thibaut and Walker's concept of process control, perceived fairness is enhanced when the employee perceives a sense of control in the procedures. Youngblood et al., (1992) have described the relationship between the employee and employer as a psychological contract in which the employee feels if he or she brings certain standards of work, loyalty and tenure, then the employer owes them fair and dignifying procedures when dealing with difficult issues. These procedures should include neutrality and lack of bias, employee input ("voice"), consistency of procedures across employees, accurate information and an appeal process (Vidmar, 1992).

## INDIVIDUAL DIFFERENCES IN LITIGIOUSNESS AND PERCEIVED FAIRNESS

In our review of research dealing with individual factors that differentially facilitate the settlement of disputes and impact perceptions of fairness in litigation, we were hard-pressed to find any factors that strongly and consistently mediated these variables. Nevertheless, we felt some individual factors should be discussed as some interesting patterns emerge in the literature, especially in regards to personality differences. We now review a series of studies and commentaries concerning individual differences in litigiousness and perceptions of procedural fairness. This review covers gender differences, personality factors, and other litigant characteristics that predict perceived fairness and litigiousness in civil proceedings. As discussed in the preceding section, the likelihood of engaging in litigation is intertwined with perceptions of fairness in that litigation system. However, it is known that individuals' perceptions of fairness in the litigation system are not static, nor are individuals necessarily similar in perceived fairness.

## GENDER DIFFERENCES

### Sexual Harassment

Individual differences in litigiousness will be discussed first in the context of sexual harassment. This literature provides a fair amount of research considering gender differences in response to such problems in the workplace. We recognize that this area may not be representative of the majority of civil disputes. As discussed below, sexual harassment is experienced and perceived quite differently by men and women, and is therefore not ideal for reviewing individual differences in litigiousness. For example, the same power differences that exist in the workforce that allow for women to be sexually harassed by men (e.g., male-dominated management structure) may also hamper women's efforts to put a stop to the problem, and these power differences may not affect sexually harassed men in the same manner. Therefore, there may be gender-related issues that effect the outcome of sexual harassment complaints that are beyond the scope of the relational justice model of claiming. That said, this literature still provides a picture of gender differences in a particular legal context.

#### PREVALENCE AND REPORTING RATES OF SEXUAL HARASSMENT

Sexual harassment (SH) litigation tripled between 1989 and 1994 in the United States, due in part to the creation of civil protection, but also by the awareness raised by the Clarence Thomas confirmation hearings (Simon, 1996). According to the model presented by Samra and Koch (this book, chapter 9), the first step in the process leading to litigation occurs when an individual responds assertively to the harassment and/or reports the behavior. Responses to harassment divide the sexes in a number of ways. First of all, there are differences in the prevalence rates of SH. Fifteen-percent of men report exposure to SH on the job, whereas women in the workforce are three times more likely (42%) to be targets (Livingston, 1982; US Merit Systems Protection Board, 1988). Second, the perception of SH and subsequent responses vary between men and women (see Blumenthal, 1998). Blumenthal (1998) conducted a meta-analysis of this literature and concluded that there are stable but small differences in men's and women's perceptions of SH. For example, women react more negatively to sexual touches and are more likely than men to rate ambiguous behavior as sexual in nature (Douglas, Nicholls, & Koch, 1997). Women are thus more likely than men to report SH, whereas men are more likely to view similar behaviors as acceptable forms of interaction (Douglas, et al., 1997; Jones & Remland, 1992). These differences may be due to power differentials between men and women. A central concern with SH is the potential threat, perceived or otherwise, on an individual's position within that organization. Accordingly, women may be more likely than men to view SH as personally threatening, or as a threat to their status in the organization. To support this, women report they do not file complaints about perceived SH because they fear retaliation, humiliation and career setbacks (Fitzgerald, Swan & Fischer, 1995). In their study comparing reporters versus non-reporters of SH, Rudman, Borgida and Robertson (1995) cite a perceived lack of procedural justice as the primary reason victims do not report episodes of harassment.

Whether due to fear of reprisals or lack of procedural justice, only a minority of cases of SH are dealt with assertively, e.g., confronting the perpetrator or filing a complaint (Douglas et al., 1997). Rather, 60–73% of female victims resort to internal coping methods to deal with the problem, such as ignoring the event or avoiding the perpetrator (Gutek & Koss, 1993; Fitzgerald et al., 1995). Those cases that are reported may be dealt with informally within an organization, thus avoiding civil redress. Therefore, despite the fact women are more likely to recommend reporting these incidents, only 1–7% of women who claim they have been sexually harassed file a complaint or lawsuit against the perpetrator or the organization in which the harassment occurred (Burnstein, 1986; Simon, 1996). This, in itself, is an important finding indicating that the majority of incidents perceived as harassment do not result in formal complaints.

In summary, since men and women perceive and experience SH in different ways, we cannot label differences across the sexes as gender differences per se. Differences in men's and women's responses to SH are probably an artifact of their different experiences and subsequent perceptions. Nonetheless, these divisions illustrate how gender plays a role in participation in workplace complaint procedures and involvement in litigation.

## Intra-Organizational Complaint Procedures

There is a paucity of data regarding employers' remedies complaints, effectiveness of those remedies, and possible gender differences in satisfaction with such remedies. There is evidence suggesting that internal complaint procedures are primarily intended to avoid litigation, at the cost of individual rights (Edelman, Erlanger, & Lande, 1993). Therefore, not only do few women act assertively to stop harassment, but those who do complain may have their complaints unjustly terminated. This is problematic if one assumes management structures that condone atmospheres of harassment may remain unchallenged because of the structure of their internal dispute procedures.

Grant and Wager (1992) examined gender differences in willingness to litigate wrongful dismissal. Their results showed that more women have their grievance and dismissal cases sustained. This is apparently not because of systematic bias against men; rather it is due to differences in how men and women rate their chances of success in litigation. Women tend to limit their grievances unless they have a very strong case, thus resulting in greater success in the courtroom.

Do men and women differ in preference for dispute resolution? Overall, gender differences in procedural preferences have not been well supported (e.g., Lee & Farh, 1999; Lind, Huo, & Tyler, 1994), nor has gender strongly divided perceptions of fairness (Lind et al., 1990). It has been hypothesized that DJ perceptions may be more important in predicting satisfaction with organizational outcomes for men; in contrast, women may demonstrate a stronger relationship between procedural justice (PJ) factors and satisfaction, given that process elements (e.g., participation in decisions) appear to be more important for women (see Sweeney & McFarlin, 1997). Sweeney and McFarlin tested this hypothesis and found that indeed there were gender differences in weightings of PJ versus DJ. Overall, women demonstrated a stronger relationship between PJ factors and a variety of organizational outcome variables (such as intent to stay with organization) than men; in contrast, men demonstrated a stronger relationship between DJ factors and outcome variables.

In conclusion, while research in procedural preferences and justice ratings do not show consistent gender effects, there are notable differences between men and women in how they perceive and manage serious relational problems in the workplace. Since the studies we reviewed did not examine possible gender differences in procedural preferences where sexual harassment was the issue, it is possible that the types of procedures presented do not capture the unique aspects (e.g., gender politics) of organizational responses to sexual harassment complaints. This provides an interesting avenue for future research.

## PERSONALITY CHARACTERISTICS

Beyond gender, are there other individual differences in litigiousness? Personality variables may affect an individual's predisposition to sue. Some research suggests the complaint base-rate (the injuries or problems the subject links to the trauma) among personal injury litigants is very high in comparison to non-litigating controls (Lees-Haley & Brown, 1993; Weissman, 1990). For example, litigants with no neuropsychological injury report symptoms associated with such impairment, such as anxiety, sleeping problems, depression and headaches (Lees-Haley & Brown, 1993). These symptoms were reported at a significantly higher rate than non-litigating controls. These writers have suggested two separate explanations for this phenomenon, which will be addressed in this section.

First, it has been suggested that the over-complaining behavior of litigating individuals is a pre-litigation personality attribute. One might consider this particular use of the construct of personality as being very broad, including not only traditional dimensions of personality (e.g., neuroticism, hostility proneness, locus of control), but also factors such as cultural identity, political affiliation, socioeconomic status, and attitudes toward corporations.

Second, it may be that involvement in litigation leads to subsequent altered self-perceptions and motivations as well as additional psychosocial stressors (c.f., Koch, et al., 1999; Weismann, 1990). This latter hypothesis is rather complex. Some authors (e.g., Weissman, 1990) suggest that personal injury litigants change their appraisal of their injury (e.g., seriousness, disabling nature) during protracted litigation. In fact, there is some research suggesting that individuals alter the pre-event (e.g., tortious injury) post-event differences in their functioning by (unconsciously) altering their retrospective estimation of their pre-event functioning (see e.g., Conway & Ross, 1984). Other authors (e.g., Koch, et al., 1999) suggest that litigation and the resulting search for evidence of harm in bodily personal injury claims produces a degree of intrusion into the lives of litigants, thus resulting in an iatrogenic effect on psychological distress and resultant physical and emotional complaints in less resilient litigants. Still other researchers provide data that suggest that implicitly held models of the cause of their physical or emotional complaints controls their retrospective recall of symptoms (e.g., McFarland, et al., 1989; Stunkard, et al., 1984).

Whether the complaint base-rate for litigants is exacerbated by the litigation process itself is an empirical question, which would require a sophisticated longitudinal design to capture potential changes in the complaint base-rate, as discussed above.

Although the impact of litigation on complaint base-rates remains unknown at the present time, there is some support that higher complaint base-rates may be the result of personality variables that lead some people to experience greater stress, more accidents, and make more frequent complaints. For example, the time urgency and aggression associated

with Type A personalities makes these individuals more prone to accidents in work places that deal with heavy machinery, such as off shore oil
rigs (Sutherland & Cooper, 1991). Type A personality is more predictive of
accident involvement and repeated accident involvement, than is Type B
personality (Magnavita et al., 1997; Sutherland & Cooper, 1991). Also,
individuals who scored high on neuroticism reported more driving accidents and traffic violations than those who scored low on these attributes
(Sutherland & Cooper, 1991). Thus, personality type can put some people
at risk for greater accident involvement. Any individual differences which
predict more frequent injuries or losses will predict greater litigation.

Once an accident has occurred, each step in the process of seeking set
tlement (initial response, complaint or claim, and litigation) may provide
unique contributions to the probability of formal litigation. Initial level of
stress from an accident has shown to vary significantly by how people
attribute responsibility for their accidents. Generally, those who believe
others are to blame for their accident were likely to be more distressed,
showed increases risk for developing Post Traumatic Stress Disorder, used
avoidance coping techniques and continued showing greater distress after
6 month follow-up (Delahanty, Herberman, Craig, Hayward, Fullerton,
Ursano, & Baum, 1997; Hickling, Blanchard, Buckley, & Taylor, 1999).
Locus of control is another personality variable that may vary an individual's post-accident coping and recovery. Those with external locus of control tend to cope less effectively with accident trauma (MacCleod &
MacCleod, 1998), and internal locus of control is related to better long-
term outcome for those with traumatic brain injury (Moore, Stambrook, &
Wilson, 1991). Most relevant to our current discussion is whether differences in locus of control varies a person's likelihood to litigate. To our
knowledge, only one study has examined this possibility. Beck (1989) surveyed injured workers who remained unemployed three years post-
injury. It appears that those with internal locus of control beliefs were
more likely to litigate than those with external beliefs. This is a rather surprising finding, considering that those with an internal locus of control
are more independent and cooperative in dealing with others (Phares,
1978). Obviously, Beck's result needs to be replicated before any conclusions can be drawn.

The initial response to an accident may also be effected by pre-
existing clinical problems such as somatoform or paranoid disorder,
whose sufferers may report more severe personal injuries than those
without such problems (Weissman, 1990, 1991). Once in the courts system,
the re-telling of the accident and the focus on defending injuries
may make individuals with hypochondriasis report their injuries with
increasing exaggeration and distortion over time (Haenen, Schmidt,

Kroeze & van den Hout, 1996; Weissman, 1991; see Samra & Koch, this book, chapter 9). There is some support that once a case makes it to formal litigation, more severely injured persons who garner more sympathy from the jury are more likely to have the defendant in their case found liable (Bornstein, 1998).

Of course, it is also plausible that specific individual differences also explain litigiousness, per se. For example, the hostility facet of Type A personality may interfere with informal dispute settlement, while neuroticism may exacerbate the functional and economic consequences of injuries, thus increasing the value of claims. Regrettably, few empirical studies track the effects of personality on response to accidents, dismissal, harassment or injury, and how these effect the likelihood of litigation. Each stage, from accident prone to accident reaction to litigiousness, may uniquely and collectively contribute to the chances of litigation. Most important in the context of the relational justice model, no research has been conducted on these personality variables in the context of a person's relationship with his or her organization. We need to understand how that relationship may exacerbate or ease problems arising from the workplace and how relationship variables interact with personality variables to vary likelihood of litigation.

## CULTURAL DIFFERENCES

To the extent that preferred methods of dispute resolution within different cultural societies reflect that society's cultural values, differences in procedural preferences across cultures may be expected (see Lind, Huo, & Tyler, 1994). Early research by Thibault and Walker indicated minimal differences across cultures (U.S. versus Western European nations) in terms of procedural preferences, leading these researchers to conclude that procedural justice was the primary predictor of procedural preferences, even across cultures (see Lind et al., 1994). Subsequent research examining the procedural preferences of Chinese students (from a "collectivist" society) versus those of American students (who are from a more "individualistic" society) found that the former groups preferred non-adversarial, conciliatory procedures (e.g., bargaining; mediation) more so than American students (Leung, 1987; Leung & Lind, 1986). However, re-analysis of this data (Lind, 1992, as cited in Lind, Huo, & Tyler, 1994) revealed that procedural fairness was the strongest predictor of procedural preferences across cultural groups. Lind et al. (1994) examined gender and ethnic (African-, Hispanic-, Asian-, and European-American groups) differences, and concluded that their data supported a universalistic theory of procedural preferences more than a cultural difference theory. Differences in conceptions of procedural fairness appeared to be more important than different values across cultures in the importance of fairness per se.

# DECISIONMAKING IN CIVIL LAW

Decisionmaking in the civil courts has been a controversial issue for a number of reasons. Primarily, legal decision-makers have come under attack due to a suspicion that civil cases are often too complex for jurors to decide, and extra-legal factors such as plaintiff sympathy guide decisions. These suspicions follow the perception that findings of liability are capricious across similar-fact cases, and that damage awards are excessive. This lack of faith in the abilities of jurors and other decision-makers has led to politically inspired reforms that target these perceived inadequacies of the civil system. For example, caps on damages aim to prevent excessive damage awards. We therefore devote the next section to examining these criticisms in light of relevant empirical research. We begin with a review of decisionmaking in complex litigation, continue with a discussion of how jurors find liability and decide damage awards, and end with a discussion on whether attitudes about the civil system influence decisionmaking.

## COMPLEX LITIGATION

One of the central concerns of the civil litigation system is the ability of courts and decision-makers to manage information in complex litigation. Decision-makers face difficult information processing challenges to the extent that they must make sense of technical information, integrate specialized, often conflicting, expert testimony, distinguish among multiple plaintiffs or defendants, and decide numerous claims or issues. Accordingly, a number of studies have addressed questions of juror decision making in complex cases (see reviews in Cecil, Hans, & Wiggins, 1991; Lempert, 1993). Researchers have examined the effects of the quantity (Heuer & Penrod, 1994; Horowitz, ForsterLee, & Brolly, 1996) and the complexity (Heuer & Penrod, 1994; ForsterLee, Horowitz, & Bourgeois, 1993; Horowitz, ForsterLee, & Brolly, 1996) of the evidence presented on juror performance. Similarly, the ability of decision-makers to disregard inadmissible evidence in civil cases has been considered (Landsman & Rakos, 1994; Cox & Tanford, 1989). The benefits and limitations of consolidation of cases in mass tort trials have also been examined (Bordens & Horowitz, 1998; Saks & Blanck, 1992). For example, Horowitz and Bordens (1988) have considered the effect of the inclusion of an outlier plaintiff (one whose injury is more severe than other plaintiffs' injuries) and of the size of the distal population on decision making.

Johnson and Wiggins (1994) compared the composition of, resources available to, and procedures required of a variety of possible alternative decision-makers for complex civil cases (e.g., judges, expert arbitrators, special juries, and panels of experts) and concluded that resources and procedures could be used to enhance the capabilities of juries in complex cases. Indeed, a number of procedures designed to facilitate decision making in complex cases have now been studied in the field and in the laboratory. For example, alternative methods of instructing jurors have been tested including pre-instruction and providing written instructions (ForsterLee, Horowitz, & Bourgeois, 1993; Heuer & Penrod, 1988; Heuer & Penrod, 1989). The effects of allowing jurors to ask questions (Heuer & Penrod), take notes (Heuer & Penrod; Rosenhan, Eisner, & Robinson, 1994), review verbatim trial transcripts (Bourgeois, Horowitz, & ForsterLee, 1993), and receive written summaries of expert testimony (ForsterLee, Horowitz, Athaide-Victor, & Brown, 2000) have all been considered. In addition, researchers have started to empirically explore the effects of structuring the jury's decision making with special verdict forms that break down the steps in the decision making task and require jurors to answer a series of questions rather than merely providing a verdict (Heuer & Penrod, 1994a; Wiggins & Breckler, 1990). While the evidence about the effects of some of these types of measures is mixed, many of these procedural reforms may enhance the jury's ability to effectively grapple with complex civil cases.

## LIABILITY JUDGMENTS

One area of tort law that has received a great deal of attention from psycholegal scholars is the determination of responsibility for injurious conduct. Numerous theories in social and cognitive psychology, such as attribution theory, event or script theories, hindsight bias, and counterfactual thinking have been applied to illuminate the ways in which individuals, including jurors, allocate responsibility for an injury (see review in Wiener, 1993).

Negligence law requires that one exercise care to avoid unreasonable risk. The required care is defined as that level of care exercised by a "reasonable person" under the circumstances. Under the reasonable person standard, the conduct of the defendant ought to influence judgments of responsibility for an injury. Several studies have demonstrated that, indeed, the carelessness of the defendant (Greene, Johns, & Bowman, 1999) and the likelihood and severity of the harm risked by the defendant (Karlovac & Darley, 1988) affect attributions of responsibility in negligence cases. In addition, experimental studies have found that increased responsibility is attributed to a party when his or her injurious act was closer in time to its outcome (Johnson & Drobny, 1985), when there were fewer intervening events between the act and its outcome (Johnson & Drobny, 1985), when the act was a prior cause of the outcome (Johnson, Ogawa, Delforge, & Early, 1989), and when the relationship between the act and the outcome is consistent with intuitive expectations about causality (Bornstein & Rajki, 1994). Relatively small effects of the severity of the actual injury on liability judgments have been found as well. Legally, while the degree of harm risked is relevant to a determination of liability, the degree of the resulting injury is not relevant to liability judgments and should only influence damage awards (Greene, Johns, & Bowman, 1999; see review in Robbennolt, in press).

The hindsight bias, exaggerating the predictability or foreseeability of past events (Fischhoff, 1975), is clearly relevant to a system in which responsibility for wrongs is evaluated in the wake of an injury. Findings of hindsight bias are robust in both legal and non-legal contexts and have been demonstrated in civil contexts as well. Kamin and Rachlinski (1995) found that many fewer participants determined that a precaution was warranted in foresight than found the failure to take a precaution negligent in hindsight. Thus, a defendant may be more likely to be held liable in a negligence action even though a reasonable person would have acted similarly in foresight. Similarly, LaBine and LaBine (1996) found that participants who were told that a psychiatric patient had committed a violent act were more likely to find that the violence had been foreseeable and that the precautions taken by the therapist had been less reasonable than were participants who were told that the patient had not become violent or who were not told the outcome. Such determinations have clear implications for the civil liability of therapists for failing to act reasonably to warn third-parties of danger (e.g., *Tarasoff v. Regents of University of California*, 1976). Rachlinski (1998) detailed these consequences of the hindsight bias for the law and concluded that courts have been quite responsive to the problems raised in specific instances (e.g., evidence rules regarding custom and subsequent remedial measures, business judgment rule). (See also Hastie, Schkade, & Payne, 1999b regarding liability for punitive damages).

Finally, researchers have begun to investigate the effects of some specific legal rules related to determinations of civil liability. For example, under the rules of comparative negligence, jurors must allocate responsibility for an incident between the defendant and the plaintiff. The court then will reduce the amount of damages awarded to the plaintiff in proportion to the plaintiff's responsibility. For example, if the plaintiff is found to be 20% at fault, the plaintiff's recovery will be reduced 20% by the judge. Thomas and Parpal (1987) found that participants' attributions of both plaintiff and defendant responsibility were influenced by those parties' evident responsibility. However, they found only low to moderate negative correlations between ratings of plaintiff and defendant responsibility, suggesting that participants were not allocating a fixed quantity of responsibility between the two parties. Psycholegal researchers have also demonstrated a "double discounting" phenomenon such that the damages assessed by mock-jurors are already lower when the plaintiff bears some responsibility for the incident and then are discounted further by the court in relation to the plaintiff's fault as required by the comparative negligence rules (Feigenson, Park, & Salovey, 1997; Zickafoose & Bornstein, 1999). Other research has examined the liability rules surrounding the negligent infliction of emotional distress on a bystander to a traumatic event (Bowen & Nordby, 1993).

## DAMAGE AWARDS

Another related concern about the functioning of tort law is how legal decision-makers determine damage awards. A number of studies have examined the process by which decision makers award damages in civil cases (see generally, Greene, 1989). Goodman, Greene, and Loftus (1989) found that many of their jury eligible participants reported arriving at their damage award by deciding upon an amount for each component of damages and then summing to get a total award amount. Others reported "picking a fair number" in order to determine an appropriate award. Zickafoose and Bornstein (1999) found no differences in award amounts between jurors who determined a total award first and those who were asked to determine each component individually and then sum to get a total award. Similarly, Wiggins and Breckler (1990) found that the damages awarded by participants who used special verdict forms did not differ in size from those made by other participants; however, those using special verdict forms allocated a greater proportion of the award to compensatory damages.

A relatively simple mechanism by which decision-makers might determine an appropriate award amount is to anchor on a number that has been provided and then adjust from that number. A number of studies have explored the effect of possible anchors on damage awards. These studies have found that the plaintiff's request for damages (Chapman & Bornstein, 1996; Hastie, Schkade, & Payne, 1999a; Hinsz & Indahl, 1995; Malouff & Schutte, 1989), testimony provided by an expert (Raitz, Greene, Goodman, & Loftus, 1990, and caps on the amount of damages allowed

(Robbennolt & Studebaker, 1999; Saks, Hollinger, Wissler, Evans, & Hart, 1997) serve as values which anchor judgments about damages.

Other factors that have been studied related to the incidence and size of damage awards include the attributes and severity of the injury to the plaintiff (Cather, Greene, & Durham, 1996; Kahneman, Schkade, & Sunstein, 1998; Wissler, Hart, & Saks, 1999; see review in Robbennolt, in press), the defendant's conduct (Cather, Greene, & Durham, 1996; Greene, Woody, & Winter, 2000; Horowitz & Bordens, 1990), the size or wealth of the defendant (Greene, Woody, & Winter, 2000; Kahneman, Sunstein, & Schkade, 1998; Vidmar, 1993); whether the defendant is a corporation or an individual (Hans & Ermann, 1989; MacCoun, 1996); the geographical locations of the plaintiff and defendant (Hastie, Schkade, & Payne, 1999a); and the injury schemas held by decision-makers (Hart, Evans, Wissler, Feehan, & Saks, 1997).

Punitive damages are a category of damages that are intended to punish a defendant for reprehensible conduct and to deter the defendant and others from engaging in similar conduct in the future. Kahneman, Sunstein, and Schkade (1998) have proposed a general model of the processes by which jurors determine punitive damage awards in particular. The model postulates that the defendant's recklessness causes jurors to experience outrage, which jurors then translate into a punitive intention, which is further translated into a punitive damage award by mapping it on to a dollar scale. The experimental research conducted by Kahneman and colleagues demonstrated a high degree of consensus among jurors about the degree of outrage felt and the appropriate severity of the penalty required. However, this consensus was not carried through into the punitive damage awards made by the jurors. Kahneman and colleagues suggested that jurors have difficulty with this mapping process because they lack experience in translating their punitive intent into dollar values and they have no modulus, or standard, to guide them.

Criticisms about the manner in which juries award damages have stimulated calls to reform the ways in which damages are determined. Psychological research has suggested that a number of these reforms may have unexpected effects (see e.g., Landsman, Diamond, Dimitropoulos, & Saks, 1998). Empirical research has shed light on the effects of many reform efforts including abolishing punitive damages (Anderson & MacCoun, 1999), placing caps on damage amounts (Robbennolt & Studebaker, 1999 (punitive damages); Saks, Hollinger, Wissler, Evans, & Hart, 1997 (compensatory damages)), bifurcating trials (Greene, Woody, & Winter, 2000; Horowitz & Bordens, 1990; Landsman, Diamond, Dimitropoulos, & Saks, 1998; Robbennolt & Studebaker, 1999); allocating a portion of any punitive damage award to the state (Anderson & MacCoun, 1999); allowing judges to determine damage award amounts (Robbennolt, in press; Vidmar & Rice, 1993; Wissler, Hart, & Saks, 1999), and scaling or scheduling damages (Saks, Hollinger, Wissler, Evans, & Hart, 1997).

While most empirical research examining how damages are awarded focuses on the damage awards of individual jurors, a few studies have examined the effects of group deliberation on damage awards. Diamond and Casper (1992) found that the median of the jury members' pre-deliberation awards was the best predictor of jury awards (see also Davis, Au, Hulbert, Chen, & Zarnoth, 1997). However, they also found that group deliberations inflated the awards (see also Landsman, Diamond, Dimitropoulos, & Saks, 1998). Diamond, Saks, and Landsman (1998) found that the damage awards of juries were higher but less variable as a percentage of the mean award than the awards of individual jurors for both economic damages and damages for pain and suffering. Schkade, Sunstein, and Kahneman (2000) found that under a rule of unanimity the punitive damage awards of juries were larger and less predictable than the awards of individual jurors. Kaplan and Miller (1987) found that the mean amounts of compensatory damages awarded by individual jurors and juries did not differ; nor did the amounts of punitive damages awarded by jurors and juries under a majority decision rule. However, they found that under a rule of unanimity, the punitive damages awarded by juries were greater than those awarded by jurors.

## ATTITUDES AND PERCEPTIONS ABOUT CIVIL LITIGATION

Appraisals of the civil litigation system provide an important input into a number of legally relevant decisions. These include the decisions of legislators considering reform of the system, the decisions of businesspeople attempting to avoid litigation, and the decisions of jurors evaluating civil cases. As such, attitudes toward and perceptions of the civil litigation system have also received attention from psycholegal researchers (see review in Hans, 1993; for a comment on the value of public opinion about the civil jury see Saks, 1998).

Perceptions of the civil litigation system may come into play when members of the public or legislators make decisions regarding the need for "tort reform," (see Songer, 1988). Appraisals of the civil litigation system may be influenced by the media, personal anecdotes, and political hype in addition to empirical research. The media, policymakers, politicians, and professionals such as lawyers and managers speculate about civil litigation run amok, and their perceptions are interpreted as empirically-based conclusions by the public (Edelman et al., 1992). Daniels and Martin (1997) suggest that those in government hungry for a political platform create a causal link between social problems and the behavior of the civil system. These politicians then provide "solutions" to a perceived or manufactured "problem", and push for tort reforms (i.e., caps for damage awards). Saks (1992) argues that we lack proper base-rates to make any claims about the functioning of most areas of the civil system. Saks argues that this lack of information (or mis-information) leads to ineffective reforms and policies that fail to achieve their aim. Further, because we lack proper base-rates, we have little empirical basis on which to evaluate the effects of tort reform or changes in organizational policy, such as those dealing with wrongful dismissal or sexual harassment complaints.

The public perception of a litigation crisis may affect expensive policy development within large organizations as well as expensive legislation. For example, subjective appraisals of the civil litigation system may influence risk management decisions of corporate officers (see Bailis & MacCoun, 1996). The fear of claims for wrongful dismissal, accident liability or harassment in organizations has sparked policy makers to investigate what aspects of an organization may exacerbate or ease the likelihood of such action by employees. Organizations, and those who manage them, learn about the law through lawyers, academics, and management and personnel managers (Edelman et al., 1992). The law is interpreted and filtered through these professionals, and organizations are faced with making decisions for their organization based on avoiding lawsuits, rather than the best interests of the business (Bies & Tripp, 1993; Saks, 1992). Edelman et al. (1992) calls this interpretation and filtration of the law by lawyers, academics and managers the "construction of the law," wherein the threat of lawsuits is often overestimated. Organizations may feel forced to budget for potential lawsuits, and take extraordinary steps to avoid litigation. Fear of defamation lawsuits has sparked protective behavior that may include a "no comment" policy on references or policies against providing reasons for dismissal (Bies & Tripp, 1993). These preventative steps are often taken without understanding the true threat of litigation by employees (Saks, 1992). Most important to the current discussion, these procedures may not actually reduce litigation because such changes may not improve the relationship between the employee and employer, or the employees' perceptions of organizational fairness in decisionmaking, two factors that appear to be important influences on employees' tendencies to litigate (see discussion above).

The public's evaluation of the civil litigation system can also affect their decisions as jurors or as voters. Hans and Lofquist (1992) found that jurors were quite suspicious of the claims and motives of plaintiffs, were troubled by what they perceived to be the potential costs of large damage awards, and had mixed view of corporations, holding generally positive views toward corporations, while harboring concerns about power and ethics abuses and holding elevated expectations for their conduct. A recent survey of potential jurors found that a majority of respondents agreed that corporate executives engaged in covering up harm, believed that lawsuits have made products both safer and more expensive, and thought that injured persons often try to blame others for their own carelessness (van Voris, 1998). Jurors who hold the view that there is a "crisis" in civil litigation are more likely to find for the defendant and to award little in damages (Greene, Goodman, & Loftus, 1991; Hans & Lofquist, 1992). Paradoxically, anecdotal information about large damage awards can also have the reverse effect and can serve to increase damage awards. Jurors who believe that large damage awards are more prevalent are more likely to award large amounts of damages themselves (Greene, Goodman, & Loftus, 1991; Robbennolt, in press).

These attitudes may not be surprising given the portrayal of civil litigation in the media. Content analyses of national magazine coverage of tort litigation (Bailis & MacCoun, 1996) and newspaper coverage of product liability cases against automobile manufacturers (Garber, 1998; see also Garber & Bower, 1999) find that there is disproportionate coverage of certain types of cases. Such cases are those involving product liability and medical malpractice, cases resulting in trials, cases culminating in plaintiff victories, cases in which the damages were relatively high, and cases in which the damage award included a punitive component. Garber (1998) also found that initial awards received more news coverage than did any subsequent reduction in the amount of the award. To the extent that individuals rely on an availability heuristic (Tversky & Kahneman, 1974), or the ease of recall, these media reports are likely to play a role in individuals' evaluation of the tort system.

In summary, decisionmaking within the civil litigation system, including legal decision-makers' abilities to decide complex cases, to make liability judgments, and to award damages, has provided a research focus for psycholegal scholars. While some research appears to provide some argument for tort reform specific to juror functioning (e.g., procedures that help jurors efficaciously handle complex cases), other reform movements (e.g., caps for damages) appear to be specious solutions to perceived problems, based on incorrect appraisals of the tort system and politically-motivated platforms. Saks (1992) persuasively argues that few conclusions can be properly drawn about the behavior of the civil justice system, because we lack proper base-rates from which to compare the effects of reforms. It appears the most important focus for future research is to compile proper base-rates of litigation and conduct prospective research on the effects of tort reforms.

## CONTRACTS AND PROPERTY LAW

Much of the research at the intersection of psychology and the civil justice system has focused quite heavily on tort law. Until recently, there had been little psycholegal scholarship in the areas of contract and property law. This new area of research is important because issues in contract and property are integral parts of public and private life, and impact most people at some point in their lives. Therefore, discerning how individuals understand contracts deserves psycholegal interest because, as we will see, these conceptions can impact fairness perceptions, and acceptance and enforcement of obligations under contract. Further, conception of property rights shows a developmental course, and those conceptions may be affected by different rights protections available. While this next section is brief, we hope it will highlight some important studies and serve to stimulate interest in the areas.

### CONTRACT LAW

Despite the pervasiveness of contractual dealings in everyday life, until quite recently, there had been little psycholegal scholarship in the area of contract law. Now there is an emerging literature focusing primarily on how individuals conceptualize legal contracts and how these contract schemas influence contract bargaining and enforcement.

Hans and Mott (2000) interviewed jurors who served in contract cases. They found that jurors utilized contract schemas in making sense out of the cases. Important components of lay contract schemas included power disparities between the parties, notions of fairness and good faith, and the notion that written documents are valid contracts. Hans and Mott also found that the jurors had trouble understanding the legal language that was used in discussing contracts.

Several other bodies of research have also examined how individuals conceptualize contractual obligations. Rousseau (Rousseau & Aquino, 1993; Rousseau & Anton, 1988, 1991; see also Rousseau & Tijoriwala, 1998; Rousseau, 1998) has conducted a program of research examining "psychological contracts" in employment settings. She has examined perceptions of employment-contract obligations and whether employment terminations are judged to be fair. In particular, she found that factors such as high seniority and formal commitments to long-term employment are most likely to give rise to a feeling that an employee should be retained. Fairness judgments were highly influenced by factors such as the offer of a severance package and appropriate notice of termination. In further support of this, Youngblood et al. (1992) noted that fairness perceptions were guided by a reciprocal psychological contract between employer and employee. These authors found employees had a sense of injustice if values such as loyalty, tenure, and hard work were not recognized in dismissal procedures.

Similarly, Schmedemann and Parks (1994) have compared how courts, employees, and expert third-party observers read employee handbooks. Specifically, they examined interpretations of the provisions for procedural protections in the case of employment termination. They found that various aspects of the language and structure of the document influence individuals' perceptions of whether contractual obligations to provide a fair process are created. The strength of the verb creating the promise and of a disclaimer of legal obligation influenced individuals' perceptions of whether a legal obligation existed. The inclusion of specific language, jargon, and a signature block also led to judgments that a legal contract had been breached (see Masson & Waldron, 1994 and Stolle, 1998 for examinations of plain language and contract comprehension). Schmedemann and Parks suggest that their participants saw a legal obligation as a subset of moral obligation, believing that procedural protections should be provided even where no legal obligation to provide such protection was created by the documents.

Kim (1997, 1999) has also studied perceptions of employment contracts by surveying individuals in a number of states about their legal rights to employment. She found that, despite variations in the applicable state laws and in individual experience, people consistently overestimated their rights, misunderstanding the default rule of employment at will and believing in a right not to be terminated without cause. She suggests that employer practices may give rise to a social norm that leads to the expectation that employees will not be terminated without cause. If employees are not sensitive to the difference between these informal social norms and their more circumscribed legal rights to employment, they are not likely to make any attempt to contract around the default rule.

The failure to contract around default contract terms has been studied more broadly by Korobkin (1998a, 1998b). Korobkin draws on several theories in social cognition to demonstrate that a bias for the status quo and a preference for inaction over action will lead contracting parties to favor default contract terms, terms in standard form contracts, and terms in negotiating drafts offered by one party. Rather than act to negotiate a change to an existing contract term, contracting parties are more likely to accept a provision when it is the default. Korobkin suggests a motivational explanation for these results, such that the parties behave so as to minimize the possible future regret that might result if action had been taken to change the default terms. Because these biases can result in agreements more often including the default term, the content of default terms becomes an important policy and fairness issue.

Stolle and Slain (1997) examined the effects of exculpatory clauses in standard form contracts. Exculpatory clauses purport to relieve one party of liability for his or her own negligence. While these clauses are often held to be unenforceable, they are still often included in contract "boiler-plate." Stolle and Slain found that, despite the fact such clauses are not enforceable, individuals are less likely to seek compensation for harm caused when such a clause is part of the contract governing the relation-ship (see also Mueller, 1970, who found that participants believed in the enforceability of exculpatory clauses). Stolle and Slain suggest that the contract schema held by laypersons includes the belief that the written terms of a contract will be enforced.

## PROPERTY LAW

Psycholegal research has also only begun to examine property law concepts. Hook (1993) examined the development of conceptions of prop-erty and found that young children have different property beliefs than do adults. While, overall, participants judged the loss or destruction of another's property to be worse than the loss or destruction of one's own property, young children did not make this distinction. Similarly, while, overall, participants judged the destruction of property to be worse than the loss of property, young children made this distinction only for one's own property. While adults categorized the manner in which the posses-sor acquired property into several levels such that acquisition by theft, by borrowing or finding, and by receipt as a gift were judged to entail increasing rights, young children did not make these distinctions. Finally, participants distinguished ownership rights from the entitlement to value created by labor. To the extent that norms and beliefs about property can and should influence legal rights involving property, an understanding of how human conceptions of property develop can provide important insight into the civil law of property.

Rachlinski and Jourden (1998) examined conceptions of property rights in the context of the remedies available to protect those rights. They posited that an important psychological aspect of ownership is the authority to sell or refuse to sell a right. Thus, they suggest that "people do not regard rights protected by damages remedies as being owned in the same way as rights protected by injunctive relief" (p. 1542) because damages do not entail the right not to sell. They found that the endow-ment effect, that people will value an item more highly when they own it than when they do not, operated when the property right was protected by an injunctive remedy but was not observed when the right was protected by a damages remedy.

The ownership of property entails the right to ultimately dispose of it. Fellows, Johnson, Chiericozzi, Hale, Lee, Preble, and Voran (1998) noted that intestacy statutes (statutes that govern the distribution of property for those who die without wills) reflect concern for donative freedom, fairness in property distribution, and support for families. With these goals as a benchmark, they examined the property distribution preferences of persons in nonmarital committed relationships and suggested statutory reforms that would reflect these preferences. Robbennolt and Johnson (1999) also examined the legal treatment of unmarried committed partners in the context of property rights. They described the long-term property and health care planning practices of persons in nonmarital committed relationships and suggested that legal practitioners should actively help these clients employ the law to achieve a distribution of their property that they deem just.


# FUTURE RESEARCH

## PERCEPTIONS OF JUSTICE

The research on economic versus irrational approaches to conflict resolution has been conducted largely in laboratory settings, using fictitious cases among undergraduate populations rather than in the context of actual legal disputes. While it is reasonable to expect such findings to generalize across a variety of settings and populations, field research could play an important role in establishing the magnitude of effects. So, for example, what is the role of legal professionals on the deviations from rationality among laypersons involved in litigation? In addition, research in-situ would invite tests of interactions among the central theoretical variables discussed above (e.g., framing differences between plaintiffs and defendants) and situational variables that have received little attention thus far (e.g., the effect of legal representation, prior experience with the legal system, criminal versus civil litigation). Such questions about generalizability, effect sizes, and interactions are likely to be particularly important when this research begins to take on a role for policy initiatives in addition to theory development.

There are critical gaps in research exploring specific elements of the relational justice model of claiming. The most important variable that is absent from the majority of the research presented in the justice section involves the individual-organization relationship. This relationship may be expressed in various ways; (a) the individual's perception of fair treatment by the organization, (b) measures of employee loyalty, (c) specific organizational behaviors or policies, or (d) interpersonal relationships within the organization (e.g., supervisor-supervisee). It may be that personality differences interact with the individual-organization relationship to influence settlement satisfaction and the probability of litigation. These variables provide numerous avenues for future studies.

More research is needed to understand the *process* of how individuals react to problems in organizations; including their identification of a problem (whether between employees or between the employee and employer), their initial emotional response, the decision to complain about procedures, factors affecting their perception of fairness of organizational policy or response to the problem, and finally factors influencing their decisions to litigate. At each stage of this process, gender, personality or cultural variables may interact with the environment in unique ways. For example, the studies we reviewed did not examine individual differences in procedural preferences where sexual harassment was the issue, and it is possible that the types of procedures presented above do not capture the unique aspects (e.g., gender politics) of organizational responses to sexual harassment complaints. Future research could examine whether there are differences in procedural preferences if they incorporate gender politics into their responses (i.e., having an external review board rather than one within the organization to handle complaints).

## DECISIONMAKING

Much of the research into the civil justice system has been done in the context of jury decisionmaking in civil (primarily tort) cases. Research in this area should continue to identify factors that effect juror decisions and to ascertain how these factors operate under differing conditions. For example, research into the mechanisms and effects of media reporting about civil justice on juror decisions and into methods for addressing these effects can serve to inform courts and attorneys. In addition, basic information about the operation of the civil justice system is sorely needed (Galanter, Garth, Hensler, & Zemans, 1994; Saks, 1992). Future research should also broaden the focus of research in the civil justice system beyond the decisions of jurors to the decisions of other parties in the process such as judges, attorneys, parties (individuals and corporate entities), and insurance companies. In particular, the effects of different legal rules on the behavior and decisions of all of these parties should be examined. For example, there is a need for research addressing the effect of new legal rules on how parties and their attorneys behave during settlement negotiations and during the post-settlement period.

The effects of alternative systems on decisionmaking ought to be evaluated. As outlined in this chapter, research in alternative systems has focused on the procedural preferences and justice perceptions of the participants. A new direction would include looking at the impact of alternative dispute resolution mechanisms such as arbitration, mediation, summary jury trials, early neutral evaluation, and settlement conferences on decisionmaking. This new research track could also extend to psychological research into alternative compensation systems such as workers' compensation.

## CONTRACTS AND PROPERTY

Research focus should continue in less-studied areas of civil law such as contract and property and should broaden its scope. Initial research has been conducted into the nature of individuals' contract schemas. Future research should explore how juror contract schemas impact their decisionmaking in contract cases and what factors might mediate those effects. This research needs to go beyond the effects of contract schemas on jury decisionmaking and should also consider how contract schemas influence the behavior of the contracting parties, both at the time of contracting and at the time of contract breach and/or enforcement. Important considerations such as what contract terms are agreed to and whether or not legal remedies are pursued in the event of breach may be strongly influenced by contract schemas and other cognitive processes.

Similarly, property law offers interesting avenues for psycholegal study. Future research might address whether or not there is congruence between people's conceptions of property and various areas of the law such as the rules surrounding adverse possession, the rights of landlords and tenants, and the law of intestacy. For example, if the law of adverse possession, which may quiet title to property in a trespasser, is not consistent with property owner's notions about property rights, property owners might be less likely to take the necessary precautions to prevent the taking of their property. Emerging property issues related to areas such as intellectual property and e-commerce will also be informative avenues of study.

## COMMERCE AND BUSINESS

A number of other areas of civil law, not directly covered in this chapter, provide a rich source of research questions. For example, future research could explore the relationship between psychology and law in the areas of commerce and business. Hans (1990) identified a number of areas of corporate law that could profit from an application of psychological theory and research. Interesting questions surround, for example, how corporate boards make business decisions, how legal rules effect such decisionmaking, and how organizations make decisions about risk. Hans (1990) noted, in particular, that the social effects of corporate takeovers on corporate decisionmaking and corporate culture might be a fruitful area of study. Related areas of study might include the effects of corporate mergers and initial public offerings on corporate and individual decisionmaking, most recently raised in the context of Internet start-up companies. Recently, questions have been raised about how corporations and the public view cost-benefit analysis and the implications of those views for the law (MacCoun, 2000; Viscusi, 2000). Moreover, areas such as product advertising (see e.g., Diamond, 1989, Stolle, 1995) and product warnings (Zuckerman & Chaiken, 1998) are fertile ground for psycholegal research. Research into the effects of product advertising on attitudes and behavior (particularly on the behavior of children), the interpretations of advertisements by consumers, and the effects of the design and content of product warnings on behavior will have significant implications for the law.

## CONCLUSION

This chapter provides a brief overview of some pertinent areas of psycholegal research in civil law. The "litigation crisis" phenomenon and its impact on public policy suggests that civil psycholegal research needs more mainstream exposure in government and organizational policy and in tort reform considerations. Litigation base-rates on both the federal and state levels are sorely needed before we can provide any definitive suggestions for reform. At this stage, policy-makers need to be convinced of what we do not yet know regarding the civil litigation system, and advised to avoid action based on public perception and political persuasion.

As we have seen, individuals are very sensitive to the procedures they encounter in civil courts and organizational contexts, which impact their sense of justice in those proceedings. Efforts to make courts responsive to the needs of those who encounter them must bring social science research into the discussion. If not, reform runs the risk of adversely affecting both sets of consumers by neglecting the known effects of human perceptions and behavior on the functioning of courts. Also, organizational policy aimed at curbing workplace problems such as wrongful dismissal and avoiding litigation needs to go beyond simple perceptions of justice and take into account important relationship-based variables that impact those perceptions. As discussed above, relationship-based variables such as voice and neutrality are important in understanding perceptions of dispute-resolution procedures. Respectful and polite treatment, the role of apologies in disagreements, and gender politics, which may impact sexual harassment complaints, are all important considerations for policy.

Finally, civil law provides a rich resource for frontier research in psychology and law. The uncharted territory outlined in the future research section above merely scratches the surface of potential future directions for scholars. Psycholegal interest in civil law should continue its forward momentum in theory, research, and practice in an effort to advance the knowledge of the field.

## REFERENCES

Anderson, M. C., & MacCoun, R. J. (1999). Goal conflict in juror assessments of compensatory and punitive damages. *Law and Human Behavior, 23*, 313–330.

Bailis, D. S., & MacCoun, R. J. (1996). Estimating liability risks with the media as your guide: A content analysis of media coverage of tort litigation. *Law and Human Behavior, 20*, 419–429.

Bebchuk, L. A. (1996). A new theory concerning the credibility and success of threats to sue. *Journal of Legal Studies, 25*, 1–25.

Bebchuk, L. A. (1988). Suing solely to extract a settlement offer. *Journal of Legal Studies, 17*, 437–450.

Bies, R. J., & Moag, J. S. (1986). Interactional justice: Communication criteria of fairness. In R. J. Lewicki, B. H. Sheppard, & M. H. Bazerman (Eds.), *Research on negotiations in organizations* (pp. 43–55). Greenwich, CT: JAI Press.

Bies, R. J. & Tyler, T. R. (1993). The "litigation mentality" in organizations: A test of alternative psychological explanations. *Organizational Science, 4*, 352–366.

Bies, R. J., & Shapiro, D. L. (1987). Interactional fairness judgments: The influence of causal accounts. *Social Justice Research, 1*, 199–218.

Bies, R. J. & Tripp, T. M. (1993). Employee-initiated defamation lawsuits: Organizational responses and dilemmas. *Employee Responsibilities and Rights Journal, 6*, 313–324.

Blumenthal, J. A. (1998). The reasonable woman standard: A meta-analytic review of gender differences in perceptions of sexual harassment. *Law and Human Behavior, 22*, 33–57.

Bordens, K. S., & Horowitz, I. A. (1998). The limits of sampling and consolidation in mass tort trials: Justice improved or justice altered? *Law and Psychology Review, 22*, 43–66.

Bornstein, B. H. (1998). From compassion to compensation: The effect of injury severity on mock jurors' liability judgments. *Journal of Applied Social Psychology, 28*, 1477–1502.

Bornstein, B. H., & Rajki, M. (1994). Extra-legal factors and product liability: The influence of mock jurors' demographic characteristics and intuitions about the cause of an injury. *Behavioral Sciences and the Law, 12*, 127–147.

Bourgeois, M. J., Horowitz, I. A., & FosterLee, L. (1993). Effects of technicality and access to trial transcripts on verdicts and information processing in a civil trial. *Personality and Social Psychology Bulletin, 19,* 220–227.

Bowen, M., & Nordby, E. C. (1993). Perceptions of liability for the negligent infliction of emotional distress to a bystander. *Behavioral Sciences and the Law, 11,* 205–211.

Burnstein, B. (1986). Psychiatric injury in women's workplace. *The Bulletin of the American Academy of Psychiatry and Law, 14,* 245–251.

Casper, J. D., Tyler, T. R., & Fisher, B. (1988). Procedural justice in felony cases. *Law and Society Review, 22,* 483–508.

Cather, C., Greene, E., & Durham, R. (1996). Plaintiff injury and defendant reprehensibility: Implications for compensatory and punitive damage awards. *Law and Human Behavior, 20,* 189–206.

Cecil, J. S., Hans, V. P., & Wiggins, E. C. (1991). Citizen comprehension of difficult issues: Lessons from civil jury trials. *American University Law Review, 40,* 727–774.

Chapman, G. B., & Bornstein, B. H. (1996). The more you ask for, the more you get: Anchoring in personal injury verdicts. *Applied Cognitive Psychology, 10,* 519–540.

Cooter, R., Marks, S., & Mnookin, R. (1982). Bargaining in the shadow of the law: A testable model of strategic behavior. *Journal of Legal Studies, 11,* 225–251.

Cox, M., & Tanford, S. (1989). Effects of evidence and instructions in civil trials: An experimental investigation of rules of admissibility. *Social Behavior, 4,* 31–55.

Daniels, S., & Martin, J. (1997). Persistence is not always a virtue: Tort reform, civil liability for health care, and the lack of empirical evidence. *Behavioral Sciences and the Law, 15,* 3–19.

Danzon, P. M., & Lillard, L. A. (1983). Settlement out of court: The disposition of medical malpractice claims. *Journal of Legal Studies, 12,* 345–377.

Davis, J. H., Au, W. T., Hulbert, L., Chen, X., & Zarnoth, P. (1997). Effects of group size and procedural influence on consensual judgments of quantity: The example of damage awards and mock civil juries. *Journal of Personality and Social Psychology, 73,* 703–718.

Delahanty, D. L., Herberman, H. B., Craig, K. J., Hayward, M. C., Fullerton, C. S., Ursano, R. J., & Baum, A. (1997). Acute and chronic distress and Posttraumatic Stress Disorder as a function of responsibility for serious motor vehicle accidents. *Journal of Consulting and Clinical Psychology, 65,* 560–567.

Diamond, S. S. (1989). Using psychology to control law: From deceptive advertising to criminal sentencing. *Law and Human Behavior, 13,* 239–252.

Diamond, S. S., & Casper, J. D. (1992). Blindfolding the jury to verdict consequences: Damages, experts, and the civil jury. *Law and Society Review, 26,* 513–563.

Diamond, S. S., Saks, M. J., & Landsman, S. (1998). Jurors judgments about liability and damages: Sources of variability and ways to increase consistency. *DePaul Law Review, 48,* 301–325.

Donohue, W. A. (1991). *Communication, marital dispute and divorce mediation.* Hillsdale, NJ: Erlbaum.

Donohue, W. A., Drake, L. & Roberto, A. J. (1994). Mediator issue intervention strategies: A replication and some conclusions. *Mediator Quarterly, 11,* 261–274.

Douglas, K. S., Nicholls, T. L. & Koch, W. J. (1997). The role of the forensic clinician in the assessment of sexual harassment victims. Unpublished manuscript.

Edelman, L. B., Abraham, S. E., & Erlanger, H. S. (1992). Professional construction of law: The inflated threat of wrongful dismissal. *Law and Society Review, 26,* 47–83.

Edelman, L. B., Erlanger, H. S., & Lande, J. (1993). Internal dispute resolution: The transformation of civil rights in the workplace. *Law and Society Review, 27,* 497–534.

Feigenson, N., Park, J., & Salovey, P. (1997). Effects of blameworthiness and outcome severity on attributions of responsibility and damage awards in comparative negligence
cases. *Law and Human Behavior, 21*, 597–617.

Fellows, M. L., Johnson, M. K., Chiericozzi, A., Hale, A., Lee, C., Preble, R., & Voran, M.
(1998). Committed partners and inheritance: An empirical study. *Law and Inequality:
A Journal of Theory and Practice, 16*, 1–95.

Fischhoff, B. (1975). Hindsight &ne; foresight: The effect of outcome knowledge on judgment
under uncertainty. *Journal of Experimental Psychology, 1*, 288–299.

Fitzgerald, L. F., Swan, S. & Magley, V. J. (1997). But was it really sexual harassment? Legal,
behavioral and psychological definitions of the workplace victimization of women. In
W. O'Donohue (Ed.), *Sexual harassment: Theory, research and treatment* (pp. 5–28). Boston,
MA: Allyn and Bacon.

ForsterLee, L., Horowitz, I. A., & Bourgeois, M. J. (1993). Juror competence in civil trials:
Effects of preinstruction and evidence technicality. *Journal of Applied Psychology, 78*, 14–21.

ForsterLee, L., Horowitz, I., Athaide-Victor, E., & Brown, N. (2000). The bottom line: The
effect of written expert witness statements on juror verdicts and information processing.
*Law and Human Behavior, 24*, 259–270.

Galanter, M., Garth, B., Hensler, D., & Zemans, F. K. (1994). How to improve civil justice
policy: Systematic collection of data on the civil justice system is needed for reasoned
and effective policy making. *Judicature, 77*, 185, 229–230.

Garber, S. (1998). Product liability, punitive damages, business decisions, and economic
outcomes. *Wisconsin Law Review, 1998*, 237–295.

Garber, S., & Bower, A. G. (1999). Newspaper coverage of automotive product liability
verdicts. *Law and Society Review, 33*, 93–122.

Gifford, D. G., & Nye, D. J. (1987). Litigation trends in Florida: Saga of a growth state.
*University of Florida Law Review, 39*, 829–85.

Goldberg, G., Green, E. D., & Sander, F. (1985). *Dispute resolution*. Boston: Little, Brown.

Goldberg, S. B., Sander, F., & Rogers, N. H. (1992). *Dispute resolution: Negotiation, mediation,
and other processes*. Boston: Little, Brown.

Goodman, J., Greene, E., & Loftus, E. F. (1989). Runaway verdicts or reasoned determinations: Mock juror strategies in awarding damages. *Jurimetrics, 29*, 285–30.

Grant, J. D., & Wagner, T. H. (1992). Willingness to take legal action in wrongful dismissal
cases: Perceptual differences between men and women. *Perceptual and Motor Skills, 74*,
1073–1074.

Greene, E. (1989). On juries and damage awards: The process of decisionmaking. *Law and
Contemporary Problems, 52*, 225–246.

Greene, E., Goodman, J., & Loftus, E. F. (1991). Jurors' attitudes about civil litigation and the
size of damage awards. *American University Law Review, 40*, 805–820.

Greene, E., Johns, M., & Bowman, J. (1999). The effects of injury severity on jury negligence
decisions. *Law and Human Behavior, 23*, 675–693.

Greene, E., Woody, W. D., & Winter, R. (2000). Compensating plaintiffs and punishing defendants: Is bifurcation necessary? *Law and Human Behavior, 24*, 187–206.

Gross, S. R., & Syverud, K. D. (1991). Getting to no: A study of settlement negotiations and
the selection of cases for trial. *Michigan Law Review, 90*, 319–393.

Gross, S. R., & Syverud, K. D. (1996). Don't try: Civil jury verdicts in a system geared to
settlement. *UCLA Law Review, 44*, 1–64.

Gutek, B. A., & Koss, M. P. (1993). Changed women and changed organizations: Consequences
of and coping with sexual harassment. *Journal of Vocational Behavior, 42*, 28–48.

Guthrie, C. (2000). Framing frivolous litigation: A psychological theory. *University of Chicago
Law Review, 67*, 163–216.

Haenen, M., Schmidt, A. J. M., Kroeze, S., & van den Hout, M. A. (1996). Hypochondriasis and symptom reporting: The effect of attention versus distraction. *Psychotherapy and Psychosomatics, 65*, 43–48.

Hans, V. P. (1990). Attitudes toward corporate responsibility: A psycholegal perspective. *Nebraska Law Review, 69*, 158–189.

Hans, V. P. (1993). Attitudes toward the civil jury: A crisis of confidence? In R. E. Litan (Ed.), *Verdict: Assessing the civil jury system* (pp. 248–281). Washington, D.C.: The Brookings Institution.

Hans, V. P., & Ermann, M. D. (1989). Responses to corporate versus individual wrong doing. *Law and Human Behavior, 13*, 151–166.

Hans, V. P., & Lofquist, W. S. (1992). Jurors' judgments of business liability in tort cases: Implications for the litigation explosion debate. *Law and Society Review, 26*, 85–115.

Hans, V. P., & Mott, N. (March 2000). How jurors construct schemas of legal contracts. *American Psychology-Law Society*, New Orleans, LA.

Hart, A. J., Evans, D. L., Wissler, R. L., Feehan, J. W., & Saks, M. J. (1997). Injuries, prior beliefs, and damage awards. *Behavioral Sciences and the Law, 15*, 63–82.

Hastie, R., Schkade, D. A., & Payne, J. W. (1999a). Juror judgments in civil cases: Effects of plaintiff's requests and plaintiff's identity on punitive damage awards. *Law and Human Behavior, 23*, 445–470.

Hastie, R., Schkade, D. A., & Payne, J. W. (1999b). Juror judgments in civil cases: Hindsight effects on judgments of liability for punitive damages. *Law and Human Behavior, 23*, 597–614.

Heuer, L., & Penrod, S. (1986). Procedural preference as a function of conflict intensity. *Journal of Personality and Social Psychology, 51*, 700–710.

Heuer, L., & Penrod, S. (1988). Increasing jurors' participation in trials: A field experiment with written and preliminary instructions. *Law and Human Behavior, 12*, 409–430.

Heuer, L., & Penrod, S. (1989). Instructing jurors: A field experiment with written and preliminary instructions. *Law and Human Behavior, 13*, 409–430.

Heuer, L., & Penrod, S. (1994b). Juror notetaking and question asking during trial: A national field experiment. *Law and Human Behavior, 18*, 121–150.

Heuer, L., & Penrod, S. (1994a). Trial complexity: A field investigation of its meaning and effects. *Law and Human Behavior, 18*, 29–51.

Hickling, E. J., Blanchard, E. B., Buckley, T. C., & Taylor, A. E. (1999). Effects of attribution of responsibility for motor vehicle accidents on severity of PTSD symptoms, ways of coping, and recovery over six months. *Journal of Traumatic Stress, 12*, 345–353.

Hinsz, V. B., & Indahl, K. E. (1995). Assimilation to anchors for damage awards in a mock civil trial. *Journal of Applied Social Psychology, 25*, 991–1026.

Hook, J. (1993). Judgments about the right to property from preschool to adulthood. *Law and Human Behavior, 17*, 135–146.

Horowitz, I. A., & Bordens, K. S. (1988). The effects of outlier presence, plaintiff population size, and aggregation of plaintiffs on simulated civil jury decisions. *Law and Human Behavior, 12*, 209–229.

Horowitz, I. A., & Bordens, K. S. (1990). An experimental investigation of procedural issues in complex tort trials. *Law and Human Behavior, 14*, 269–285.

Horowitz, I. A., ForsterLee, L., & Brolly, I. (1996). Effects of trial complexity on decision making. *Journal of Applied Psychology, 81*, 757–768.

Houlden, P. (1980). Plea bargaining. *Law & Society Review, 15*, 267–291.

Houlden, P., LaTour, S., Walker, L., & Thibaut, J. (1978). Preference for modes of dispute resolution as a function of process and decision control. *Journal of Experimental Social Psychology, 14*, 13–30.

Huo, Y. J., Smith, H. J., Tyler, T. R., & Lind, E. A. (1996). Superordinate identification, sub-group identification, and justice concerns: Is separatism the problem; is assimilation the answer? *Psychological Science, 7*, 40–45.

Johnson, J. T., & Drobny, J. (1985). Proximity biases in the attribution of civil liability. *Journal of Personality and Social Psychology, 48*, 283–296.

Johnson, J. T., Ogawa, K. H., Delforge, A. & Early, D. (1989). Causal primacy and compara-tive fault: The effect of position in a causal chain on judgments of legal responsibility. *Personality and Social Psychology Bulletin, 15*, 161–174.

Jones, T. S., & Remland, M. S. (1992). Sources of variability in perceptions of and responses to sexual harassment. *Sex Roles, 27*, 121–142.

Kahneman, D., & Tversky, A. (1979). Prospect theory: Analysis of decision under risk. *Econometrica, 47*, 263–291.

Kahneman, D., & Tversky, A. (1984). Choices, values, and frames. *American Psychologist, 39*, 341–35.

Kahneman, D., Schkade, D., & Sunstein, C. R. (1998). Shared outrage and erratic awards: The psychology of punitive damages. *Journal of Risk and Uncertainty, 16*, 49–86.

Kamin, K. A., & Rachlinski, J. J. (1995). Ex post &ne; ex ante: Determining liability in hind-sight. *Law and Human Behavior, 19*, 89–104.

Kaplan, M. F., & Miller, C. E. (1987). Group decision making and normative versus informa-tional influence: Effects of type of issue and assigned decision rule. *Journal of Personality and Social Psychology, 53*, 306–313.

Karlovac, M., & Darley, J. M. (1988). Attribution of responsibility for accidents: A negligence law analogy. *Social Cognition, 6*, 287–318.

Katz, A. (1990). The effect of frivolous lawsuits on the settlement of litigation. *International Review of Law & Economics, 10*, 3–27 page number.

Kelly, J. B. (1989). Mediated and adversarial divorce: Respondents' perceptions of their processes and outcomes. In J. B. Kelly (Ed.), *Empirical research in divorce and family medi-ation* (pp. 71–88). San Francisco: Jossey-Bass.

Kelly, J. B. (1996). A decade of divorce mediation research: Some answers and questions. *Family and Conciliation Courts Review, 34*, 373–385.

Kim, P. T. (1997). Bargaining with imperfect information: A study of worker perceptions of legal protection in an at-will world. *Cornell Law Review, 83*, 105–156.

Kim, P. T. (1999). Norms, learning, and law: Exploring the influences on workers' legal knowledge. *University of Illinois Law Review, 1999*, 447–515.

Kitzmann, K. M. & Emery, R. E. (1993). Procedural justice and parents' satisfaction in a field study of child custody dispute resolution. *Law and Human Behavior, 17*, 553–567.

Koch, W. J., Shercliffe, R, Fedoroff, I., Iverson, G., & Taylor, S. (1999). Malingering and liti-gation stress in road accident victims. In E. Hickling & E. Blanchard (Eds.), *The International Handbook of Road Traffic Accidents and Psychological Trauma: Current Understanding, Treatment and Law*. Oxford, England: Pergamon Press.

Korobkin, R. (1998a). The status quo bias and contract default rules. *Cornell Law Review, 83*, 608–687.

Korobkin, R. (1998b). Inertia and preference in contract negotiation: The psychological power of default rules and form terms. *Vanderbilt Law Review, 51*, 1583–1651.

Korobkin R., & Guthrie, C. (1994). Psychological barriers to legal settlement: An experimen-tal approach. *Michigan Law Review, 93*, 107–192.

Korobkin, R., & Guthrie, C. (1997). Psychology, economics and settlement: A new look at the role of the lawyer. *Texas Law Review, 76*, 77–141.

Kurtz, S. T., & Houlden, P. (1981). Determinants of procedural preferences of post court-martial military personnel. *Basic and Applied Social Psychology, 2*, 27–43.

LaBine, S. J., & LaBine, G. (1996). Determinations of negligence and the hindsight bias. *Law and Human Behavior, 20*, 501–516.

Landis, J. M., and Goodstein, L. (1986). When is justice fair? *American Bar Foundation Research Journal, Fall*, 675–707.

Landsman, S., & Rakos, R. F. (1994). A preliminary inquiry into the effect of potentially biasing information on judges and jurors in civil litigation. *Behavioral Sciences and the Law, 12*, 113–126.

Landsman, S., Diamond, S. S., Dimitropoulos, L., & Saks, M. J. (1998). Be careful what you wish for: The paradoxical effects of bifurcating claims for punitive damages. *Wisconsin Law Review, 1998*, 297–342.

LaTour, S. (1978). Determinations of participant and observer satisfaction with adversary and inquisitorial modes of adjudication. *Journal of Personality and Social Psychology, 36*, 1531–1545.

LaTour, S., Houlden, P., Walker, L., & Thibaut, J. (1976). Some determinants of preference for modes of conflict resolution. *Journal of Conflict Resolution, 20*, 319–356.

Lee, C., & Farh, J. L. (1999). The effects of gender in organizational justice perception. *Journal of Organizational Behavior, 20*, 133–143.

Lees-Haley, P. R. & Brown, R. S. (1993). Neuropsychological complaint base rates of 170 personal injury claimants. *Archives of Clinical Neuropsychology, 8*, 203–209.

Lempert, R. (1993). Civil juries and complex cases: Taking stock after twelve years. In R. E. Litan (Ed.), *Verdict: Assessing the civil jury system* (pp. 181–248). Washington, D C · The Brookings Institution.

Leung, K. (1987). Some determinants of reactions to procedural models for conflict resolution: A cross-national study. *Journal of Personality and Social Psychology, 53*, 898–908.

Leung, K., & Lind, E. A. (1986). Procedural justice and culture: Effects of culture, gender, and investigator status on procedural preferences. *Journal of Personality and Social Psychology, 50*, 1134–1140.

Levi, D. L. (1997). The role of apology in mediation. *New York University Law Review, 72*, 1165–1210.

Lind, E. A. (1997). Litigation and claiming in organizations: Antisocial behavior or quest for justice? In R. A. Giacalone & J. Greenberg (Eds.), *Antisocial behavior in organizations* (pp. 150–171). Thousand Oaks: Sage.

Lind, E. A., & Tyler, T. R. (1988). *The social psychology of procedural justice.* New York: Plenum Press.

Lind, E. A., Huo, Y. J., & Tyler, T. R. (1994). &ellipsis;and justice for all: Ethnicity, gender, and preferences for dispute resolution procedures. *Law and Human Behavior, 18*, 269–290.

Lind, E. A., Kanfer, R., & Earley, P. C. (1990). Voice, control, and procedural justice: Instrumental and noninstrumental concerns in fairness judgments. *Journal of Personality and Social Psychology, 59*, 952–959.

Lind, E. A., Lissak, R. I., & Conlon, D. E. (1983). Decision control and process control effects on procedural fairness judgments. *Journal of Applied Social Psychology, 13*, 338–350.

Lind, E. A., Erickson, B. E., Friedland, N., & Dickenberger, M. (1978). Reactions to procedural models for adjudicative conflict resolution: A cross-national study. *Journal of Conflict Resolution, 22*, 318–341.

Lind, E. A., MacCoun, R. J., Ebener, P. A., Felstiner, W. L. F., Hensler, D. R., Resnik, J., & Tyler, T. R. (1990). In the eye of the beholder: Tort litigants' evaluations of their experiences in the civil justice system. *Law and Society Review, 24*, 953–989.

Livingston, J. A. (1982). Responses to sexual harassment on the job: Legal, organizational, and individual actions. *Journal of Social Issues, 38*, 5–22.

MacCleod, L., & MacCleod, G. (1998). Control cognitions and psychological disturbance in people with contrasting physically disabling conditions. *Disability and Rehabilitation, 20,* 448–456.

MacCoun, R. J. (1996). Differential treatment of corporate defendants by juries: An examination of the "deep pockets" hypothesis. *Law and Society Review, 30,* 121–161.

MacCoun, R. J. (2000). The costs and benefits of letting juries punish corporations: Comment on Viscusi. *Stanford Law Review, 52,* 1821–1828.

MacCoun, R. J., Lind, E. A., Hensler, D. R., Bryant, D. L., & Ebener, P. A. (1988). *Alternative adjudication: An evaluation of the New Jersey automobile arbitration program.* Santa Monica, CA: Institute for Civil Justice, RAND Corporation.

Magnavita, N., Narda, R., Sani, L., Carbone, A., De Lorenzo, G., & Sacco, A. (1997). Type A behavior pattern and traffic accidents. *British Journal of Medical Psychology, 70,* 103–107.

Malouff, J., & Schutte, N. S. (1989). Shaping juror attitudes: Effects of requesting different damage amounts in personal injury trials. *Journal of Social Psychology, 129,* 491–497.

Masson, M. E. J., & Waldron, M. A. (1994). Comprehension of legal contracts by non-experts: Effectiveness of plain language redrafting. *Applied Cognitive Psychology, 8,* 67–85.

McEwen, C. A., & Maiman, R. J. (1986). The relative significance of disputing forum and dispute characteristics for outcome and compliance. *Law and Society Review, 20,* 439–447.

Moore, A. D., Stambrook, M., & Wilson, K. G. (1991). Cognitive moderators in adjustment to chronic illness: Locus of control beliefs following traumatic brain injury. *Neuropsychological Rehabilitation, 1,* 185–198.

Mueller, W. (1970). Residential tenants and their leases: An empirical study. *Michigan Law Review, 69,* 247–298.

Phares, E. J. (1978). Locus of control. In H. London & J. E. Exner (Eds.), *Dimensions of personality.* New York: Wiley-Interscience.

Polinsky, A. M. & Rubinfeld, D. L. (1993). Sanctioning frivolous suits: An economic analysis. *Georgetown Law Journal, 82,* 397–435.

Posner, R. A. (1973). An economic approach to legal procedure and judicial administration. *Journal of Legal Studies, 2,* 399.

Priest, G. L. (1985). Reexamining the selection hypothesis: Learning from Wittman's mistakes. *Journal of Legal Studies, 14,* 215–243.

Priest, G. L., & Klein, B. (1984). The selection of disputes for litigation. *Journal of Legal Studies, 13,* 1–55.

Rachlinski, J. J. (1996). Gains, losses, and the psychology of litigation. *Southern California Law Review, 70,* 113–185.

Rachlinski, J. J. (1998). A positive psychological theory of judging in hindsight. *University of Chicago Law Review, 65,* 571–625.

Rachlinski, J. J., & Jourden, F. (1998). Remedies and the psychology of ownership. *Vanderbilt Law Review, 51,* 1541–1582.

Raiffa, H. (1982). *The art and science of negotiation.* Harvard University Press: Cambridge, MA.

Raitz, A., Greene, E., Goodman, J., & Loftus, E. F. (1990). Determining damages: The influence of expert testimony on jurors' decision making. *Law and Human Behavior, 14,* 385–395.

Robbennolt, J. K. (in press). Punitive damage decision making: The decisions of citizens and trial court judges. *Law and Human Behavior.*

Robbennolt, J. K. (in press). Outcome severity and judgments of "responsibility": A meta-analytic review. *Journal of Applied Social Psychology.*

Robbennolt, J. K., & Johnson, M. K. (1999). Legal planning for unmarried committed partners: Empirical lessons for a preventive and therapeutic approach. *Arizona Law Review, 41,* 417–457.

Robbennolt, J. K., & Studebaker, C. A. (1999). Anchoring in the courtroom: The effects of caps on punitive damages. *Law and Human Behavior, 23*, 353–374.

Rosenberg, D., & Shavell, S. (1985). A model in which suits are brought for their nuisance value. *International Review of Law & Economics, 5*, 3–13.

Rosenhan, D. L., Eisner, S. L., & Robinson, R. J. (1994). Notetaking can aid juror recall. *Law and Human Behavior, 18*, 53–61.

Ross, L. H. (1980). *Settled out of court: The social process of insurance claims adjustments* (2nd ed.). New York: Aldine.

Rousseau, D. M. (1998). The "problem" of the psychological contract considered. *Journal of Organizational Behavior, 19*, 665–671.

Rousseau, D. M., & Anton, R. J. (1988). Fairness and implied contract obligations in job terminations: A policy capturing study. *Human Performance, 1*, 273–289.

Rousseau, D. M., & Anton, R. J. (1991). Fairness and implied contract obligations in job terminations: The role of contributions, promises, and performance. *Journal of Organizational Behavior, 12*, 287–299.

Rousseau, D. M., & Aquino, K. (1993). Fairness and implied contract obligations in job terminations: The role of remedies, social accounts, and procedural justice. *Human Performance, 6*, 135–149.

Rousseau, D. M., & Tijoriwala, S. A. (1998). Assessing psychological contracts: Issues, alternatives, and measures. *Journal of Organizational Behavior, 19*, 679–695.

Rudman, L. A., Borgida, E., & Robertson, B. A. (1995). Suffering in silence: Procedural justice versus gender socialization in university harassment grievance. *Basic and Applied Social Psychology, 17*, 519–541.

Saks, M. J. (1992). Do we really know anything about the behavior of the tort system—and why not? *University of Pennsylvania Law Review, 140*, 1147–1289.

Saks, M. J. (1997). Injuries, prior beliefs, and damage awards. *Behavioral Sciences and the Law, 15*, 63–82.

Saks, M. J. (1998). Public opinion about the civil jury: Can reality be found in the illusions? *DePaul Law Review, 1998*, 221–245.

Saks, M. J., & Blanck, P. D. (1992). Justice improved: The unrecognized benefits of aggregation and sampling in the trial of mass torts. *Stanford Law Review, 44*, 815–851.

Saks, M. J., Hollinger, L. A., Wissler, R. L., Evans, D. L., & Hart, A. J. (1997). Reducing variability in civil jury awards. *Law and Human Behavior, 21*, 243–256.

Schkade, D., Sunstein, C. R., & Kahneman, D. (2000). Deliberating about dollars: The severity shift. *Columbia Law Review, 100*, 1139–1175.

Schnedemann, D. A., & Parks, J. M. (1994). Contract formation and employee handbooks: Legal, psychological, and empirical analyses. *Wake Forest Law Review, 29*, 647–687.

Sheppard, B. (1985). Justice is no simple matter: Case for elaborating our model of procedural fairness. *Journal of Personality and Social Psychology, 49*, 953–962.

Shuman, D. W. (2000). The role of apology in tort law. *Judicature, 83*, 180–189.

Simon, R. I. (1996). The credible forensic psychiatric evaluation in sexual harassment litigation. *Psychiatric Annals, 26*, 139–148.

Songer, D. R. (1988). Tort reform in South Carolina: The effect of empirical research on elite perceptions concerning jury verdicts. *South Carolina Law Review, 39*, 585–603.

Stolle, D. P. (1995). The FTC's reliance on extrinsic evidence in cases of deceptive advertising: A proposal for interpretive rulemaking. Kraft, Inc. v. FTC, 970 F.2d 311 (7th Cir. 1992), cert. denied, 113 S. Ct. 1254 (1993). *Nebraska Law Review, 74*, 352–373.

Stolle, D. P. (1998). A social scientific look at the effects and effectiveness of plain language contract drafting. Doctoral dissertation, University of Nebraska, Lincoln.

Stolle, D. P., & Slain, A. J. (1997). Standard form contracts and contract schemas: A preliminary investigation of the effects of exculpatory clauses on consumers' propensity to sue. *Behavioral Sciences and the Law, 15,* 83–94.

Sutherland, V. J., & Cooper, C. L. (1991). Personality, stress and accident involvement in the offshore oil and gas industry. *Personality and Individual Differences, 12,* 195–204.

Sweeney, P. D., & McFarlin, D. B. (1997). Process and outcome: Gender differences in the assessment of justice. *Journal of Organizational Behavior, 18,* 83–98.

Tarasoff v. Regents of University of California, 551 P.2d 334 (1976).

Thibaut, J., & Walker, L. (1975). *Procedural justice: A psychological analysis.* Hillsdale, NJ: Erlbaum.

Thibaut, J., & Walker, L. (1978). A theory of procedure. *California Law Review, 66,* 541–566.

Thibaut, J., Walker, L., LaTour, S., & Houlden, P. (1974). Procedural justice as fairness. *Stanford Law Review, 26,* 1271–1289.

Thomas, E. A. C., & Parpal, M. (1987). Liability as a function of plaintiff and defendant fault. *Journal of Personality and Social Psychology, 53,* 843–857.

Trubek, D. M., Sarat, A., Felstiner, W. L. F., Kritzer, H. M., & Grossman, J. B. (1983). The costs of ordinary litigation. *UCLA Law Review, 31,* 72–127.

Tversky, A., & Kahneman, D. (1974). Judgment under uncertainty: Heuristics and biases. *Science, 185,* 124–1131.

Tversky, A., & Kahneman, D. (1981). The framing of decisions and the psychology of choice. *Science, 211,* 453–458.

Tversky, A., & Kahneman, D. (1986). Rational choice and the framing of decisions. *Journal of Business, 59,* S251–S278.

Tversky A., & Kahneman, D. (1991). Loss aversion in riskless choice—A reference-dependent model. *Quantitative Journal of Economics, 106,* 1039–1106.

Tversky, A., & Kahneman, D. (1992). Advances in prospect theory: Cumulative representation of uncertainty. *Journal of Risk & Uncertainty, 5,* 297–323.

Twaite, J. A., Keiser, S., & Luchow, A. (1998). Divorce mediation: Promises, criticisms, achievements and current challenges. *Journal of Psychiatry and Law, 26,* 353–381.

Tyler, T. R. (1984). The role of perceived injustice in defendant's evaluations of their courtroom experience. *Law and Society Review, 18,* 51–74.

Tyler, T. R. (1987). Conditions leading to value expressive effects in judgments of procedural justice: A test of four models. *Journal of Personality and Social Psychology, 52,* 333–344.

Tyler, T. R. (1989). The psychology of procedural justice: A test of the group value model. *Journal of Personality and Social Psychology, 57,* 830–838.

Tyler, T. R., & Bies, R. J. (1990). Beyond formal procedures: The interpersonal context of procedural justice. In J. S. Carroll (Ed.), *Applied social psychology in business settings.* Hillsdale, NJ: Erlbaum.

Tyler T. R., & Degoey, P. (1995). Collective restraint in social dilemmas: Procedural justice and social identification effects on support for authorities. *Journal of Personality and Social Psychology, 69,* 482–497.

Tyler, T. R., & Folger, R. (1980). Distributional and procedural aspects of satisfaction with citizen-police encounters. *Basic and Applied Social Psychology, 1,* 281–292.

Tyler, T. R., & Lind, E. A. (1992). A relational model of authority in groups. In M. Zanna (Ed.), *Advances in experimental social psychology* (Vol. 25, pp. 115–191). New York: Academic Press.

Tyler, R., Rasinski, K., & Spodick, N. (1985). Influence of voice on satisfaction with leaders: Exploring the meaning of process control. *Journal of Personality and Social Psychology, 48,* 72–81.

United States Merit Systems Protection Board. (1988). *Sexual harassment in the federal government: An update.* Washington, DC: U.S. Government Printing Office.

van Koppen, P. J. (1990). Risk taking in civil law negotiations. *Law & Human Behavior, 14,* 151–164.

van Voris, B. (1998, November 2). 1998 juror outlook survey. Civil cases: Jurors do not trust civil litigants. Period. *The National Law Journal,* A24.

Vidmar, N. (1992). Procedural justice and alternative dispute resolution. *Psychological Science, 3,* 224–228.

Vidmar, N. (1993). Empirical evidence on the deep pockets hypothesis: Jury awards for pain and suffering in medical malpractice cases. *Duke Law Journal, 43,* 217–266.

Vidmar, N., & Rice, J. J. (1993). Assessments of noneconomic damage awards in medical negligence: A comparison of jurors with legal professionals. *Iowa Law Review, 78,* 883–903.

Viscusi, W. K. (2000). Corporate risk analysis: A reckless act? *Stanford Law Review, 52,* 547–596.

Walker, L., LaTour, S., Lind, F. A., & Thibaut, J. (1974). Reactions of participants and observers to modes of adjudication. *Journal of Applied Social Psychology, 4,* 295–310.

Wagatsuma, H., & Rosett, A. (1986). The implications of apology: Law and culture in Japan and the United States. *Law & Society Review, 20,* 461–498.

Weissman, H. N. (1990). Distortions and deceptions in self presentation: Effects of protracted litigation in personal injury cases. *Behavioral Sciences and the Law, 8,* 67–74.

Weissman, H. N. (1991). Forensic psychological assessment and the effects of protracted litigation on impairment in personal injury litigation. *Forensic Reports, 4,* 417–429.

West, R., & Hall, J. (1997). The role of personality and attitudes in traffic accident risk. *Applied Psychology: An International Review, 46,* 253–264.

Wiener, R. L. (1993). Social analytic jurisprudence and tort law: Social cognition goes to court. *St. Louis University Law Journal, 37,* 503–551.

Wiggins, E. C., & Breckler, S. J. (1990). Special verdicts as guides to jury decision making *Law and Psychology Review, 14,* 1–41.

Wissler, R. L., Hart, A. J., & Saks, M. J. (1999). Decisionmaking about general damages: A comparison of jurors, judges, and lawyers. *Michigan Law Review, 90,* 751–826

Wittman, D. (1985). Is the selection of cases for trial biased? *Journal of Legal Studies, 14,* 185–214.

Yngvesson, B., & Hennessey, P. (1975). Small claims, complex disputes – Review of small claims literature. *Law and Society Review, 9,* 219–274.

Youngblood, S.A., Trevino, L., & Favia, M. (1992). Reactions too unjust dismissal and third-party dispute resolution: A justice framework. *Employee Responsibility and Rights Journal, 5,* 283–307.

Zickafoose, D. J., & Bornstein, B. H. (1999). Double discounting: The effects of comparative negligence on mock juror decision making. *Law and Human Behavior, 23,* 577–596.

Zuckerman, A., & Chaiken, S. (1998). A heuristic-systematic processing analysis of the effectiveness of product warning labels. *Psychology & Marketing, 15,* 621–642.

# 11

# Evaluating Published Research in Psychology and Law

*A Gatekeeper Analysis of Law and Human Behavior*[1]

## RICHARD L. WIENER, RYAN J. WINTER, MELANIE ROGERS, HOPE SEIB, SHANNON RAUCH, KAREN KADELA, AMY HACKNEY, AND LAURA WARREN

[1]This work was supported by grant no. SBR #9515451 from the Law and Social Science Program at the National Science Foundation.

RICHARD WIENER • Department of Psychology, Baruch College and Graduate Center, City University of New York, New York, New York 10010.     RYAN J. WINTER • Department of Psychology, Brooklyn College and Graduate Center, Brooklyn, New York 11210.     MELANIE ROGERS • Department of Psychology, Brooklyn College and Graduate Center, Brooklyn, New York 11210.     HOPE SEIB • Department of Psychology, Saint Louis University, St. Louis, Missouri 63101.     SHANNON RAUCH • Department of Psychology, Saint Louis University, St. Louis, Missouri 63101     KAREN KADELA • Department of Psychology, Saint Louis University, St. Louis, Missouri 63101.     AMY HACKNEY • Department of Psychology, Saint Louis University, St. Louis, Missouri 63101.     LAURA WARREN • Department of Psychology, Saint Louis University, St. Louis, Missouri 63101.

## LAW, PSYCHOLOGY, AND A STANDARD OF REVIEW

In 1993, the United States Supreme Court announced its momentous ruling in *Daubert v. Merrell Dow Pharmaceuticals*, which shifted the burden of evaluating the quality of scientific research offered in testimony at trial from general acceptance in the field (*Frye v. United States*, 1923) to the guided discretion of the trial judge. Psychologists immediately began to analyze the implications of this most important procedural change for research, practice, and ultimately for psychological testimony. In fact, the third edition of Monahan and Walker's influential case book, *Social Science in Law: Cases and Materials* (1994), which was published before the case appeared in the West reporter system, included a slip copy of the case accompanied by an analysis of its meaning for social science research. Others quickly joined in the debate to determine the likely impact of the *Daubert* ruling on the status of psychological knowledge in the courts. For example, Faigman (1995) reviewed the new standard for traditional (e.g., eyewitness testimony) and controversial (e.g., repressed memory) areas of psychological testimony and concluded that while some forms of testimony may very well meet the standard and pass the hurdle imposed by the Court to disallow junk science, the more controversial evidence might very well not qualify under the new rule of admission. At about the same time, Zonana (1994) applied the *Daubert* criteria to psychiatric testimony and was unsure how the new reliability standard would play out with expert opinion based upon psychiatric interviews, medical history, and psychological testing.

In the years since the *Daubert* ruling, this debate in the courts as well as in the social sciences has only grown in depth and breadth. The Supreme Court expanded its holding in *Daubert* when it held in *Kumho Tire, Inc. v. Carmichael* (1999) that trial judges had broad discretion to determine the admissibility of not only "scientific testimony" but also the admissibility of "technical or other specialized knowledge" (p. 1194). The Justices also expanded the *Daubert* holding by acknowledging that other systems of scrutiny beside the approach adopted for scientific research in *Daubert* might be useful in examining the reliability of other types of specialized knowledge. Thus, it may be incumbent upon those who offer specialized testimony that is not entirely based upon scientific research to present a system of analysis that will allow the courts to evaluate the reliability of that testimony. This flurry of activity and interest is mirrored on the psychological side of expert testimony. In fact, a recent search of the psychological literature found 54 articles, books, edited chapters, and other psychological treatises devoted to the application of the trial judge's expanded gatekeeper role to the work of psychologists. Psychological scholars have examined the implications of a *Daubert* type analysis for their testimony in areas as diverse as general psychiatric/psychological testimony (Gutheil, 1999; Gutheil & Stein, 2000), facilitated communication among the developmentally disabled (Gorman, 1999), child sexual abuse accommodation syndrome (Heath, 2000), psychodiagnostic assessment of posttraumatic stress disorder and multiple personality disorder (Grove & Barden, 1999), sexual predator testimony in commitment hearings (Schopp, Scalora, & Pearce, 1999), evaluations in child custody hearings (Krauss & Sales, 1999), social science evidence in business litigation (Lipton, 1999), jury simulation studies in child abuse cases (Bull-Kovera & Borgida, 1998), and eyewitness research and jury decision making (Penrod, Fulero, & Cutler, 1995).

Psychologists working in the legal system have a lot to say about how *Daubert* ought to be applied to their work and the implications of *Daubert* type analyses for their proffered testimony. They have reacted, debated, and written extensively, adding their considered opinions to those of the appellate level judges to try to shape the admissibility debate. It appears to us that this debate, at least from the social scientist's perspective has started at the end of the epistemological process rather than at the beginning of that process. It is the role of judges to evaluate the reliability and relevance of psychological testimony from the point of view of the law and legal procedure. It is certainly appropriate for psychologists to comment on that analysis. However, how much more weighty would be the psychologists' input if they began by evaluating their own literature with regard to its reliability and relevance? In other words we believe the place to begin is a consideration of the quality of the research literature that psychologists produce. After all, this literature provides the basis for the testimony that ultimately is judged admissible or inadmissible at trial. The purpose of this chapter is to focus the spotlight back on the research literature of psychology and law and evaluate its strengths and weaknesses rather than to examine its fit to the *Daubert* type standards, which so many have already done.

We focus our attention primarily on the work that has been published in the official journal of the American Psychology-Law Society, *Law and Human Behavior*. To help evaluate our literature we find it useful to adopt an epistemological standard, as the Supreme Court has done in its reliance on reliability and fit in examining the quality of scientific research offered by experts in the courts. For that standard, we turn to the program evaluation literature, which is unified not by its substantive content, but rather by its emphasis on method and procedure. One approach that has been extensively applied to quantitative research in that area goes under the rubric of critical multiplism or planned critical multiplism (Blankertz,

1998; Houts, Cook, & Shadish; 1986; Shadish, 1986). Critical multiplism begins with the assumption that no single method or theory captures the entirety of phenomenon of interest in most fields. This is especially true in applied areas of research where investigations are most sensitive to measurement and manipulation of the constructs, as they exist not only in the laboratory environment but also in the real world. Any single method of investigation is associated with not only random error (lack of reliability) but also with systematic error (actual bias). As Blankertz (1998) writes, "the central tenet of critical multiplism is that there is no firm foundation of knowledge ... each paradigm, theory, research question, methodology, data analysis and interpretation is inherently biased" (p. 208).

Consider line-up investigations, an area that many regard as the most methodologically rigorous of all the research paradigms in psycholegal science. Line-up studies that present crime scenes in the form of photographs or videotaped sequences have no alternative other than to incorporate the random noise produced by the ease (or difficulty) of recognition associated with the facts and scenes in specific target cases. However, even more limiting is the systematic variance associated with the method of presenting photographs or even videotapes. The form of the pictorial depictions limits the type of information available for the target descriptions. The target scenes restrict the range of focus, narrowly directing the attention of the viewer. Visual scanning is normally free to vary across the distribution of events and circumstances that make up an actual episode; however, photographic simulation directs the attention of the viewer toward or away from the most important particulars of the event as recorded by the camera. As a result, eyewitness identification studies that present crime scenes in this manner are biased in the sense that they simplify the task for the observer in accordance with the perspective of the researcher, or at least that of the cameraperson.

Results from eyewitness programs of research are most believable when they report findings that rely on both live and recorded target scenes. Each methodology is tainted by its own systematic error. However, because these errors are not shared by the presentation styles, results found across studies rule out systematic bias. For example, live but fabricated crime scenes (e.g., a confederate walks into a room of waiting research participants and walks out with a laptop computer) allow observer perceptions to operate freely. The attention distortions that are present in videotaped target sequences do not operate in live performances. However, to collect enough data such performances need to be carried out repeatedly. As a result practice effects and fatigue effects bias the presentations of the confederates and likely create systematic differences in the both the early and later experimental trials. If the target scene is presented only once, there are still systematic attributes uniquely associated with the actors' performance and emotional experience. Replicated findings across maximally different types of target presentation gain in validity because the systematic errors inherent in each replication tend to cancel each other out.

Planned critical multiplism (Houts, Cook, & Shadish, 1986; Shadish, 1986) is the constant search for new and alternative methods for testing research hypotheses. Research is conducted with the knowledge that uncertainty is the rule rather than the exception and that every methodology introduces its own set of plausible explanations that offer alternative conclusions to those reached by the researcher. The goal of the scientist is to propose models of psychological reality that pass increasingly more difficult tests until the models fail. When a model fails it is altered, modified, and resubmitted to this most rigorous and demanding process. As a result of this iteration of tests and theory modifications, the quality of our research efforts and the status of our substantive findings are interconnected. It is not possible to totally separate our methodologies from current findings and ultimately from our views of psycholegal reality.

Blankertz (1998) describes three steps that constitute the planned critical multiplism recipe for scientific inquiry in a program of research. First, the researcher must assess the biases in each available method. Second, the investigator critically examines each method to ascertain the limitations imposed by each potential bias and to determine if some methods are more suitable for the purpose of the current inquiry than are other methods. Finally, if all methods are biased in some manner, the researcher selects methods that are biased in different directions so that results that withstand multiple tests gain in veridicality. Applying a similar recipe to psycholegal investigations, Wiener and Hurt (1999) point out that researchers who intend their work to be used in court are under a double burden to critically examine their own work. Advocates, those who examine the results of their research looking for confirmation and ignoring alternative explanations of their hypotheses and conclusions, do so at great risk of attack not only from journal reviewers but also from attorneys, perhaps aided by opposing experts, during cross examinations both in depositions and in court. As a result, it behooves the research community to apply a higher standard to the research literature than the reliability and relevance criteria adopted by the courts. In fact, research published in scientific journals like *Law and Human Behavior* must not only meet the criteria suggested in *Daubert* (1994) (i.e., the hypothesis is testable, the results survived peer review, the research demonstrated an acceptable error rate, and the methodology is generally accepted in the field), it should also meet the higher standard of pluralistic critique. This standard exists independent of the law. It does not originate from theories of jurisprudence but rather from theories of scientific epistemology. After all, the researchers themselves are the final gatekeepers in the scientific enterprise and it is their role to scrutinize most carefully the methodologies in their science. Wiener and Hurt (1999) point out that psychology and law researchers constitute a research paradigm in the sense described by Kuhn (1970) and Lachman, Lachman, & Butterfield (1979). In other words, "there exists a collection of psycholegal scientists who share a common commitment to a set of scientific beliefs and values and who agree on common problems and appropriate methodologies to study substantive and procedural issues that are relevant to the law." (Wiener & Hurt, 1999, p. 569). We posit that the true gatekeepers in the psychology and law arena are the members of this research paradigm and the standard that should be applied to the product of their science is the standard of planned critical multiplism.[2]

## THE SAINT LOUIS CONFERENCE

In the Spring of 1999, 23 researchers with backgrounds in clinical, cognitive, social, and developmental psychology and who regularly publish and review papers for *Law and Human Behavior* gathered at Saint Louis University, to take stock of the direction that our paradigm had taken and to offer some suggestions for the future work in the area.[3] *Law and Human Behavior* is the official journal of the American Psychology-Law Society,

---

[2]At this point a short digression is in order to introduce a caveat to our approach. As the law recognizes that not all specialized and technical knowledge can be categorized "scientific" (see, *Khumo Tire, 1999*), we recognize that not all work in social science and law fits the paradigmatic system that is generally adopted in *Law and Human Behavior*. While the journal does publish a small number of qualitative research reports, the major emphasis in the journal is experimental or correlational investigation, usually in the tradition of what has come to be known as quantitative research. We recognize that there is a substantial role for qualitative research and, in fact, the cover page of the journal invites this type of work. Regardless, researchers submit few qualitative studies. As a result, the dominant paradigm in psychology and law relies upon quantitative methodologies. Therefore, our analysis applies a standard that is designed to evaluate this type of research. Our approach parallels the logic outlined in *Khumo Tire*. We acknowledge that other systems of analysis should be offered to examine the suitability of qualitative research efforts just as the Supreme Court acknowledged the need for schemes to evaluate the reliability of skilled and technical knowledge outside the realm of science. However, here we do not develop such a system because the amount of qualitative work published in psychology and law does not yet justify devoting a lengthy analysis to establishing such a framework.

[3]The St. Louis Conference was funded by grant SBR #9515451 from the Law and Social Science Program at the National Science Foundation.

Division 41 of the American Psychological Association. The journal publishes 6 peer reviewed editions each year consisting mostly, but not exclusively of empirical studies. Although mostly psychologists author the articles, a variety of other social scientists (e.g., sociologists, criminologists, anthropologists, and psychiatrists) write papers for the journal. The publication policy found on the front cover of each edition states that the journal is "a multidisciplinary forum for the publication of articles and discussions of issues arising out of the relationship between human behavior and the law, legal system, and legal process." As journal editor, the first author of this chapter wrote a brief supplement to the editorial policy in 1997 (Wiener, 1997) in which he stated:

> The best manuscripts will be those that present analyses of legally relevant issues from a theoretical and empirical base within the social sciences. Articles that are empirical should report data collected in accordance with current standards of rigorous scientific investigation... the best work goes beyond sophisticated social science methodology applied to problems of law and legal process. The best work is truly interdisciplinary in that it begins with a careful analysis of law, the legal system, or legal process, and proceeds by offering a meaningful social scientific analysis of the problem. The most interesting and persuasive empirical investigations are those that use our most powerful empirical methods to test insights drawn from social scientific theory and research.

The focus of the conference was to examine the content, methodology, and current direction of articles published in *Law and Human Behavior*, identify areas of scholarship that are lacking, and develop a strategy for encouraging the future submission of diverse manuscripts to the journal. As a result, this working group developed some interesting insights that can be thought of as a critical analysis of the research literature in the area of law and psychology. Before the conference began, we content analyzed the abstracts published in *Law and Human Behavior* from 1994 to 1998 (mostly articles submitted from 1993 through the middle of 1998) and those submitted for publication in 1998 through 1999. We begin our current analysis, as we began the St. Louis Conference, with a presentation of those results.

We coded 185 abstracts on 39 variables that described the methodology and content of the publications. Initially we collected reliability data (percent agreement across the 39 variables) on a sample of 20 abstracts selected at random and evaluated by each of the 6 independent coders. Agreement rates across all six coders ranged from 86% to 100% on each of the 39 factors.[4] For every abstract we evaluated: the topic of the investigation (e.g.,

---

[4]Chance agreement rates across the factors was equal to 50%.

jury decision making, eyewitness identification, assessment of psychological status, etc.), the gender of authors, whether special populations were
involved (i.e., minorities, women, and children), whether the topic
involved criminal or civil law, and whether the topics were clinical in
nature.[5] For the empirical articles only, we coded the type of independent
or exogenous factors, the type of dependent or endogenous factors, the type
of the sample (whether it was representative of the legal actors studied),
and the use of psychological mechanisms to predict or explain legally relevant actions.

Overall, the median number of authors listed on articles published in
the journal equaled 2 (1 male and 1 female author). However, across all
5 years, 63% of first authors were male and 37% were female. This number varies by year showing an increasing number of female first authors
from 1994 to 1998 (with 34%, 39%, 47%, 20%, and 44%, respectively and
46% of submitted articles from 1998 to 1999). The journal appears to be
doing reasonably well at including articles from female as well as male
authors. On the other hand, the number of articles that focused on special
populations with the exception of papers relating to children in the law
was not overwhelming. Although 19% of published articles during the
target years and 15% of submitted papers in 1998 to 1999 pertained to
children and law only 6% of published articles in the target years focused
on minorities and only 8% on gender issues. This is especially troubling
given that these figures appear not to be increasing, i.e., 6% of submitted
articles from 1998 to 1999 pertained to minority issues and 9% to gender
topics. Further, of the published articles on minority issues, 7 of 11 were
in a special edition on minorities and of the published articles on gender
8 of 15 were in a special edition on gender in the law. Thus, while children,
families, and the law seem to be a well-researched and published topic,
gender and minority issues in the law remain underdeveloped.

Turning to the specific topics of interest, Figure 11.1 displays the percent of articles published during the investigative window (1994–1998)
organized according to topic.

First, most of the articles published in *Law and Human Behavior* are
empirical investigations (82% or 150 of 183 published papers). Still, a significant number are legal or social science commentaries (18% or 33 of 183).
Authors devote a great deal of their effort to reporting empirical investigations of jury decision making (34% or 63 of 183 published papers). This
is followed by forensic psychology (clinical topics including assessment,
risk of dangerousness, and treatment) (18% or 27 of 183), eyewitness
identification (12% or 22 of 183), and corrections research (combining

---

[5]Clinical topics were any that pertained to assessing risk of dangerousness, assessment of
psychological status (including competencies and insanity), or treatment issues.

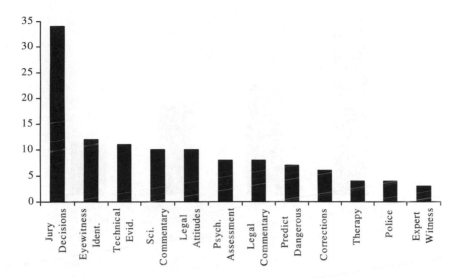

FIGURE 11.1. *Law and Human Behavior:* Topics of Publication 1994–1998 Percent of Total.

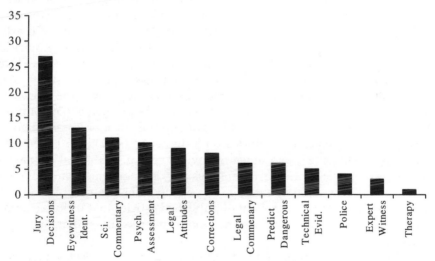

FIGURE 11.2. *Law and Human Behavior:* Topics of Submissions 1998–1999 Percent of Total.

corrections and policing) (10% or 20 out of 183). Figure 11.2 reports a similar figure for articles submitted during 1998 through 1999. Again, the most frequent topics of empirical investigation were jury decision-making, forensic psychology, eyewitness identification, and corrections research.

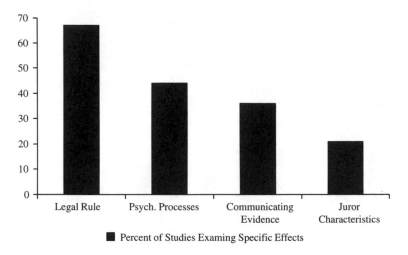

FIGURE 11.3. *Law and Human Behavior:* Investigations of Jury Decision Making 1994–1998.

Papers on jury decision-making are the most frequently published and the number of publications has remained relatively stable across the window of investigation (34%, 42%, 34%, 34%, 28% of the published articles in 1994, 1995, 1996, 1997, and 1998, respectively were empirical reports of jury decision making studies). Therefore, we examined in more detail the types of jury studies that appear in press. Figure 11.3 shows that among published jury studies the most frequent topic was the effects of specific legal rules on verdicts and evaluation of arguments (65% of published articles). Second were the effects of psychological processes such as scripts, stories, schemas, attitudes on judgments, (42%), third were the effects of methods of communicating evidence (e.g., statistical vs. narrative depictions) (36%) and last were social or demographic characteristics on juror and jury decision making (e.g., age, gender, attitude bias) (21%). The figure represents the percent of published articles that included some mention of at least one of these topics; many included more than one topic of investigation.

While the last several editions of *Law and Human Behavior* included several empirical studies of civil law, and the new decade submissions impressionistically appear to include more civil law papers, the data from the last years of the 1990s suggest that the journal has published and continues to publish many more criminal law pieces. To be coded as a civil or criminal law topic, the abstract needed to either mention a specific area of criminal or civil law or to use the words civil or criminal law as a description of the paper's topic. Some abstracts did neither. Forty-six percent of

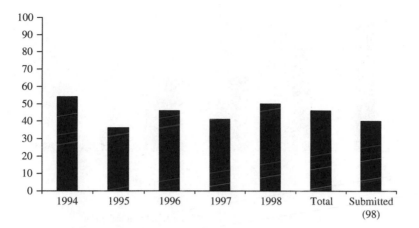

FIGURE 11.4. *Law and Human Behavior*: Percent of Criminal Law Abstracts 1994–1998.

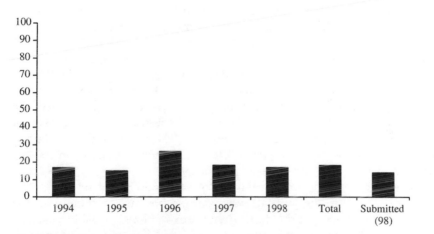

FIGURE 11.5. *Law and Human Behavior*: Percent of Civil Law Abstracts 1994–1998.

those published in the 1994 to 1998 window were easily identified as criminal topics, as were 40% of the submitted papers. However, only 18% of published articles concerned civil law and only 14% of the submitted papers pertained to that topic. As Figures 11.4 and 11.5 show, the emphasis of criminal over civil law has been stable over the 5 year window. The first author (the journal's current editor) suspects that there has been a recent increase in interest in the civil law among psycholegal researchers; it will be interesting to see if data from the first few years of the new decade bear out this impression.

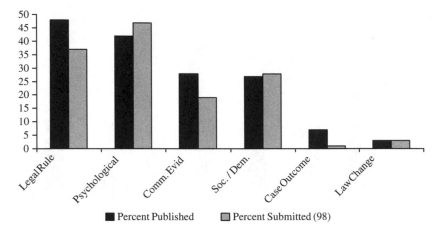

FIGURE 11.6. *Law and Human Behavior:* Independent Variable Definitions 1994–1998.

While some have expressed concern that *Law and Human Behavior* de-emphasizes clinical topics of interest in favor of social science articles, our data suggest that this is not the case. Figure 11.2 shows that about 17% of submissions pertained to clinical topics and our content analysis of published abstracts show that about 18% of published papers over the 1994 to 1998 years were concerned with assessing risk of dangerousness, assessment of psychological status (including competencies and insanity), or treatment issues. If anything, over the years the number of clinical papers has been steadily increasing from 10% in 1994 to about 20% in 1998. Overall, 18% of published articles in *Law and Human Behavior* from 1994 to 1998 were concerned with forensic psychology.

Turning now to the empirical investigations (167 of 185 or 90% of the published papers in the journal), we examine both the independent (or exogenous) variables and the dependent (or exogenous) variables, each in turn.[6] Figure 11.6 shows that presentations of different formulations of legal rules (50% of published papers) (e.g., type of line-up and standard of proof) and psychological factors (40% of published papers) classify most of the independent variables in our paradigm. Not withstanding, a substantial number of articles pertain to how the nature of evidence presentation (e.g., statistical versus narrative format) and demographic factors (e.g., gender, age, and ethnic background) influence legally relevant judgments, evaluations, and perceptions. Very few researchers report studies of the effects of changes in statutory law or outcomes of judicial rulings

[6]It should be noted that abstracts coded for empirical content often included more than one type of independent variable, dependent measure, or psychological explanation. As a result, the percentages in this section of the chapter may exceed 100%.

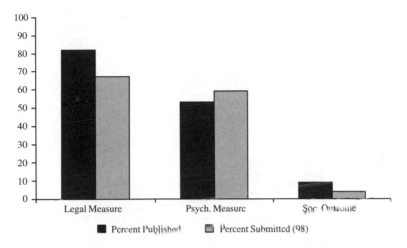

FIGURE 11.7. *Law and Human Behavior:* Dependent Variable Definitions 1994–1998.

on cognition, affect, or behavior. On the dependent variable side of our research, almost all empirical studies include some legal measure (e.g., verdict, punishment, and culprit identification) and many, if not most, include a psychological measure (e.g., memory, judgment of credibility, and attitudes). Very few researchers who publish in *Law and Human Behavior* study social outcomes or community level variables (see Figure 11.7). In summary, while many have argued that psycholegal studies should focus on the effects of law on culture and everyday human behavior (Melton, 1988, 1990; Finkel, Fulero, Haugaard, Levine, & Small, 2001; Wiener, 1990, 1993), the research community has not yet responded with increased efforts in this direction.

Perhaps, most interesting to researchers are the types of psychological mechanisms that our paradigm uses to account for the legal behavior of research participants. Here our estimates are a bit low because it is not uncommon for discussions of psychological interpretations of research findings not to include such a summary in the articles' abstracts. Nevertheless, as displayed in Figure 11.8, the most frequent psychological topic is some form of social cognitive mechanism (e.g., social perception models, attribution theory, story and script models, and attitude theory). Thirty-seven percent of the abstracts discussed social cognitive mechanisms to either predict or explain findings. Another 16% relied upon more purely cognitive mechanisms, such as memory models and decision strategies, online vs. offline processing theories to predict or explain findings. Together then, our work emphasizes the cognitive aspects of human behavior and focuses much less on personality (including motivation),

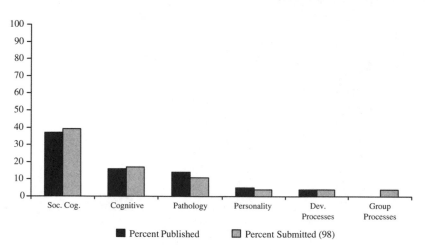

FIGURE 11.8. *Law and Human Behavior:* Psychological Theory Explanations 1994–1998.

group processes, and developmental processes to study human behavior in its legal context. As would be expected by the sizeable contribution that forensic psychology makes to *Law and Human Behavior* there is a healthy representation of theories of psychological pathology. Perhaps, future years will see an increase in studies of motivation and motivated errors in legal judgment now that the wider discipline is refocusing so much of its effort on these issues.

Finally, our content analysis did try to examine the types of samples that are typically used in empirical work reported in *Law and Human Behavior*. This is probably the least informative measure, however, because it proved to be very difficult to code the representativeness of samples from published abstracts. Only 106 of 167 empirical abstracts discussed the type of sample employed. Of the empirical pieces, 94 claimed to have collected a representative sample (e.g., eligible jurors, civilly committed patients, offenders, attorneys, etc.) and 12 reported not using representative participants in the abstracts (i.e., most used college students as samples of convenience). Assuming that an author would likely indicate in an abstract the make up of the sample studied if it were other than a college student sample or some other sample of convenience, then it may be reasonable to assume that authors who failed to discuss this issue in empirical studies likely collected data from an unrepresentative sample. If we make this conservative assumption, then we can estimate that about 56% of our samples are representative of the legal actors that are under investigation. This is in fact similar to the result that Haugaard (1999) came up with in his full analysis of the all the papers published in the 1998 edition of the journal (49% of empirical articles used representative samples). On the other hand, if we do not assume that researchers include information about samples in their abstracts when they are, in fact, representative, then we estimate that 89% of articles (94 out of 106) use representative samples. Thus, the use of representative samples ranges between 56 and 89%. Even the lower, more conservative measure, suggests that our work is taking seriously the criticisms that the courts (and our own colleagues) some-times raise about using samples of convenience.[7]

## DETAILED ANALYSIS OF EMPIRICAL RESEARCH: A STANDARD AND SOME EXAMPLES

Our content analysis presents an overview of the research paradigm that makes up the content of *Law and Human Behavior*. However, this overview does not illustrate any specific pieces of work in which psy-holegal scholars engage. To be complete, our gatekeeper analogy requires a more in-depth view of at least some illustrative works that appear in press in *Law and Human Behavior*. The task of reviewing even one or two years of publications is a formidable one. The result of this enterprise would produce more in terms of an overview of the substantive content of our work and less exemplifying the types of methodologies in our par adigm. Instead of engaging in an exhaustive review of published manu-scripts, we examine eight articles that have been published in the journal from 1997 to 2000. We selected two articles from each of the four areas most frequently represented in our 1999 content analysis: jury decision making, eyewitness identification, forensic psychology, and corrections and police studies.

Following the standard of planned critical multiplism, we chose arti-cles that were maximally different in methodology and approach within each of these categories. We present each research report not as a sum-mary of the substantive content in the area but rather as an analysis of the type of research conducted in that area. We selected articles based upon their capacity to illustrate different strengths in our research enterprise. To evaluate those strengths we relied on the validity analysis offered by Cook and Campbell (1979) in their classic work, *Quasi-Experimentation: Design and Analysis for Field Settings*. Although the approach is not new, it is still the gold standard for research in the social sciences. We examine

---

[7]Note that a recent meta-analysis (Bornstein, 1999) suggests that college students acting as mock jurors do not perform much differently than do jury eligible citizens.

each of our illustration articles from the perspective of construct validity, internal validity, statistical conclusion validity, and external validity (Cook and Campbell, 1979) and compare the two articles in each area looking for evidence of critical multiplism, that is, differences in method-ological and substantive approaches to similar problems. Although indi-vidual researchers obviously did not plan the multiplism that we emphasize, our review does represent planned practices across investiga-tors who presumably took into consideration other approaches from other studies in the sub-field when designing their research.

It is helpful to describe each type of validity at the outset of our illus-trative analysis. Construct validity refers to two separate inferences that researchers make regarding the substance of their work: (1) the construct validity of the intended causes and (2) the construct validity of the intended effects (Cook and Campbell, 1979). With regard to causes, we ask how well the manipulated (or exogenous) variables represent the con-ceptual labels that the investigator intended. The issue is one of represen-tativeness, do the operations represent the factors of interest not only in the laboratory but also in the real world contexts (here legal contexts) in which the construct exists? Construct validity of cause is often tested in experimental studies with manipulation checks or checks on the take of the independent variables. To the extent that the manipulations (or meas-ures) under-represent (i.e., fail to include operations that capture the core) or over-represent (i.e., include operations that are extra to the core) the concept, the researchers err in inferring that they have isolated the essence of the exogenous variable under investigation. For example, consider a jury investigator who varies the expertise of an expert witness by pre-senting different experts with systematically varying levels of training, skill, and education. The researcher may test the participants' judgments about those factors (i.e., training, skill, and education) along with their evaluations of the expert's personality, favorableness, and overall like-ability to demonstrate that the manipulation influenced the earlier vari-ables but not the later ones. Such an outcome would demonstrate that the manipulation fit the concept well, neither under- nor over-representing witness expertise.

With regard to construct validity of the effect, the issue is whether the purported dependent (endogenous) constructs were measured (Cook & Campbell, 1979) as intended. The approach of multiplism is to measure the construct with independent operations that converge on the same con-struct, each measure correlating highly with the others. This process, known as convergent validity, is complemented with discriminant or divergent validity if measures of other unintended constructs do not cor-relate highly with the first set of measures intended to map on to the